Office and SharePoint 2007 User's Guide

Integrating SharePoint with Excel, Outlook, Access, and Word

Michael P. Antonovich

Apress®

Office and SharePoint 2007 User's Guide: Integrating SharePoint with Excel, Outlook, Access, and Word

Copyright © 2008 by Michael P. Antonovich

ISBN-13 (pbk): 978-1-59059-984-6

ISBN-10 (pbk): 1-59059-984-5

ISBN-13 (electronic): 978-1-4302-0632-3

ISBN-10 (electronic): 1-4302-0632-2

Printed and bound in the United States of America 9 8 7 6 5 4 3 2 1

Lead Editor: Tony Campbell
Technical Reviewer: David Pyke
Editorial Board: Clay Andres, Steve Anglin, Ewan Buckingham, Tony Campbell, Gary Cornell, Jonathan Gennick, Matthew Moodie, Joseph Ottinger, Jeffrey Pepper, Frank Pohlmann, Ben Renow-Clarke, Dominic Shakeshaft, Matt Wade, Tom Welsh
Project Manager: Richard Dal Porto
Copy Editor: Ami Knox
Associate Production Director: Kari Brooks-Copony
Production Editor: Liz Berry
Compositor: Susan Glinert Stevens
Proofreader: Linda Seifert
Indexer: Julie Grady
Artist: April Milne
Cover Designer: Kurt Krames
Manufacturing Director: Tom Debolski

Distributed to the book trade worldwide by Springer-Verlag New York, Inc., 233 Spring Street, 6th Floor, New York, NY 10013. Phone 1-800-SPRINGER, fax 201-348-4505, e-mail orders-ny@springer-sbm.com, or visit http://www.springeronline.com.

For information on translations, please contact Apress directly at 2855 Telegraph Avenue, Suite 600, Berkeley, CA 94705. Phone 510-549-5930, fax 510-549-5939, e-mail info@apress.com, or visit http://www.apress.com.

Apress and friends of ED books may be purchased in bulk for academic, corporate, or promotional use. eBook versions and licenses are also available for most titles. For more information, reference our Special Bulk Sales–eBook Licensing web page at http://www.apress.com/info/bulksales.

The source code for this book is available to readers at http://www.apress.com. You may need to answer questions pertaining to this book in order to successfully download the code.

For my wife of 30 years, Susan, and our wonderful daughter, Natasha. I love you both.

Contents at a Glance

About the Author xv

About the Technical Reviewer xvii

Acknowledgments xix

Introduction xxi

CHAPTER 1   An Introduction to SharePoint 1

CHAPTER 2   SharePoint Lists 53

CHAPTER 3   Creating Content Pages 99

CHAPTER 4   Using Your Document Library with Microsoft Office 133

CHAPTER 5   Using Outlook 167

CHAPTER 6   Managing Lists with Access 211

CHAPTER 7   Managing SharePoint Lists from Excel 261

CHAPTER 8   Publishing Excel with Excel Services 287

CHAPTER 9   An Introduction to Creating Forms with InfoPath 335

CHAPTER 10   Publishing InfoPath Forms in SharePoint Libraries 381

CHAPTER 11   Peer-to-Peer Collaboration with Groove 423

CHAPTER 12   Additional Supporting Libraries 455

INDEX 507

Contents

About the Author xv

About the Technical Reviewer xvii

Acknowledgments xix

Introduction xxi

■CHAPTER 1   **An Introduction to SharePoint** 1

Site Collections, Sites, and Subsites 2
    Collaboration Site Templates 3
    Meeting Templates 6
    Enterprise Site Types in MOSS 2007 8
    Publishing Sites 9
    Library Types 11
    Permissions and Groups 13

Adding a Document Library 19

Knowing Your Document Templates 21

Adding Your First Document to Your New Library 22
    Uploading a Document 26
    Editing Documents Stored in Your Library 33
    What Is a Concurrency Problem? 36
    Why Use Check-Out and Check-In? 36
    Tracking Document Versions 41
    Promoting a Prior Version to the Current Version 43
    Publishing Documents to Your Document Library 45
    Requiring Document Approval to Hide Drafts: A Simple Workflow 48
    Recovering Accidental Deletions with the Recycle Bin 50

Summary 51

■CHAPTER 2   **SharePoint Lists** 53

Exploring SharePoint's Built-in List Types 53
    Communications Lists 53
    Tracking Lists 57
    Other Lists 69

Creating a New SharePoint List Based on an Existing Template 70
Adding Items to Your New List 75
Building a Custom List 77
Modifying the Columns in Your List 83
Using Alerts to Notify You When Your List Is Changed 87
Creating RSS Feeds for Your List 89
Defining Views for Your List 93
Sorting and Filtering Lists 96
Summary 98

▪CHAPTER 3   **Creating Content Pages** 99

Adding a Page to Your Site 99
Placing Simple Content on Your New Page 101
Adding an Image to Your Content 103
Adding a Hyperlink to Your Content 104
Copying Text from a Word Document 104
Adding a Table to Your Content 105
Your Final Content Page 106
Adding Functionality with Web Part Pages 107
Creating a New Web Part Page 107
Modifying the Page Title Bar 108
Adding a Web Part to a Web Part Zone 110
Adding Content to the Content Editor Web Part 111
Modifying the Generated HTML 113
Adjusting the Appearance of the Web Parts 115
Using Web Parts to Display Libraries and Lists 118
Creating Master-Detail Relationships Between Your Lists 119
Editing Existing Pages with Check-Out and Check-In 123
Tracking Page Versions 126
Publishing Pages to Your Site 126
Recovering Accidental Deletions with the Recycle Bin 130
Summary 131

▪CHAPTER 4   **Using Your Document Library with Microsoft Office** 133

Opening a SharePoint Document from Within Microsoft Office 134
Editing and Saving a Document to a Document Library 140
Saving a New Document 142
Saving a Document to an Existing Library 142

Creating a New Document Workspace......................143

What Is Metadata? 145

Using Metadata with the Document Information Panel 146

Uploading Existing Documents into a Library Prompts
for Required Metadata 147

Working with Document Metadata.........................149

Managing Your Documents with the Document
Management Panel 151

Other Document Management Panel Features 154

Searching Your Documents 154

Using Word to Contribute to Your Blog Site 156

Creating a Blog Site 157

Defining Categories for Your Blogs.........................158

Creating a New Blog Posting.............................159

Editing Blogs 162

Setting Blog Permissions................................162

Understanding Word's New Open XML File Format 164

Summary 165

CHAPTER 5   Using Outlook 167

Synchronizing Your Contacts Lists Between SharePoint
and Outlook 167

Connecting Your SharePoint Contacts List to Outlook 167

Adding SharePoint Columns That Will Synchronize
with Outlook..170

Managing Update Conflicts 171

Deleting Contacts 173

Recovering Deleted Contacts 174

Moving Contacts Between Lists 175

Synchronizing Your Calendars Between SharePoint and Outlook 176

Adding a SharePoint Calendar to Outlook 176

Overlaying Calendars 180

Making Changes to Calendar Items 182

Copying and Moving Items Between Calendars 183

Deleting Items from the Calendar.........................183

Synchronizing Tasks Between SharePoint and Outlook 184

Adding Tasks Lists to Outlook............................185

Editing Tasks from Outlook 187

Using Outlook to Work Offline with Content 188

Letting Alerts Notify You of SharePoint Changes 193
    Configuring Your Alerts 194
    Correcting/Modifying Alerts................................... 196
Using Outlook's RSS Reader to Subscribe to SharePoint RSS Feeds .. 198
    Adding an RSS Feed to Internet Explorer 7.0 198
    Adding an RSS Feed to Outlook 2007 201
    Deleting Items from an RSS Feed............................. 204
    Viewing Other List Items Not in the RSS Feed................ 205
Sending E-mail to Lists 207
    Sending a Message to a SharePoint Group 207
    Sending a Message to a List or Library 207
Sending Links via Send To 209
Summary 209

■CHAPTER 6   **Managing Lists with Access** 211

Exporting SharePoint Lists to Access 211
    Saving Your Export Steps.................................... 217
    Transfer Issues 218
Linking SharePoint Lists to Access 225
    Editing Linked Data 226
    Using Access to Make Mass Updates........................... 227
Use Multivalued Fields in Lists 230
    Creating a Multivalued Column in SharePoint................. 230
    Opening a List with Multivalued Columns in Access 234
    Some Reasons Not to Use Multivalued Columns 236
Creating Access Forms and Reports from a SharePoint List 237
    Creating a Simple Form 237
    Creating a Split Form 239
    Creating a Custom Form Using a Subform 241
    Creating a Simple Report.................................... 245
Working with Offline Lists Within Access 246
    Taking Your List Data Offline............................... 246
    Returning to Online Mode and Synchronization 249
    Resolving Conflicts... 250
Controlling Which Forms and Reports Are Available in SharePoint ... 252
Can Recycle Bin Recover Deleted List Records? 259
Summary 260

CHAPTER 7   Managing SharePoint Lists from Excel 261

Exporting a List from SharePoint to Excel 261
  The Role of the IQY File 262
  Choosing How to Display Your Imported List. 264
  How Views Affect the Data Exported to Your List 266
  Using Hyperlinks in Your List. 266
  Other Table Tools in Your Excel Workbook 268
Exporting Data from an Excel Spreadsheet into a Custom List 269
  Defining a Table Within Your Excel Worksheet 270
  Exporting the Excel Table. 271
  Viewing the Exported Excel Data in the New SharePoint List 274
A Quick Look at Excel 2003 and Synchronization 276
  Exporting a SharePoint List to Excel 2003. 276
  Exporting Excel 2003 Worksheets to SharePoint 277
What Happened to Synchronization? 279
Linking a List in Excel to SharePoint 280
Summary 285

CHAPTER 8   Publishing Excel with Excel Services 287

Configuring Excel Services 288
Publishing an Excel Form to Excel Services 289
  Adding an Excel Workbook to Your Document Library
    from SharePoint. 289
  Navigating Around Your Worksheet 291
Why You Need Parameters to Make Your Excel Form Interactive 292
Defining Parameters for Your Excel Form 293
  Publishing Your Excel Workbook. 295
  Viewing Uploaded Excel Documents 300
Using the Excel Page Web Part 301
Viewing Data from External Sources in Excel Using a
  Data Connection 305
  How to Create an External Connection. 306
  Importing the SharePoint List to a Workbook 311
  Formatting a Pivot Table to Look Like a Worksheet 313
  Publish Your Formatted Workbook 315
Working with the Report Center 317
Introduction to KPIs 317
  KPI Types Defined. 318
  Creating a KPI List 318

Creating Dashboards with Excel and KPIs 324
    Building a Dashboard from the Dashboard Template
      in the Report Center 325
    Organizing Web Parts in the Dashboard Web Part Zones 326
    Adding KPIs to Your Dashboard. 328
Summary 332

◾CHAPTER 9 An Introduction to Creating Forms with InfoPath 335

Why You Should Use InfoPath 336
Exploring the InfoPath Interface 337
Creating a Simple Form 338
    The Task Group: Layout. 340
    The Task Group: Controls 343
    The Task Group: Data Sources 347
    The Task Group: Design Checker 348
    The Task Groups: Views and Publish Form Template 349
    Steps to Build the Request for Absence Report 349
Migrating Your Existing Word Forms into InfoPath 354
Migrating Your Existing Excel Workbook into InfoPath 356
Defining InfoPath Views 360
    Viewing Properties 360
    Generating Your Second View. 362
Building Data Connections for Forms 365
Connecting InfoPath Forms to Data 370
Creating and Reusing Form Sections with Template Parts 375
Summary 379

◾CHAPTER 10 Publishing InfoPath Forms in SharePoint Libraries 381

Publishing InfoPath Forms to a Network File Share 381
    Publishing a Form to a Network Location 384
    Using Your Published Form 387
    Saving Your Completed Form 388
Using InfoPath Forms Services for Customers Without InfoPath 390
    Publishing to a SharePoint Server. 390
    Defining Metadata for the Document Library 394
    Additional Library Settings. 397
    Using the Published Form 399
    Changing Submit Options for a Form. 400
    Saving the Data from a Form 401

Publishing a Form to a Content Type 403
Installing and Using Site Collection Content Types 408
    Adding a Content Type to a Library 408
    Changing the Default Content Type 409
    Working with a Library That Has Multiple Content Types 410
Building Custom Workflows for InfoPath Forms Using
   SharePoint Designer 411
    What Is a Workflow?...................................... 411
    Beginning a Simple Approval Workflow 412
    Defining Workflow Details 414
    Configuring an E-mail Message 415
    Adding Multiple Actions 416
    Adding Conditions to Actions.............................. 417
    Adding Additional Steps................................... 418
    Restructuring Your Conditions............................. 420
Summary 422

■CHAPTER 11   **Peer-to-Peer Collaboration with Groove** 423

Getting into the Groove 424
A Quick Look at Groove's Other Tools 430
    Chat 430
    Pictures 430
    Sketchpad 431
    Notepad 431
    Discussion 431
    Files 431
    Calendar... 432
    Issue Tracking.. 432
    Meetings 432
    Forms... 433
    InfoPath Forms 434
    SharePoint Files 434
Sharing Your Files Using Groove: Simple Group Collaboration 435
    Using Subfolders.. 436
    Editing Your Shared Files.................................. 437
    Dealing with Conflicts.................................... 438
    Deleting Files... 438
    Saving Files 439
    Creating a New File 439
Setting Up a SharePoint Document Library Connection 440

Setting Permissions for the SharePoint Files Folder 441
Working on SharePoint Documents Offline 443
Protecting Changes with Check-Out and Check-In
    Along with Versioning 443
Collaborating with People Outside Your Organization 445
Synchronizing Files Between Groove and SharePoint
    Document Libraries 446
        Scheduling Synchronization 448
        Managing Synchronization 449
Who Is the Synchronizer? 450
Summary 452

■CHAPTER 12   **Additional Supporting Libraries** 455

Creating a Records Management System to Archive
    Your Documents 455
        Creating Site Columns 456
        Creating a Content Type for RFB Documents 458
        Creating a Site Library to Collect RFB Documents 462
        Creating the Records Center Site 468
        Creating the External Service Connection 469
        Creating the Archival Library in the Records Center........... 471
        Creating a Policy for the Archival Library................... 472
        Creating a Record Routing Rule 474
        Archiving Your Documents 475
Creating a Picture Library in SharePoint 477
        Uploading Pictures to SharePoint Using Picture Manager 481
        Using the Microsoft Office Picture Manager 483
        Using Windows Explorer to Upload Pictures 486
        Downloading Images from Your Picture Library 487
        Sending Images to a Microsoft Office Application 490
        Viewing the Pictures in a Picture Library 492
Creating a Slide Library in SharePoint 496
        Uploading Pictures to Your Slide Library
           from PowerPoint 2007 499
        Copying Slides from Your Slide Library to
           PowerPoint Presentations............................. 504
Summary 505

■INDEX 507

About the Author

MICHAEL P. ANTONOVICH graduated from Lehigh University with a bachelor's degree in chemical engineering in 1976 and an MBA in 1980, but his career almost from the start evolved toward computers and application development. He started working with large mainframe systems but quickly developed a keen interest in microcomputers when Apple introduced its Apple II, for which he wrote his first book in 1983. Over the years, he has learned many different systems, applications, and programming languages, but the first development environment he felt really strong about was FoxBase and later FoxPro. During the '90s, he published four books on FoxPro before the Internet and SQL Server bug bit him.

In addition to his full-time jobs developing applications, Michael has conducted dozens of different computer training classes for companies and universities. In 2003, he joined the IT team of Orange County Public Schools as they prepared to launch a major new student tracking system. But the lure of the Internet along with a "little" product called SharePoint pulled him back into Internet development in the fall of 2006, when he took on the task of heading up the technical team to develop a new SharePoint portal for the school district that would provide all users with a single consistent, easy-to-use interface. While portions of that project have been completed, others are still being worked on, and some are still in planning. However, the eventual goal is to support all district Internet and intranet sites via SharePoint, as well as to encourage greater collaboration through a single portal that students, parents, staff, and the community can access anywhere, anytime.

About the Technical Reviewer

■**DAVID PYKE** is a director of Inta Networking Ltd., an established company providing enterprise content management, public key infrastructure, and process improvement consultancy to both businesses and the public sector. He has been engaged as a consultant on several Microsoft SharePoint–based projects from the very earliest versions of the product to the latest, and has a particular understanding of how to exploit the powerful Microsoft Office portfolio to provide effective information management environments. He has one wonderful son, Herbie, and lives with his lovely and ever-patient girlfriend, Liz, in the Georgian market town of Farnham in Surrey, England.

Acknowledgments

Even though a book may get published with a single name on the cover, many people are actually involved in getting that book into your hands. I'd like to thank Jonathan Hassell for taking a chance on this book concept. I was sorry to see you move on to other opportunities, but I wish you the best. Thanks to Richard Dal Porto, my project manager, for stepping into a project half started and taking over when Jonathan left, and for trying to keep me on schedule. Sorry for the confusing order in which I worked on the chapters, but I guess I just don't think linearly anymore; everything is a separate object, it seems. Thanks to Tony Campbell, my lead editor, and David Pyke, my technical reviewer, for pointing out the technical things I assumed everyone would know but needed to include. To Ami Knox, thanks for helping me make this text more readable and fixing my grammar mistakes. And Liz Berry, thanks for catching everything the rest of us missed. This team did a wonderful job catching problems, so any errors that you may still find in this book are undoubtedly mine.

Thanks to Kevin Goff, a good friend since my early days of FoxBase work, whose own recent book for Apress convinced me that it was time for me to give it a go again. I'm watching for your next one, buddy.

A huge thanks must go to the entire SharePoint team at Microsoft for creating such a tremendously powerful and solid application platform like SharePoint. It was a job well done. It brings together the best of the Internet with the best of Microsoft Office in a way that can boost productivity to unbelievable heights. I have been more excited about working with SharePoint than any other product since my old FoxPro days.

A great big thank-you goes out to Charles Thompson, our former CIO at Orange County Public Schools, for having the vision to see the value of a single portal for all district information access and for giving me the opportunity to get in on the ground floor of that vision.

I'd also like to shout out a huge thank-you to Scott Tarnell. We brought Scott in to handle the administration of SharePoint, and he dove into the product, becoming an expert at not only the hardware requirements, but also the software configuration, branding, security, and countless other details. I rely on the ability to bounce ideas off Scott every day to make sure we can meet our user needs even before they know what they are.

To the rest of my SharePoint Team, special thanks to Mike Healey for helping us understand web parts and workflows, a big thanks to Shelly Henriott for making sure all the pages look good and for helping the users learn how to support their own content, and huge thanks to Serena Wright for holding us all together and keeping us moving in one direction, rather than the fifty thousand we might try if left to our own devices.

The biggest thanks, though, has to go to my wife for understanding that writing a book takes a lot of time away from other things, not just for a few days, but month after month.

Finally, thanks to all the production people at Apress for their parts in making this book happen.

Introduction

SharePoint may be the biggest thing to affect the way you and I work in our offices since . . . well . . . since Microsoft Office. Word showed us how to write and edit our writing more efficiently on a computer screen than we ever could before with a typewriter. Similarly, Excel showed us how to manipulate numbers more accurately than any accounting sheet created with pencil and paper. (Okay, I know there were some word processors before MS Word and spreadsheets before MS Excel, but just go with me for a second.)

Over the years, Microsoft Office has become so pervasive that it is almost impossible to get an office job today if you do not have a firm understanding of at least Word and Excel. But we still store hundreds of files in dozens of different directories and even different servers across our companies. Documents are created and printed and then carried from one office to another. Sometimes, dozens of copies are made and distributed. Some get lost. Some find their way into file folders in people's desks. Others get archived into boxes and stored offsite in the fear that someday, someone may want to see them again.

The electronic revolution of the 1990s and early 2000s did not free us from paper. Rather, it seems to have buried us deeper in a rising tide of paper that comes into our inbox faster than we can file it, much less read it.

We've all heard of the utopia of a paperless society where information flows at the speed of light from its point of creation to each user who must review and approve it. Perhaps the tools were just not ready before. Perhaps we were simply missing that keystone piece that makes it all come together into a compelling argument for a new way of working with information. The Internet was not the solution, although it was an enabling piece of technology that may make our vision of the office of the future possible.

So what is the next revolution that will bring our dream of a paperless environment into reality?

I believe that SharePoint collaboration and content management is that next revolution.

Oh, you say you have heard of SharePoint, but thought that it was a portal for a company's web site. Yes, that is true, but that is only one facet of a many-faceted tool.

SharePoint sits on top of the many technologies of the past. It borrows a lot from web development. But it also integrates tightly into many of the Microsoft Office products, giving them the ability to accomplish goals like the following:

- Create shared document libraries that can be accessed from anywhere a person can get an Internet connection.

- Present electronic forms for people to interactively fill in, rather than having to print the form, write on the form, send it back, and then have someone enter the data into a computer program interface.

- Store multiple versions of documents so a revision history can be retained.

- Display business information in Excel-style pages that you can even change interactively to help managers make better decisions.

Currently, a large number of IT people worldwide are beginning to use SharePoint. They are creating web sites and collaboration sites. And that is all good. However, SharePoint will not reach its full potential until every computer user who knows how to use Microsoft Office becomes as familiar with SharePoint from a user perspective as they currently are with their favorite Office application, such as MS Word or MS Excel.

No, this does not mean you need to know how to install SharePoint or even how to configure it (although understanding a little of the configuration would not hurt). However, it does mean that you need to know how to create and use libraries, lists, and many other features. It means that you should learn how to use Office tools like Word, Outlook, Excel, and Access to not only create and maintain your own files on a SharePoint site, but also store files on a centralized server at your company that you can access from anywhere you can get an Internet connection. It should not matter whether you are at home connected through your home computer or on vacation using your laptop and wireless connection at your resort. You could even be at your local library using its computer. Anywhere. Anytime. The dream of having access to your corporate data is only a connection away.

But there is more to it than just accessing your files. You can share your files with colleagues or even the project consultant who works in a different city. I will show you how you can share files with people who do not have access to your network. You can also create workflows without programming so that when a document is created, you can automatically send it to someone else to review or approve. You will see how you can consolidate your lists, calendars, and tasks from multiple sources. You will discover how easy it is to create forms for others to use through their browser. But most of all, you will see how you can become more productive and efficient using your favorite Microsoft Office tools together with SharePoint, without needing to learn programming first.

The revolution has begun. You already know how to use the basic tools. Now, let me show you how you can capitalize on those tools to take you to a new level of productivity and freedom from that paper avalanche on the side of your desk.

Who This Book Is For

This book is for anyone who wants to reap the benefits of working with SharePoint and Microsoft Office without having to learn programming. Sure, there are many additional things you can do with SharePoint if you have programming skills. There are many other books on the market that take you down that road. When you are ready to get more into programming, I recommend *Pro SharePoint Solution Development: Combining .NET, SharePoint, and Office 2007* by Ed Hild and Susie Adams (Apress, 2007), and *Microsoft SharePoint: Building Office 2007 Solutions in VB 2005* and *Microsoft SharePoint: Building Office 2007 Solutions in C# 2005*, both by Scot P. Hillier (Apress, 2007). However, there are far more office workers out there who use Microsoft Office every day who can benefit from using SharePoint without necessarily going into programming. You know who you are. You are the power users of Microsoft Office. You are the ones other people in the office come to when they need to do something in Office but don't quite know how. You are ready to take the next step in Office productivity to promote increased collaboration between members of a project or department, to build the content for intranet and even Internet sites, to replace the passing of paper in your office with electronic forms driven by workflows from person to person. You dream of a day when you will not need a single sheet of paper on your desktop to get your work done. If this sounds like I'm describing you, then this book is your starting point toward that future.

Contacting the Author

You can contact the author by e-mail at mike@micmin.org. I will be establishing a blog to go along with this book at http://mpantonovich.spaces.live.com/default.aspx. From time to time I will post additional tips and tricks related to collaboration between Microsoft Office and SharePoint.

CHAPTER 1

■ ■ ■

An Introduction to SharePoint

SharePoint is Microsoft's enterprise-level application solution for organizations wanting to deploy any combination of an internet, intranet, or extranet with a consistent user experience. By heavily leveraging other Microsoft Office family products, SharePoint allows teams to work together and collaborate when separated across the country or even the globe. SharePoint is currently one of Microsoft's fastest growing products with over 75 million licenses sold. Perhaps most important to business planners is that Forrester lists SharePoint as the number one portal product on the market and Gartner places SharePoint 2007 as a leader in their "Magic Quadrant for Horizontal Portal Products in August 2007."

Microsoft envisions SharePoint as the single portal that an organization needs to deploy for its internet, intranet, and extranets. Tight integration with other Microsoft Office family products enables SharePoint to boost the productivity of employees by reducing the time and effort needed to create and maintain sites. It allows more people to participate in the creation of site content. It provides a framework from which everyone within an organization can share information, conduct meetings, and track tasks. It enables you to work remotely while storing files centrally, yet work on them anywhere you have access to the Internet; and even when you don't have access to the Internet, you can check out documents ahead of time, work on them while disconnected, and then synchronize your changes when you connect to the Internet again.

While no single book can cover everything there is to know about SharePoint, this book focuses on helping you to work with SharePoint using many of the common Microsoft Office tools such as Outlook, Word, Excel, PowerPoint, and Access. You will even get a look at some of the newer Office tools such as InfoPath and Groove. This book concentrates more on collaboration-type activities as opposed to Internet site development. However, many of the same techniques for working with web pages, web parts, libraries, and lists apply to both areas.

In this chapter, you will look at how to create a SharePoint site and come to understand the flexibility of building a hierarchy of sites within a site collection. You will also see how to define permissions for users, allowing some users to create new content and edit existing content while restricting other users to viewing the published content. Next, you will build a document library and learn how to use Microsoft Word to add and edit documents stored in that library. Then I will show you how to preserve the integrity of your editing through the use of the check-out and check-in facility for documents. Finally, you will explore the use of versioning to control the publishing of information that others can view.

In subsequent chapters, you will explore SharePoint's other features, from lists through web pages, from the point of view of how to integrate your current knowledge of Microsoft Office tools. My goal is not to make you a SharePoint administrator. Rather my goal is make you a power user when it comes to working with SharePoint through Microsoft Office.

Site Collections, Sites, and Subsites

Think of a *site* within SharePoint as a group of related pages, libraries, and lists that you can view using a web browser such as Internet Explorer, Firefox, or several others. A department within an organization may want to have a site on the Internet to publish information about what services or products that department provides. Similarly, a *site collection* is a collection of sites. For example, the company internet might be a site collection consisting of individual department sites. At the site collection level, you can store common objects that all sites within it can use. For example, you might store the organization's logo at the site collection level so that all department sites can reference that logo from one place.

A site typically focuses on specific topics, groups of people, or activities. Just like a web site, a SharePoint site has a home page, sometimes called its *default page*, which links to other pages in the site. This page can provide navigation to the other pages in the site either through menus or links. Each page supports content of various types ranging from lists to libraries to simple text and images, all organized in what could look like a regular web page found on the Internet.

As a content creator within SharePoint, you have the freedom to control the appearance and content of pages within a site. No longer must you submit content changes to a web design person and then wait for him to incorporate the changes into your organization's web pages. You can collaborate with any number of people in your organization, from one to many thousands who have direct access to updatable lists, documents, and even content pages on your intranet or internet sites.

A site can also have one or more *subsites*. While a subsite inherits many of its properties from its parent site, it also can have its own identity, properties, and objects. Subsites further subdivide the focus of the higher-level site. If a site represents a department, a subsite might represent a project or a team.

For example, suppose you create a SharePoint site for your entire organization. In this top-level site, you create content pages that pertain to your organization as a whole. However, since each group within your organization wants to create its own set of pages and content, you create subsites for each division, department, or workgroup beneath this top-level site. Each subsite may have additional subsites beneath it representing individual projects, groups, or activities. You may even build subsites that represent projects that cross department or division boundaries.

Each subsite in the preceding scenario represents a unique and distinct area or portion of the entire organization. This group of sites and subsites forms a hierarchy referred to as a site collection. By dividing your information into multiple sites and subsites, you control the features, access rights, and settings appropriate for each one. But by placing all of them under a single umbrella, you can provide a single entry point or portal for all content as well as inheritance of selected features from the top site. No longer will each department, project, or group need to store its information in a separate database, file structure, or server completely separate from all others. This type of data silo inhibits the cross-flow of information and makes searching for specific information difficult or impossible. A single portal approach for all of an organization's information facilitates features like document searching, provides a common look and feel, simplifies navigation and support, and encourages collaboration and agility to respond quickly between members of ad hoc groups.

SharePoint also stores the information for all the sites within a site collection within a single SQL Server database. The site collection lets you share objects among the sites it contains. For example, you can share images, templates, site columns, content types, and permissions defined at the site collection level with any site within the site collection. Since each site collection represents a separate SQL Server database, you can provide separate backup and restore operations for the collection.

Tip If you are using SQL Server Express as your back-end database engine, you might also consider using separate site collections due to the current limit of 4GB on the size of individual databases.

Creating a site from scratch may sound a little intimidating at first. Indeed, before SharePoint, the prospect of creating sites across an entire organization would probably require a team of developers and months of time. However, SharePoint simplifies the process by providing a collection of *templates* for various object types to get you started. Of course, as you progress in your SharePoint knowledge, you can add to these templates with your own or those from third-party developers. While the book will explore some of these in more detail later, here I'll give you a quick overview of the types of sites you can create out of the box with SharePoint, starting with collaboration sites, which exist in both Windows SharePoint Services (WSS) 3.0 and Microsoft Office SharePoint Server (MOSS) 2007.

Collaboration Site Templates

WSS 3.0 and MOSS 2007 supply five major collaboration site templates as shown in Figure 1-1. Each template provides a unique starting point for creating a new site. However, just because site templates initially define specific unique features and web parts does not limit what you can do to customize a site. SharePoint allows you to customize a site based on one template with features that may be found in another. In fact, you can create your own custom templates starting from one of the supplied templates. So let's take a brief look at what each collaboration site template provides.

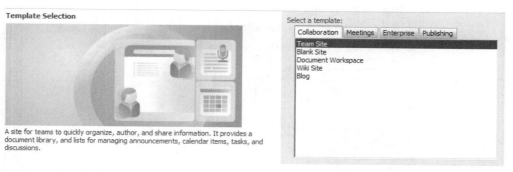

Figure 1-1. *Collaboration site templates*

Team Site

The Team Site template serves as a fast, out-of-the-box starting point for work teams that center around projects. It provides for creating and sharing of information through document libraries, establishing project calendars, tracking of individual and project tasks, and facilitating of discussions among the site members.

Figure 1-2 shows a WSS 3.0 team site that I will use as the basis to illustrate many of the examples in the next few chapters. This figure identifies several key areas that you need to become familiar with, as I will refer to them often in the following text.

Note A team site created within MOSS 2007 may also include a **My Site** link and a **My Links** link in the upper-right corner of the screen if those features are enabled. Also in both MOSS 2007 and WSS 3.0, the **Site Actions** button appears only for those users who have permission to edit site content. Users who can only view the site will not see this button. The examples will assume that you have the necessary permissions to edit site content.

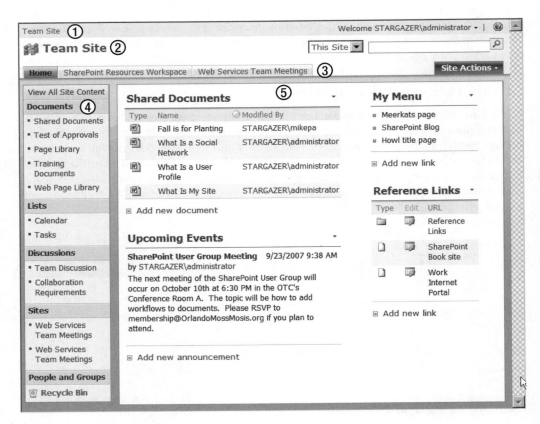

Figure 1-2. *The major sections of a SharePoint page*

1. The **Global Links Bar** contains a reference to the home page of the top-level site on the left. On the right, a **Welcome** menu displays the name of the current user. The arrow to the right of the user's name displays a menu with options to personalize the current page, change user settings, send the site administrator a request for more permissions, and log on with a different account if you have more than one or allow a different user to log in. The last item on the far right is the **Help** link icon. Click this icon at any time to find help topics via a **Contents** list or by typing in keywords in a search engine.

■**Tip** The site developers in some organizations have multiple accounts representing different permission sets so that they can log in and view pages as other users would see them.

---

2. The **Title** area displays the name of the site along with a site logo (image). On the right side, the **Search** feature allows you to search for content by keywords either in the current site and subsites or when using MOSS 2007 across all sites in your enterprise.

3. The **Navigation Bar** normally lists the sites available to the user. On the right side, the **Site Actions** button displays a menu of site management options available to the user.

4. The **Quick Launch** area located on the left side of the page provides one-click access navigation to selected sites, documents, and lists. Depending on your permissions, you can customize what appears in this area and the **Navigation Bar**.

5. The **Main Content** area takes up the rest of the page. SharePoint divides this area into one or more sections called *web part zones* depending on the site template. You can add content in each zone consisting of libraries, lists, and other web parts to customize your page.

Blank Site

The Blank Site template is like a blank piece of paper. The person creating the site has total control over what appears on the site and where it appears. Until you have developed some familiarity with the other site templates and have customized them, you may not want to begin with a blank site. On the other hand, experienced site developers often prefer the Blank Site template because they do not have to waste time deleting or moving web parts and features that they do not want to use or that they want to appear elsewhere. Instead, they can focus on adding what they do want.

Document Workspace

SharePoint provides a Document Workspace template designed around creating a place where groups of people can work collaboratively on documents. It facilitates this through a document library and adds task lists for to-do items and link lists to track resources consisting of people and things.

Wiki Site

Wiki means *quick* or *fast* in Hawaiian, and therefore the Wiki Site template provides a quick way for teams to share and discuss information. The users of these sites can easily edit the content and link new pages using keywords in the topic text. Wiki sites generally consist of a set of collaborative web pages that users can easily contribute content to. Links between the pages of a wiki site allow readers to branch from the main topic to related topics as they appear in the text as hyperlinks. For example, you might use a wiki to publish tricks and tips for various applications within your organization. Links might refer to similar tricks described on other pages. You can also use pages to present definitions for technical terms your organization uses, organizational information, project definitions, and many more useful pieces of information.

Blog

While SharePoint administrators design wiki sites so anyone who can access them can contribute, edit, and add to them, blog sites, which you can create through the Blog template, generally exist for an individual or team to post major ideas or observations. Blog sites do not allow users to edit prior postings by others, but you can always post comments to any blog entry. Also unlike wiki sites, blog sites cannot easily be linked together based on topic words. Blog entries typically appear in reverse chronological order, making it easier for readers to see the most recent entries, whereas most newsgroups use a chronological hierarchy beginning with the initial entry and flowing down to more recent entries.

Bloggers (as some people refer to blog site contributors) use blog sites to discuss their projects or favorite subjects, or to provide additional information or viewpoints. In some ways, you might consider blogging as an alternative to using newsgroups based on a news server. Some organizations use internal blog sites to document the work effort on projects by creating daily or weekly entries detailing the progress made since the last entry. For those *Star Trek* fans out there, a blog site corresponds to a kind of Captain's Log.

Meeting Templates

Meeting templates provide predefined configurations that include different web parts in the default site template. SharePoint refers to these sites as *workspaces* rather than sites because they provide tools, web parts, and resources specifically oriented toward facilitating the activities of workgroups. Meeting workspaces include lists and documents, links, and team member information. While each template has a unique combination of web parts that defines its character, always remember that you can customize the appearance of your meeting workspace to include web parts contained in other templates. So let's take a look at the provided templates as listed in Figure 1-3.

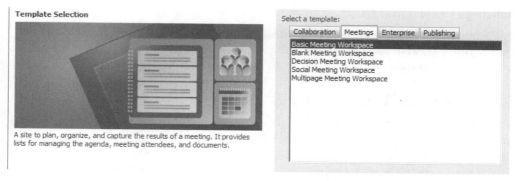

Figure 1-3. *Meeting templates*

Basic Meeting Workspace

Most meetings have common requirements to help members plan, conduct, and document them, and the Basic Meeting Workspace template takes these into account. Things like agendas, attendee lists, and libraries for documents reviewed in preparation for the meeting, during the meeting, or as follow-up to the meeting define a few of the important components of a basic meeting workspace.

Blank Meeting Workspace

The Blank Meeting Workspace template, like its name implies, starts with no predefined pages containing specific web parts. This template best suits the experienced site designer who prefers to start with a clean site rather than spending time deleting web parts from a predefined template.

Decision Meeting Workspace

People call meetings for a variety of purposes. You might hold some meetings to brainstorm new ideas or plan out the steps of a project. You could hold informational meetings to inform your staff about activities in other groups or departments. You might even call a meeting to evaluate lessons learned after a project ends. But you probably also call many meetings to make a decision.

   The Decision Meeting Workspace template includes web parts to document objectives, agendas, and attendees. It includes a document library that holds documents relevant to the decision at hand. It also provides a means to document the decision as well as to create follow-up tasks or even tasks needed prior to the decision meeting such as research or testing tasks.

Social Meeting Workspace

The Social Meeting Workspace template includes features that help plan for special events such as company picnics and awards presentations, or even prepare for a company conference. This workspace includes discussion boards, picture libraries, directions to the event, and lists of things to bring.

Multipage Meeting Workspace

The Multipage Meeting Workspace template includes many of the features found in a basic meeting workspace but is organized over multiple pages. Of course, the other workspace templates permit the addition of more pages, but you may like to start with preconfigured pages.

Enterprise Site Types in MOSS 2007

All the previously mentioned, site templates come with both WSS 3.0 and MOSS 2007. However MOSS 2007 adds additional templates applicable to larger organizations. I will touch on some of these later, but for now let's take a quick look at what MOSS 2007 adds to the prior template list to help the enterprise user. Figure 1-4 shows the enterprise templates added by MOSS 2007 to SharePoint.

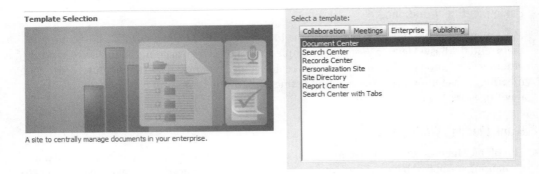

Figure 1-4. *Enterprise templates*

Document Center

The Document Center template is used to manage from a central location documents with a large volume of content and/or a large number of documents.

Search Center

The Search Center site template allows users to perform searches. This site does not include other content such as lists or libraries. Rather it allows users to define search criteria and to return the results of that search.

Records Center

The Records Center template supports records routing and can track and route records based on rules. It can hold records based on a date or approval status, store records with incomplete information separately so you can address them manually, and store records separately that do not match any existing routing rules. Unlike content added to most other SharePoint sites, you cannot edit records after you add them to the Records Center repository.

RECORDS CENTERS

Most organizations have a Records Center—a central repository where documents are sent for long-term storage. These documents typically must be retained either for legal reasons or tax reasons for a specified number of years so that they can be retrieved at a future time.

Users do not create records in a Records Center. They create records in document libraries. Once they no longer actively need the document, they can send it to the Records Center where it will be stored and managed until such time as it can be destroyed. Typically your organization's legal department will have some level of control over the operation of the Records Center.

Personalization Site

The Personalization Site template allows users to create custom views of available site information. Users of a personalized site can define navigation to pages important to them, bypassing the navigation of the main site to which it belongs.

Site Directory

The Site Directory template lists and categorizes sites within the SharePoint installation. It includes the ability to list the top sites, the sites deemed the most important. It also supports a site map to provide a visual depiction of the sites within the entire SharePoint installation.

Report Center

The Report Center site template gathers together in one place reports, dashboards, and presentations of key performance indicator information as well as metrics and business intelligence data.

Search Center with Tabs

The Search Center with Tabs site template extends the capabilities of the Search Center site by adding tabs that allow different search scopes. For example, out of the box, SharePoint provides a tab that searches content and another that searches for people. However, you can add tabs for custom search scopes unique to your site.

Publishing Sites

In addition to enterprise sites, MOSS 2007 adds three special sites, shown in Figure 1-5, related to publishing content that can be inserted into a site collection, and two portal templates, shown in Figure 1-6, that can only be used as the top-level site for a site collection. These site templates apply primarily to those organizations creating internet or intranet sites either for the entire organization or for specific groups within the organization. These templates support features such as the page editing toolbar, content editor, and web parts specific to creating internet and intranet portals. While this book does not focus on creating web portals, it may be useful to know what publishing sites offer so you know when to use them.

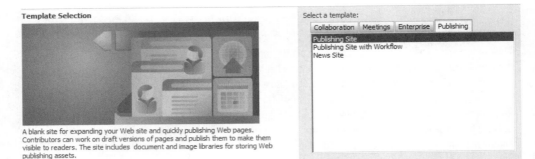

Figure 1-5. *Site publishing templates*

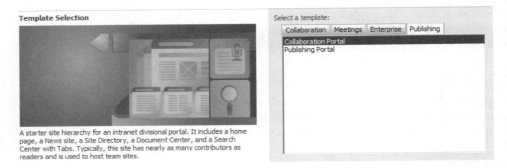

Figure 1-6. *Top-level site publishing templates*

Publishing Site

SharePoint designed publishing sites specifically to display basic content on web pages. Developers of internet or intranet sites often use the Publishing Site template as a starting point. However, you can include document and image libraries as well as lists and other web part objects.

Publishing Site with Workflow

SharePoint bases the Publishing Site with Workflow template on the Publishing Site template but adds the ability to include workflows. Workflows might require documents to have approval before making them available for the general user to view.

■**Note** Within a Publishing Site with Workflow, you can only build subsites using the Publishing Site with Workflow template.

News Site

The News Site template manages all types of news from basic news article pages to RSS feeds and photos. It also supports archiving of old news items rather than deleting them so they can always be searched later.

If it is the case that you do not have the Create Subsite permission, you will not be able to create your own sites. However, if you are responsible for content and working within one or more sites to add and maintain content, you should still have a basic understanding of the available site templates. For the purposes of much of this book, I will focus on several of the basic web site types that specialize in collaboration and interaction using Microsoft Office. By specifying the capabilities you need in a site and perhaps even the web part features, you can select the best site template for your needs.

Collaboration Portal

You must use the Collaboration Portal template to create the first site in a new site collection. Collaboration portals can form the framework around building an organization's intranet. They can include subsites, news sites, Search Centers, team sites, and others where the organization's employees can collaborate on projects and publish documents and lists of information that they want only other employees of the organization to see.

Publishing Portal

The Publishing Portal template differs from the Collaboration Portal template in that it has an outward-facing orientation or internet pages. Often SharePoint developers will customize the look and feel of these sites to establish a "branding" through the use of themes, custom master pages, and CSS files. Being outward facing, organizations use the Publishing Portal template to publish information that they want the general public to see.

■**Note** The top-level site publishing templates described here can only be created from SharePoint's Central Administrator site.

Library Types

One of the most basic objects that you can add to most sites is a library. Libraries store documents, images, reports, and other objects. Some libraries serve as a general collection point for many different types of documents. You can create other libraries for very specific purposes with only particular file types allowed. Thus the type of library you need depends on what type of information you want to store in the library. Let's examine the basic library types shown in Figure 1-7 and how you can use them.

Libraries
▫ Document Library
▫ Form Library
▫ Wiki Page Library
▫ Picture Library
▫ Translation Management Library
▫ Data Connection Library
▫ Slide Library
▫ Report Library

Figure 1-7. *Library templates*

Document Library

The Document Library is the most common library type. It can hold any document type that you would normally find in a directory on your computer's hard disk. A document library, like a disk directory, typically stores various file types with little or no relationship to each other. However good file management applies as much to SharePoint libraries as it does to your hard disk. Just as you would create different directories for different types of files, projects, or applications, you should consider organizing your document libraries so all files in one document library have a common focus, perhaps even a common type.

Form Library

The Form Library stores the XML source documents for forms created with Microsoft Office InfoPath. Users with InfoPath installed on their local computer can form definitions stored here and then publish them as templates for other libraries. I cover working with InfoPath and form libraries in more detail in Chapters 9 and 10.

Wiki Page Library

The previous section briefly described wiki sites, and you saw that they provide a forum for users to add their own content on individual topics. So it should come as no surprise that wiki sites need a special type of library to support that user collaboration. SharePoint uses the Wiki Page Library as the storage container to hold all wiki page content.

Picture Library

The Picture Library provides a common place to store images for content pages in your site. You might also use a picture library to store images or photographs for your sales or marketing staffs to help them provide a consistent message. Picture libraries also provide a storage location for pictures used in web pages. You will learn more about picture libraries in Chapter 12.

Translation Management Library (MOSS 2007 only)

The Translation Management library is found only in MOSS 2007, where advanced site designers use it to manage translation workflows. A Translation Management workflow manages the process of routing a document to designated translators read from a Translators List. The workflow notifies each translator for the document of the task. As each translator finishes the translation of their copy of the document, they can mark their part of the workflow as complete. The entire workflow is not complete until all translators for the document have finished their translations.

Data Connection Library

When Office documents created with InfoPath or Excel need to interact with back-end data sources, you can store connection definitions centrally in using the Data Connection Library.

Slide Library

SharePoint provides the Slide Library to work specifically with PowerPoint 2007 to store individual slides. You will examine slide libraries in greater detail in Chapter 12.

Report Library (MOSS 2007 only)

The Report Library stores Excel Services reports, KPIs, and dashboards. You will examine report libraries in greater detail in Chapter 8.

Permissions and Groups

When your SharePoint administrator sets up a top-level site, she needs to determine who can view, edit, and design pages and content on the site. You may have a very simple site that everyone can view, or you may want to limit your site to only the people in your company, your department, or your project. You also need to decide who can contribute content to your site and who can make design changes or can approve content before making it visible to all. You may at first think you can do this on a person-by-person basis, but for most sites, you typically will have groups of people that you want to assign the same rights to. In fact, you may only have a small number of groups that require unique rights. For that reason, SharePoint allows you to associate users together in groups and then assign permission levels to those groups. Then when you need to assign permissions to a new user, you can simply determine which group he should belong in and assign him to that group to define his permissions.

You will encounter the site owner group first. When your SharePoint administrator creates a new site, he can associate up to two site owners to it. A site owner has all rights to the site, allowing her to add users and groups to the site, to customize or delete items within a site, and to create subsites under the current site.

The SharePoint administrator also determines when he creates the site whether the site allows anonymous access and whether anonymous access applies only to users authenticated through the domain or all users.

After the SharePoint administrator creates the site, the site owner can go into the site and add additional users to one of the default site groups. New sites begin with the three default groups listed here. Notice that each group name begins with the site name.

<Site Name> Visitors This group defines the lowest default security group, and SharePoint associates it with the Read permission level, which allows the group members only to view pages and items. They cannot contribute content. They may have the ability to create a Self-Service Site if the SharePoint administrator activated that feature. They then serve as administrators in these sites. The Read permission level grants the following individual permissions:

- View Items

- Open Items

- View Versions

- Create Alerts

- View Application Pages

- View Pages

- Browse User Information

- Use Remote Interfaces

- Use Client Integration Features

- Open a Web Site, List, or Folder

While your SharePoint administrator typically handles the creation of permission levels and security groups, you might be interested to know that SharePoint supports 32 different individual permissions, which you can combine in various ways into permission levels. The default Read permission level includes just the ten permissions previously listed.

<Site Name> Members SharePoint associates this group with another predefined permission level: Contribute. Compared to the Visitors group, this permission level has the additional rights to add, edit, and delete items and pages. Users in this group can work with web parts and create content. However, they cannot create new lists or libraries. Depending on how the SharePoint administrator defined the site, their content updates may require approval by a person with approval rights before others can see them.

<Site Name> Owners SharePoint associates the Owners group with the Full Control permission level. By default, this level includes all 32 individual permissions. Users assigned to this group can view, add, update, delete, approve, and customize all aspects of the site. They also have the ability to add new users and groups, as well as assign permissions and create new sites.

Should you decide not to include a new user in one of the predefined site groups, you can assign her to a permission level directly using the options in the **Give Permission** section of the **Add Users** page shown in Figure 1-8. Initially, SharePoint defines the following four permission levels, of which three are directly associated with one of the site groups just discussed:

- **Full Control**: Users with this permission level usually share the same permissions as the Owners group.

- **Design**: Designers can manage lists and libraries, create pages, and customize them. They may approve pages created by the Members group. They can also override check-out locks on lists and library items created by contributors.

- **Contribute**: Contributors can view, add, update, and delete content on the site, but they cannot approve that content on sites that require approval. Therefore, visitors to the site cannot see their changes until someone with the permission to approve them does so.

- **Read**: Readers can only view data on the site. They cannot contribute or change any content.

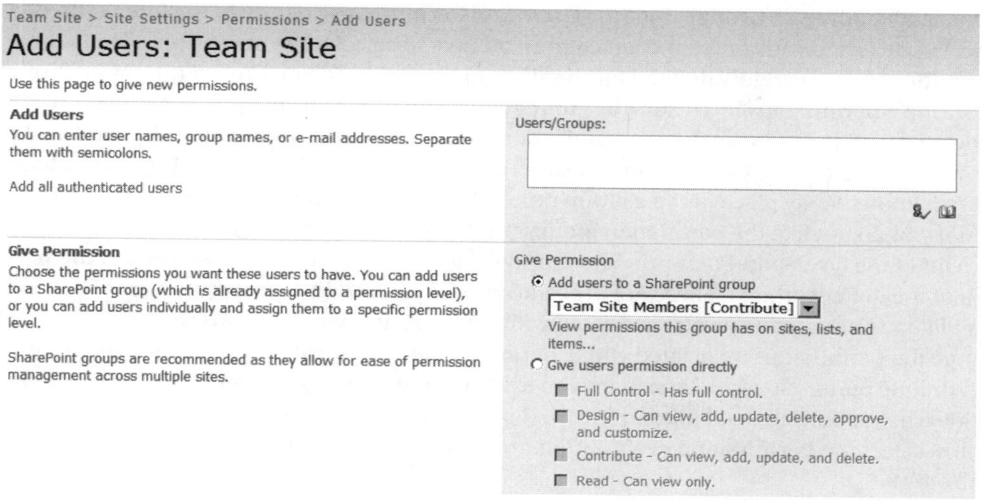

Team Site > Site Settings > Permissions > Add Users
Add Users: Team Site
Use this page to give new permissions.
Add Users
You can enter user names, group names, or e-mail addresses. Separate them with semicolons.
Add all authenticated users
Users/Groups:
Give Permission
Choose the permissions you want these users to have. You can add users to a SharePoint group (which is already assigned to a permission level), or you can add users individually and assign them to a specific permission level.
SharePoint groups are recommended as they allow for ease of permission management across multiple sites.
Give Permission
Add users to a SharePoint group
Team Site Members [Contribute]
View permissions this group has on sites, lists, and items...
Give users permission directly
Full Control - Has full control.
Design - Can view, add, update, delete, approve, and customize.
Contribute - Can view, add, update, and delete.
Read - Can view only.

Figure 1-8. *Permission options*

In addition to the default groups, you can add other groups or edit the permissions of existing groups. For example, you may want to create a separate group that has permission only to edit and approve list items, pages, and documents, but cannot add anything new. To do this, begin by opening the **Site Actions** drop-down menu on the upper right of the page and select **Site Settings**. Figure 1-9 shows this menu.

Site Actions
Create
Add a new library, list, or web page to this website.
Edit Page
Add, remove, or update Web Parts on this page.
Site Settings
Manage site settings on this site.

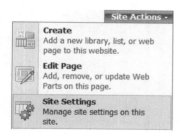

Figure 1-9. *Site Actions menu*

The **Site Settings** page displays options that change the way a site and the objects within the site look and react to users. SharePoint breaks down these options into five groups:

- **Users and Permissions**: Define users and their permissions.
- **Look and Feel**: Define the site's appearance. An option allows you to create a new site template from the current site.
- **Galleries**: Add reusable components here that can be used to build your sites.
- **Site Administration**: Manage the features of the site.
- **Site Collection Administration**: Options to manage the entire site collection. These options only appear when you open the **Site Settings** page from the top-level site.

Select **People and Groups** from the **Users and Permissions** column of the **Site Settings** page. On this page, look down the left column menu and select **Site Permissions**. This page shows the groups currently defined for the site and their permissions. You can see details of any group's permissions by clicking its group name. You can even change the permissions associated with the group, or you can add new groups with unique permissions by clicking the arrow to the right of the **New** button and selecting **New Group** or **Add Users**. If you add a user, you can immediately place her in a group rather than assign permissions to individuals. But what if you do not like the permission groups predefined by SharePoint?

Out of the box, SharePoint provides four permission levels and associates one of them to each of the default groups. These are the same groups you would add new users into. If you don't like the permission levels associated with these groups, you have two choices: either change the permissions associated with a permission level or create a new permission level with unique permissions and assign it to an existing or new group. However, before you can decide what to do, you need to examine what permissions make up each permission level. To do this, select the **Permission Levels** option from the **Settings** drop-down menu as shown in Figure 1-10.

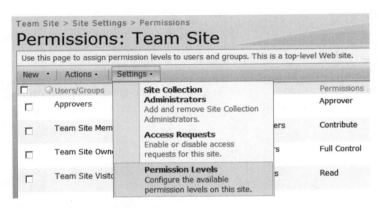

Figure 1-10. *Selecting the Permission Levels option*

The **Permission Levels** page shown in Figure 1-11 lists the permission levels that have been defined. Notice that you cannot access the Full Control and Limited Access permission levels, because these levels must always exist, and their definitions cannot change. The Full Control level belongs to site owners. The Limited Access level belongs to site guests who only have limited access to specific lists or documents libraries, not the entire site.

Suppose you decide to add a new permission level called **Approver**. Click the **Add a Permission Level** menu option near the top of the page to display the page shown in Figure 1-12. The first section asks you to provide a name and description for the new level. Then you can select from the possible permissions. SharePoint splits permissions into three major groups:

- **List Permissions**: Permissions related to list objects, including libraries

- **Site Permissions**: Permissions related to sites

- **Personal Permissions**: Permissions related to personalization

Team Site > Site Settings > Permissions > Permission Levels

Permission Levels

This Web site has unique permission levels.

⌸Add a Permission Level | ✕ Delete Selected Permission Levels

	Permission Level	Description
▣	Full Control	Has full control.
☐	Design	Can view, add, update, delete, approve, and customize.
☐	Contribute	Can view, add, update, and delete.
☐	Read	Can view only.
▣	Limited Access	Can view specific lists, document libraries, list items, folders, or documents when given permissions.

Figure 1-11. *Reviewing permission levels*

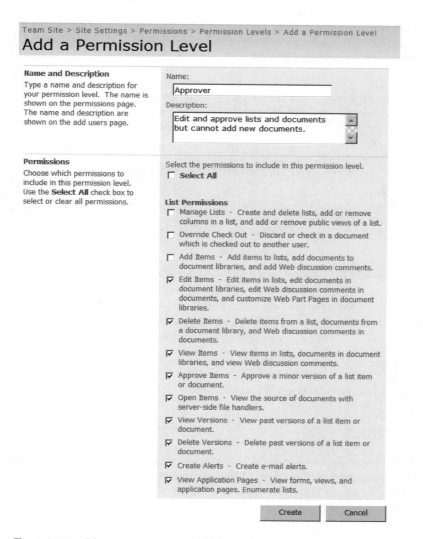

Team Site > Site Settings > Permissions > Permission Levels > Add a Permission Level

Add a Permission Level

Name and Description

Type a name and description for your permission level. The name is shown on the permissions page. The name and description are shown on the add users page.

Name:

    Approver

Description:

    Edit and approve lists and documents
    but cannot add new documents.

Permissions

Choose which permissions to include in this permission level. Use the **Select All** check box to select or clear all permissions.

Select the permissions to include in this permission level.

☐ **Select All**

List Permissions

☐ Manage Lists - Create and delete lists, add or remove columns in a list, and add or remove public views of a list.

☐ Override Check Out - Discard or check in a document which is checked out to another user.

☐ Add Items - Add items to lists, add documents to document libraries, and add Web discussion comments.

☑ Edit Items - Edit items in lists, edit documents in document libraries, edit Web discussion comments in documents, and customize Web Part Pages in document libraries.

☑ Delete Items - Delete items from a list, documents from a document library, and Web discussion comments in documents.

☑ View Items - View items in lists, documents in document libraries, and view Web discussion comments.

☑ Approve Items - Approve a minor version of a list item or document.

☑ Open Items - View the source of documents with server-side file handlers.

☑ View Versions - View past versions of a list item or document.

☑ Delete Versions - Delete past versions of a list item or document.

☑ Create Alerts - Create e-mail alerts.

☑ View Application Pages - View forms, views, and application pages. Enumerate lists.

[Create]   [Cancel]

Figure 1-12. *Adding a permission level definition*

Of course, you can select all of them by either clicking each check box individually or checking the **Select All** option. However, for your version of the Approver level, you want to selectively choose permissions that allow the user to view, edit, and approve items, but not create them or override a checkout. Therefore, you might make the permission selections shown in Figure 1-12.

When satisfied with the permissions selected for your new level, click **Create** to build the new permission level definition. Returning to the **Permission Levels** page, you will now see the Approver permission level.

At this point, you might go back to the **People and Groups** page for your site and add a group specifically for approvers: using the **New** drop-down menu at the top of the page, select **New Group**. In the **New Group** page, add the group name (**Approvers**) along with a description. You will see other options that allow you to add an owner for the group, change group settings, and handle membership requests. I will not detail these options here because your SharePoint administrator typically defines most of this for you. However, the last series of options allows you to define the permission level you want to give to this group for this site. As shown in Figure 1-13, you can see that a new permission level now appears, verifying the successful addition of the Approver level that you just created.

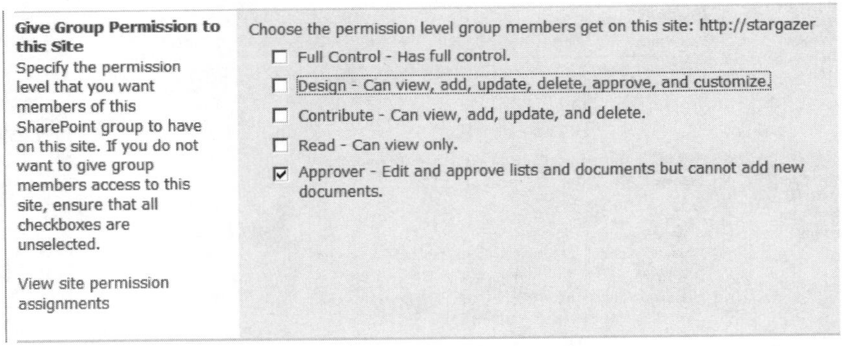

Give Group Permission to this Site
Specify the permission level that you want members of this SharePoint group to have on this site. If you do not want to give group members access to this site, ensure that all checkboxes are unselected.

View site permission assignments

Choose the permission level group members get on this site: http://stargazer

☐ Full Control - Has full control.

☐ Design - Can view, add, update, delete, approve, and customize.

☐ Contribute - Can view, add, update, and delete.

☐ Read - Can view only.

☑ Approver - Edit and approve lists and documents but cannot add new documents.

Figure 1-13. *Your new permission level appears when defining a new group.*

When you click **Create**, you will see the **Approvers** group in the **Groups** list along the left side of the **People and Groups** page. You can now add individual users or other groups to this new group.

■**Tip** You can nest one group inside another group. This can be faster than removing users from one group and adding them to another.

In summary, before adding users to a group, you need to determine what groups you need and what permissions those groups should have. Then you can work with your SharePoint administrator to create those groups and ensure that he adds users to the appropriate group.

Adding a Document Library

In most cases, when you first create a site, you get a default document library called **Shared Documents**. However, you may want to add your own document library with its own name. In fact, just like you would use multiple directories on your local hard disk or your file server for different file types or projects, you should use multiple document libraries in SharePoint to organize your documents.

To create a new document library for your specific document needs, click **View All Site Content** or **Documents** from the **Quick Launch** area to show your current document libraries. If someone has already created document libraries other than the **Shared Documents** library, you will see them here. Next, click the **Create** menu item at the top of the **Document Libraries** list as shown in Figure 1-14.

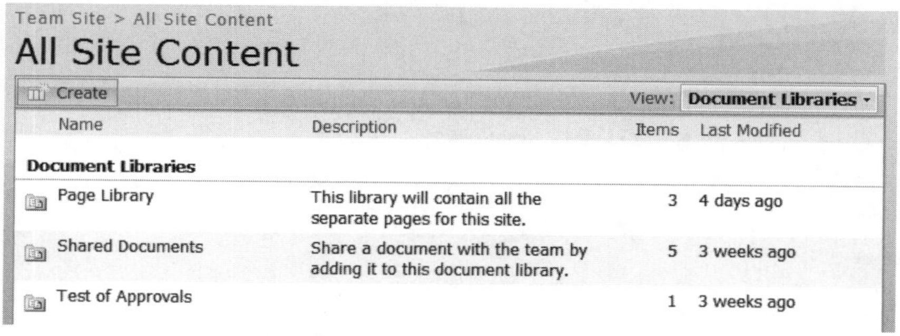

Team Site > All Site Content

All Site Content

	Name	Description	Items	Last Modified
Document Libraries				
	Page Library	This library will contain all the separate pages for this site.	3	4 days ago
	Shared Documents	Share a document with the team by adding it to this document library.	5	3 weeks ago
	Test of Approvals		1	3 weeks ago

View: Document Libraries ▾

Figure 1-14. *Adding a new document library*

The **Create** page lets you create several different object types for your site. SharePoint divides these object types into five categories:

- Libraries

- Communications

- Tracking

- Custom Lists

- Web Pages

Locate and click **Document Library** under **Libraries**. Figure 1-15 shows the options that you can define for a new document library. Besides specifying a name for your new library, you can supply a description for the library and define whether the library appears in the **Quick Launch** menu.

By default, the library does not support versions. In other words, when you make changes to documents in the library, the changes replace the previous versions. This document mode uses the least amount of storage space, but it leaves you unable to retrieve a previous document version to compare changes or to revert back to a previous version.

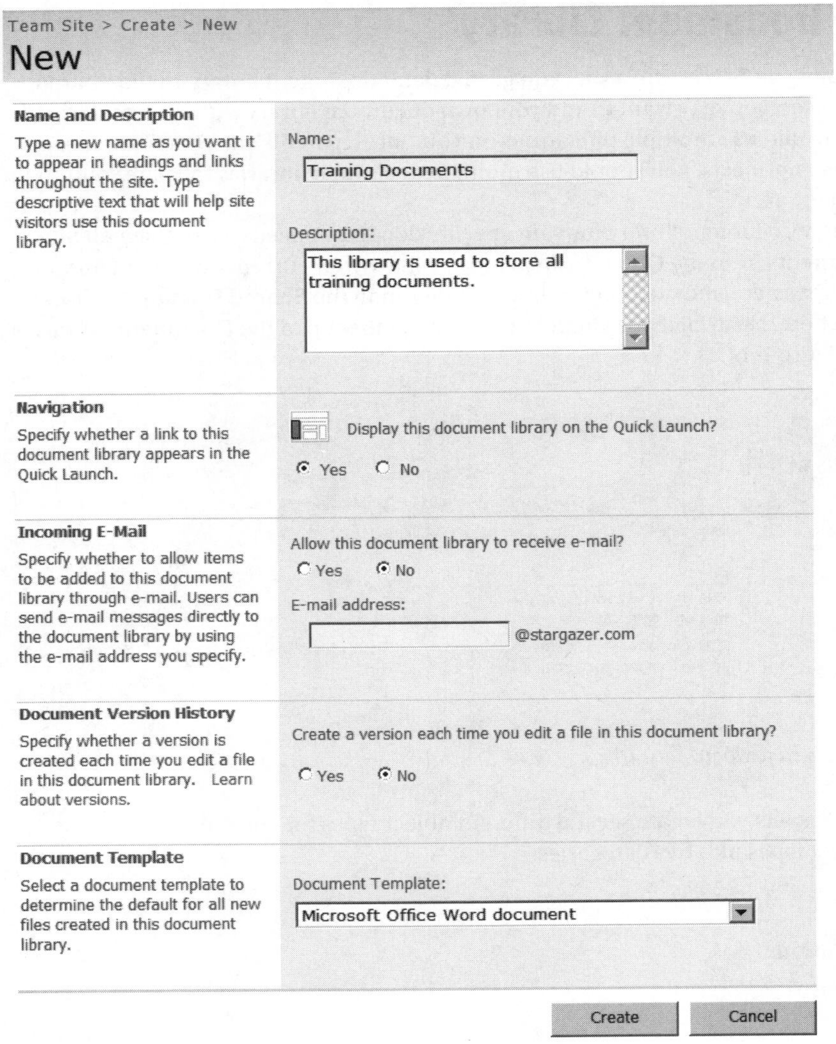

Team Site > Create > New
New

Name and Description

Type a new name as you want it to appear in headings and links throughout the site. Type descriptive text that will help site visitors use this document library.

Name:

    Training Documents

Description:

    This library is used to store all
    training documents.

Navigation

Specify whether a link to this document library appears in the Quick Launch.

    Display this document library on the Quick Launch?

    ⦿ Yes   ○ No

Incoming E-Mail

Specify whether to allow items to be added to this document library through e-mail. Users can send e-mail messages directly to the document library by using the e-mail address you specify.

Allow this document library to receive e-mail?

    ○ Yes   ⦿ No

E-mail address:

    [   ] @stargazer.com

Document Version History

Specify whether a version is created each time you edit a file in this document library.   Learn about versions.

Create a version each time you edit a file in this document library?

    ○ Yes   ⦿ No

Document Template

Select a document template to determine the default for all new files created in this document library.

Document Template:

    Microsoft Office Word document   ▾

                                            [Create]   [Cancel]

Figure 1-15. *Defining document library properties*

The last option lets you select a default document template when creating a new document within SharePoint for this library. Each library can have only one default template, so you should select the most likely document template for the library. Some SharePoint site designers create a separate library for each document type needed when they define custom templates. In Chapter 10, you will see how to define multiple content types for a single library.

After defining the options for your new library, click **Create** to build it. You can then add documents from your local or network drives (using the **Upload** option from the menu at the top of the library) or create new documents using the default template from within SharePoint (using the **New** option from the same menu).

■**Tip** While you can upload documents of different types into a single library, you may consider creating a separate library for each major document type you need to store, especially if you add a custom template to your document library. There are several advantages to this. First, users do not have to decide on a content type. They just click **New**. Second, you don't have to define different views to support the different metadata that might be associated with different content types. This topic is covered in later chapters when discussing metadata with libraries and multiple content types, with a particular emphasis in Chapter 10 on supporting multiple content types.

Knowing Your Document Templates

The **Document Template** section shown previously in the page in Figure 1-15 allows you to define a default template to use when you choose to create a new document directly from within the library. My default list of available templates includes the following:

- Microsoft Office Word 97–2003 document

- Microsoft Office Excel 97–2003 spreadsheet

- Microsoft Office PowerPoint 97–2003 presentation

- Microsoft Office Word document

- Microsoft Office Excel spreadsheet

- Microsoft Office PowerPoint presentation

- Microsoft Office OneNote section

- Microsoft Office SharePoint Designer Web page

- Basic page

- Web Part page

In this list, the difference between the two Word templates is that the template named Microsoft Office Word document defaults to the Word 2007 format, whereas the other defaults to earlier versions. A similar difference explains the multiple Excel and PowerPoint entries.

Each of these predefined templates represents blank Office templates or web pages. However, your SharePoint administrator may have also preinstalled document templates from which you can choose. For example, a folder for expense reports may have a blank formatted expense report form created in Word or Excel. These templates do not limit what you can save within the library. They merely define a default document type when you create a new document directly from within the library.

Adding Your First Document to Your New Library

When most people start using SharePoint for collaboration, they create a document library as one of their first tasks so they can store the files that they want to share with others. If you had your SharePoint administrator create a site for you or if you created it yourself, you probably noticed that a **Shared Documents** library already exists in your site. This library appears under **Documents** in the **Quick Launch** menu along the left side of the main site screen.

To open the **Shared Documents** library, click it. SharePoint opens a screen that displays a list of your shared documents. Of course, a new library has no documents in it. To create your first document, open the **New** menu at the top of the library list by clicking the down pointing arrow and then click **New Document** as shown in Figure 1-16.

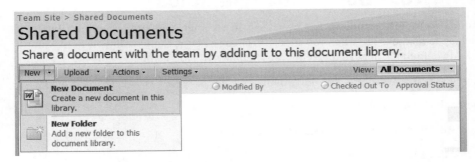

Figure 1-16. *Creating a new document*

■**Tip** You can also just click the **New** button to create a new document using the default content type.

This menu lets you create a new document or a new folder within the library to organize your documents. Let's continue by creating a new document.

If you select this option, SharePoint by default attempts to open a new Word document based on the default document template defined for the library. Even after you create the library, you can change the document template by pointing to a different file in the Forms folder of the library. You can place any Microsoft Office document in this folder and select it as the document template. For example, if you have a standardized expense report, you can create a separate document library, and add a blank expense report created in Word to the Forms folder of the library. Then point the document template URL for the library to that form. Now when you click **New** in this library, SharePoint displays a blank expense report for you to fill in rather than just a blank Word document.

CHANGING THE DEFAULT TEMPLATE FOR A DOCUMENT LIBRARY

In twelve easy steps, you can change the default template for any of your existing document libraries.

1. First create the document you want to use as a default template.

2. In SharePoint, open the library from the **Quick Launch** area or click **View All Site Content** if your library does not appear as a separate entry, and then click your library.

3. Open the **Actions** menu and select **Open with Windows Explorer**.

4. Browse to the template you created in step 1 (use the address bar to point back to your computer).

5. Right-click the file and select **Copy**.

6. In the Explorer view, click the **Back** button until you get back to the library's Forms folder.

7. Right-click a blank area and paste your document in this folder.

8. Close the **Explorer** window.

9. Select the **Settings** menu of the document library.

10. Click **Document Library Settings**.

11. Click **Advanced Settings** under the **General Settings** column.

12. Change the template URL to point to the file you pasted. The URL will look like

    /<LibraryName>/Forms/<TemplateName>

    where <LibraryName> is the library name and <TemplateName> is the name of the document pasted into the Forms folder in step 7.

The next time you create a new document in this library, it will default to the new template. In Chapter 10, you will learn how to set the default library template to an InfoPath form.

Assume for the moment that you want a new default document on this site, and you click **New Document**. Using the new document created by the default template, create a document. When finished, click **Save** in the **Office Button** menu of Word. Notice that when the **Save As** dialog box appears, it does not display files from your local directories. Rather, it displays a reference to the **Shared Documents** site.

Next enter a name for the document. Notice at the bottom of the **Save As** dialog box shown in Figure 1-17 that the document type is a Word 2007 document as identified by the .docx extension. When I created my site and the document library within it, I selected the default document type for the **Shared Documents** library; on my machine, which has Office 2007 installed, Word 2007 is correctly selected. Your installation default may vary depending on the version of Office you have installed on your machine.

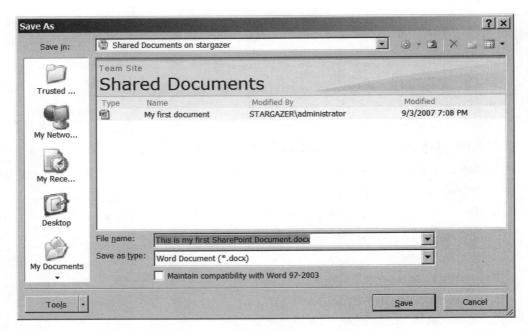

Figure 1-17. *Saving your new document to SharePoint*

If your **Shared Documents** library defaults to Word 2007 like mine, but you must share documents with people who have not yet switched to the new Word 2007 format, you should save your document in the 97–2003 format by clicking the check box **Maintain compatibility with Word 97–2003**. After entering a file name, click **Save** and then close Word.

Figure 1-18 shows that on returning to the Shared Documents folder in SharePoint, you will see your new document. SharePoint displays at least three default properties for each document. The first column displays an icon representing the document type. These are the same icons you see in Windows Explorer for different file types. Clicking the icon opens the file or folder. The second column displays the document name. Notice the green text after your file name: !NEW. SharePoint automatically adds this text to new documents as an indicator that the document has recently been added. This indicator displays for about 1 or 2 days, and then SharePoint automatically removes it. But in the meantime, it helps you identify new documents, especially if you have many people adding documents to the library.

In the third column, SharePoint displays the date and time that the file was last modified. SharePoint displays the name of the person who made the modification in the fourth column. If you click the person's name, a screen appears with information about that user. If the site administrator who added the new user included her e-mail address, you can send an e-mail to that person by clicking that e-mail address.

In addition to the user's name and e-mail address, this screen can include the person's photo, department, job title, and Session Initiation Protocol (SIP) address, which is an address used to uniquely identify the user.

The fifth column tracks who has a document locked for editing; you will learn more about this property in Chapter 2. SharePoint may not show this column. For now know that SharePoint tracks this information, but does not display it by default.

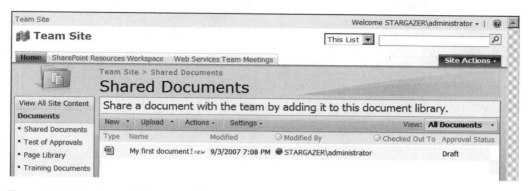

Figure 1-18. *Viewing your first saved document in the library*

The sixth column shown in Figure 1-18 only appears if the document library has the **Require content approval for submitted items** setting from the library's **Versioning Settings** page enabled and shows the current status of the document. In this figure, a status of **Draft** indicates that the document creator has not yet finished editing and preparing the document for publication. You'll learn more about approval of content in the section "Requiring Document Approval to Hide Drafts: A Simple Workflow" later in this chapter.

ADDING COLUMNS TO A VIEW

Documents have many more properties than shown in Figure 1-18. In fact, as with the **Checked Out To** column, SharePoint does not display many document properties unless you ask it to. After all, a screen row only has so much horizontal space.

To add another property to the **Document Libraries** list, click **Settings** in the top menu bar and then select **Document Library Settings**. Then scroll down to the **Views** section and click the **All Documents** view. The displayed page allows changes to the view name, columns, sort, filter, and many more properties. For now, focus on the **Columns** group. Notice that it displays over a dozen possible columns, of which only a few have their check box selected. Scan through the list until you find **Checked Out To**. Select this column by clicking the check box to its left.

You may have also noticed the drop-down lists to the right of each of the columns. The numbers in these fields define the column order from left to right. To change the order, click the column you want to reposition and change the position value. SharePoint adjusts affected columns between the old and the new value by one to make room for the moved column.

Now when you return to the **Shared Documents** library, you will see a new column telling you who checked out the document. As with the **Modified By** column, you can use the information stored about the user to send an e-mail to him asking when he might finish using the document.

If the person also uses MSN Messenger, Live Messenger, or a compatible presence aware-ness application such as Microsoft Office Communicator, an icon appears before the person's name. The color of the ball indicates the user's status as shown in Table 1-1. When you hover over the colored ball, it opens a menu as shown in Figure 1-19.

Table 1-1. *Messenger Status Indicator*

Color of Icon	Status
Green	Online
Orange/Red	Busy/In a call
Yellow	Be right back/Away/Out to lunch

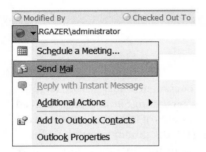

Figure 1-19. *Options for Modified By person*

Uploading a Document

If you previously created documents to upload to your **Shared Documents** site, click the **Upload** button in the library's menu bar. Figure 1-20 shows the **Upload Document** screen.

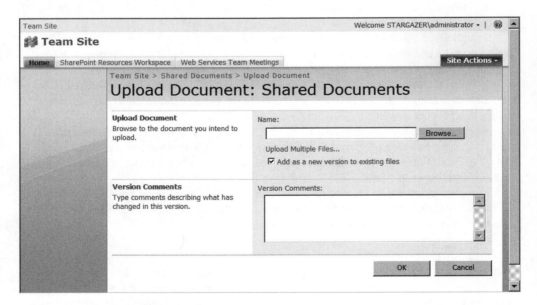

Figure 1-20. *Uploading a document*

In this screen, you have three options for selecting files to upload:

- You can directly enter the name of the document that you want to upload.

- You can click the **Browse** button to open a browse window to find and select the file to upload.

- You can click the **Upload Multiple Files** option to upload more than one file in a single operation.

I'll let you explore the first two options on your own. However, the third option proves rather useful when uploading groups of existing documents. When you click this link, the window shown in Figure 1-21 appears.

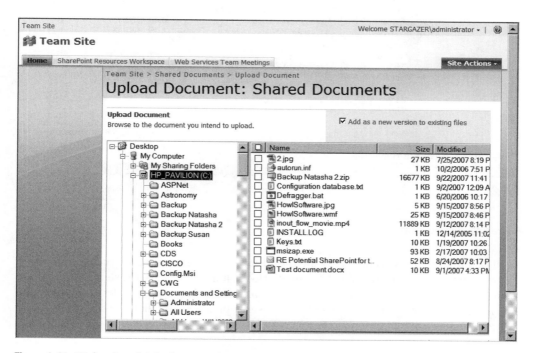

Figure 1-21. *Upload multiple documents screen*

Note that this screen consists of two parts. Use the tree structure on the left to navigate the drives and directories you have rights to. You can even open **My Network Places** to retrieve files stored on another computer. The list on the right side of the screen displays the files in the selected folder. A check box precedes each file name. To upload a file, click the check box before the name. By clicking the double check box in the title bar of the file list to the left of the column header **Name**, you can quickly select all files in the current directory for upload. This saves you time if you build your SharePoint site from previously created documents. Note also that you can check the box to overwrite existing files already in the SharePoint directory. If you do not check this option and you select a file that already exists in the library, SharePoint will not upload the file, even if the file selected has a more recent modified date than the version SharePoint already has. Finally, you can select multiple check boxes but only within the currently selected folder. Figure 1-22 shows several files marked for upload.

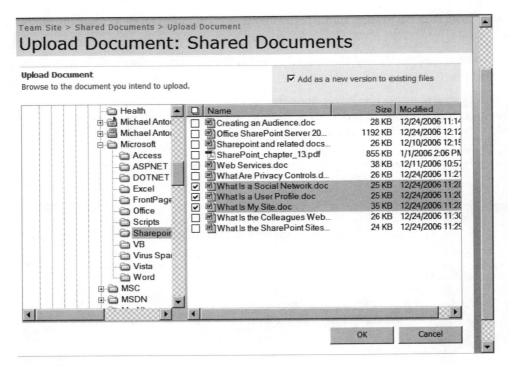

Figure 1-22. *Selecting multiple files to upload*

To complete your selection, click the **OK** button. SharePoint prompts you with a message box to confirm your desire to upload documents to the library. Click **Yes** to execute your upload request. SharePoint then takes a few moments to retrieve and upload your files. The amount of time needed depends on the number of files you are uploading and their sizes.

■**Note** By default, sites limit uploads to 50MB for the entire upload, whether it consists of a single file or multiple files. However, this setting can be changed by your SharePoint administrator by going into **Central Administration**, selecting the **Application Management** tab, and then selecting **Web Application General Settings** under the group **SharePoint Web Application Management**. On the resulting page, she can update the field associated with the **Maximum Upload Size** option. Therefore, your maximum upload size may be different from the default.

Figure 1-23 shows the **Shared Documents** library after uploading the selected documents from Figure 1-22.

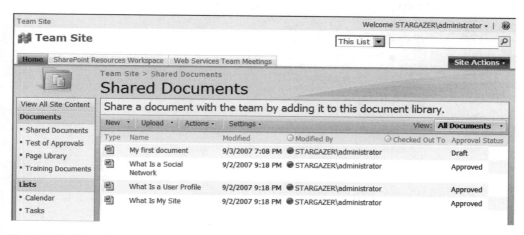

Figure 1-23. *Shared Documents library after uploading multiple documents*

You may not have noticed that the uploaded documents were Word 2003 files in the DOC format. Looking at the list of four Word documents in the **Shared Documents** library, how can you tell a Word 2003 document from a Word 2007 document? The icons to the left of the file name do have a small difference, but an easier way exists. When you hover over the document icon with your mouse, a tooltip style box appears below the cursor with the full file name, which also displays in the **Status Bar** at the bottom of the window. Either way, the file's extension suggests the version of Word used to create that document.

You can change the sort order of your document list by clicking the column header by which you want to sort. The first time you click the column header, SharePoint sorts that column in ascending order, and it displays a small up arrow to the right of the column name. The second time you click the column header, SharePoint sorts that column in descending order and adds a small down arrow to the right of the column name.

You can also sort a column by hovering over a column header to highlight it. On the right side of the column header, a drop-down arrow appears. Click this arrow to open a menu of options that allow you to sort the column. In addition to sorting, the drop-down list allows you to filter the list based on values in the selected column. Figure 1-24 shows that you can filter document types based on their extension.

■**Note** You cannot filter the **Name** column.

If you select the .doc filter from the **Type** column, the library displays only the three documents stored as Word 2003–style documents. SharePoint does not delete the Word 2007–formatted document when it applies a filter, it merely hides it. You could add an additional filter on another column, in which case SharePoint displays only documents that match the filters from both columns.

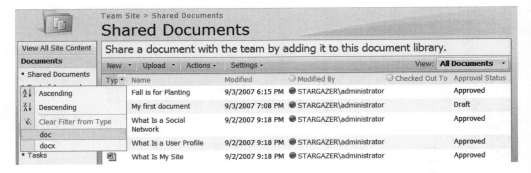

Figure 1-24. *Filtering the shared documents in a library*

■Note A column with an active filter displays a funnel to the right of the column name.

To remove filters, open the drop-down for each column that has a filter and select the **Clear Filter** option.

Displaying Documents in the Datasheet View

Before looking at how to edit a document in the library, let's look at two other ways to view your documents. You can access both methods from the **Actions** menu at the top of the **Shared Documents** page.

Figure 1-25 shows the first alternative view: **Edit in Datasheet**.

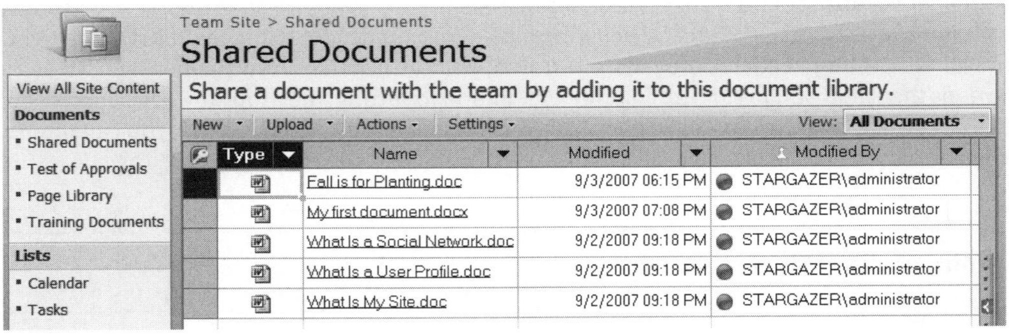

Figure 1-25. *Library displayed in Datasheet View mode*

As you can see, this view displays the same information as the **Standard View**. In **Datasheet View**, notice the icon in the upper-left corner of the table. This icon resembles the icon used by Access. In fact, SharePoint displays the list of documents as a table because that is exactly how it stores document information in SQL Server.

This view also supports the ability to sort and filter the information displayed. However, rather than hovering over the column header, click the down arrow to the right of the column header name as shown in Figure 1-26 to open the menu.

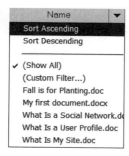

Figure 1-26. *Sorting and filtering in Datasheet View mode*

Notice that the sort options appear at the top of the list in this figure. Beneath the sort options you will find the filter options. In addition to filtering on specific values found in the selected column, you can define a custom filter. This feature can help you find documents in large libraries when you only remember a part of their file names. Figure 1-27 creates a custom filter in which the values in the **Name** column must begin with the word "What."

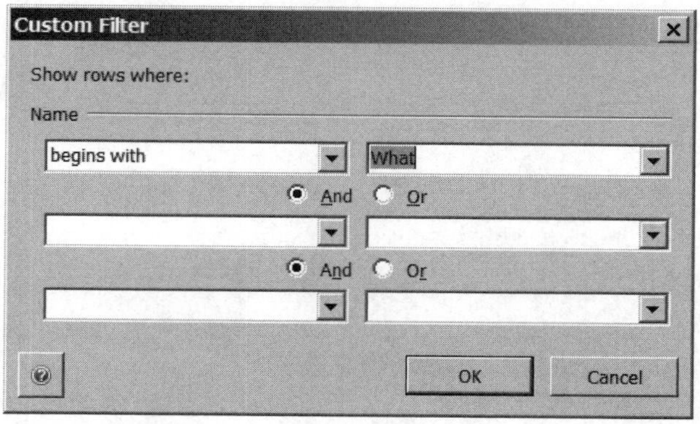

Figure 1-27. *Defining a custom filter*

Note You can filter on any displayed column within the library using this method. For example, if the document list displays a **Created By** column, you can filter on documents created by a specific person.

When defining a custom filter, you can specify up to three expressions for the filtered column. You can then connect each of these expressions with either an **And** or an **Or**. When you connect expressions with **And**, the expressions on either side must be true for that document to appear in the library list. When you connect expressions with **Or**, only one of the two expressions must be true for the document to appear. If you use expressions connected with both **And** and **Or** connectors, SharePoint executes the expressions from the left to the right. The **And** expression does not have precedence over the **Or** expression.

Tip Use the **Datasheet View** if you have to make changes to a custom column across many of the documents in the library. You can edit the data in the columns in this mode just like you edit data in an Excel spreadsheet.

Displaying Documents in Windows Explorer

The last way you will look at the document library in this chapter begins by opening the **Actions** drop-down menu and selecting **Open with Windows Explorer**. This action opens a separate window and displays the documents using Windows Explorer. This view has an interesting feature. If you open a second Windows Explorer session from your desktop, you can drag and drop files between the two windows. In other words, this view provides another way to upload documents into SharePoint libraries. In Figure 1-28, you can see two separate Windows Explorer sessions. The figure shows that I have just selected the file `Fall is for Planting.doc` from a directory in my local machine and dragged it into the **Shared Documents** library.

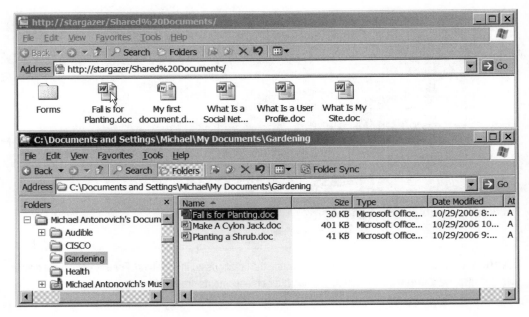

Figure 1-28. *Dragging and dropping documents into SharePoint*

When you return to your SharePoint session, you may need to refresh your page, but you will see that the new file now appears in the **Shared Documents** list.

Editing Documents Stored in Your Library

After you have saved several documents to your library, you probably at some point want to edit them. You can choose from several ways to edit a document depending on your currently selected library view.

Editing a Word Document from Standard View

Suppose you want to edit one of the Word documents previously added to the library. Open the **Shared Documents** library. Hover the cursor over the name of the document you want to edit. Notice that SharePoint surrounds the document name with a box and a drop-down arrow to the right. It also underlines the document name, changing it to a hyperlink. You can edit this document by either clicking the document icon or its hyperlinked name. This action opens the dialog box shown in Figure 1-29 that lets you open the document for editing or just view it in **Read-Only** mode.

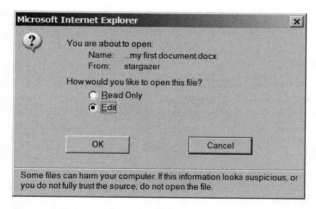

Figure 1-29. *File download prompt*

By default, SharePoint tries to open documents as read-only files. You should open documents this way if you only want to view, download, or print a copy of the document. This allows other people to open the document for editing. However, if you need to edit the document, click the **Edit** option before clicking **OK**.

Even if you forget to select **Edit** and open the document as read-only, Word displays a bar across the top of the opened document that allows you to switch to **Edit** mode as shown in Figure 1-30.

Figure 1-30. *Switching a document to Edit mode*

Once in **Edit** mode, you can make changes to the document and save them by clicking **Save** in the **Office Button** menu.

You can also begin editing a document by clicking the down arrow displayed to the right of the document name when you hover over the name to open the drop-down menu. This drop-down menu shows options available for that document. Select **Edit in Microsoft Office Word** as shown in Figure 1-31 to edit the document.

Figure 1-31. *Choosing to edit in Microsoft Word*

Editing a Document from Datasheet View

If you prefer to use the **Datasheet View** of your documents, you can also initiate editing of a document by right-clicking in the **Name** field of the document you want to edit. This opens a drop-down menu of available options. Move down to the **Document** option to display a submenu. This submenu, shown in Figure 1-32, presents options to open the document in **Read-Only** or **Edit** mode.

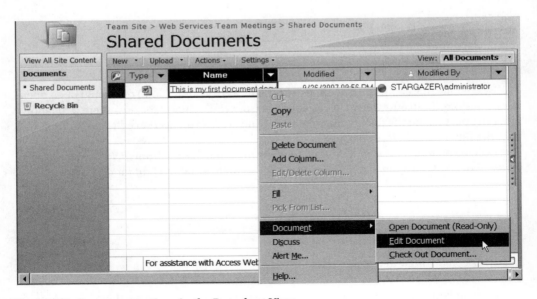

Figure 1-32. *Document options in the Datasheet View*

The **Edit Document** option opens the document in **Edit** mode assuming no one else has the document open for editing. If they do, SharePoint can only open the document in **Read-Only** mode.

Under the **Actions** menu, you can also display your document library using Windows Explorer. While Windows Explorer does not directly show all the document options presented in either the **Standard View** or the **Datasheet View**, it still recognizes when someone else has the document open and by default tries first to open the document in **Read-Only** mode.

So now you know several different methods of opening a document for editing. But what happens when someone attempts to open your document while you have it open in **Edit** mode?

Simple Locking of Documents

When you open a document in **Edit** mode with one of the preceding methods, the document is temporarily locked. If another user attempts to open the document while you have it open, he receives a warning message like the one shown in Figure 1-33.

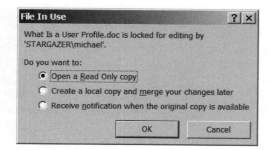

Figure 1-33. *"File in Use" message*

When SharePoint locks a file, it gives you three choices of what to do (actually four if you count closing the dialog box and going away):

- Open a read-only copy.

- Create a local copy and merge your changes later.

- Receive notification when the original copy is available.

Let's assume that you really do need to edit the document, not just view or print it. In that case, you could select either the second or third option. I will cover option two in Chapter 4. Option three provides an interesting alternative. With this option, you can ask SharePoint to notify you when the other person closes her copy of the document so you can open it. With this option, you do not have to even keep the read-only version of the document open. You can focus on another task, and when the document becomes available for editing, SharePoint sends you a message like the one shown in Figure 1-34.

When you receive this message, click the **Read-Write** button to begin editing the document, or if you no longer need to make the changes, click the **Cancel** button to make the file available to others.

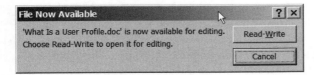

Figure 1-34. *"File Now Available" message*

For most quick changes, working in **Edit** mode as described in this section with the automatic locking that SharePoint provides may not pose a problem. However, the default SharePoint locking does not last forever. In fact, depending on the operating system used by the person editing the document, the lock may only guarantee exclusive use of the document for 15 to 30 minutes. Thus, if you need more time than that to edit the document, you could have a concurrency problem.

What Is a Concurrency Problem?

A concurrency problem occurs when two or more people open a document for editing at the same time. As an example, say you open a document in the **Shared Documents** library. After 30 minutes, suppose that you still have the document open, but you leave for lunch without closing the document. Now Natasha from the office down the hall opens the same document. Since more than 30 minutes have passed, SharePoint no longer maintains the lock on the document. So Natasha opens the document, makes her changes, and saves them. Finally, you come back from lunch an hour later and realize that you have not closed your document. So you click **Save** and close the document.

Later that same day, Natasha goes back into the document to check one of her changes and discovers that she cannot see her changes. Furthermore, the document looks entirely different from the one she edited. She wonders, did someone delete her changes?

Well actually yes, someone did delete her changes, but not intentionally. When you came back from lunch and saved the document, SharePoint happily overwrote the existing version in the library, the one containing Natasha's changes.

Because Windows XP holds a lock on a file for only 15 minutes by default, relying only on this basic lock functionality when opening a document can lead to problems. If you have Windows Vista, you can keep a file open for 30 minutes while the automatic lock remains in place. For quick changes, 15 to 30 minutes should provide adequate editing time. However, when you need to make major changes to a document, you may want to use a feature called Check-Out first before you edit the document.

Why Use Check-Out and Check-In?

Using Check-Out results in a more secure way to lock a document before opening it for editing. This manually applied lock stays in place until you decide to check the document back in. That means you can keep a document checked out for an hour, a day, or even longer without worrying about someone else making changes to the document while you have it. Think of Check-Out as getting exclusive control over a file, like checking a book out of a physical library. While you have it checked out, no one else can check it out. (Well, almost no one—I'll get to that in a moment.) But unlike your public library down the street, when you check out a document from a SharePoint library, other people can come in and open a read-only copy of the last saved version.

Checking out a document has other advantages. Both the **Standard View** and the **Datasheet View** can show you the name of the person who has the document open. Therefore, if you really need to get to that document, you can just walk down the hall, call him, or instant message him to ask when he will finish editing the document so you can open it to make your changes.

How to Check Out a Document

To check out a file when using **Standard View**, open the drop-down menu for the document and select **Check-Out** as shown in Figure 1-35.

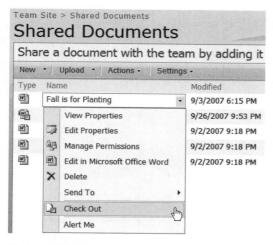

Figure 1-35. *Checking out a document in Standard View*

After you check out a file, you still must return to the drop-down menu to select **Edit** in Microsoft Office Word to open the document in Word. However, from the time you check out a file until the time that you check it back in, you have exclusive access to the file. Remember, if you choose to display the **Checked Out To** column in your **Shared Documents** view, you will see who has documents checked out. This feature does not exist if you rely on the automatic locks provided by simple document editing. However, if you attempt to edit the document, the **File in Use** dialog box shown earlier in Figure 1-33 will display the name of the user who has the file open for editing. Figure 1-36 shows an example of how the **Standard View** looks when someone has checked out the document "Fall is for Planting."

If you check out a document and realize you picked the wrong document or you no longer need to make changes to that document, select the **Discard Check Out** option, which only appears in the drop-down menu after you have a document checked out.

When you check out a document, SharePoint asks whether you want to save a copy of the document in your local drafts folder as shown in Figure 1-37. If you do not click this option, SharePoint creates a copy on the server that you can edit. However, saving intermediate changes to the server takes more time, and only by saving a copy in your local drafts folder can you work on the file offline, a topic that I will cover in Chapter 4.

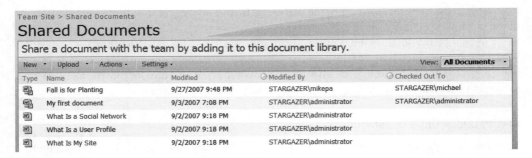

Figure 1-36. *Checked out files listed in Standard View*

Figure 1-37. *Saving a copy in your local drafts folder*

■**Note** You may need to make your SharePoint site a trusted site in your Internet Explorer Security options before you can use your local drafts folder.

Once you check out a document, you can edit the document for hours or even days if necessary. When you are done, make sure that you save your changes, close Word, and then check the document back in. Saving your changes and closing Word does not automatically check in the document. Good office etiquette requires that you only check out a file for as long as necessary to make your changes. Keeping a file checked out longer than necessary merely prevents others from getting their work done.

If someone were to not notice the checked out information in the **Shared Documents** listing and attempt to edit this document anyway, she would receive the warning shown in Figure 1-38.

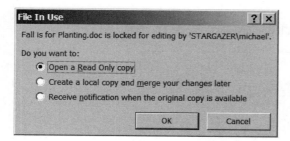

Figure 1-38. *"File in Use" warning*

Checking Documents Back into the Library

When versioning is not turned on, SharePoint does not make visible your intermediate changes until you check the document back into the library. This functionality differs from editing a document without checking it out. In that case, every time you save the document, whether you close Microsoft Word or not, other users can see your changes.

When versioning is turned on and you edit a document directly, each time you save your changes, SharePoint creates a minor version of the document. When you check in the document, other users with permission to edit can open your document and make further edits. Minor versions of the document may or may not be visible to users with only Read permission, depending on the **Draft Item Security** setting in the library's **Versioning Settings**. Thus, you can use this setting to determine whether users with Read permissions can see minor versions of the document. When you check out a document to your local drafts folder, SharePoint hides all changes until you check the document back in because you are working with a local copy of the document. At that time, the user saving the document can assign the update a minor or a major revision number and provide revision comments.

When you close the Word session used to edit the document, a message prompt reminds you that SharePoint does not make changes visible to other users until you check the document in. If you have not finished with your changes but merely want to go to lunch, click **No**. However, if you have finished, click **Yes** to check your document back in as shown in Figure 1-39.

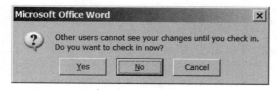

Figure 1-39. *Prompt to check in changes*

When you check in changes with versioning turned on, SharePoint provides several alternatives to label your new version as shown in Figure 1-40.

> ■**Note** You will not see the **Check In** dialog box if your site does not use versioning.

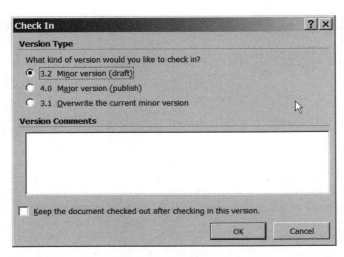

Figure 1-40. *Select check-in version and add comments via the Check In dialog box.*

By default, SharePoint labels your checked-in version with the next available version number. If your site only uses major versioning (whole numbers), SharePoint increments the version by 1. If your site uses minor versioning, SharePoint increments the version by 0.1. If your site supports minor versions, you must decide when to accept the next available minor version number or instead use the next major version number. How you decide depends on you, but if you made major changes to a document, you probably should go with the next major version number. Alternatively, if you started from a previous draft version and only made a few spelling corrections, you could simply replace the current version. How your SharePoint administrator has set versioning in your library may also affect which option you can choose.

In addition to selecting the version for your changes, you can enter comments about the new version. In the comments section, you should include information about the changes you made, who requested them, who approved them, or what impact the change will have on your organization. You can view these comments when you display a document's version history (which you'll learn more about in the upcoming section, "Tracking Document Versions").

Overriding a Check-Out

Previously I stated that a document checked out by a user cannot be edited by anyone else. However, suppose you absolutely must get into a document, but the person who checked it out has left for a two-week Mediterranean cruise. If you have administrator rights to the document library, you can right-click the document and select **Check-in** to bring up a dialog box asking you to confirm you want to override the check-out as shown in Figure 1-41.

> **Tip** If you do not have the rights to override a checked-out document, contact your SharePoint administrator or the site owner. She can either check in the document or modify your rights to allow you to override a check-out.

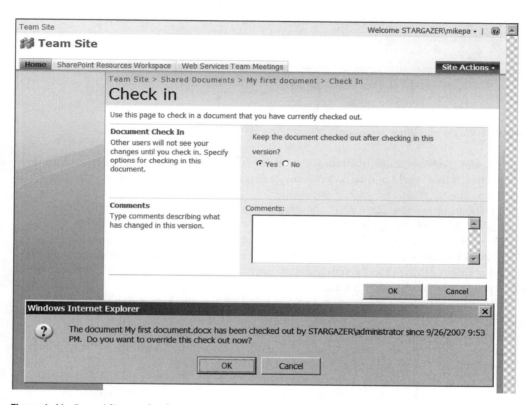

Figure 1-41. *Overriding a check-out.*

When an administrator overrides a checked-out document, the user who had originally checked out the document may lose some of his changes unless he edited it from his local drafts folder. Therefore, it is good office etiquette to let the other user know that you had to override his checked-out document while he was out of the office.

Tracking Document Versions

When your SharePoint administrator turns on document versioning, SharePoint stores multiple copies of each document, representing saved changes to the document. To see the versions for a document, click the down arrow when hovering over a document name in a library and select **Version History**. Figure 1-42 displays the versions for the document Fall is for Planting.doc in the Shared Documents folder.

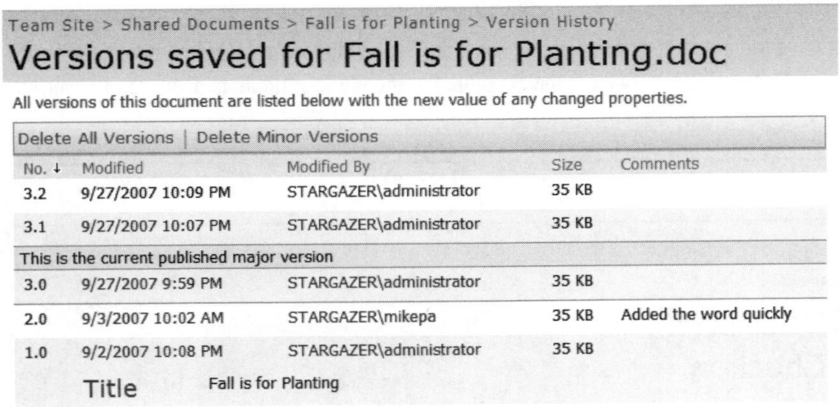

Team Site > Shared Documents > Fall is for Planting > Version History

Versions saved for Fall is for Planting.doc

All versions of this document are listed below with the new value of any changed properties.

Delete All Versions	Delete Minor Versions			
No. ↓	Modified	Modified By	Size	Comments
3.2	9/27/2007 10:09 PM	STARGAZER\administrator	35 KB	
3.1	9/27/2007 10:07 PM	STARGAZER\administrator	35 KB	
This is the current published major version				
3.0	9/27/2007 9:59 PM	STARGAZER\administrator	35 KB	
2.0	9/3/2007 10:02 AM	STARGAZER\mikepa	35 KB	Added the word quickly
1.0	9/2/2007 10:08 PM	STARGAZER\administrator	35 KB	
	Title	Fall is for Planting		

Figure 1-42. *Displaying a document's version history*

Notice the version history of the selected document includes both major and minor revisions. Recall that whole numbers define major versions, and minor versions contain decimal portions like 2.1.

Depending on how you use your **Shared Documents** library, you may not want to track minor versions. Including an approval process for content is the primary reason to consider tracking minor versions. When doing this, you might only allow a specific group of people defined as content creators to have the ability to view and edit both major and minor versions of a document. However, only a content approver can publish a new version of a document. Everyone else may only view the most recently published version.

In the case of using document approvals, consider a major version to be one ready for the general public to read. Within an organization, you might designate a project group to have access to both major and minor versions of a document. However, the rest of the organization sees only major versions representing finished documents from the group that only change periodically.

Your SharePoint administrator may also limit the number of both major and minor versions that SharePoint stores. After all, the more versions you track, the more disk space you need. Therefore, a SharePoint administrator may allow you to store only the last three major releases and the minor releases made from the current release. Figure 1-43 shows how a SharePoint administrator might configure versions so that only users with permission to edit can view minor releases, and minor versions are kept only since the last major version.

■**Tip** To change the version settings, select **Document Library Settings** under the **Settings** drop-down menu of the **Standard View** of the library. On the **Customize Shared Documents** page that appears, select **Versioning settings** in the **General Settings** section.

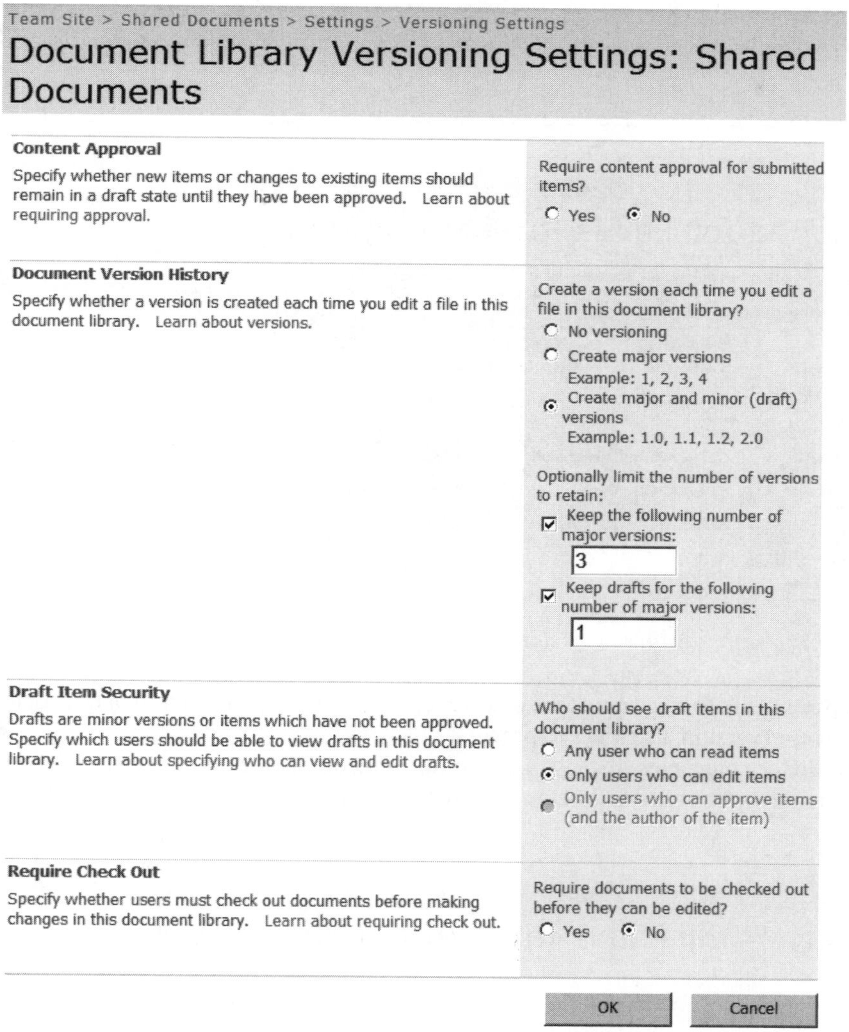

Team Site > Shared Documents > Settings > Versioning Settings

Document Library Versioning Settings: Shared Documents

Content Approval

Specify whether new items or changes to existing items should remain in a draft state until they have been approved.   Learn about requiring approval.

Require content approval for submitted items?

○ Yes   ⦿ No

Document Version History

Specify whether a version is created each time you edit a file in this document library.   Learn about versions.

Create a version each time you edit a file in this document library?

○ No versioning

○ Create major versions
Example: 1, 2, 3, 4

⦿ Create major and minor (draft) versions
Example: 1.0, 1.1, 1.2, 2.0

Optionally limit the number of versions to retain:

☑ Keep the following number of major versions:

[3]

☑ Keep drafts for the following number of major versions:

[1]

Draft Item Security

Drafts are minor versions or items which have not been approved. Specify which users should be able to view drafts in this document library.   Learn about specifying who can view and edit drafts.

Who should see draft items in this document library?

○ Any user who can read items

⦿ Only users who can edit items

○ Only users who can approve items (and the author of the item)

Require Check Out

Specify whether users must check out documents before making changes in this document library.   Learn about requiring check out.

Require documents to be checked out before they can be edited?

○ Yes   ⦿ No

[OK]   [Cancel]

Figure 1-43. *Defining versioning settings*

Promoting a Prior Version to the Current Version

Occasionally, you may need to return to a previous version of a document. Perhaps the change you added to a policy document has been rescinded by management, and they want the previous policy statement reinstated. Of course, you could edit the current document and hope to reverse all the changes, returning the document to its previous content. That could entail a major effort fraught with the potential of missing a change. It is far easier to simply view the version history for the document and select the prior version, making it the current version.

To do this, first check out the document from the **Standard View**. Then select **Version History** in the document's drop-down menu. Next, hover over the **Modified Date/Time** of the version you want, and click the **Restore** option in the menu as shown in Figure 1-44.

■**Note** If you do not first check out the document, SharePoint displays an error message informing you to first check out the document.

Team Site > Shared Documents > Fall is for Planting > Version History

Versions saved for Fall is for Planting.doc

All versions of this document are listed below with the new value of any changed properties.

Delete All Versions	Delete Minor Versions			
No. ↓	Modified	Modified By	Size	Comments
3.2	9/27/2007 10:09 PM	STARGAZER\administrator	35 KB	
3.1	9/27/2007 10:07 PM	STARGAZER\administrator	35 KB	
This is the current published major version				
3.0	9/27/2007 9:59 PM	STARGAZER\administrator	35 KB	
2.0	9/3/2007 10:02 AM ▾	STARGAZER\mikepa	35 KB	Added the word quickly
1.0	9/2/200	View	STARGAZER\administrator	35 KB
	Title	Restore	Planting	
		Delete		

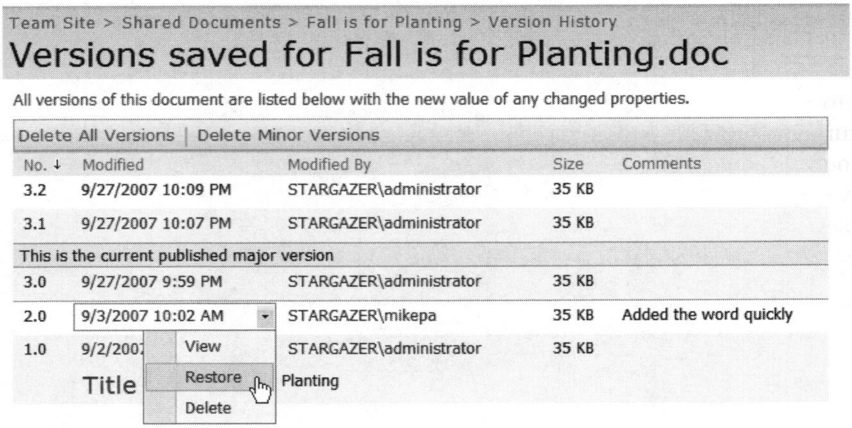

Figure 1-44. *Restoring a prior document version*

SharePoint prompts with a warning that you are replacing the current version of the document with the selected version. Click **Yes** to proceed.

The **Version History** page now displays a new minor version of the document as shown in Figure 1-45. When you open this document, you see that it is a copy of version 2.0 selected in Figure 1-44.

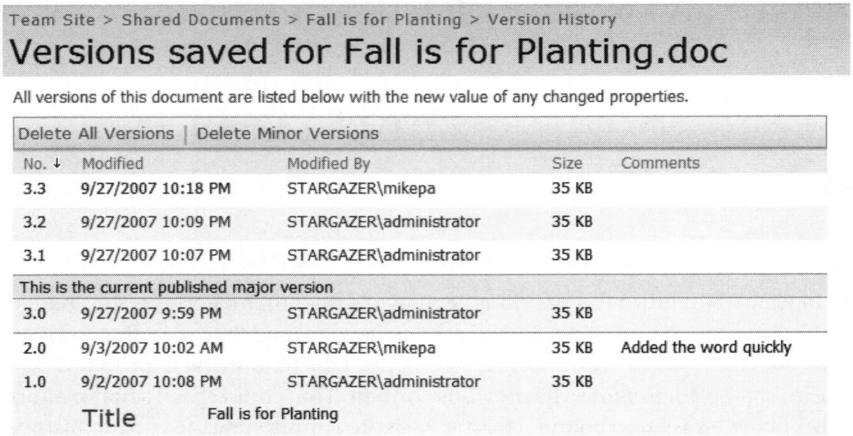

Team Site > Shared Documents > Fall is for Planting > Version History

Versions saved for Fall is for Planting.doc

All versions of this document are listed below with the new value of any changed properties.

Delete All Versions	Delete Minor Versions			
No. ↓	Modified	Modified By	Size	Comments
3.3	9/27/2007 10:18 PM	STARGAZER\mikepa	35 KB	
3.2	9/27/2007 10:09 PM	STARGAZER\administrator	35 KB	
3.1	9/27/2007 10:07 PM	STARGAZER\administrator	35 KB	
This is the current published major version				
3.0	9/27/2007 9:59 PM	STARGAZER\administrator	35 KB	
2.0	9/3/2007 10:02 AM	STARGAZER\mikepa	35 KB	Added the word quickly
1.0	9/2/2007 10:08 PM	STARGAZER\administrator	35 KB	
	Title	Fall is for Planting		

Figure 1-45. *New version created from a prior version*

Publishing Documents to Your Document Library

If your site requires content approval, you can only approve and publish major versions of a document. So when you promote a prior document version as shown in the last section, or when you add minor version changes to your document, your changes may not be immediately visible to everyone. In fact, even without content approval, users other than the content creators and approvers may not be able to see minor versions based on the version settings in the library. Obviously, you do not want to publish every minor version. To avoid this, you could ask your SharePoint administrator to turn off minor versioning, thus effectively turning every saved version into a major version.

When you turn off all versioning, management of the document library becomes informal. Only do this if you do not need to save previous versions. This practice reduces the amount of space needed by your site. However, if you ever need a prior version of a document, you may be out of luck unless you can restore one from a backup copy of the database. However, retrieving documents from a backup copy of the database requires time and a separate place to restore it. Such extra work will not earn you bonus points with your SharePoint administrator.

To publish your most recent document, return to your `Shared Documents` folder and open the drop-down menu associated with that document. Notice that it shows the document as still checked out because the **Check In** option appears. Click the **Check In** option, and the page shown in Figure 1-46 appears. This page allows you to determine whether you want to keep the document as a minor version or publish it to the next major release number.

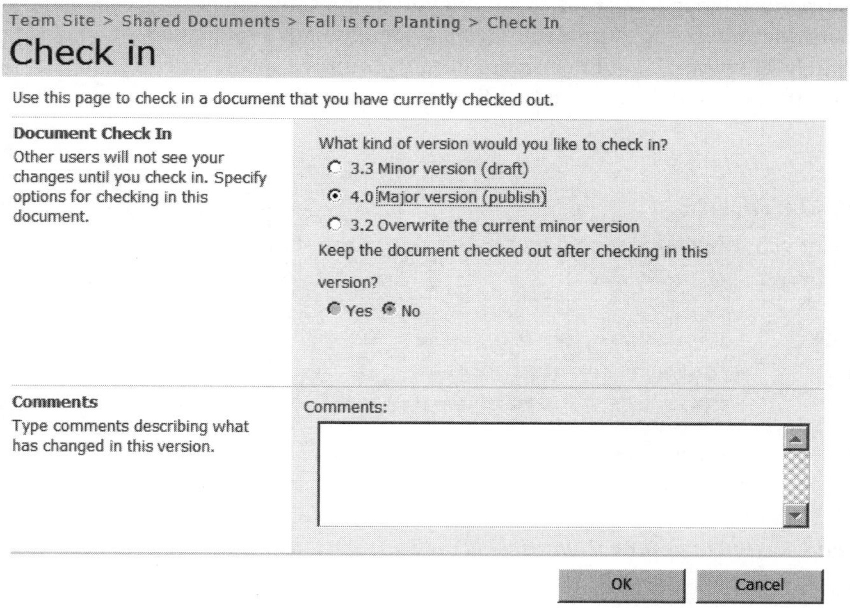

Team Site > Shared Documents > Fall is for Planting > Check In

Check in

Use this page to check in a document that you have currently checked out.

Document Check In

Other users will not see your changes until you check in. Specify options for checking in this document.

What kind of version would you like to check in?

- ○ 3.3 Minor version (draft)
- ◉ 4.0 Major version (publish)
- ○ 3.2 Overwrite the current minor version

Keep the document checked out after checking in this version?

○ Yes ◉ No

Comments

Type comments describing what has changed in this version.

Comments:

| OK | | Cancel |

Figure 1-46. *Publishing a restored document during check-in*

If you choose to leave the document as a minor version, you can always return to the document later in the **Standard View**, open the drop-down menu, and click **Publish a Major Version**. As shown in Figure 1-47, you can add comments when you publish a major version, documenting what has changed since the last major version.

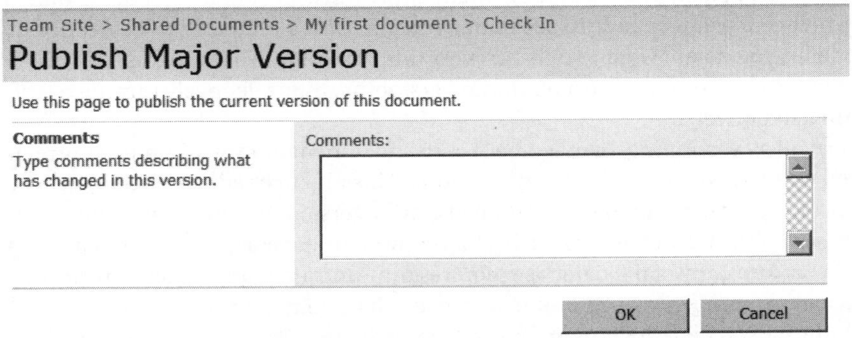

Team Site > Shared Documents > My first document > Check In
Publish Major Version

Use this page to publish the current version of this document.

Comments	Comments:
Type comments describing what has changed in this version.	

OK   Cancel

Figure 1-47. *Publishing a major version*

Notice the message at the top of Figure 1-47. If your **Shared Documents** library requires approval of major document changes before the public can view the latest document version, SharePoint displays this message. Click **OK** to submit your request to publish this version for approval. If the site does not require approval, saving a document as a major version makes it public immediately. However, if your document library requires approval, saving a major version merely sets the status of the page to **Pending** as shown in Figure 1-48.

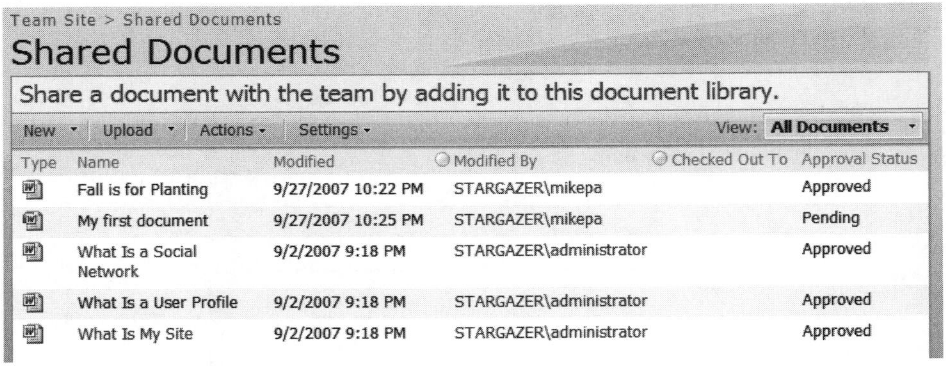

Team Site > Shared Documents
Shared Documents

Share a document with the team by adding it to this document library.

New ▾ Upload ▾ Actions ▾ Settings ▾   View: **All Documents** ▾

Type	Name	Modified	○ Modified By	○ Checked Out To	Approval Status
📄	Fall is for Planting	9/27/2007 10:22 PM	STARGAZER\mikepa		Approved
📄	My first document	9/27/2007 10:25 PM	STARGAZER\mikepa		Pending
📄	What Is a Social Network	9/2/2007 9:18 PM	STARGAZER\administrator		Approved
📄	What Is a User Profile	9/2/2007 9:18 PM	STARGAZER\administrator		Approved
📄	What Is My Site	9/2/2007 9:18 PM	STARGAZER\administrator		Approved

Figure 1-48. *Viewing document approval status*

SharePoint adds the column **Approval Status** automatically when your SharePoint administrator requires documents on your site to be approved before publishing them.

To approve the content, log in as someone with approval permission. If you have approval permission, go to the **Shared Documents** page and open the drop-down menu for the document. Notice you now have a new option: **Approve/reject**. Clicking this option displays the page shown in Figure 1-49.

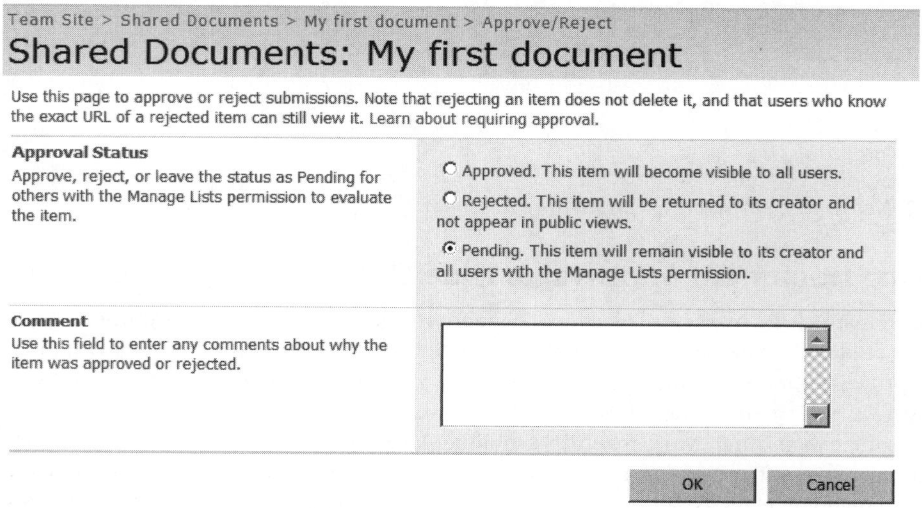

Figure 1-49. *Approving a document for publishing*

As you can see in this figure, approvers have three possible actions they can select for this request:

- **Approve:** The document becomes visible to all users.

- **Reject:** The document does not become public. This option returns the current source to its creator.

- **Pending:** The document remains in its current state. This option can be used by approvers when asking for further clarification.

No matter what action the approver selects, she can include a comment. An approver should always include comments when rejecting a document or sending it back pending additional work, information, etc. When the approver selects **Approve** and clicks **OK**, SharePoint publishes the page, making it available to all viewers of the site, and in the **Shared Documents** page, the approval status is changed to **Approved.**

Figure 1-50 looks at the version history for this document. You see a new major release (2.0) now listed and all the minor releases from version 1.0 have been removed. This occurs because the version setup defined in Figure 1-43 tells SharePoint to retain only minor releases for the current major release.

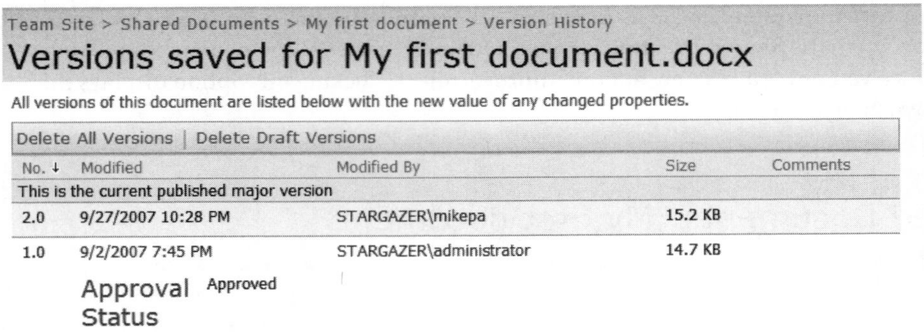

Figure 1-50. *New major release after publishing document*

Requiring Document Approval to Hide Drafts: A Simple Workflow

Workflows constitute an important feature of collaboration. Most business environments pass documents created by one person to two or more people for review, further editing, and ultimately approval before publishing them. In the past, organizations implemented workflows by physically transferring a document from one office to another via interoffice mail or by walking it from one office to another. More recently, e-mail replaced the need to physically move most documents between offices. However, even with e-mail, organizations have an inherent need for the person who receives a document to know who to send the document to next. Workflows can automate that entire process.

Workflows manage the flow of documents through various stages and, based on the action taken at any stage, determine who should receive the document next. Workflows also manage the development of a document from initial draft through editing, approval, and finally publishing. Also, since SharePoint carries out all steps in the workflow electronically, it is possible to locate where each document exists in the flow and where bottlenecks slow down the process.

For simple document approval, use the document library's **Versioning settings**. Open the library you want to work with and choose **Document Library Settings** from the **Settings** drop-down menu at the top of the **Library** list. From the settings page, click **Versioning settings** in the **General Settings** group. Define the versioning settings similar to those shown in Figure 1-51. These settings turn on content approval for new and edited items. Use major and minor version history to track multiple draft versions prior to publishing a major version. Then set the **Draft Item Security** so that only the content author and people who have approval permission can view the draft documents. Finally, select the **Require Check Out** option to force SharePoint users to check out the document before editing it.

A simple workflow begins with the content creator. While working on a document, SharePoint sets the document status to **Draft**. Once the content creator completes a document, he submits it for approval, which changes the status to **Pending**. An approver may approve, reject, or leave a document in a pending state (refer back to Figure 1-49). Some approvers may have permissions to perform basic editing tasks, or their rights may limit them to verifying the information in the document. If the approver rejects the document, SharePoint sets the status to **Rejected**. Similarly, SharePoint changes the status of an approved document to **Approved**.

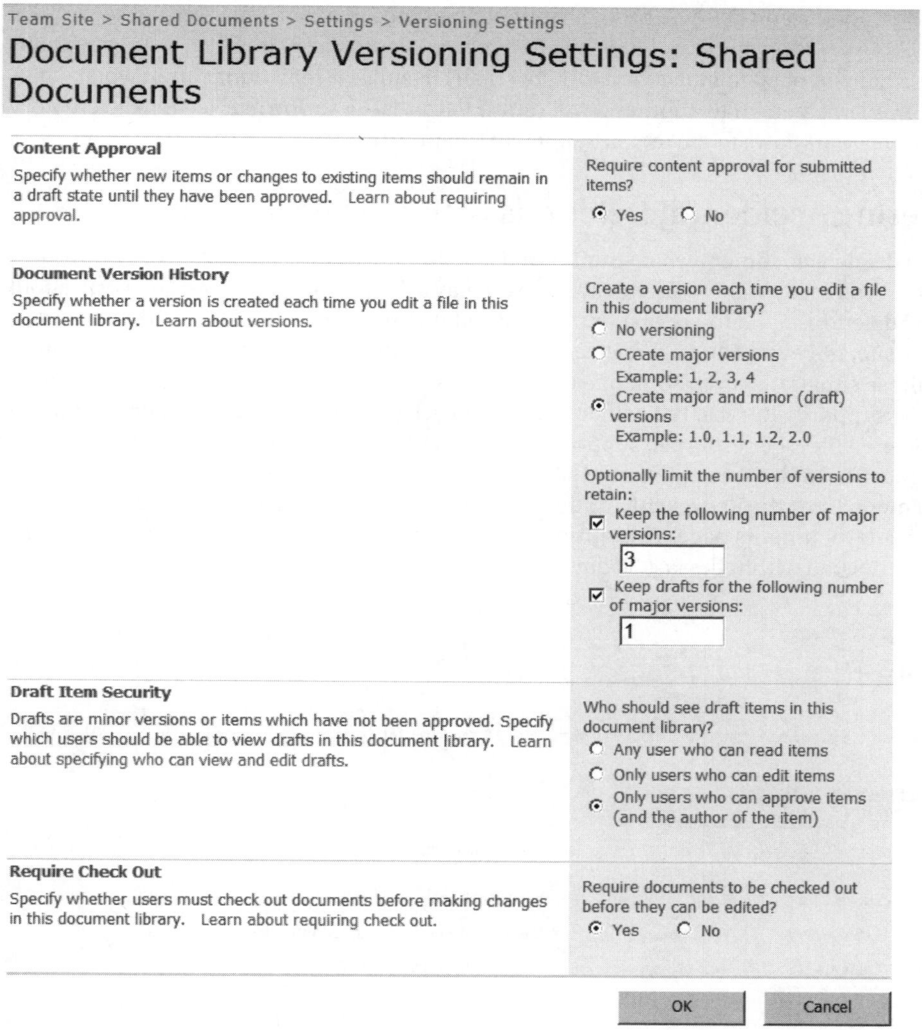

Team Site > Shared Documents > Settings > Versioning Settings

Document Library Versioning Settings: Shared Documents

Content Approval

Specify whether new items or changes to existing items should remain in a draft state until they have been approved.   Learn about requiring approval.

Require content approval for submitted items?

◉ Yes   ○ No

Document Version History

Specify whether a version is created each time you edit a file in this document library.   Learn about versions.

Create a version each time you edit a file in this document library?

○ No versioning

○ Create major versions
Example: 1, 2, 3, 4

◉ Create major and minor (draft) versions
Example: 1.0, 1.1, 1.2, 2.0

Optionally limit the number of versions to retain:

☑ Keep the following number of major versions:

`3`

☑ Keep drafts for the following number of major versions:

`1`

Draft Item Security

Drafts are minor versions or items which have not been approved. Specify which users should be able to view drafts in this document library.   Learn about specifying who can view and edit drafts.

Who should see draft items in this document library?

○ Any user who can read items

○ Only users who can edit items

◉ Only users who can approve items (and the author of the item)

Require Check Out

Specify whether users must check out documents before making changes in this document library.   Learn about requiring check out.

Require documents to be checked out before they can be edited?

◉ Yes   ○ No

[OK]   [Cancel]

Figure 1-51. *Library Versioning settings for document approval*

This simple workflow for a document allows documents to remain hidden while in draft mode, usually requiring a person other than the content creator to approve the document. However, at this level, SharePoint provides no dynamic notification to approvers when a document has been submitted for approval. Nor does SharePoint provide notification to the content creator when the approver changes the document status to approved or rejected. Rather all parties must constantly monitor the status of documents in the various libraries. If you only have a single library, this may not seem like a major inconvenience. However, if you support several sites, each of which has multiple document libraries and lists, manually checking the status of documents and lists will probably not happen on a regular basis. You will see in Chapter 2 how to set up alerts and RSS feeds, which you could use to monitor changes to your libraries. What you need to make this workflow really useful is e-mail notification when a task is passed from one person to another. I will return to this issue so you can see how to create more complex workflows to make this happen in Chapter 10.

Recovering Accidental Deletions with the Recycle Bin

When you delete a document from your **Shared Documents** library, SharePoint prompts you to confirm that you really want to delete the file. You may ask why you would need to worry about accidental deletions. I did too at first, until I realized that with more than one person having access to a site, not everyone may realize the value of the documents you decide to publish.

For those situations when someone accidentally deletes a document, both WSS 3.0 and MOSS 2007 support a Recycle Bin, which like the Recycle Bin on your desktop, allows you to recover deleted files. For example, suppose you accidentally deleted the file My first document.docx from the Shared Documents folder and then realized that you really need to keep that document. Click the **Recycle Bin** option at the bottom of the **Quick Links** menu on the left of the **Shared Documents** page. This option, shown in Figure 1-52, displays a page listing all documents deleted within the last 30 days.

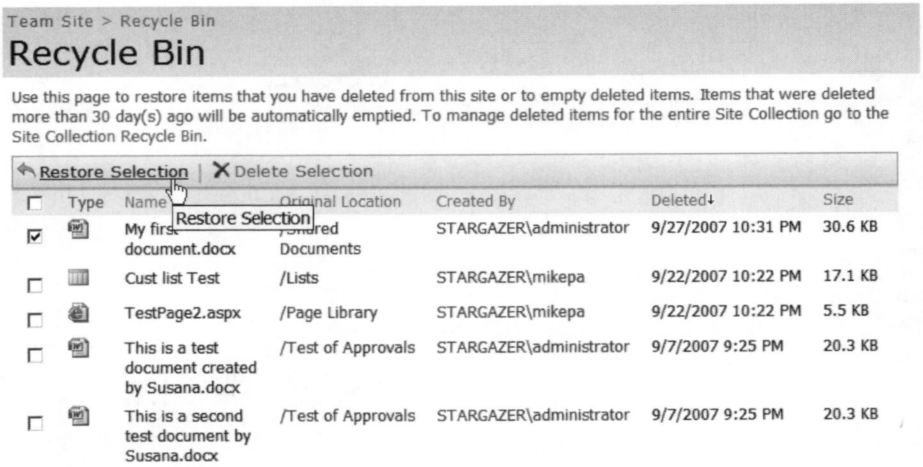

Team Site > Recycle Bin
Recycle Bin

Use this page to restore items that you have deleted from this site or to empty deleted items. Items that were deleted more than 30 day(s) ago will be automatically emptied. To manage deleted items for the entire Site Collection go to the Site Collection Recycle Bin.

↶ **Restore Selection** | ✕ Delete Selection

	Type	Name	Original Location	Created By	Deleted↓	Size
☑		My first document.docx	/Shared Documents	STARGAZER\administrator	9/27/2007 10:31 PM	30.6 KB
☐		Cust list Test	/Lists	STARGAZER\mikepa	9/22/2007 10:22 PM	17.1 KB
☐		TestPage2.aspx	/Page Library	STARGAZER\mikepa	9/22/2007 10:22 PM	5.5 KB
☐		This is a test document created by Susana.docx	/Test of Approvals	STARGAZER\administrator	9/7/2007 9:25 PM	20.3 KB
☐		This is a second test document by Susana.docx	/Test of Approvals	STARGAZER\administrator	9/7/2007 9:25 PM	20.3 KB

Figure 1-52. *The Recycle Bin collects all deleted documents.*

To recover a document, click the check box to the left of the document and click the **Restore Selection** option at the top of the page.

When you delete a document, you delete all versions of that document as well. You may be surprised to learn that when you recover a document from the Recycle Bin that you also recover all versions of that document as well. So rather than thinking of files in your document library as single files, think of them as a small collection of files with the same name.

■**Tip** You can ask your SharePoint administrator to change the length of time items stay in the Recycle Bin. She can go into Central Administration and select the **Application Management** tab. Then by selecting the **Web Application General Settings** page, the administrator can scroll down to the **Recycle Bin** section and change the number of days items are kept in the Recycle Bin.

Summary

This chapter began by looking at how SharePoint organizes sites into a hierarchical structure starting with a top-level site and nesting additional sites within it. If you are using WSS 3.0, you can choose from ten collaboration and meeting site templates. If you are using MOSS 2007, you have additional templates grouped under the group titles of enterprise and publishing templates. Remember that a template just provides a starting point for building your site. You can find many of the features that are available in one template in other templates as well. This allows you to customize a template no matter which one you start with.

Next, I showed you how to add users and permissions to a site. By default, when you create a new site under the top-level site or even another site, you can simply inherit the permissions used on that site from its parent. This can save you a lot of time. However, if you need to customize the permissions or the users who have access to your site, you can add users for specific sites as well as assign them to custom group definitions having custom permission levels.

After defining which users can access a site, you typically will start building content for the site. Therefore, the text examined one of the library types provided by SharePoint, document libraries. A document library can hold just about any type of file. However, most Microsoft Office users think first of Microsoft Word documents. Therefore using Microsoft Word, you saw how to create new documents in the library as well as upload existing documents. With respect to editing these documents, anyone with a compatible client application can edit a document stored in a library. However, unless the library forces documents to be checked out or you manually check out the document first, you could have concurrency problems. Also, if you check out a document, remember to check the document back in so others can see your changes and to allow others to make further changes to the document.

Document versions allow you to track changes made to the document. You can track both major and minor versions. Keep in mind that visitors to your site may only be able to read major versions. Therefore, you can use minor versions as working documents within your team until you are ready to publish the final version, and then save the document as the next major version.

You can also use the document approval feature to allow documents to remain hidden until someone with approval permission can release the document. Organizations often use this model when publishing information that the general public can view on internet pages. They may allow nearly everyone in the organization the permission to create new documents or to edit existing documents. However, until an approver reviews those documents, the general public cannot see them.

Finally, the chapter closed with a brief look at the Recycle Bin. This feature helps you recover documents accidentally deleted. However, as you will see in later chapters, it works with many other SharePoint objects, including objects shared with Microsoft Office tools.

The next chapter extends this introduction to SharePoint to lists and Chapter 3 to content web pages.

SharePoint Lists
Everything Is a List

Well, perhaps not everything. But SharePoint stores most content information for collaboration sites in lists, or some may say variations of lists. That should come as no surprise considering that SharePoint uses SQL Server as a storage container for all content information as well as for information used to define the appearance of your site. Lists translate well into the table paradigm of databases.

This concept brings up an interesting observation. One could say that SharePoint even stores the document libraries discussed in Chapter 1 in a special type of list. By adding unique attributes to those of a basic list, SharePoint can create not only libraries, but also many other types of lists. In this chapter, we will examine SharePoint's built-in lists and then explore how to create and use custom lists.

Exploring SharePoint's Built-in List Types

SharePoint provides a variety of predefined lists grouped by two or more categories (depending on whether you are using WSS 3.0 or MOSS 2007). First we will explore the communications lists.

Communications Lists

A communications list generally facilitates the exchange of information between the users of a site. It coordinates basic interaction between the columns and the items of the list. You can create one of these lists by choosing **Create** from the **Site Actions** menu. The **Create** page divides the objects that you can create into five categories. Under the **Communications** group, you see three list types:

- **Announcements**
- **Contacts**
- **Discussion Boards**

Announcements List

Many collaboration templates include by default an announcements list. Announcements list upcoming events or activities that you want your site readers to know about. An announcement consists of a title, a body, and an expiration date, the last being supported because most announcements have time sensitivity.

Figure 2-1 shows a list with four announcements. The first one refers to a breakfast meeting with the new CIO on September 10. This announcement expires on September 11 because after the 10th, it serves no purpose. You should use expiration dates to ensure that your announcements remain timely and to eliminate the need for you to manually monitor your lists on a daily basis to remove announcements for past events. Although SharePoint does not remove expired announcements, when you use the **Expires** field together with a filter on the view, you can automatically hide expired items from display. This way, you can always go back and view historical announcements should you need to.

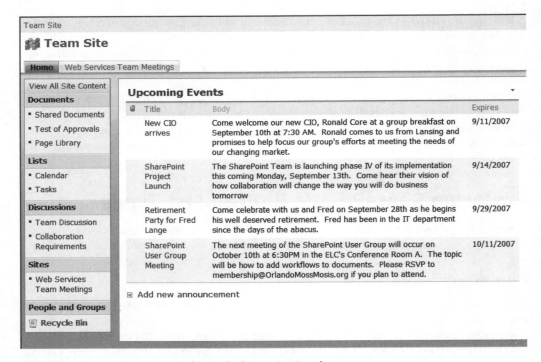

Figure 2-1. *This announcements list includes expiration dates.*

Tip   In the view definition used to display announcements, open the **Filters** section, select the **Expires** column, and set it to be greater than or equal to **[Today]**. This filter hides expired announcements automatically.

Perhaps you have visited web sites that contain notices for past events. Not only does this annoy visitors to the site, but it places an additional burden on the site support staff to constantly monitor the site content and remove expired information. Let SharePoint perform this task for you.

Contacts List

A contacts list lets you place the names and important contact information about people you work with in a convenient-to-reference spot on your site. Figure 2-2 shows a typical contacts list labeled as **Office Contacts**. It displays the first and last name of each contact along with his business phone and e-mail address.

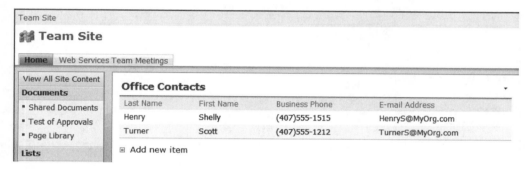

Figure 2-2. *Using a list to display your contacts*

If you're a newcomer to SharePoint, you may wonder if you must display all columns in a list. The simple answer is no. A list consists of a collection of columns (think of columns as fields) arranged by items (think of items as rows). Then you create or modify views of that list to display the specific columns you want displayed. You can also sort and filter the list if desired. A list can have many views, with each one displaying a different column subset, a different sort order, or a different filter. In this contacts list example, the view only shows four columns. Not only are there other fields available to you that are not displayed on this list, but you can also add custom fields to your list specific to your needs, and I'll show you how to add new columns in the section "Building a Custom List" and modify existing columns in the section "Modifying the Columns in Your List" later in this chapter.

The contacts list includes two hyperlinks. The first hyperlink, on the contact's last name, displays a page containing additional data for this contact. Here you can update the contact's information or set an alert to notify you if the contact's information changes. The second hyperlink, on the e-mail address field, opens your e-mail application and creates a blank message form for this contact.

WHAT IS AN ALERT?

An *alert* is a flag set within SharePoint to notify you via e-mail when a change occurs to the selected item. You can define when you want to receive alerts and for what types of changes you want them. Of course, their real value is that they alleviate the need to take time to monitor lists and libraries where you have an interest in tracking changes or additions.

Discussion Board List

Some people associate the discussion board list for internal use within a company with an Internet-style newsgroup used across companies. Both support multiple messages related to each topic. Both allow you to group messages chronologically or by thread subject. A SharePoint discussion board supports columns such as the discussion subject and body, the name of the user who created the message and the creation date, as well as user-defined columns. You might implement a discussion board list on topics where you want feedback from members of your organization or when you need to provide a place where they can post comments, questions, or concerns. Figure 2-3 shows a discussion board for a new collaboration project used to obtain opinions from the staff concerning features needed for collaboration.

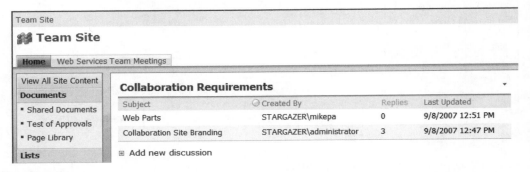

Figure 2-3. *Showing subjects in a discussion board list*

Figure 2-3 shows a subject listing of the discussion topics. Note that the first discussion thread has no replies at the moment, while the second topic already has three replies. To view these replies, click the subject. This action displays a new page with only the messages related to the selected subject displayed in a hierarchy view called a *thread view*.

In a thread view, SharePoint indents a message reply a small amount from the message it replies to. Multiple replies to the same message have the same indent. In Figure 2-4, users MikePA and SusanA respond to the original message from the administrator. User NatashaA responds to SusanA's message. Note that from this view, you can reply to any message at any level within the thread by clicking the **Reply** button to the right on the reply header.

Over time, a single message thread spawns multiple branches off the main thread as people explore different issues. The thread approach to displaying messages helps organize what might otherwise be a confusing chronological sequence of messages into a rational conversational sequence.

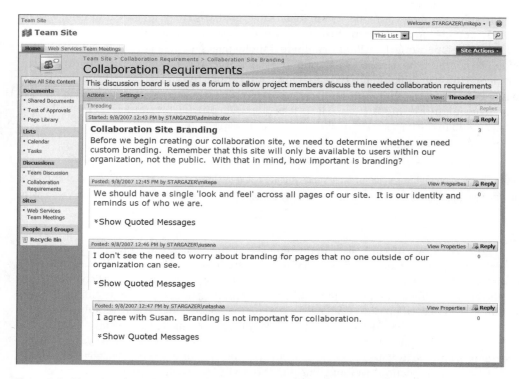

Figure 2-4. *Showing threaded messages within a discussion board subject*

Tracking Lists

You can create a variety of tracking lists by clicking **Create** from the **Site Actions** menu. These lists help you to keep track of pieces of information such as links to other pages or sites, calendar events, tasks, issues, or even surveys. In fact, when you look under the **Tracking** group, you will find these six list types:

- **Links**

- **Calendar**

- **Tasks**

- **Project Tasks**

- **Issue Tracking**

- **Survey**

- **Agenda**

Links List

You might think of the links list as the simplest of the lists in the **Tracking** group, as it consists of a collection of links to other pages. Once you have more than about a dozen links, you might want to start grouping your links within folders to organize them. With a custom field, which I'll show you how to add later in the chapter, you can also create views to filter the links.

Site developers often use links to point to popular pages on their site or when they need to reference content from several places or to reference other related subsites within their environment. However, links do not have to point within your site—in fact, they do not even have to point within your organization. Links can also reference other sites on the Internet that publish related or supporting information. A links list could even provide the framework for building a simple menu to the pages on your site or a menu of related sites.

■**Tip** Depending on the version of SharePoint you are using (MOSS 2007 vs. WSS 3.0), you may also have alternative ways to build menus such as the Table of Contents, Site Aggregator, and Content Query web parts.

Figure 2-5 shows two links lists on the right side of the page. The top one, called **My Menu**, displays links using the built-in **Summary View** for this list type. The second list uses the **All Links** view and includes a few additional columns in a customized view. The first column identifies the item type (folder or link) using different icons for each, and the second column displays an **Edit** button that, when clicked, allows you to edit the selected item. This example illustrates one of the important features of views in SharePoint. You can display data from a list using a view provided by SharePoint, or you can create your own custom views to display not only information entered by your site's creators, but also information SharePoint itself tracks for the object. Later in the section "Defining Views for Your List," you will see how to customize existing views and create new views.

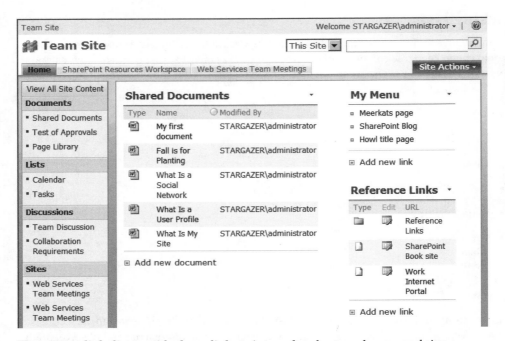

Figure 2-5. *A links list provides hyperlinks to internal and external pages and sites*

Calendar List

The calendar list shares some similarities to the announcements list. Both display events and activities. However, the calendar list extends this functionality by letting you define items as recurring events just like in Outlook. In fact, the calendar list integrates with Outlook 2003 and later. Chapter 5 explores the calendar list's capabilities more fully.

Figure 2-6 shows a basic calendar list with three upcoming events. The default view displays the date and time of the events along with the event title and description. The calendar list includes several built-in views including the following:

- **All Events**: This view displays all past, present, and future events.

- **Current Events**: This view displays all present and future events only.

- **Summary View**: This view displays only the date and the event title for present and future events.

Figure 2-6. *Calendar list using the All Events view*

In addition to list-style views, the calendar list includes special views that display calendar data by month, by week, or by day. Figure 2-7 shows an example of the month view of the events shown in Figure 2-6.

The calendar list has another interesting feature. It can share its events with the events in your local copy of Outlook so you can access your schedules no matter where you store your events, meetings, and appointments. For example, you might use a SharePoint site to track information about your project. Within this site, your project manager maintains a single calendar of major events related to the project. You can merge this site calendar with your Outlook calendar to build a single consolidated view of all your events. Chapter 5 explores in depth how to work with calendar lists through Outlook.

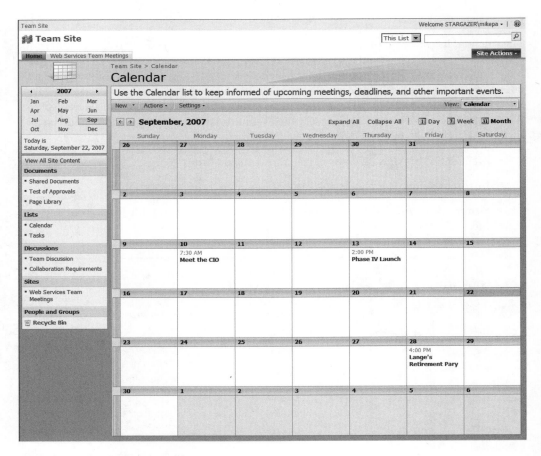

Figure 2-7. *Calendar list monthly view*

Tip Don't like your list view? Change it! Click the small down arrow to the right of the list name and select **Modify Shared Web Part**. A dialog box appears to the right of your page. Find the **Selected View** property and choose a different view from the drop-down list. Click **OK** to apply and exit this dialog box. Click **Exit Edit Mode** immediately beneath the **Site Actions** button to return to a normal page view mode.

Tasks List

If you use the Tasks list in Outlook to manage your to-do lists or the to-do lists of your staff, you have some idea of how such lists can help organize your work day. The SharePoint tasks list also includes columns that let you enter task titles, descriptions, start dates, due dates, status, and task percent completion. You can (depending on your permissions) assign tasks to other users. Then you can change the view to see all tasks, just tasks assigned to you, tasks due today, or all active tasks.

■**Tip** You can define an alert to receive notification by e-mail when a new task is added and assigned to you.

If you manage work for other users, the tasks list might help you better organize your staff's work. Since even completed tasks remain in the list, you might filter the list to show your boss all the tasks completed by your staff in the last reporting period. With a few custom fields, you could track hours expended per task. Tracking actual time to complete tasks can help you estimate required time for similar tasks in the future. You can also use this information to bill back your group's time if you manage a consulting group. By adding a field for completion dates, you could compare the difference from the task due dates to determine whether your staff can keep up with the workload or whether you need to request additional staff or simply extend your expected due dates.

Figure 2-8 shows a simple tasks list.

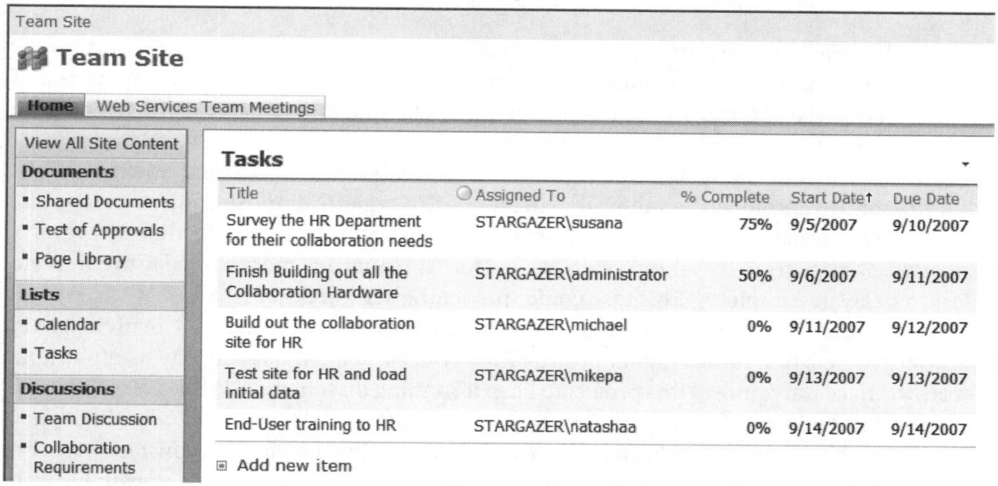

Figure 2-8. *Tasks list for a project in progress*

As with the calendar list, you can integrate the tasks list with Outlook. We will explore these capabilities in Chapter 5.

Project Tasks List

The project tasks list at first looks similar to the tasks list in that it supports the same basic fields. However, while the items in the tasks list might represent tasks from multiple independent projects, the items in the project tasks list generally represents tasks for a single project. In fact, as you enter items in this list, the start and due dates define a bar in a Gantt chart that SharePoint automatically generates in the list's default view.

GANTT CHARTS

A **Gantt chart** is often used in project management as a way to visually show the sequence of tasks in a project along a horizontal timeline. It also attempts to show the status of the project by shading each task line based on its percent completion, which when compared to the current date on the horizontal timeline gives a visual estimate of the project's status.

On the left of the chart you will find a list of the major tasks in a project. The right of the chart consists of a timeline depicting days or weeks in the project, depending on the time scale. Each row on the Gantt chart identifies one specific task within the project. To the right of the task name, a horizontal line identifies the start and end of the project along the timeline. If one task depends on another task, lines from the end of the first task connect to the start of the next task to indicate that the second task cannot begin until the first task completes. Typically, the chart shows the position of the current date as a vertical line. Shading of the task lines or even the use of different colors often depicts the percent completion of each task. This can be visually compared to the vertical line representing the current date to indicate the status of the project.

If you also track the percent completion of each item, SharePoint displays the portion of the bar from the start date to the percent completion point in a different color from the rest of the bar. With this visual cue, you can identify behind-schedule tasks by comparing where the bar color changes to the current date on the Gantt chart.

Figure 2-9 shows a Gantt chart for a simple project with five items to implement a collaboration site for the Employee Relations department of an organization. Suppose that today is 9/8/2007. We can visually see that the first task is probably close to being on schedule. However, the second task appears to be behind schedule. In fact, with only one more work day to complete this task, a delay in completing this task could impact the start of other tasks.

Of course, this Gantt chart for a single project does not show user SusanA's involvement in three other projects that have a higher priority than your project. As a result, she won't be able to devote the necessary time to this project to keep it running on schedule. While you can create separate project tasks lists for each project, SharePoint currently does not include a built-in web part to combine information from multiple projects to facilitate seeing relationships between projects. However, in a quick Internet search, you can find several commercially available web parts for SharePoint to enhance your project management support. Alternatively, if your organization includes a development staff, you might convince them to build a custom project web part just for you.

■**Note** Another alternative for managing the resources across multiple projects might be Microsoft's Project Server.

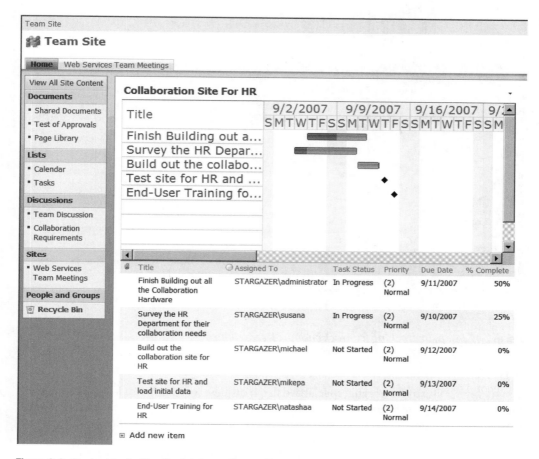

Figure 2-9. *Project tasks list displaying a Gantt chart*

Issue Tracking List

The issue tracking list also looks similar to the tasks list in that it tracks independent activities that typically cross multiple projects or activities. Your organization may use an issue tracking list to track customer support calls, risk mitigation activities, or other activities that do not directly relate to one project. In addition to the fields supported by the tasks list, the issue tracking list classifies items by categories. A category might represent a department, application, team, or any grouping you want. You can also associate an item in the list with other items already in the list by category. Figure 2-10 shows a typical issue tracking list created by a Customer Care unit within an organization.

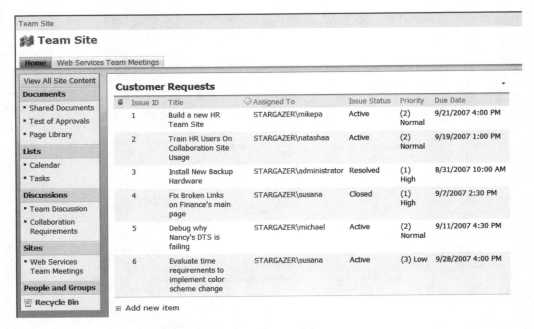

Figure 2-10. *An issue tracking list tracks nonproject activity.*

Survey List

The survey list illustrates a highly specialized list. It displays its columns as a questionnaire for the reader to complete rather than a list to display data. As in other lists, you assign a name and description to a new survey. But surveys have two additional options that you must set when you create the list.

First you must decide whether to display the respondent's name in the survey. Some people like to have the respondent's name in the survey so they can contact her for additional comments related to her responses. On the other hand, if your survey asks questions such as the respondent's satisfaction with current management policies or the effectiveness of her immediate supervisor, the respondent may not be totally honest in her responses unless you use an anonymous survey.

The second option you must specify lets you decide whether a single user can respond to a survey only once (no stuffing the ballot boxes here, please). Even if the user responds anonymously, a hidden field tracks which users have responded to the survey so you can still limit users to one response to the survey.

Next you create your survey questions. SharePoint provides ten built-in question types to choose from. The question types range from simple text responses to multiple choice and even rating scale questions using a Likert scale. Each question type has its own unique settings. You can make individual questions required. Some question types allow multiple value selections. You can also set minimum and maximum value limits to numeric questions.

THE LIKERT SCALE

A Likert scale survey attempts to determine the respondent's level of agreement with a statement by selecting a value from 1 to n based on how strongly he agrees or disagrees with the statement. A simple example might be as follows:

SharePoint provides a good collaboration framework for the work environment.

1. Strongly Disagree

2. Disagree

3. Neither Agree nor Disagree

4. Agree

5. Strongly Agree

Some scales do not include a central choice like the third one where the respondent does not really have to make a choice on one side or the other of the question. Other scales might include more values. However, the more values that separate the two extremes of the scale, the more difficulty respondents have deciding between the choices.

A concept known as *central tendency bias* refers to a respondent who avoids extreme responses. In a scale of only 1 to 5, such a bias forces a respondent's answers to the three middle values. This bias provides one argument for scales with more choices.

Other common biases in Likert scales include the *acquiescence bias*, where respondents tend to agree with all statements, and the *social desirability bias*, in which respondents tend to select answers based on what they think the surveyor expects. This latter bias appears often as a problem with nonanonymous surveys in a work environment where respondents feel that their responses could affect their careers.

All questions support branching logic. Rather than building a survey in which the user answers every question, you can create a questionnaire that branches to different questions depending on how the user responds to a question, thus customizing the survey based on early question responses.

Figure 2-11 shows the user view of an available survey. The user initially sees only the name of the survey along with a brief description and its creation date. The user also sees the number of responses already submitted. To respond to the survey, she should click the link **Respond to this Survey** found at the bottom of the survey or click the title of the survey. Both actions open a separate page with the survey. The menu bar of this screen also has the option **Respond to this Survey**.

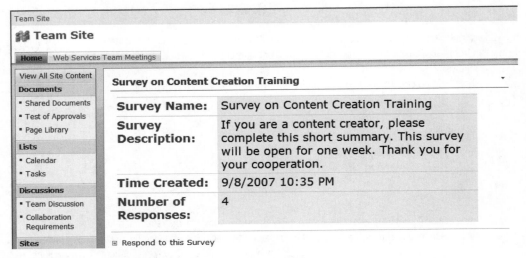

Figure 2-11. *Displaying a notification of survey availability*

When the user responds to this example survey, SharePoint displays a page with the questions as shown in Figure 2-12. Notice that for yes/no questions, SharePoint uses a check box which when checked indicates **Yes** and when left blank indicates **No**. Although you can set the default value to either **Yes** or **No**, neither choice really guarantees that the respondent actually made the response you retrieve later in his saved responses. A more accurate way to ask even a simple yes/no question might use the **Choice** question type. When using this question type, include a default option **NA** to indicate that the respondent has not made a choice or simply leave the default value blank.

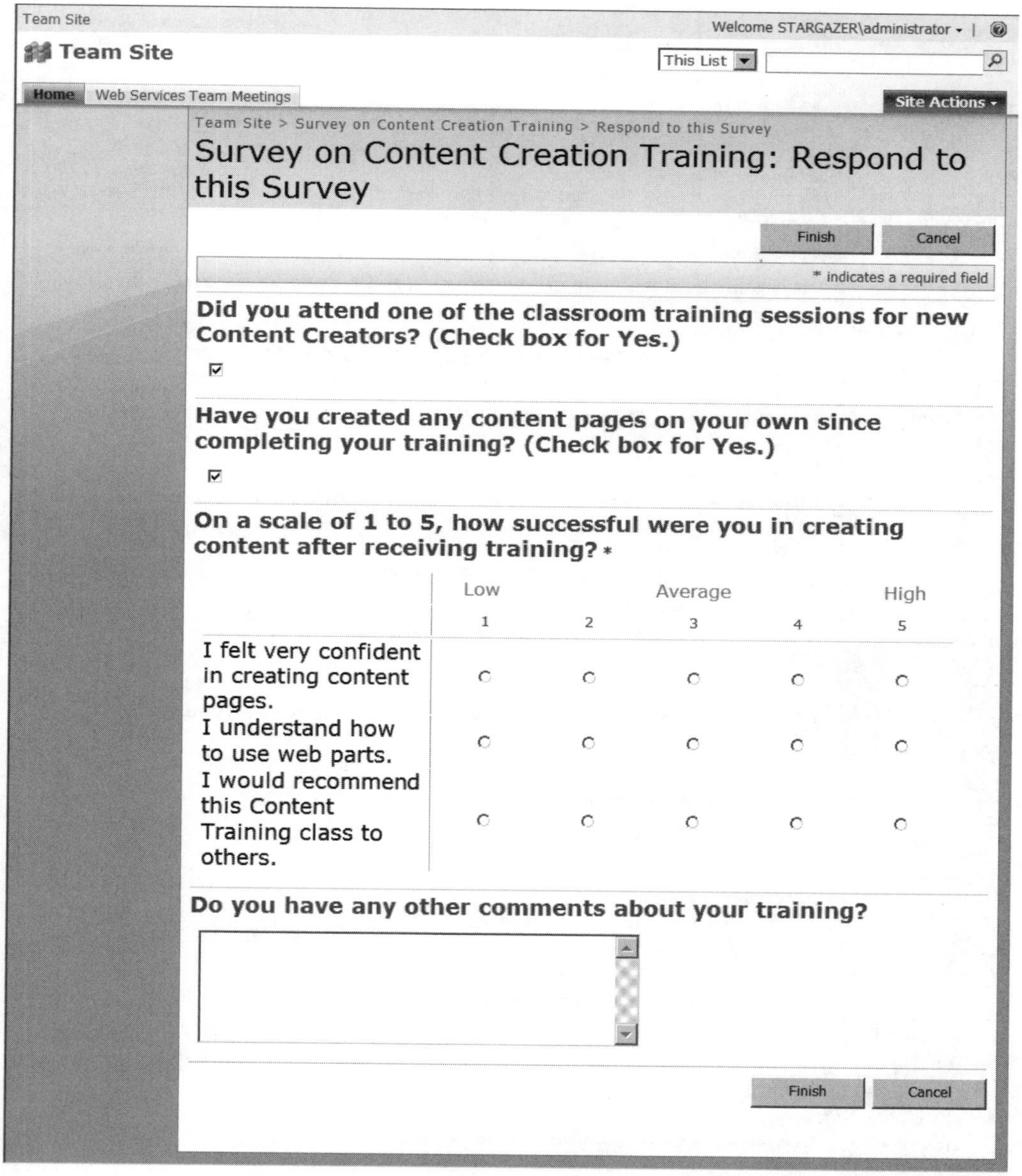

Figure 2-12. *Responding to a survey*

As I mentioned previously, you can click the survey title to open a separate page displaying only the survey. This page has a menu bar across the top. On the right side of the menu bar, the **View** option lets you select the **All Responses** view, which displays all previous responses to the survey in a list format. Use this view format if you want to perform additional analysis on the survey results and need to export the data. The second built-in view option, **Graphical Summary**, displays previous responses summarized graphically as shown in Figure 2-13. This view makes it easy to interpret the survey results.

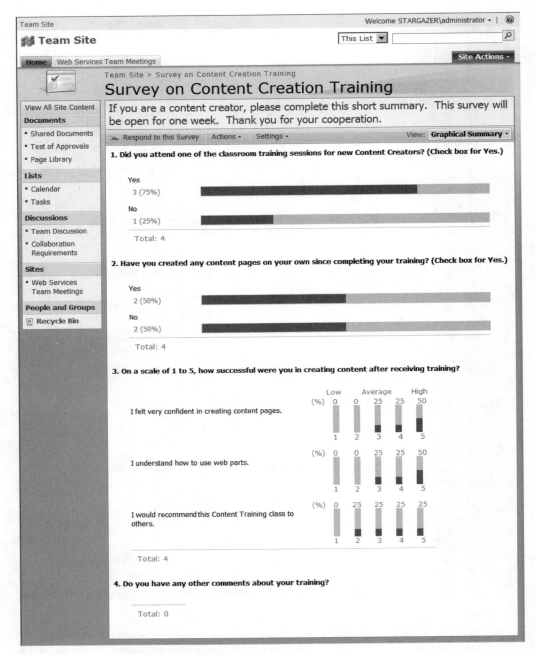

Figure 2-13. *Displaying survey results graphically*

Note One of the survey's **Advanced Setting** options allows the survey builder to determine whether other users can see responses or just their own. Of course, the survey builder as well as the site owners can always view all of the survey results. However, allowing potential respondents to first view prior results might distort their responses (see the sidebar "The Likert Scale" for types of bias in surveys). They may even decide that, based on the overwhelming direction of current responses, their opinion may not matter and thus not take the survey.

Agenda List

The agenda list only becomes an available choice when using a meeting site. You can use this list to create a unique agenda for each meeting. On the other hand, if you use the same agenda items for each meeting, you might want to turn the items into a series that defaults for each new meeting agenda instance. Of course, you can make adjustments to the items in any instance of the meeting agenda as necessary. Figure 2-14 shows a simple meeting agenda list.

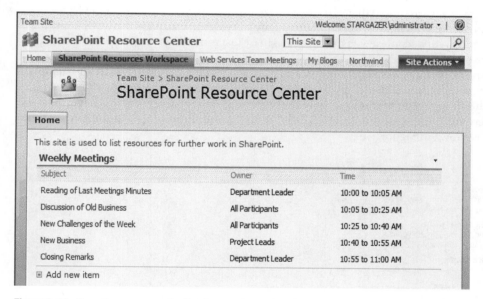

Figure 2-14. *Creating an agenda list for your meetings*

Other Lists

SharePoint makes several other lists available under **Custom Lists** when you select **Create** from the **Site Actions** button on a meeting site. The four lists described here provide fairly basic features.

- **Decisions**
- **Objectives**
- **Text Box**
- **Things to Bring**

Microsoft SharePoint Server 2007 (MOSS 2007) includes two additional and very specialized lists. The first is the Key Performance Indicator (KPI) list. This list type displays the current status of quantifiable business measurements. KPIs range from monthly sales data to counts of the number of issues that come into your company's help desk and how many have been satisfactorily resolved. In addition to manually entered data, you can build KPIs based on data in other lists, Excel workbooks, or SQL Server.

MOSS 2007 also adds a Languages and Translators list. This list works with the Translation Management workflow to assign translation tasks based on the languages involved.

Creating a New SharePoint List Based on an Existing Template

Now that you've read through the descriptions of the many available SharePoint lists and understand the variety that SharePoint provides out of the box for those built-in lists, it's time to see how to create new list instances from these base lists and even add columns or views. The steps for doing so are common to all lists.

You may have assumed that you can add list objects directly to the site home pages as shown in these earlier figures, but SharePoint only lets you add web parts to a site's home page. So how does a list become a web part? You begin by instantiating or creating a copy of the list from a list template.

Think of list templates as patterns used to make copies of themselves. If you take a template and stamp out a copy of that template, you create an instance of that template. For example, to create the announcements list you saw at the beginning of the chapter, you first navigate to the site where you want to use the list. Once there, open the **Site Actions** menu and click the **Create** option as shown in Figure 2-15.

Figure 2-15. *Creating a new list based on an existing list template*

■**Note** This concept also applies to creating libraries from library templates or sites from site templates as shown in Chapter 1.

This action opens the **Create** page shown in Figure 2-16. This page displays all library and list templates that you can create within the current site. If you see additional templates on your **Create** page, check with your SharePoint administrator to find out whether a Microsoft service pack or upgrade to SharePoint provided them or whether the administrator installed a third-party template.

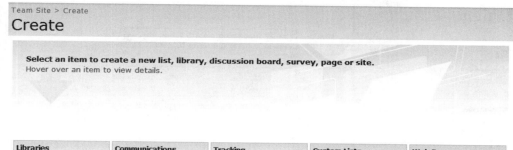

Figure 2-16. *Selecting a template to instantiate a copy*

■Note Although not covered here, you can save a custom list as a template by selecting the **List Settings** option from the list's **Settings** drop-down menu. Then select **Save list as template** from the **Permissions and Management** group.

Notice that different types of objects appear in columns categorized by object type. The **Communications** and **Tracking** columns contain the predefined list templates that you can use out of the box. The **Custom Lists** group provides templates to create your own lists. However, you can also customize any of the predefined lists while retaining their unique functionality.

To create a new announcements list, click **Announcements** under **Communications** to create an instance of the list as shown in Figure 2-17. In this screen, you can define overall list settings. The first and most important setting is the list name. Once you save a list name, SharePoint defines all future references to that list through that name, which also forms part of that list's URL. Therefore, you must supply a unique name for each list within a site.

In addition to the list name, you should enter a list description. After creating dozens of lists for your site, these descriptions help users select which list they want to use.

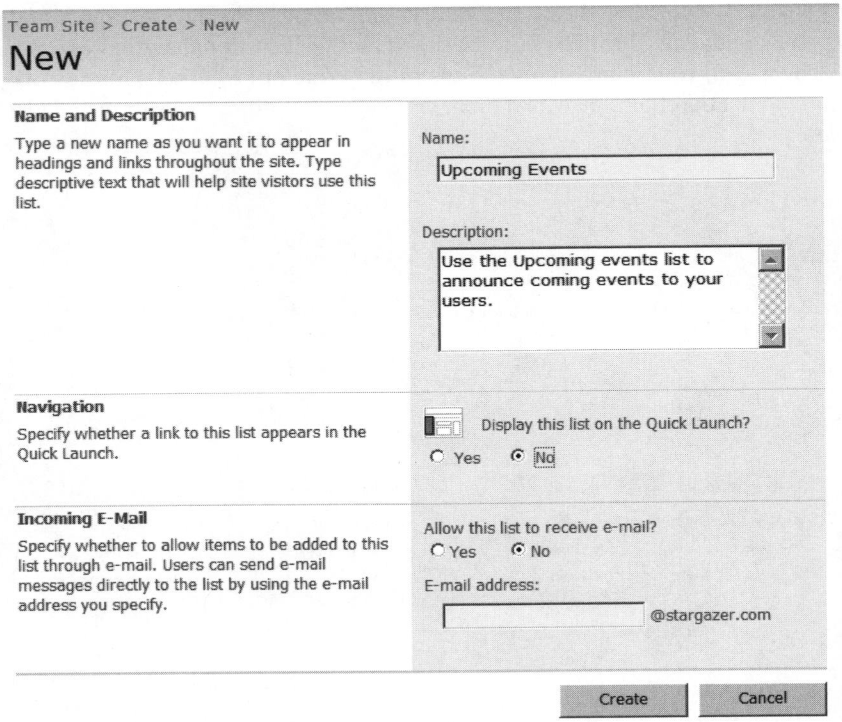

Team Site > Create > New
New

Name and Description

Type a new name as you want it to appear in headings and links throughout the site. Type descriptive text that will help site visitors use this list.

Name:

Upcoming Events

Description:

Use the Upcoming events list to announce coming events to your users.

Navigation

Specify whether a link to this list appears in the Quick Launch.

Display this list on the Quick Launch?
○ Yes   ● No

Incoming E-Mail

Specify whether to allow items to be added to this list through e-mail. Users can send e-mail messages directly to the list by using the e-mail address you specify.

Allow this list to receive e-mail?
○ Yes   ● No

E-mail address:

_____ @stargazer.com

[Create]   [Cancel]

Figure 2-17. *Creating an instance of the announcements list*

You then can determine whether you want users to access your list directly from the **Quick Launch** area on the left side of the screen. Adding your list to the **Quick Launch** area provides quick access to the list unless, of course, your site has hundreds of lists. If you have many lists in your site, you probably don't want every one in the **Quick Launch** menu. After all, users can always click the **Lists** header in the **Quick Launch** menu to access the entire list collection. They can also click **View All Site Content** at the top of the **Quick Launch** area to see instances of all templates. Another alternative to the **Quick Launch** menu for accessing a list involves adding the list to a page in your site (see Chapter 3).

The last setting on this page enables the list to receive e-mail if this capability has been enabled by your SharePoint administrator. If you allow the list to receive e-mail, you must supply a unique e-mail address that can accept incoming e-mail for this server. When you enable this feature, users can send an e-mail to the specified address. SharePoint opens the e-mail, extracts the contents of the message, and places it in the list.

When you finish specifying the list settings, click the **Create** button. Other lists have a similar settings screen.

Figure 2-18 shows the **All Site Content** page that includes each library and list instantiated along with its description, the number of items it contains, and when someone last modified it.

You can open a list directly from this page. However, you may not want to have users poking around your site to find your list in this way. Rather, you might want to display your lists on one or more of the site's web pages. Your SharePoint site's home page is an example of a web page created with SharePoint.

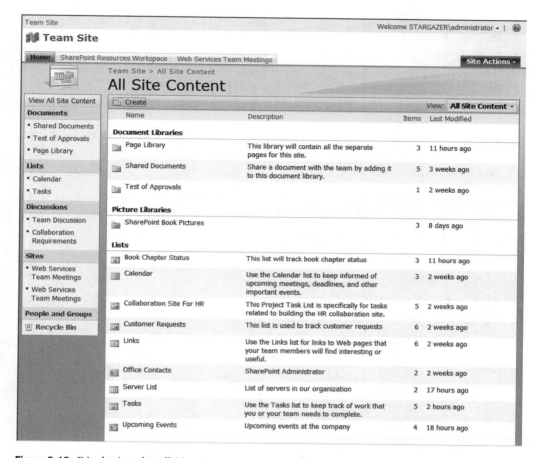

Figure 2-18. *Displaying the All Site Content page to locate your new list*

WEB PAGES

SharePoint displays everything through web pages. Sites consist of collections of web pages of which one page serves as the default or home page for the site. Most sites include individual pages focused on specific functional areas of the site or different types of content or collaboration groups.

While Chapter 3 focuses on adding pages to your site, the concepts explored here and in Chapter 1, working from the site's home page to display libraries and lists, apply to any pages that support the inclusion of web parts.

To add a new list to the site's home page, return to the home page and click **Edit Page** in the **Site Actions** menu. Figure 2-15 showed this menu earlier.

Your page now shows separate areas called *web part zones*. The default team site home page includes two zones, one labeled left and the other labeled right.

■**Note** Other web page templates may have different zone definitions. A web page template is a predefined page layout consisting of headers, footers, web part zones, and content areas. For example, one template may have a single web part zone, while another may have two web part zones defined as columns. Some web part zones add web parts horizontally, while others may add web parts vertically.

The top of each zone consists of a bar that displays the text **Add a Web Part**. Select the Left web part zone and click this header. Figure 2-19 shows the dialog box that lets you choose a web part to add to the selected zone.

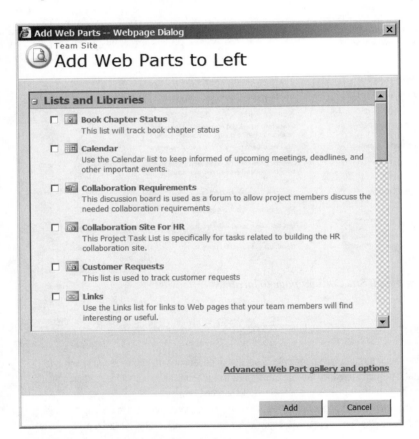

Figure 2-19. *Adding a web part to the home page*

Notice that each list and library you instantiated becomes an available web part for you to add to any page in your site. Click the check box in front of each list you want to add. You can select multiple web parts to add at one time. Then click **Add** to complete the addition of the selected web part to the Left web part zone. Figure 2-20 shows the web page after adding the **Upcoming Events** list to the Left web part zone.

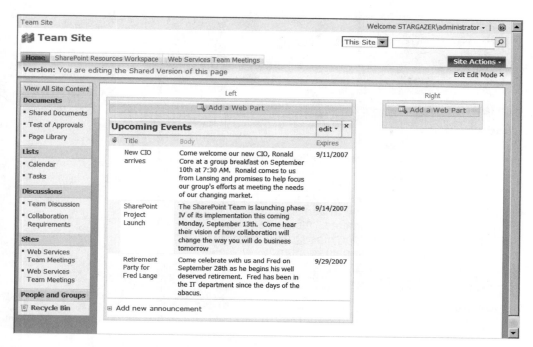

Figure 2-20. *The announcements list appears in the Left web part zone.*

By default, a newly added web part always appears at the top of the zone. If you would prefer to rearrange the order of the web parts in the zone, click and drag the web part by its header to another position within the zone. You can also click and drag the web part to another zone by dragging it to the position in that zone where you want it to appear.

When you have your web parts arranged the way you like, click the link in the upper-right portion of the screen below the **Site Actions** button labeled **Exit Edit Mode**. You can now see how your site's home page displays the new list.

Adding Items to Your New List

Now that you have a new list inserted on your site's home page, how do you add items to it?

One way uses the **Add new announcement** link at the bottom of the list that appears if the user has permission to add announcements to the list. When you click this link, a new window opens as shown in Figure 2-21 and displays the fields used by the announcements list. The first field, named **Title**, has a red asterisk after the name. This asterisk indicates that an announcement item must have a title before SharePoint will save it. You can optionally enter data into the other fields. As you saw in the first part of this chapter, each list type supports its own unique set of defining fields.

Click the **OK** button when you have finished entering the data for the list item. SharePoint automatically returns you to the previous page where you can see the new item at the top of the **Upcoming Events** list as Figure 2-22 shows.

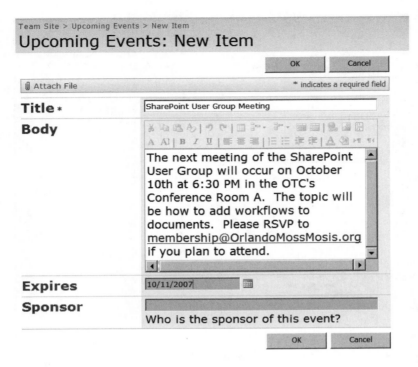

Figure 2-21. *Adding a new announcement item*

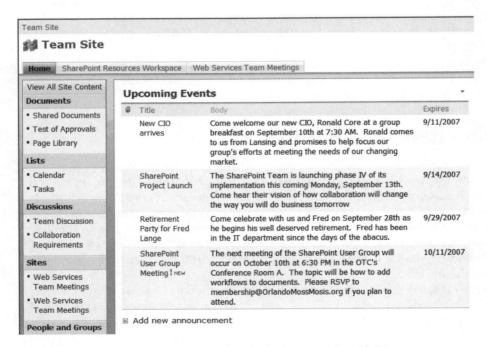

Figure 2-22. *Updated Upcoming Events list displaying a newly added item*

Building a Custom List

Even though SharePoint provides a variety of lists out of the box, you may have a requirement that none of them completely satisfies. If one of the templates comes close to meeting your needs, you may want to add a few additional columns, modify a few, or even delete a few to build exactly what you want. However, if your requirements differ greatly from any of the available templates you saw in the first part of this chapter, then creating a custom list can usually satisfy your specific needs.

If you have **Create** permissions, you may find creating a new list easier than editing an existing one. Many people find adding to an empty list definition to be easier than deleting from an existing one. To begin a new list, click **Create** from the **Site Actions** menu as shown earlier in Figure 2-15. On the **Create** page, shown previously in Figure 2-16, select **Custom List** from the **Custom Lists** section.

Figure 2-23 shows the **New** screen SharePoint displays when creating a custom list. Like any other list, you must provide a unique list name within your site. You should also provide a description that informs your site readers about the focus of your list.

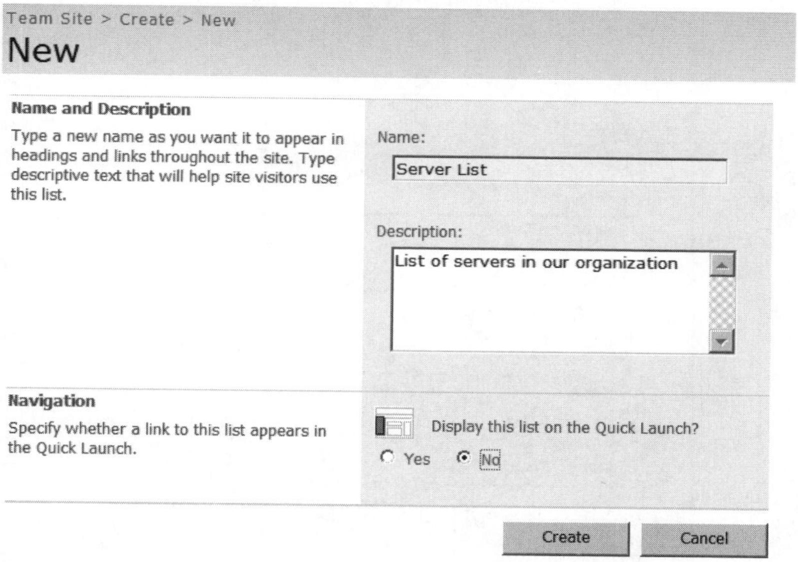

Figure 2-23. *Naming your list*

Under the **Navigation** section, choose whether to include the list in the **Quick Launch** area. If you do not, users can still find your list by clicking either **Lists** or **All Site Content** in the **Quick Launch** area. Remember also that list instances become web parts that you can add to any page within a web part zone.

But first, you must add columns to your list. After you click **Create** on the **New** page, SharePoint displays an empty list. By default, a list must have at least one column, which SharePoint names by default **Title**. In fact, if you only need a single column, you can use that one column, perhaps renaming it to something more appropriate. In most cases, you will add a few columns to that initial list.

From the menu bar across the top of the list, click **Create Column** from the **Settings** drop-down menu. The top portion of the **Create Column** page, shown in Figure 2-24, lets you name your new column and select the field type.

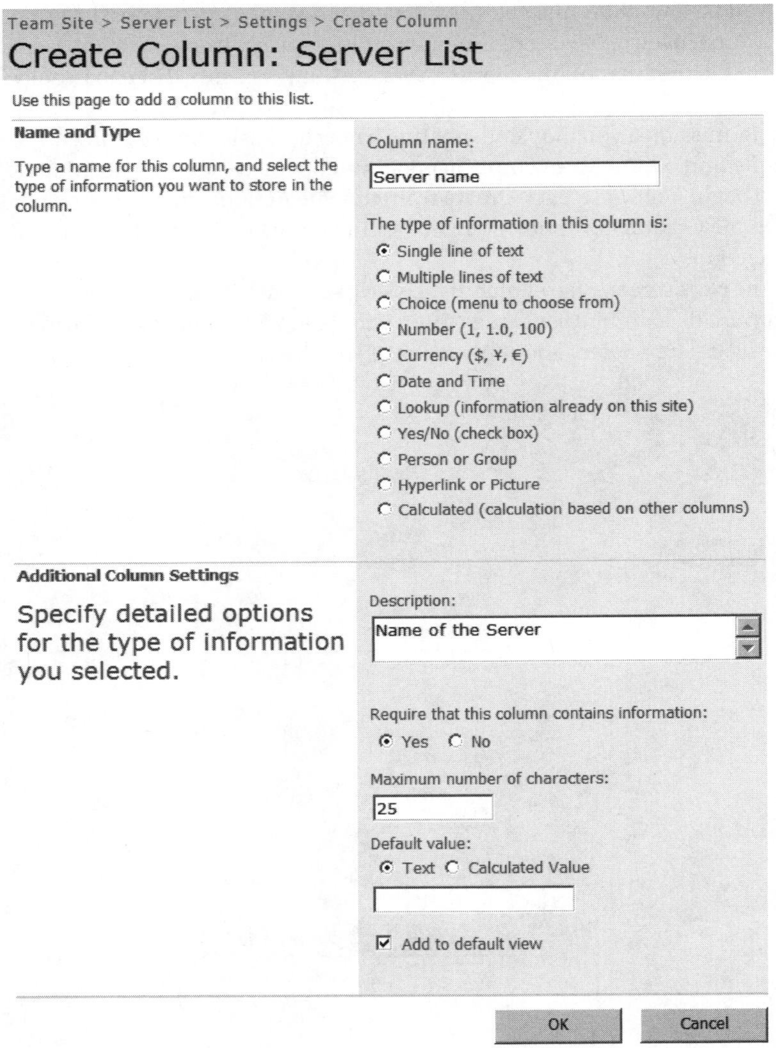

Team Site > Server List > Settings > Create Column

Create Column: Server List

Use this page to add a column to this list.

Name and Type

Type a name for this column, and select the type of information you want to store in the column.

Column name:

Server name

The type of information in this column is:

○ Single line of text
○ Multiple lines of text
○ Choice (menu to choose from)
○ Number (1, 1.0, 100)
○ Currency ($, ¥, €)
○ Date and Time
○ Lookup (information already on this site)
○ Yes/No (check box)
○ Person or Group
○ Hyperlink or Picture
○ Calculated (calculation based on other columns)

Additional Column Settings

Specify detailed options for the type of information you selected.

Description:

Name of the Server

Require that this column contains information:
○ Yes   ○ No

Maximum number of characters:
25

Default value:
○ Text   ○ Calculated Value

☑ Add to default view

OK   Cancel

Figure 2-24. *Adding a column to the list*

You must define unique column names within a list instance. However, you can use the same name for columns in different list instances. SharePoint provides a collection of column types:

- Single line of text
- Multiple lines of text
- Choice

- Number

- Currency

- Date and time

- Lookup

- Yes/No

- Person or group

- Hyperlink or picture

- Calculated

- Business data (MOSS 2007 only)

- Publishing (Image, HTML, Schedule end date, Schedule start date, available only as site columns)

- Audience targeting (This is automatically added if you turn on audience targeting for a list or library. Not selectable as a user-defined column type.)

■**Tip** If you plan on using the column as a linking field in a master-detail relationship, it helps clarify your design intent to use the same column names in both tables.

All these field types do not occur in every list. In fact, some only appear in lists available through MOSS 2007 or when adding site columns to your list or library.

Depending on the selected column type, the second half of this page prompts for additional settings for that column. These settings include whether to make the column required, to limit the maximum length of strings, to provide minimum and maximum values for numeric fields, and more.

When defining a column, the last setting determines whether this field appears on the default view maintained behind the scenes by SharePoint.

■**Note** The default view is not the same as the form displayed by SharePoint when you add a new item to the list. The form that SharePoint creates to enter new list items or edit existing ones always displays all columns defined in the list, and you cannot edit it. However, the default view consists of a unique combination of columns, filters, sort orders, and other characteristics used to display a subset of the list on a page. SharePoint builds the default view for you as you define the columns in your list. You can always create additional views for a single list. But you can only define one view as the default view.

After you click **OK** to add your new column, SharePoint returns to the default list view shown in Figure 2-25. You can repeat the process to add more columns by clicking **Create Column** in the **Settings** drop-down. In fact, you can add up to several thousand columns in a standard list. After you add more than a couple columns, the value of the last setting that asks whether to add the column to the default view becomes clear. You should only display the most important columns in the default view. Readers can always click the item's title field, which serves as a link to display a page with all the item's columns. Use the view to help users identify and select the item. They can click the item's title field to view or edit the column data or even to delete the item.

Figure 2-25. *Default list view*

LIMITS AND PERFORMANCE

The latest release of SharePoint does not have limits as restrictive as prior versions on lists and columns within lists. However, practical concerns related to performance still affect how you design lists. Several blogs and web sites have suggested that building lists with over 2,000 columns can work. However, they all agree that long before you reach a hard limit, performance declines rapidly. Of course, you might ask whether you really need a list with more than 2,000 columns. One possible workaround may involve creating two or more lists that you link in a master-detail relationship as described in Chapter 3.

On the other hand, a limit of 2,000 items in a list might seem a bit more restrictive. Lists with more than around 2,000 items also appear to seriously impact performance. While indexing a list can help performance issues, displaying a view based on a filtered list using an indexed column still degrades performance when you have thousands of records.

For those of you with a web background, talk of performance limits when displaying lists may come as no surprise. The performance of web pages also degrades as the size of a table displayed on the page increases. Formatting a web page is a very intensive task. The key to improving performance for large tables involves splitting tables into smaller formatted units. You can accomplish this with a set of separately filtered views or with a view that uses the paging capability to display a limited number of items at a time. Using the properties of views, you can also limit the number of items displayed at a time.

In any case, the best approach avoids large lists as much as possible, either in terms of columns or items.

After you finish adding the columns you need for your list, you can begin adding items by clicking the **New** option in the **List** menu. Regardless of how many columns you include in the default view, SharePoint includes all columns from the list in a form that it generates when adding a new item. Figure 2-26 shows the form generated to maintain a list named **Server List**.

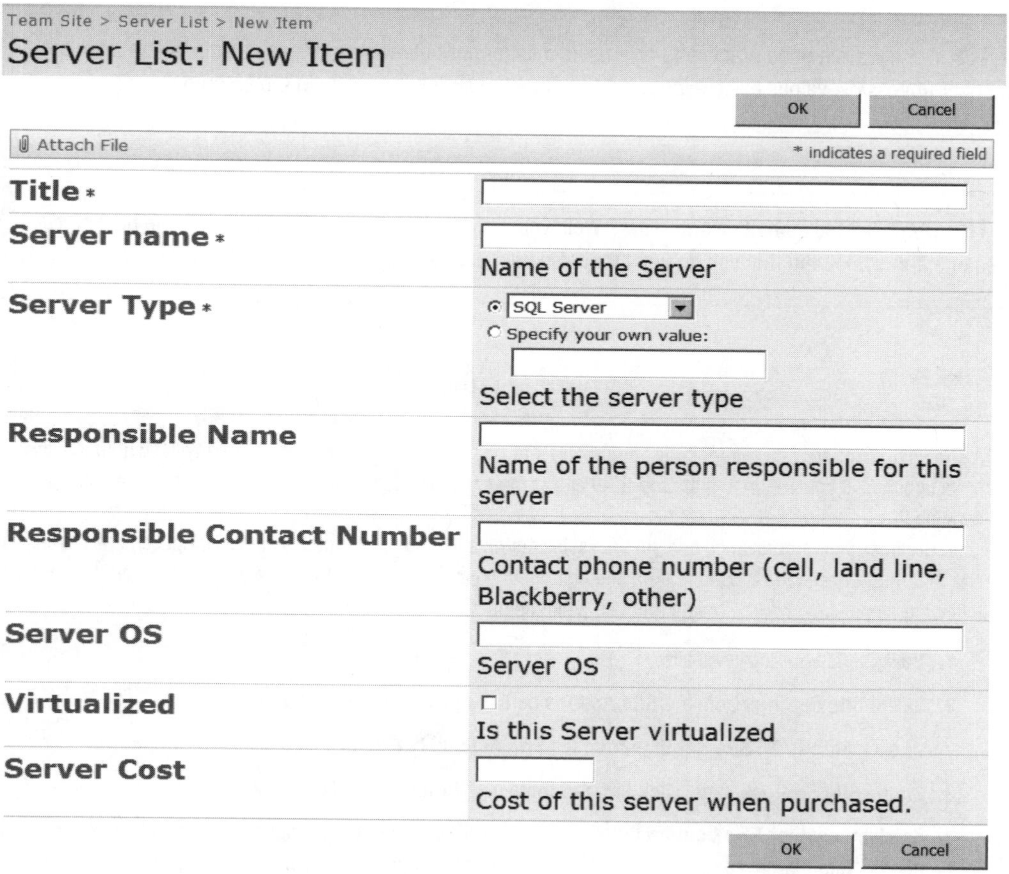

Team Site > Server List > New Item

Server List: New Item

	OK	Cancel

⋃ Attach File	* indicates a required field

Title *	

Server name *	
	Name of the Server

Server Type *	⦿ SQL Server ▾
	○ Specify your own value:
	Select the server type

Responsible Name	
	Name of the person responsible for this server

Responsible Contact Number	
	Contact phone number (cell, land line, Blackberry, other)

Server OS	
	Server OS

Virtualized	☐
	Is this Server virtualized

Server Cost	
	Cost of this server when purchased.

	OK	Cancel

Figure 2-26. *Item entry form for the Server List*

Note The description for a column appears beneath the data entry controls.

After you see the new item data form used to enter data for the first time, you may decide to change the data type description or the name of one or more of the list columns. In this case, perhaps you realize that rather than letting the user enter the Server OS, you prefer to give the user a list from which to select a value.

Tip It is always a good practice to give users a list of possible values for any column where a limited number of possible values exist, especially if you must ensure the spelling of the entered values.

Tip Don't like the default column **Title**? Well, you cannot remove it. So why not make the best of it? Rename it to something that you do want that also happens to be a text field.

SITE COLUMNS

A *site column* differs from a regular list column in that you can access the column from any list within the site or its subsites. If you create it in the top-level site of the site collection, any list within the entire site collection can use it.

Suppose your organization has multiple sales districts. Rather than create a sales district column in every site that might need it, you can create a site column in your top-level site to define your sales districts. The following steps show how to create and use a site column:

1. Navigate to your top-level site.

2. Select **Site Settings** from the **Site Actions** button if you are using WSS 3.0.

   Or click **Modify All Site Settings** from the **Site Actions** button if you are using MOSS 2007.

3. On the **Site Settings** page, click **Site Columns** in the **Galleries** option group.

4. Scroll through the **Site Column Gallery** page to verify that no existing site column would serve your needs. Note that this page organizes site columns into groups. Make sure you select **All Groups** from the **Show Group** drop-down (should be the default) when verifying the need for a new column.

5. Click **Create** to start defining a new site column.

6. Enter a name for the new site column and then choose a type.

7. Associate the new site column with an existing group or define a new group.

8. Complete any additional column settings such as a description, default value, required field flag, and any other type-specific settings.

9. Click **OK** to create the site column definition.

10. Create a new list (or modify an existing one) in your site.

11. Select **List Settings** or **Document Library Settings** from the **Settings** drop-down of the list or document library.

12. In the **Columns** section of the list **Customize** page, click **All from existing site columns**.

13. Find the new site column in the scrollable list of the **Available site columns** section and click the **Add** button. If you have a large number of site columns, filter the list by selecting the site column group using the drop-down list at the top of this page.

14. Click **OK** to add the site column to the list.

Now click back on the list name using the breadcrumb path at the top of the **Customize** page. Add a new item to see your site column list in the page used when you enter and edit item information.

Modifying the Columns in Your List

Whether you want to modify the columns in the instance of a SharePoint list or a custom list that you or a colleague created just yesterday, you proceed the same way. First, open the list. Then select **List Settings** from the **Settings** drop-down in the list menu shown in Figure 2-27.

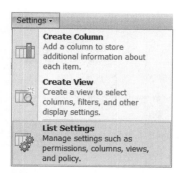

Figure 2-27. *Modifying a column*

This menu option opens the **Settings** page for the selected list as shown in Figure 2-28. Locate the column you want to modify in the **Columns** section of this page and click the column name. SharePoint then displays a page with possible changes you can make to the column. For many columns, you can change the column name as well as its type.

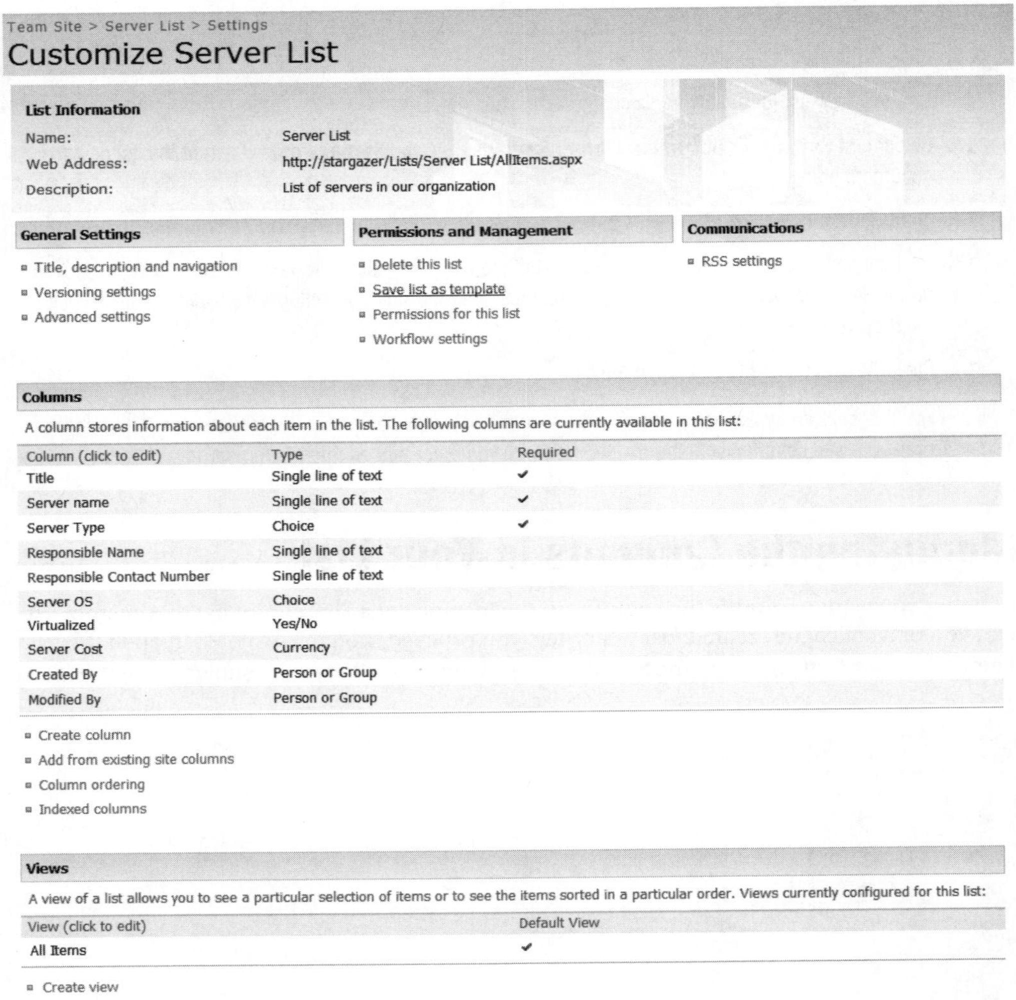

Team Site > Server List > Settings

Customize Server List

List Information

Name:	Server List
Web Address:	http://stargazer/Lists/Server List/AllItems.aspx
Description:	List of servers in our organization

General Settings	Permissions and Management	Communications
▫ Title, description and navigation	▫ Delete this list	▫ RSS settings
▫ Versioning settings	▫ Save list as template	
▫ Advanced settings	▫ Permissions for this list	
	▫ Workflow settings	

Columns

A column stores information about each item in the list. The following columns are currently available in this list:

Column (click to edit)	Type	Required
Title	Single line of text	✔
Server name	Single line of text	✔
Server Type	Choice	✔
Responsible Name	Single line of text	
Responsible Contact Number	Single line of text	
Server OS	Choice	
Virtualized	Yes/No	
Server Cost	Currency	
Created By	Person or Group	
Modified By	Person or Group	

▫ Create column
▫ Add from existing site columns
▫ Column ordering
▫ Indexed columns

Views

A view of a list allows you to see a particular selection of items or to see the items sorted in a particular order. Views currently configured for this list:

View (click to edit)	Default View
All Items	✔

▫ Create view

Figure 2-28. *Modifying a list's settings*

■**Note** You cannot change the column type of the **Title** column. However, as mentioned previously, you can change its name. In addition, several other column types such as multiline text fields and date and time fields cannot be converted to other types. Data types that you can convert to other types include the single line of text, number, currency, and yes/no column types.

Figure 2-29 shows the **Server OS** column converted to a choice type column. A choice type must have a set of possible drop-down values. SharePoint can display a choice type as a drop-down list, a set of radio buttons, or a set of check boxes.

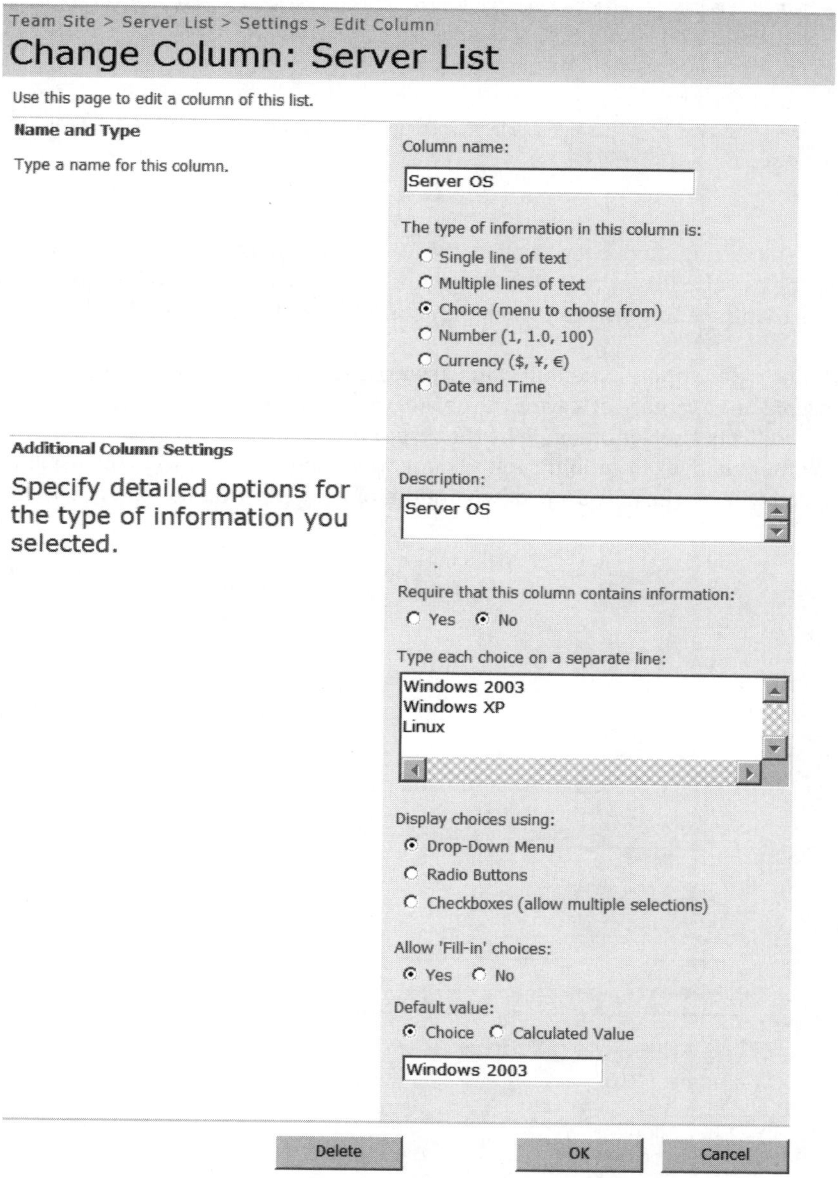

Team Site > Server List > Settings > Edit Column

Change Column: Server List

Use this page to edit a column of this list.

Name and Type

Type a name for this column.

Column name:

[Server OS]

The type of information in this column is:

- ○ Single line of text
- ○ Multiple lines of text
- ● Choice (menu to choose from)
- ○ Number (1, 1.0, 100)
- ○ Currency ($, ¥, €)
- ○ Date and Time

Additional Column Settings

Specify detailed options for the type of information you selected.

Description:

[Server OS]

Require that this column contains information:
○ Yes ● No

Type each choice on a separate line:

[Windows 2003
Windows XP
Linux]

Display choices using:
- ● Drop-Down Menu
- ○ Radio Buttons
- ○ Checkboxes (allow multiple selections)

Allow 'Fill-in' choices:
● Yes ○ No

Default value:
● Choice ○ Calculated Value

[Windows 2003]

[Delete]   [OK]   [Cancel]

Figure 2-29. *Modifying a column type*

BUILDING CHOICE LISTS FOR COLUMNS

In many lists, the reader selects values for a column from a drop-down list. You define drop-down lists when you create the column definition using the choice type. You then display possible values for a choice in one of three ways: a drop-down menu, a set of radio buttons, or a group of check boxes.

Only the check box option allows the user to select multiple values for the column.

Developers use a drop-down list to save space when the number of choices exceeds more than four or five.

Radio buttons save keystrokes by displaying all values without needing to open a drop-down but only allow the user to select single values.

Notice also that the settings in this figure allow the user to fill in her own value rather than selecting one from the list. Use this option only if you do not know all possible values the user might enter. Beware of misspelling entries, which may complicate filtering and selecting the data later.

Finally, the choice type supports a default value. If you do not want to force a default value, leave the text box blank. An advantage of leaving the default value blank is that any value returned by the list absolutely reflects a selection made by the responder.

You can make other changes to columns in the same way. When you return to the list and add the next item, you will see the new drop-down option for the **Server OS** column as shown in Figure 2-30.

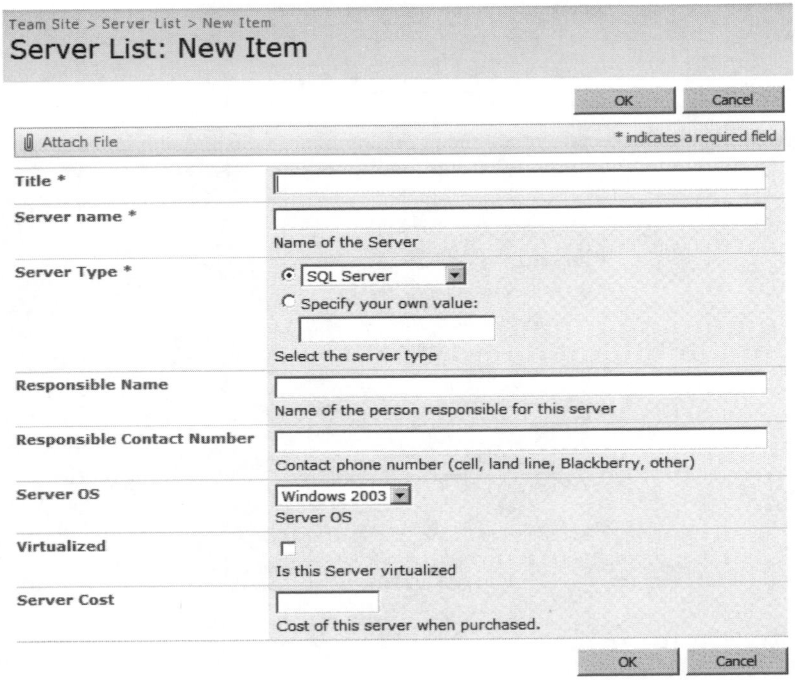

Figure 2-30. *Updated item entry form*

■**Caution** SharePoint allows you to change the columns of a list at any time. However, with a survey list, changing the survey questions or possible answers after several respondents have taken the survey can invalidate the initial results. That reasoning should also govern changes made to the columns of any list.

Using Alerts to Notify You When Your List Is Changed

Did you want to know when someone makes changes or additions to a list, but you dread having to spend time reviewing each list every day? What if SharePoint could notify you of changes or additions made to the list? Well, it can. With the Alert Me feature of lists and libraries, you can have SharePoint send you an e-mail whenever someone modifies or adds an item to any list.

To set up an alert for a list, first open the list. If you set an alert when you create a new list, you can monitor all changes to it from its beginning. With the list page displayed, open the **Actions** menu and select **Alert Me** from the drop-down menu as shown in Figure 2-31.

Figure 2-31. *You define an alert by first selecting Alert Me.*

You must name every alert. To make it easier to identify your alerts, you might include the name of the list in the alert name. You can even define alerts that get sent to multiple people as shown in Figure 2-32.

■**Tip** If you are a site administrator or owner, you can review the alerts by user by going to the **Site Settings** page, selecting **User Alerts**, and then selecting the user from the **Display alerts for** drop-down list.

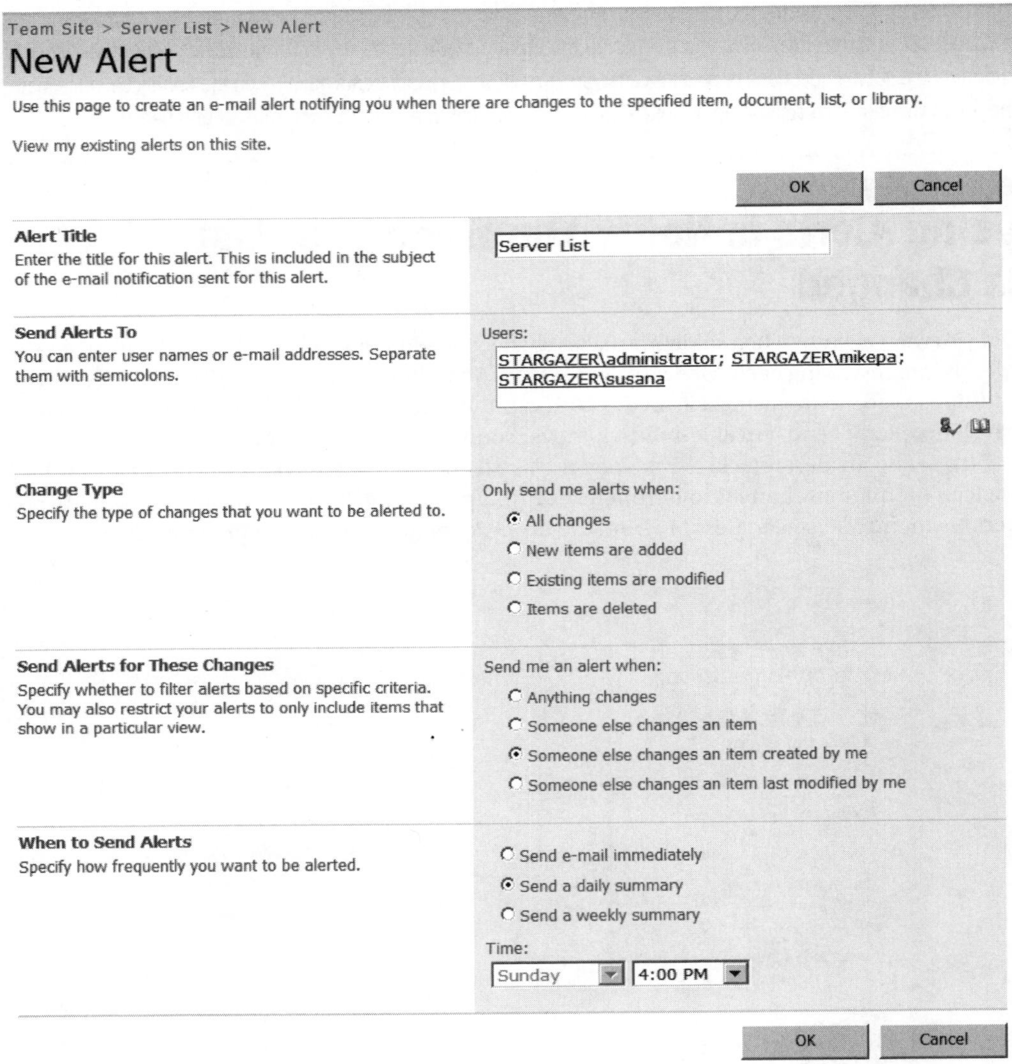

Team Site > Server List > New Alert
New Alert

Use this page to create an e-mail alert notifying you when there are changes to the specified item, document, list, or library.

View my existing alerts on this site.

| | OK | Cancel |

Alert Title

Enter the title for this alert. This is included in the subject of the e-mail notification sent for this alert.

> Server List

Send Alerts To

You can enter user names or e-mail addresses. Separate them with semicolons.

Users:

> STARGAZER\administrator; STARGAZER\mikepa; STARGAZER\susana

Change Type

Specify the type of changes that you want to be alerted to.

Only send me alerts when:

- ⦿ All changes
- ○ New items are added
- ○ Existing items are modified
- ○ Items are deleted

Send Alerts for These Changes

Specify whether to filter alerts based on specific criteria. You may also restrict your alerts to only include items that show in a particular view.

Send me an alert when:

- ○ Anything changes
- ○ Someone else changes an item
- ⦿ Someone else changes an item created by me
- ○ Someone else changes an item last modified by me

When to Send Alerts

Specify how frequently you want to be alerted.

- ○ Send e-mail immediately
- ⦿ Send a daily summary
- ○ Send a weekly summary

Time:

> Sunday ▼   4:00 PM ▼

| | OK | Cancel |

Figure 2-32. *Setting the properties of the alert*

When defining an alert, you must specify the type of changes you want to monitor. Perhaps you only want to know when someone adds, deletes, or modifies items. Unfortunately, if you want more than one of the notification types just listed, you must either create separate alerts for each notification type or select **All Changes**.

You can further fine-tune your alert to only fire when someone else changes an item in the list. After all, do you really need notification when you make the change yourself? Similarly, you may only want notification when someone changes an item that you created or perhaps an item that you were the last person to modify. If you have overall responsibility for the list, you may prefer notification of any changes made by anyone to any item in the list.

Finally, you can decide when you want SharePoint to send your alerts. Do you really need to know about changes immediately? Perhaps you only need a daily summary of alerts. If so, you can even specify the time that you want SharePoint to send the alerts. If you only have an interest in monitoring the list, perhaps a once-a-week e-mail with changes will satisfy your curiosity. Again, you can define the day and time to receive your weekly alerts.

That's all you need do other than to click **OK** to start receiving alerts when things change in your lists.

■**Tip** There are several third-party web parts available on the Internet that expand on the built-in capabilities of SharePoint's alert model.

Creating RSS Feeds for Your List

RSS feeds provide another way to track changes to a list or library. RSS, which stands for *Really Simple Syndication*, has gone through several changes in the past 10 years since the idea of content syndication across the Internet got its start. Web designers wanted a way to publish frequently updated information such as news that people could subscribe to and receive automatically without forcing them to return to their site. Originally, to read an RSS feed, you needed to find and download or purchase a program that could receive the RSS feeds and display their content as readable text. Today, you can use IE 7.0 or Microsoft Office 2007 or later versions to subscribe and read RSS feeds. In addition, dozens of freeware programs that can read RSS feeds exist on the Internet.

Setting up RSS feeds in SharePoint requires you to first open your list. Then click **List Settings** in the **Settings** drop-down menu. Figure 2-33 shows the settings page for the **Upcoming Events** list. Click **RSS Settings** under the **Communications** area to define your RSS feed.

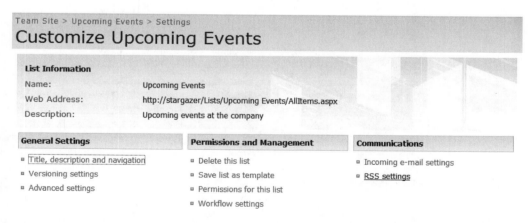

Figure 2-33. *Starting a list RSS feed*

When defining options for the RSS feed, you begin with a simple prompt asking whether you want to allow RSS for the current list. Of course, to create a feed, you need to select **Yes**.

Under **Channel Information**, you also need to define feed properties such as the title, the description, and an optional image URL. Notice you have the option of limiting multiline text fields to 256 characters. This option trims long feeds that may consist of entire news stories to just enough text to entice the viewer to click the item's title to read the entire story. As you will see in a moment, the title of the list item serves as a hyperlink to open the details of the item.

In the **Columns** section, you decide which columns to include in the feed. The RSS feed in Figure 2-34 includes a text column named **Body** along with the expiration date for the item. However, RSS feeds can include any or all columns from a list, including not only other custom columns you may have added, but also columns that SharePoint includes like **Title**, **Modified By**, and **Modified**.

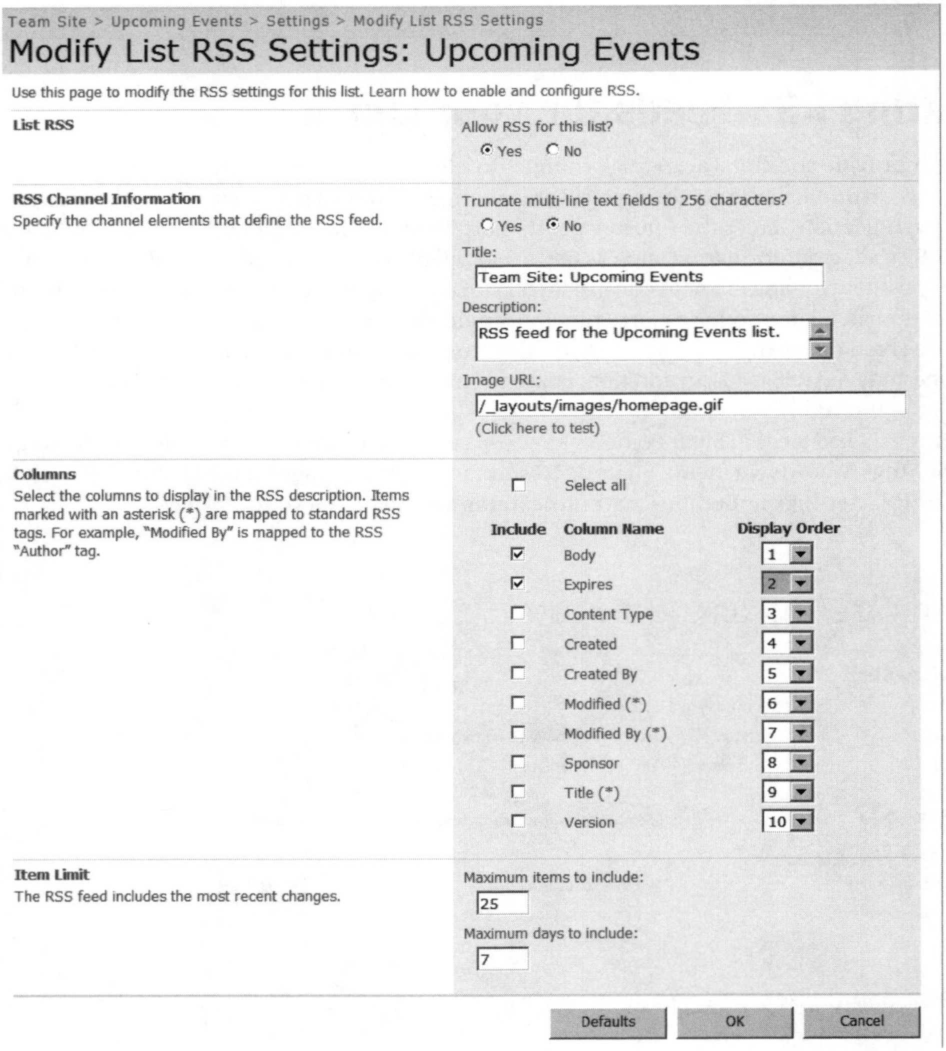

Team Site > Upcoming Events > Settings > Modify List RSS Settings

Modify List RSS Settings: Upcoming Events

Use this page to modify the RSS settings for this list. Learn how to enable and configure RSS.

List RSS

Allow RSS for this list?
◉ Yes   ○ No

RSS Channel Information
Specify the channel elements that define the RSS feed.

Truncate multi-line text fields to 256 characters?
○ Yes   ◉ No

Title:

> Team Site: Upcoming Events

Description:

> RSS feed for the Upcoming Events list.

Image URL:

> /_layouts/images/homepage.gif

(Click here to test)

Columns
Select the columns to display in the RSS description. Items marked with an asterisk (*) are mapped to standard RSS tags. For example, "Modified By" is mapped to the RSS "Author" tag.

☐   Select all

Include	Column Name	Display Order
☑	Body	1
☑	Expires	2
☐	Content Type	3
☐	Created	4
☐	Created By	5
☐	Modified (*)	6
☐	Modified By (*)	7
☐	Sponsor	8
☐	Title (*)	9
☐	Version	10

Item Limit
The RSS feed includes the most recent changes.

Maximum items to include:
> 25

Maximum days to include:
> 7

[Defaults]   [OK]   [Cancel]

Figure 2-34. *Defining settings for the RSS feed*

Next, you can decide how many items to include in the feed and the maximum number of days to include an item in a feed. Both of these settings help keep your feed fresh and constantly displaying only the newest changes to your list. Based on the frequency of changes to your list, you should set both of these options so as to not overwhelm the reader with too many items while focusing on items changed most recently. Finally, click **OK** on the settings screen to enable your RSS feed.

If you use IE 7.0 or better, you should now see the RSS icon in your browser's menu bar turn from gray to orange when you display this list. This button remains inactive and gray when you view pages that do not support an RSS feed. However, when you navigate to a page that does support an RSS feed, this button turns orange.

Click this button within IE to display a view of the RSS feed as shown in Figure 2-35. With SharePoint lists, this view displays the site name along with the list name as the title. It then tells you that you can subscribe to the feed. Subscribing automatically downloads information from the feed to your computer, where you can display it in IE or add it to any other program that supports an RSS reader.

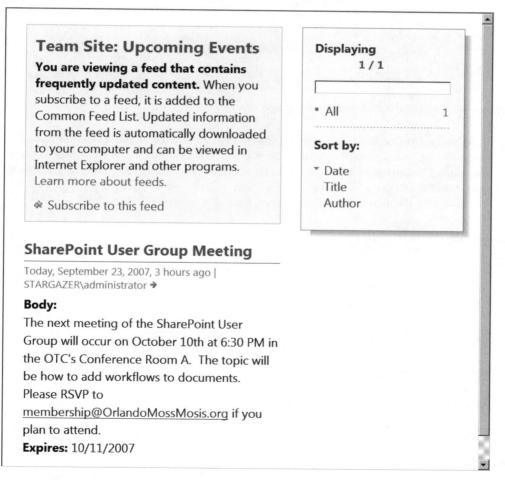

Figure 2-35. *Subscribing to a feed*

The sample feed view shows you the current contents of the feed. In a box in the upper right of the screen, the feed displays a count of the number of items currently in the feed. You can also sort the feed items by date, title, or author by clicking the links under the **Sort by** section. Note the small blue arrow to the left of the selected sort field. If you click the field multiple times, this arrow changes from pointing up to pointing down and back again. This indicates the sort direction of the feed items based on the selected field.

When a user subscribes to a feed using IE, a dialog box prompts him for the name he wants to use on his computer to identify the feed. The default name includes the site name and the list name separated with a colon as shown in Figure 2-36. But the user can provide any name for the feed. Next, define a folder in which to store the feed. Just like favorites in IE, you can create a hierarchy of folders to organize your feeds.

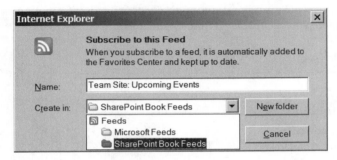

Figure 2-36. *Naming the feed and placing it in a new or existing folder*

After you subscribe to the feed, you can open it by clicking the **Favorites Center** option in IE. You will see, in addition to your other bookmarked URLs stored under **Favorites**, a button named **Feeds**. Click this button to see the folders and feeds within them. Figure 2-37 shows two folders under **Feeds**: Microsoft Feeds and SharePoint Book Feeds. Opening the SharePoint Book Feeds folder displays two RSS feeds added from lists created in this chapter.

Figure 2-37. *Selecting the feed from within IE's Favorites Center to view the feed contents*

■**Note** A **Refresh** button appears to the right of each feed. The **Refresh** button consists of two green arrows pointing up and down as shown in Figure 2-37. Click this button to refresh your RSS with the latest feeds from the RSS site.

Defining Views for Your List

Perhaps you don't like the default view's look. Or maybe you want to create different views of the same list to use on different pages within the site. For lists like tasks lists, project tasks lists, and issue tracking lists, you might want multiple views of the list data to examine tasks or issues by person, project, status, or other criteria.

In any case, the path to a new view begins by clicking the drop-down menu on the right side of the list labeled **View** as shown in Figure 2-38. This drop-down menu first displays all views currently defined for the list. You can switch from one view to another by clicking the one you want. While displaying any view, you can return to this drop-down and click **Modify the View** to make changes to the selected view. If none of the existing views meet your needs or even come close enough to be worth editing, you can create a new view by clicking **Create View** at the bottom of the **View** drop-down.

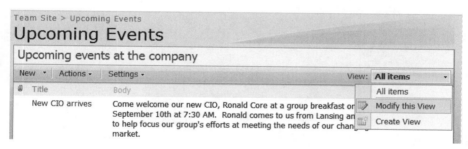

Figure 2-38. *Using the View drop-down to manage your views*

Alternatively, you can go through the **List Settings** option of the **Settings** drop-down menu to bring up the page shown in Figure 2-39. Either way, you will arrive at the list **Customize** page that shows all the list options. It lists the defined views at the bottom of the page and identifies one view as the default view. You can modify a view by clicking its name, or you can create a new view by clicking the link **Create View**.

■**Tip** You can delete any view, except the default view, by clicking it to display its **Edit View** page and then clicking the **Delete** button. But what if you really want to delete the default view? Select one of the other views, and in the **Edit View** page promote it to the default view. Then return to the original view, which SharePoint no longer identifies as the default, open its **Edit View** page, and delete it. Keep in mind that a list must have at least one view, and that one view must serve as the default view until you create another view.

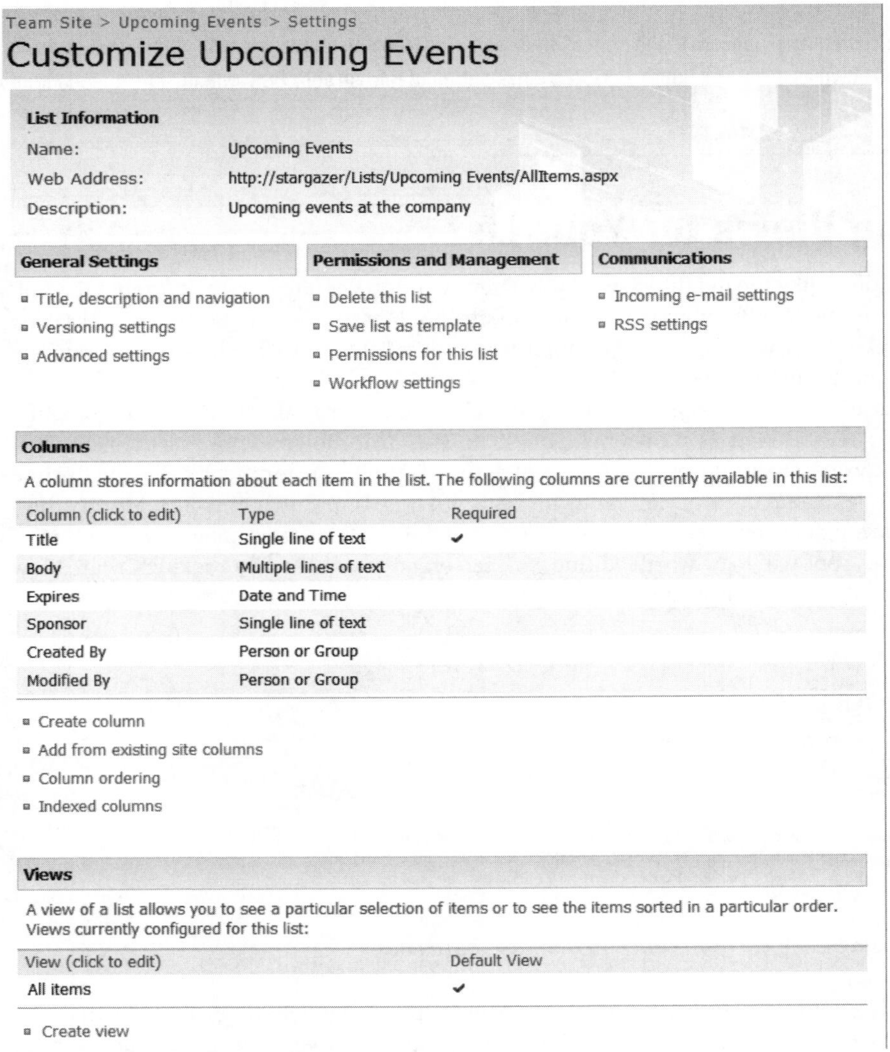

Team Site > Upcoming Events > Settings

Customize Upcoming Events

List Information

Name:	Upcoming Events
Web Address:	http://stargazer/Lists/Upcoming Events/AllItems.aspx
Description:	Upcoming events at the company

General Settings	**Permissions and Management**	**Communications**
▫ Title, description and navigation	▫ Delete this list	▫ Incoming e-mail settings
▫ Versioning settings	▫ Save list as template	▫ RSS settings
▫ Advanced settings	▫ Permissions for this list	
	▫ Workflow settings	

Columns

A column stores information about each item in the list. The following columns are currently available in this list:

Column (click to edit)	Type	Required
Title	Single line of text	✔
Body	Multiple lines of text	
Expires	Date and Time	
Sponsor	Single line of text	
Created By	Person or Group	
Modified By	Person or Group	

▫ Create column
▫ Add from existing site columns
▫ Column ordering
▫ Indexed columns

Views

A view of a list allows you to see a particular selection of items or to see the items sorted in a particular order. Views currently configured for this list:

View (click to edit)	Default View
All items	✔

▫ Create view

Figure 2-39. *The List Settings page lets you define columns and views.*

SharePoint displays a screen like the one shown in Figure 2-40 when you create or edit a view. Actually, this figure only shows the top two sections of the view definition. In the top section, you can enter the view name. What if you decide later that you don't like the name you previously gave the view? Don't worry. Generally, you can change a view name at any time with no adverse affects. In fact, SharePoint automatically updates any references to the view name automatically. The same applies if you change the URL, as long as you store the URL in its own field. If you embed the URL in other content, SharePoint may miss it. But as a general rule, try to minimize your changes to names and URLs after you start including references to them in other parts of your site.

Team Site > Upcoming Events > Settings > Edit View

Edit View: Upcoming Events

To customize this view further, use a Web page editor compatible with Windows SharePoint Services.

OK	Cancel

Name

Type a name for this view of the list. Make the name descriptive, such as "Sorted by Author", so that site visitors will know what to expect when they click this link.

View Name:

All items

Web address of this view:

http://stargazer/Lists/Upcoming Events/ AllItems .aspx

This view appears by default when visitors follow a link to this list. If you want to delete this view, first make another view the default.

⊟ Columns

Select or clear the check box next to each column you want to show or hide in this view. To specify the order of the columns, select a number in the **Position from left** box.

Display	Column Name	Position from Left
☑	Attachments	1
☑	Title (linked to item with edit menu)	2
☑	Body	3
☑	Expires	4
☐	Content Type	5
☐	Created	6
☐	Created By	7
☐	Edit (link to edit item)	8
☐	ID	9
☐	Modified	10
☐	Modified By	11
☐	Sponsor	12
☐	Title	13
☐	Title (linked to item)	14
☐	Type (icon linked to document)	15
☐	Version	16

Figure 2-40. *Creating the view name and columns*

If, rather than adding a view, you decide to edit the default view, this top section reminds you that you cannot delete the current view. As mentioned in the previous tip, if you have more than one view, you can set any one of them as the default view and delete any of the others.

The second section shows the available columns in the list. The check box to the left of the column name indicates whether to include the column in the current view. To add or remove a column from the view, toggle the check box. The drop-down box to the right with a number in it defines the order of the fields from left to right. To change the order of the columns, change the number in the drop-down of the column you want to move, selecting the numeric value of its new position. For example, to move the column **Attachments** to the fourth position, open its drop-down list and select the number **4**. All other columns from **2** through **4** automatically move to positions **1** through **3**, making room for the repositioned **Attachments** column.

Sorting and Filtering Lists

The third section of the **Edit View** page lets you define the sort order for the items in the view. You can sort by no more than two columns. However, you can independently sort each column in ascending or descending order. Figure 2-41 shows a view sorted first by **Expiration Date** in ascending order. When more than one item has the same expiration date, it sorts by **Title** in ascending order.

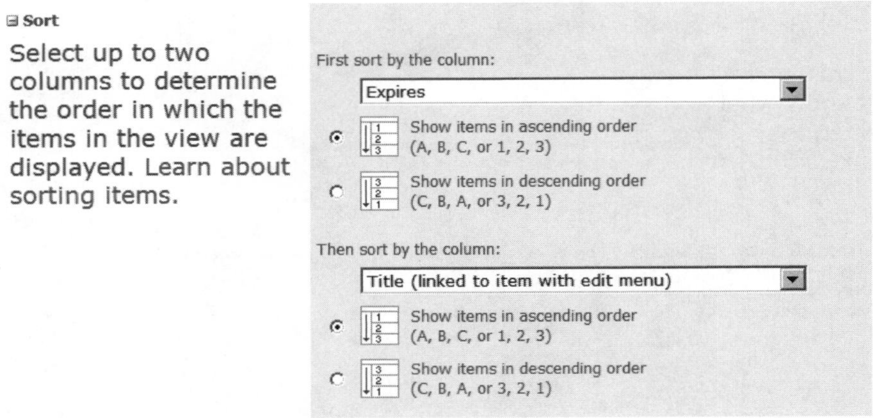

Figure 2-41. *Sorting your list on up to two columns*

As your list grows, you may want to define a filter for a list to focus on different item groups. For example, you could create a custom view of upcoming events that automatically hides items with expiration dates prior to today by adding a filter that compares the column **Expires** to the current date as shown in Figure 2-42.

There are other sections on this page to further define a view. For example, the **Group By** section allows you to group items in the list using up to two columns. The advantage of using groups over merely sorting your items is that you can expand and collapse groups to let users see just a portion of the list without needing a different filtered view for each group.

■**Note** **Group By** works best on columns that have only a limited number of values such as choice fields.

The **Totals** section lets you add totals on your list. For example, if your **Upcoming Events** list includes a **Department** column to associate events with their hosting department, you could create a total while grouping by department to see how many events each department hosts.

In the **Style** section, you can select from a predefined set of styles for your list. For example, the **Shaded** style alternates the items with shading to make the list more readable.

Because lists can include folders, the **Folders** group lets you decide whether to navigate through folders or to view all items as if there were no folders.

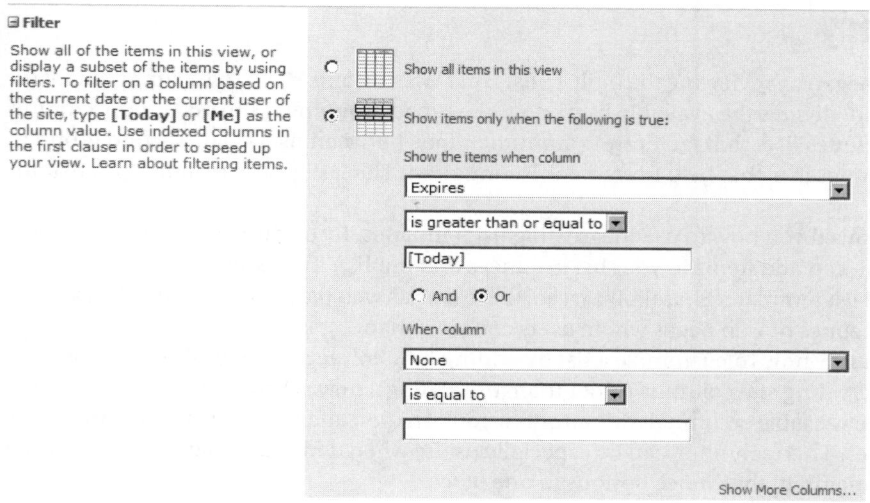

⊟ **Filter**

Show all of the items in this view, or display a subset of the items by using filters. To filter on a column based on the current date or the current user of the site, type **[Today]** or **[Me]** as the column value. Use indexed columns in the first clause in order to speed up your view. Learn about filtering items.

○ ⊞ Show all items in this view

◉ ⊞ Show items only when the following is true:

Show the items when column

| Expires | ▼ |

| is greater than or equal to ▼ |

| [Today] |

○ And   ◉ Or

When column

| None | ▼ |

| is equal to ▼ |

| |

Show More Columns...

Figure 2-42. *Defining a filter for your list*

As your list grows, you may discover that it suddenly stops displaying all its items. You may find the answer to that problem in the list setting **Item Limit**. First, I would not recommend that you try to display a list with thousands of items as a single screen. Not only will performance degrade, but your readers will not want to scroll through a list that large. Rather, use **Item Limit** along with the option to display items in batches. For example, if your list has 345 items and you specify an item limit of 100, your list begins by displaying the first 100 items. You can then select the next page of the list to display the second set of 100 items. In this way, your readers can page through all items in the list, 100 items at a time, until they reach the end.

Finally, you can define views for mobile devices. These typically include fewer columns and items than their PC screen cousins.

■**Tip** Consider using filtered views to limit the number of items in a list's view. This will improve page performance. You could also use the **Group By** (collapsed) option to limit the number of items displayed, yet easily allow users to expand the groups for which they want to see the details.

■**Tip** When sorting or filtering a large list, index the column used by the filter. You can create indexed columns by clicking the **Indexed columns** hyperlink at the bottom of the **Columns** section of the list's **Customize** page.

Summary

This chapter began by reviewing the built-in lists that WSS 3.0 and MOSS 2007 supply out of the box. SharePoint divides the available lists into three broad groupings. The first group, communications, includes lists that facilitate communications between users. The second group, tracking, includes lists that help users track information. The last group includes the custom list template.

I then showed you how to use the existing list templates. By creating instances of these templates, you can add items to your list instances and publish the resulting lists. By creating instances of a list template, SharePoint treats these lists as web parts that can then be inserted into web part zones of web pages where users can view them.

You then saw how to customize a list by adding new columns and modifying existing columns. By creating site columns rather than just adding a new column to an individual list, you can create reusable column definitions that you can then add to any list in the current site and its subsites. This technique can be especially useful when defining choice columns so you only need to maintain the choice options in one place.

Next you looked at using alerts to keep informed via e-mail of changes or additions made to a list or library. You can customize how often you receive alerts and for what events you want to receive alerts. Rather than having to physically visit each list or library and try to determine which, if any, items were updated, alerts can save you time by keeping you notified about changes.

Lists and libraries also support RSS feeds as a way to publish additions to a list or library. Both IE 7.0 and Microsoft Outlook 2007 support reading RSS feeds directly, making it easy for users to monitor updates to lists and libraries while they check their e-mail or browse the Internet.

Finally, you learned how to define multiple views for a list. Each view can support a different combination of columns, sorts, and filters. It is also possible to group a list by a "slowing changing" column (a column that only supports a few unique values) and use an expand/collapse feature to make it easier to see subsets of your list items without creating separate views for each group.

In later chapters, I will show how to access and work with lists directly from Microsoft Office products such as Excel, Access, and Outlook.

■ ■ ■

CHAPTER 3

Creating Content Pages
All Content Pages in SharePoint Are Really Web Pages

Surprised? You shouldn't be. If you accessed SharePoint libraries and lists as you read Chapters 1 and 2, you already know this because you used a web browser like IE, Firefox, or another to open and view your site. When you create a new site with one of the site templates, SharePoint creates an initial home page for that site, and that page is a web page.

Fortunately, you do not need to cram everything you want to display on your site on that one page. First, doing so would make your page rather long, and it could take a while to load. But more importantly, readers of your page would have a difficult time finding the information they needed if you forced them to scroll through dozens of libraries, lists, and other content to find a particular item. So, you want to model your SharePoint site after a traditional web site, where the home page serves as a landing page or an introduction to the site and then provides links or navigation aids to other pages.

Adding a Page to Your Site

In the previous chapters, you saw how to create libraries and lists by going to the **Site Actions** button in the upper-right corner of your site and clicking the **Create** option. Creating a new page for your site begins the same way.[*] On the **Create** page, five columns group the types of objects you can create on your site. The last group, shown in Figure 3-1, is the **Web Pages** group. In this group, you can choose to create a basic page or a web part page. The primary difference between the two is that a basic page does not include any web parts. That means that you cannot display lists or libraries like the ones created in Chapters 1 and 2 in these pages.

---

[*] This chapter's examples add pages to nonpublishing templates. However, the techniques apply to web pages added to any site.

 - Basic Page
 - Web Part Page
 - Sites and Workspaces

Figure 3-1. *Creating a new web page*

If you select the **Basic Page** option, specify a name for the page you are creating and a location where you want to save the page. Figure 3-2 shows the definition screen for a basic page. Notice that you store pages in a document library. While you can store pages in any library, including the **Shared Documents** library created when the SharePoint administrator created the site, you may want to create a separate page library just for your web pages. This figure shows a page called **SPBook** being saved in a library called **Page Library**.

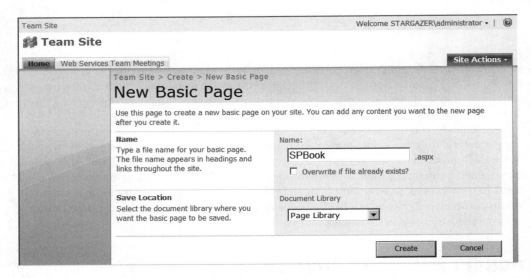

Figure 3-2. *Specifying name and location for a new basic web page*

■**Note** If you are starting from a publishing portal, an additional option not shown in Figure 3-1 appears at the bottom of the **Web Pages** group: **Publishing Page**. When you select this option, you must still supply a page title along with an optional description. You must also select a page layout. Some of the page layouts contain web parts, and some have just rich text fields and images. Advanced users can create additional page layouts that content creators can then use when creating new web pages. Once you have created your page, placing content on that page follows rules similar to those discussed in the next section.

When you click **Create**, SharePoint builds the new page and opens it for editing. It also opens a window shown in Figure 3-3 with the title **Rich Text Editor—Webpage Dialog**. Using this dialog box, you can create content for your new web page using an interface very similar to what you find in Microsoft Word. In fact, if you can create a Word document, you can create content for a web page. No longer do you have to send your content to a web master to encode it as HTML or build your page using some complex program that only he can use or understand. You now have the freedom to create content (and as we will see shortly, edit any content) anytime you wish. Furthermore, you can post your changes immediately. Okay, it may not be visible to others immediately if your site requires page approval, but we will get to that later as well.

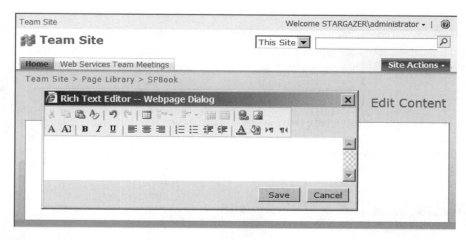

Figure 3-3. *Creating content using the Rich Text Editor*

Placing Simple Content on Your New Page

Once you have the Rich Text Editor open, enter your content as you normally would in any Word document. In fact, if you look at the toolbar at the top of the dialog box shown in Figure 3-3, you see many of the tools already familiar to Word users. For any tools unfamiliar to you, simply hover your mouse over the icon until a tooltip appears below your cursor. Some of the text formatting features you have when creating text include the following:

- Fonts

- Font sizes

- Font styles (bold, italic, underlined)

- Font colors

- Text highlighting

- Alignment (left, center, and right)

- Lists (unnumbered and numbered)

- Indenting (and outdenting)

- Copying and pasting text

- Clearing all formatting

- Do and undo

- Tables and manipulation of tables and their cells

- Hyperlinks

- Images

■**Caution** While you can choose any font you have installed on your machine when you create your web pages, the actual font that displays still depends on the fonts your site's reader has on her machine. Therefore, the best practice suggests using common fonts such as Arial, Times New Roman, Courier, or Helvetica.

With these text tools, you can create web pages like a professional web designer. Figure 3-4 shows the rich text design for a web page I created called Meerkats, where I include one of the pictures I took at a local theme park. I also used some of the formatting options to change font size, color, and style of some of the text.

Figure 3-4. *Creating content in the Rich Text Editor*

Adding an Image to Your Content

Deciding where to save the images I wanted to use and learning how to reference them within the page may have been the most challenging part of creating the page in Figure 3-4.

Picture libraries provide the answer to the first part of that challenge. You need to create a picture library if you do not already have one. Write down the name of the picture library, as you will need that later to reference your image. In this example, I named the picture library **SharePoint Book Pictures**. Like web pages, picture libraries can be created from the site **Create** page. Look for the **Picture Library** option beneath the **Libraries** group. You do not have to display the picture library link in the **Quick Launch** menu. In fact, I recommend that you don't if the sole purpose of the picture library is to provide a storage location for images used on your web pages. Also, you probably don't need to track versions of your pictures because you only care about the most recent version.

■Note You must upload your images to a SharePoint picture library because you are publishing pages to a web server. Web servers typically reside on a different physical box from the one on which you work. Therefore, the web server must have local access to the image to display it. It cannot reference a local image on your machine. Also, if you later delete the image from the picture library, the web page on which you displayed it will now display a box with a red "x" in it, indicating that it cannot locate the image.

Within a picture library as with any library, you can create folders to store your images. As previously suggested, creating folders helps to organize items you save, and that applies to pictures as well. To create the previous example, I named the folder `SharePoint Pictures`. Within this folder, I can upload images that I want to use on my SharePoint site. Suppose my picture has the name `AK030714_Meerkat.jpg`; the URL I need to reference this picture looks like this:

```
http://stargazer/SharePoint Book Pictures/SharePoint Pictures/AK030714_Meerkat.jpg
```

which is generally defined as follows:

```
http://<servername>/<picture library>/<library folder>/<filename>
```

You need to know where to store your images and how to reference them because the dialog box that the Rich Text Editor uses to prompt for the image address does not allow you to browse to the image location. Figure 3-5 shows the dialog box used to insert an image into your rich text content. Notice that the spartan dialog box provides you with no assistance if you forget your image's URL.

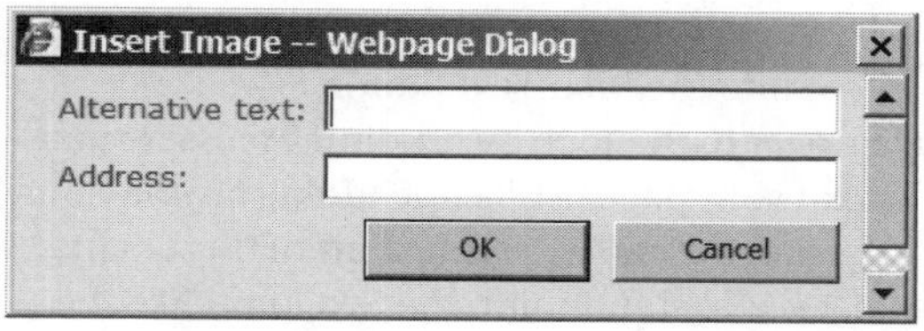

Figure 3-5. *Dialog box used to insert an image into your content*

The other property in this dialog box allows you to specify an alternative text string. Most web browsers display the alternative text string when users turn off image downloading within their browser. Fewer users do this anymore, but you can still find users who do this if they have slower Internet connection speeds. The practice of eliminating images may also apply to small form devices such as BlackBerry devices and other handhelds. Alternative text also appears when you hover the mouse cursor over an image, causing a tooltip to appear beneath the cursor. This text may also help sight-impaired people experience your site if they have software that can perform text-to-voice operations.

Adding a Hyperlink to Your Content

The Rich Text Editor has the ability to add a hyperlink to another page on your site or any site on the Internet. Suppose you find some useful information on the popular site Wikipedia about meerkats and want to add a link to that site so readers can get additional information.

To create a hyperlink from within your content, begin by selecting the text that you want readers to click. Then click the **Insert Hyperlink** button in the rich text toolbar. As with the image dialog box, the hyperlink dialog box, shown in Figure 3-6, only has two property fields. The first field echoes the text highlighted before clicking the **Insert Hyperlink** tool. You then need to enter the page URL to link to using the second field. Note that this field does not support a **Browse** button either. You must locate the page you want to link to, copy the link to your clipboard, paste the link in the **Address** field, and click **OK**.

Figure 3-6. *Inserting a hyperlink to an Internet site*

After you add a link, test it from **Edit** mode by pressing the Ctrl key while you click the left mouse button. The linked page should pop up in a separate browser window. If, however, you save your edited content first, you can test your link by clicking it normally. This time, however, the destination page replaces the window in which you were viewing your page. To return to your SharePoint site, you need to click the **Back** button in your browser menu.

Copying Text from a Word Document

Perhaps you already have Word documents containing the text you want to add to your site. The Rich Text Editor contains copy and paste tools. Thus you might be tempted to simply copy your text from the Word document and then paste it into the Rich Text Editor.

This technique works. However, it also carries over to the Rich Text Editor excess formatting information from Word that increases the size of your page, while not adding any obvious formatting to it. Figure 3-7 shows the **SPBook** page created earlier with a draft of this chapter pasted from Word into the Rich Text Editor. From a visual standpoint, the text looks like the Word document, except for losing the paragraph indent on the second paragraph. However, behind the visual text, the copy-and-paste operation carried along many of Word's formatting commands. You cannot easily see the overhead problem in this dialog box because there is no option to show the raw text. Therefore, we will revisit this issue in the sidebar "What Pasted Word Text Really Looks Like" later in this chapter. In the meantime, if the speed of copying text from Word documents outweighs the extra storage requirements of the hidden formatting information, this technique can quickly convert your Word documents to SharePoint web pages.

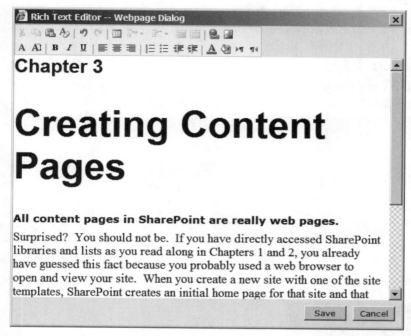

Figure 3-7. *Copying text from Word and pasting it into the Rich Text Editor*

■**Note** You could select all the copied text and click the **Clear Format** button to remove all existing formatting. However, the time required to reformat a document may not justify the slight increase in space needed by the page when you directly copy it from Word.

Adding a Table to Your Content

A similar trade-off between time to reformat and increased space exists when working with tables. You could of course create a new table directly from within the Rich Text Editor using the **Create Table** tool. Figure 3-8 shows the only two settings you can define for a table: the number of columns and the number of rows.

After you create the table, the Rich Text Editor does not provide any additional formatting options. However, when you create a table in Word, you can apply any of the many predefined table styles or create your own. In this case, if you want to control the table's appearance, you may want to create your table in Word and then cut and paste it into the Rich Text Editor, which preserves most if not all of the formatting defined through Word.

Figure 3-8. *Inserting a table into your rich text content*

Your Final Content Page

Figure 3-9 shows how the Meerkat page might look to a visitor to your site after adding a table that scientifically identifies the meerkat. Note that the visitor does not have page edit rights and therefore does not have the **Site Actions** button in the upper-right corner of the page. Thus she can view the page, but not edit it.

Figure 3-9. *How the Meerkat page looks to a visitor*

Adding Functionality with Web Part Pages

In the previous section, you saw how easily you can create basic web pages within SharePoint using the Rich Text Editor. However, basic web pages do not let you display your libraries or lists.

Creating a New Web Part Page

As shown earlier in Figure 3-1, you can create a web part page by clicking **Create** within the **Site Actions** menu and then selecting **Web Part Page** from the **Web Pages** section. Figure 3-10 shows the new web part page. In addition to naming the page, you must select a page layout, of which SharePoint includes several. These layouts consist of various combinations of zones or content areas, including header, footer, left column, right column, body, multiple center columns, and top rows. When you highlight any of the layout templates, a sample layout appears on the left side of the page illustrating the position, size, and orientation of the web part zones.

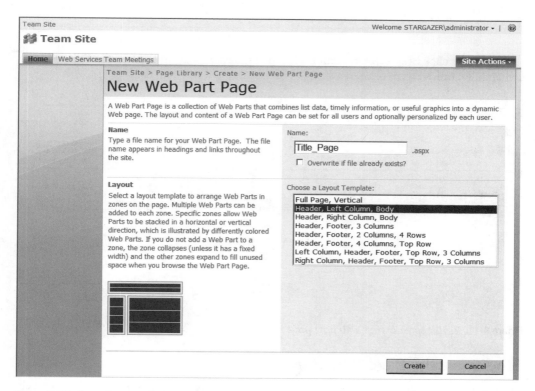

Figure 3-10. *Creating a web part page*

■**Tip** Do not include spaces in page names. If you want to separate words within a name, use an underscore character (_) between the words. Web pages translate a space in a name to the string %20, making referencing them a little more complex.

Even with such a large selection of templates, you may not find one you like. Following are two ways you can increase your template options:

1. You can ask your SharePoint administrator to create a new page template for you. This option may take some time, but after installing it, you can create web part pages with it just like using any of the built-in templates. You need to use this method if you require a totally different zone layout.

2. You can manipulate the appearance of the various web part zones by leaving selected zones empty and/or physically changing the width or height of web parts in adjacent zones. However, this method does not let you add or redefine where zones appear.

■**Note**   You cannot apply a new page template to an existing page. You can only use new page templates to create new pages.

After you click **Create**, SharePoint builds the requested page and opens it in **Edit** mode as shown in Figure 3-11.

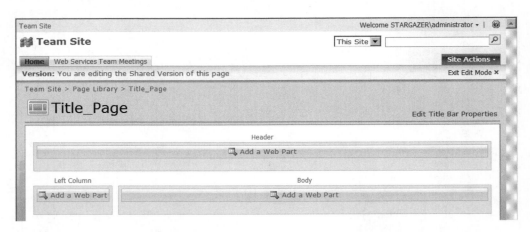

Figure 3-11. *Building your first web part page*

Modifying the Page Title Bar

The created page includes a title bar across the top and three web part areas. The Header web part zone spans the entire width of the page. The Left Column web part zone appears as a narrow area that you could use to create a navigation or menu area for other pages in the site.

■**Tip**   If you have a library of documents or even a page library that you want your viewers to access, you can use the Content Query web part in MOSS 2007 to create a menu of those documents. In WSS 3.0, you must build your menu manually.

The Body web part zone occupies the rest of the page width. You might use this zone to hold general information for your site such as libraries or lists. It can also display a web part that allows HTML-based content to appear on the page.

You may have noticed that the title bar by default includes the page title as well as an icon of a generic web part page. To change one or both of these defaults, click the **Edit Title Bar Properties** link to the right of this area.

Editing the title bar properties displays the panel shown on the right side of Figure 3-12.

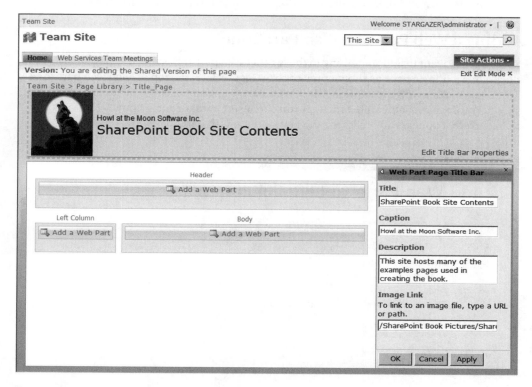

Figure 3-12. *Modifying the page title bar properties*

■**Caution** If you do not see the title bar properties, your screen resolution may be hiding this area. Check whether the browser displays a horizontal scrollbar at the bottom of the window. Move the scroll thumb to the right or click the right side of the horizontal scrollbar to expose the properties area.

In the **Title Bar** properties panel, you can change the page title as well as add a caption that actually appears above the title, but in a smaller font size. In Figure 3-12, I've added the company name in the caption field. You can also provide a different image for this area. Here, I add the logo of the fictitious Howl at the Moon Software Inc.

As in the Meerkat web page, I first upload the company logo into a picture library for the current site. Then for the URL, I include the path to this logo. However, this time, I use a relative

URL path rather than an absolute path. Since this site is my server's default site or top site, I can make an absolute URL path a relative URL path by trimming off the initial server name. As a result, I can define my relative URL as follows:

```
/<picture library>/<library folder>/<filename>
```

Relative URLs add mobility to a site. I can move the site to a different server, and it will find the company logo without making a single change to this page. On the other hand, coding the absolute reference and then moving your site to a different server will break the page.

Adding a Web Part to a Web Part Zone

Next you may want to add something in those other web part zones that this page makes available. While editing a page as shown previously in Figure 3-12, the top of each web part zone contains a header with the caption **Add a Web Part**. Click any of these headers to display a dialog box of the available web parts that you can insert in that zone. Figure 3-13 shows the dialog box that appears after clicking the Left Column web part zone.

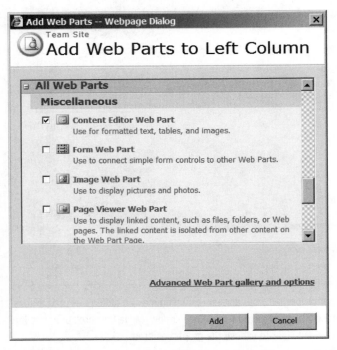

Figure 3-13. *Selecting a web part from the Add Web Parts dialog box*

The available web parts list consists of at least two major sections. The first section has the title **Lists and Libraries**. If you scroll through this portion of the list, the names of the web parts should look familiar, as it includes the lists and libraries that you have created. In fact, everything that I talked about creating in Chapters 1 and 2 appears in this list if you have been following along on your site. If you want a special list or library to appear on a web page, just create it using the methods in the previous chapters. Then you can add it as a web part to a page. You can even define special views for lists or libraries and use those views, rather than the default views, on your page.

However, SharePoint also provides additional web parts out of the box that allow you to customize your page further. You can find these web parts in the **All Web Parts** section. Subsequent chapters will examine several of these web parts. However, for now, select the **Content Editor Web Part** option as shown in Figure 3-14.

Figure 3-14. *Adding a Content Editor web part to a web zone*

This web part allows you to enter plain text or formatted text to create content for the page. You can also create tables and add images relatively easily. Content can be directly entered using an interface similar to Word, making the creation of your own content web pages nearly as easy as creating a Word document.

This web part should interest you because it provides a very customizable platform to create just about any text area. In an earlier section, you saw how easily you could add text to a page using the Rich Text Editor. The Content Editor web part allows you to do the same thing. However, the Content Editor web part also allows you to add formatted HTML text. As an example, let's see how to create a menu for this page using a few lines of text and a little bit of HTML.

Adding Content to the Content Editor Web Part

To start adding content to the Content Editor web part, notice the **Edit** button in the web part's title bar. You open the web part to edit its properties by either clicking this button or by clicking the text "open the tool pane" in the default paragraph of the part. SharePoint then opens a properties panel for the web part as shown in Figure 3-15.

Note Depending on the width of your screen and the size of the window you have open, you may click the **Edit** button and think at first that nothing has happened. The properties panel for the web part appears to the right of the page window. If this panel materializes off the right edge of your screen, you may not see it at first. However, by examining the horizontal scrollbar at the bottom of the window, you should notice that the scrollbar's thumb has changed in size to indicate that there is additional information off the right side of the screen. Click in this blank area in the scrollbar, drag the scrollbar thumb, or use the arrow at the end of the scrollbar to move your view to the right. Now you should see the panel as shown in Figure 3-15.

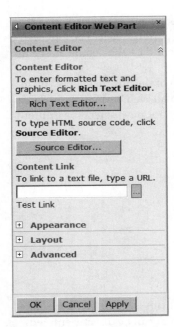

Figure 3-15. *Properties for the Content Editor web part*

The properties panel begins by giving you the option to enter formatted text using the Rich Text Editor or to enter HTML source code using the Source Editor. You select an editor depending on how you plan to create your content. If you plan to enter content just like you would enter text in a Word document, select the Rich Text Editor. You saw the interface for the Rich Text Editor earlier. If you have precreated content, select and copy the content from your original document and then paste it within this editor.

On the other hand, if you have experience creating web pages using HTML, you may want to either directly enter your content using HTML tags for formatting text in the Source Editor or, if you have another program to generate HTML documents, copy and paste your HTML formatted content into the Source Editor.

And you can switch back and forth between editors. In other words, you can start entering your content using the Rich Text Editor, perhaps even making some formatting changes, and then switch to the Source Editor to add a few custom HTML tags as finishing touches. In fact, I will walk you through that technique to create a simple menu for the current page.

To begin, open the Rich Text Editor and create a title for the menu such as Howl Menu. Select the title, and if you want, change its formatting by enlarging the font, switching its color, and perhaps even making it bold. Next, drop down a line or two and add each menu item as a separate line of text. Figure 3-16 shows a very simple start of a menu created in the Rich Text Editor.

Next, you'll convert each of these lines into a menu link or a hyperlink: select the text from the first line, and then click the tool button that looks like a small globe with a chain link beneath it. This action pops up a dialog box to define the hyperlink properties similar to those seen previously for images. Figure 3-17 shows this dialog box.

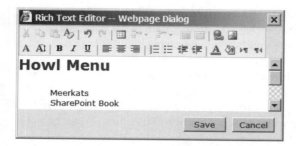

Figure 3-16. *Using the Rich Text Editor to create your raw menu content*

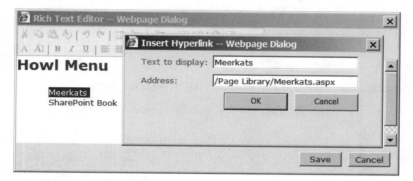

Figure 3-17. *Adding hyperlinks to each menu item*

The text that you selected before clicking the Hyperlink tool appears in the first text box. The second text box allows you to enter the address for the hyperlink. Again, this text box requires that you know the URL and can type it in. It provides no browse option. To easily add a hyperlink to a page or site that already exists, follow these steps:

1. Open the page.

2. Copy the URL that appears in the address bar.

3. Paste the URL into the **Address** field.

After you finish building your menu, click the **Save** button to close the Rich Text Editor. This action does not close the properties panel for the web part, so your changes do not imme-diately appear in the web part. However, you can force the web part to update by clicking the **Apply** button at the bottom of the properties panel. Once you have updated the web part, you can test the link by clicking it.

Modifying the Generated HTML

In this example, if you test one of your menu links by clicking it, you notice that the linked page replaces your current site page. This may be exactly what you want so users can navigate to other pages. However, if you want the linked page to appear in a separate browser window, you need to make a small adjustment to the web part content. That change requires you to edit the content with the Source Editor so you can adjust the raw HTML. You may be thinking that you did not write any HTML because you used the Rich Text Editor. You may not have directly added any HTML; however, by changing text formats and by applying hyperlinks to text, you did add HTML to the raw text.

To see the HTML that you generated while creating your menu, edit the web part again, but this time rather than selecting the Rich Text Editor, choose the Source Editor. The HTML shown in Figure 3-18 defines not just the content to display in the Content Editor web part, but also how to format that text and what to do when a user clicks one of the menu links.

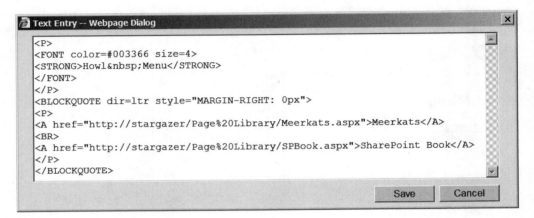

Figure 3-18. *Viewing the HTML created for the menu*

We will not attempt to analyze the HTML here. Many good books can be found in your local bookstore to help you understand HTML if you need assistance. Instead, I want to show how a simple addition to one of the menu links can force the referenced page or site to open in a new browser window.

Notice the two menu lines begin with the following text:

```
<A href=...
```

This line of text begins an anchor tag definition. *Anchor tags* define a hyperlink and include two required parts: a reference URL that the link points to and one or more characters to visually display the link and allow the user to click it. Without at least a single character to click, the user would not have any way to execute the link. Notice that the text that we originally entered in the Rich Text Editor to represent the menu item appears between the <A> and </A> tags. The URL for the link occurs within the <A> tag and begins with the element

```
href =
```

However, by adding another element to the <A> tag, you can tell the browser to display the page in a separate instance of the browser window. (If you use a tabbed browser, this may open a separate tab rather than a separate window.) You only need to add the following element:

```
Target = "_blank"
```

Thus, you could cause the second menu item to open in a separate window by changing the line

```
<A href="http://stargazer/Page%20Library/SPBook.aspx">SharePoint Book</A>
```

to

```
<A href="http://stargazer/Page%20Library/SPBook.aspx" target="_blank">
SharePoint Book</A>
```

Adjusting the Appearance of the Web Parts

When you look at the finished menu in Figure 3-19, you may wonder why the menu web part stretches all the way across the screen and where the content from the other column would appear. Or you may wonder why you see the header **Content Editor Web Part**.

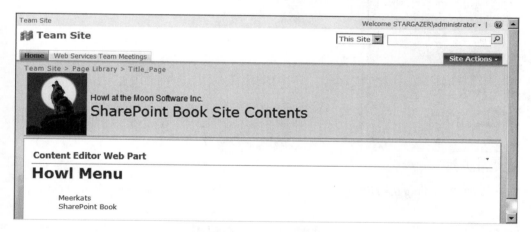

Figure 3-19. *A menu defined with the Content Editor web part*

To answer the first question, the reason why the menu stretches the full width of the page lies in the fact that the Right Column web part zone has no content yet. When you do not add a web part to a zone, that zone collapses in view mode as if it does not exist. The zones that do exist then expand to fill in that empty space by default unless you fix their height and width. This effect also explains why no gap appears at the top of the page for the Header web part zone. When you add a list, library, or other web part to the Right Column web part zone or the Header web part zone, those areas appear and cause the repositioning and resizing of the menu automatically.

The top of the menu still says **Content Editor Web Part** because you did not change the web part **Title** property but rather added a separate title to the content area. To correct this "double" title, edit the page again as well as the web part and remove the **Title** value. While in the properties panel, change the border type to **Border Only** to display a thin borderline around the menu part to set it off from the rest of the page. Figure 3-20 shows the settings changed to create the page in Figure 3-21.

Of course, this page still needs additional content. Next, you'll add a few lists.

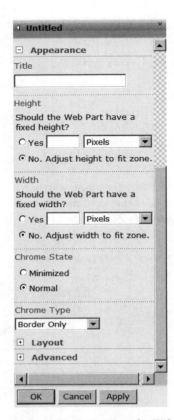

Figure 3-20. *Removing the Title value and changing the Chrome Type setting to Border Only*

Figure 3-21. *View of the modified page with menu*

WHAT PASTED WORD TEXT REALLY LOOKS LIKE

Earlier in the chapter, I mentioned that you could copy and paste text directly from a Word document into the Rich Text Editor. I also suggested that this practice could bring a lot of unnecessary overhead into your page. To see this for yourself, add some text into a Content Editor web part by performing these steps:

1. Open a Word document and copy a portion of the text.

2. Add a Content Editor web part to a page as described earlier in this section.

3. Edit the properties of the Content Editor web part.

4. Open the Rich Text Editor.

5. Paste the text you copied from Word.

6. Click the **Save** button to save the content and close the editor window.

7. Open the Source Editor by clicking the **Source Editor** button.

You now see your content with the formatting interpreted as HTML. Depending on the text you copied, you will see various HTML tags used to format the text. The following illustration shows the beginning of the text I copied for Figure 1-7 earlier in this chapter in the Source Editor. You can see many tags that as HTML will have little or no meaning since these classes and styles have not been defined in the web site. For example, the class and style elements of paragraph tags have no effect on the displayed page. Other tags such as the `<SPAN style="mso-spacerun: yes">` tags appear to preserve two or more consecutive spaces, and other whitespace appears between words because HTML generally ignores extra whitespace. Your content may include other tags that take up space but do nothing, especially if you copied text from a highly formatted page. This extra "stuff" will not hurt your page, but it does make your page larger than it needs to be, thus increasing the transfer time across the Internet and the rendering time needed by your browser.

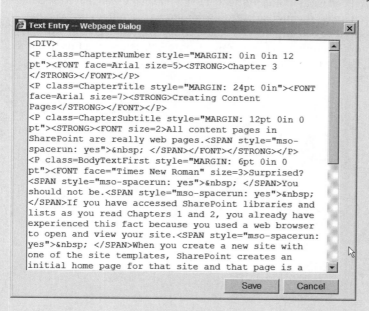

How significantly these issues affect you depends on your individual circumstances. Just be aware that this occurs.

Using Web Parts to Display Libraries and Lists

To add a list to one of the web part zones, edit the page again. Select the web part zone to which you want to add the list. Suppose you want to add a previous list to the Right Column web part zone. Click the zone header. When the Add Web Parts dialog box appears (as shown back in Figure 3-13), scroll through the Lists and Libraries section to find a list you want to display on the page. In this example, I will demonstrate adding the **Upcoming Events** list, used in Chapter 2. Remember that you can change properties of existing lists. In the discussion of lists in the previous chapter, you saw how to create multiple views from the same list. Each view might contain a different subset of columns, or you might sort or filter the items in the view in a different way. You can even create a special view just for this page if none of your other views displays the data the way you want.

While editing the web part, you can also edit other properties, including its title, height, width, chrome state, chrome type, and other layout characteristics.

In the Left Column web part zone, let's add a second web part. Suppose you need a team contacts list using a custom view that displays only each contact's first and last name along with his business telephone number. Using what you learned in Chapter 2, first create the new view of your contacts list. Then add the list to the Left Column web part zone. The **Selected View** property in the web part's properties panel lets you select the view displayed on the page.

After you add this second web part, notice that SharePoint places it above the menu added to the page earlier. In fact, every time you add a web part to a web part zone, SharePoint adds it to the top of the zone. Suppose you want the menu at the top of the page, not the contacts list. How do you order your web parts the way you want?

While still in page **Edit** mode, click the header of any web part and drag that web part to another location. In this case, click the menu header of the web part, which now says "Untitled" if you removed the title as discussed earlier. Drag the header to the top of the web part zone beneath the zone header. When you release the mouse button, SharePoint rearranges the web parts. You can even drag a web part that you initially placed in a different web part zone from its current position to a position in another web part zone. Figure 3-22 shows the finished web part page with two lists and a Content Editor web part for a menu.

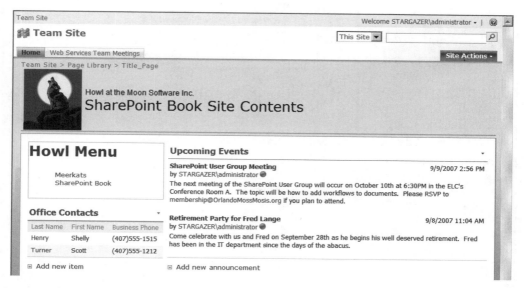

Figure 3-22. *Completed web part page*

Creating Master-Detail Relationships Between Your Lists

One of the more interesting things you can do with lists is to define master-detail relationships between two or more lists. A *master-detail relationship* between lists looks a lot like the parent-child relationship between tables in a database. Basically, it means that a list designated as the master has items that relate to one or more items in a second list called the detail list.

One example of a master-detail relationship might involve a list of the departments in your organization. Since departments consist of one or more staff members, you might build a detail list of staff and include their names, titles, telephone extensions, and related information.

Another example might list your employees in a master list and the projects they work on in the detail list. In fact, the staff detail list of the first example might serve as the master list for the second example.

In SharePoint, when you create a master-detail relationship between lists, the master list controls the items you can see in the detail list. In other words, the master list displays all its items. However, the item you select from the master list determines which items, if any, appear in the detail list.

Figure 3-23 shows two lists on one page. The top list displays a list of authors for different genres of computer books. The bottom list displays a list of books written by each of the authors. You probably noticed that author names provide a common element between these two lists. You must have a common or linking field between your two lists to create a master-detail relationship. Thus you can create a master-detail relationship between these two lists using the author field.

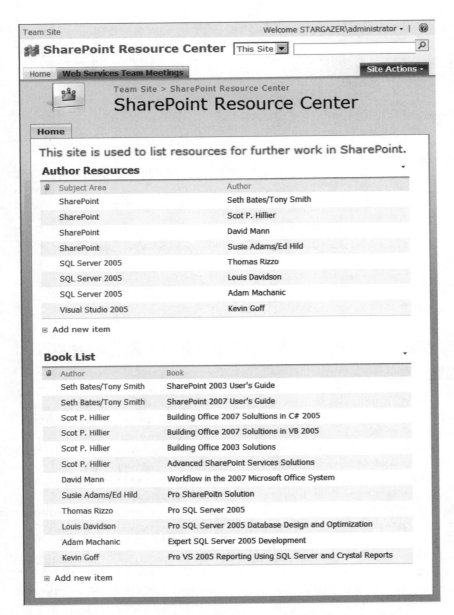

Figure 3-23. *Initial two lists before defining a master-detail relationship*

Once you place both lists on the page, you can define the relationship between them starting from either list. If you begin with the **Author Resources** list, drop down the menu from the **Edit** button in the list header. You will see the option **Connections** at the bottom of menu. As you hover your cursor over the word **Connections**, a secondary menu pops out to the side that defines the possible connection types. From this menu, move your mouse over the **Provide Row To** option. You use the **Provide Row To** option when you begin from the master list side. You use the **Get Sort/Filter From** option when you begin with the detail list. Another menu appears listing the other available lists on the current page. In this case, select **Book List** from the menu. Figure 3-24 shows this sequence of selections.

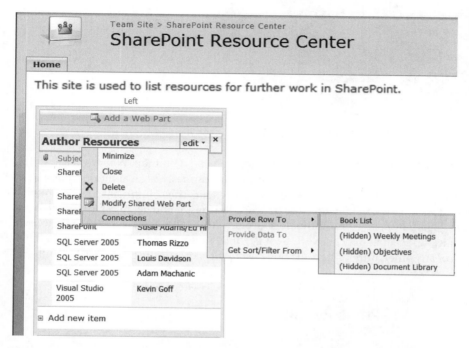

Figure 3-24. *Defining the connection from the master list*

SharePoint displays a dialog box asking you to select the column from the master list to use to filter (link) the detail list. Figure 3-25 shows this dialog box, prompting for the **Author Resources** column to use and the selection of the **Author** column.

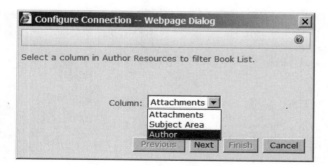

Figure 3-25. *Selecting the linking field from the master list*

After you select the column from the master list, you must select the connecting column from the detail list. Figure 3-26 shows the selection of the detail list column, **Author**.

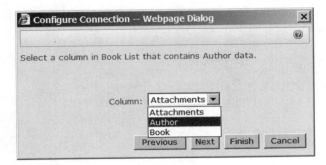

Figure 3-26. *Selecting the linking field for the detail list*

Now click the **Finish** button to complete the relationship definition. When you exit **Edit** mode for the page, you see that the master list, **Author Resources**, has an additional column at the beginning of the list. This column has no column header. The column has a radio button before each list item. To see the relationship between the master and detail list, click any of the radio buttons. Figure 3-27 shows the **Author Resources** list with the author Scot P. Hillier selected. In the **Book List**, notice that only books by Scot P. Hillier now appear. Similarly, clicking the radio button of any other author filters the book list to display only the books for that author.

Team Site > SharePoint Resource Center

SharePoint Resource Center

Home

This site is used to list resources for further work in SharePoint.

Author Resources

	Subject Area	Author
○	SharePoint	Seth Bates/Tony Smith
◉	SharePoint	Scot P. Hillier
○	SharePoint	David Mann
○	SharePoint	Susie Adams/Ed Hild
○	SQL Server 2005	Thomas Rizzo
○	SQL Server 2005	Louis Davidson
○	SQL Server 2005	Adam Machanic
○	Visual Studio 2005	Kevin Goff

⊞ Add new item

Book List

	Author	Book
	Scot P. Hillier	Building Office 2007 Solultions in C# 2005
	Scot P. Hillier	Building Office 2007 Solultions in VB 2005
	Scot P. Hillier	Building Office 2003 Solutions
	Scot P. Hillier	Advanced SharePoint Services Solutions

⊞ Add new item

Figure 3-27. *Filtering books by author*

Editing Existing Pages with Check-Out and Check-In

In the first portion of this chapter, I did not mention the need for Check-Out or Check-In in regards to web pages. However, just like documents in a document library, you need to be concerned about locking your web pages while you edit them. Say you open a web page to make changes, and while you have it open for an extended time, another staff member opens the same web page to make changes; whoever saves their changes first loses because the second person to save could overwrite the changes saved by the first.

So what can you do to protect your web page while you have it open for editing? You check the page out just like you do with documents. Depending on whether your SharePoint administrator has configured your site to automatically check out pages, you may need to perform the check-out as a separate step as shown in Figure 3-28.

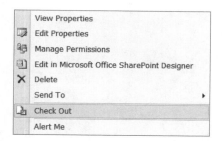

Figure 3-28. *Manually checking out web pages before editing*

Figure 3-28 shows the options available from the drop-down menu when you view your available pages in a page library. In this particular case, suppose the site does not force a check-out before opening the page for editing. If you want to safely edit the page and do not know how long it will take you to edit it, you need to first select the **Check Out** option before manually editing the page. If you have Microsoft Office SharePoint Designer installed on your system, you can use the option to edit your page via this tool. If you do not have Microsoft Office SharePoint Designer, you can still edit the page after checking it out by clicking the page name.

When you check out a web page, the page icon before the name displays a small box with an arrow in it (which will appear green on your screen) like the one shown in Figure 3-28 next to the **Check Out** option. If you attempt to open a checked-out page and edit the document, you will get one of two possible warnings that you cannot save your changes depending on what you attempt to change. If you attempt to change text in a content area such as a plain web page or the text in a Content Editor web part, SharePoint displays the dialog box shown in Figure 3-29.

While both of these examples show that SharePoint protects the integrity of the checked-out page, you may wish that SharePoint had warned you of the document's status before you started editing it. Well, actually it did. You just must be aware of that little green box in the bottom corner of the page icon when you view the pages in the **Page Library**.

Figure 3-29. *Warning that you cannot save content changes to a checked-out page*

On the other hand, if you attempt to edit the properties of a web part, SharePoint displays the message shown at the top of Figure 3-30 when you attempt to apply your changes or click the **OK** button in the properties panel.

Figure 3-30. *Warning that you cannot save changes to a web part*

Earlier in this section, I mentioned the possibility that your SharePoint administrator may have configured the site to automatically check out pages when you edit them. To see how she does that, return to the **Page Library** and select **Document Library Settings** from the **Settings** tab. Then on the **Customize Page Library** page, click **Versioning Settings** under the **General Settings** group of options. The resulting page, shown in Figure 3-31, has four settings groups.

The first group has a single setting that asks whether you want someone to approve all new and changed items. When you select **Yes** to this setting, you must select an option from the **Draft Item Security** group. When you require approval, SharePoint places all new and changed documents in draft mode. While in draft mode, you may not want other visitors to your site who just have read-only rights to see the page. Perhaps you want to allow anyone with edit rights to view the new or changed pages, even if that person did not create the changes or new pages. This security mode represents a collaboration mode to editing. In the most restrictive mode, SharePoint limits access to new and changed pages to users who have approval rights so that they can approve the pages. Of course, in any of these security modes, the person who makes the changes or creates the new page has rights to view and further edit the page.

Going back to the second settings group, **Document Version History**, the SharePoint administrator can define how many versions of a page SharePoint should retain. The next section discusses versions in more detail.

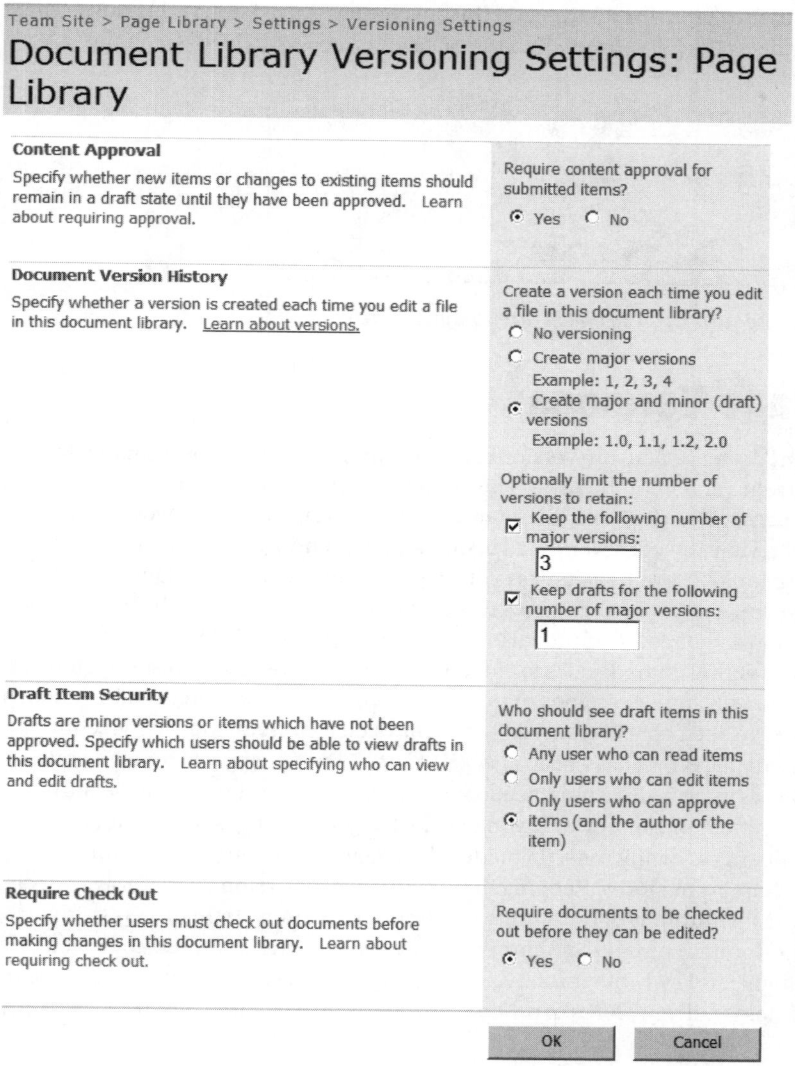

Team Site > Page Library > Settings > Versioning Settings

Document Library Versioning Settings: Page Library

Content Approval

Specify whether new items or changes to existing items should remain in a draft state until they have been approved.   Learn about requiring approval.

Require content approval for submitted items?

⊙ Yes   ○ No

Document Version History

Specify whether a version is created each time you edit a file in this document library. Learn about versions.

Create a version each time you edit a file in this document library?

○ No versioning

○ Create major versions
   Example: 1, 2, 3, 4

⊙ Create major and minor (draft) versions
   Example: 1.0, 1.1, 1.2, 2.0

Optionally limit the number of versions to retain:

☑ Keep the following number of major versions:

[3]

☑ Keep drafts for the following number of major versions:

[1]

Draft Item Security

Drafts are minor versions or items which have not been approved. Specify which users should be able to view drafts in this document library.   Learn about specifying who can view and edit drafts.

Who should see draft items in this document library?

○ Any user who can read items

○ Only users who can edit items

⊙ Only users who can approve items (and the author of the item)

Require Check Out

Specify whether users must check out documents before making changes in this document library.   Learn about requiring check out.

Require documents to be checked out before they can be edited?

⊙ Yes   ○ No

| OK | Cancel |

Figure 3-31. *Setting your Page Library to require check-out of edited pages*

Finally, the last group on the settings page, **Require Check Out**, allows the SharePoint administrator to require check-out of pages before you can edit them. When set, this option checks whether you first checked the page out before you can open it for editing. If you attempt to edit a page without first checking the page out, SharePoint displays the dialog box shown in Figure 3-32.

If you click **OK** in this dialog box, SharePoint automatically checks out the page and opens it for editing. When you complete your changes, remember to check your changes back in. If you forget to check your pages in, other staff members cannot edit the page. Also, content approvers cannot approve the page and make it available to site readers. Of course, if you have administrator rights to the site, you can override the check-out. However, use this power only as a last resort, as it causes the person who had the page checked out to lose her changes.

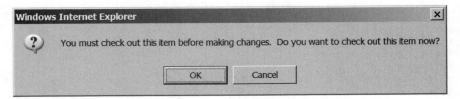

Figure 3-32. *SharePoint requires you to check out a page before editing it.*

Tracking Page Versions

By default, SharePoint does not activate versioning. In versionless mode, every change to a page updates the current version of the page. This mode uses the smallest amount of storage space for your site's pages. Whether your site maintains versioning for your pages or not, all visitors to your site can view the current major version and, depending on the Draft Item Security setting, minor versions of your page unless you require content approval. Only by using content approval can you guarantee that pages under revision remain hidden from your site visitors until you submit the page for approval and a content approver publishes the page.

If your SharePoint administrator decides to allow SharePoint to save version histories, he must decide whether to store only major versions or both major and minor versions. Major versions represent pages that have been checked back in (and approved if content approval is required). Minor versions represent pages that have been checked back in, but not approved. So you might think of minor versions as intermediate modifications or drafts to a page either because multiple people have made modifications or because you checked in your changes more than once as you worked on your changes. In any case, if you decide to keep versions, you can limit the number of versions SharePoint stores. Keeping in mind that each version uses storage space, you may want to limit the number of both major and minor versions. In Figure 3-31, the SharePoint administrator has configured SharePoint to store only the last three approved versions (major versions) and only the minor versions since the most recent major version. In other words, it only retains current works in progress as well as the last three published versions.

Publishing Pages to Your Site

When you edit a page with versioning turned on, your changes may not be visible to everyone depending on how your SharePoint administrator defined the **Draft Item Security** and **Content Approval** settings for your library. To be visible to everyone, your pages must be published. If your site does not use versioning and approval, SharePoint publishes pages by default when you check them back in.

If your site uses versioning, SharePoint publishes only major versions of pages. However, if your site also requires approval, checking in a page to save your changes from your current session does not necessarily make it visible to anyone other than yourself and users with approver rights. Therefore, if you check in a page but still have more work to do on it, you should either assign it the next minor version number or reuse the current minor version number if the page already had a minor version when you opened it to edit. Keep in mind that if you reuse the current version number, you cannot back out your changes by merely restoring the prior versions. If you expect to make further changes before publishing your page or if you expect other members of your team to make changes, you should check the page back in using a minor version number. If your check-in completes the changes you want to make before publishing, save the changes with the next major version number. No matter whether you intend to check the page in as a major or minor version, SharePoint tracks the versions of the page and automatically assigns the next available major or minor number for you.

Perhaps you do not need to keep intermediate versions between major changes to the page. You could ask your SharePoint administrator to turn off minor versioning. This guarantees that every checked-in version is a major version.

You can also turn off all versioning if the **Page Library** is informal and you do not need to save each version. This selection saves storage space required by your site. However, if you ever need a prior version of the page, you may be out of luck unless your SharePoint administrator can get one from a backup copy of the database. Retrieving pages from a backup copy of the database is a very time-intensive task. If you do this too often, you may discover your SharePoint administrator hiding when she hears you coming toward her office.

To publish your most recent page update, you must assign the next major version number to it when you check it in. To check in your page, open the **Page Library** and right-click the page. Select **Check In** from the drop-down list of options. Figure 3-33 shows the **Check in** dialog box. Notice that in addition to assigning your updated page either a minor or major version number, you can determine whether you want to keep the modified page checked out, but only if you save the updated page as a minor version.

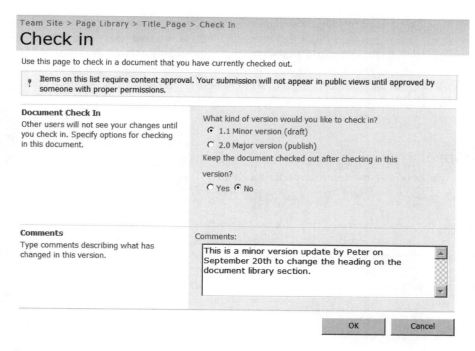

Figure 3-33. *Checking in a modified web page*

Anytime you check a page back in, you have the option of adding comments to the version. You may want to use comments to document who made the change and when, and provide a change summary.

If you choose to assign the updated page a minor version, you can always return to the document through the **Page Library**, open the drop-down menu for the page, and click **Publish a Major Version**. When published this way, you still have the option of adding comments as shown in Figure 3-34.

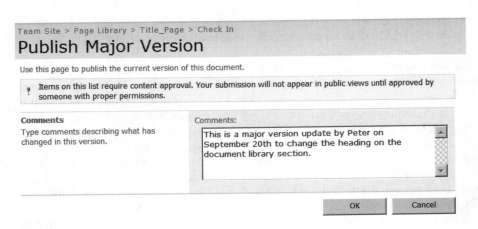

Figure 3-34. *Publishing a major version directly from the Page Library*

Note the message at the top of Figure 3-34. If your **Page Library** requires approval of major changes before the public can view them, this message reminds you that your updates must still receive approval, even though you just saved the page as a major version. Click **OK** to check in your page and mark it as pending approval as shown in Figure 3-35. SharePoint updates the **Approval Status** column automatically from **Draft** to **Pending**, indicating that you have saved a major version release of the page that needs approval before others can see it.

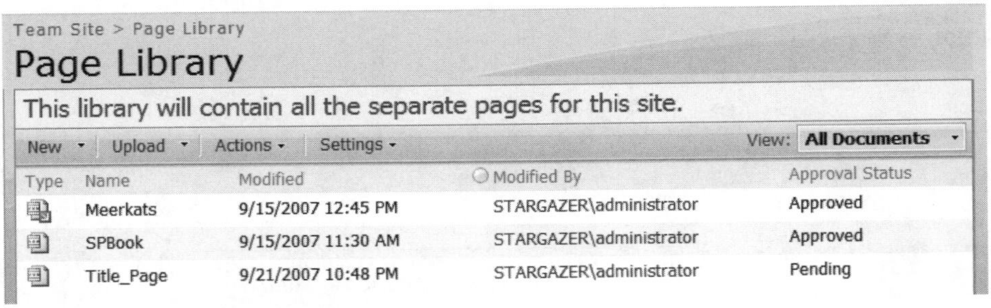

Team Site > Page Library

Page Library

This library will contain all the separate pages for this site.

New ▾   Upload ▾   Actions ▾   Settings ▾   View: **All Documents** ▾

Type	Name	Modified	◯ Modified By	Approval Status
	Meerkats	9/15/2007 12:45 PM	STARGAZER\administrator	Approved
	SPBook	9/15/2007 11:30 AM	STARGAZER\administrator	Approved
	Title_Page	9/21/2007 10:48 PM	STARGAZER\administrator	Pending

Figure 3-35. *Pages checked in as major versions have a status of Pending.*

To approve the page, you need to have the site administrator or another user with approval rights open the **Page Library**. He can then click to the right of the page name to open the drop-down menu for the page and select **Approve/Reject**. Clicking this option displays the page shown in Figure 3-36.

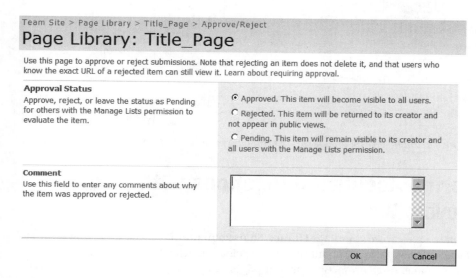

Team Site > Page Library > Title_Page > Approve/Reject

Page Library: Title_Page

Use this page to approve or reject submissions. Note that rejecting an item does not delete it, and that users who know the exact URL of a rejected item can still view it. Learn about requiring approval.

Approval Status

Approve, reject, or leave the status as Pending for others with the Manage Lists permission to evaluate the item.

◉ Approved. This item will become visible to all users.

○ Rejected. This item will be returned to its creator and not appear in public views.

○ Pending. This item will remain visible to its creator and all users with the Manage Lists permission.

Comment

Use this field to enter any comments about why the item was approved or rejected.

[OK]   [Cancel]

Figure 3-36. *Approvers can approve or reject a major version.*

As you can see in this figure, approvers have three possible actions they can select on this request:

- **Approved**: The newest page version is made visible to all users.

- **Rejected**: The newest page version does not become public. If the page has a previously approved version, it remains the public version.

- **Pending**: The page remains in its current security state and is not published. The approver typically uses this option when asking for further clarification on the change.

No matter what option the approver selects, she can leave a comment. However, approvers should use comments when rejecting a page or sending it back pending additional clarification or work. When the approver clicks **OK** on this page, SharePoint executes the page action, changing the status of the page in the **Page Library** to **Approved**, **Rejected**, or **Pending** based on the selection made.

If you were to look at the version history for this page as shown in Figure 3-37, you would see that a new major release (2.0) is now listed after approving the page, and all of the minor releases from version 1.0 have been removed because the version setup as defined in Figure 3-31 only requires SharePoint to save minor releases within the current major release.

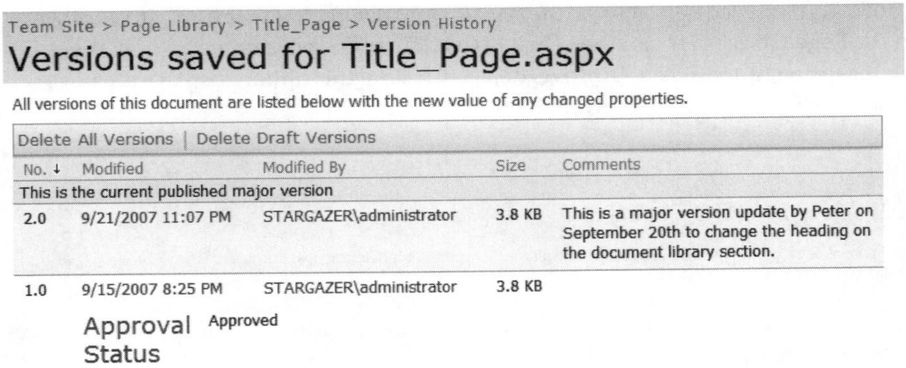

Team Site > Page Library > Title_Page > Version History

Versions saved for Title_Page.aspx

All versions of this document are listed below with the new value of any changed properties.

Delete All Versions	Delete Draft Versions			
No. ↓	Modified	Modified By	Size	Comments
This is the current published major version				
2.0	9/21/2007 11:07 PM	STARGAZER\administrator	3.8 KB	This is a major version update by Peter on September 20th to change the heading on the document library section.
1.0	9/15/2007 8:25 PM	STARGAZER\administrator	3.8 KB	

Approval   Approved
Status

Figure 3-37. *The version history for a page can tell you who made each change and when he made it.*

Recovering Accidental Deletions with the Recycle Bin

When you delete a page from your **Page Library**, SharePoint prompts to confirm your desire to delete it. If you only had to worry about your own accidental deletions, this dialog box may seem like more than enough protection for your pages. However, you probably have several people with edit rights on your site. In some large organizations, you may have dozens of people with edit rights, perhaps even hundreds. So what happens when they delete a page because they don't think they need it, a page you worked on for hours and for which you have no other backup? I suppose you could read them the riot act, otherwise known as corporate policy. Of course, if they sit higher in the organization than you, that could limit your career potential.

Fortunately, if someone accidentally deletes a page, SharePoint provides a safety net. Both WSS 3.0 and MOSS 2007 support a Recycle Bin, which like the Recycle Bin on your desktop temporarily stores deleted files. For example, suppose someone with no appreciation for your concern about animals deletes your Meerkat page from the **Page Library**. Rather than rant and rave, you can recover that page with just a few mouse clicks. Begin by clicking the **Recycle Bin** option at the bottom of the **Quick Launch** menu on the left of the **Page Library** page. The Recycle Bin, shown in Figure 3-38, displays a listing of all the documents deleted within the last 30 days.

To recover a deleted object, click the check box to the left of the object to select it. Then click the **Restore Selection** option at the top of the page.

When you delete a page, you delete all of the versions of that page as well. SharePoint keeps all versions together as a single item in the Recycle Bin so that when you recover an object from it, SharePoint recovers all versions of that document.

■**Tip** You can ask your SharePoint administrator to change the length of time items stay in the Recycle Bin. She can go into Central Administration and select the **Application Management** tab. Then by selecting the **Web Application General Settings** page, she can scroll down to the **Recycle Bin** section and change the number of days items are kept in the Recycle Bin.

Team Site > Recycle Bin

Recycle Bin

Use this page to restore items that you have deleted from this site or to empty deleted items. Items that were deleted more than 30 day(s) ago will be automatically emptied. To manage deleted items for the entire Site Collection go to the Site Collection Recycle Bin.

↰ Restore Selection | ✕ Delete Selection

	Type	Name	Original Location	Created By	Deleted↓	Size
☑	📄	SPBook.aspx	/Page Library	STARGAZER\administrator	9/21/2007 9:03 PM	9.4 KB
☐	📄	Title_Page.aspx	/Page Library	STARGAZER\administrator	9/15/2007 8:21 PM	4.1 KB
☐	📄	TitlePage.aspx	/Page Library	STARGAZER\administrator	9/15/2007 8:18 PM	3.7 KB
☐	📰	Announcements	/Lists	STARGAZER\administrator	9/13/2007 9:36 PM	13.4 KB
☐	📰	Get Started with Windows SharePoint Services!	/Lists/Announcements	STARGAZER\administrator	9/13/2007 9:36 PM	< 1 KB
☐	▥	test	/Lists	STARGAZER\administrator	9/10/2007 9:20 PM	13.4 KB
☐	📄	This is a test document.docx	/Test of Approvals	STARGAZER\administrator	9/7/2007 9:35 PM	20.3 KB

Figure 3-38. *The Recycle Bin collects all deleted objects.*

Summary

This chapter took a look at creating content pages within SharePoint. We focused on basic pages and web part pages, which are available in both WSS 3.0 and MOSS 2007. MOSS 2007 also supports a third type of page called publishing pages. Although publishing pages weren't discussed in this chapter, if you can work with basic and web part pages, you will have no trouble with publishing pages.

You first learned how to create a basic page and saw how to work with images and hyperlinks. In both cases, you must be careful when entering the URL of the image or hyperlink site, because you must directly enter the value without the help of a browse feature. Furthermore, you must store your images in a picture library. You also saw that you can take a Word document and copy the text directly into the content area of a web page while preserving most of the formatting of the page. In fact, copying a table created in Word may be the best way to create a formatted table.

You then looked at working with the web part page template. These pages contain one or more web part zones in which you can add web parts that SharePoint provides or any of the libraries or lists you created using the skills covered in Chapters 1 and 2. After adding two or more lists to a web part page, you might be able to define a master-detail relationship between the web parts if they have common fields. After you have defined such a relationship, users can select a record from the master list and display only those records in the detail list related to the master record.

When working with either basic or web part pages, you want to use the Check-Out and Check-In features as described when working with libraries to protect the integrity of your changes until you are done. You can also use page versioning to track changes to a page so that you can return to a prior version of the page by simply selecting it from the version history of the page. When working with versions, the total storage requirement of your page grows because of the number of versions you have. You can determine by individual library the number of major and minor versions of a page you want to retain. You can determine who can view minor versions. However, most people limit the viewing of minor versions to only those people with content creation rights and approvers (if approvers are used).

If your library has content approval turned on as well, even saving a major version of the page does not make it visible to the average site visitor. Rather, the page must first be reviewed by an approver who must approve the page before it is officially published to your site. Content approval is used most frequently on published sites in which the department or company wants to ensure that the content is accurate and appropriate for distribution to the public.

Finally, you saw that the Recycle Bin you encountered previously for libraries also works for web pages. It allows you to recover accidently deleted pages 30 days after they have been deleted, depending on how your SharePoint administrator has set up your site.

While this introduction to SharePoint provided in the first three chapters does not cover everything you can do with libraries, lists, and pages, it lays a framework for the next group of chapters, which focus on how to work with these objects using several Microsoft Office tools.

CHAPTER 4

■ ■ ■

Using Your Document Library with Microsoft Office

Chapter 1 introduced material showing how to use Microsoft Word with your SharePoint document library. In that chapter, I covered many of the basic concepts for working with Word documents stored in SharePoint. However, SharePoint does not limit you to Word documents. You can also store other Microsoft Office document types in your document library, including Excel, PowerPoint, and OneNote. Furthermore, SharePoint does not limit you to Microsoft Office tools. You can store almost anything in SharePoint, with the only limitation being that the applications they depend on may not integrate with SharePoint as well as Office does.

Some details of what has been discussed related to Word 2007 documents may vary from one Office tool to the next. However, most features discussed here work the same across them all. While you would not expect the integration with earlier versions of Office to be as strong as with Office 2007, you can use SharePoint as a file store for documents from earlier Office versions. However, because of SharePoint's enhanced integration with Office 2007, most of the discussions from this point forward will focus on Office 2007 unless otherwise stated.

Table 4-1 shows some of the integration points between SharePoint and Office 2003 vs. Office 2007. In some cases, it is hard to draw the line between what can be done in an older version via some complex manual method as opposed to an easier-to-use automated process in Office 2007. It is sort of like deciding whether to drive from New York City to Los Angeles rather than flying there. Both transportation methods work, but flying is clearly more efficient. On the other hand, if you are only going from New York to Boston, the decision on how to get there is significantly less clear. The same is true for some of the feature differences between Office 2003 and Office 2007: some are quite clear, others may not be. In any case, the following table is my interpretation of some of the SharePoint feature integration with Office 2003 and Office 2007.

Chapter 1 focused primarily on how to work with Word documents from the SharePoint point of view. This chapter takes an expanded look at additional integration features from the Microsoft Office point of view.

Table 4-1. *Comparing Integration Points Between SharePoint and Office 2003 vs. Office 2007*

Feature	Office 2003	Office 2007
Create, edit, save documents from SharePoint sites	Yes	Yes
Check-in/Check-out documents	Yes	Yes
Automated record management	No	Yes
Alert integration	Yes	Yes
RSS feeds	Not integrated with Outlook	Integrated with Outlook
Synchronize calendars, tasks, and contacts with Outlook	Read-only	Bidirectional
Use Excel Services	Limited	Yes
Parameterized browser-based spreadsheets	No	Yes
Use Business Data Catalog (BDC)	No	Yes
Require InfoPath client to fill in forms	Yes	No
Use of workflows within client	No	Yes
Compose and publish wikis and blogs with MS Word	No	Yes
Document Information panel to manage metadata	No	Yes
Groove synchronization to work with documents offline	No	Yes
OneNote integration to allow shared notebooks	No	Yes
Access integration with SharePoint sites	Limited	Yes
Slide library integration with PowerPoint	No	Yes

Opening a SharePoint Document from Within Microsoft Office

Beginning from Microsoft Office Word, your first challenge might be how to access SharePoint document libraries from within Word 2007. If the document you want to open exists on a SharePoint site that you previously visited, you may see a reference to that library in your My Network Places folder of Windows Explorer. At least that statement is true if you use Windows XP as your client operating system and you previously visited the site. Unfortunately, Windows Vista does not automatically add references to places you visit in SharePoint in its equivalent of My Network Places. For a moment, let assume you use Windows XP. Open the My Network Places folder to display the files stored there as shown in Figure 4-1.

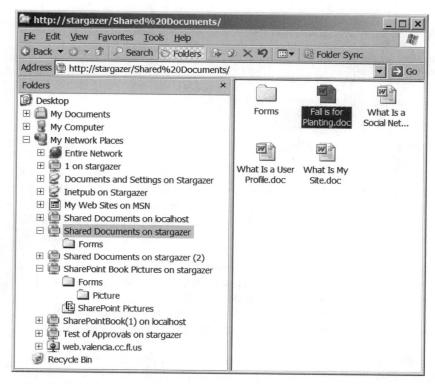

Figure 4-1. *Opening a SharePoint document from Windows Explorer*

WHERE DOES VISTA STORE REFERENCES TO SITES YOU VISITED?

Since web folders have been removed from Vista, some of the steps I list here for XP won't work if you use Vista. However, with just a few changes, you can do virtually the same thing in Vista.

Create a new Internet shortcut:

1. Using your browser, navigate to the site you want to quickly access in the future.

2. Copy the URL to your clipboard.

3. Click the Windows icon and then click your profile name. This opens Windows Explorer to your profile folder.

4. On the right side of the folder contents, right-click a blank area and create a new folder named Sites.

5. Open the new folder by double-clicking it.

6. Right-click a blank area and create a new shortcut.

7. Paste the URL from the web site into the text box and click **Next**.

8. Provide a name for the shortcut and click **Finish**.

Next you will add this folder to Vista's taskbar so you can easily access its contents:

1. Display Vista's taskbar and right-click a blank area of the taskbar.

2. Navigate to **Toolbars** and select **New Toolbar.**

3. Click the Desktop folder in the left pane.

4. Open your profile folder.

5. Locate the folder Sites you created earlier.

6. Click **Select Folder.**

Now, you can virtually do the same thing for other web sites in Vista! From any web site, click the icon found at the beginning of the address text box and drag it into the **Sites** toolbar in your taskbar. When you release your mouse button, Vista adds the shortcut to the **Sites** toolbar. The next time you open the **Sites** toolbar, the new shortcut will appear.

Looking at your SharePoint document folders from within Windows Explorer reveals several advantages to exploring the library contents this way. First, you can rename documents in the library, move documents from one library to another, make copies of a document from one library to another, and even delete documents from the library. From a single Windows Explorer instance, you can copy and paste documents from your local hard drive or any network drive you can access to a SharePoint library. Of course, you can also copy files from that library back to your local hard disk. But if you open a second Windows Explorer instance, you can easily drag and drop files from one folder to another, even two different SharePoint folders. Finally, to edit any Office document stored in a SharePoint library, just double-click it.

All the rules about editing documents discussed in Chapter 1 apply to documents opened directly from Windows Explorer. If the document requires you to check it out before you can modify it, you will see a bar at the top of the document asking you to check out the document as shown in Figure 4-2.

Of course, if you only want to read the document or print it, you do not need to check it out. Should you decide to check out the document to edit it, you have the option of editing the copy within SharePoint directly, or you can copy the document to your local computer and edit it offline, as shown in Figure 4-3. If you only have a quick change, it may not seem to make sense to have to download a copy of the document, make the change, and then upload the document again when you save it. However, by downloading the document, you can disconnect from the SharePoint site, edit the document, and then reconnect to SharePoint to save your changes at a later time.

Why would you do this? Perhaps you can only connect to your SharePoint site from your network at the office. To work on that document at home or to take it with you on that long cross-country plane flight, you need a local copy of the file on your hard disk.

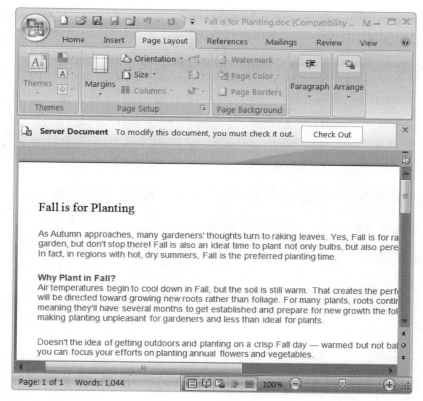

Figure 4-2. *Opening a SharePoint document from Microsoft Word*

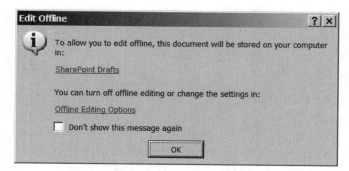

Figure 4-3. *Defining the SharePoint Drafts folder*

Notice the link named **SharePoint Drafts** in Figure 4-3. If you point to this link, you can see in the pop-up tooltip the current folder on your hard drive where your computer stores Share-Point drafts. By default, Windows XP creates a folder named

```
C:\Documents and Settings\YourUserId\MyDocuments\SharePoint Drafts\
```

In Windows Vista, SharePoint uses a local drafts folder found at

`C:\Users\Your_Profile_Name\Documents\SharePoint Drafts\`

If you want to define a different location for your drafts, click the second link on Figure 4-3, **Offline Editing Options**. This link opens the **Word Options** dialog box (because the document is a Word document), shown in Figure 4-4. In the **Save** page of this dialog box, find the section **Offline editing options for document management server files**. In this section, select whether to check out files to a local draft folder or edit them on the SharePoint server. If you choose to use a local folder, you can specify its location or use the **Browse** button to navigate to a folder you want to use.

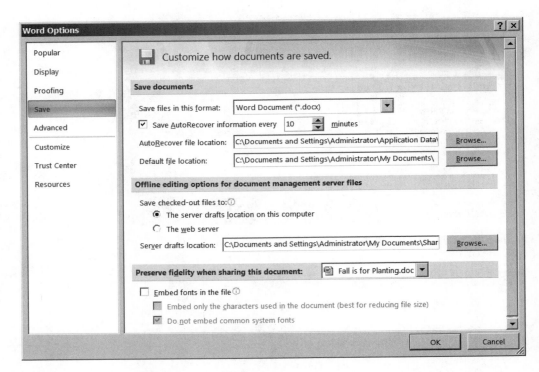

Figure 4-4. *Defining offline editing options*

■**Tip** If you haven't already done so, now would be a good time to define a frequency for saving an AutoRecovery copy of your documents as you work on them.

If you want to define these settings ahead of time, you can open the options dialog box for any Microsoft Office 2007 tool by clicking the **Office Button**. Then select the **Options** button in the lower right of the pop-up menu next to the **Exit** button.

Suppose, however, that you do not see folders in Windows Explorer for your SharePoint libraries. You can still open documents from your SharePoint library directly from within the relevant Microsoft Office 2007 tool if you know both the SharePoint site URL and the library names. Figure 4-5 shows the **Open** dialog box from within Word. Notice in the **File name** combo field, you can enter the name of the SharePoint site URL along with the **Shared Documents** library rather than the name of a file.

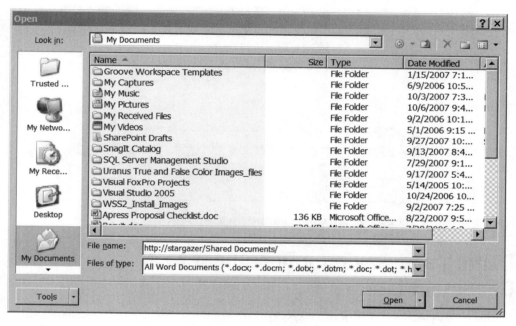

Figure 4-5. *Referencing a SharePoint library in the Open dialog box*

■**Note** You must precede the site URL with either `http://` or `https://`, depending on whether your SharePoint site uses a secure connection or not. If you do not know which to use, you can try both, or you can ask your system administrator.

Do not change the contents of the **File of type** field. Word fills in this field, as will most applications, based on the types of files the application recognizes. If you change this field to display other file types, any attempt to open those files may fail. When you click **Open** with only the URL of a library specified as shown in Figure 4-5, Word displays the Word documents stored in that library as shown in Figure 4-6.

Now you can open any document by double-clicking its name. You can also click the document to select it and then click **Open**.

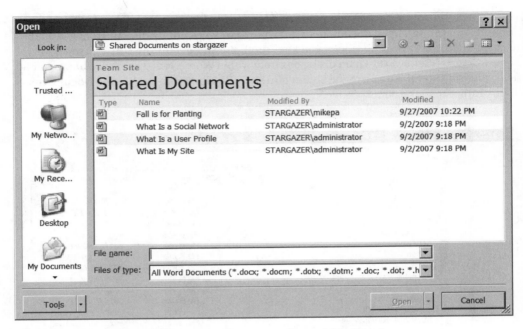

Figure 4-6. *Viewing the SharePoint library contents from within Word*

Editing and Saving a Document to a Document Library

In the previous section, you saw two ways to open a Word document stored in a SharePoint library without first opening a SharePoint site. You should note that security defined in Share-Point for checking out documents still applies even when you open the document from Windows Explorer or from within Word. That means you can only open the document to edit it if you have edit rights and it is not checked out to someone else. Remember that while these examples use Microsoft Word documents, these techniques apply to any file type recognized by Share-Point and registered in the operating system to an installed application.

CONCURRENCY PROBLEMS

For those readers who skipped the first three chapters, the importance of using the Check-Out and Check-In features when editing documents derives from the need to prevent concurrency problems. Concurrency problems occur when two or more people edit the same document at the same time.

The potential for concurrency problems increases as the number of users on the site increases. However, generally, concurrency problems decrease as more content gets saved to the site. Unfortunately, no statistic on usage will matter much to you if you lose all your changes because someone else modified the same document as you and saved his changes after you saved yours.

When editing documents directly from Windows Explorer as described earlier, you receive no visual cues that someone else may have the file open for editing until you try to check it out. On the other hand, when you use a Microsoft Office 2007 tool like Word, the file icon in the type column of the **Open** dialog box displays a green box with a white arrow in the lower-right corner, indicating that someone has the file checked out.

If you attempt to open a file that someone else has checked out, the **File in Use** dialog box shown in Figure 4-7 appears. Notice that this dialog box also tells you who has checked out the file.

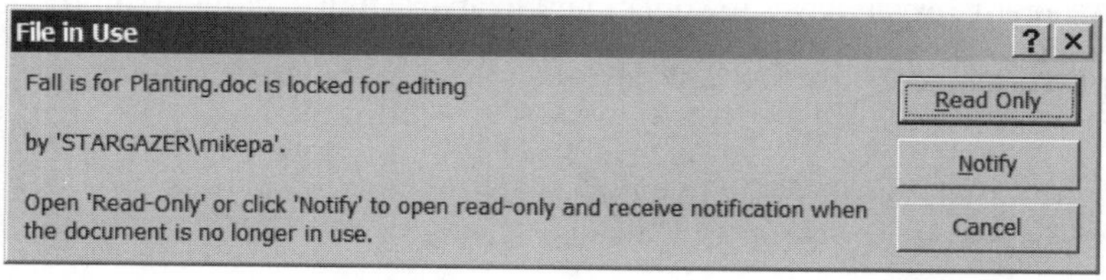

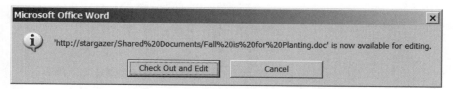

Figure 4-7. *File in Use dialog box*

As shown in this dialog box, you can choose to continue opening the file in **Read-Only** mode. If you only need to view the document or print it, this mode will not restrict these actions. However, if you really must edit the document, click the **Notify** button. This option tells Share-Point to notify you when the document becomes available. While waiting, leave the copy of Word open, although it does not have to be the active window (you can minimize it). When the other user closes and checks in the document, a pop-up dialog box appears as shown in Figure 4-8, notifying you that you can check out the current version to edit it.

Figure 4-8. *Notification that the file is now available for editing*

When you finish editing the document, save it and close the application used to edit it. If you checked out the document, you must also check it back in. Otherwise, it remains checked out to you. This feature supports working on documents offline while periodically updating your changes back to SharePoint. It should not be used so you can keep the document permanently checked out.

Each of the previous examples involve opening, editing, and resaving documents that already exist in SharePoint. But suppose you want to create a new document and save it. Again, I will demonstrate using Microsoft Office Word as the application tool, but remember that techniques that apply to one Office product typically apply to others as well.

Saving a New Document

To begin, create a new document in Word 2007. For this example, call your document "Hello World." When finished, save the document by clicking the **Office Button**. Rather than clicking **Save**, choose **Publish** as shown in Figure 4-9. This option has three suboptions:

- **Blog**: Posts the contents of the new document as a new blog entry (We will return to this topic later in this chapter in the section "Using Word to Contribute to Your Blog Site.")

- **Document Management Server**: Saves the document to an existing document library

- **Create Document Workspace**: Creates a new document workspace (see Chapter 1)

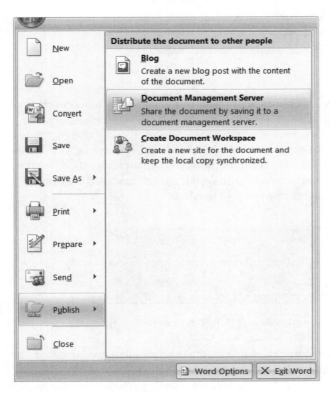

Figure 4-9. *Publish options in the Office Button menu*

Saving a Document to an Existing Library

Let's continue by saving a new document to an existing document library by selecting the **Document Management Server** option. When you select this option from among Word's **Publish** selections, the **Save As** dialog box appears as shown in Figure 4-10.

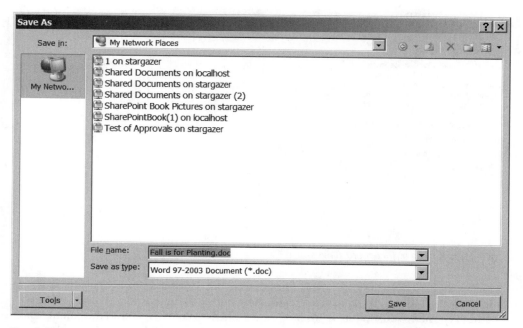

Figure 4-10. *Previously visited SharePoint libraries on a Windows XP platform*

Notice that the entries in this figure show the path to several previously visited document libraries. Select the library where you want to save the new document by double-clicking its name. If you never saved anything to a document library previously, you can still save to an existing document library if you know the SharePoint server name and the path to the document library. To save the new document in the **Shared Documents** library of the top-level site in the Stargazer SharePoint server, you would enter a URL like the one shown earlier in Figure 4-5.

After selecting a library or entering the URL for one and clicking **Save**, you should see a listing of the documents in that library. Next, specify the name for the new document, and click **Save** to add your new document to the selected library.

Creating a New Document Workspace

If instead you choose to create a new document workspace, a new panel named **Document Management** appears as shown in Figure 4-11. To build the document workspace, you also need to supply a name for your new document workspace and the location of the workspace.

■**Note** You must have site creation rights in order to create a new document workspace.

First you need to supply a name for the document workspace. By default, Word may try to use the name of your new document. Don't do this. In most cases, you probably want a more general name for your site than your document's name. Within this site, SharePoint creates a **Shared Documents** library and saves your new document as the first document in it.

Figure 4-11. *Creating a document workspace*

The location of the workspace may appear in the drop-down for this field if you have visited it before. However, if you plan to create a new workspace within SharePoint, you must select the **(Type new URL)** option in this drop-down and then enter the URL of the parent Share-Point Site. My SharePoint server has the name Stargazer. Therefore, on my server, to create a new document workspace within my top-level site, I would enter

```
http://stargazer
```

When SharePoint completes the creation of the new document workspace, you will see the contents of the **Document Management** panel change to something like Figure 4-12. Notice that the top of this panel displays the name of your new workspace. Beneath the name, click the text **Open site in browser.** This text serves as a link to your new document workspace.

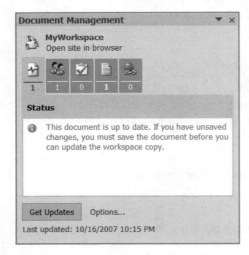

Figure 4-12. *The Document Management panel after selecting a site*

In this new document library, you can add other documents, edit existing documents directly from SharePoint, or continue to work within Word. Over the next few sections of this chapter, we will explore the **Document Management** panel to see how you can manage SharePoint libraries without leaving Word.

What Is Metadata?

In simple terms, *metadata* is data about data. When you save a file in Windows Explorer and then view the directory, you do not see only the file name. In Windows XP and most prior versions of the Windows operating system, Windows Explorer shows the date modified, file type, and size of each file. By default, Vista's Windows Explorer also includes the date modified, type, size, and tags. These additional pieces of information represent metadata for the file; that is, they provide you with more information about the file. In addition to these fields, you can right-click the header of the Explorer list to see additional available columns or metadata that Windows Explorer supports. In Vista, folders that focus on different types of files might use different sets of columns. For example, if you open a folder that contains music files such as My Music, you may see column headers such as **Name**, **Artists**, **Albums**, **#**, **Genre**, and **Rating**.

Metadata exists in documents created by most Office tools such as Word, Excel, PowerPoint, and others, allowing you to define additional properties for your documents. To add values to these properties in a Word 2007 document, click the **Office Button**, and then point to **Prepare**. Click **Properties** in the menu that appears, and Word displays the default properties it supports in a panel across the top of the document window. Click **Advanced Properties** in the **Document Properties** drop-down menu to display the **Document Properties** dialog box from Office 2007. Here you can create custom properties for the current document and assign them values.

SharePoint retains these properties when you upload the documents to a library. However, SharePoint also allows you to add more properties to the document. But rather than adding properties to individual documents, it adds custom columns to your document library. Every column in a document library then becomes metadata for each document added to the library.

Now that you know that metadata has been included in everything you do in Microsoft Office, what can you do with it? Metadata can help search, filter, or sort the data it refers to, such as the items in your library. You already have been using metadata associated with files in your Windows directories to sort the files in the directory. The same concept applies to the documents in a SharePoint library or the items in a list. Metadata can help you associate documents in one library or information in a list to those in another. It can also help automate workflows.

Metadata can enhance your SharePoint experience, just like indexes can enhance your database experience. However, too much metadata can become a burden for users to enter, like too many indexes can negatively affect database performance. You don't want metadata to become such a burden that users stop entering it. To illustrate the value of metadata, the next section explores the use of metadata within a custom library.

Using Metadata with the Document Information Panel

Your company probably uses purchase orders to buy the items it uses. On a very basic functional level, you could use a custom shared document library to store the purchase orders after you create them. At a slightly higher level, you might take a blank purchase order form built with Word and save it as a template. Then you could upload that Word template into your SharePoint site and modify your purchase order library to use that template as its default document type when creating a new document. I discussed how to change your default document template in Chapter 1.

But you can leverage SharePoint further. When you create a new document library, it generates a list structure with three or four base properties: **Title**, **Created By**, **Modified By**, and possibly **Checked Out To**. The same would apply to a new custom library named **Purchase Orders**. After creating the library, you might go into the document library settings page and rename the **Title** column to **Purchase Order Number**. While there, you can select other columns that SharePoint automatically tracks to display in your list, or you could add your own custom columns.

■**Note** **Purchase Order Number** makes an ideal replacement for the **Title** column because it uniquely defines each purchase order. You should never have two purchase orders with the same number.

Because this library only holds purchase orders, you might consider adding a few special columns to track information to help sort, filter, or group your purchase orders. Let's add the following three columns to this custom library:

- **Date Created**: The date someone entered the purchase order

- **Department**: The department requesting the purchase order

- **Purchase Amount**: The total amount of the purchase order

When defining the **Department** column, consider making it a Lookup-type column using a department custom list so that you can add new departments on the fly without modifying the library settings. Of course, you could add more than these three fields. However, let's limit the custom columns to these for now.

Each of these new columns represents metadata for the purchase order. That means that they define additional information about the document. It also means that each time you create a new document in this library, you may need to define values for these columns when you save the new document. In fact, when you open a new document, Word 2007 displays these document properties in a banner-like panel across the top of the document as shown in Figure 4-13.

Notice that the four fields across the banner prompt for values for each of your custom purchase order columns. You can fill in these fields at any time from when you first open the purchase order to when you complete it. In fact, except for the field with the red asterisk (**Department**), the other fields do not even need values for you to save the document.

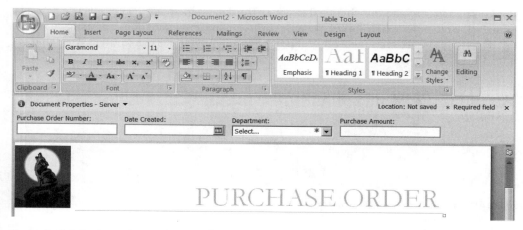

Figure 4-13. *Word 2007's metadata displayed in a panel at the top of the page*

■**Tip** If you plan to use the metadata to sort, group, or filter your purchase orders later, return to your column definition and make each of these columns required. If you already have saved purchase orders without these columns, SharePoint does not raise an error unless you edit and resave those purchase orders after making the custom columns required.

When you require values for any of the metadata fields, you cannot save the purchase order until you supply values for each required column. The text after the word **Location** tells you whether SharePoint has saved the document in the library.

You may have also noticed that the text on the left side of the first line of the banner says **Document Properties – Server**. This tells you that SharePoint, acting as a server, not Word, requires the properties displayed in the banner. If you click the down arrow to the right of this text, you see two other options. If you select **Document Properties**, the banner displays properties supported directly by Word. SharePoint shares some information with these fields. For example, notice that the **Title** field on this banner contains the same value as the **Purchase Order Number** field on the **Server** properties banner. This apparent linking of differently named fields occurs because you renamed the **Title** column in the SharePoint library to **Purchase Order Number**. The new name acts as more of a display characteristic rather than changing the nature of the **Title** field. Therefore, you could think of the display name as metadata for this column, which itself serves as metadata for the document. The **Advanced Properties** option opens the standard properties dialog box used by Word. Using this dialog box, you can access other metadata that Word supports or add new metadata fields within the current document.

Uploading Existing Documents into a Library Prompts for Required Metadata

Rather than creating a new document directly from the library, say you need to upload existing purchase order documents into the library; you can accomplish this task following the same steps discussed earlier in this chapter. First open the document in Word and then use the **Save As** dialog box to point to the library. Because the uploaded document does not yet have values for the required SharePoint metadata columns, SharePoint notifies you through Word that some required properties are either missing or invalid as shown in Figure 4-14.

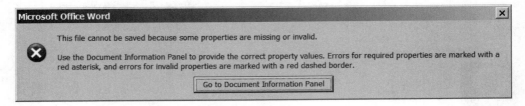

Figure 4-14. *Notice of missing properties*

To supply these values, click the button **Go To Document Information Panel**. When you do this, Word displays the panel across the top of the document shown in Figure 4-15, which already has some values entered. Notice the red dashed line around the box for the **Purchase Amount** field. This indicates that the field violates a constraint placed on the field. Remember that numeric columns in a SharePoint list or library support a minimum and a maximum value constraint. In this case, the original constraint limited the maximum value for this column to $5,000. Perhaps someone entered this limit incorrectly, or perhaps it represents an old limit that needs to be updated. Or perhaps purchase orders above a certain threshold need to go through a different process, and you must add them to a different library. In any case, you must resolve this problem before you can save this document.

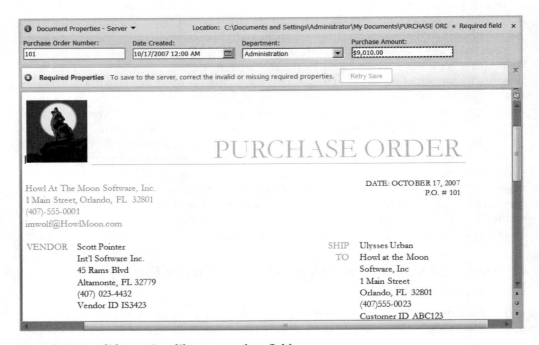

Figure 4-15. *Invalid entry in a library metadata field*

When you return to your SharePoint library and click a document to open and edit it, you may not automatically see the metadata for the document. You can turn on the **Document Properties** panel by clicking the **Office Button**, pointing to the **Prepare** option, and then clicking **Properties**. This selection displays the same panel shown in Figure 4-15 with the current values of each property. Remember to always save your document after any changes, even if you only make changes to the metadata.

■**Caution**   You need IE 6.0 or greater to edit a document directly from SharePoint.

Working with Document Metadata

By adding metadata to a document library, you can more easily sort, filter, and even perform simple aggregate functions across the documents it contains. The following example examines the steps needed to view only the purchase orders from a single department, Administration, counting the number of purchase orders and calculating a grand total amount.

1. Click the **View** drop-down in the upper-right corner of the page.

2. Select the **Create View** option.

3. From the first **Create View** page, select the **Standard View** format.

4. In the second **Create View** page, name the view **Administration Purchase Orders**. Do not make this the default view.

5. Create this view as a public view. You can also create a personal view that only you can see. However, for the purpose of this example, I will assume that the permissions to this library have already limited the potential audience to an appropriate subset of all users.

6. Next, select the columns you want to display. For this example, include at least the following:

   • **Type Icon**

   • **Purchase Order Number**

   • **Date Created**

   • **Department**

   • **Purchase Amount**

7. Define the primary sort to be **Date Created** in ascending order.

8. Define a secondary sort by ascending **Purchase Order Number** in case you have more than one purchase order a day per department.

9. Filter on column **Department** equal to **Administration**.

■**Caution** Notice that when defining a filter, you must enter the value of the filter directly, not select it from a list of possible values. Therefore spelling counts. However, the value's case does not affect the result.

---

10. Expand the **Totals** section. Notice this displays each column in the library with a drop-down of possible values.

11. Select **Count** for the **Purchase Order Number** column.

12. Select **Sum** for the **Purchase Amount** column.

13. Click **OK** to create the new view.

SharePoint returns you to the library view as shown in Figure 4-16. Notice that the list now contains only the purchase orders for the Administration department. Also at the top of the library list, the **Purchase Order Number** column contains the text **Count=2** and the **Purchase Total** column contains the text **Sum = $9,000.00**.

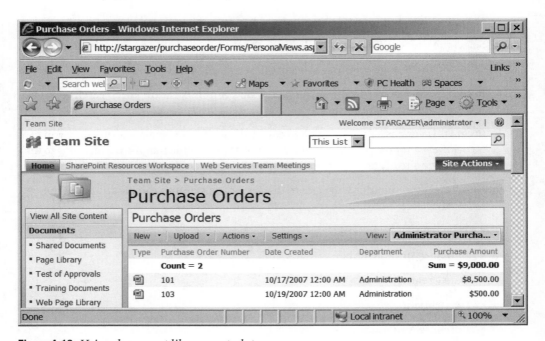

Figure 4-16. *Using document library metadata*

This example uses metadata for the document library to sort the documents, filter on a department, and then count the number of purchase orders while totaling the amounts. Notice also that with RSS feeds turned on, you can subscribe to this library and receive notifications when someone makes changes to it through your favorite news aggregator, IE 7.0, or Outlook 2007, or better. Similarly, you can also subscribe to alerts for changes. Now that is something that a simple Windows Explorer view of a directory of purchase order documents cannot do.

Managing Your Documents with the Document Management Panel

Earlier in this chapter, you learned how to create a new document workspace. In the process of setting up this site, Word 2007 opened the **Document Management** panel. Word 2007 makes this panel available only when working with a document opened from a SharePoint library. If the panel does not automatically appear, you can manually open it by clicking the **Office Button** followed by **Server** and then **Document Management Information**. Figure 4-17 shows the open **Document Management** panel for one of the purchase order documents.

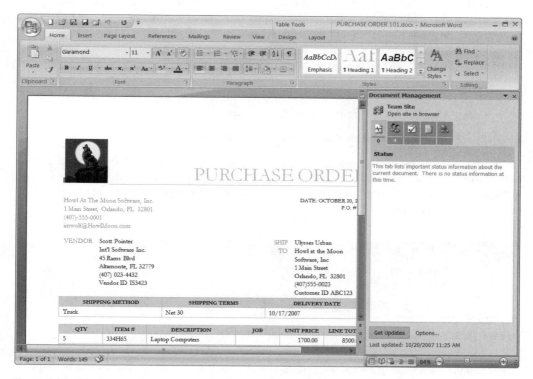

Figure 4-17. *Displaying the Document Management panel when editing a SharePoint library document*

■**Note** If you want the **Document Management** panel to automatically display when you open a document saved in SharePoint, click the **Options** button at the bottom of the panel and click the first check box in the **Document Management** panel section.

The top of the panel displays the library name where the current document belongs. Beneath the name is a link that takes you to the root of the site, but not necessarily the library. Beneath the link you will find one to five icons, each with a number beneath it.

The first icon identifies the check-out status of the documents you have open. If you check out a document before you edit it, this may be the only icon displayed in the panel. If no one including yourself has checked out the document you currently have open, you will see the following text:

```
This tab lists important status information about the current document. There
is no status information at this time.
```

However, if you or someone else has checked out the document, it shows you who has the document checked out. Since you probably opened a copy of the document in **Read-Only** mode or as a new copy that you plan to merge back later, you can use this status indicator to know when the other person checks the original document back into the library.

Suppose you attempt to open for edit a document that someone else has checked out. Word displays the **File in Use** dialog box containing three options:

- **Open a Read Only copy**

- **Create a local copy and merge your changes later**

- **Receive notification when the original copy is available**

Let's select the second option. After you make your changes, click the **Save** option in the **Office Button**. If someone else still has the file checked out, Word displays the message shown in Figure 4-18, suggesting that you save your changes in a different location and attempt to merge them at a later time.

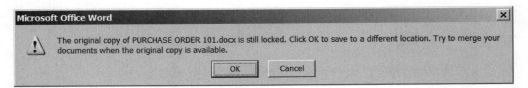

Figure 4-18. *Word's message that someone else has the file checked out*

If you click **OK** to save a local copy of the document, Word displays the **Save As** dialog box and shows your My Documents folder. It also appends the text - for merge to your file name to remind you that you should merge this document at a later time with the original. You can save the document multiple times as a merge document. Each time Word saves it, it appends a sequential number to the end of the name to uniquely identify it.

If the first person checks in the document while you still have your copy open, Word displays a message that the document is now available and that you can merge your changes into the original copy. Figure 4-19 shows this message.

When you click the **Merge** button, Word combines your changes with those in the original document using different colors. Figure 4-20 shows that two different people made a change to the **Shipping Terms** field with one person entering **60** and the other person entering **31**. (Black-and-white screen images do not render color differences well, but trust me or try it for yourself. The 60 and the 31 appear in different colors.)

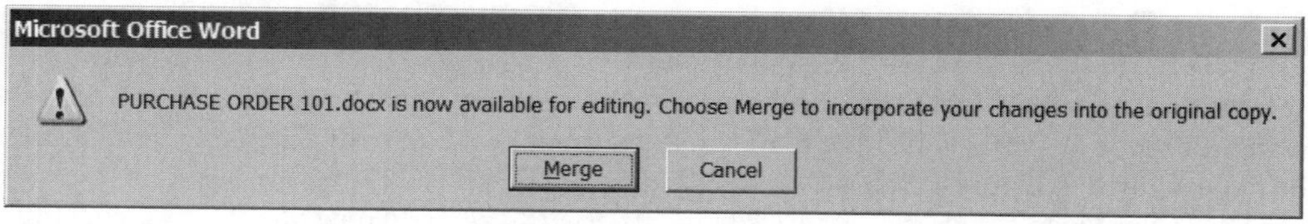

Microsoft Office Word   ☒

⚠ PURCHASE ORDER 101.docx is now available for editing. Choose Merge to incorporate your changes into the original copy.

[Merge]   [Cancel]

Figure 4-19. *Document is available for editing message*

SHIPPING METHOD	SHIPPING TERMS	DELIVERY DATE
Truck	Net 6031	10/27/2007

Figure 4-20. *Word displays merged changes for acceptance.*

If you respond to this image like most users, you probably have no idea which color represents the changes you made. To resolve this confusion, open the **Review** tab in the **Word** Ribbon and click the **Reviewing Pane** button in the **Tracking** section. Word displays this pane by default in a vertical orientation. However, you can also display it horizontally across the top of the page. Either way, it displays each change and who made it as shown in Figure 4-21.

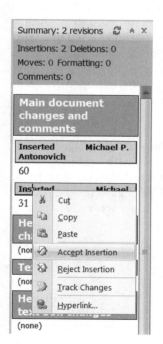

Figure 4-21. *Review pane for merged documents*

From this pane, you can right-click the versions you want to keep and select the **Accept** option. You can also achieve the same result by right-clicking directly on the revision you want to keep. Once you are done accepting the changes, select **Reject All Changes in Document** from the **Reject** drop-down in the **Changes** section to remove the remaining unaccepted changes. Then save the document.

Other Document Management Panel Features

Now that you have seen how to use the **Document Management** panel to work with Word documents, let's look at some of its other features. Remember I said up to five icons can appear in the panel shown in Figure 4-17.

The second icon shows the current site members. You can add new members by clicking the **Add new members** option at the bottom of the detail section for this tab. When adding members, you must know either their e-mail address or their SharePoint user names. You can assign a permission level to each person or group of people you add.

The third icon displays tasks from the oldest (or only) SharePoint tasks list of the selected site. The box at the beginning of each task indicates its status.

- *Empty box*: Not started

- *Solid filled box*: In-progress task

- *Box with a check mark*: Completed task

If the task box indicates that it has not been started or is in progress, you can click the check box to add the check mark indicating that the task has been completed.

When you click each of the tasks, a pop-up displays the columns defined for the task list. Notice that the drop-down in the upper right of this control lets you select the column by which you want to sort the tasks. You can also add new tasks from here by clicking the **Add new task** option. The option **Alert me about tasks** lets you define an alert for the current library. You can pick the change type of the alert and when you want to receive alerts.

The fourth icon displays all the documents in the selected library. You can open the document using Word, delete the document, or define an alert for changes made to just that one document. In the additional options shown at the bottom of the panel, you can add new documents and folders to the library.

Finally, the last icon shows the links from the oldest (or only) links list of the selected site. Note that the number shown beneath the link icon may appear to differ from the actual number of links shown in the detail section below. The detail section only shows actual links, not the folders in which you might organize them or the contents within those folders. Again, the bottom of the panel provides options to add links and to define alerts when changes occur to any items in the links folder.

Searching Your Documents

When you only have a few documents in your SharePoint site, finding the one you want may not seem like a big challenge. But what happens after your site grows to hundreds of files in dozens of libraries and nested folders? Trying to remember where you stored a document and searching for it may make looking for a needle in a haystack seem easy. But even finding a needle in a haystack can be made easy with the right tool, such as a strong magnet. Similarly, you need a strong tool to find that one document out of hundreds in the libraries on your site. Fortunately, SharePoint provides that tool in the form of the Search feature.

The Search feature typically appears in the upper-right corner of every page in WSS 3.0 and MOSS 2007. Of course, if someone branded your pages, they may have moved or even deleted this feature. Hopefully that did not happen, because the Search feature in SharePoint can help you find anything in your site quickly and easily.

WHAT IS BRANDING?

While you can quickly change the appearance of your SharePoint site by changing the theme you apply to it, SharePoint provides only a limited number of themes. You can also directly modify the appearance of individual pages through tools like SharePoint Designer among others. However, you would have to manually customize each new page you add to the site using this method. That would not be very efficient. Also, if your organization has provided a limited set of themes to preserve some consistent look and feel across all sites, you may not be permitted to add your own themes or customized pages made with the existing themes. You could also create your own custom master pages or define new CSS files to customize the appearance of the master pages, but these methods lie beyond the scope of this book.

Creating a new set of master pages or CSS files to customize the appearance of your master pages allows the changes to be put into place one time. Then all new pages created within the site will automatically inherit the look and feel they define. Microsoft defines SharePoint branding as the technique of customizing your site so that each page has a custom look that you define.

If you go to the home page of your top-level site or the default page of any subsite, the Search feature, shown in Figure 4-22, will search the entire site and any subsite. This is the search scope or the definition of the content that SharePoint searches. Place the words or phrases you want to search for in the text box to the right of the search scope box. Then press the button with the magnifying glass icon to start the search.

Figure 4-22. *SharePoint's Search feature*

The text box search string cannot exceed 255 characters. You do not have to worry about simple variations of words such as whether to enter "class" or "classes." SharePoint automatically accounts for plurals if you enter the singular form. Nor should you worry about case, as SharePoint performs all searches as case-insensitive. If you include common words such as "the" or "it," SharePoint ignores them. SharePoint also ignores the order of words, making a search on "United States" the same as "states united." So don't waste time and characters entering "flags of the United States" when you can just as easily enter "United States flags."

Search does not understand Boolean connectors like AND or OR between words or phrases. However, you can put a plus sign in front of a word to qualify the search. For example, "Software +Microsoft" returns only documents that reference software and Microsoft. But beware of the fact that the Search feature has no real intelligence. The preceding search could return a document with the title "The 20 Best Software Products Not Produced by Microsoft" because the title contains both the words "Software" and "Microsoft." You did not specify that you wanted "Microsoft software" (to do so, you would have to enter it just like that, with double quotes around the phrase).

Similarly, SharePoint ignores wildcards that some search engines allow such as the asterisk (*), which allows partial word searches. Finally, Search does not search attachments to list items, only the list items themselves.

So how do you decide what text to enter in the Search box? Try to think of one or two unique words that might appear in the text of only the document you want.

Tip Search also searches the document or list metadata. Therefore, if you know a unique value that can be found in the document's metadata, you can use it to search and find the document even if the document itself does not contain that text string.

You can even search for every document or list a specific user has created or modified by searching on her SharePoint user name, which SharePoint stores in the **Created By** and **Modified By** metadata fields.

Instead of starting your search from a web page within a site, you could start a search while you have a specific list or library open. This means that you have opened the library or list from the **Quick Launch** menu or you clicked the library or list's title so that it displays by itself in the browser window. When in a library or list, the Search scope drop-down includes two options: **This Site** and **This List**. The **This List** option limits the search scope to only the current library or list.

Figure 4-23 shows the results page of a search from my top-level site home page for the word "Autumn." Notice that it returns the document "Fall Is For Planting," which contains the word "Autumn" in the document's text but not in the document's title.

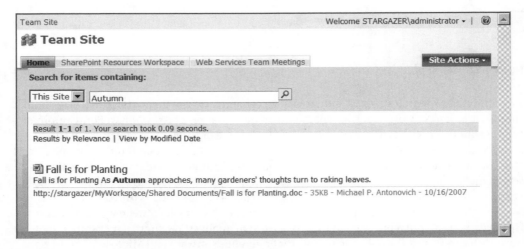

Figure 4-23. *Search results for the word "Autumn"*

Using Word to Contribute to Your Blog Site

Blog sites have become increasingly popular in the last few years. Many companies support blogs to provide news about their company or their company's products. They may even encourage specific individuals with a flair for writing to post blogs favorable to the company or its products. Many individuals use blogs as personal diaries. Developers and consultants use blogs to document their work and to provide a place to post downloadable information about their current projects. Speakers and authors often use blogs to post additional information for their attendees or readers such as sample code or their slide presentation.

Before you begin contributing to a blog, you must have a hosted blog site. Thousands of blog sites already exist on the Internet. Most allow visitors to the site to contribute to them after registering on their site. But you may want to have your own blog site not associated with another company or organization. If you have a SharePoint site, and if you have permission to create sites on it, you can follow the steps in the next section to create your own blog site. If you do not have permission to create sites, talk with your SharePoint administrator to see if he can set up a blog site for your use. Of course, if your administrator built the SharePoint installation as an intranet site only, your blog will only be visible to users within your company. If that satisfies your need for fame, great! Otherwise, you may have to consider one of those public sites such as Microsoft's Live Spaces to host your blog.

Creating a Blog Site

You can create a blog site as a subsite to any site. Some people may create a personal blog site in their **My Site** area. However, you may want a department or project blog. The following instructions step you through creating a blog site beneath a top-level site:

1. Begin by clicking your top-level site name in the **Global Links Bar**.

2. Select **Create** from the **Site Actions** menu.

3. Under the **Web Pages** column, select **Sites and Workspaces**.

4. Enter a name for your blog site along with a description.

5. Enter a web site address for the blog. Notice that SharePoint provides the first part of the address, defining the root address for the site.

■Tip In addition to trying to keep your blog address short and easy to remember, I recommend that you use the blog title just entered, removing any special characters or blanks.

---

6. Select a template for your site. You can find the blog template in the **Collaboration** tab.

7. Define permissions for your blog site. You can inherit the permissions from the parent site, the top-level site in this case, or you can create unique permissions to your blog site. Remember that defining unique permissions means that you will have full responsibility for creating all permissions to your blog. If you want just a personal blog for yourself, your close friends, or the other members of your department or project, unique permissions may be exactly what you want.

8. Define the navigation into and out of your site.

In the **Navigation** section, you first define navigation into your blog site. You can determine whether a link to the blog appears in the **Quick Launch** menu and whether to display the blog site in the top link bar of the parent site. While these two navigation options provide users with ways to get to your blog site, they are not the only methods you have at your disposal. You could also add links on your site's home page pointing to your blog. If every user in your company or every product has their own blog site, a **Links** list on your site's home page may be a good way to help visitors navigate to one of dozens of blog sites in your SharePoint installation.

The navigation section also includes a method to help users navigate away from your blog site. SharePoint asks whether the blog site shares the top link bar with its parent or whether it starts the top link bar all over again with just the blog site listed. By sharing the top link bar with the parent site, the user can navigate back to the parent site. However, even if you do not share the top link bar, users can still return to the top-level site by clicking the link in the **Global Links Bar** at the top of the page.

After defining the properties for your site, click the **Create** button. SharePoint creates the site and displays its main page. You see a default welcome message provided by SharePoint. If you have rights to add, edit, and delete list items, you will see a column to the right of the blog entries with administration options for the blog. The following list presents the available options:

- **Create a Post**: Create a new blog entry.

- **Manage Post**: Edit/Delete blog entries.

- **Manage Comments**: Edit/Delete comments associated with blog entries.

- **All Content**: Same as clicking **View All Site Content** in the **Quick Launch** menu.

- **Set Blog Permissions**: Modify users or their permissions to the blog site.

- **Launch Blog Program to Post**: By default, this option loads Word.

Defining Categories for Your Blogs

In the **Quick Launch** menu, you also see three categories generically named **Category 1**, **Category 2**, and **Category 3**. Within a blog site, you can separate entries by category to organize them by topics or types. For example, you might use a different category to post code updates, discussions on configuration settings, or posts of instructions on how to use application features. You might even keep separate categories to post FAQs or to report bugs.

While you do not need to have all your categories predefined before people start to add posts to the blog site, you want to define at least a few major categories so that all posts do not get lumped together in one category.

■**Tip** A person with administrator rights for the blog site can go into individual posts and reassign them to a different category. Administrators often do this when posts start to diverge from the intended purpose of the category. They also do this if they later split categories into smaller divisions.

To define your own initial set of categories, click **Categories** in the **Quick Launch** menu. SharePoint defines categories as a simple list of items in which the **Title** column defines the category. As with many lists, when you click a title, SharePoint opens the view that displays all columns for the selected item. Of course, this list only has one column. To change its value, click **Edit Item** in the menu bar and enter your desired category text.

In a similar way, update each of the category items, adding or deleting items as necessary to build the complete list of categories you need. When finished, return to your blog site's home page by finding its reference in your breadcrumbs. Before leaving this page to create blog posts from within Word, take note of the URL in the address bar of your browser. Commit to memory, copy to the clipboard, or write down this address because you will need to reference it to tell Word where to send your blog posts. You can ignore the portion of the URL at the end that says `default.aspx`.

Creating a New Blog Posting

To create your first blog post, return to Word 2007 and open the **Office Button** menu. Click **New**. You should see **New blog post** in the **Blank and Recent** template section. Select this template and click the **Create** button. If you never created a blog post before, you may get a dialog box asking you to register your blog account as shown in Figure 4-24. You can skip registration for now, as Word prompts you again when you attempt to post your first blog.

Figure 4-24. *Register a Blog Account dialog box*

Word then displays a blank document with a text field at the top of the page that prompts [**Enter Post Title Here**]. Click anywhere between the square brackets, and enter your post title. Then click beneath the horizontal line below the title and enter your blog text. By creating your blog entry with Word, you can take advantage of all the formatting features Word offers. When you finish, click the **Publish** button in the **Blog** section of the **BlogPost** Ribbon in Word. Figure 4-25 shows a blog post about to be published.

When you click **Publish** for the first time, you must register an account if you did not do so when you first created the document. Remember, you skipped registration earlier, so you must do it now. Click the **Register an Account** button. A **New Blog Account** dialog box appears as shown in Figure 4-26. This wizard provides a drop-down list of available blog sites you could publish to. Maybe you already used one of these blog sites but did not know that you could publish directly to them from within Word 2007.

To publish to your SharePoint blog, select **SharePoint blog** and click the **Next** button. The **New Blog Account** dialog box needs one more piece of information to post your text, the blog URL. This URL refers to the address I asked you to commit to memory or write down earlier. Hopefully you wrote it down, placed it on the clipboard, or memorized it. Enter it in the **Blog URL** text box, as shown in Figure 4-27, and click the **OK** button.

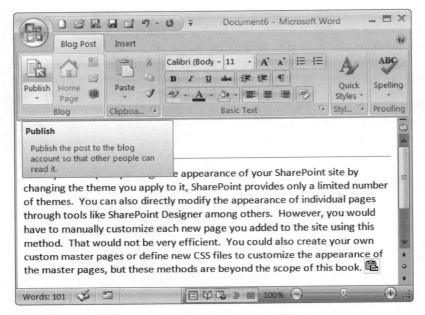

Figure 4-25. *Publishing a blog entry from Word 2007*

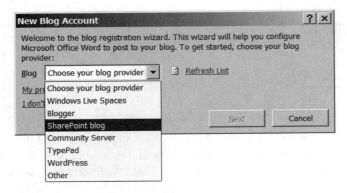

Figure 4-26. *Creating a new blog account*

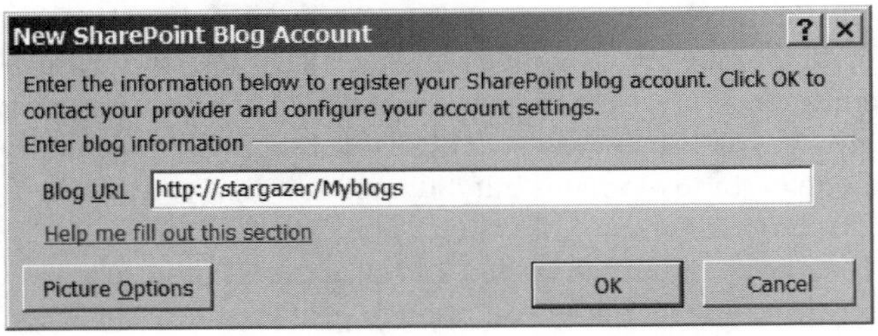

Figure 4-27. *Creating a new SharePoint blog account*

Word then prompts you that it is sending information to the blog service provider and that other people may see it. Setting up a SharePoint blog site on your company's SharePoint server exposes you to little risk, especially if your servers and you sit behind the company's firewall. So click **YES** to continue. When Word successfully registers with SharePoint, a dialog box displays, confirming its success and also informing you that you can go to the **Blog Posts** tab within Word 2007 and click **Manage Accounts** to remove, modify, or add other accounts.

When Word returns to the document page, a banner across the top of the page tells you that the post was published to the blog site at the specified URL. Switching back to your browser, you can navigate to your blog site to see the post as shown in Figure 4-28.

Figure 4-28. *Viewing a published blog entry in SharePoint*

■**Note** If you had already pointed your browser to the blog page before starting this process, you may need to refresh the page in order to see the posting.

Notice also in Figure 4-28 that RSS feeds have been enabled for this site. Actually, you may not easily see this from the figure, but when your browser displays the RSS feed icon in orange, the feed has been enabled. That means that you and your users can subscribe to the RSS feeds and receive notification when someone posts new entries to this blog.

Editing Blogs

To add a comment to an existing blog post, click the **Comments** link beneath the post. This adds a small form to the screen prompting for an optional title and the body of the comment. Comments automatically include the SharePoint user name of the person adding the comment as well as the date and time she added it. Comments do not display by default, but if you click the **Comments** link when the number in parentheses is greater than zero, you can view those comments and add your own.

Remember, only people with administrator rights can manage posts and comments. On many public blog sites, people who can create and post blog comments cannot edit or delete the blog after they submit it. So be sure you want others to see what you have written before you submit your posts or comments. As an administrator for the blog, you might need to delete blog or comment entries if they become inflammatory, abusive, discriminatory, or constitute a character attack.

Setting Blog Permissions

Before leaving this discussion on blogs, let's look at the permissions that affect what a user can see and do. Begin by using the **Admin Links** on the blog page and select **Manage Posts**. This displays the **Posts** list, a list like many of the other lists you have examined. From **Settings** in the menu bar select **List Settings**, then select **Advanced Settings** under **General Settings**.

The top section of this page, shown in Figure 4-29, begins with the item-level permissions. Notice that you can control whether users can read all posts or just their own. If users can only read their own blogs, your blog site becomes more like a private diary than a public blog.

More importantly, you can define whether users can edit all posts, their own posts only, or none. If you select none, you can effectively block all attempts to edit or delete a post once it has been submitted. Only an administrator can then edit or delete posts. You need to decide whether you should use that setting or not.

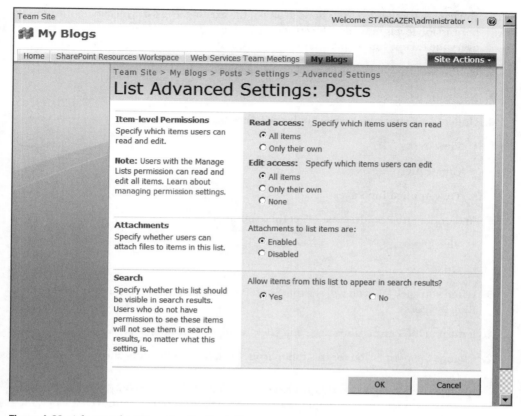

Figure 4-29. *Advanced settings for the Posts list*

Another way to look at permissions is by individual user or group. You saw in Chapter 1 how to assign permissions to permission levels and then associate a permission level with a group or an individual. When you create a blog site, you have the option of inheriting permissions for groups from the parent site. This might be fine if you want to treat the blog like any other list and use the list permissions from the parent site. But if you want to assign special permissions for your blog sites, you need to select the **Use Unique Permissions** options. Fortunately, you can change your mind even after you build the blog site.

1. Navigate to the blog site and then select **Site Settings** from the **Site Actions** button. Under the **Users and Permissions** column, select **Advanced Permissions**.

2. On the **Permissions** page, open the **Actions** menu and select **Edit Permissions**. This option breaks the inheritance from the parent site after making a copy of the parent permissions.

3. Click **Permission Levels** in the **Settings** menu that now appears.

4. Click **Edit Permission Levels**.

5. You can now edit the permissions in any of the existing levels or you can define unique permission levels for use with your blog site. For example, you might want to place everyone except your department staff in a group that only has read rights to blogs.

6. On the **Permission Levels** page, click **Add a Permission Level**.

7. Name the permission **Blog Readers**.

8. Under **List Permissions**, select only the following options:

   • **View Items**

   • **Create Alerts**

   • **View Application Pages**

9. And under **Site Permissions**, select these options:

   • **View Pages**

   • **Open**

10. When you click **OK**, you will see that SharePoint created a new permission level named **Blog Readers**.

11. Return to the **Permissions** page and click **Team Site Visitors**.

12. Change the permission for this group from **Read** to **Blog Readers** and click **OK**.

Now when users assigned to this group visit the blog site, they can only view the existing blogs. They can also view the comments associated with them, but they cannot create new blog entries or add comments to existing entries. In a similar way, you can define custom permissions for all groups who can access your blog site.

If at a future time you decide you would rather inherit rights from the parent site, you can do so by returning to the **Permissions** page of the blog site and selecting **Inherit Permissions** from the **Actions** menu.

Understanding Word's New Open XML File Format

Since the first mention of Word documents in this book, I have tried to emphasize the difference between Word 2007 documents and documents created with earlier versions of Word. Perhaps at one point you discovered that you could not open a Word document you received from a coworker who already had Word 2007 because you still had only Word 2003.

When Microsoft released Office 2007, it changed the default file format for Office documents. To avoid confusion between different formats, Microsoft also changed the extension name for Office 2007 documents by adding an "x." Thus, .doc becomes .docx, .xls becomes .xlsx, and .ppt becomes .pptx.

You might ask, what is with the "x" added to the end of each document extension? Why not an "a" or maybe even "7" for 2007? The reason lies in the format now used for the Office files. Office saves all files as XML files. By abandoning the proprietary format of the older versions of Word, Microsoft allows any application that can open and read XML files to read Office documents.

Perhaps you heard this before and tried to open a Microsoft 2007 document in your XML editor, but found that it still did not look like something you could read. Before you can open the document in XML, you must first unzip the document. That's right. Each final Office 2007 document file actually consists of a collection of files zipped together into the final file that you see. For example, if you have a Word document containing images, you will find each of the image files you inserted into the document stored as a separate file within the zipped collection. The primary file containing the text of your document can be found in document.xml. Word also includes separate XML files to store styles, themes, numbering styles, fonts, and more. Figure 4-30 shows a portion of the contents of a Word document file. While not a major factor when working with Word, we will see in Chapters 7 and 8 how the difference between the old and new Excel formats affects the way Excel integrates with SharePoint.

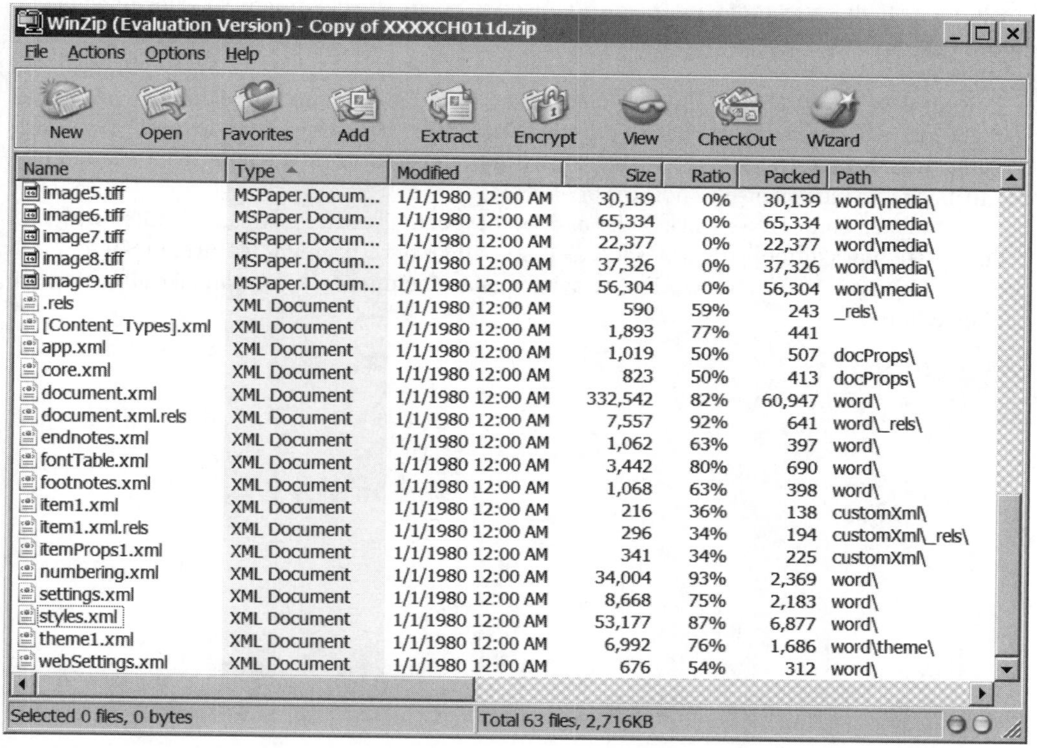

Figure 4-30. *Contents of a Word DOCX file*

Summary

In Chapter 1, you saw how to create documents using Word for your document libraries and how to define default templates for those libraries. In this chapter, you took a deeper dive into using Microsoft Word with your SharePoint site. You saw how you can work with documents in Word and then save them directly to existing SharePoint libraries and even how to create new libraries from Word.

You also looked at metadata. Office products such as Word have supported the additional file properties for some time. SharePoint makes use of those properties by allowing you to associate them with columns in a library view. Once exposed as columns in a view, you can customize the view to aggregate the information found in those columns to create counts, sums, filters, etc.

You also looked at how you can use the **Document Information** panel to tell you more about the status of the document and your library site. You saw that the SharePoint Search feature can help locate documents in your libraries because it can search for words not only in the document's title, but also in the document's content as well as its metadata. You can also create entries to your blog sites directly from within Word and post those entries without ever directly logging into SharePoint. Finally, I peeled back the covers of the new Office 2007 document format structure to show you that it consists of a collection of files zipped together that includes XML files together with image files used to create the document. This format change affects SharePoint's integration with Excel but has little effect on SharePoint's integration with Word.

Microsoft Word 2007 strongly complements SharePoint and opens the door to web-based collaboration support to people with normal Office skills. Most users knowledgeable in Word can become productive in a collaborative environment supporting document libraries and contributing to blog sites in a short time.

In the next chapter, we will explore a different tool in the Microsoft Office Suite, Outlook. You will see how Outlook integrates its calendar and tasks with similar features in SharePoint. You will also learn how to use Outlook to synchronize documents so you can take advantage of offline editing.

CHAPTER 5

∎ ∎ ∎

Using Outlook

This chapter focuses on using Outlook 2007. Outlook 2003 has limited integration with Share-Point. In fact, it only allows you to view copies of SharePoint lists such as the tasks list, the contacts list, and calendar list. You cannot edit the data in these copied lists and send the changes back to SharePoint. Outlook 2003 can receive alerts generated by SharePoint when someone makes changes to these lists, but it cannot use RSS (Really Simple Syndication) feeds.

Outlook 2007 expands on all these limitations, turning Outlook 2007 into a virtual front-end client for SharePoint. Not only can you copy these lists to Outlook 2007, but changes you make in Outlook are shared with SharePoint. In addition, Outlook 2007 supports RSS feeds, workflow integration, records management, and more.

Let's begin by taking a look at sharing your SharePoint contacts lists with Outlook.

Synchronizing Your Contacts Lists Between SharePoint and Outlook

Suppose you have one or more SharePoint sites that you regularly visit in your organization. They may be departmental or project sites, it does not matter. What does matter is that each of these sites has multiple contacts lists that you might need to reference on a regular basis. But going online and finding which site the contact is in each time you need a phone number, physical address, or an e-mail address just takes too long. Of course, you could just reenter the information you frequently use into Outlook yourself, but who has time for that? Fortunately, SharePoint can simplify your life.

Connecting Your SharePoint Contacts List to Outlook

To begin organizing your contacts in one place, open your favorite SharePoint site, one that has a contacts list that you frequently access. For the purposes of the following discussion, I'm going to open the list **My Work Contacts** located in my top-level team site.

1. Open the list in a separate page as shown in previous chapters so the list menu appears across the top of the list.

2. Open the **Actions** drop-down menu and select **Connect to Outlook**. By now you may have noticed that the **Actions** menu provides you with operations you can perform on the current list, while the **Settings** menu lets you define properties of the list.

At this point, SharePoint attempts to connect to Outlook on your local computer. Outlook recognizes this attempt and raises a warning message box asking you whether you know and trust this source. To help you decide this vital security question, the message box, shown in Figure 5-1, displays the name of the site and the list. It also includes the list's URL. The buttons at the bottom of the box let you accept the connection by clicking **Yes** or reject it by clicking **No**. Of course, in this case you trust the source, so click **Yes**.

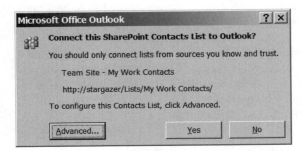

Figure 5-1. *Connecting to a trusted SharePoint contacts list*

In most cases, you will not need to open the **Advanced** dialog box. However, if you are curious and do click the **Advanced** button, it displays the dialog box shown in Figure 5-2. This dialog box allows you to change the folder name where Outlook stores the transferred contacts list. By default, SharePoint concatenates the site name with the contacts list name, using a hyphen between them. This usually defines a unique tasks list name in Outlook. However, you can supply your own name if you prefer. You can also provide a description for the folder. Outlook displays this description when you look at the properties of the created folder. This dialog box also displays other properties for informational purposes such as the list name, list type, and its URL.

After you click **OK**, SharePoint transfers all items from the SharePoint list to the new folder in Outlook. If the SharePoint list has columns that do not have corresponding fields in Outlook, Outlook ignores them. Table 5-1 shows a list of the default SharePoint contact columns and their corresponding Outlook contact fields.

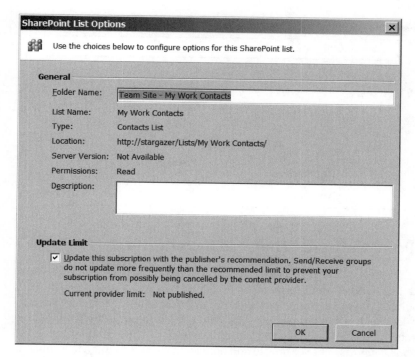

Figure 5-2. *Defining the folder name and description for a shared contacts list*

Table 5-1. *Mapping SharePoint Contact Columns to Outlook Columns*

SharePoint Column	Outlook Column
Last Name	Last Name
First Name	First Name
Full Name	Full Name
E-mail Address	Email
Company	Company
Job Title	Job Title
Business Phone	Business
Home Phone	Home
Mobile Phone	Mobile
Fax Number	Business Fax
Address	Business Address
City	Business City

Table 5-1. *Mapping SharePoint Contact Columns to Outlook Columns (Continued)*

SharePoint Column	Outlook Column
State/Province	Business State/Province
Zip/Postal Code	Business Zip/Postal
Country/Region	Business Country
Web Page	Web Page
Notes	Notes
Created By	<Not mapped>
Modified By	<Not mapped>

Adding SharePoint Columns That Will Synchronize with Outlook

Perhaps you realized that Outlook supports many other fields than those shown in Table 5-1. Can you use those too? Yes, you can use them on the Outlook side without affecting the synchronization of the other data fields with SharePoint. SharePoint ignores these additional fields.

However, remember from Chapter 2 that you can add columns to a list. To add some of the other fields that Outlook supports, let's see how to add home address information to a contact.

1. Begin by opening the linked contacts list in SharePoint.

2. Open the **Settings** menu and select **List Settings**.

3. In the **Columns** section, click **Add from existing site columns** at the bottom of this section.

4. Select **All Groups** from the first drop-down combo box if not already selected.

5. Scroll down through the list of fields until you find the home address fields. Select the following fields:

   - **Home Address City**

   - **Home Address Country**

   - **Home Address Postal Code**

   - **Home Address State or Province**

   - **Home Address Street**

6. Be sure to check the box **Add to default view** if you want to see these values in the list view.

7. Click **OK**.

SELECTING MULTIPLE ITEMS

When selecting multiple items as in step 5, you can

- Select each one by clicking it and then clicking the **Add** button.

- Double-click each item.

- Click the first item. With the Shift key pressed, click the last item. (Use this technique when selecting a contiguous range of values.) Then click the **Add** button.

- Click the first item, and then while holding down the Ctrl key, click each additional item. (Use this technique when selecting items scattered throughout the list.) Then click the **Add** button.

Now when you return to your list, you can edit any or all of your contact items to add home address information. However, just because you clicked **OK** to save your changes in SharePoint doesn't mean those changes will immediately appear in Outlook. To force a refresh, open the **Actions** menu and again select the **Connect to Outlook** option. This forces SharePoint and Outlook to resynchronize the changes made.

Similarly, you can make a change to contact information in Outlook. Again, the change to the fields visible or not visible in the default view of the list may not appear immediately in SharePoint. Why can't you see the changes? Actually, in this case, Outlook has passed the changes to SharePoint, but web pages do not automatically refresh. To see the updated values, click the **Refresh** button in the browser menu. Also, if you edit an item in the list, any pending updates from Outlook for that list item appears when the **Edit** form appears.

Managing Update Conflicts

What if someone updates a contact in Outlook at the same time that someone else updates the same item in SharePoint? What happens to both sets of changes? It depends on who saves his changes first. If the Outlook user saves his changes first, then you as the SharePoint user get an error message when you attempt to save your changes that says

---

```
Save Conflict. Your changes conflict with those made concurrently by another user.
If you want your changes to be applied, click Back in your Web Browser,
refresh the page, and resubmit your changes.
```

What this statement does not make clear is that you must reapply your changes to the refreshed page. Consider that refreshing a web page updates all fields on the page, including those fields just changed by the Outlook user. This, of course, erases all your changes.

If the SharePoint user saves her changes first, the Outlook user gets an error message when he attempts to save his changes. The dialog box that appears says

The item cannot be saved because it was changed by another user or in another window. Do you want to make a copy in the default folder for this item?

If you click **Yes** after this message, Outlook saves a copy of your contact with your changes in the default folder, probably the `Contacts` folder. In either case, you will need to reenter your changes if you want to update the fields that sync to the SharePoint list and try to save the changes again.

Figure 5-3 shows an example of what a list synchronized from SharePoint looks like. Notice that Outlook places synchronized lists in a folder named `Other Contacts` in the **Navigation** panel of the **Contacts** page. However, you can click and drag contacts lists between folders, also referred to as *groups*. If you do not like these groups, you can create a new group by right-clicking any of the group headers and selecting **New Group**.

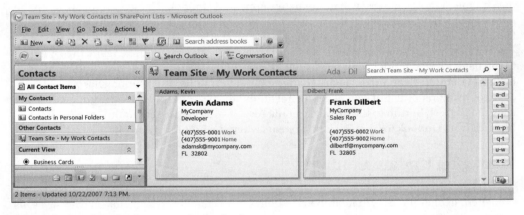

Figure 5-3. *Synchronized contacts in Outlook*

With each contacts list, you can right-click the list name to display its properties. The property dialog box consists of six tabbed pages. Click the **General** tab to see the description you entered back in the **SharePoint List Options** dialog box in Figure 5-2 when initially synchronizing the SharePoint list to Outlook.

You also have the ability to show or hide a contact folder from the e-mail **Address Book** drop-down shown in Figure 5-4. Even if you hide the contacts list from the Address Book on the e-mail page, you can still open the **Contacts** page and click the desired list. Then locate the contact you want to e-mail. Finally, right-click the contact and select **Create ➤ New Message to Contact** from the pop-up menu.

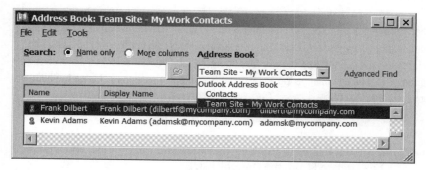

Figure 5-4. *Synchronized lists appear in Outlook's Address Book.*

Deleting Contacts

Just as you can edit information on a contact in either Outlook or SharePoint, you can delete contacts from either location as well. If you start from SharePoint, follow these steps:

1. Open the contacts list you want to edit.

2. Locate the contact you want to delete.

3. Hover your mouse over the contact to activate the drop-down menu button to the right of the contact.

4. Open the drop-down menu (see Figure 5-5).

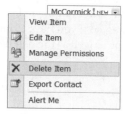

Figure 5-5. *Deleting a contact from SharePoint*

5. Click **Delete Item**.

As with documents and other lists, SharePoint prompts you with a dialog box to ensure that you really want to delete the item. Remember that even when you delete items from lists, SharePoint first places them in the site Recycle Bin for a limited time, from where you can restore them later.

Tip Remember that you can ask your SharePoint administrator to change the length of time items stay in the Recycle Bin. By default, they stay there 30 days. But your administrator can change this by going into **Central Administration** and selecting the **Application Management** tab. Then by selecting the **Web Application General Settings** page, she can change the value in the **Recycle Bin** section to change the number of days items are kept in the Recycle Bin.

If you open the **Outlook Contacts** page and view the shared SharePoint list, you will find that the contact has also been deleted from the Outlook list.

Recovering Deleted Contacts

If you accidentally delete the wrong contact, open the site Recycle Bin found at the bottom of the **Quick Launch** menu. You may need to scroll through the items previously deleted to find the contact record, or you can sort on the **Deleted** date field by clicking it. However, after you find it, click the box to the left of the name and click **Restore Selection** from the menu bar at the top of the Recycle Bin.

After 30 days or whatever number of days your Recycle Bin has been set to have passed, SharePoint removes the item from the site Recycle Bin so it doesn't continue to grow indefinitely. However, even after that time, you can contact your SharePoint administrator and ask him to retrieve the item from the site collection Recycle Bin. SharePoint holds deleted items here for an additional time period, depending on the settings made by your SharePoint administrator, before permanently deleting them.

Figure 5-6 shows that the first item in the Recycle Bin selected for restoration just happens to be the deleted contact. Notice this figure also shows a deleted document in the Recycle Bin. The Recycle Bin holds everything from lists to libraries to web pages, so if you have trouble finding a deleted item, you may also find it useful to sort by item type as well as the deleted date and time to help locate the item you want.

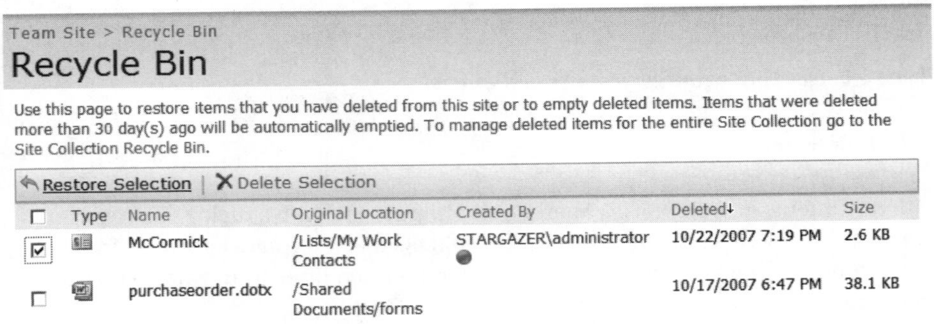

Team Site > Recycle Bin

Recycle Bin

Use this page to restore items that you have deleted from this site or to empty deleted items. Items that were deleted more than 30 day(s) ago will be automatically emptied. To manage deleted items for the entire Site Collection go to the Site Collection Recycle Bin.

	Type	Name	Original Location	Created By	Deleted↓	Size
☑		McCormick	/Lists/My Work Contacts	STARGAZER\administrator	10/22/2007 7:19 PM	2.6 KB
☐		purchaseorder.dotx	/Shared Documents/forms		10/17/2007 6:47 PM	38.1 KB

Figure 5-6. *Restoring a deleted contact from the Recycle Bin*

After you click the **Restore Selection** link, SharePoint prompts to confirm the item by name that you want to restore. When you click **OK**, SharePoint restores the item from the Recycle Bin, returning it to the list it originally came from. You may be surprised to learn that the process of restoring the contact from the SharePoint Recycle Bin also places the contact back in Outlook's shared list. You can verify this by opening Outlook and looking at the shared contacts list.

So what happens when you start by deleting the contact from within Outlook? In this case, SharePoint recognizes that the contact has been deleted through Outlook and moves the contact information from the list to the Recycle Bin. From that point, the story remains the same. You can go into the Recycle Bin in SharePoint and restore the contact to both the SharePoint list and the Outlook contacts list.

Moving Contacts Between Lists

SharePoint does not really provide a way to move or copy a contact from one list to another. However, if you share both contacts lists through Outlook, Outlook can accomplish this task quickly and easily by following these steps:

1. With both contacts lists synchronized in Outlook, open the list you want to copy the contact from to show the individual items it contains.

2. Click and drag the contact to the destination contacts list title in the **Navigation** panel on the left side of the screen.

3. When you release the mouse button, Outlook moves the contact from the original list and places it in the new list. You can verify this by returning to your SharePoint window and viewing the items in each contacts list. Remember to refresh the list displays if you already had them open.

■**Tip** This ability to copy between contacts lists extends to all contacts lists in Outlook, not just those linked to SharePoint. As a result, you can use this technique as an easy way to populate a new SharePoint list from your main contacts list in Outlook.

If you work at a company that uses Exchange Server, your main Outlook contacts list already contains all the people in your organization. You can transfer that information to a custom SharePoint list for a department or project by following these steps:

1. Open SharePoint and create a new empty contacts list in the desired site.

2. Open the list after creating it.

3. Select **Connect to Outlook** from the **Actions** menu.

4. Open the main **Contacts** list in Outlook using the **Contacts** page.

5. Locate the people you want to add to the SharePoint list.

6. Right-click and drag the contacts to the SharePoint list.

7. Release the mouse button and select **Copy** from the pop-up menu. In this case, you don't want to move the contacts from one list to another.

8. Repeat Step 5 to copy each additional contact to the SharePoint list.

9. When finished, return to SharePoint and open the new list, or if you still have it open from before, refresh the page.

You now can populate a list without retyping the entries.

Synchronizing Your Calendars Between SharePoint and Outlook

Calendars seem to be springing up everywhere. If you have been a Microsoft Office user, you probably already use Outlook's calendar to track your appointments, meetings, task due dates, and more while in the office. You may also add your personal events such as doctor appointments, birthdays, anniversaries, and your son's or daughter's school events.

With the introduction of SharePoint collaboration, it has become easy for project managers and group managers to create shareable online calendars with events that affect everyone in the project or group. Like contacts lists, the more projects you belong to, the more calendars you must check on a regular basis to make sure that you do not miss an event, a deadline, or a meeting. With so many places to check for the information you need, you can easily miss something critical.

To solve this problem of having too many calendars, you can join calendars from Share-Point and Outlook into a common view. Functionally, this technique works similarly to viewing calendars from multiple people. Besides being able to view multiple calendars together on the screen, sharing calendars between SharePoint and Outlook lets you manage multiple Share-Point calendars from Outlook.

Adding a SharePoint Calendar to Outlook

To add a SharePoint calendar to Outlook, begin by opening the calendar within SharePoint as shown in Figure 5-7.

It does not matter which calendar view you begin from, as SharePoint synchronizes all calendar items with Outlook. Information that SharePoint synchronizes includes these columns:

- **Item Title**

- **Location**

- **Start Time**

- **End Time**

- **Description**

- **All Day Event**

- **Recurrence**

Next open the **Actions** drop-down menu as shown in Figure 5-8 and select the option **Connect to Outlook**.

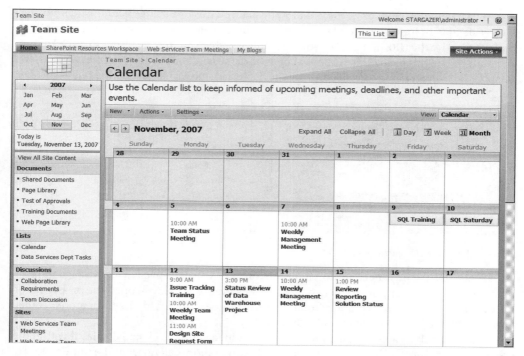

Figure 5-7. *Typical calendar list in calendar view*

Note While calendar events in Outlook supports scheduling options such as selecting attendees, setting reminders, and adding flags and categories, these features do not exist in SharePoint. This difference in supported elements limits what information SharePoint can synchronize.

Figure 5-8. *Choosing to connect a calendar list to Outlook*

As with contacts, Outlook needs you to verify that you trust the source before synchronizing with a calendar list from SharePoint or any other source. In the dialog box shown in Figure 5-9, Outlook displays the URL of the list so you can verify whether you trust the list. If so, click **Yes** to continue. Also in this dialog box, Outlook shows the name it intends to assign to the calendar. By default, the calendar name concatenates the site name with the list name separated with a hyphen.

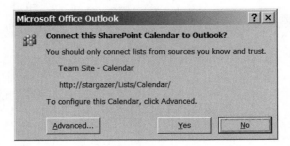

Figure 5-9. *Confirming that you trust the calendar source*

If you click the **Advanced** button in this dialog box, you can specify your own calendar name as well as a description. You can view this description when you open the properties of the Calendar folder within Outlook. You might use this description to provide a more detailed explanation of the purpose of the calendar.

After Outlook creates the folder for the SharePoint calendar, you can display it within the **Calendar** page. Outlook has the ability to display two or more calendars at the same time. To display more than one calendar, open the **Navigation** panel, shown in Figure 5-10, if not currently open. You can do this through Outlook's **View** menu.

Figure 5-10. *The Navigation panel in Outlook for calendars*

In the top portion of the **Navigation** panel, a calendar appears. Use this calendar to select the month, week, or day you want to view. Beneath this calendar you will find a section entitled **All Calendar Items**. This section contains one or more subsections. By default, the subsection named **My Calendars** represents standard calendars created within Outlook. In this subsection, you should have at least one calendar named **Calendar,** which represents your primary Outlook calendar. If you have attached additional files to Outlook such as archived Outlook files from the current or different machines, you may see additional calendars from these archives as well. In addition, Outlook allows you to create additional calendars.

CREATING A NEW OUTLOOK CALENDAR

You can create a new Outlook calendar for a project or other special purpose by selecting **New ➤ Calendar** from Outlook's **File** menu.

1. In the dialog box that appears, supply a name for your new calendar.

2. Make sure that the **Folder Contains** drop-down has the option **Calendar Items** selected.

3. Select where you want to create the calendar.

4. Once created, the new calendar will appear in the **My Calendar** subsection of the **Navigation** panel.

    To display the calendar, click the check box to the left of the name.

A second subsection, named **Other Calendars,** holds calendars linked to Outlook from SharePoint. I use the term "linked" here rather than "copied" to emphasize that the SharePoint calendar can be updated in either SharePoint or Outlook and have those updates displayed in the other system.

You can display any combination of the calendars from these two subsections by selecting them using the check box to the left of their names. While you can display several calendars at once, the physical width of your monitor will determine how many calendars you can reasonably view. Generally, more than two or three at a time makes it difficult to read the events and appointments. However, by positioning your mouse over an item in the calendar, a tooltip style window appears beneath your cursor with the item's time and subject.

Figure 5-11 shows two calendars side by side. The default Outlook calendar appears on the left, and a SharePoint calendar appears on the right.

Outlook lets you display one day, one week, or a full month of each calendar using the buttons across the top of the calendar area. You can also change the detail level displayed. Table 5-2 lists the three available detail settings and explains each one.

You can quickly move between months by clicking the **Previous** and **Next** buttons, represented by left and right arrows respectively, at the top left of the calendar area. Each click moves your view one month at a time.

Tip You can also move through your calendar one week at a time if you have a scroll wheel on your mouse.

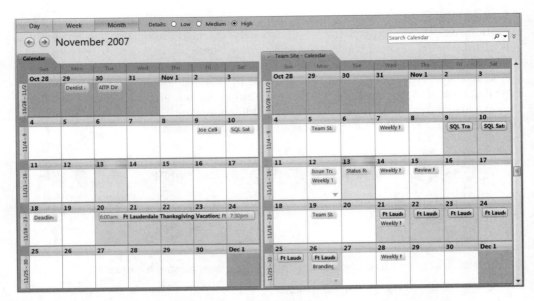

Figure 5-11. *An Outlook calendar and a SharePoint calendar displayed side by side*

Table 5-2. *Calendar Detail Levels*

Level	Description
Low	This mode shows only full-day events.
Medium	In addition to full-day events, this mode displays a horizontal bar for each appointment. The thickness of the bar represents the duration of the appointment. The bar's relative vertical position indicates the start time during the day. Outlook adds a thin bar at 12 noon as a reference point for midday.
High	This mode displays all events and appointments with their start times and subjects.

Overlaying Calendars

While displaying two calendars at a time side by side allows you to visually compare events and appointments on common days, you can make this process easier by overlaying the calendars on top of each other. To do this, click the arrow to the left of the calendar name tab of any calendar after the first one. When you do this, Outlook overlays the calendars, showing a single view of your events and appointments.

Alternatively, you can select the **View in Overlay Mode** option in the **View** drop-down menu as shown in Figure 5-12.

Figure 5-12. *Switching view modes in the Navigation panel*

When Outlook overlays calendars, it displays a tab for each calendar at the top of the combined calendar. Click the tab of the calendar you want to appear on top of the others. The events and appointments of the top calendar appear in bold black text compared to the events and appointments beneath the top calendar. You should also notice that events for calendars beneath the top calendar use a font color that matches the tab color so you can easily identify to which calendar an event belongs when overlaying three or more calendars. Clicking between the tabs illustrates this point. Figure 5-13 shows two overlayed calendars.

■**Tip** If you can see the calendars of your coworkers, you can use this technique to overlay them to quickly spot times when you can have group meetings.

To display each calendar separately again, click the arrow to the left of any calendar name in the tab area. You can also select **View in Side-by-Side Mode** from the **View** drop-down menu.

Figure 5-13. *Two overlayed calendars*

Making Changes to Calendar Items

You can change any of the properties for an event or appointment in a synchronized Share-Point calendar by double-clicking it in Outlook to open the item's property form. Then click the **Save and Close** button to save those changes.

Outlook synchronizes changes to the original SharePoint calendar so that someone viewing the calendar item directly from SharePoint sees your changes. Similarly, changes made in the SharePoint calendar update the view in Outlook the next time you open the calendar page (or when you press F9).

■**Caution** When editing an event or appointment from a SharePoint calendar within Outlook, you can set properties that will not synchronize back to SharePoint such as categories, flags, reminders, and several others. While Outlook saves these properties for use within Outlook, SharePoint ignores them.

Copying and Moving Items Between Calendars

If you have appointments in more than one calendar, you might want to display multiple calendars to help visually organize your day. You can also look for conflicting appointments or free time. You might even want to move appointments or events from one calendar to another.

To move an event or appointment when you have two or more calendars displayed, click and drag an item from one open calendar to the next. While you can easily change the day of an appointment within a single calendar displayed in month mode, you cannot change the start or end times of the appointment by simply dragging the item; you must manually edit the times. This method, however, is much faster than reentering the appointment.

■**Caution** Remember, any calendar event you copy to a SharePoint calendar will not only be seen by anyone with access to that SharePoint calendar, but also will synchronize with their Outlook if they connect that calendar to their Outlook. So you may not want to share your personal appointments.

You may want to create a separate calendar in Outlook to plan a project schedule. Then when you have worked out the details, you can link to a SharePoint calendar on a project collaboration site and transfer your milestone dates by dragging them from one calendar to another.

You can copy items in either direction to or from SharePoint. Thus you could also use this technique to copy important events or appointments from a shared calendar to your personal calendar. However, once copied, the copy in your personal calendar will not show changes made to the SharePoint event or appointment or vice versa.

If, rather than copy, you want to move the item from one calendar to another, you could proceed exactly like the copy method I just outlined. Then after making the copy, delete the item from the original calendar. Alternatively, you can perform the operation in a single step by holding down the right mouse button while you drag the item. When you release the button, you can decide from a pop-up menu whether to copy or move the item to the new location.

■**Tip** Need to create a project calendar but feel more comfortable working with Outlook's calendar inter-face? No problem. Build your project calendar in a separate Outlook calendar, link to the project calendar in SharePoint, and copy the events from your local calendar to SharePoint.

Deleting Items from the Calendar

When you delete an item from an Outlook calendar, you can restore it by selecting **Undo** from the **Edit** drop-down menu as long as you have not closed Outlook. But after you close Outlook, you cannot recover it.

On the other hand, if you delete an item from a SharePoint calendar, even if you perform the delete on a synchronized calendar within Outlook, SharePoint places the deleted item in the site's Recycle Bin. You can recover the item by opening the Recycle Bin and selecting the item to restore as shown in Figure 5-14. Then click the **Restore Selection** option.

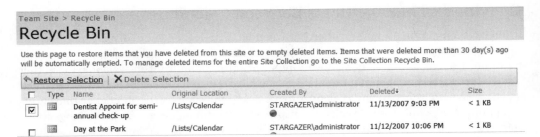

Figure 5-14. *Recovering a deleted item from SharePoint's Recycle Bin*

After confirming that you want to restore the item, SharePoint puts the item back in the calendar. You will also see the restored item in the Outlook synchronized copy the next time you open Outlook. If you have Outlook open while restoring the item, you may need to click off the **Calendar** page, perhaps going to the **Mail** page, and then return to the calendar page to see the restored item. You can also press F9 to perform a send-receive update.

Synchronizing Tasks Between SharePoint and Outlook

Sharing tasks may be as important as sharing contacts for many people when they begin using SharePoint together with Outlook. If you already use Outlook to plan your day, you know how valuable it can be to keep all your tasks in one place where you can monitor start and due dates, group tasks by priority, categorize your tasks by percent completion, and set up reminders as deadlines approach. If you work as a consultant, you can use Outlook's **Tasks** tool to track hours that can be used to support billing information. You can even use the large text area Outlook tasks provide as a task journal. For nonconsultants, these features can help document your work effort required to complete tasks. You might even document external factors that affect your ability to meet deadlines. For example, you might include a note in the text area that the reason you completed the installation of the new billing system three days late was because it took two weeks for the CIO to approve the purchase of the servers needed to run the new system.

No matter the specifics, using the **Tasks** feature in Outlook can help you organize and document your work. For many of these same reasons, your immediate manager or your project managers will also use the tasks list and project tasks list features of SharePoint as a convenient way to plan workloads and assign tasks to you. The problem you have is that you now must view tasks lists scattered in several different places across one or more SharePoint installations. Your boss keeps his tasks list in the department work site, while each of the project managers you support have their own project sites with their individual tasks lists. In addition, you have your own personal tasks list stored in Outlook on your desktop. You may have wondered how you can keep up with changes to these individual tasks lists stored in different places to determine what you really need to focus on today. Of course, you could periodically open each list one at a time and check for new tasks or changes to your existing tasks. However, as you become busy and focused on any one task, you may forget to check the other tasks lists for the latest crisis. Fortunately, Outlook can serve as a collection point for multiple SharePoint tasks lists and can display them together with your own personal tasks list through a single page.

WHAT ABOUT THE ISSUE TRACKING LIST?

Perhaps you remember from Chapter 2 that another list exists that tracks tasks that I did not mention in this section: the issue tracking list. Your help desk staff might use the issue tracking list to log issues called in to them. They could use this list to assign issues that they could not directly resolve to the appropriate development staff. You might even use the issue tracking list on your personal, project, or department site to track problems.

You might think that it would be great to combine these tasks with other tasks gathered from other SharePoint tasks lists and project tasks lists. Unfortunately, neither WSS 3.0 nor MOSS 2007 supports connecting to Outlook from an issue tracking list. I'm hoping that Microsoft can address this oversight in a future release.

In the meantime, you could set up an alert in the list by clicking **Alerts** in the **Actions** menu of the list. Then in the section **Send Alerts for These Changes**, select the option **A task is assigned to me**. This will send you an e-mail when a new task is added and assigned to you.

Adding Tasks Lists to Outlook

To begin organizing your tasks, open SharePoint and identify the names and locations of each tasks list you want to synchronize with Outlook. For the purpose of the discussion in this section, I'm going to load tasks from three tasks lists to show how Outlook gathers your tasks in one place. These tasks lists include the following:

- **Data Services Dept Tasks:** A basic tasks list created by a department manager, as shown in Figure 5-15.

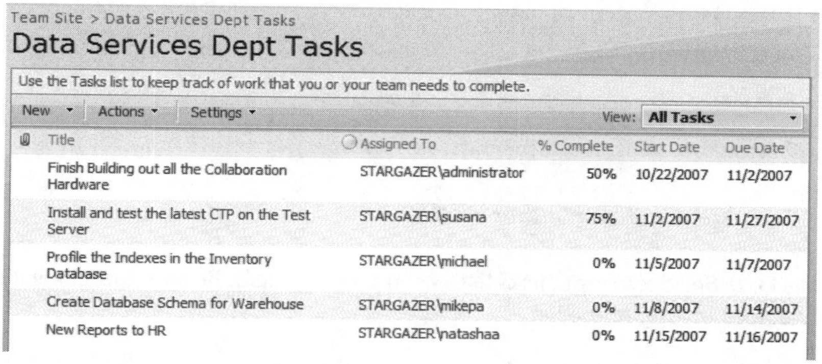

Figure 5-15. *The Data Services Dept Tasks list*

- **My Help Desk Calls:** A tasks list updated by the company's help desk, as shown in Figure 5-16.

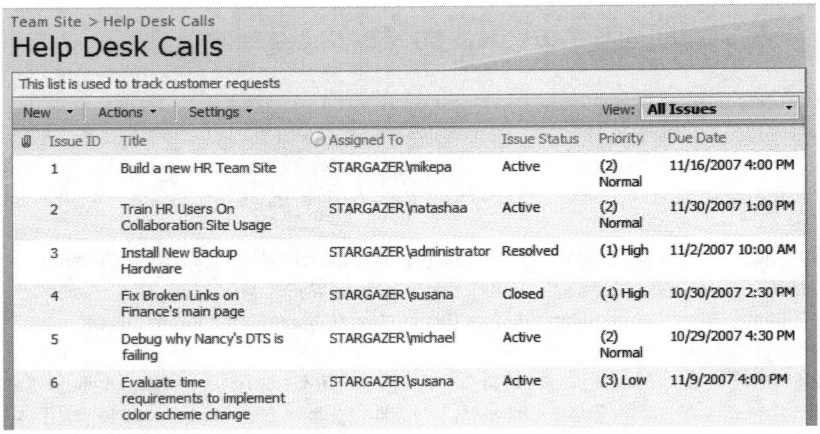

Figure 5-16. *The Help Desk Calls list*

- **Collaboration Site for HR**: A project tasks list created by the collaboration project manager, as shown in Figure 5-17.

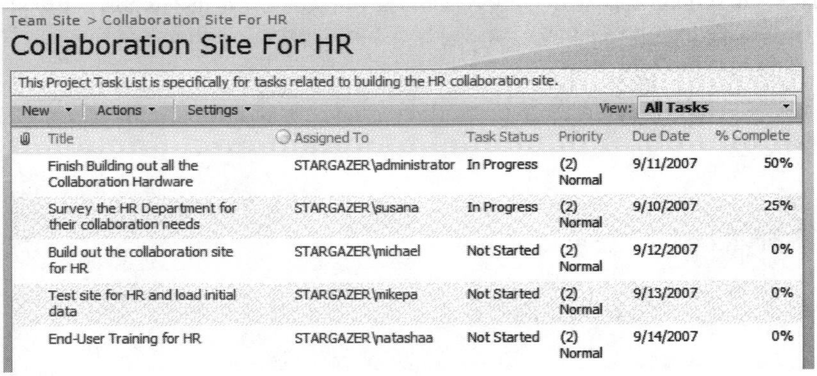

Figure 5-17. *The Collaboration Site for HR list*

1. Open the **Data Services Dept Tasks** list as shown previously. Be sure that the list menu appears across the top of the list.

2. Open the **Actions** drop-down menu and click **Connect to Outlook**. The **Actions** menu includes the operations you can perform on the current list.

   When you select this option, SharePoint attempts to connect to Outlook on your local computer. As you saw earlier with synchronizing contacts, Outlook tries to protect you from outside applications writing to Outlook and thus displays a warning message when it detects such an attempt. In this message box, you can accept or reject the connection. In this case, you should trust the connection and accept the default name for the new tasks list SharePoint creates in Outlook for the transferred data.

In a similar fashion, you can open each of the other two lists and transfer them to Outlook, accepting their default names. Figure 5-18 shows the **Navigation** panel on Outlook's **Tasks** page after attaching these three lists.

Figure 5-18. *Outlook's Tasks page Navigation panel*

Editing Tasks from Outlook

After you have connected to project or department tasks lists, you could edit these tasks within Outlook and have those edits appear in SharePoint, just like with contacts. However, unless you are the project manager or department manager and own the tasks list, I would recommend caution about making changes. On the one hand, your manager may want you to update selected fields such as the **% Complete**, **Finish Date**, **Completed Flag**, and **Notes** fields. On the other hand, that manager would not appreciate your changing the details of the task or the due date. At this point, SharePoint does not provide custom column-level security, so if users need edit permissions on some fields, they get edit permissions on all fields.

Of course, if you manage the list, not only can you edit existing tasks, but you can also create new tasks and delete tasks from within Outlook. You can even monitor the status of tasks, their progress, and their completion from within your Outlook **Tasks** page, even as your staff updates their task status through their Outlook **Tasks** pages.

So what if you want to prevent unintended changes to your tasks by your staff? Lists support an approval process like we saw earlier for documents. When turned on, the approval process hides the publishing of changes to the tasks list until a person with approval rights, such as you, approves the changes. The use of approvals provides two benefits. First, you can simply deny any unintended changes that might modify or delete the task. Second, you can review the legitimate updates to the tasks by your staff to monitor what they have accomplished.

Before you activate the approval process, make sure that Approval permissions for lists have been properly assigned to managers of the lists. Then follow these steps to turn on the approval process for a tasks list:

1. Open the tasks list where you want to enable the approval process.

2. Open **List Settings** in the **Settings** drop-down menu.

3. Click **Versioning Settings** in the **General Settings** section.

4. In the **Content Approval** area, select **Yes** to require content approval.

5. You can also choose to keep both major and minor versions. I recommend keeping at least two major versions with draft versions made to the most recent approved version. These settings provide basic version protection without consuming a huge amount of additional storage space. Plus they let you see what the current data was changed from. Change these settings in the **Item Version** history section to suit your needs.

6. In **Draft Item Security**, I recommend only allowing users with approval rights and the author to view the changes. That way everyone else sees only the most recently approved versions.

7. Click **OK** to accept these changes.

8. Click the name of your list in the breadcrumbs at the top of the page to return to the list view.

■**Note** Draft versions of tasks may not be as common as draft versions of documents, but you may encounter them, especially when managers build tasks lists for large projects.

You can now connect the list to Outlook. Select **Connect to Outlook** from the **Actions** menu and tell Outlook that you trust the SharePoint list when the message box appears.

Using Outlook to Work Offline with Content

You can work on documents in a document library by connecting the SharePoint library to Outlook as described previously for contacts and tasks. With one additional step, you can check the document out from within SharePoint to protect your changes.

Open the library that contains the document you want to work on. If your document is in a folder within the library, open the folders until you see the document list containing the document you want.

From within the document library, right-click the documents you want to work with offline and check them out. You do not have to check out every document in the library, just the ones you plan on working with offline. This allows other users to work with the documents you have not checked out.

Select the **Connect to Outlook** option in the **Actions** menu. Outlook opens on your local computer, if not already open, and prompts you to respond whether you trust the source attempting to connect to it. Since you know the source is your SharePoint document library, check **Yes** to continue.

Outlook then creates a folder named `SharePoint Lists` if one does not already exist in your **Mail Folders** list. It then adds a folder for the site library using the naming convention `<site name> - <library name>`. Within this folder, it builds any additional folder structure needed to match the folder hierarchy within the library down to the folder containing your document. In the last folder, the one you said to connect to Outlook from SharePoint, Outlook displays a list

of all files. Figure 5-19 shows an example of the Digital Signatures folder found within the
Shared Documents library of a site named **Web Services**.

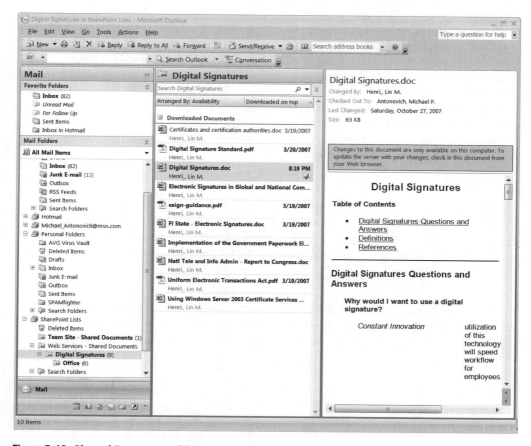

Figure 5-19. *Shared Documents library referenced through Outlook*

When you look at the files in this folder, you may see one or more with a small icon in the
lower-right side of the individual file listing. This icon, which shows a page with a red upward
pointing arrow in it, identifies the file as having been checked out. If you position your mouse
over the file, the tooltip text beneath the title also tells you that the file has been checked out
and who has checked it out. Finally, if you click the file and have the document preview window
open, it says

```
Changes to this document are only available on this computer.
To update the server with your changes, check in this document from
your Web browser.
```

This message reminds you that you have checked out the document to edit it offline. Only
documents that you have checked out are copied to your local drafts folder. If there is another

document that you did not check out before connecting the library with Outlook, you can double-click it within Outlook to open the document if you are still connected to your network. When you do this, a dialog box asks whether you want to open the document or save it to your computer.

If you choose to open the document, Word opens the document (assuming it is a DOC or DOCX file) in **Read-Only** mode. However, you can edit the document by clicking the **Edit Offline** button immediately beneath the Ribbon. When you click this button, Word retrieves a copy of the document, placing it in your local SharePoint drafts folder. You can now disconnect and edit the document.

If you choose to save the document to your computer when you double-click it from Outlook, a copy of the file is downloaded to the directory of your choice. However, this action breaks the link between SharePoint and Outlook. Thus, when you edit this copy of the file, Word does not transfer the changes back to SharePoint.

■**Tip** Outlook 2007 provides a great preview feature for Office files such as Word, Excel, and PowerPoint. When you click an e-mail message with an attachment from one of these applications, you can preview the attachment by clicking it. Similarly, when you use Outlook to work offline on SharePoint libraries with these file types, you can preview their content when you select the individual items in the linked library.

If you double-click the file, Outlook opens the document for editing. It also opens the **Document Management** panel as shown in Figure 5-20. The **Document Management** panel indicates that the file has been checked out and provides a link for you to check the document back in.

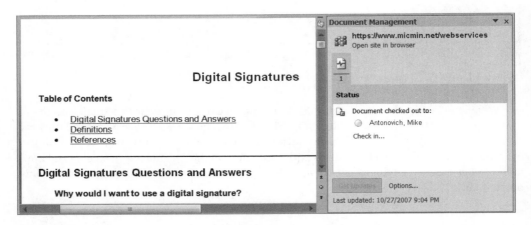

Figure 5-20. *Opened document edited offline*

But let's assume that you want to work on the document later. After you have disconnected from your network, you can edit the local copy of the document saved in the SharePoint Drafts folder even if you have disconnected from your network. You can open the file stored here either by double-clicking it through Outlook or by opening your SharePoint Drafts folder and double-clicking the file directly. In fact, you can open, edit, and save the document repeatedly while disconnected from the network. Word stores your changes in the local copy of the file.

The next time you connect to the network and open one of the files you edited while disconnected, a message box pops up as shown in Figure 5-21. Outlook remembers that you edited this file offline, and now that you have reconnected to the network, wants to know if you want to update the server version of the document with your changes.

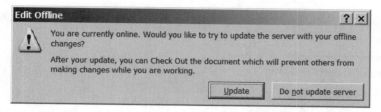

Figure 5-21. *Request to resync after reconnecting to network*

Even if you want to keep the document checked out, you may want to update the document version on the server. Saving the offline changes does not automatically check the document back into the server. It only saves the changes back to your SharePoint library. On the positive side, saving your changes back to the server protects them, assuming that your system administrator regularly backs up your SharePoint servers. On the negative side, depending on whether the library requires document approval or not, updating the server could make your recent changes visible to other people opening the document from the library. In that case, if you want to keep your changes private until you have completed all your changes, click the **Do not update server** option. You can continue to update the document on your local machine, saving your intermediate changes to your Drafts folder even when you are connected to your network. When you finish making changes, use the **Check in** link in the **Document Management** panel shown in Figure 5-22. If your document library tracks versions, a dialog box allows you to enter comments about the current version. Use this opportunity to describe the reasons for the changes made to the document.

■**Tip** If you are not done with all of your changes, but just want to save what you have changed until later, click the check box at the bottom of the **Check In** dialog that says **Keep the document checked out after checking in this version**. This option saves your changes back to SharePoint as if it checked it in and then immediately checked it back out again. If you have minor versioning turned on, this increments the minor version count.

When you click the **OK** button, Outlook first saves the document to the server. It then checks the document back into the library and attaches the version comments to the most recent version.

When you look at your file list in Outlook, you will see that the icon of the page with the red arrow has now been removed. Also, if you go into SharePoint, the small green box with the arrow in it that identifies checked-out documents has also been removed.

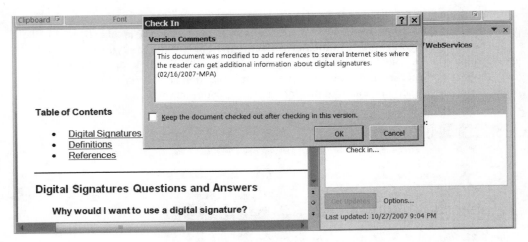

Figure 5-22. *During check-in, adding comments describing changes made to this revision*

Does this mean that you cannot edit the checked-in document again? No. Actually you have two choices. You can check out the document again from SharePoint, and then click **Connect to Outlook** in the **Actions** menu to update the information in Outlook if you don't want to wait for the periodic automatic resync. However, as long as you remain connected to the network, you can simply double-click the document from within Outlook to open it again in Word. Word opens the document in **Read-Only** mode. Notice that even though you have not checked out the document, you can still download a copy of it to edit offline. Of course, without checking out the document, someone else could edit the document while you work on it offline, creating a conflict when you attempt to save your changes. If you choose to proceed anyway, click the **Edit Offline** button shown in Figure 5-23.

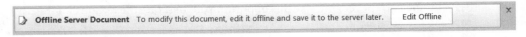

Figure 5-23. *The Edit Offline button lets you edit a document without first checking it out.*

This option opens the document in **Edit** mode. However, you still have not checked out the document. Word stores the changes you make here in the local drafts folder when you click the **Save** option in Word. When you close Word though, it prompts you to upload the changes to the server. If no one else has opened the document to make a change, Word allows you to save your changes. Thus you can make a quick change without going through the check-out process using this method. However, if anyone else has opened the document and saved her changes while you had your offline copy open for editing, Word displays the message shown in Figure 5-24 that you need to resolve a conflict between the changes someone else made to the document and the changes you made.

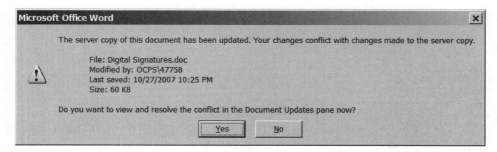

Figure 5-24. *A conflict was detected during an update.*

If you click **Yes**, you need to know where to find the **Document Updates** panel. In Office 2007, click the **Office Button** and select **Server**. From the server options, select **Document Management Information**. The **Document Management** panel, which you saw in Chapter 4, opens on the **Document Updates** panel. Here you can open both documents to compare their differences. You can then choose to keep either the server copy or your copy. If you choose to keep your copy, then the pop-up shown in Figure 5-25 appears, reminding you that this action replaces the server version with your copy.

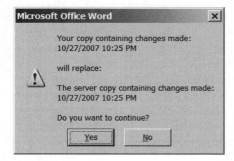

Figure 5-25. *Replacing a server copy with your copy of document changes*

■**Note** This is an all-or-nothing choice. You cannot choose individual updates from different versions.

Letting Alerts Notify You of SharePoint Changes

An alert is a feature of SharePoint that you can use to notify you of changes made to libraries and lists via e-mail so that you do not have to constantly return to the library or list to see if anything was changed. With a manual check, you might spot new additions or deletions to the library or list. However, unless you were to track the modified dates of individual items in the library or list, it would be difficult to determine when they were modified. Alerts can do this work for you. I first discussed alerts in Chapter 2 in the context of our initial exploration of lists. You can turn alerts on by opening the **Actions** drop-down menu in libraries or lists and selecting the **Alert Me** option as shown in Figure 5-26.

Figure 5-26. *Selecting the Alert Me action*

Configuring Your Alerts

The **Alert Me** action opens the **New Alert** page shown in Figure 5-27. The first property you must define is the **Alert Title**. You can create hundreds of alerts within a SharePoint site. So naming the alert carefully and uniquely helps you manage your alerts later. Case in point, SharePoint uses the alert title as the subject text when sending you the alert via e-mail. SharePoint also uses the alert title when it lists your alerts, should you decide to delete some of them later.

After the alert title, you can specify who should receive the alert. By default, SharePoint places your SharePoint user ID in this field, which links to your e-mail address defined in your user account. However, you can create alerts for other people if you have administrator rights by deleting your name and adding e-mail addresses for others separated with semicolons. If several people need to receive the same alert, this feature can save you time by not having to create individual alerts for each person.

Next, you need to select for which types of changes you want to send alerts. Of course, you could send alerts for all changes, but that might create too many e-mails. You can also limit alerts to just additions, modifications, or deletions. Unfortunately, you cannot select both additions and deletions, but not modifications. Radio buttons only allow mutually exclusive selections.

You can also specify whether you want to see alerts when someone else other than yourself changes any document. Department and project managers may want to choose this option so SharePoint notifies them of all changes made to documents under their responsibility. You can also limit alerts to when someone makes changes to documents you created or modified last. With tasks lists, you can set your alert to notify you of only those tasks that have been assigned to you.

The final section in defining alerts lets you define the frequency with which you want to receive the alerts. You could receive the alert as soon as the event monitored occurs. This may be important when SharePoint immediately publishes changed documents.

On the other hand, maybe you only want to receive a daily notification of events that occurred. When using this option, you can specify the time of day to receive the alert. SharePoint then delivers alerts on a 24-hour cycle. So if you specify that you want to receive alerts at 4:00 p.m. and someone updates or deletes a document at 4:30 p.m., you will not receive that alert until 4:00 p.m. the next day.

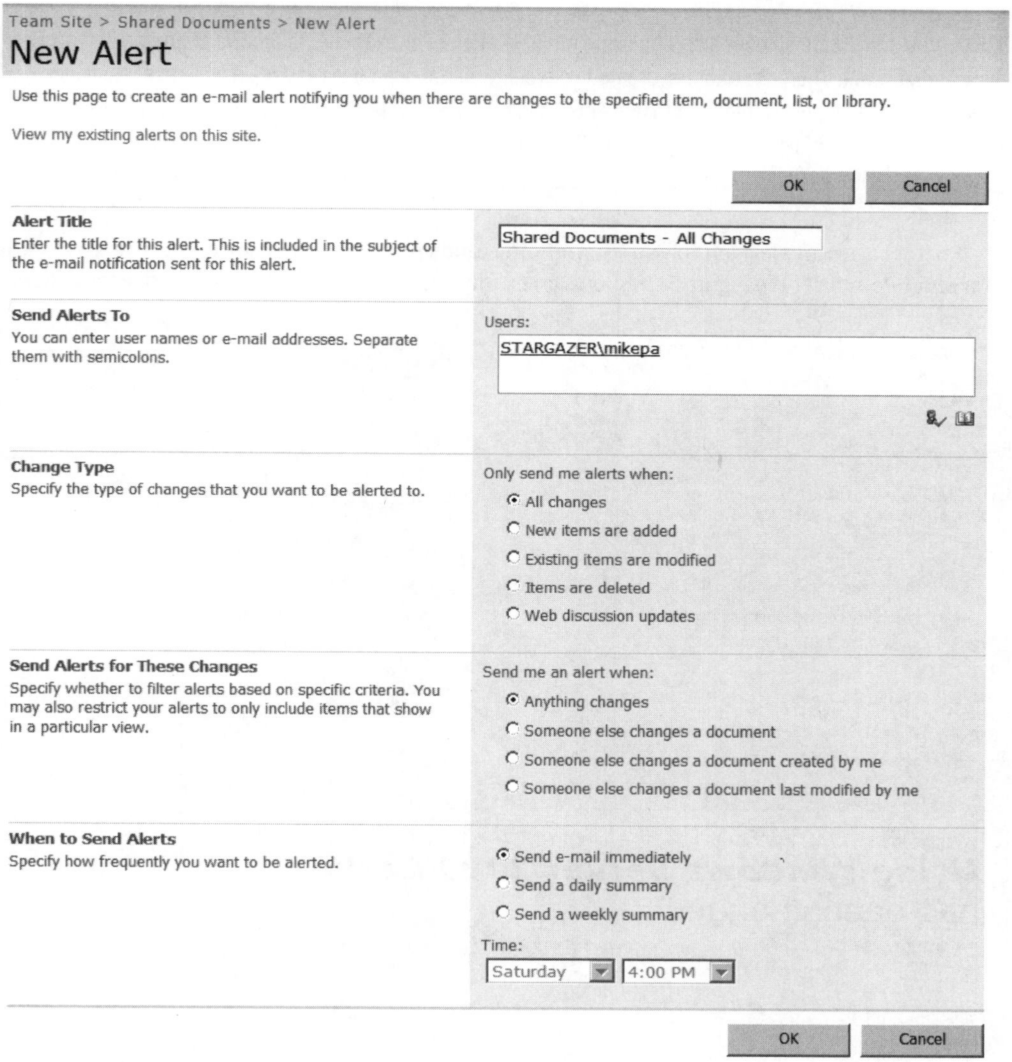

Team Site > Shared Documents > New Alert

New Alert

Use this page to create an e-mail alert notifying you when there are changes to the specified item, document, list, or library.

View my existing alerts on this site.

[OK] [Cancel]

Alert Title

Enter the title for this alert. This is included in the subject of the e-mail notification sent for this alert.

Shared Documents - All Changes

Send Alerts To

You can enter user names or e-mail addresses. Separate them with semicolons.

Users:

STARGAZER\mikepa

Change Type

Specify the type of changes that you want to be alerted to.

Only send me alerts when:

- ⊙ All changes
- ○ New items are added
- ○ Existing items are modified
- ○ Items are deleted
- ○ Web discussion updates

Send Alerts for These Changes

Specify whether to filter alerts based on specific criteria. You may also restrict your alerts to only include items that show in a particular view.

Send me an alert when:

- ⊙ Anything changes
- ○ Someone else changes a document
- ○ Someone else changes a document created by me
- ○ Someone else changes a document last modified by me

When to Send Alerts

Specify how frequently you want to be alerted.

- ⊙ Send e-mail immediately
- ○ Send a daily summary
- ○ Send a weekly summary

Time:

[Saturday ▼] [4:00 PM ▼]

[OK] [Cancel]

Figure 5-27. *New Alert dialog box*

You might also choose to see alerts only once a week on a specific day and time. For example, you might want to see alerts first thing Monday mornings for changes made the previous week. As previously stated, events that occur immediately after the alert notice goes out must then wait until the end of the new cycle, even if that means waiting for 6 days, 23 hours, and 59 minutes.

You can define multiple alerts for the same list. Perhaps each one notifies you of different actions performed on the list and may be delivered to you at different time intervals. For example, you may want to be notified immediately of inserts, daily of deletes, and weekly of updates.

■Tip You can create custom alerts by using multiple alerts. For example, to receive change notifications every Tuesday and Thursday at noon, create two weekly alerts, one for each day. In this case, each alert works independently of the other so that events typically appear in both lists. For example, an event on Monday will appear in both the Tuesday and Thursday alerts.

So how does an alert get to you? SharePoint sends it to the e-mail address associated with your SharePoint user ID. Figure 5-28 shows an example of what a typical alert message looks like.

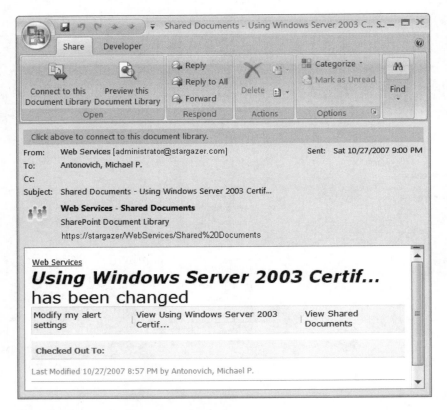

Figure 5-28. *Sample alert sent to Outlook*

Correcting/Modifying Alerts

If you make a mistake entering your alert or just want to modify it, how can you change it? Well, the bad news is that you cannot change it. The good news is that you can delete the original alert and replace it with a new one having the same name, but that does what you want. To remove an alert, follow these steps:

1. Select the **Site Settings** option after clicking the **Site Actions** button.

2. Select **User Alerts** from the **Site Administration** section. You must have administration rights to the site to see and select these options. If you do not, you must contact your administrator for his assistance.

3. In the **Display Alerts For** drop-down, select the **User ID** of the person from whom you want to delete an alert and click the **Update** button to show her alerts.

Note Only users with alerts appear in this drop-down list.

---

4. From the list of alerts, find the one you want to remove and click the check box to the left of the alert name. You can select multiple alerts for the person by selecting their respective check boxes.

5. Click the **Delete Selected Alerts** link at the top of the list to remove the chosen alerts.

Figure 5-29 shows the **User Alerts** page with a few alerts selected. Notice the value of using unique names here to identify which alerts to delete, especially when multiple alerts exist for the same list.

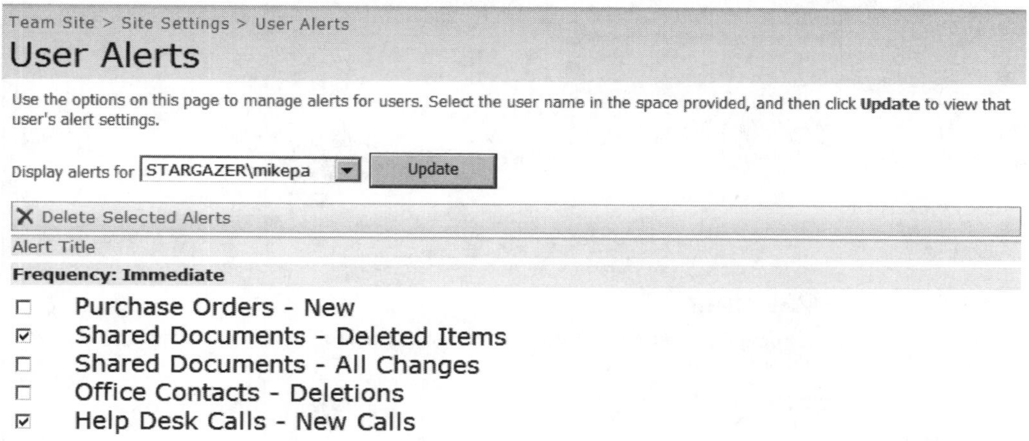

Team Site > Site Settings > User Alerts
User Alerts

Use the options on this page to manage alerts for users. Select the user name in the space provided, and then click **Update** to view that user's alert settings.

Display alerts for STARGAZER\mikepa ▼   Update

✗ Delete Selected Alerts

Alert Title

Frequency: Immediate

☐   Purchase Orders - New
☑   Shared Documents - Deleted Items
☐   Shared Documents - All Changes
☐   Office Contacts - Deletions
☑   Help Desk Calls - New Calls

Figure 5-29. *Dialog box for deleting alerts*

Tip A good practice might be to name alerts by the list they apply to, the events they track, and perhaps even their delivery schedule.

Using Outlook's RSS Reader to Subscribe to SharePoint RSS Feeds

Both Internet Explorer and Outlook 2007 have an RSS aggregator that displays links to your subscribed RSS feeds directly from their respective menus.

Adding an RSS Feed to Internet Explorer 7.0

To add a new RSS feed, navigate to a page in a SharePoint site that supports RSS. You can easily identify those sites by looking at the RSS feed icon in Internet Explorer 7.0's menu bar. Figure 5-30 shows the RSS feed icon.

Figure 5-30. *The RSS feed icon*

When Internet Explorer displays this icon in orange, the page supports an RSS feed. By clicking the down arrow to the right of the icon, the drop-down displays the page components that support the RSS feed. Figure 5-31 shows the **Calendar** page from a SharePoint site with an enabled RSS feed.

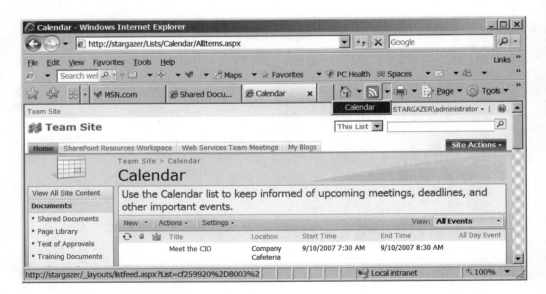

Figure 5-31. *Calendar page with active RSS feed*

If the page only has a single RSS feed component, you can select it by either clicking it in this drop-down list or simply clicking the RSS icon itself. In either case, SharePoint displays a window containing information about the feed, as shown in Figure 5-32. The upper-left portion of this window identifies the source of the feed using the site name and the library name separated with a colon. The box on the right displays the number of items available in the list or library and lets you sort these items by date, title, or author. Beneath these two areas appear the current items in the list.

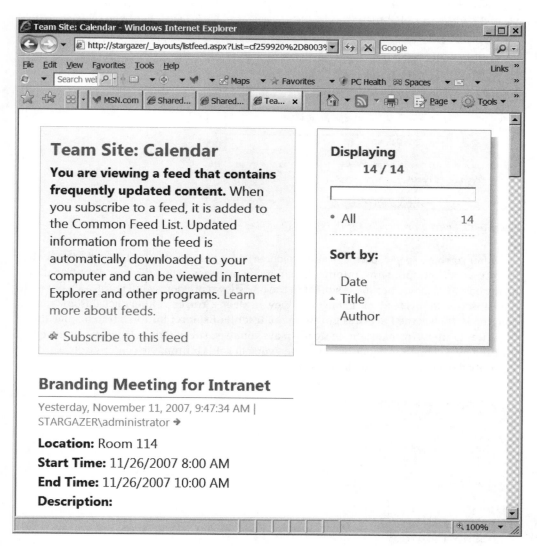

Figure 5-32. *Subscription page for a typical RSS feed*

To subscribe, you could click the link **Subscribe to this feed**. While this option adds the feed to your **Favorites Center** in Internet Explorer, it may not add it to Outlook directly (see the upcoming section "Adding an RSS Feed to Outlook 2007"). When you click the **Subscribe to this feed** link, Internet Explorer displays the subscription box, which requires the feed name and the location where you want to create the feed. By default, the feed name combines the site name and the library or list name separated by a colon. If you have never created an RSS subscription before, the **Create In** text box displays an empty Feeds folder. You can add your subscription directly to this top-level folder, or you can first create a new folder under Feeds. When you add a new folder, you can, of course, name it something appropriate to the type of feeds you intend to store in it. Figure 5-33 shows that two folders have already been created under Feeds, and the second folder, SharePoint Book Feeds, has been selected to hold the new subscription.

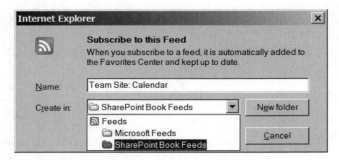

Figure 5-33. *Setting properties for the subscribed feed*

After you have specified a name and a folder in which to store your feed, click the **Subscribe** button. After a few moments, Internet Explorer creates the feed and displays a confirmation dialog box. This dialog box looks similar to the one shown previously in Figure 5-32, but with the **Subscribe to this feed** link changed to **View my feeds**. You can either click this link to view your feeds or click the **Favorites** button in the Internet Explorer button bar to display the **Favorites Center**. Normally, the center displays your web site favorites. However, at the top of the list, you will find the **Feeds** button. When you click this button, the center displays your subscribed feeds as shown in Figure 5-34.

Figure 5-34. *RSS feeds shown in the Feeds section of Outlook's Favorites Center*

Adding an RSS Feed to Outlook 2007

You can save yourself a lot of time by letting the feeds added in IE automatically populate the feeds list in Outlook. If you want IE and Outlook to share RSS feeds, and you add a feed to IE 7.0 or better and it does not update Outlook 2007 or better, follow these steps:

1. Go to the **Tools** menu of Outlook.

2. Click **Options** to display the **Options** dialog box.

3. Click the **Other** tab.

4. Click the **Advanced Options** button in the **General** section.

5. On the **Advanced Options** page, find the option **Sync RSS Feeds to the Common Feed List** and make sure that the check box has been selected.

6. Close Outlook and reopen it.

7. When you reopen Outlook, it will ask whether you want to use the **Common Feed List**. Verify that you do.

If you don't want to automatically populate the RSS feeds in Outlook 2007 with the feeds from IE 7.0, you will have to manually add RSS feeds to Outlook. There are several ways to do this. If Outlook is not open, open it now and arrange your Windows as shown in Figure 5-35, with Outlook beneath and to the side of Internet Explorer so you can see both the **Favorites Center** in Internet Explorer and the Outlook left-side menu.

Figure 5-35. *Dragging an RSS feed from the Favorites Center to Outlook's RSS Feeds*

■**Tip** You might need to follow similar steps if you are using a different RSS aggregator.

Then locate the feed you want to add to Outlook. Right-click and drag the feed over to the RSS Feeds folder in the Outlook menu. When you release the right mouse button while pointing to RSS Feeds, a pop-up menu appears with the options **Cancel** or **Copy Here as Message with Text**. Choose the copy option. This opens the message form as shown in Figure 5-36.

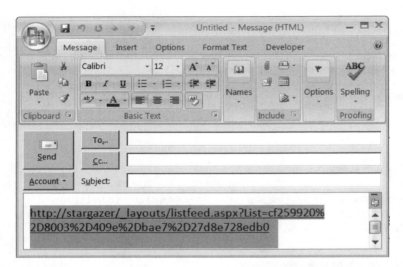

Figure 5-36. *Message created by dragging an RSS feed to Outlook*

While you really do not want to send a message with the RSS feed link, you do want to copy the link from this message to the clipboard. Once you have the URL for the RSS link on the clipboard, right-click the RSS Feeds folder in Outlook and select the option **Add a New RSS Feed**.

This option opens a small dialog box asking you to enter the location of the RSS feed you want to add to Outlook. Paste the contents of the clipboard (the link from the message) here and click **Add**.

Outlook recognizes that this subscription link could be a potential risk to your system and prompts you with another dialog box asking whether you know and trust the site from which the feed originates. If you do, as in this case, you would click **Yes**. Otherwise, click **No**. After a few moments, Outlook connects to the RSS source using the supplied URL and populates your new RSS feed folder as shown in Figure 5-37.

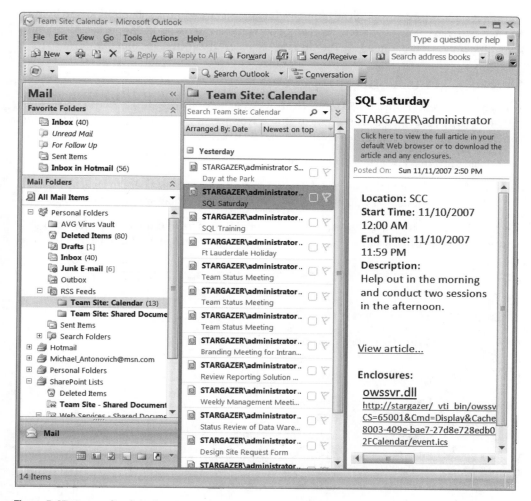

Figure 5-37. *Items displays from an RSS feed in Outlook*

A FASTER METHOD TO MANUALLY SPECIFY THE RSS FEED IN OUTLOOK 2007

After you create the RSS subscription in Internet Explorer, you can, of course, use that feed link directly as found in the **Favorites Center**. As you saw in Figure 5-32, when you finish defining a new feed or when you click one of your existing feeds, Internet Explorer opens a page with the current RSS items.

You may not have noticed that the text in your browser's URL field at the top of this page displays the feed link. You can also copy this URL to the clipboard. Then as before, right-click RSS Feeds in Outlook, select **Add a New RSS Feed**, and paste the copied URL into the dialog box that appears.

Notice that each item in the calendar appears as a separate entry in this Outlook folder. If you click the **Arrange by** button at the top of the list, you can sort the items by any of the columns in the calendar list. You can also group the items based on the sort.

Since an RSS feed automatically updates the items shown in the subscription and bolds any item you have not yet opened, you can easily spot new items added to the list. After you open an item to view it, the text in the Outlook list reverts to normal for that item.

Deleting Items from an RSS Feed

You can delete items from the RSS list by right-clicking them and selecting **Delete**. Unlike other lists, this has no effect on the subscription's source. However, if you really want to delete the item, you can click it to display a preview of the item and then perform one of the following actions:

- Click the link **View article** from the preview pane.

- Click the banner at the top of the preview pane that says "Click here to view the full article in your default web browser or to download the article and any enclosures."

In either case, these actions display the SharePoint item in your browser as shown in Figure 5-38. This form uses the default edit form for columns in a SharePoint list.

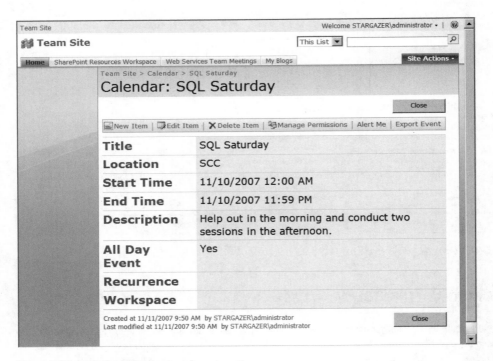

Figure 5-38. *Edit form for an item's properties*

At the top of this form, you have the standard options to edit or delete the current item, assuming you have these permissions for list items in the current site. If you delete the item here, SharePoint asks you to confirm that you want to send the item to the Recycle Bin. If you click **OK**, SharePoint deletes the item from the list, but it may still appear in the RSS subscription in Outlook, at least until the next synchronization.

As with other deleted items, you can recover items deleted within SharePoint. Go to the Recycle Bin, select the item you want to recover, and click the **Restore Selection** button.

When viewing an RSS feed to a document library, this method still begins by showing the properties of the individual library item as shown in Figure 5-39. To view the document associated with the item, click the document name. In this figure, clicking **The Perfect Day** retrieves the document from SharePoint and opens a local copy of it.

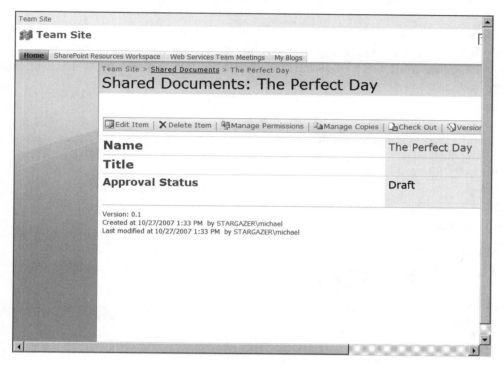

Figure 5-39. *Viewing an item from a document library through an RSS feed*

■**Tip** Don't want the RSS feed anymore? Just right-click it and select **Delete**. If you delete the RSS feed from Outlook, it does not delete it from IE. However, if you want to add the RSS feed back to Outlook, you may need to use one of the manual methods discussed in this section.

Viewing Other List Items Not in the RSS Feed

Remember that the RSS feed will only display relatively recent additions to the reference list or library. You will not necessarily see all the documents in the RSS feed.

■**Note** You can specify how long documents or list items remain in the RSS feed by going to the library or list in SharePoint and selecting **Document Library Settings** or **List Settings** from the **Settings** drop-down menu. On the **Settings** page, select **RSS Settings** from the **Communications** option group. On the **RSS Settings** page, find the section labeled **Item limit** at the bottom of the page.

By selecting any one item and displaying its edit page, you can navigate to the full list or library. With the item's edit page open, locate the breadcrumbs at the top of the page. Typically, the entry immediately before the name of the current item represents the list or library from which the entry originates. Click this name to display the full list or library. From this page, you can then open and edit any item in the list or library, even those no longer referenced in the RSS feed.

■Tip For libraries or lists that add new items only occasionally, you may want to limit the RSS feed based on the number of items displayed. If instead item additions occur frequently, consider using the maximum day option to determine how many items to display in the feed.

Simply point your mouse over the desired document. When the drop-down menu button appears to the right of the name, click it to open the menu. For example, you would click **Edit in Microsoft Office Word** to open and edit a Word document from a library as shown in Figure 5-40.

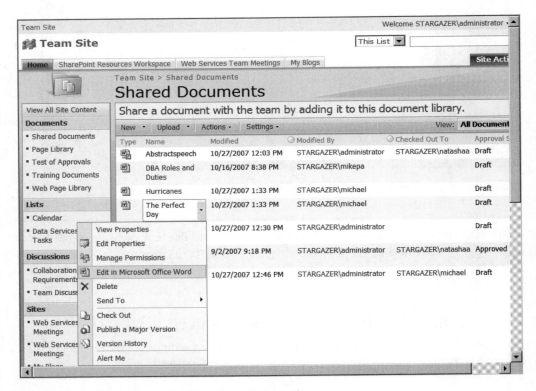

Figure 5-40. *Editing a document from the full library list*

Sending E-mail to Lists

So far in this chapter, I demonstrated several ways to use Outlook to connect to various lists and libraries in SharePoint. You also saw that SharePoint can send e-mail messages when someone adds items to a list, changes items in a list, or deletes items from a list. However, you can also send e-mail messages to groups of SharePoint users as well as several of SharePoint's lists.

Sending a Message to a SharePoint Group

Not only can you send alerts via e-mail to SharePoint users, but you can also send messages to any of the SharePoint groups that have been set up by the administrator. Suppose you want to send an e-mail to all content approvers reminding them to check for any documents that they must review and approve before anyone can see those documents on your site. To accomplish this task, create your e-mail and then include the e-mail address for the content approvers.

If their address does not appear in your e-mail application's Address Book, ask your administrator for the information. Then place the address in either the **To** or **Cc** field of the e-mail and send it.

Sending a Message to a List or Library

Not all SharePoint lists can receive e-mail, and even those that do handle it in different ways. Lists that can accept e-mail include

- Announcements

- Blogs

- Calendars

- Discussion boards

- Document libraries

- Form libraries

- Picture libraries

The ability to send e-mail to these lists depends on the settings your SharePoint administrator applied in the SharePoint Central Administration site. It also depends on settings added to your lists when your site administrator created the site and its lists. To enable and configure e-mail at the list or library level, you must have the **Manage Lists** permission. Site owners have this permission by default. Thus, even though these lists have the potential of receiving e-mail as defined at the site level, their current configuration may not allow e-mail.

To determine whether your list can receive e-mail messages, first check the site settings for the list assuming you have the appropriate rights. Alternatively, check with the site administrator to ask whether the list supports e-mail and what e-mail address you must use to send content to the list.

HOW E-MAIL IS ENABLED

To add e-mail support to a SharePoint site, your SharePoint administrator must enable e-mail support at the web application level in the SharePoint's **Central Administration** site. Your site administrator may also decide to allow or not allow incoming e-mail at the site level. However, even then, unless you specify an e-mail address for individual lists, the lists cannot receive e-mails.

You enable e-mail through the e-mail link for individual site lists and libraries that you want to receive e-mail by going to their **Settings** page and selecting **Incoming e-mail settings** from the **Communications** option group. If this option does not appear, you must see your SharePoint administrator. Either you do not have the necessary permissions to configure this setting or you must have your administrator turn e-mail on through the **Central Administration** site.

■**Tip** If you have the right to create lists, you should consider adding the e-mail address to the list description if you have e-mail enabled for the list. Because the description text appears immediately beneath the list title when displayed in SharePoint, this practice might reduce the number of calls you will get asking for the e-mail addresses of your lists.

After you determine whether a list supports e-mail, create a new message in Outlook. You can place the list e-mail address in either the **To** or the **Cc** field. You can send the message to one or more lists, people, or groups from a single message entry. Then refer to Table 5-3 to see how to add content to the lists via your message.

Table 5-3. *Sending Content to a SharePoint List*

List/Library	Where to Place Content
Announcements	Include your announcement text as an attachment. SharePoint takes your message title as the title of the announcement.
Blogs	Include your blog text in the main body of the message.
Calendars	Send a meeting request or appointment to the list.
Discussion boards	Include your text in the main body of the message.
Document libraries	Include the document you want to add as an attachment to the e-mail.
Form libraries	Include the form you want to add as an attachment to the e-mail.
Picture libraries	Include the picture as an attachment to the e-mail.

If you send an e-mail with both a blog entry and a document file that you will reference within your blog, you can send both with a single e-mail. Include both the blog list and the document library list e-mail address in the **To** field of the message. SharePoint will extract the text from the main body of the message and send it to the blog site while taking the attachment and sending it to the document library. It does this because each list type can only accept information from specify parts of the e-mail message.

When you are ready to send your content, include the appropriate SharePoint e-mail address in the **To** or **Cc** box and then click **Send**.

Sending Links via Send To

SharePoint can send a link for any document, image, or form to anyone via e-mail. You can find this option by opening the drop-down list for any item in a library or list. In the drop-down menu, point to **Send To** to open the secondary flyout menu. In this menu, select the option **E-mail a link**. This opens a normal e-mail message with the link to the item in the body of the message.

When the e-mail recipient receives the e-mail message, she can click the link to open and edit the document, resulting in a more efficient, smaller e-mail message than sending the entire file. The user initially opens a read-only version of the document pointed to by the link. However, she can choose to edit the document and of course send her changes back to SharePoint.

Summary

This chapter showed you several ways to use Outlook 2007 together with SharePoint, beginning with a look at organizing multiple contacts lists in different SharePoint sites with your Outlook contacts list. By adding links to two or more SharePoint contacts lists, you saw that you can copy and move contacts between any of the lists including the Outlook **Contacts** list itself.

In a similar way, you can use Outlook to consolidate multiple SharePoint calendars with your own Outlook calendar to plan your daily schedule as well as build SharePoint calendars by copying events from your Outlook calendar to them. Outlook lets you overlay two or more calendars so you can see when events conflict, when available time exists, and the relative sequence of events from different calendars.

Next you looked at combining tasks from multiple SharePoint lists within Outlook. As with contacts and calendars, the ability to consolidate information from multiple tasks lists can help ensure that events from one calendar do not get overlooked.

Outlook also lets you work with documents as if they were e-mail messages. It supports the ability to check out documents so you can edit them offline and then resync your changes with the original documents in SharePoint the next time you connect.

Alerts create a notification capability to let you know when items are added, deleted, or modified in libraries and lists. You can also determine how frequently you want to see the alerts. By monitoring changes within SharePoint libraries and lists, alerts can save you a tremendous amount of time so that you do not have to monitor each of the libraries and lists for changes that might pertain to you or be of interest to you.

SharePoint libraries and lists have the ability to support RSS feeds as a way to distribute news, blogs, library, and list additions, and other information feeds. Both IE 7.0 and Outlook 2007 have built-in RSS readers and can have independent RSS feed lists, or you can synchronize the feeds that appear in both programs using the **Common Feeds** list.

Finally, you can send e-mails to most blogs, lists, and libraries to update information stored in them. This may require some additional configuration from your SharePoint administrator in both the **Central Administration** site as well as the communication settings of the individual libraries and lists you want to send e-mail updates to. You can also send an e-mail to others with the URL of an item in a library or list. The recipient of that e-mail can then click that link to open and edit that item.

Thus you can see that Outlook provides many ways to work with several SharePoint features to better organize your work and personal activities. Outlook can change the way you work with documents, lists, and tasks. It can help you share your thoughts through discussions and blogs. You can use the combination of alerts, RSS feeds, and Outlook to stay informed about changes to lists and libraries.

CHAPTER 6

■ ■ ■

Managing Lists with Access

It must be a law of the universe that over time most SharePoint lists will grow. At some point, you may decide that some of your lists have grown too large to work with in SharePoint. Maybe it takes you too long to scroll through the data to find the items you want. Maybe the list contains mostly obsolete data. Whatever the reason that is important to you, you know that the time has come to remove some of the older list items; but you don't want to lose the data, just archive it in case you need it later. Perhaps you want to generate reports from the archived data. You might even want to move the data from one list in one site to another list in another site. Whatever your reason for needing to move items out of one of your SharePoint lists, Access can help you achieve your desires.

I stated in the beginning of Chapter 2 that you can think of lists in terms used by database systems: items represent rows, and columns represent fields. In this chapter, I will prove how well SharePoint lists translate into databases by demonstrating how you can manage your lists using a database application, Microsoft Access.

Note Again, the text will focus on Access 2007, because previous versions of Access do not support many of the features described here.

Exporting SharePoint Lists to Access

To export a SharePoint list into Access, you can start from SharePoint or Access. Let's first start from SharePoint. Navigate to your SharePoint site, and open the list you want to export. From the menu bar at the top of the list, click **Actions** to open the drop-down menu and select **Open with Access** as shown in Figure 6-1.

A message box, shown in Figure 6-2, prompts you for two pieces of information. First, you must specify a location and name for a new or existing database. Access stores each database as a separate file. Further, it can store the file in any directory. By default, SharePoint attempts to create a database in your Documents and Settings folder under My Documents. Also by default, SharePoint wants to use the list name as the database name. You can change either of these defaults by entering a different file name and/or path. You can also use the **Browse** button to locate a directory. However, you may find the real advantage of the **Browse** button occurs when you need to find an existing database into which you want to add the SharePoint list.

Figure 6-1. *Exporting a SharePoint table to Access*

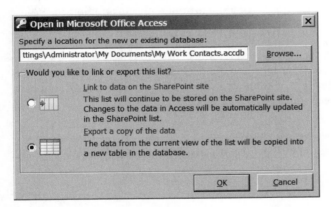

Figure 6-2. *You can either export a copy of a SharePoint list to Access or create a link to the list in Access.*

If you export a copy of your SharePoint list to a new Access database, SharePoint tries to name both the database and the table within the database using the list name. If you select an existing database with a different database name, SharePoint still tries to name at least the table with the list name. If you attempt to export the same SharePoint list a second time to the same database, SharePoint recognizes this and assigns a sequential number as a suffix to the table name. It even increments the sequential number with each save. Of course, you could override this automatically generated name and save the table in the existing database with your own unique name. If the database already has a table with that new name, SharePoint again appends the next available number as a suffix to the table name. It will never let you replace an existing table.

So how do you replace an existing Access table in a given Access database with the updated contents of the same SharePoint list? The simple way would be to delete the Access table first, and then export the SharePoint list. This may not be feasible if you established links to other Access tables or use the table as a data source for view definitions, reports, or forms within Access. You have several programmatic alternatives at this point, the details of which are beyond the scope of this book. Most begin with exporting the SharePoint list to a table with a different name. Then you can update the original table from the second table using SQL statements.

If you prefer not to work with SQL, you can modify the connection properties of each object that uses the original table to point to the new table. The risk here of missing a reference to the original table may be high depending on the complexity of your database.

SYNCHRONIZING THE DATA IN TWO VERSIONS OF AN ACCESS TABLE

Suppose you have two tables called Table1 and Table2, in which Table2 is a more recent copy of Table1 and has changes in it that Table1 does not have. How can you programmatically synchronize the changes from Table2 back to Table1?

From within Access, you can quickly update Table1 to look exactly like Table2 if you make a few assumptions. First, assume that if Table1 and Table2 use any other related tables for lookup values, nothing in those tables has changed that would require those tables to be updated first. Second, assume that Table1 uses a unique ID field consisting of a sequential number and that the value has no additional meaning other than to uniquely define the rows of the table.

The first step updates all of the fields in Table1 with values from Table2 where the unique ID field in Table1 equals Table2. The complexity of this SQL UPDATE expression comes from the SET clause, which must include an expression for every field in the table.

```
UPDATE Table1
INNER JOIN Table2
ON Table1.ID = Table2.ID
SET Table1.[Field1] = [Table2].[Field1],
Table1.[Field2] = [Table2].[Field2],
Table1.[Field3] = [Table2].[Field3];
```

Next, you eliminate any records in Table1 that do not have a corresponding ID value in Table2.

```
DELETE *
FROM Table1
WHERE Table1.ID NOT IN (SELECT Table2.ID FROM Table2);
```

Finally, you add any records from Table2 that do not exist in Table1.

```
INSERT INTO Table1
SELECT *
FROM Table2
WHERE Table2.ID NOT IN (SELECT Table1.ID FROM Table1);
```

At this point, the data in Table1 should exactly match the data in Table2.

■**Tip** To change the Access table used by a form, open the **Property Sheet** for the form. Click the **Data** tab and then locate the **Record Source** property. Open the drop-down list for this field and select the new table.

■**Caution** If you update an object such as a report or form with a new record source, beware of fields deleted or renamed from the original table schema. This will cause the form to fail unless you remove such a field from the form or table or associate it with a different table field.

Getting back to the second decision you must make in Figure 6-2, you must decide whether you want to link the SharePoint list data with the Access table or export a copy of the list data to the table. The main advantage of linking the data between Access and SharePoint involves editing. When you link the list and table, changes made to a record/item on either side of the link are updated on the other side the next time you refresh the screen view. Linking your Share-Point list to Access eliminates the complexity of the last several paragraphs caused by list updates when you only export a copy of the list to Access.

There are other advantages of linking the SharePoint list to an Access table, but first let's see what happens when you copy the list to an Access table.

After you click **OK** in Figure 6-2, SharePoint takes a few moments to transfer the selected columns to Access. After completing the transfer, Access opens and displays the new table as shown in Figure 6-3.

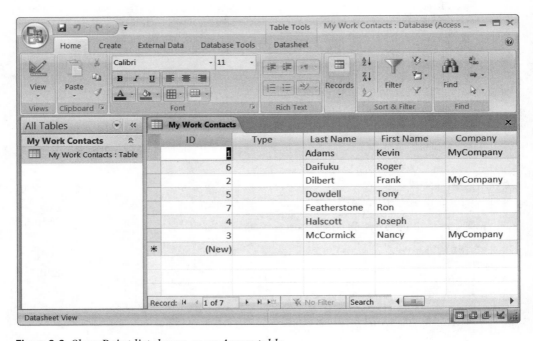

Figure 6-3. *SharePoint list shown as an Access table*

Notice that when copying a SharePoint list to Access, only the rows and fields included in the SharePoint view appear in the table. Thus you can determine not only the items/rows transferred to Access, but also the columns/fields transferred.

Tip Use the copy data option when you want to archive selected items from the list. To perform the archive, first define a new view in SharePoint to filter the records you want to archive. Then switch to this view when you display the list. This view does not have to be the default view, but it must be the current view. Then select **Open with Access** as before, selecting **Export a copy of the data**. Place this data in a database where you want to store archived data. You could use a different database each time you download the list, perhaps including the date to identify the archived date range, or you could add sequentially numbered tables or tables that include a date in the name for a single archived database.

After transferring the data, you can save the database in one of the three most recent Access data formats:

- Access 2007

- Access 2002–2003

- Access 2000

Thus, you can share list data with those unfortunate associates who have not upgraded to Access 2007, or with someone who does not have access to your SharePoint site.

But what if, after you copy data to an Access table, you decide to transfer it back to SharePoint? Can you do that? Yes, you can export data from Access not only to Excel, but also to a SharePoint list.

Figure 6-4 shows the **Access** Ribbon with the **External Data** tab selected. Within the **Export** section, find the button **SharePoint List**.

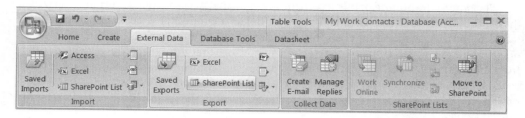

Figure 6-4. *External Data tab in the Access Ribbon*

When you click this button, a dialog box opens. You must first specify the name of the SharePoint site where you want to publish the data. In Figure 6-5, I have selected the site address `http://stargazer`, the URL of the top-level site of my SharePoint test server.

Next, you must specify the name of the list you want to copy the Access data into. Note that you can only export your Access table to a new SharePoint list. If you attempt to specify the name of an existing list, SharePoint adds a sequential number to the end of the list name.

Also, the check box at the bottom of this figure lets you immediately open the new list after you create it. I personally like to see the list after creating it to verify that everything transferred correctly. It's a "Trust but Verify" rule I encourage developers to adopt. If you feel lucky and trust Access to transfer your table to a SharePoint list, I suppose you could leave this option unchecked.

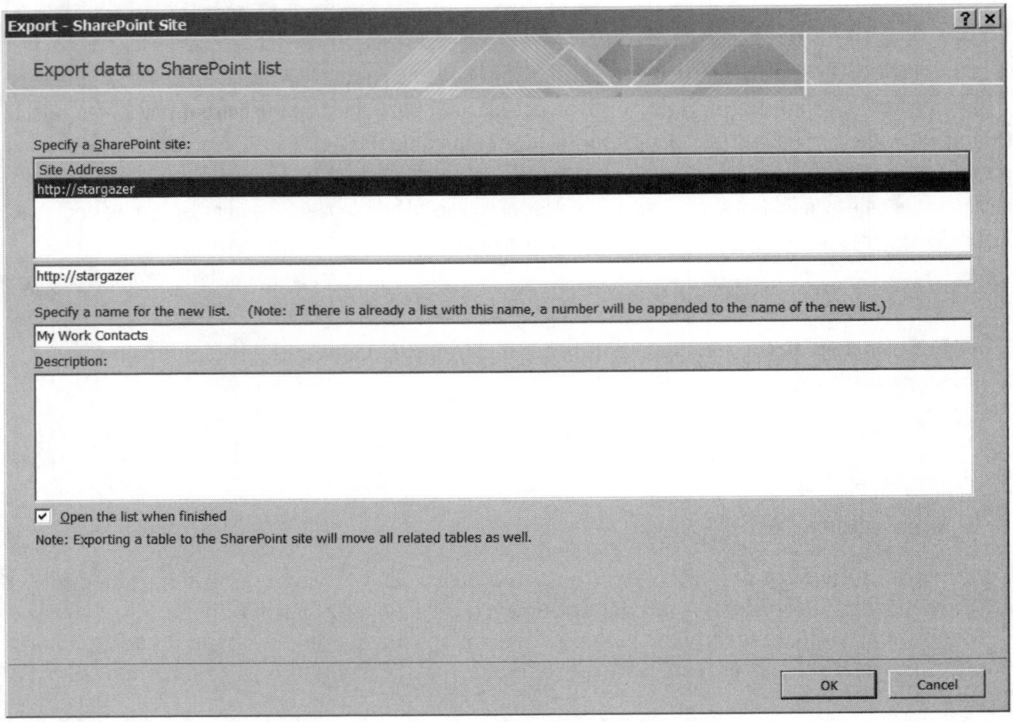

Figure 6-5. *Dialog box that prompts for SharePoint site and list names*

The note at the bottom of this screen informs you that Access exports any tables related to the exported table to their own SharePoint lists. In fact, not only does Access upload all related tables to individual SharePoint lists, but SharePoint automatically converts the foreign key fields in the parent table to lookup type fields to ensure that the user can select values only from the child table. However, SharePoint does not support true referential integrity, as illustrated by the ability to modify or even delete values from the lookup lists without SharePoint raising any warnings or errors caused by existing records in the parent list that might refer to the old values.

For example, suppose you have two tables in Access. The first table, **Depts**, lists each department in your organization with related information about that department, such as the department name, department head, and perhaps the department's primary phone number. In the second table, **Employees**, you list employees in your organization. Besides the obvious fields such as the employee's name, phone number, start date, and others, you include the department ID from the **Depts** table. Let's also assume that you have formalized this relationship on **Department ID** between the two tables using referential integrity.

Now when you attempt to export the **Employees** table to SharePoint as a new list, SharePoint recognizes the relationship between the **Employees** and **Depts** tables and uploads both as new lists on the selected site. Opening the **Employees** list settings, you can see that the **Department ID** field definition uses a lookup field type that points to the **Department ID** field in the **Depts** list.

Saving Your Export Steps

When you click **OK** as shown in Figure 6-5, another dialog box, shown in Figure 6-6, appears asking whether you want to save your export steps.

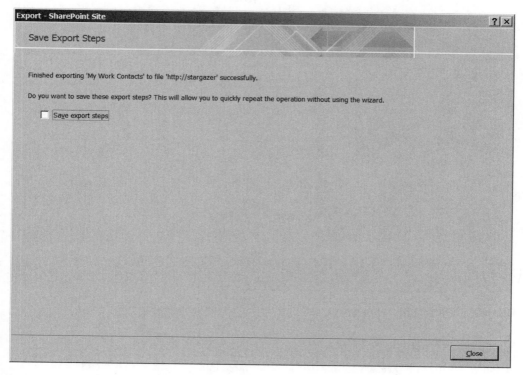

Figure 6-6. *Prompting to save export steps*

If you plan on performing this export only one time, you may not want to select this option. On the other hand, if you think you might perform this task frequently, you may want to save these steps. If you select this option, Access displays the dialog box shown in Figure 6-7.

This Access dialog box asks you to enter a name and a description to identify your export steps. You must enter a name, because Access uses this name to identify this set of export steps from others you may define, as you will see shortly. While Access considers the description optional, it appears in Access's list showing available exports and can help further identify different exports.

You also have the option of creating an Outlook task. While you cannot rerun the export directly from this task, you can use the task as a reminder to run the export on a future date. You can even set up a recurring reminder to run the task periodically.

When you click **Save Export**, SharePoint performs the export, creates the saved steps in Access, and creates the task in Outlook. This shows another example of the power of SharePoint and Office 2007 integration, as it updates three separate MS Office products with one action.

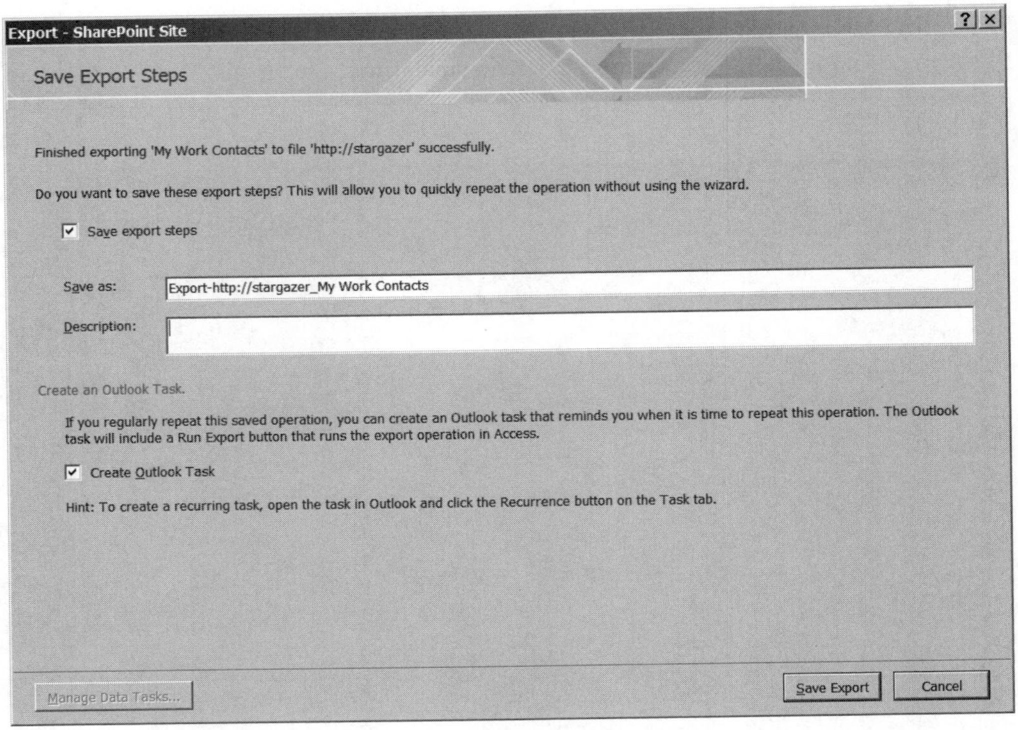

Figure 6-7. *Defining the name and description of the export steps*

Transfer Issues

When you return to Access, you may see another table in the **Navigation Bar** called **Move to SharePoint Site Issues**. Open this table to examine any problems with the export to SharePoint. Figure 6-8 shows the issues generated when moving the **My Work Contacts** table back to SharePoint.

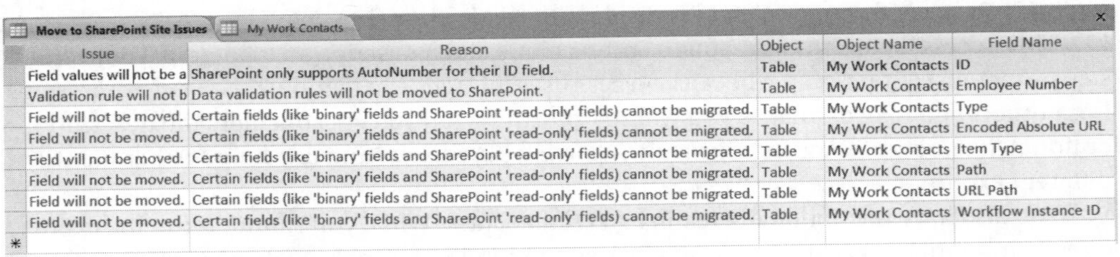

Issue	Reason	Object	Object Name	Field Name
Field values will not be a	SharePoint only supports AutoNumber for their ID field.	Table	My Work Contacts	ID
Validation rule will not b	Data validation rules will not be moved to SharePoint.	Table	My Work Contacts	Employee Number
Field will not be moved.	Certain fields (like 'binary' fields and SharePoint 'read-only' fields) cannot be migrated.	Table	My Work Contacts	Type
Field will not be moved.	Certain fields (like 'binary' fields and SharePoint 'read-only' fields) cannot be migrated.	Table	My Work Contacts	Encoded Absolute URL
Field will not be moved.	Certain fields (like 'binary' fields and SharePoint 'read-only' fields) cannot be migrated.	Table	My Work Contacts	Item Type
Field will not be moved.	Certain fields (like 'binary' fields and SharePoint 'read-only' fields) cannot be migrated.	Table	My Work Contacts	Path
Field will not be moved.	Certain fields (like 'binary' fields and SharePoint 'read-only' fields) cannot be migrated.	Table	My Work Contacts	URL Path
Field will not be moved.	Certain fields (like 'binary' fields and SharePoint 'read-only' fields) cannot be migrated.	Table	My Work Contacts	Workflow Instance ID

Figure 6-8. *Issues generated when moving a table back to SharePoint*

Issues with Auto Increment Fields

The first issue in this list refers to the field **ID**. SharePoint automatically adds this field to contacts lists and issue tracking lists to uniquely identify records, and defines it as an autoincrement field.

AUTOINCREMENT FIELDS

Every table in a relational database should have a primary key. Most relational systems do not allow you to update existing data without a primary or unique key to identify which record to update. When possible, you should always use existing table fields to create a "natural" key. But at the same time, you should avoid long "natural" keys or keys that require the concatenation of many individual fields. One solution to long keys uses a "created" key called an *autonumber field*. Access uses this field type to create a unique integer field for each record. You should add this field to the table schema before adding any records to the table. However, you can add it later by prefilling the field with sequential values for each record and then appropriately setting the field's start value property.

The start value for a new table typically begins with 1, and each record added to the table increments this value by 1. However, you can start an autoincrement field using any value, and you can define increment values other than 1. If you delete a record, the database does not reuse that number. Also, autoincrement fields generally cannot be edited.

In addition to serving as indexes, autoincrement fields often make ideal choices as relational fields between tables. Since this field cannot be edited, the referential link cannot easily be broken.

When used, the autoincrement field should not imply any significance other than to provide a unique identifier for a record that may or may not also serve as a linking field between two tables.

Due to all of the preceding characteristics of autoincrement fields, you normally cannot include this field when you copy a table with one of these fields to another table, regardless of whether you create a new table or intend to append to an existing table.

Surprisingly, the import of a list from SharePoint to Access does appear to import the **ID** field. You can prove this by taking an issue tracking list and deleting a few items from the middle of the list. Then import the list into Access. If you open the table in design mode, you will discover that the **ID** field has been defined as an autonumber field. But when you open the corresponding Access table, you will see a gap in the ID sequence exactly representing the positions of the deleted items from SharePoint.

However, exporting the table back to SharePoint does not transfer the autonumber field. If you were to export the issue table with the deleted records from the middle of the table, the new SharePoint list displays a new **ID** field with no gaps in the sequence. In other words, the transfer back to SharePoint reassigns new ID values to all items, closing the previous gap.

■**Caution** Based on the way SharePoint and Access treat the **ID** field when they transfer information back and forth, I would not recommend using the autogenerated **ID** field in the issue tracking list as a lookup field or a linking field to another list, because the values could change if someone exports the list to Access and then imports it back to SharePoint.

Issues with Validation Rules

The second transfer issue refers to a validation concern with the **Employee Number** field. In SharePoint, this field has a maximum of 10 characters. When you export the list to Access, the SharePoint size restriction on the field becomes an Access validation rule. Unfortunately, the export of tables from Access back to SharePoint does not convert this validation rule back into a maximum ten-character restriction.

All the other issues refer to read-only fields that originated in the SharePoint list. While the transfer of the list to Access includes these fields, Access does not normally display them. As read-only fields that SharePoint generates, Access cannot export these fields back to SharePoint.

■**Caution** Review the issue list when you transfer an Access table back to a SharePoint list. Some issues you cannot do anything about. However, if the transfer drops validations that you need on fields, you should open the list settings and see whether the SharePoint column properties support a similar style of validation.

Issues with Transferring Referential Tables

Another example of issues that you might encounter when you transfer data from Access back to SharePoint occurs when you have two or more related tables in Access. If you established referential integrity definitions between these tables, and you attempt to export them back to SharePoint, you might observe one or more of the following issues:

- Referential integrity will not be enforced.

- Deletes will not be cascaded to related records.

- Updates will not be cascaded to related records.

While SharePoint supports lookup columns using other lists, and while this looks like referential integrity, it does not support the enforcement characteristics found in a true relational model. That means that after you add an employee to the **Employees** list and assign a department to him, you could go back to the **Depts** list and change and/or delete the department, with no warnings about employee items that refer to that department. In other words, SharePoint does not define a permanent relationship between the lists like true referential integrity requires. It only uses the lookup list to supply values while adding or modifying an employee record.

Dealing with Duplicate Lists

Figure 6-9 shows the lists in my SharePoint site. Notice that because I added the list **My Work Contacts** a second time, SharePoint adds a "_1" suffix to the list name to make it unique. I now have essentially two lists with the same name and content, less any minor changes made while in Access.

If this happens to you and you want to keep both lists, you should rename one of them to avoid confusion. But let's assume that you don't want to keep both. You could delete the original list and rename the new list back to the original name by deleting the "_1". This technique effectively represents a manual way to update a SharePoint list using Access. However, a better way to deal with updates links the Access table to the SharePoint list so you can perform continuous synchronization between them.

	Name	Description	Items	Last Modified
			View: **Lists**	
	Name	Description	Items	Last Modified
Lists				
	Book Chapter Status	This list will track book chapter status	3	5 days ago
	Calendar	Use the Calendar list to keep informed of upcoming meetings, deadlines, and other important events.	3	2 months ago
	Collaboration Site For HR	This Project Task List is specifically for tasks related to building the HR collaboration site.	5	2 months ago
	Data Services Dept Tasks	Use the Tasks list to keep track of work that you or your team needs to complete.	5	5 days ago
	District Area	District areas	4	3 weeks ago
	Help Desk Calls	This list is used to track customer requests	6	5 days ago
	My Help Desk Issues	My help desk issues	4	4 days ago
	My Site Menu	Links to pages on my site	3	5 weeks ago
	My Work Contacts	My Work Contacts	7	7 days ago
	My Work Contacts_1	This is my revised contacts list from Access.	7	4 minutes ago
	Office Contacts	SharePoint Administrator	3	7 days ago
	Reference Links	Use the Links list for links to Web pages that your team members will find interesting or useful.	6	5 weeks ago
	Server List	List of servers in our organization	2	3 weeks ago
	Stores	Stores	1	3 weeks ago

Figure 6-9. *SharePoint lists after exporting tables back from Access*

The Outlook Task for the Export Steps

If you create a task in Outlook for the export steps, you can open your **Tasks** panel to see the task with the name you defined. In Figure 6-10, you can see that this task does not currently have a due date and has a status of not started.

To customize this task, double-click it to open the task details. You can now define a start date and a due date as well as set a reminder to perform the task. In the **Task** Ribbon, click the **Recurrence** option in the **Options** panel to define a recurrence schedule if you must perform this export on a regular basis.

■**Tip** You might want to set up tasks to remind you to archive old data from lists such as issue tracking lists to prevent such lists from growing too large with completed tasks and degrading performance.

Unfortunately, you cannot run the export task directly from the Outlook task. However, Access automatically includes text in the task instructing you how to execute the saved export operation from within Access.

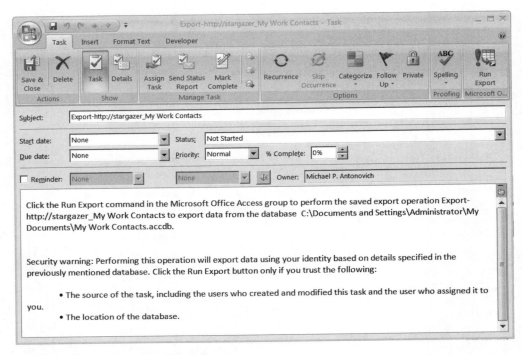

Figure 6-10. *Details of the export task in Outlook*

Reusing Saved Export Steps

To execute a saved export, open Access and click the **External Data** tab of the **Access** Ribbon. In the **Export** panel, click the **Saved Exports** option to display a window like the one shown in Figure 6-11.

In this tabbed window, you can see all your saved imports and exports. Click the **Saved Exports** tab and select the export you want to run. Notice that you can create an Outlook task from here if you did not do so when you created the original export. You can also delete any of the saved exports you no longer need, as well as edit the name or the description of the saved export by clicking its respective text. If you did not include a description when you originally saved the export, click beneath the SharePoint server name on the text **Click here to edit the description**. A text box appears allowing you to enter a description.

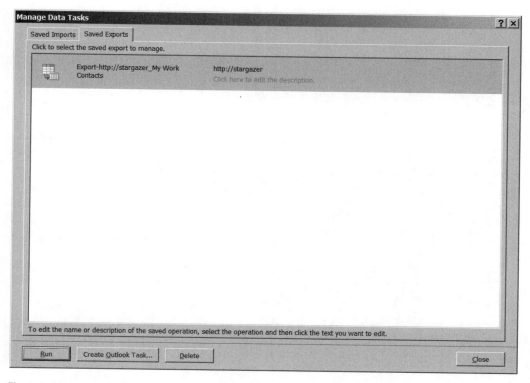

Figure 6-11. *Saved Exports tab in the Manage Data Tasks dialog box in Access*

Importing a SharePoint List Directly from Access

You began this section by exporting the SharePoint list by opening the list in SharePoint. However, you can perform the same operation directly from Access without first going to SharePoint. Start by opening Access and then follow these steps:

1. If you get the **Getting Started** screen, select **Blank Database** and click **Create**.

2. Select the **External Data** tab in the **Access** Ribbon.

3. Click the **SharePoint list** button in the **Import** panel.

This action opens the dialog box shown in Figure 6-12, which is similar to the dialog box shown earlier in Figure 6-2. You must specify the SharePoint Server site address. Then you can choose to either import the source data, creating a new Access table, or create a linked table. Let's begin with the import option.

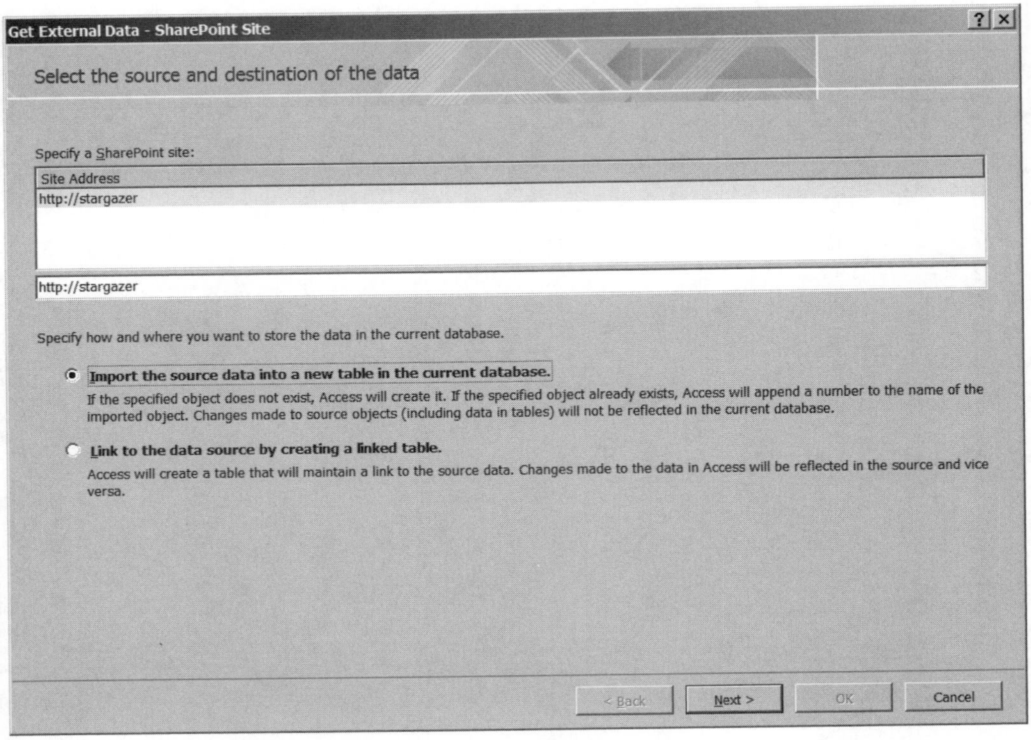

Figure 6-12. *Selecting the source and destination of data*

The next dialog box displays all lists in the selected SharePoint site. Each list has a separate check box, which allows you to select multiple lists to import at one time rather than exporting them one at a time as you did from within SharePoint. Notice that after selecting a list, the **Items to Import** column changes to a drop-down list from which you can select a view to use. Remember that not only do views control which columns SharePoint exports to Access, but the view's filter also defines which items (rows) to transfer. Figure 6-13 shows an example of transferring three lists using selected views.

Access then allows you to save the import steps just like you did when you exported data from Access. If you choose to save your import steps, you must specify a name for the operation. By default, Access creates a name that begins with "Imports - " followed by the name of the first list. You can also create an Outlook task to remind you to perform this operation later. When you click **OK**, Access imports the lists.

You may have noticed that in Figure 6-13 the list of objects that Access could import includes all the SharePoint libraries as well as the lists. When importing into Access from a library, Access only imports the metadata for each library item. The actual document itself does not transfer to Access. However, if you only want to manipulate the metadata from the library, this may be okay with you. For example, after importing the metadata from the **Purchase Orders** library into an Access table, you could easily create an Access report using the table as the data source. This report might sum the purchase amounts by department for each month in the most recent fiscal period.

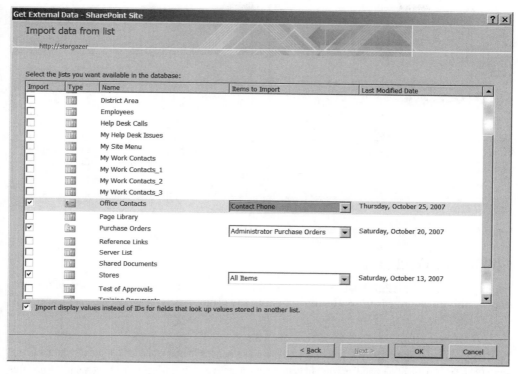

Figure 6-13. *Importing multiple SharePoint lists using selected views*

Linking SharePoint Lists to Access

In the examples discussed in the previous section, you imported a copy of the SharePoint list data into an Access table. Before continuing with some other ways to work with SharePoint data from Access, let's see how linking to the SharePoint lists differs from simply copying the data into an Access table.

Because you have already seen how to begin a transfer of a list from SharePoint to Access in the previous section, let's pick up the transfer at the point where you have to decide whether to link to SharePoint or simply copy the data. Figures 6-2 and 6-12 earlier illustrate this point in the process beginning with SharePoint or Access, respectively. However, this time, rather than copying the list data to the Access table, select the link option.

For this illustration, suppose I select only the **Employees** list to transfer to Access. However, remember that the **Employees** list uses a lookup list to select the department to which the employee belongs. While SharePoint does not directly support relational integrity between lists, it does recognize when transferring a list with a lookup to Access that it should also transfer the lookup list. This process mirrors the way Access includes relational tables when transferring data back to SharePoint. Figure 6-14 shows that both the **Employees** and **Depts** tables have been transferred to Access. In addition to these two tables, SharePoint adds a third table labeled **User Information List**. This table includes a row for every user account or group defined in the site.

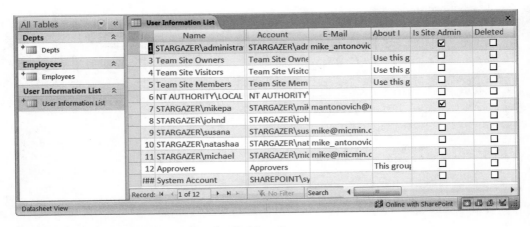

Figure 6-14. *Employees and Depts lists loaded into Access*

Editing Linked Data

When you link a SharePoint list to an Access table, you can edit items in either SharePoint or Access, and the changes automatically appear in the other.

■**Tip** As a standard practice, you probably would not use Access to edit individual elements of data in a SharePoint list. On the other hand, you might want to use Access and its linking ability to make mass updates to data, move data between lists, or even move data between lists on different servers.

As long as everyone works on different items/rows, no one knows that others might be editing the same list. But when two or more people edit the same item at the same time, a conflict situation arises. As expected, the first person to save her changes to the item succeeds. The second person to save his changes sees an error message such as the one shown in Figure 6-15.

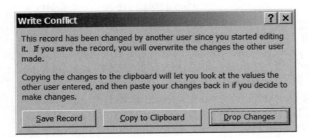

Figure 6-15. *Edit conflict on a list linked to SharePoint*

In this case, Access raises the message box because it recognizes that one or more columns in the row have changed since you began editing it. Access gives you three options to resolve this conflict. First, you could save your record anyway. This option blindly overrides the previous changes to the fields with your values. One objection to this option might be that you do not know which fields the other person updated, much less the changes she may have made.

The second option lets you copy your changes to the clipboard while updating the record in Access with the most recent values. You can at least use the **Clipboard Viewer** or paste the clipboard contents into an instance of WordPad to see and evaluate the changes. If you still want to use your values, you can reupdate the fields with your values and save the record by navigating to another record. Figure 6-16 shows an example of conflict data from the **Depts** table. The conflicting data has been added to the clipboard and then displayed in a WordPad document.

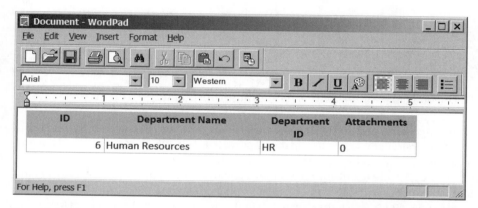

Figure 6-16. *Contents of an update conflict added to the clipboard and viewed in WordPad*

The third and final option drops your changes. When you select this option, Access updates the table with the values entered by the other person and ignores all your changes.

You might be thinking that you could avoid conflict problems if you check out the list before you begin making changes. Unfortunately, the Check-Out feature does not exist for lists edited from a linking Access table. However, if you link to the metadata associated with a document library, you can check out items in a document library. This prevents anyone else from making changes to the metadata. You can also edit metadata for a checked-out Word document through Word 2007 itself.

Using Access to Make Mass Updates

SharePoint has trouble making mass updates to lists. As an example, suppose the purchase orders previously created in Chapter 4 do not include sales tax. You could go back into each item, open the document and update the metadata for the document, and then save the document. If that sounds like a lot of work, you are right. You might even pull out your calculator, determine the new order total based on the new sales tax, and update the metadata using the **Datasheet View** of the library.

However, if you have a lot of records, a faster way to update the metadata for all the purchase orders begins by linking the metadata for the **Purchase Orders** library to an Access table. From within the Access table, a single update statement can add the sales tax to the **Purchase Amount** field for all items. When finished, you can simply delete the Access table, and the metadata in the SharePoint library shows the new totals.

Let's begin by looking at the **Purchase Orders** library again before making any changes. Figure 6-17 shows the first four items in the library. You can see the **Purchase Amount** column for the first item displays a total of $7010.00.

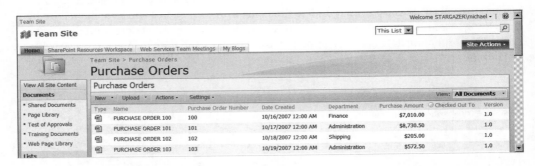

Figure 6-17. *Original purchase amounts in the Purchase Orders library*

Next, open Access and create a blank database. From the **External Data** tab on the **Access** Ribbon, select the **SharePoint List** button in the **Import** section. In the subsequent dialog boxes, define the SharePoint site and select **Purchase Orders** from the list of objects that you can import into Access. Be sure to link the SharePoint list to the Access table. After you have loaded the metadata into an Access table, you can create a query to update the data.

To create a new query, select the **Create** tab in the **Access** Ribbon. Then select **Query Design** from the **Other** section of the **Access** Ribbon. The first step in creating a query displays a dialog box to select the tables you want to include in the query. In this case, select the newly added **Purchase Orders** table by clicking it and then clicking **Add**. If you have other tables to include in your query, you could add them here. If you do not, close this dialog box by clicking the **Close** button.

Next, scroll through the list of fields until you find the field **Purchase Amount**. Double-click the field to select it, and add it to the grid in the lower half of the query builder screen. By default, Access assumes that you want a SELECT query. However, you need to use an UPDATE query to change the values of the **Purchase Amount** field. Therefore, click the **Update** button in the **Query Type** panel of the **Design** Ribbon. This also changes the other information you must provide for the selected field so you can add an update formula. Next, you can specify a filter criterion so that your update only acts on some of the rows in the table. If you want to change all the rows, do not include a filter. However, you still must supply a formula to add sales tax to the **Purchase Amount** field. Figure 6-18 shows the formula needed to add a 7% sales tax to this field.

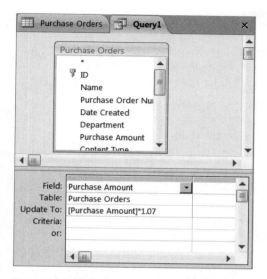

Figure 6-18. *Adding a 7% sales tax to the Purchase Amount field*

When you use an UPDATE query, Access reminds you that you cannot undo the changes made by the query to the linked table. Therefore, the first dialog box that Access pops up lets you cancel the update by clicking **No** or proceed with your action query by clicking **Yes**.

The second dialog box that Access displays tells you how many rows it will update in the table. Again, you can cancel the update by clicking **No** now. If you click **Yes**, Access performs the update to the table. Because you linked the SharePoint list to Access, the changes also apply to the metadata in the **Purchase Orders** library on your SharePoint site. If you open the Share-Point site and view the **Purchase Orders** library, you will see the **Purchase Amount** fields have been updated. Figure 6-19 shows the first four items in the library, where you can verify that the first item now has a purchase amount of $7,500.70, representing the original amount of $7,010 plus a 7% sales tax of $490.70.

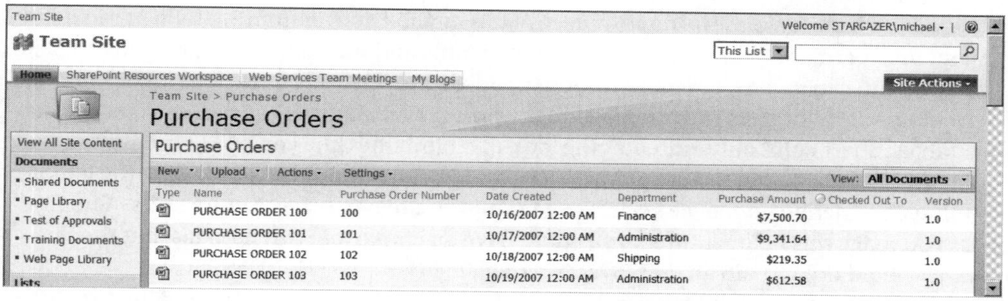

Type	Name	Purchase Order Number	Date Created	Department	Purchase Amount	Checked Out To	Version
	PURCHASE ORDER 100	100	10/16/2007 12:00 AM	Finance	$7,500.70		1.0
	PURCHASE ORDER 101	101	10/17/2007 12:00 AM	Administration	$9,341.64		1.0
	PURCHASE ORDER 102	102	10/18/2007 12:00 AM	Shipping	$219.35		1.0
	PURCHASE ORDER 103	103	10/19/2007 12:00 AM	Administration	$612.58		1.0

Figure 6-19. *Updated purchase amounts in the SharePoint Purchase Orders library*

Use Multivalued Fields in Lists

Multivalued fields allow a single field to have more than one value. Microsoft added this capability to the most recent version of Access as well as to SharePoint. Many people believe that this feature violates data normalization rules, which call for atomicity of field values.

■**Note** *Atomicity* means that a field should have one and only one value.

If a record in a table has a field that needs more than one value for any field, data normalization requires that you remove that field and make a related table for it. On that basis, people do not believe that a database field should have more than one value. On the other hand, simple lists do not have to follow such rules. Therefore, it may have been SharePoint's use of multivalued fields that drove the change in Access, and not the other way around. Or maybe they are not related at all.

Rather than debate the pros and cons of multivalued fields, let's look at an example of a SharePoint list that uses them and see how you can enter and maintain that data. You will also look at how SharePoint and Access exchange data with these types of fields.

Creating a Multivalued Column in SharePoint

In SharePoint, you have two ways to create a multivalued field. The first way uses the choice column type. If you remember the discussion on this column type, you might recall that you must specify the possible values for this field when you define it. You can then display the values either as radio buttons, a drop-down list, or check boxes on the default edit form when adding or modifying items in the list. When displayed with check boxes, the user can select one or more of the values. If the user selects multiple values, SharePoint displays them in the **Standard View** concatenated together with a semicolon to separate them.

Alternatively, you could use a lookup column type to create a multivalued field. The key advantage to using this method lies with the ease in which you can maintain the list used to supply values to the lookup. The disadvantage of this method derives from SharePoint's inability to maintain a permanent link between the lookup table and the table having the lookup field. As a result, you can make changes to the lookup table after creating a few records, removing used lookup values or changing them without warning of the effect the changes may have on other tables. SharePoint only evaluates the lookup table at the time you add or modify the item.

Figure 6-20 shows a new list column being added to the **Employees** list using the lookup column type to define employee skills. Each employee can have one or more skills. Actually, unless you make this field required, you could have an employee with no skills, but then he probably would not remain an employee for long. Right?

Notice that I selected the **Allow multiple values** check box at the bottom of the **Create Column** page. If you do not select this option, the user can only select one skill from the list. This might be okay if the field description asks for the employee's primary skill rather than her skills in general.

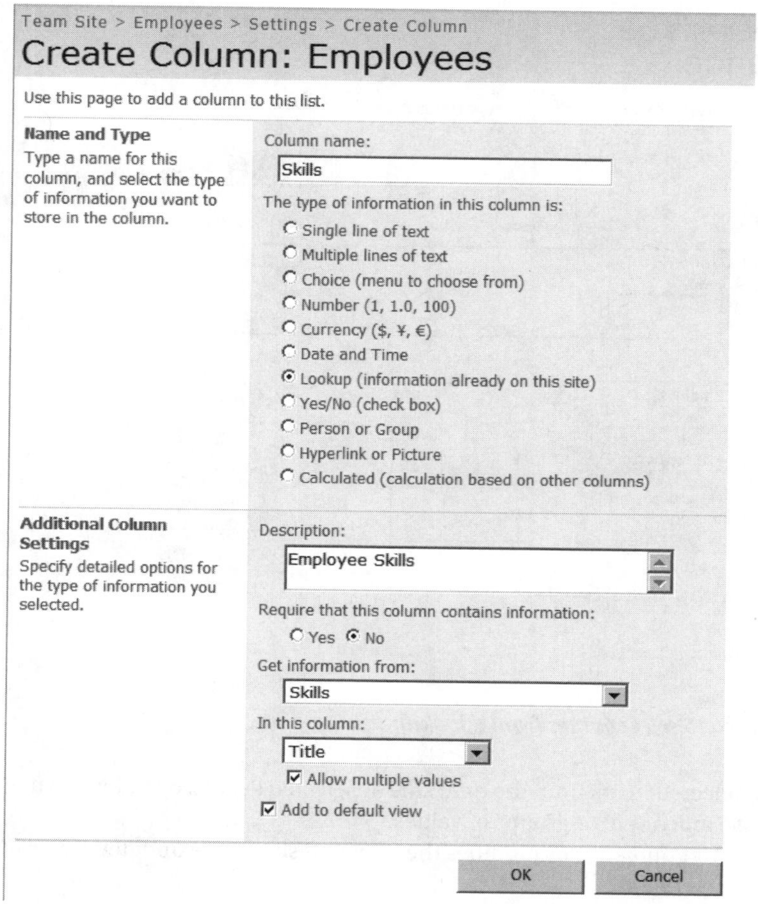

Team Site > Employees > Settings > Create Column

Create Column: Employees

Use this page to add a column to this list.

Name and Type

Type a name for this column, and select the type of information you want to store in the column.

Column name:

Skills

The type of information in this column is:

○ Single line of text
○ Multiple lines of text
○ Choice (menu to choose from)
○ Number (1, 1.0, 100)
○ Currency ($, ¥, €)
○ Date and Time
◉ Lookup (information already on this site)
○ Yes/No (check box)
○ Person or Group
○ Hyperlink or Picture
○ Calculated (calculation based on other columns)

Additional Column Settings

Specify detailed options for the type of information you selected.

Description:

Employee Skills

Require that this column contains information:

○ Yes ◉ No

Get information from:

Skills

In this column:

Title

☑ Allow multiple values

☑ Add to default view

OK   Cancel

Figure 6-20. *Defining a multivalued column*

Lookup fields always display in the add/modify form SharePoint automatically generates for a list, using a dual list box sometimes referred to as *mover boxes* because you want to move values from one list to the other. Mover boxes also generally take less space on a form than the corresponding radio buttons or check boxes for situations that have more than just a few options. The list box on the left typically shows the available values from which you can select. The list box on the right shows the values you have already selected. Buttons between the two list boxes help facility moving items from one list to the other. Figure 6-21 shows an example of how SharePoint implements a lookup field.

To add a skill, you can double-click the skill name in the skill box on the left side. You can also click the value and then click the **Add** button found between the lists. Both methods add the skill to the list box on the right side containing your selected skills.

You can also select multiple skills from the available skill list by clicking the first skill, and then pressing the Shift key while you click the last skill you want to select. This technique selects not only the two skills you clicked, but all the skills between them. If rather than holding the Shift key you hold the Ctrl key, only the skills you click are added to the selection.

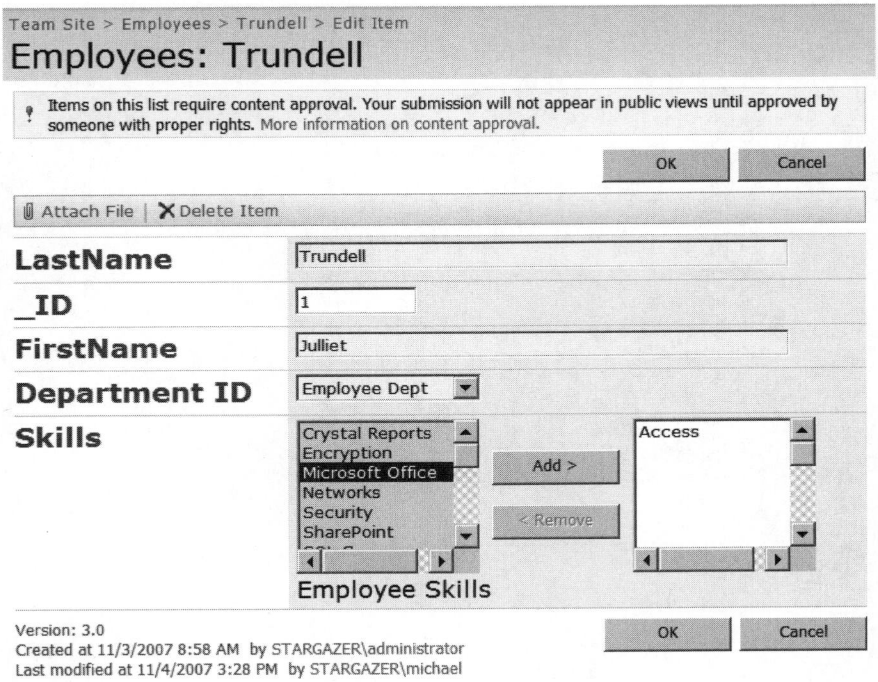

Team Site > Employees > Trundell > Edit Item

Employees: Trundell

> Items on this list require content approval. Your submission will not appear in public views until approved by someone with proper rights. More information on content approval.

OK   Cancel

📎 Attach File | ✗ Delete Item

LastName	Trundell
_ID	1
FirstName	Julliet
Department ID	Employee Dept ▼
Skills	Crystal Reports / Encryption / **Microsoft Office** / Networks / Security / SharePoint Add > < Remove Access

Employee Skills

OK   Cancel

Version: 3.0
Created at 11/3/2007 8:58 AM by STARGAZER\administrator
Last modified at 11/4/2007 3:28 PM by STARGAZER\michael

Figure 6-21. *Mover boxes used to select values from a lookup list*

You can also remove selected items from the right side or selected list box by following the same techniques to remove individual or groups of values.

When you click **OK**, SharePoint adds or modifies the item and shows the updated list as shown in Figure 6-22.

Team Site > Employees

Employees

New ▼   Actions ▼   Settings ▼   View: **All Items** ▼

EmployeeID	LastName	FirstName	Skills	Department ID	Approval Status	Modified By
1	Trundell	Julliet	Access; Microsoft Office; Vista	Employee Dept	Pending	STARGAZER\administrator
2	Shandeau	Rivoli		Legal	Approved	STARGAZER\administrator
3	Chapman	Alex		Devices	Approved	STARGAZER\administrator
4	Powell	Max		Network Services	Approved	STARGAZER\administrator
5	Anders	Susan		Purchasing	Approved	STARGAZER\administrator
6	Antonovich	Michael		Web Services	Approved	STARGAZER\administrator

Figure 6-22. *Employees list with multivalued Skills column*

Notice that the selected skills for Julliet Trundell appear in the **Skills** field separated with semicolons. Another thing to notice about this list focuses on the column header, **Skills**.

It appears slightly dimmer than the other column headers. This occurs because you cannot sort the list items by this field. In fact, if you click the header, the first line of the drop-down menu reminds you that it cannot sort on this column. Figure 6-23 shows this drop-down menu.

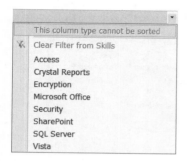

Figure 6-23. *Drop-down menu for a multivalued column*

Notice, however, that you can filter the list by individual values in the field. For example, if you select the value **SQL Server**, SharePoint refreshes the list, applying the filter to display only those employees with SQL Server as a skill. Opening the drop-down menu for the **Skills** column a second time displays an option to clear the filter from the column, and thus displaying all employees again. While a column has an active filter, a funnel-shaped icon appears in the header to the right of the name.

Note You cannot select more than one filter for a column at a time. However, you can select filters on two or more columns at once.

Tip If you switch to the **Datasheet View**, you can create custom filters that can include more than one filter for a single column.

In addition to the **Skills** column, suppose you added a choice type column, named **Language**, so you can track the languages each employee knows. Since an employee might know multiple languages, you decide to make this field a multivalued field as well.

Figure 6-24 shows this field after you have added it to the list and specified values for each employee. On your screen, you might notice that the font appears in a different color from the **Skills** column. When you create a multivalued column using the choice column type, the way you define the field fixes the possible values. However, the **Skills** column links to the **Skills** list, building the list of possible values dynamically, and thus appears as a hyperlink value rather than just text. In either case, you cannot sort on a multivalued column no matter how you create it. You can verify this by clicking the column header to open the drop-down menu. However, you can filter the lists by individual values used in the multivalued column.

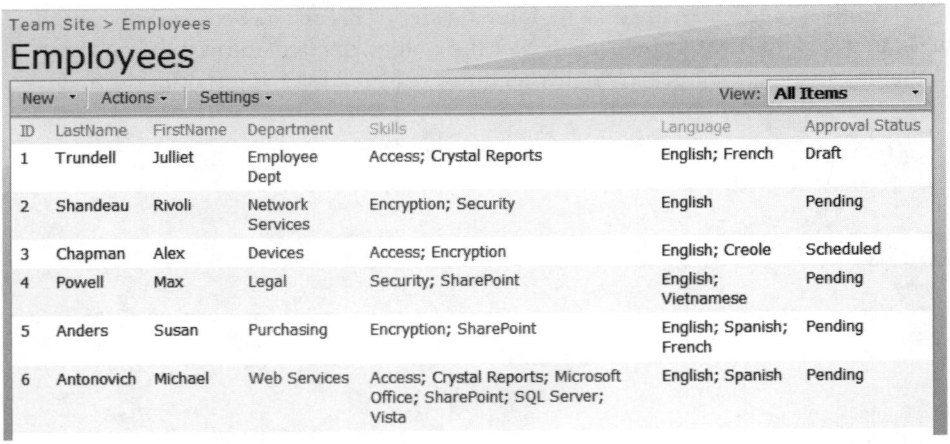

Figure 6-24. *Employees list with Skills and Language multivalued columns*

At first, you may think that either method of adding a multivalued column should effectively result in the same end-user experience. The primary difference between the two methods is that users with the rights to add and modify items in a list can maintain the skills lookup list, but they cannot add or modify the items in the language choice list unless they also have the Manage Lists permission. But that is not the only difference.

Opening a List with Multivalued Columns in Access

Let's open the **Employees** list in Access to see how Access treats these two column types.

1. Open the **Employees** list in SharePoint.

2. Select **Open in Access** from the **Actions** menu.

At this point, Access opens a dialog box asking whether you want to link to the data in SharePoint or export a copy of the data. This dialog box appeared originally in Figure 6-2. Let's see what happens when using each method beginning with a simple export.

3. Select **Export a copy of the data** and click **OK**.

After a few moments, Access opens with a copy of the employee data as shown in Figure 6-25. If the table does not immediately open, you may need to open the **Employees** table from the **Navigation** panel by double-clicking it.

You should first notice that the skills in the **Skills** column have been replaced with their corresponding skill ID, making it rather difficult to interpret and use the **Skills** column. This does not happen to the **Language** column defined as a choice type column. Thus copying a list to Access treats lookup columns differently from choice columns. Furthermore, if you click in the **Skills** column of any row in the Access table, the drop-down only includes the ID values already used for that employee. Thus the drop-down for each of the employees differs. Nor can you manually enter other ID values, even if you know what skills each ID value represents. Figure 6-26 shows a typical skills drop-down for an employee.

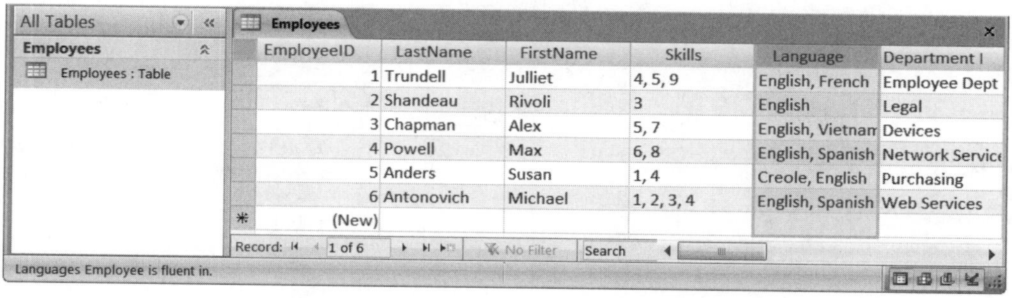

Figure 6-25. *Employees table after copying the list*

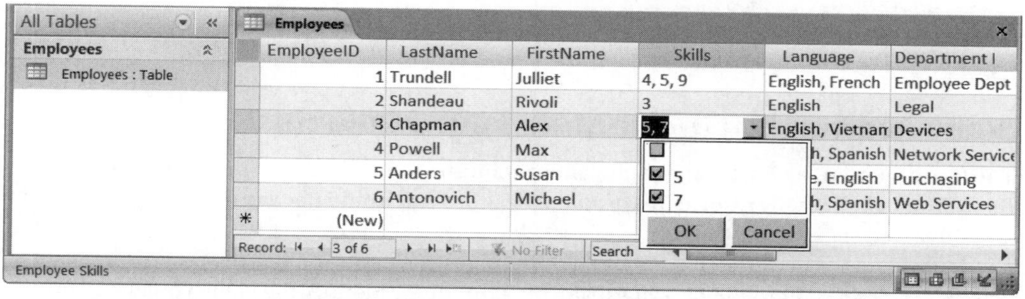

Figure 6-26. *Skills drop-down list that appears when you copy the Employees table*

On the other hand, the **Language** column displays the selected languages just as it did within SharePoint, except commas separate the values rather than semicolons. Also, if you edit this field by opening the drop-down list of values for any employee, you will see the complete list of possible values exactly as defined in SharePoint. Using this drop-down, you can modify the languages associated with any employee by clicking the check box before each language. However, changes to any of these columns do not resynchronize with the original SharePoint list because you chose the copy option to create this table.

Instead of choosing **Export a copy of the data** when you open the SharePoint list in Access, suppose you open Access using the **Link to data on the SharePoint site** option. When you select this option, SharePoint not only creates a link in Access from the **Employees** table to the **Employees** list in SharePoint, but also includes links to all the lookup tables. Figure 6-27 shows that in addition to the **Employees** table, Access also creates links to the **Skills** and **Depts** tables. As a result, you now see the skill names, not just the skill ID values. Furthermore, if you click in the **Skills** column for any employee and open the drop-down menu, you will see all the available skills from the **Skills** list.

For this reason alone, you may choose to use the links option rather than the copy option to view SharePoint lists in Access. But wait, there is more.

When you link to the SharePoint list rather than copy from it, you can make changes in either SharePoint or Access and have your changes appear in the other platform. When you copy the list from SharePoint to Access, changes you make in either platform remain only in the platform in which you make them. This means that by using links to your lists, you can use Access to manage your SharePoint lists, even those with multivalued columns.

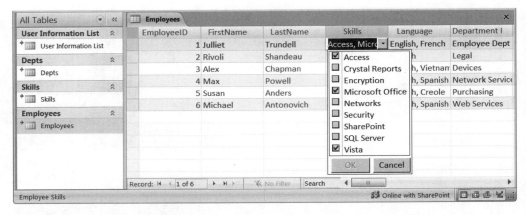

Figure 6-27. *The skills drop-down is complete when linking to the Employees list.*

Some Reasons Not to Use Multivalued Columns

The first argument against using multivalued columns comes from the inability to sort by them. You cannot easily resolve this problem because you would need to decide which value in a multivalued set controls the sort.

Filtering poses a different problem. While you may be able to filter the records in a table using a "contains" filter, the filtering string must uniquely identify the value you want and no other value. For example, if you used the two languages French and French Creole, you might encounter problems if you attempted to filter or search the records for employees who could speak French. A "contains" filter on the text "French" would return employees who spoke either French or French Creole.

Another potential problem occurs when you want to link the **Employees** table to another table on a multivalued field. For example, suppose you have a table of projects that includes a field which defines the skills needed by the project. You might want to relate these two tables to see which employees you could assign to each project based on matching their skills to the skills needed for the project. However, if you define the **Skills** field in either or both tables as multivalued fields, you cannot use that field to link the tables.

Before leaving this discussion on multivalued fields, let's take a quick look at the schema for these fields in Access. Figure 6-28 shows the field properties for the **Skills** field. In the **Lookup** tab, you can see that the row source uses a SELECT statement that pulls data from the **Skills** table. It defines the bound column as the ID column (remember that the copy option shows only the ID values), but defines the width of the first column as 0 so that the skill name (Title) appears, not the ID. Notice also the property **Allow Multiple Values** must show **Yes** to allow multiple values in the field.

To conclude this section, I would recommend that you exercise caution when using multi-valued columns, with full knowledge of the limitations they create.

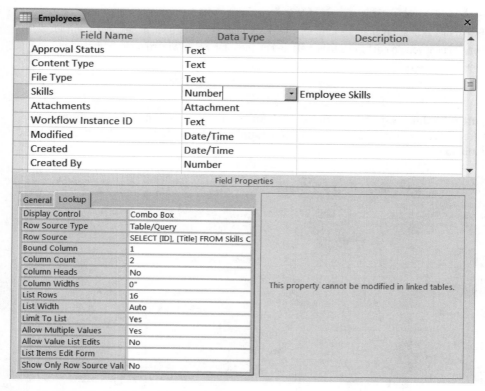

Figure 6-28. *Skills field definition in the Access version of Employees*

Creating Access Forms and Reports from a SharePoint List

Once you bring your first list into Access, a natural question might be, "Can I create forms and reports from the list data?" The answer is yes.

Suppose you start with the **Employees** list. If you remember from earlier in this chapter, the **Employees** list uses two fields that define their values using items found in two other lists, the **Depts** and the **Skills** lists. Thus when you link the **Employees** SharePoint list to Access, it also links these two lists.

Creating a Simple Form

With the three employee-related tables linked into Access, you can generate a simple form for displaying and using just the data from the **Employees** table. The fastest way to create a new form for a single table uses the **Form Wizard**, which you can find by clicking the **Create** tab of the **Access** Ribbon and looking for **Form** in the **Forms** section.

■**Tip** By default, Access generates a form for whichever table you have open or selected in the left-side **Navigation** panel. If you do not have a table selected or open, the **Form Wizard** appears grayed-out and unavailable.

Figure 6-29 shows an example of a default form generated by Access for the **Employees** table. Like all Access forms, you can further customize the form after using the wizard to build the base form.

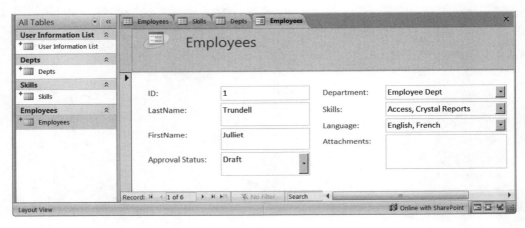

Figure 6-29. *A simple form for the Employees table*

■**Tip** If you do not like the default form generated by Access using the **Form Wizard**, you can abandon this form by closing it without saving it, and then create a new form from scratch using the **Form Design** option from the **Forms** section of the **Create** menu. You could also generate a form, save it, and then use **Form Design** to edit the appearance and/or functionality of the form.

Notice that all fields originally created as lookup or choice fields in SharePoint now appear as drop-down lists. Of course, only the **Skills** and **Department** drop-downs link to other tables in the Access database, while the **Approval Status** and **Language** drop-downs reference a fixed selection of values. In addition, the fields for **Skills** and **Languages** display the multivalued format discussed earlier in this chapter when you click open their drop-down lists.

If you like the way a form appears; you can save it for future use by right-clicking the highlighted tab at the top of the form and selecting **Save** from the menu that appears. This action opens a simple dialog box that prompts for the form name. Access supports form names that have any combination of letters and numbers. However, you should never use special characters. I do not recommend using spaces in table or field names either, although both are possible because you then must delimit those names when you reference them.

As to how long table or field names should be, you should always use as many characters as necessary to fully describe your Access tables and forms up to the limit of 64 characters, but don't make long names just because you can. You can even save a form or report with the same name as the table on which you base it, although that can lead to some confusion. At least when the form appears in the **Navigation** panel on the left, you can always differentiate between the table, form, and report by the icon that appears to the left of the name as shown in Figure 6-30. The word "Form" after the form name is another good clue.

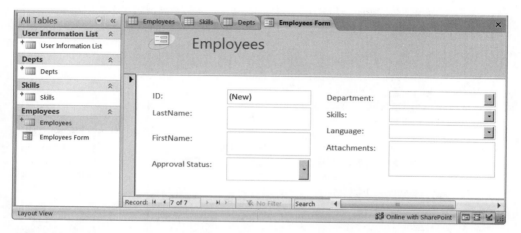

Figure 6-30. *A saved form appears in the Navigation panel with its own icon.*

In addition to the basic form shown in Figure 6-29, Access provides wizards to help you create several other types of forms, including the following:

- Split Form

- Multiple Items

- PivotChart

- PivotTable

- Modal Dialog

- Datasheet

- Custom forms

It is beyond the scope of this book to examine each of these form types. However, let's take a look at two form variations beginning with the Split Form.

Creating a Split Form

The Split Form can give you two views of the same data on the same form. Figure 6-31 shows a Split Form for the **Employees** table, in which the top portion of the form shows the fields laid out similar to those of Figure 6-30. However, the bottom of the form displays the table records in a grid format, in which each record displays as a row in the grid.

Figure 6-31. *A Split Form provides two ways to edit records.*

You can change the record shown in the top portion of this form by scrolling through the records using the grid in the lower portion and clicking anywhere in the row of the desired record. Once you select the record, you can then edit the fields in either portion of the form. When you move off the record, Access automatically saves the changes you made to that record.

If you do not like the way a form generated by the wizard looks, you can edit the form design by right-clicking the form's highlighted tab and selecting **Design View** from the drop-down menu. You can also select **Design View** from the **View** option of the **Views** section of the **Home** Ribbon.

Figure 6-32 shows the **Depts** form displayed in **Design View**. A form like a report in Access consists of a series of bands. In a form, the default bands include a **Form Header**, **Detail**, and **Form Footer** section. Not shown in this figure are **Page Header** and **Page Footer** bands. You probably will use these latter two bands infrequently when designing forms. However, you may find them quite useful when designing reports. Note that you do not need to use each of these bands. You can create a form that only uses the **Detail** band. You can turn on or off any of these bands, as well as access other band features, by right-clicking the band's title bar.

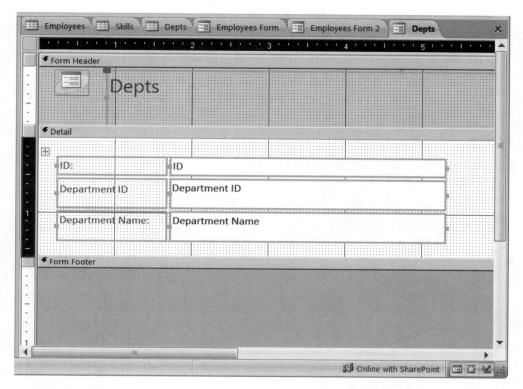

Figure 6-32. *Design View lets you customize your form's appearance.*

Creating a Custom Form Using a Subform

The last form type you will briefly explore here is the custom form, which uses a subform to display data from a related table. You would use this type of form to show a parent-child relationship between two tables. For example, suppose you want to display a list of employees by department. In this case, the **Depts** table acts as the parent, as each employee belongs to only one department, but each department can have multiple employees.

To begin a form that displays this relationship, create a simple form for the **Depts** table. Then after the **Form Wizard** finishes, choose the **Design View** for the form. Next find the **Subform** icon in the **Controls** section of the **Design** Ribbon as shown in Figure 6-33.

After selecting this design tool, move back into the form and draw a rectangle to represent the area where you want the subform to appear. When you release the mouse button, Access prompts for more information to tie the main portion of the form to the subform using a series of dialog boxes.

The first dialog box, shown in Figure 6-34, asks whether you want to use an existing table or query or if you want to use an existing form. I recommend that you create the subform first and then just reference it from the list of available forms.

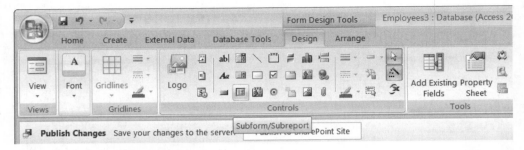

Figure 6-33. *The Design Ribbon with the Subform tool selected*

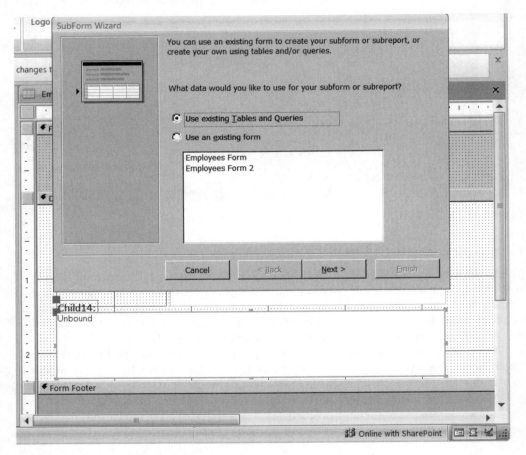

Figure 6-34. *Creating your subform from tables, queries, or existing forms*

Tip Use tools and wizards as much as possible to reduce the amount of work you must perform manually.

If you have not created a subform ahead of time, you can always go directly to a table or query. In that case, you must begin by selecting the table or query you want to use in the subform. Then select the fields you want to appear in the subform. Figure 6-35 shows an example of the dialog box that lets you select fields from the list of available fields in the selected table or query and move them into the **Selected Fields** list. The order in which you select fields for this list determines the order in which the fields appear in the subform. Therefore, select the order carefully. While Access lets you rearrange fields in **Design View** mode, you can save yourself time by giving the order of the fields some thought before you select them rather than spending time later moving them around.

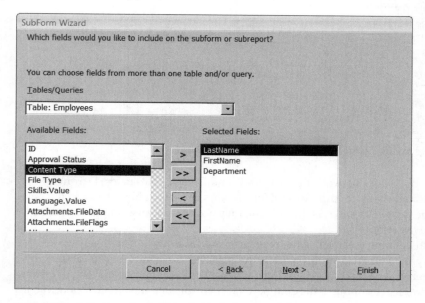

Figure 6-35. *Selecting the fields to include in the subform*

After you have defined the fields in your subform, you still need to define how you want to link the main form to the subform. Access attempts to help by providing some suggestions in the next dialog box of the wizard. However, if nothing in this list seems correct to you, you can define your own connection.

Figure 6-36 shows the dialog box used to define your own link between the main form and the subform. In this case, you want to use the **ID** field as the connecting field between the **Depts** table and the **Department** field in the **Employees** table. Remember, you saw earlier that when you bring a list from SharePoint over to Access, the lookup columns in the list contain the ID of the record in the lookup table.

■**Caution** When you define your own link, the field type on both sides of the link must be the same. In other words, if you select an integer field on the main form side, you must select an integer field on the subform side.

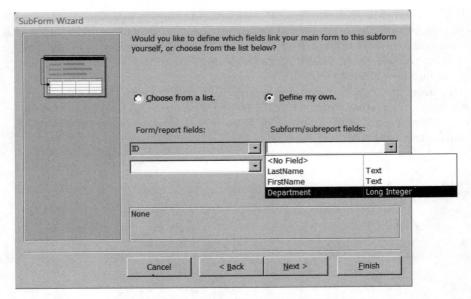

Figure 6-36. *Defining the link between the main form and the subform*

While you can build links between the form and subform using two fields, I strongly recommend using single fields for primary and foreign keys between tables. If you do not have a natural unique single field to serve as the key, you may want to use an autonumber field on the primary side of the relationship.

After you finish defining the link between the form and subform, you are ready to save the subform. However, first you must supply a name for it. As with table names, you can use any combination of letters and numbers as long as the total length of the name has less than 64 characters. Figure 6-37 shows an example of the completed form displaying the employees within a department.

So why did you go through all of this trouble to create an Access form based on tables that represent links to lists in SharePoint? The answer rests with the fact that you linked the Share-Point lists to Access. Because the Access tables represent links, you can modify the data in the Access table or any forms created from those tables, and Access synchronizes your changes back to the SharePoint list. The next time someone opens the SharePoint list, she will see your changes. Thus, you have an alternative way to maintain your lists. Rather than go through the SharePoint interface to edit your lists, you could create a series of Access forms and organize them into an Access application that anyone can use to maintain your SharePoint lists.

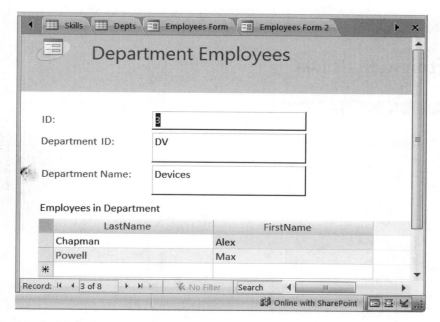

Figure 6-37. *Example of finished Split Form*

Creating a Simple Report

In a similar fashion, you can create Access reports to display data from multiple SharePoint lists. In fact, the technique for designing reports uses many of the same concepts and similar wizards that you used when creating forms. For illustration purposes, the report shown in Figure 6-38 displays the employees in each department.

Again, I want to emphasize that learning how to use Access to create forms and reports goes beyond what we have time for here. There are many books available for Access 2007 that can provide you with further assistance in learning how to create forms and reports if you so need it.

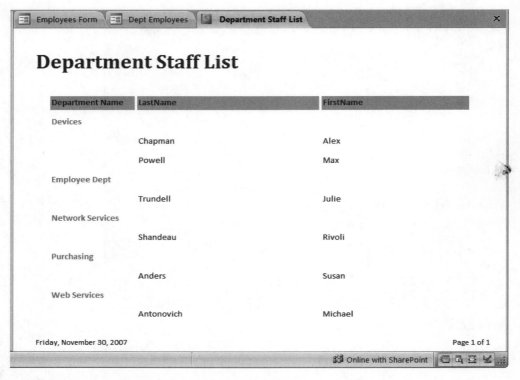

Figure 6-38. *Sample of an Access report created from linked SharePoint lists*

Working with Offline Lists Within Access

When you share a SharePoint list in Access, you can disconnect from your network and work with the list data offline. You can have queries and reports that use the list data to make it easier to display, edit, and report on the list data. If you add other tables to the database not derived from a SharePoint list, you can create forms and reports that combine both the SharePoint-derived data with the non-SharePoint data. But the most interesting feature is that with offline data, you can edit your SharePoint list data even when not connected to your network. You can then upload your changes to the lists the next time you connect to the server.

However, simply creating a linked list in Access does not allow you to work with disconnected data, at least not if you want to protect the integrity of your changes. Just like working with documents, you need to "check out" the data so that SharePoint knows you may be working with it. When it comes to linked lists in Access, that means taking your data offline.

Taking Your List Data Offline

When you work with list data online, the active link between Access and SharePoint continually looks for conflicts between your updates and updates others may create within SharePoint. When a conflict occurs, Access or SharePoint can immediately notify you. But if you want to work on your list data while disconnected from your network, perhaps while you sit on that cross-country flight, you need a way to track the changes you make to the data. Access provides that tracking ability through a technique called *working offline*. While offline, Access tracks all changes made to the linked lists so you can synchronize your changes back with the original lists the next time you connect with your network. Let's see how that happens.

To work offline with your linked SharePoint lists, you must start the process while you are still connected to your network. Let's use the **Employees** list previously discussed in this chapter with its two related tables, **Depts** and **Skills**. Figure 6-39 shows this database already open in Access.

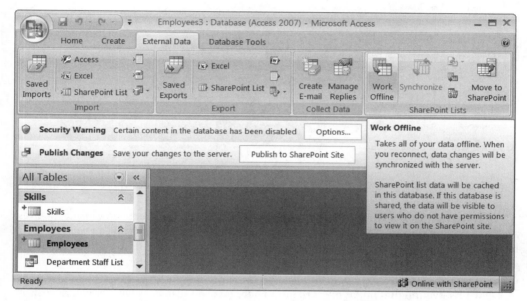

Figure 6-39. *Working offline to track changes to tables when not connected to the network*

Next, perform these steps:

1. Open the Access database in which you have linked your SharePoint lists.

2. Click any of your SharePoint list tables in the Access **Navigation** panel to select it. Do not open it.

3. Click the **External Data** tab on the **Access** Ribbon.

4. In the **SharePoint Lists** section, click the button **Work Offline**.

When you do this, two changes occur to indicate that you can now work with these tables offline. First, the **Work Offline** button now says **Work Online**. This button toggles between the **Work Online** and **Work Offline** states. Second, the icon to the left of the table names in the **Navigation** panel changes. The new icon looks like it has a shadow table behind the original icon. Figure 6-40 shows the tables in offline mode. Compare the icons in this figure to those in Figure 6-39.

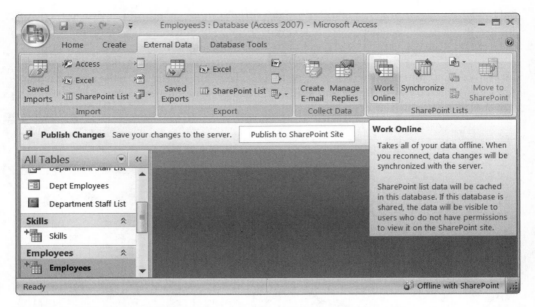

Figure 6-40. *Different icons before table names identify them as offline tables.*

You can now work with the data from your lists offline. You can create new forms, queries, and reports while offline. You can even edit the data in the lists. In fact, you can treat these tables just like any other table you might find in an Access database. For reasons previously mentioned, I will not go into detail here about how to create forms, reports, or even queries using these tables, as there are many books that cover these skills for Access users.

One observation that might merit mention here involves visually seeing which records in a linked list you have modified since taking the data offline. When you modify the contents of a record contained in a linked list, Access tracks your changes, regardless of whether you make those changes through a form or an update query, or directly by opening the table, clicking on fields, and changing them. To see which records you have made changes to, open the Access table in **Datasheet View**. You will notice that some rows have a pencil icon at the beginning of the row. Access uses this icon when you click a row and begin editing any column in that row. However, now it uses a shadow version of this icon to indicate which rows have changed since taking the data offline. Figure 6-41 shows the **Employees** table after changing several rows.

■**Note** It does not matter how many times you modify a row or even if you reverse your changes back to their original values. The row retains the icon, indicating that a potential change has occurred to that row, and Access will try to synchronize the data in that row with the SharePoint list data the next time you connect to your network.

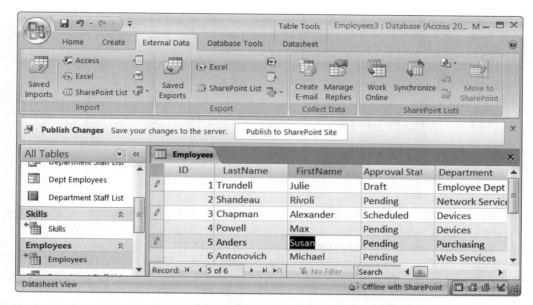

Figure 6-41. *Edited records in offline tables are marked with the icon shown here.*

Returning to Online Mode and Synchronization

The next time you connect to your network after working offline, you may want to return to working online. To return to online mode, follow these steps:

1. Open the Access database in which you have the linked data.

2. Click any of your SharePoint list tables in the Access **Navigation** panel.

3. Click the **External Data** tab on the **Access** Ribbon.

4. In the **SharePoint Lists** section, click the button **Work Online**.

Access then attempts to synchronize your data with the list data in SharePoint. If it succeeds, the button reverts to the **Work Offline** text, and the icon to the left of the table name reverts to the single grid image. The synchronize action succeeds without any additional intervention as long as no one edited any of the list items you edited while you had the list offline.

Note If someone edited a different list item from the one you edited, synchronization will still succeed. Remember that merely taking a table offline does not mark it as exclusive to your use.

If you want to synchronize your offline changes but remain offline, use the **Synchronize** button instead of the **Work Online** button. This button performs only the synchronization of the data, leaving the table marked as offline.

Resolving Conflicts

You might think that update conflicts can only occur when you take an Access table offline and make changes to it. However, conflicts can occur even when you make changes to a record while working online. Suppose you open an Access table and begin editing a record at the same time that someone else opens the corresponding SharePoint list. You make your change to the Access table and move off the record. In Access, moving off a record tells Access to write your change back to the database. In the case of a linked table, this also writes the change back to the SharePoint list. Suppose another person begins to edit the same field in SharePoint, opening the list just prior to your change being sent back to SharePoint. Therefore, he sees the old values for the item. A web page does not refresh automatically when the underlying data changes. Thus the other SharePoint user will attempt to make his change and move off the item. Only at that point does SharePoint recognize that the underlying data has changed and flags the record with a conflict indicator.

Figure 6-42 shows a SharePoint-side conflict. Notice that the first item in the list has a yellow diamond-shaped icon in the first column with two red arrows pointing toward each other. This visually indicates that this item has been changed by two different processes. To resolve this conflict, click the icon in the row it occurs or click the word "Resolve" found in the message at the bottom of the grid.

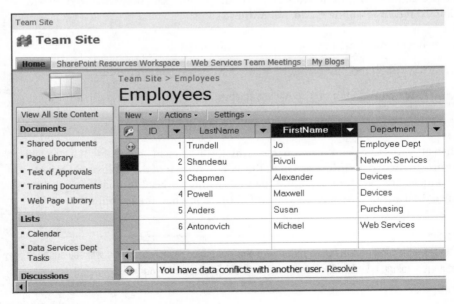

Figure 6-42. *Conflict identified by SharePoint list*

Using either method, SharePoint pops up a dialog box to help resolve the conflict. I cover this dialog box next.

Conflicts also occur when you make changes to a record in Access while working offline and someone else makes a change to one of the items in the corresponding list in SharePoint. When you attempt to synchronize your Access tables with the SharePoint lists, Access recognizes a conflict and displays a dialog box to help resolve it. This dialog box, shown in Figure 6-43, displays a separate page for each conflict record detected. If more than one conflict exists, you can navigate between them using the **Next** and **Previous** buttons in the upper-right corner of the dialog box. Because only one record has a conflict, these buttons appear disabled in Figure 6-43.

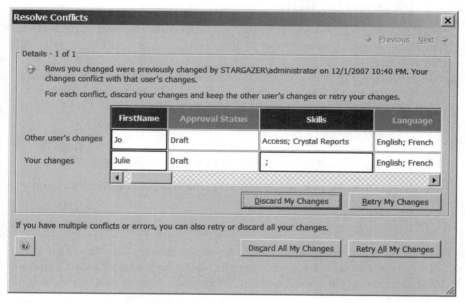

Figure 6-43. *Resolve Conflicts dialog box*

As seen in this dialog box, each column from the table appears in a small table. The columns with conflicts appear highlighted in a different color. The top row of the grid displays the table's column names to help identify the fields with problems. The next row shows the values for each field/column in the conflicting version of the data. The last row shows your values for each field/column.

Unfortunately, you cannot use this grid to edit the values in either the Access table or the SharePoint list. You can, however, choose to address each conflict individually or act on all conflicts as a group. If you only have a single conflict item, either method addresses that conflict.

If you have multiple conflicts, you might want to address each one separately using the **Discard My Changes** and the **Retry My Changes** buttons immediately beneath the conflict grid. If you click the **Discard My Changes** button, the SharePoint list's conflicting value replaces your value for all columns in the row being addressed. In other words, you cannot retain your changes to some columns while also retaining the conflicting values made by the other person for other columns. You cannot resolve multiple conflicts in the same table row using different methods. On the other hand, the **Retry My Changes** button updates the table and linked list with your values.

If you have multiple records with conflicts, you can address all conflicts at one time by using the buttons at the bottom of the dialog box. Click the **Discard All My Changes** button if you want to throw out your changes and keep the data someone else saved. Clicking the **Retry All My Changes** button overrides all conflicting data with your data.

Controlling Which Forms and Reports Are Available in SharePoint

Not only can you publish an Access database to SharePoint, but you can control which forms and reports SharePoint users can directly access. To illustrate this concept, let's begin by looking at the Northwind database.

Even if you have Office 2007 installed on your machine, you may not have the latest, greatest version of the Northwind database, the one specifically designed for Access 2007. However, Microsoft has made it easy to obtain and install it. Just follow these steps:

1. Open Access.

2. Click the **Office Button**. Then select **Database Properties** in the **Manage** section.

3. From the **Getting Started** screen, select **Sample** in the **From Microsoft Office Online** section.

4. Northwind 2007 should appear in the sample list as shown in Figure 6-44. Select it.

5. The right column of the screen updates with information about the selected sample database. Notice the check box near the bottom of this column that offers to **Create and link your database to a Windows SharePoint Services site**. Save yourself some time and select this option.

6. Click the **Download** button.

You may be asked to verify that you are running a genuine version of Microsoft Office. After that, it may take a few seconds to a few minutes to download the database file, depending on the speed of your network connection and the size of the file. But when it finishes, you will see a screen asking for the URL of the site where you want to create corresponding lists from Northwind. For illustration purposes, I created a blank collaboration site named Northwind under my top-level site. Therefore, my URL for this site is http://stargazer/Northwind/. Figure 6-45 shows this step.

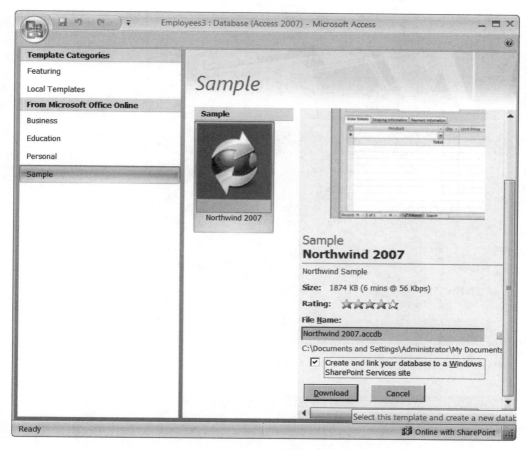

Figure 6-44. *Downloading a copy of the Northwind 2007 sample database*

Notice the last line in the dialog box in Figure 6-45. It asks for the name of a document library to save a copy of the Access database in the SharePoint site. Since I started with a blank collaboration site, I would need to jump back into SharePoint to create a document library for my Northwind site. If I call this library **Northwind Documents**, I can come back to this dialog box, click the **Browse** button, and select the library before clicking **Next** to continue.

Clicking **Next** starts the process of building the Northwind database and site. This process takes several minutes, so after starting it, you may want to grab a cup of coffee. When it finishes, you will see a screen, shown in Figure 6-46, hopefully telling you that your tables have been successfully shared with your SharePoint site.

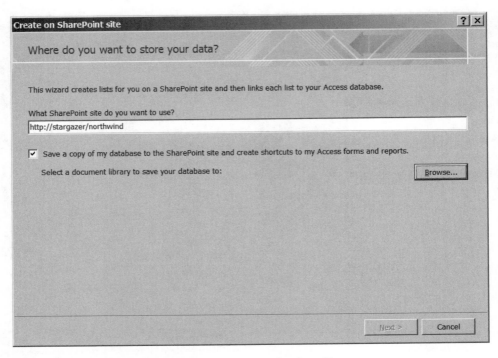

Figure 6-45. *Identifying where to store your Access database lists*

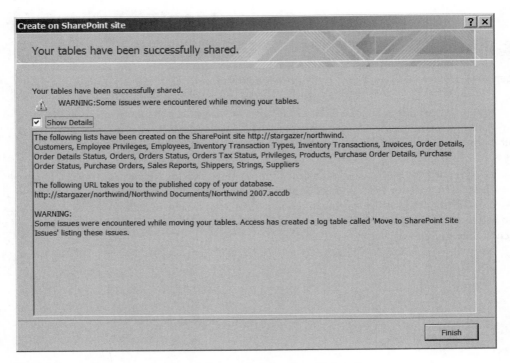

Figure 6-46. *Notification of successfully creating the SharePoint site*

The dialog box probably also includes a warning that some issues were encountered while setting up the SharePoint site. If you click the check box before the text **Show Details**, you will see some additional information, but the real core of the issues can be found in the log table that Access generates called **Move to SharePoint Site Issues**. Figure 6-47 shows a portion of the records in this table after installing the Northwind database. Earlier I showed you a similar table for issues when publishing individual tables to SharePoint lists. The types of issues described there largely apply here as well. You should always review this log. However, don't get too concerned over most of the issues, especially when the move drops referential integrity or the enforcement of unique indexes or autonumber fields. On the other hand, you may want to look at cases where data validation rules or default values do not transfer to SharePoint to see whether you can determine a way to create similar validation rules or set appropriate default values. After you finish checking the issues, you can delete this Access table.

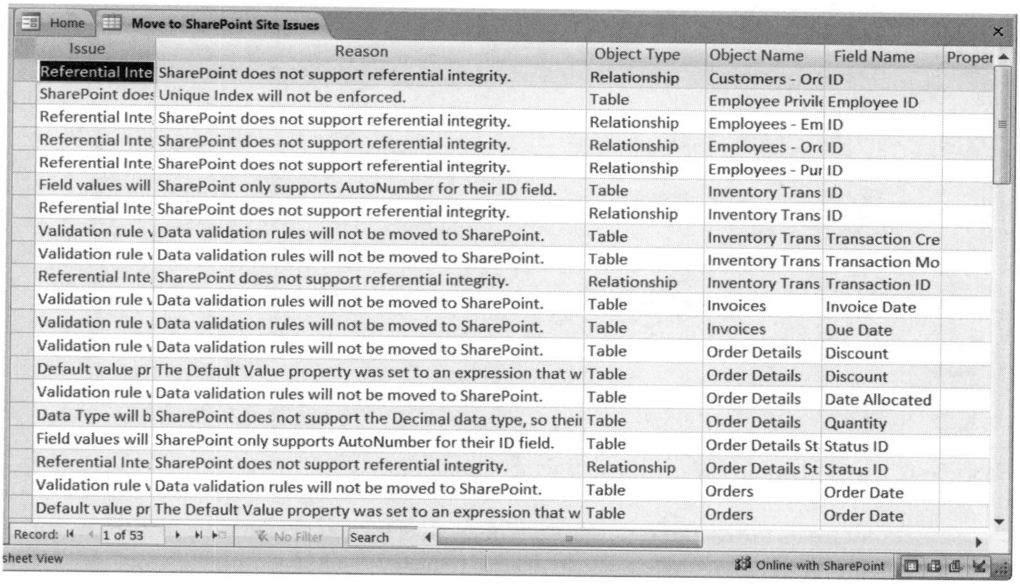

Figure 6-47. *Example of some of the issues involving moving tables to SharePoint sites*

Next, you probably want to see what has happened to the Northwind site on SharePoint. Opening the site, you may at first think that nothing happened. From the **Home** page of the site, the **Quick Launch** menu looks rather empty, having only a single entry in the **Documents** section created earlier. If you open this document library, you will find a copy of the Access database. You need to have a copy of the Access database in the SharePoint site as you will see in a moment.

Click **Lists** in the **Quick Launch** menu or click **View All Site Content** as shown in Figure 6-48. As you can see, the site has quite a number of lists. In fact, there should be a separate list for every table in the Northwind database. But where, you might ask, are all the forms and reports from the database?

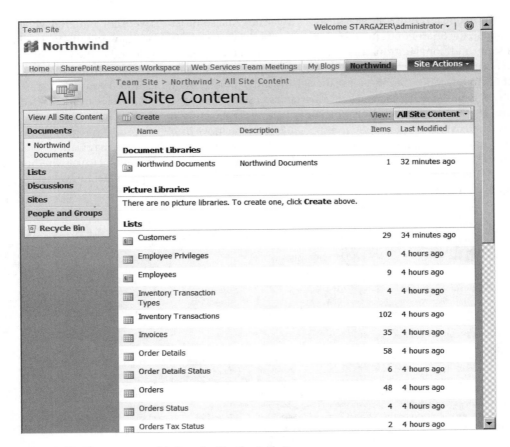

Figure 6-48. *The content added to the Northwind site*

SharePoint treats forms and reports as a type of view associated with the list. To see this, open the **Customers** list as shown in Figure 6-49. Then click the **View** drop-down in the upper right. In the drop-down menu, you can find all the forms and reports that use the **Customers** table. If you click any of these, SharePoint attempts to open a copy of Access on your machine and uses the copy of the Northwind database stored in the site's document library to display the selected form or report in a separate window. If you do not have Access 2007 on your local machine, SharePoint will not be able to open the selected view or report.

■**Tip** Examining the available views associated with a list is an interesting way to quickly see which forms and reports use that table in the Access database.

In the view's drop-down for any list, you can also add your own views and modify Share-Point views as described earlier in the Chapter 2 when I discussed working with custom views. In fact, the view **My Customers** represents a custom view built within SharePoint against the list data.

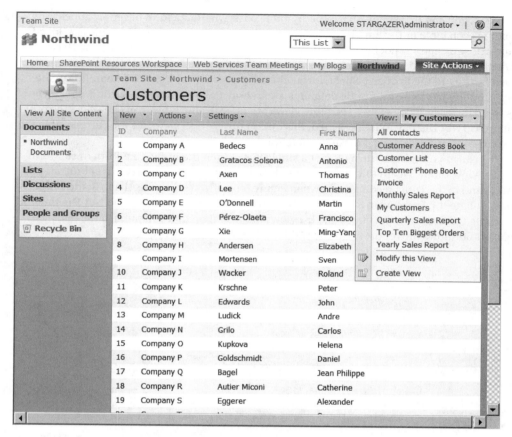

Figure 6-49. *Forms and reports appear as views in SharePoint lists.*

However, even with each list having multiple views available, you may still identify forms and reports that do not appear associated with any list. The reason is that you can control which lists, forms, and reports get published to SharePoint.

Starting with the 50,000-foot look at publishing Access databases to SharePoint, you can control at the database level whether you want any forms or reports to appear at all. To do so, follow these steps before you publish the database:

1. Open the Access database you want to publish back to SharePoint.

2. Select **Database Properties** from the **Manage** group.

3. In the **Properties** dialog box, click the **Custom** tab.

4. In the **Properties** field, click the name **DisplayAllViewsOnSharePointSite**.

5. Set the **Value** of this property to **0** if you do not want associated views representing forms and reports added to the SharePoint site. Otherwise, set this property to **1**.

Next, you can determine on a table-by-table basis whether a form or report appears by opening each table in **Design View**. You may get a pop-up warning that the table is a linked table whose design cannot be modified. Click the **Yes** button to open it anyway. The **Design** tab of the Ribbon should automatically open. Within the **Show/Hide** section, click the **Property Sheet** button. In the **Property Sheet**, locate the property **Display Views on SharePoint Site**. This property has two options. By default, it should say **Follow Database Setting**, which you just set. However, if you want to turn the views off for a specific table, you can select the other option, **Do Not Display**. When selected, this option turns off all views for the current table the next time you publish the database to SharePoint.

If instead you want to turn off just a single view, open the individual form or report in **Design View** mode. Again under the **Design** Ribbon, locate the **Property Sheet** button, this time found in the **Tools** section as shown in Figure 6-50. If you select the **All** tab in the **Property Sheet**, locate the **Display on SharePoint Site** option and set the value to **Do Not Display** to eliminate the form or report from any list views the next time that you publish the database. Figure 6-50 shows the report **Customer Address Book** being turned off.

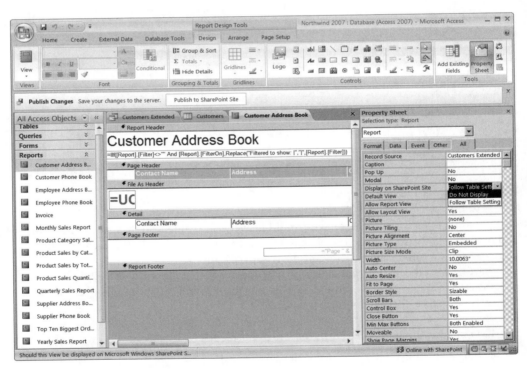

Figure 6-50. *Determining whether to display a report in SharePoint as a view*

Even though you have made changes to the properties of the database itself, the individual tables, or the forms or reports, the changes do not synchronize with SharePoint the way changes to data synchronize. In order to have these changes updated in SharePoint, you must republish the database. Access makes this step easy by providing a button to publish changes to the SharePoint site as shown in Figure 6-50 immediately below the **Access** Ribbon commands. When you click this button, it could take a few seconds to a few minutes depending on the number of changes you made since the last time you published the database as well as the size of the database itself. However, when it finishes, you can open your SharePoint site and check the changes in the views available for each of the lists.

Tip This section showed how to select forms and reports and publish them back to the SharePoint site using the Northwind database. However, the same technique applies to any database, even one that may have started from a set of SharePoint lists. Simply build your forms and reports in Access, and then publish the database to SharePoint.

Can Recycle Bin Recover Deleted List Records?

By now, it should not come as a surprise that when you delete a record in an Access table that links to a SharePoint list, SharePoint also deletes the record from that list. However, unlike deleting a record from a stand-alone table in Access, when you delete just about anything in SharePoint, it gets sent to the Recycle Bin. Therefore, if you happen to delete the wrong record while in Access, you can recover it through SharePoint.

To recover a deleted record, open SharePoint and navigate to the site. You do not need to first go to the list that links to the Access table. Just follow these steps:

1. Scroll down through the **Quick Launch** area on the left to **Recycle Bin** found at the bottom.

2. Click **Recycle Bin**.

3. When the Recycle Bin opens, it shows all the items deleted in the last 30 days (by default). Locate the deleted record (see Figure 6-51).

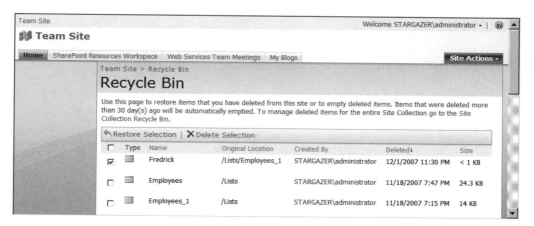

Figure 6-51. *Recovering a deleted Access record using the SharePoint Recycle Bin*

4. Click the check box to the left of the record you want to restore.

5. Click the **Restore Selection** button at the top of the recycle list.

If you now return to the list, the deleted record again appears in the list. Furthermore, if you go to Access and open the table corresponding to the linked list again, you see that the deleted record appears there again as well.

Summary

In this chapter, you saw how to use Access to work with SharePoint lists. You began by performing simple tasks to export SharePoint lists to Access and to publish Access tables to SharePoint. You learned that by linking lists from SharePoint to Access, you could edit data from either platform. Furthermore, within Access, you could build forms to edit the linked tables. You also looked at using multivalued fields, a new and controversial feature to Access, as it violates the first rule of data normalization—to keep all data fields atomic.

Until this point, you had performed all editing while remaining online with the SharePoint server. However, the advantage of using Access to manage your lists comes from its ability to work with lists offline. Therefore, I showed you how to take Access tables offline and then resynchronize your changes with SharePoint's list values. Of course, anytime more than one person can modify data from two or more platforms, conflicts can and will occur if multiple people attempt to update the same record at the same time. Therefore, I also demonstrated how to resolve conflicts.

Finally, you looked at how to selectively publish tables, forms, and reports from Access back to SharePoint. Using all these techniques together, you could start from a set of SharePoint lists, link them to an Access database, build forms to maintain them and reports to report on them, and then publish the entire collection back to SharePoint, where the forms and reports become views for the corresponding lists.

■ ■ ■

CHAPTER 7

Managing SharePoint Lists from Excel

Along with MS Word, MS Excel is one of the oldest products in the Microsoft Office Suite. Microsoft developed Excel in the early days of PCs after the wildly successful introduction of Lotus 1-2-3, which was one of the great early productivity tools that helped to justify using PCs in many business offices. But even before Lotus was introduced, VisiCalc and MultiPlan, an early predecessor to Microsoft Excel, tested the spreadsheet waters. The ability to work with rows and columns of numbers took advantage of a familiar paradigm for accountants and finance departments to work within. And since finance departments often controlled the use of computers at many companies, the speed of developing a usable accounting application using a spreadsheet along with an intuitive interface that users quickly adapted to showed that the PC was not a toy or a passing fad, but a real technology tool that businesses could benefit from.

Thus several early competitors played in this market, hoping to make PCs respectable in corporate environments where large mainframe computers ruled the day. It wasn't until 1985 that Microsoft finally introduced Excel; even then, it was only for the Macintosh. In fact, it took until 1987 for the first Windows version of Excel to appear.

Of course today, Microsoft Excel is as synonymous with Microsoft Office as Microsoft Word. In fact, with the possible inclusion of Microsoft Outlook, these three products form the central core around which users at most offices that use Microsoft products spend the majority of their day. So when Microsoft introduced SharePoint, integrating collaboration features with these three Office products would seem to be a no-brainer. Why force users already familiar with several of your other products to learn a new product paradigm, when they could leverage their existing skills to take advantage of that new product?

For Microsoft Word, Outlook, and even the relatively new kid on the block, Access, integration with collaboration has been a priority with SharePoint. But is the same true for Excel? In this chapter and the next, you will explore how SharePoint works with Excel.

Exporting a List from SharePoint to Excel

The last couple chapters have covered exporting lists from SharePoint to Outlook and Access. So it should not surprise you that you can export a SharePoint list to Excel. In fact, if you have been checking out the options in SharePoint's list and document menus, you probably already have a good idea of how to start.

To show that document libraries act very much like lists, let's start with the **Purchase Orders** library. You previously used this library to learn how you could use library metadata in other Microsoft Office applications. You even created a custom view to sum the **Purchase Amount** column by department to produce a "report" within SharePoint showing how much each department spent during a specified time period defined by a filter.

Begin as always by navigating to the library or list you want to use from your SharePoint site. Next, open the **Actions** menu from the menu bar at the top of the **Purchase Orders** library. Figure 7-1 shows this drop-down menu. Notice that while it has the options **Connect to Outlook** and **Export to Spreadsheet**, it does not have an option you might expect, **Open with Access**.

Figure 7-1. *Opening the Export to Spreadsheet menu option*

■**Note** Access can only open lists, not libraries.

This difference between lists and libraries defines one of the differences in terms of how you work with them. I will mention others as you proceed through this chapter.

Taking a closer look at Figure 7-1; notice another subtle difference in the options shown in this menu. While the **Connect to Outlook** option includes descriptive text that talks about synchronizing items and working with them offline, the **Export to Spreadsheet** option uses no such language in its description. Rather it simply refers to the ability to analyze items within a spreadsheet application. Let's continue on to see what this change in terminology means with respect to our ability to collaborate.

The Role of the IQY File

After selecting the **Export to Spreadsheet** option, a dialog box pops up with the title **File Download**. Figure 7-2 shows this dialog box. It asks whether you want to open or save a file with the rather odd extension of .iqy. According to the **Type** description, this file type represents a Microsoft Office Excel Web Query File. If you click **Save**, the **Save As** dialog box appears, letting you select where to save this file. However, by itself, the **Save** option does not open the file in Excel or even open Excel. It merely saves a file to your local hard drive. Interestingly, if you double-click this file after saving it, it opens Excel and begins the process of retrieving data from the SharePoint library. If you open the IQY file using Notepad, you will discover that this small file contains some very cryptic text. I will not try to decipher this text here. However, you should be able to read enough of it to learn that this file contains information pointing back to your SharePoint site and specifically to the library you want to export to Excel.

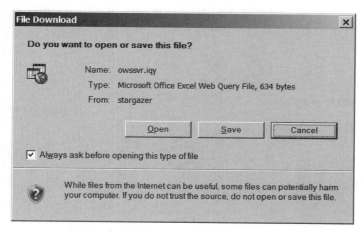

Figure 7-2. *The File Download dialog box saves the Excel Web Query File that retrieves the SharePoint List.*

Regardless of whether you try to open the query file immediately or decide to later open a copy of the query file saved to your local hard drive, you will first see a security notice generated by Excel. This security concern occurs because the query file attempts to command Excel to make a connection with another server. With ever-increasing concerns about viruses, Trojan horses, and other nasty things getting into your computer, all software vendors by default lock down connections between machines but allow you to decide which connections to allow and when to allow them. Figure 7-3 shows the **Microsoft Office Excel Security Notice** dialog box that appears when the IQY file tries to connect Excel to SharePoint.

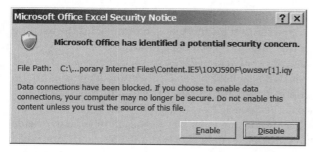

Figure 7-3. *Microsoft Office Excel Security Notice dialog box before making a data connection*

In any situation when you attempt to connect to another server, always verify that you trust the connected source. If you have any doubts about a content source, click the **Disable** button. But if the server resides inside your corporate firewall, you can probably trust it and safely click the **Enable** button to continue.

Choosing How to Display Your Imported List

In the next dialog box that appears, the **Import Data** dialog box shown in Figure 7-4, you get to make two decisions on how to display your exported list data. In the top portion of this dialog box, you receive up to four options on how to view your data:

- **Table**

- **PivotTable Report**

- **PivotChart and PivotTable Report**

- **Only Create Connection**

Figure 7-4. *The Import Data dialog box lets you decide where to place your data.*

By default, most lists export to tables. The second half of the dialog box lets you choose whether to place the list in an existing worksheet, a new worksheet, or a new workbook. If you start the export process with Excel open, you can select any of these options. But if you begin your export without first opening Excel, SharePoint skips this dialog box and adds the list data to a new workbook with a single sheet containing the list data beginning in cell A1.

Before clicking **OK** to begin the actual export of data to Excel, you can click the **Properties** button in this dialog box. This button opens a dialog box named **Connection Properties**. At the top of the dialog box, you can find the connection name along with an optional description. The rest of the dialog box consists of two tabbed pages.

In the first tab, you cannot edit most of the data fields. However, you should find two fields in the **Refresh** control area that you can edit. The first field allows you to enable background refresh. Basically, this option allows you to continue to use Excel while the query executes. Unless you have a very large list from which to refresh your Excel data, the query execution time may not matter much to you.

The second option that you can set is **Refresh the data when opening the file**. If you do not select this option, Excel stores a local copy of the current data when you save the spreadsheet and displays that same data the next time you open the spreadsheet, regardless of what changes have occurred in the original SharePoint list. Of course, you could always manually refresh the data by clicking the **Refresh** button in the **External Table Data** group of the **Table Tools Design** Ribbon. But by selecting this option, you could save time and reduce uncertainty of the current data values by telling Excel to refresh the data automatically each time you open the spreadsheet.

■**Note** Excel does not automatically refresh data from a SharePoint list. That accounts in part for the use of the term "export" in the SharePoint menu selection **Export to Spreadsheet**. Thus your first clue: SharePoint does not maintain a continuous link to the data in Excel.

The second tab, titled **Definition**, contains information about the connection between Excel and the SharePoint list so that manual refreshes of the data know how to access the list data. You can also save a copy of the connection definition by clicking the **Export Connection File** button and selecting a location to save the file.

■**Caution** Do not change the connection definition unless you have a deep understanding of how to define connection strings, and even then think twice.

When you click **OK** to begin the import of data into Excel, Excel uses the information in the IQY file to import the list data into a spreadsheet. For the **Purchase Orders** library, Figure 7-5 shows the resulting worksheet after exporting and opening the list data within Excel.

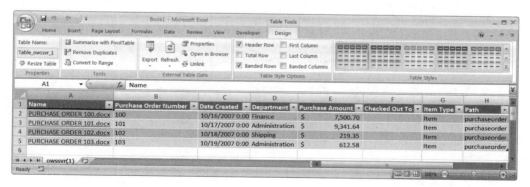

Figure 7-5. *Excel worksheet displays the exported SharePoint list.*

How Views Affect the Data Exported to Your List

When you export a list to a spreadsheet, the items you export as well as the specific columns you export depend very much on the view open at the time you choose to export. For example, looking at the data in Figure 7-5, suppose you had a view that included only purchases by the Administration department, and you only included as columns in that view **Purchase Order Number**, **Date Created**, and **Purchase Amount**. Then the export to Excel would include only those two items with the three selected columns each.

You may have noticed that the data in this worksheet is not just simple spreadsheet data. Rather, it appears structured within a table, with each column representing a separate field and each row representing a separate list item. Your other clue that this is not just a collection of cells with data in them should have been the title of the Ribbon, **Table Tools**.

Using Hyperlinks in Your List

If you include one of the instances of the **Name** field linked to the document in a shared documents library as you did in this case, that field displays in Excel as a hyperlink. That means that you can click the document name, and through the URL associated with the hyperlink, the document opens using the appropriate Microsoft Office product, such as MS Word in this case.

Note Clicking a link to the document can only open the original document if a) you have an appropriate application that can open the document installed on your desktop, and b) if you have an active network connection. Opening a link cannot work when you work offline.

Figure 7-6 shows a dialog box that may pop up when you click a hyperlinked **Name** field from a document library. When accessing an internal SharePoint site at your company, you probably can trust the files to be virus free. However, you should have a virus scanning program on your local desktop computer or network to ensure that harmful programs cannot get to your files when you open them from a shared location.

Figure 7-6. *Warning dialog box that pops up when opening a document from a SharePoint library*

When you open a document, it appears no different than had you opened it directly from the SharePoint library. In the case of an MS Word document, the **Document Management** panel also opens, as shown in Figure 7-7. With the document open, you can make changes and then close the document. You can then save those changes, and they will be sent back to the SharePoint library because you effectively performed a remote edit directly to that file. Remember, the file itself does not become a part of your Excel worksheet.

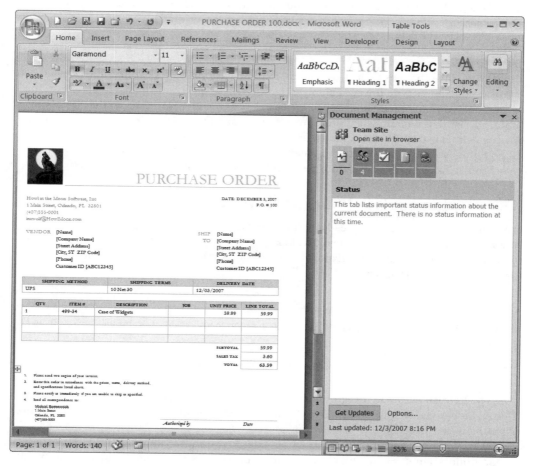

Figure 7-7. *The opened MS Word document also opens the Document Management panel.*

However, while you have the document open for editing, it may not be checked out. You can verify this fact by looking back at the document library from within SharePoint and noticing that the document icon does not contain the green box with the arrow in the lower-right corner, as you have previously seen indicating a checked-out document. Therefore, someone else could check out and edit the same document while you edit it. For that reason, I do not recommend editing documents linked to an Excel list.

■**Tip** That is true unless you go into **Document Library Settings** for the SharePoint library first, select **Version Settings**, and change the **Require Check Out** option to **Yes**. If you do this first, when you attempt to open the document from Excel and it is not checked out, you can open the document to read it, but you will be prompted to check the document out before you can edit it. On the other hand, if the document is already checked out by someone else, and you attempt to open it, you will get the **File in Use** notification dialog box that allows you to open the document in **Read-Only** mode or be notified when the document becomes available for editing.

If you make changes to the document, MS Word asks you to save your changes when you close the document with unsaved changes. However, while you can open, edit, and save the document, you cannot edit and save changes to any of the metadata back to the SharePoint library or list. The data transfer between SharePoint and Excel occurs in two separate paths. You can either export a SharePoint list or library to Excel or export an Excel spreadsheet to a SharePoint list. You can even refresh the Excel data from SharePoint. However, you cannot synchronize Excel changes back into the original SharePoint list.

Other Table Tools in Your Excel Workbook

You can export your changed spreadsheet to a new SharePoint list. You can verify this by clicking the **Table Tools** tab, as shown previously in Figure 7-5. The **External Table Data** group only contains two options under the **Export** button to support exporting from Excel to SharePoint lists and Visio Pivot Diagrams.

■**Note** If you do not have Visio installed, the option to export to Visio Pivot Diagrams will be grayed out and unselectable.

The **Refresh** button in this group lets you refresh the Excel data using the original connection created to transfer the data to Excel. However, neither of these options let you synchronize data changes in Excel back to SharePoint.

Furthermore, you can only export Excel tables to lists, not to libraries. That means the export option cannot re-create a library from the purchase orders, even though they originally came from a library. It can, however, create a standard list in which the item's **Name** field displays as a hyperlink, letting you open the Word document almost like you would in a library. I say "almost" because as it is a list, you do not have the ability to check out documents while you edit them. Thus, if you start with a SharePoint library and export it to an Excel table, you can only import it back into SharePoint as a new list, not as a replacement for the existing library or even a new library.

The **Refresh** button, mentioned previously, allows you to refresh the data in the Excel spreadsheet with data from the source SharePoint library or list, updating changes to the items and columns displayed. This includes not only items that have changes, but also new items and removed items. This refresh, however, overwrites any changes you made in the Excel worksheet with the current information from the SharePoint library.

The **Properties** button allows you to select some of the properties that affect how the table responds to new and deleted rows.

The **Open in Browser** button opens the library or list page from the SharePoint site.

The **Unlink** button permanently removes the connection from the worksheet. While the worksheet remains intact with all its data after you select this option, you can no longer update the data from the SharePoint library or list by clicking the **Refresh** button.

■**Caution** When you unlink a table from its corresponding SharePoint library or list, you cannot restore the link or the connection.

The crucial concern about exporting your lists to Excel comes down to the lack of synchronization of changes. While you can refresh your Excel table as often as you like by using the **Refresh** button in Excel to get the latest and greatest values from the SharePoint list, this process is one-way only, and a manual process at that unless you use the **Refresh the data when opening the file** option mentioned earlier. Also, this refresh process overwrites any changes to the Excel data you made from within Excel, as it completely replaces the Excel data with data from the SharePoint list. The consequences of the refresh option also limit your ability to reorganize the information in the spreadsheet.

■**Note** Excel 2003 had the ability to update SharePoint lists. However, this feature has been deprecated in favor of using Access 2007. I will return to this issue in the section "What Happened to Synchronization?" later in this chapter to show a way to resolve this limitation.

Exporting Data from an Excel Spreadsheet into a Custom List

In the last section, you saw that when you export a SharePoint list to Excel, you can manually update the Excel spreadsheet with changes made in SharePoint, but you cannot update SharePoint with changes made to the Excel spreadsheet. Let's now take a look at what you can do when you start from Excel 2007.

For the example shown here, I've created an Excel table that lists the top 30+ brightest stars in the evening skies. The table includes the name of the star, the name of the constellation in which the star can be found, and the star's apparent magnitude.

ABSOLUTE VS. RELATIVE BRIGHTNESS FOR THE LAYMAN

Apparent magnitude defines the relative brightness of the stars when you view them. However, similar stars appear to vary in brightness when you look at them not only because some are bigger or hotter, but also because they may exist at different distances from the Earth. If you could place all stars at the same distance from the Earth, you could then refer to their absolute brightness.

Figure 7-8 shows the beginning of this worksheet.

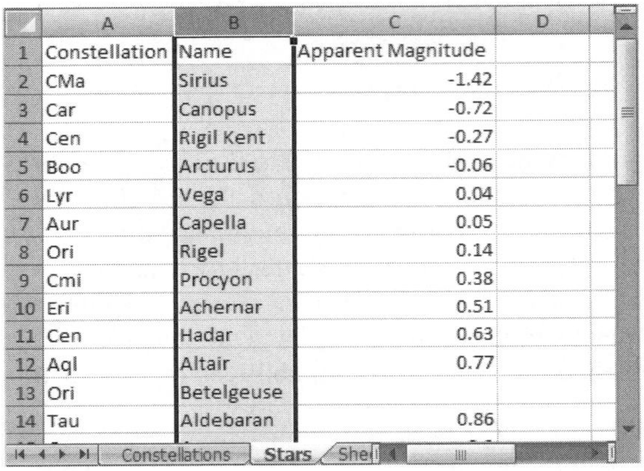

	A	B	C	D
1	Constellation	Name	Apparent Magnitude	
2	CMa	Sirius	-1.42	
3	Car	Canopus	-0.72	
4	Cen	Rigil Kent	-0.27	
5	Boo	Arcturus	-0.06	
6	Lyr	Vega	0.04	
7	Aur	Capella	0.05	
8	Ori	Rigel	0.14	
9	Cmi	Procyon	0.38	
10	Eri	Achernar	0.51	
11	Cen	Hadar	0.63	
12	Aql	Altair	0.77	
13	Ori	Betelgeuse		
14	Tau	Aldebaran	0.86	

Figure 7-8. *Portion of the 30+ Brightest Stars spreadsheet*

Defining a Table Within Your Excel Worksheet

Next, before you can export this Excel worksheet to SharePoint, you need to define the data that you want to transfer as a table. A table can include all the data in a worksheet, or it can include a subset of the data. To define a table within a worksheet, follow these steps:

1. Go to the **Insert** Ribbon and select **Table** from the **Tables** section.

2. Select the cells you want to include in the table. Do this by clicking in any corner of the data block you want to use and, while holding the left mouse button down, drag through the data to the diagonal corner.

3. When you reach the diagonal corner, release the mouse button. Excel circumscribes the selected data with a dotted border and lightly shades the cells of the selected range.

4. After releasing the mouse button, a pop-up dialog box appears showing you the range of the selected cells, as displayed in Figure 7-9. You can edit this range manually. However, if you carefully chose your starting and ending points when dragging through the data, this range should accurately represent the data you want to use.

Figure 7-9. *Defining the cell range you want to export by creating a table*

■**Caution** While it is possible to define multiple data ranges for some commands, the **Create Table** command does not support multiple data ranges.

In addition to defining the cell range for the table, you can determine whether your data range includes headers. When copying data to SharePoint, the headers from the Excel data range become the column names. Therefore, including them lets you determine the column names. If you do not include column names, then SharePoint generates a set of default names for the columns such as **Column1**, **Column2**, etc.

Exporting the Excel Table

Once you have defined a table, a new tab appears above the **Excel** Ribbon named **Table Tools**. This tab contains only a single subtab named **Design**. This Ribbon displays only those commands that act on tables, not worksheets. In this Ribbon, locate the **External Table Data** section and click the **Export** button. This button's action displays a drop-down menu of the types of exports that Excel supports for tables. In Figure 7-10, you can see that this workbook supports two exports, one for SharePoint and one for Visio. In this case, you want to export the table to a SharePoint list, so select the first option.

Figure 7-10. *Exporting the table to a SharePoint list*

Before Excel can export the table, it needs additional information. First, it needs the address to the SharePoint site. For this example, I will again use the top-level site on my SharePoint server named Stargazer. Figure 7-11 shows this dialog box.

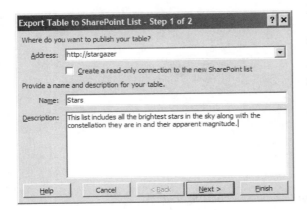

Figure 7-11. *Defining the SharePoint server to publish to and selecting a list name*

Immediately beneath the **Address** field you see a check box that asks whether you want to create a read-only connection to the SharePoint list. This option may confuse you because if you do not select it, no connection between the SharePoint list and the Excel worksheet will exist after Excel publishes the data to SharePoint. The thing to remember is that this statement is from Excel's point of view. Therefore, by checking this box, you create a one-way data synchronization that allows Excel to read changes made in the SharePoint list to update the Excel worksheet, but does not allow Excel to write changes made in Excel back to SharePoint. Next, you must supply a name for the new SharePoint list. This name cannot be the name of any existing list in your SharePoint site. If a list already exists with the name you supply, Excel displays a message that says "The specified list name is already in use on this server. You must rename the list before publishing it to the server."

Note You must have permission in SharePoint to create lists to export data from Excel to SharePoint.

You can also supply a list description. This description appears when you display the lists on the site. Therefore, supply a meaningful description that would help visitors to the site determine what type of data to expect in the list.

The second page of this dialog box, shown in Figure 7-12, displays how it associates each table field with a data type recognized by SharePoint. Excel tries to assign appropriate data types to each field. However, if it does not, you may need to cancel the current operation, return to the data in the worksheet, and change the data formatting of individual cells to a type that converts to the SharePoint data type you want.

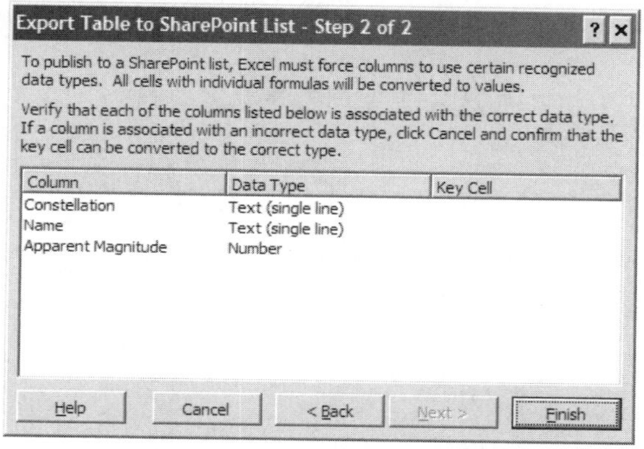

Export Table to SharePoint List - Step 2 of 2   ? ✕

To publish to a SharePoint list, Excel must force columns to use certain recognized data types. All cells with individual formulas will be converted to values.

Verify that each of the columns listed below is associated with the correct data type. If a column is associated with an incorrect data type, click Cancel and confirm that the key cell can be converted to the correct type.

Column	Data Type	Key Cell
Constellation	Text (single line)	
Name	Text (single line)	
Apparent Magnitude	Number	

Help   Cancel   < Back   Next >   Finish

Figure 7-12. *Verifying the data types selected for the SharePoint columns*

■**Note** You cannot directly change the data types shown in the **Export Table to SharePoint List** dialog box. You can only change the underlying Excel cell formatting to affect the selected data types.

To begin the actual data export, click the **Finish** button. Depending on the size of your table, this operation can take from a few seconds to a few minutes. However, when it finishes exporting the data, the dialog box shown in Figure 7-13 tells you whether it was able to publish the table successfully or not. If the publishing task succeeds, this dialog box also contains a clickable hyperlink to display the new SharePoint list.

Windows SharePoint Services   ? ✕

The table was successfully published and may be viewed on:
http://Stargazer/Lists/Stars/Allitemsg.asp

OK

Figure 7-13. *Dialog box announcing the successful publishing of the table*

Tip You may want to click this link before you click **OK** to finish this publishing process. Then you will not have to manually open SharePoint and navigate to the new list to verify the data transfer. Just be sure to eventually click the **OK** button to finish the publishing process.

Viewing the Exported Excel Data in the New SharePoint List

Figure 7-14 shows the lists in my SharePoint site. Notice that the list **Stars** appears along with the description supplied in the **Export Table** dialog box from Figure 7-11.

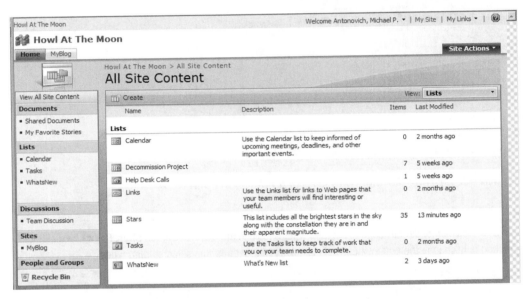

Figure 7-14. *All Site Content page displaying all lists in the current site*

If you click the **Stars** list, SharePoint opens the list using the default view as shown in Figure 7-15. Notice that the transfer adds two columns at the beginning of the list that define the item type and allow attachments.

Tip If all the values in a column typically remain empty, you should consider modifying the view to eliminate that column from displaying in the default view and any other views you might subsequently create.

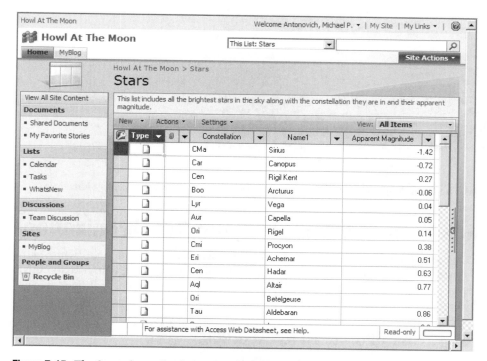

Figure 7-15. *The Stars data after being imported to a SharePoint list*

Another change you might notice is that SharePoint changes the name of the column defining the star names. In Excel, you identified this column in the header as **Name**. However, SharePoint reserves this name and therefore renames the column by adding a "1" to the end of the column name. If you do not like this, you can always go to the list properties and change the column name to something you do like that is potentially more meaningful, such as **Star Names**.

If you did not check the box to create a read-only connection to the SharePoint list, any changes you make in this SharePoint list cannot be synchronized back to the Excel spreadsheet. On the other hand, if you did select this option, you can make changes to the SharePoint list, and then with the Excel spreadsheet open, navigate to the **Table Tools Design** Ribbon. In the **External Table Data** group, click the **Refresh** button and select the option **Refresh** or **Refresh All** as shown in Figure 7-16. These options use the stored connection information between the SharePoint list and Excel created when you exported the original SharePoint list to Excel. You can now reuse this connection to update Excel with the current values in the SharePoint list.

While you can update the Excel table with changes made to the SharePoint list that you exported from Excel, you cannot make changes to the Excel table and automatically synchronize those changes to the SharePoint list. As mentioned before, Microsoft deprecated this feature in Excel 2007. One solution would be to downgrade your Office installation and use Microsoft Excel 2003, which can synchronize data changes in both directions. However, if you think of downgrading your copy of Microsoft Office as something on par with giving up your fully loaded BMW for a Yugo Koral 45, read on to the next sections.

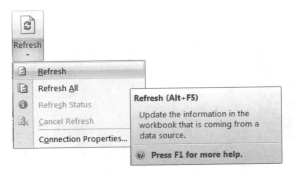

Figure 7-16. *The Refresh options available when using a read-only connection to SharePoint*

A Quick Look at Excel 2003 and Synchronization

Because I've mentioned several times that Excel 2003 provides more functionality with Share-Point than Excel 2007, you may be discouraged about Excel's role in SharePoint's collaborative future. Before presenting a solution for the Excel 2007 user, let's take a quick look back at Excel 2003 and SharePoint.

Exporting a SharePoint List to Excel 2003

To export a SharePoint list to Excel 2003, you begin by selecting the SharePoint list you want to use and choosing **Export to Spreadsheet** from the **Actions** menu. As before, your computer first displays a dialog box asking whether you trust the source when SharePoint tries to send the IQY file. Click **Open** to allow your computer to download the file.

Excel may also prompt you with a similar question about whether you trust the query used to import external data. Since you trust the source in this case, click **Open** to continue.

You might receive one more dialog box asking you for your user name and password to access the data on SharePoint, depending on the integration of your network security. After you click **OK** on this dialog box, you should see the list appear in an Excel worksheet as shown in Figure 7-17. Notice that during this process, you only have the option of selecting where to load the list, such as into a new workbook or a new worksheet, or where on an existing worksheet to place the list if you have Excel open before you start the export from SharePoint. Excel 2003 also does not support the **PivotChart** option found in Excel 2007.

The **List** toolbar in Excel 2003 allows you to work with the downloaded list. Let's look first at the third and fourth buttons from the left.

The third button synchronizes the Excel list with the SharePoint list. When you click this button, it sends changes made to data rows in Excel back to SharePoint, and changes to SharePoint items overwrite the existing data in Excel. If someone makes changes to both the SharePoint item and the Excel row of the same item, the synchronize action displays a **Resolve Conflicts and Errors** dialog box showing both sets of changes and allows you to determine which set of changes you want to keep.

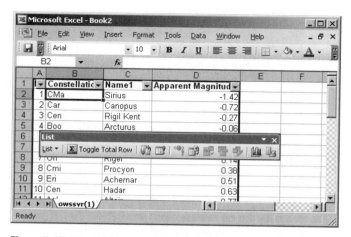

Figure 7-17. *Excel 2003 uses the List toolbar to work with synchronized lists.*

The fourth button lets you discard your changes and refresh your Excel list with current data from the SharePoint list. Use this option if you made accidental changes to the Excel list or changes that you do not want to keep.

The first button in the toolbar opens a drop-down list of options that allow you to

- Insert rows and columns into the list.

- Delete rows and columns from the list.

- Sort the list.

- View and edit the list data with an Excel-generated form.

- Publish the list to SharePoint.

- Resize the list.

- View the list on server.

- Convert the list back to a normal range of data.

- Unlink the list (from SharePoint).

- Define other data range properties and connection properties.

Exporting Excel 2003 Worksheets to SharePoint

One of the first differences you will notice when starting an export from Excel 2003 is how to begin the process. In Excel 2007, you had to define the range of cells you wanted to use as a table before you could export the data to SharePoint. In Excel 2003, the proper terminology defines a **List** instead. You still must select the range of data you want to define in your Excel list the same as you do in Excel 2007. However, to create the list, open the **Data** drop-down menu. From this menu, select **List** and then **Create List** as shown in Figure 7-18.

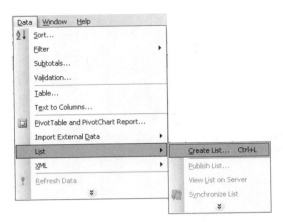

Figure 7-18. *Creating a List in Excel 2003 before you can export data to SharePoint*

The **Create List** option opens a dialog box that confirms the data range you want to use for the list. You can manually adjust this list by either entering a new range directly or clicking the button to the right of the range displayed and dragging through the cells you want to use. You should always include headers as the first row of the list. SharePoint uses these headers as your column names. Otherwise, SharePoint creates default names for the columns: **Column1**, **Column2 . . . Column***N*. Figure 7-19 shows that this dialog box looks similar to the one used in Excel 2007 except that it replaces the word "Table" with "List."

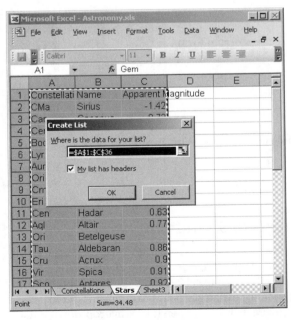

Figure 7-19. *Confirming the list data range and whether it has headers*

Having defined a list, you can now use the **List** toolbar. Open the **List** drop-down menu to find and select the **Publish List** option as shown in Figure 7-20.

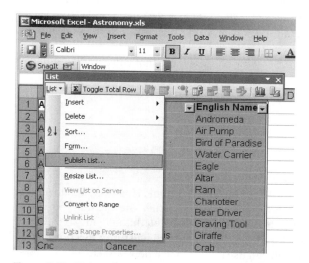

Figure 7-20. *Using the Publish List option from the List toolbar to publish to SharePoint*

The rest of the process for publishing the list parallels what you saw earlier using Excel 2007, with the exception that the word "List" replaces the word "Table" in the dialog boxes. The next dialog box that appears asks you for the site address where you want to publish your list. Instead of a check box asking you to create a read-only connection to the SharePoint list, Excel 2003 displays a check box asking whether you want to link to the new SharePoint list. If you do not select this check box, you cannot synchronize changes between the two lists after the publication process completes. But if you do select it, you can synchronize data in both directions.

If the publication of your Excel 2003 worksheet succeeds, you should see a dialog box similar to the one in Figure 7-21.

Figure 7-21. *Successfully published Excel worksheets display a link to the new list.*

What Happened to Synchronization?

As mentioned at the end of the last section, Microsoft chose to deprecate the ability for Excel to synchronize data with a SharePoint list. While Excel proponents are quick to point out that a large number of Office users feel very comfortable working with Excel spreadsheets and manipulating its data, Access supporters counter that they have a superior development platform that allows for the easy creation of forms and reports that can manipulate data and can appear as SharePoint views when exported back to SharePoint. After carefully considering where to place its efforts, Microsoft made the decision to deprecate synchronization from Excel 2007.

So out of the box, Excel 2007 no longer supports synchronization. However, all is not lost. Another alternative has become available.

Microsoft has published an add-in for Excel 2007 that allows it to synchronize data with the corresponding SharePoint list. The only caveat is that you may first need to save the Excel spreadsheet using the older 2003 format, load the add-in from Microsoft, and then open the spreadsheet again to use the new add-in.

You can currently find this add-in at the following address (note that you should enter it as a single line):

```
http://www.microsoft.com/downloads/details.aspx
?FamilyId=25836E52-1892-4E17-AC08-5DF13CFC5295&displaylang=en
```

or just enter

```
http://tinyurl.com/yvw8g5
```

Hopefully that URL will not change by the time you read this book. However, if it does, you may be able to use your favorite Internet search engine to find the file. The site that this URL takes you to includes full instructions on how to download and install this add-in. Therefore, I will skip going over installation procedures for this add-in. Instead, I will jump to a point after you have installed the add-in to show how you can use it to upload a new table to a new Share-Point list and then maintain the list data from either SharePoint or Excel.

Linking a List in Excel to SharePoint

In this section, I will assume that you have successfully installed the Excel add-in mentioned in the previous section that allows you to synchronize Excel 2007 tables with SharePoint. In fact, I will start with a basic spreadsheet shown in Figure 7-22 that contains some data on America's fleet of space shuttles that NASA has built and flown for the past 30 years.

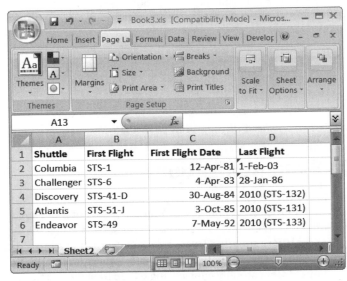

Figure 7-22. *Shuttle list created in Excel 2007 but saved in 2003 format*

As you can see in this figure, the worksheet contains a simple set of data consisting of four columns and five rows. (If you're a space enthusiast who is wondering what happened to the *Enterprise*, note that I'm only including shuttles that have actually flown into space.) But you cannot simply point at a spreadsheet and upload the data from it into a SharePoint list. I suppose this apparent limitation derives from the fact that a worksheet by itself does not have any boundaries. How many rows does it really have? How many columns does it really have? You can resolve these questions by selecting the columns and rows you want to define as a list and then formatting them as a table within Excel 2007. To do this in Excel 2007, follow these steps:

1. Click in one of the corners of the spreadsheet and, while pressing the left mouse button, drag through the cells to the diagonal corner.

2. Click the **Insert** tab of the Ribbon.

3. Select the **Table** option in the **Tables** group of the **Insert** Ribbon.

4. A small dialog box appears allowing you to verify the data range for the table. You can also select whether this data range includes headers as its first row. These headers when present define the names of the columns in the SharePoint list.

When you click **OK**, you have defined a limited area of a worksheet. You can have other data on the spreadsheet that is not part of this table. In fact, you can have several different tables defined on the same worksheet. If you click anywhere within the table you want to publish, a new Ribbon tab appears named **Table Tools Design**. Click this tab to open this Ribbon. The add-in mentioned at the beginning of this section creates a new group named **SharePoint**. This group has a single button labeled **Publish and allow Sync**. Click this button to publish the table you have selected.

Excel opens another dialog box that asks where you want to publish your table. In the **Address** field, enter the URL of the site where you want to publish the data. Then supply a list name in the **Name** field along with a description. These latter two pieces of information help you identify your new list from other lists you may already have in your SharePoint **Lists**. Figure 7-23 shows this first dialog box along with the new SharePoint section of the **Table Tools Design** area in the background.

As before, a second dialog box asks you to confirm the data types that SharePoint uses for each of the table fields. When you proceed, Excel publishes the table to SharePoint, and a dialog box appears at the completion of the process letting you know whether it succeeds. When successful, this dialog box also displays a link to the new SharePoint list. If you click this link, SharePoint displays the new list as shown in Figure 7-24.

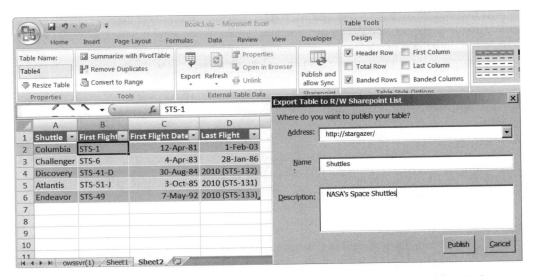

Figure 7-23. *Using Publish and allow Sync to publish Excel 2007 spreadsheets to SharePoint*

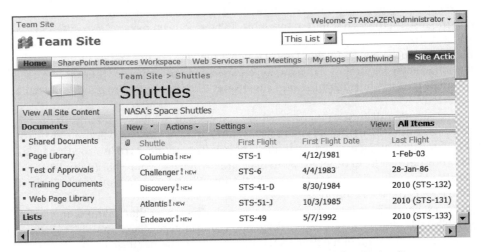

Figure 7-24. *Published Excel spreadsheet table displayed in a SharePoint list*

Now suppose you discover that you have to make a change to the data for one of the shuttles. You can open the Excel spreadsheet of your shuttle information, and find and edit the specific cell. In fact, you can make several changes. But when you are done making changes, you can now synchronize your changes back to the SharePoint list by right-clicking anywhere within the table. This opens the drop-down menu shown in Figure 7-25. Find the **Table** option in this menu. As you hover over this menu option, a submenu flies out to display options specific to tables. Look for and select the option **Synchronize with SharePoint**.

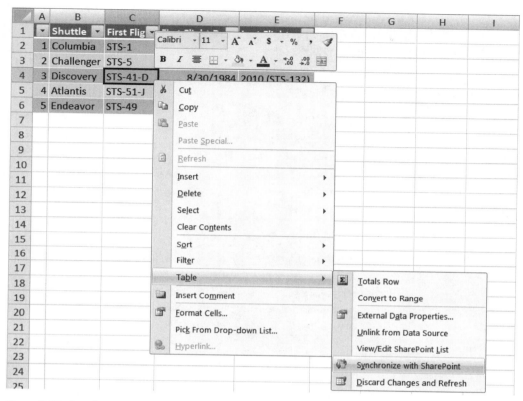

Figure 7-25. *Synchronizing Excel changes with SharePoint*

When you select this option, Excel synchronizes its changes with SharePoint and vice versa. As long as no one tries to edit the same item/row, this process completes after a few seconds. If a conflict does occur, a dialog box appears with both sets of changes, and you can select how you want to resolve the conflict.

■**Note** With this add-in to allow synchronization, you can no longer click the **Refresh** button in the **External Table Data** section of the **Table Tools Design** Ribbon.

If you have been making changes in Excel and decide before you synchronize those changes that you really want to discard them and refresh your spreadsheet with the data from the SharePoint list, you can right-click anywhere within the table and select the **Table** option as shown in Figure 7-26. Then click the **Discard Changes and Refresh** button.

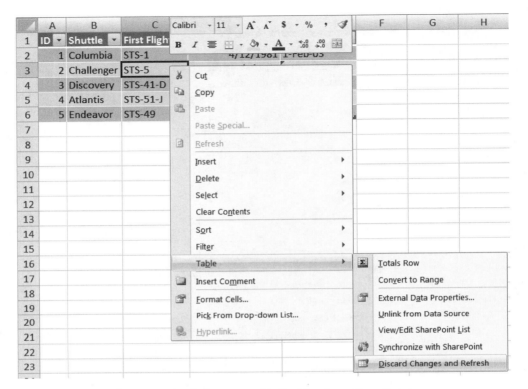

Figure 7-26. *Discarding your Excel changes and refreshing from SharePoint*

This action updates the Excel table with values from the SharePoint list. You cannot select which of your changed Excel values SharePoint will update. Therefore, the dialog box shown in Figure 7-27 reminds you that refreshing your data from the SharePoint list erases any changes you made in the Excel table, preventing you from updating SharePoint with any of them. In other words, unlike synchronizing, this option performs a one-way overwrite of everything in your Excel worksheet using data from the SharePoint list, just like the old **Refresh** button would.

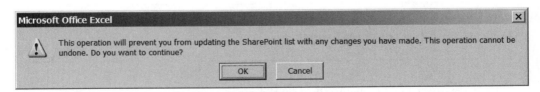

Figure 7-27. *Refresh replaces all Excel data with SharePoint data.*

Summary

In this chapter, you examined the basic collaboration features between SharePoint and Excel 2007. You started by exporting the metadata from a document library to an Excel worksheet. If you include a SharePoint column that also includes a link to the document itself, you can open the document from Excel by clicking the link.

While at first it may seem that the collaboration between these two products works like SharePoint's collaboration with other Office products such as MS Word, you quickly discovered that it actually has at least one serious limitation. While you can export data from SharePoint to Excel, and you can refresh Excel with changes made in SharePoint, you cannot send changes made to the Excel worksheet back to the SharePoint list. The synchronization between these two products only works in one direction.

Taking a look back at Excel 2003, you see that SharePoint did support bidirectional synchronization of changes made on either platform. Fortunately, while Microsoft chose to deprecate bidirectional synchronization between SharePoint and Excel 2007, Microsoft does provide an add-on to Excel that restores this capability. In the last section of this chapter, you saw how to use this add-in with Excel 2007 to synchronize changes between Excel and SharePoint.

Microsoft hopes that users will switch from Excel to Access for manipulating SharePoint lists while also creating additional functionality through forms and reports. However, SharePoint still has a special role for Excel, as you will see in the next chapter. SharePoint combines Excel spreadsheets with a new service called Excel Services that allows the publication of spreadsheets across the Web. It also provides limited functionality to users of these spreadsheets, even for users who do not have Excel on their desktops.

■ ■ ■

CHAPTER 8

Publishing Excel with Excel Services
Why Should I Use Excel Services?

You saw in the last chapter that, by itself, Excel does not bring as much capability to the table of collaboration as Word, Outlook, and Access. With the decision to deprecate synchronization between Excel and SharePoint lists, your initial impression may be that the only value Excel can offer might lie in its ability to help you create lists from other data sources. Perhaps if you can export other data into an Excel format or maybe read it into Excel, you might subsequently export it to a new SharePoint list. Similarly, you might transfer the data from a SharePoint list to an Excel worksheet so that you can save it perhaps as a CSV file that other applications might then import. Not to say that these capabilities do not add value, but for a tool as popular as Excel has become, perhaps you expect more.

The good news is that there is more. The bad news is that to use the features discussed in this chapter, you need to be running MOSS 2007 with Excel Services turned on. You cannot run Excel Services on WSS 3.0 alone. Therefore, if you are fortunate enough to have MOSS 2007, you'll want to read this chapter, which examines how to publish Excel spreadsheets to Share-Point. Then from within SharePoint, not only can you view the data already in the worksheet, but you can also update the data in the worksheet while protecting your format and calculation formulas through the use of parameters. Some of the other benefits of publishing an Excel spreadsheet using SharePoint's Excel Services include the following:

- You can now make your spreadsheet available to anyone who has access to your Share-Point site through a browser. Users with access do not need to have Excel on their desktops.

- You can publish just the parts of your spreadsheet that you want others to see. You can hide your staging data and formulas.

- You can limit viewers' interaction with your spreadsheet to selected cells through the use of parameters.

I will also demonstrate how you can create dashboards with Excel and work with data cubes. Finally, I will close this chapter with a brief look at the Report Center and how it plays with Excel Services, KPIs, and more.

Configuring Excel Services

Typically, the task of configuring Excel Services falls to your SharePoint administrator. However, you may be curious about how to turn Excel Services on just in case you need to go to your SharePoint administrator with additional requests to expand your use of Excel Services to new sites and libraries. Therefore, this section briefly lists the steps required to accomplish this task.

1. First, your SharePoint administrator must open your SharePoint **Central Administration** site.

■Tip On the **Home** screen of **Central Administration**, you can bypass steps 2 through 4 by clicking the link to the farm's shared services found in the **Quick Launch** menu under **Shared Services Administration**.

---

2. There are two main tabbed pages within **Central Administration**, **Operations** and **Application Management**. Open the **Application Management** page.

3. Options on this page appear in groups separated by highlighted section headers. Find the **Office SharePoint Server Shared Services** group.

4. Within this group, click the option **Create or configure this farm's shared services**.

5. Unless your administrator has created a very unusual site, look for the shared service provider (SSP) that has **(Default)** after its name. While the default name may be SharedServices1, your administrator may have renamed it, so just locate the default SSP and click it.

6. On the SSP page, locate the **Excel Services Settings** section and click **Trusted file locations**. Basically, you need to tell SharePoint the location of the library that holds the Excel files so that IIS trusts opening and displaying those files.

7. On the **Excel Services Trusted File Location** page, click **Add Trusted File Location**.

8. On this page, the **Address** section expects the URL of the document library or network folder where you will store the Excel files you plan to access. With whatever address you enter, you must select a location type. If you plan on storing your Excel files in a Share-Point document library, select **Windows SharePoint Services**. If you are using a network folder or a web folder, use the UNC or HTTP options, respectively.

9. You can leave most of the other options on this page on their default settings. However, you should change the setting **Allow External Data** to the option **Trusted data connection libraries only**.

10. Click the **OK** button to complete your definition of the Trusted File Location.

■**Note** If you have different sites that need their own document library for storing Excel files for use with Excel Services, you must repeat the preceding steps, creating a Trusted File Location for each one.

At this point, your administrator has enabled Excel Services for your document library. If you plan to use simple Excel workbooks with self-contained data, you are set to continue. However, if you want to use an Excel workbook that connects to an external data source, first you must create a data connection library. Also, data connection libraries only exist when building sites from MOSS 2007, thus you will also be able to use Excel workbooks that reference external data. I will talk more about working with data connections later in this chapter.

Publishing an Excel Form to Excel Services

Before you publish your spreadsheets to Excel services, you should know that Excel Services supports all the layout and formatting features found in Excel 2007, but only when you save your spreadsheets in XLSX or XLSB format. What the user sees after you publish your spreadsheet visually matches what you designed within Excel. Therefore, do not be afraid to create visually appealing layouts with formatting to emphasize different aspects of your spreadsheet. All of your formatting work translates to Excel Services.

To publish a form to Excel Services, you only need to add it to the document library defined when you activated Excel Services and specified as a Trusted File Location. You can do this from SharePoint by adding a new document to the document library, or you can publish the workbook from within Excel to your SharePoint library. Let's take a look first at simply adding a new document to the document library.

Adding an Excel Workbook to Your Document Library from SharePoint

For this method, suppose you previously created and saved a workbook that calculates the month-by-month interest and principal portion of a loan payment. A portion of this spreadsheet is shown in Figure 8-1.

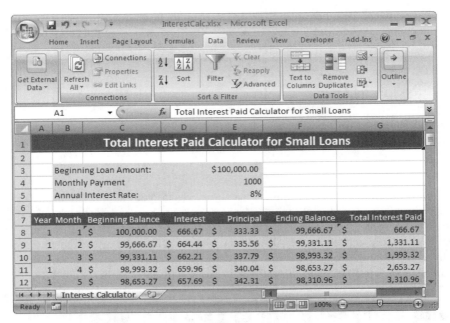

Figure 8-1. *An interest paid calculator built in Excel*

You can begin by opening the document library where you want to store your Excel workbook. For the purpose of this example, suppose you plan to store your Excel workbook in the **Shared Documents** library of a site named **Web Services** within a server named Stargazer. Simply open the library and click the **Upload** option in the library's menu bar.

This option opens the **Upload Document** dialog box you saw earlier in this book in Figure 1-20, which allows you to either locate the file you want to upload by using the **Browse** button or upload multiple files by clicking the **Upload Multiple Files** link. For a single workbook, you could enter the file name by typing it in the **Name** text box, but to ensure that you do not misspell the name, I recommend using the **Browse** button to select the file using the standard Windows **Open File** dialog box.

With the file to upload selected, click the **OK** button to continue. SharePoint now loads the file, and it appears in the **Shared Documents** library looking like any other file. You can now view the file either by directly clicking the file name in the library list, or, if you display the library using the **Standard View**, by positioning your mouse over the file name to display the drop-down menu arrow to the right of the file name and selecting **View in Web Browser**.

■**Caution** Clicking directly on the file name in the library may open the Excel workbook in your web browser or in your local copy of Excel, depending on the setting of the library. To find out how your library has been set up, open **Settings** for your library and choose **Advanced Settings**. Then in the section titled **Browser-enabled Documents**, select the option **Display as a Web page** to open your Excel document within the web browser by default.

When you open the workbook within your browser using Excel Services, it should look similar to Figure 8-2. Note that it looks similar to the workbook opened in Excel.

Web Services > Previous Page					My Site	My Links ▾	
Open ▾	Update ▾	Find			◀ ▷ ▸ · ▲ · ▼ ▾	⊘

	A	B	C	D	E	F	G
1			Total Interest Paid Calculator for Small Loans				
2							
3		Beginning Loan Amount:			$ 100,000.00		
4		Monthly Payment			1000		
5		Annual Interest Rate:			8%		
6							
7	Year	Month	Beginning Balance	Interest	Principal	Ending Balance	Total Interest Paid
8	1	1 $	100,000.00	$ 666.67	$ 333.33	$ 99,666.67	$ 666.67
9	1	2 $	99,666.67	$ 664.44	$ 335.56	$ 99,331.11	$ 1,331.11
10	1	3 $	99,331.11	$ 662.21	$ 337.79	$ 98,993.32	$ 1,993.32
11	1	4 $	98,993.32	$ 659.96	$ 340.04	$ 98,653.27	$ 2,653.27
12	1	5 $	98,653.27	$ 657.69	$ 342.31	$ 98,310.96	$ 3,310.96
13	1	6 $	98,310.96	$ 655.41	$ 344.59	$ 97,966.37	$ 3,966.37
14	1	7 $	97,966.37	$ 653.11	$ 346.89	$ 97,619.48	$ 4,619.48

◀ ▶ ▶ Interest Calculator

Figure 8-2. *The interest paid calculator worksheet displayed using Excel Services*

Navigating Around Your Worksheet

You can scroll through your workbook both horizontally and vertically. Depending on the size of your workbook, you may see the entire content. However, if your workbook has more than 75 rows or 20 columns, you may see only a portion of your workbook.

■Caution Don't panic if you open a large spreadsheet using your browser from a SharePoint library and only part of it appears. This behavior occurs by design to optimize the time needed to render the web page.

Rendering large tables within a web page can seriously and adversely affect performance. Therefore, Excel Services only displays a section of the workbook typically configured to 75 rows by 20 columns to display at a time. However, the balance of the workbook still exists, and you can view it by using the paging controls found at the top right of the browser grid. Figure 8-3 shows these paging controls.

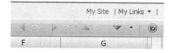

Figure 8-3. *Paging controls to view entire spreadsheet*

SharePoint automatically enables the paging controls when it determines that it can only display a portion of your worksheet at a time. When the controls are enabled, you can click them to move your 75-row by 20-column window on your workbook from one section to the next. By default, these controls move to the next section down, up, right, or left. However, if you open the drop-down menu next to any of the active paging buttons, you can set a different scroll increment from the fixed values shown.

On the top left of the Excel grid, you see three additional sets of options. The first of these options opens a drop-down menu that lets you open a copy of the Excel workbook if you have Excel installed on your local computer.

The second drop-down menu provides several options to refresh selected or all connections in the workbook, recalculate the cells of the workbook, or reload the workbook. Refreshing a connection basically instructs the spreadsheet to read the data from its external data connection, check for new values, and update the spreadsheet appropriately. Recalculating the workbook recalculates cells based on formulas, but does not check if any data in its data source has changed. The reload option updates the file stored in the SharePoint library from its source, retrieving any new values as well as changes to formulas, content, formatting, etc., of the workbook.

The third option set provides the ability to find text strings anywhere within the spreadsheet. For example, you can look for a specific text string representing characters or even numbers in the values of the spreadsheet cells. Unfortunately, you cannot search using Boolean expressions on cell values. Nor can you search within the formulas used to calculate the cells.

You can even navigate between worksheets of your workbook if you have more than one by using the controls in the lower-left corner of the grid. Notice that just like within Excel, you can move to the first, previous, next, or last worksheet in your workbook using the first four controls. You can also click the worksheet tabs in this section to jump directly to any of the worksheets in the workbook.

What you cannot do is directly edit any of the cell values in the grid.

■**Caution** If recalculating the workbook does not appear to update the cells you expect, contact your SharePoint administrator to find out whether the field **Type of Toolbar** is set to **None** or **Navigate only**. Another possible setting to check is the **Calculate Workbook** setting.

Why You Need Parameters to Make Your Excel Form Interactive

Providing a static spreadsheet for users to view in the browser may have its place, but overall, most users want to change data in a spreadsheet, re-sort the data, or even filter the data to better serve their needs. After all, spreadsheets are all about what-if analysis and making business decisions after evaluating data.

While you cannot provide total access to all the features users might normally use directly within Excel, you can at least provide users with the option to change values associated with specific cells while viewing the spreadsheet. Besides, if they really need to have total control over the design of the spreadsheet and change the formatting, structure, or even the formulas used by the spreadsheet, they can always click the **Open in Excel** option mentioned earlier and work with the spreadsheet using their desktop copy of Excel. Just be sure to limit their permissions so they cannot save changes back to the library that potentially change the functionality of your workbook.

When you define parameters for your Excel worksheet, users can enter values for each of the parameters and then recalculate the worksheet the same as if they entered the values directly in the spreadsheet. Basically, a parameter defines an input value that updates a named cell, which in turn updates all dependent cells. In the next section, you will see how to define parameters that allow users to "update" the browser view of the spreadsheet.

Defining Parameters for Your Excel Form

When you decide to publish a spreadsheet with Excel Services, you must decide which field(s) users would most likely need to manipulate. If you begin with the example of the simple interest calculation program mentioned earlier, you can quickly determine that the user only needs to vary three values:

- The initial loan amount

- The loan interest rate

- The monthly payment

With these three pieces of information, you can calculate each month's payment, determining the portion that pays the interest due and the amount used to reduce the loan's principal amount. You can then create a running total of these two numbers to display by month the amount in interest you paid to the bank for the privilege of borrowing the money and the remaining amount due on the loan. It then makes sense to define one row in the table for each month, with the columns representing the various calculated sums. In fact, once you have designed the formulas that you need to calculate for the first month, you can copy them for any number of months.

In the sample spreadsheet created for the examples in this chapter, I stopped the calculations after 10 years for the loan. But that does not mean that it will take 10 years to pay off the loan or that you will necessarily pay off the loan on the last month of the tenth year. In working with loans, you really need four pieces of information: the three specified previously and the length of the loan. You can specify any three, but you cannot force the fourth to a specific value without calculating it. A different example would be to create a spreadsheet in which you start with an initial loan amount, an interest rate, and a fixed number of months to pay off the loan, and then calculate the amount of the monthly payment you need to make given the other three constraints. This latter example illustrates how a bank determines your monthly mortgage payment amount when you buy a house for $200,000 with a 30-year 6% annual interest rate loan. By adding a few more rows to the interest calculator used here, you could see how much sooner you could pay off your loan by making an extra $200-a-month payment and how that reduces the total amount of money you ultimately pay to the bank.

To create a parameter, you need to create a named range, or in this case a named cell. To do that, click the cell you want such as the **Beginning Loan Amount** from Figure 8-1. Then simply go to the **Name Box** to the left and immediately above the column headers of the grid. By default, the **Name Box** currently displays the cell name. When you click in the **Name Box**, the cell reference should become selected. You can simply type the name you want to give to the cell, replacing the cell reference. For example, after clicking in the loan amount cell (E3), you might enter the name **LoanAmt**.

You can repeat this process for each cell you want to define with a name. In fact, you can name any cell or cell range and then use those names in your formulas rather than the cell reference. This technique makes returning to your spreadsheet months later and attempting to figure out what your formulas mean a lot easier. Just because you named a cell or a cell range does not mean that it will become a parameter for your spreadsheet. However, to become a parameter, you must begin with a named cell.

Note As you will see later, you can create named cell ranges that you can then use in the Excel web part SharePoint provides to display a portion of a spreadsheet.

Another way to define the name for the cell begins again by selecting the cell or cell range you want to use. Then open the **Formulas** Ribbon. In the **Defined Names** group, select the button **Define Name**. A dialog box appears, shown in Figure 8-4, that lets you define a name. Names can consist of up to 255 characters. However, like any object name, you want to use only as many characters as necessary to clearly and uniquely identify the object. A name must begin with a letter, underscore, or backslash. Excel treats the name **Interest** the same as **interest**, so don't try to differentiate cell names merely on the basis of case. You cannot name a cell the same as another cell reference. You cannot include spaces in a name. However, using an underscore in place of a space makes the name just as readable.

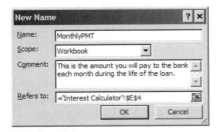

Figure 8-4. *Naming a cell or cell range*

Next in the dialog box, select a scope. By default, Excel assumes the entire workbook as the scope of the name. However, you can limit the name's scope to just the current worksheet.

The third item in the dialog box lets you document the cell by adding a comment. While adding a comment to a name might define why the cell or range was important enough to name, this information does not appear anywhere when working on the spreadsheet itself. You can, however, see your comments when you open the **Name Manager** dialog box, also found in the **Defined Names** group of the **Formulas** Ribbon.

The last option identifies the cell or cell range that the name references. You can change this value either by entering the cell or range reference manually or by clicking the button to the right of this field, which lets you select the cell or range by clicking and dragging (if you want to define a range) through the cells you want to reference. When you finish, click **OK** to create the name.

If you forget what names you have already used or which cell or cell range they apply to, you can view a dialog box that shows all the defined names within the current workbook by clicking the **Name Manager** button. Figure 8-5 shows an example of the **Name Manager**.

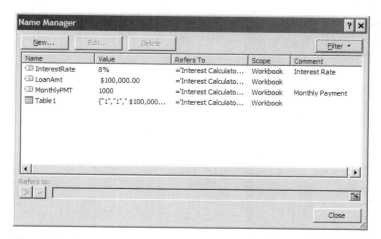

Figure 8-5. *The Name Manager shows all named cells and ranges.*

You can also use the **Name Manager** to edit properties of a name or delete a name. You can even create a new name definition by clicking the **New** button.

Ideally, you should define named cells that you want to use as parameters before you begin creating your spreadsheet. A good practice groups these parameter cells in a single place, perhaps at the top of the spreadsheet as shown in this example, or on a different worksheet dedicated to only prompting for parameters. Then as you lay out the rest of your spreadsheet, you can reference the named cells and named cell ranges in your formulas rather than using cryptic cell references.

Publishing Your Excel Workbook

Once you have finished building your spreadsheet, first save the spreadsheet before you begin the steps to publish it to SharePoint. You can choose from two different ways to publish your spreadsheet. You already saw one way earlier in this chapter: you can simply open the library where you want to publish your Excel files and upload the file to the library.

But you can also publish the workbook from within Excel itself. Open the **Windows** menu in Excel and position your mouse over **Publish** to display the publishing options. Figure 8-6 shows this menu, which resembles the menu you saw when publishing documents from Microsoft Word.

In the main **Save As** dialog box, click **My Network Places** along the left side. If you previously published a document to the library where you want to save the Excel spreadsheet, you probably will find a reference to the library here. If so, double-click it to select and open the library. If you have folders already set up for different types of files, open the folder by double-clicking it also. When you reach the folder where you want to save your file, enter a file name that you want to use. By default, Excel assumes that the SharePoint file name will match the name of the file on your local file system if you previously saved the file locally. Also make sure that you save the file as an Excel workbook (*.xlsx) type file.

Figure 8-6. *Publishing the Excel worksheet to Excel Services*

If you have not previously saved anything to the document library where you want to save the workbook, you must enter the URL of the library directly into the **File Name** box. Figure 8-7 shows an example of entering the URL. Notice that when you enter the URL, you must include the server name, as well as all folders up to and including the name of the library where you want to save the file.

■**Tip** How do you know the URL you need to enter? Simple. Open SharePoint and navigate to the document library where you want to save your workbook. With the library open, capture the URL from the **Address** bar at the top of your browser. This URL contains some additional information at the end to display the contents of the library. Therefore, you can remove anything after the name of the library itself, but leave the last slash at the end of the URL so that Excel knows that you have only defined a directory, not a file.

After you select the library name from your **Network Places** or have manually entered the URL for the library, press the Enter key. This displays the contents of the library. Again, navigate through any subfolders if necessary to open the folder where you want to save the workbook.

With the folder selected, you could save the spreadsheet at this point by entering a file name and clicking the **Save** button. However, you would only wind up with a noneditable spreadsheet again, just as if you had used the upload option from within SharePoint. Instead, click the **Excel Services Options** button at the bottom of the **Save As** window before uploading the file. This button opens the **Excel Services Options** dialog box shown in Figure 8-8.

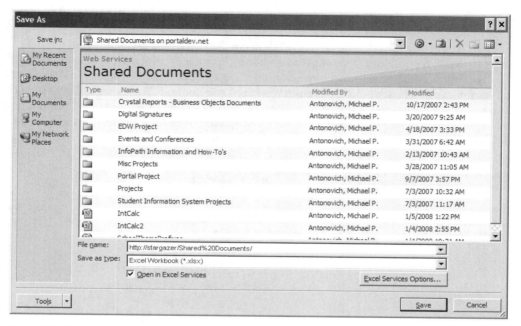

Figure 8-7. *Entering the URL of the document library in SharePoint where you want to publish the workbook*

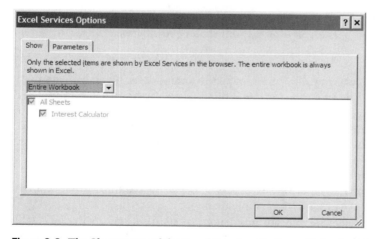

Figure 8-8. *The Show page of the Excel Services Options dialog box determines what users see.*

This dialog box consists of two pages. The first page lets you define what parts of the workbook you want to display. By default, the entire workbook, with all its worksheets and items, will display. Therefore, there are no additional options to select in the selection area beneath the drop-down list that displays the text **Entire Workbook**.

If you only want to display selected worksheets from the workbook, open the drop-down menu and select **Sheets**. This option displays each worksheet in the workbook with a check box before it. Remove the check from the check box for sheets you do not want to publish from the document. You can select individual worksheets, or you can return back to the **All Sheets** option to automatically select them all.

A third option in the drop-down named **Items in the Workbook** lists tables and named ranges in the workbook. Thus, you can limit publication to a section of a worksheet defined by a specific table or a named cell range and ignore anything else that might appear in the workbook.

For this example, leave the option **Entire Workbook** selected and click the second tab, named **Parameters**. Excel does not assume any of the named cells should be parameters. Thus the parameter list begins empty as shown in Figure 8-9, and you must click the **Add** button to begin adding named cells that you want to use as parameters to the list.

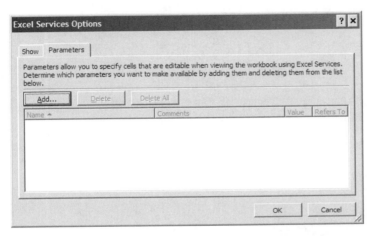

Figure 8-9. *The Parameters page of Excel Services Options shows which named ranges to treat as parameters.*

When you click the **Add** button, you see a list of all the named cells. If you have named ranges or named tables, these do not appear. Only individual cells can serve as parameters. Thus, if you have 20 cells that you want to let users update when they interact with your spreadsheet online, you need to have 20 separate named cells. You cannot simply create a single named range and use it as your parameter. I know that this would make your development life easier. In fact, in some cases, it may even make sense when the values form a series. However, the parameter feature does not support that capability at this time.

On the other hand, as shown in Figure 8-10, you can select all the parameters you want to add at one time. You do not have to select them individually.

Now click **OK** to save the **Excel Service Options** dialog box settings, and finally you can click **Save** to publish your workbook. Once you have published your workbook, you can open it in your browser by going to the SharePoint library, locating the workbook file, right-clicking the file to open the drop-down menu, and selecting the option **View in Web Browser**. After the few moments it takes Excel Services to open the workbook and format the web page, you should see a page that looks like Figure 8-11.

Notice that, unlike the first time when you uploaded an uneditable version of the spreadsheet, this time you get a panel on the right side that displays the parameters that you defined. If you want to change any of the parameters, simply enter the new values you want to use in the text boxes to the right of the parameter names. You do not have to enter all the parameters. You only need to enter the parameters that you want to change from their current value.

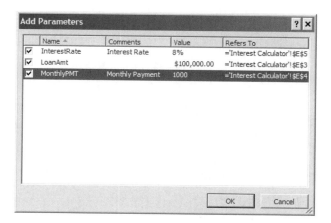

Figure 8-10. *Selecting the named ranges you want to use as parameters*

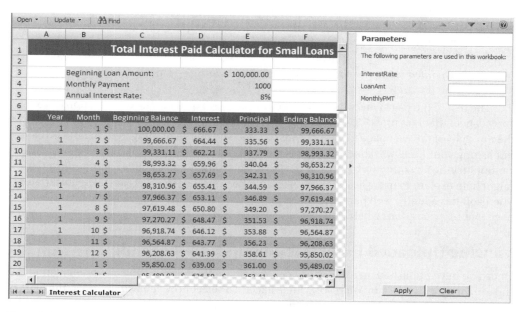

Figure 8-11. *Initial values for the interest paid calculator*

■**Tip** If you do not include the cells referenced by your parameters in a visible part of the spreadsheet, you will not easily know which parameters changed. Therefore, be sure to include them in your displayed range.

Then click the **Apply** button at the bottom of the **Parameters** panel to recalculate the spreadsheet using your new parameter values. Figure 8-12 shows an updated screen image after changing the monthly payment amount from $1,000 to $1,400.

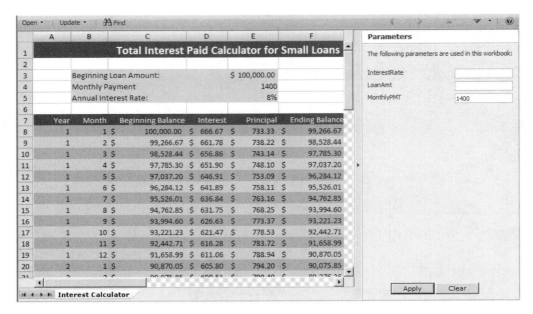

Figure 8-12. *Updated values for the interest paid calculator using parameter values*

The rest of the page works the same as noted earlier. You still see only a section of your spreadsheet that is at most 75 rows long by 20 columns wide. You can use the page controls at the top right of the web page to view other sections. The one remaining item to note is that by publishing your Excel workbook using this method, you use an entire page to display it. You cannot include any other web parts on the page. You cannot add a header or other text that might help explain to users how to use the parameters for the Excel spreadsheet. Fortunately, Microsoft has added a web part that allows you to include an Excel spreadsheet on any web page that has web zones where you can add web parts.

Viewing Uploaded Excel Documents

Once you have published an Excel workbook to a SharePoint library, you can open it either in the web browser itself or in Microsoft Office Excel. To select how you want to open the workbook, open the workbook's drop-down menu as shown in Figure 8-13.

Users who have Microsoft Office Excel installed on their local machines can gain access to the full functionality of the spreadsheet by opening the Excel document in Edit mode. When opened this way, users can edit any cells within the spreadsheet, not just the cells identified as parameters. They can also make changes to the spreadsheet. If those users also have the necessary permission to write files back to the library, they can then save those changes back to the document in the document library. You can control this ability through the option **Permissions for this document library** under the **Permissions and Management** section of the library's **Settings**.

Also under **Settings**, select **Advanced Settings** and change the option for **Browser-enabled Documents** to **Display as a Web page**. Then if the user simply clicks the document from the library, it will open by default in their browser rather than in their local copy of Excel.

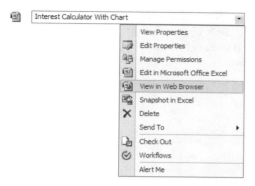

Interest Calculator With Chart

View Properties
Edit Properties
Manage Permissions
Edit in Microsoft Office Excel
View in Web Browser
Snapshot in Excel
Delete
Send To ▶
Check Out
Workflows
Alert Me

Figure 8-13. *To view an Excel document, open the document drop-down menu.*

Using the Excel Page Web Part

Viewing an Excel workbook from a SharePoint library either in the browser using Excel Services or by downloading and opening it in a local copy of Microsoft Excel provides a quick way to view the spreadsheet. However, it does not let you include the workbook with other SharePoint features. Fortunately, SharePoint provides a web part that allows you to include an Excel workbook or portion of a worksheet inside any web page.

Suppose you start with a simple web page such as the one shown in Figure 8-14. In this page, you want to add an Excel spreadsheet to the Left web part zone to display the interest paid calculator created in the last section.

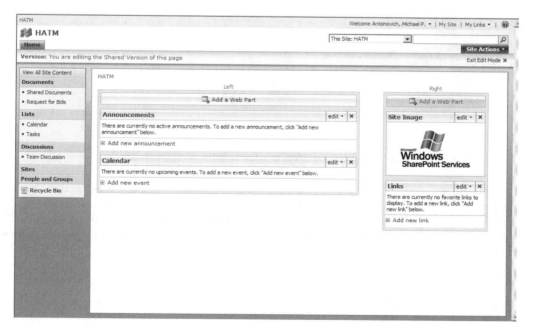

Figure 8-14. *Beginning with a basic web page with two web part zones*

This page has two web part zones. By clicking the header on either zone, you can add web parts from the list of available web parts shown in Figure 8-15. Scroll through this list to find the **Business Data** section. In this section, find the web part **Excel Web Access**. Select this web part and click the **Add** button at the bottom of the window.

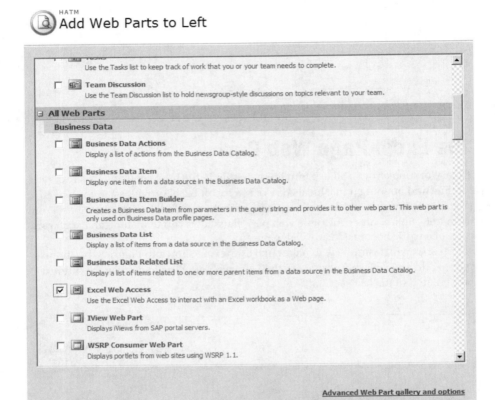

Figure 8-15. *Adding a web part from the available parts list*

You will now see a new web part at the top of the Left zone titled **Excel Web Access**. The initial contents of this web part tells you that you must select a workbook for the web part to display by opening the tool pane for the web part. Do this by opening the **Edit** drop-down menu and selecting **Modify Shared Web Part**. You can also simply click the link in the web part: **Click here to open the tool pane.**

When the tool pane opens, as shown in Figure 8-16, in the first text box after the label **Workbook**, enter the URL of the workbook from the library where you published it. If you do not remember the name or if you want to make sure that you get the path correct, click the button with the ellipses to the right of the text box.

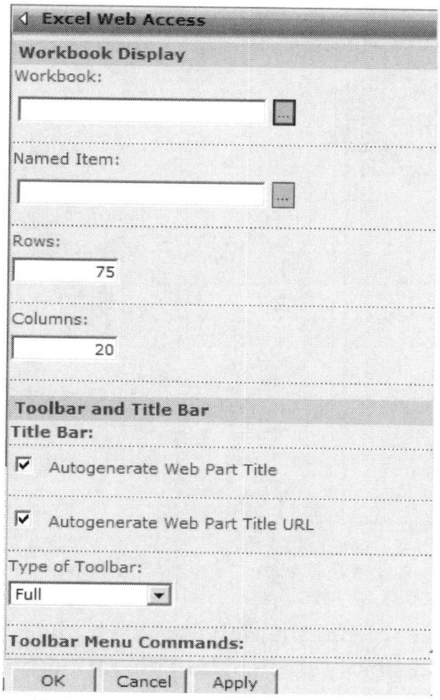

Figure 8-16. *Defining the properties of the Excel Web Access web part.*

Clicking the ellipses button for the URL displays the **Select a Link** dialog box shown in Figure 8-17. Use this dialog box to navigate the folders of your SharePoint site to locate the folder containing the spreadsheet you want to display. When you find it, double-click it, or click it once and then click the **OK** button at the bottom of the dialog box to place the URL in the **Workbook** text field.

Under **Named Item** in the tool pane, you can also choose a specific named item from the workbook to display. When you do this, only that named area appears within the web part when you display it. This feature eliminates the user's ability to move around the workbook to other areas on the worksheet or to different worksheets. You create a named item just like creating named cells for parameters in an earlier section of this chapter. While in Excel, select the range of cells you want to treat as a single object for display purposes and give it a name. Then when you add the workbook to the web part, use the **Named Item** field to select the named range. Unlike the **Workbook** field, which lets you search for the workbook, the named item field does not provide you with an easy list to select from available named ranges in the current workbook.

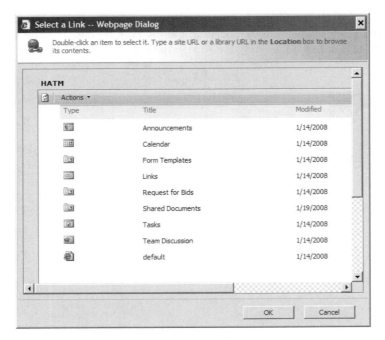

Figure 8-17. *Navigating to your workbook*

By default, the Excel web part automatically generates a title for the web part. To replace this title with your own title, you might think that you could simply change the **Title** property in the **Appearance** section of the tool pane. After all, this technique works for many other web parts. However, it will not work here unless you also uncheck the option **Autogenerate Web Part Title** in the top section as well. If you do not uncheck this option, the web part continues to autogenerate its title, overwriting the changes you make to the **Title** field when you attempt to apply your changes.

As you saw before, SharePoint always adds web parts to the top of the web part zone. However, you can click the web part's header and drag it to a different position in the zone or even to a different zone.

■**Caution** Always turn off the **Close** option in the **Appearance** section of a web part if you do not want users to accidently remove web parts from the page.

Figure 8-18 shows an example of how you might include a web part in the middle of a web page while including other web parts around it. In this case, above the Excel web part, you add the **Content Editor** web part, which describes the Excel web part and explains its use.

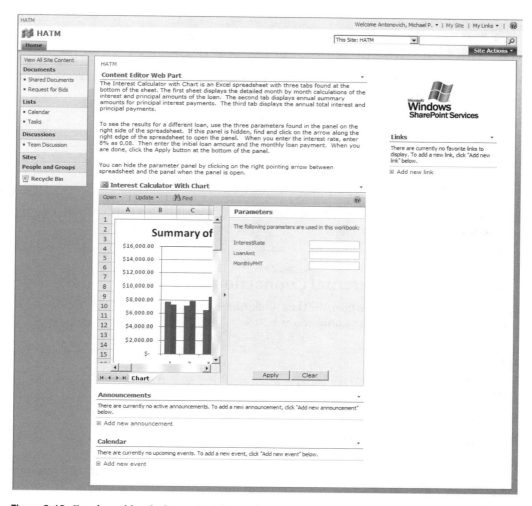

Figure 8-18. *Excel workbook shown inside a web part*

Viewing Data from External Sources in Excel Using a Data Connection

In all the Excel examples so far, the data for the cells have been entered directly into the cells of the worksheets. However, you can create Excel worksheets to display and manipulate data from external data sources. By external data sources, I am primarily referring to the use of databases such as Access and SQL Server. However, you can connect to many other data sources as well.

For this section, let's use the PUBS database for SQL Server 2005.

■**Tip** If you have Visual Studio, you can create the PUBS database for SQL Server 2005 from `C:\Program Files\Microsoft Visual Studio 8\SDK\v2.0\Samples\Setup\InstPubs.sql`.

If you do not have Visual Studio, you can also download PUBS for SQL Server 2000 from Microsoft's Download Center at the following site (be sure to enter the URL as one line):

`http://www.microsoft.com/downloads/details.aspx?`
`FamilyID=06616212-0356-46A0-8DA2-EEBC53A68034&displaylang=en`

or simply enter

`http://tinyurl.com/yzx6lz`

If you start with the original SQL 2000 PUBS database, you can still use it, but you may need to set the compatibility level using the Tipcommand `EXEC sp_dbcmptlevel 'Pubs','90'`.

How to Create an External Connection

Start a new Excel workbook and open the **Data** Ribbon as shown in Figure 8-19. In the **Connections** section of this ribbon, click the **Connections** button.

Figure 8-19. *Beginning a connection definition*

This button opens the **Workbook Connections** dialog box, which shows any connections currently defined for the workbook. As seen in Figure 8-20, this dialog box initially has no defined connections for a new workbook.

To create a connection, click the **Add** button. This action first displays a list of all existing connections within your workbook, your computer, and your network. Figure 8-21 shows the existing **Data Connections** dialog box. If a connection already exists on your network or on your computer that you can use, you can save time by reusing it. Let's assume that none of the existing connection definitions point to the databases and tables that you want.

When you click the **Browse for More** button, the **Select Data Source** dialog box appears. In addition to displaying the same connections seen in the **Existing Connections** dialog box, you also have what looks like two folders called

- **Connect to New Data Source.odc**

- **New SQL Server Connection.odc**

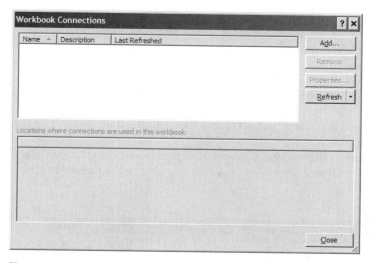

Figure 8-20. *Initially, the workbook displays no connections.*

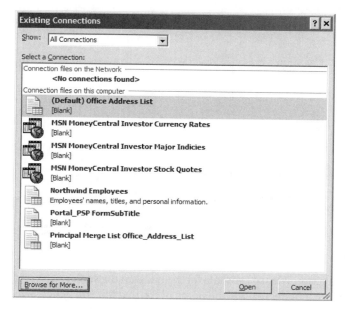

Figure 8-21. *Select from existing connections or browse for more.*

If you double-click either of these, they open additional dialog boxes to let you define a new connection. While it is possible to create a data connection from the **Connect to New Data Source.odc** option, I recommend using the **New SQL Server Connection.odc** option directly if your data resides in a SQL Server database. You can use the **Connect to New Data Source.odc** option when creating a connection to non-SQL Server data sources. For example, you can create ODBC data connections to many applications including Crystal Reports, dBase, and Access. However, you should use OLE DB connections whenever available for your data source. Therefore, check the **Other/Advanced** option in the **Data Connection Wizard** first to see whether you have access to an OLE DB driver. For example, here you will find the latest data link driver for Microsoft Access called **Microsoft Office 12.0 Access Database Engine OLE DB Provider**. There are also OLE DB providers for SQL, Analysis Services, OLAP Services, Oracle, and more. If you do not see the provider you need in this list, contact your system administrator to see if he can locate and install a driver that you can use.

Choosing the **New SQL Server Connection.odc** option, shown in Figure 8-22, takes you directly to the **Data Connection Wizard** where you can enter the information needed to create a connection to SQL Server.

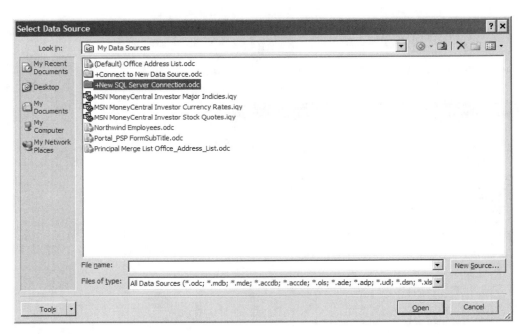

Figure 8-22. *Creating a new SQL Server connection*

The first page of the **Data Connection Wizard** prompts for the name of the server you want to access. This is the SQL Server name, not necessarily the name of the machine on which SQL Server runs, although they are often the same. You can enter the server name as localhost when creating the connection from the machine on which SQL Server runs. However, you cannot use these connections from other machines, because localhost will not resolve to the correct server. Therefore, always enter the name of the server.

You can supply credentials to SQL Server either by using your Windows Authentication information or by supplying a specific user name and password. Using Windows Authentication generally provides a more secure method of defining your connection, since you do not include your user name and password in the connection information, and unencrypted user names and passwords do not get sent across the network by the operating system. Figure 8-23 shows the dialog box that prompts for your server information.

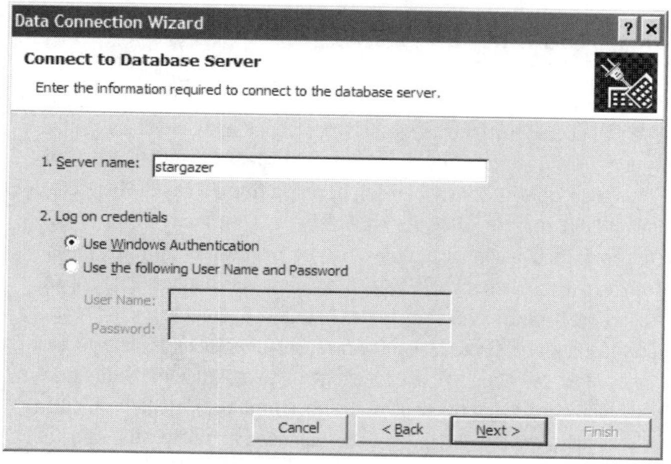

Figure 8-23. *Selecting the database server*

When you click the **Next** button, the **Data Connection Wizard** contacts the server you specified and uses the logon credentials you indicated. If it succeeds in connecting to the server, it returns in the next page with information asking you to which database, table, or cube you want to connect.

The first prompt uses a drop-down list to display all the databases on the referenced server. It initially selects the default database for the server. However, opening the drop-down list, you can select any of the databases on the server.

Once you have selected a database, you can select the specific table, view, or cube you want to use. Figure 8-24 shows that after selecting the PUBS database, I select a view named **AuthorRoyalty**. Because you can only select a single table for a connection to an Excel worksheet, you may find that views provide the only way to access fields from multiple tables, especially in a normalized database where you want to display descriptive text for users to read, rather than ID values that serve as pointers back to their parent tables.

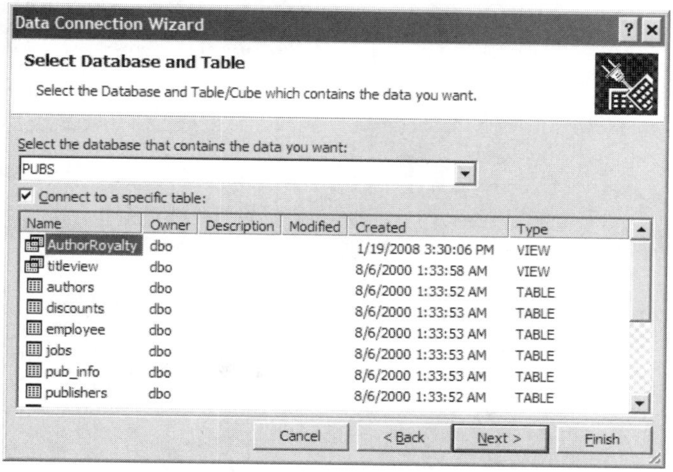

Figure 8-24. *Selecting the table or view*

THE AUTHORROYALTY VIEW

Here I'll give you a closer look at the **AuthorRoyalty** view, in case you want to try re-creating it on your machine. I created a view in the PUBS database so that I could retrieve the sales for each book and then calculate the sales for the book along with the royalty due to each author. This information spans five different tables within PUBS beginning with the **Sales** table. The **Sales** table identifies the book by only a **title_id** value. Therefore, I have to link this ID to the **title_id** value in the **Titles** table. Then the **Titles** table forms a many-to-many relationship with the **Authors** table. Therefore, you need a connecting table named **TitleAuthor** between these two tables to create two one-to-many relationships. Then if you also want to know which states sold books, you need to link the **Sales** table to the **Stores** table using the **stor_id** field found in both tables.

Next, you need to look at the fields you want in the spreadsheet and see whether those fields exist as individual fields in the tables selected or whether you need to calculate some of them. While the **Sales** table provides the quantity of books sold by title, you need to get the price of the book from the **Title** table to calculate the value of the books sold. Similarly, to calculate the author's royalty, you need to multiply the value of the books sold by the author's royalty percentage, which can be found only in the **Authors** table.

Thus the definition for the view can be written out as follows:

```
USE [PUBS]
GO
/****** Object:  View [dbo].[AuthorRoyalty]
*******Script Date: 01/20/2008 13:39:41 ******/
SET ANSI_NULLS ON
GO
SET QUOTED_IDENTIFIER ON
GO
CREATE VIEW [dbo].[AuthorRoyalty]
AS
SELECT stores.stor_name
     , stores.state
     , sales.ord_date
     , sales.qty
     , titles.title
     , titles.type
     , titles.price
     , titles.royalty
     , authors.au_lname
     , authors.au_fname
     , sales.qty * titles.price AS Amount
     , sales.qty * titles.price * titles.royalty / 100 AS AuthorRoyalty
  FROM dbo.sales INNER JOIN
       dbo.stores ON sales.stor_id = stores.stor_id INNER JOIN
       dbo.titles ON sales.title_id = titles.title_id INNER JOIN
       dbo.titleauthor ON titles.title_id = titleauthor.title_id INNER JOIN
       dbo.authors ON authors.au_id = titleauthor.au_id

GO
```

Once created, you can access views from a database, in most cases using the same methods as you would to access a table. If you need a special view for your Excel table and do not feel comfortable defining the view yourself, contact your database administrator for further assistance.

After you have selected the table or view you want to use in the connection, the next page of the wizard prompts you for a file name for the data connection. As with most files, you should choose a file name long enough to fully describe the content or purpose of the file, while trying to keep the name as short as possible. One advantage data connection files have that most other files do not have is a *friendly name*. The friendly name appears in dialog boxes such as the **Workbook Connections** and the **Existing Connections** dialog boxes, making it easier to identify which connection file you want to use. Figure 8-25 shows the final page of the **Data Connection Wizard**.

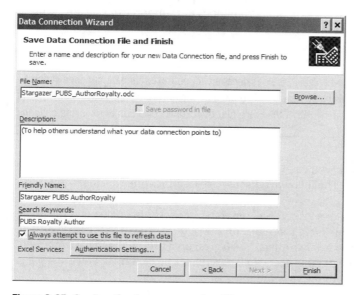

Figure 8-25. *Saving the data connection file*

Click the **Finish** button after finishing this last page of the **Data Connection Wizard**. You then return to the **Workbook Connections** dialog box, where you see the name of the new connection listed. Click the **Close** button on this dialog box.

Importing the SharePoint List to a Workbook

You should now see the **Existing Connections** dialog box again. If you do not, open the **Existing Connections** dialog box from the **Data** Ribbon. You can find it in the **Get External Data** group. Click the connection you just created followed by the **Open** button. You now can import the data from your external connection into Excel. But first you must choose how you want to view the data, selecting from the options **Table**, **PivotTable Report**, and **PivotChart and PivotTable Report**. Figure 8-26 shows the **Import Data** dialog box.

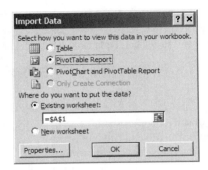

Figure 8-26. *Placing data in a PivotTable Report*

Your first inclination might be to select **Table** because you want to view the columns and rows of the data. However, Excel Services in SharePoint does not support external data ranges. Fortunately, it does support pivot tables.

■**Note** The technical details behind why Excel Services does not support external data but does support pivot tables are beyond the scope of this book. However, in general terms, the difference lies in the way pivot tables organize and sort data as a hierarchy rather than as a two-directional collection of rows and columns.

Fortunately, with a little work, you can make most pivot tables look similar to the original tables or views they started from. The following discussion describes one way to reformat the pivot table.

After exporting the view data to a PivotTable Report, your Excel screen displays the pivot table on the left and the **PivotTable Field List** panel on the right, as shown in Figure 8-27. The **PivotTable Field List** panel consists of five areas. The largest area lists all the fields from the table or view used to create the pivot table. Each field has a check box before it. You must select each field that you want to use from the view or table.

If you simply go down the list of fields, selecting them in the order displayed, the pivot table assumes that you want to create a hierarchy with the fields in that order. If you select the fields in a different order, the hierarchy that Excel builds will change accordingly.

For example, if you select **Title** before **State** or book **Type**, Excel will assume that you want to display different states within each book title and different book types within each state. Depending on the author, this could mean that while the pivot table lists each book separately, two books classified as Business may be separated by a book classified as Fiction just because you defined the book's **Title** higher on the hierarchy.

On the other hand, if you select the **Type** field before selecting the book's **Title**, all books of the same type for an author will appear together. Similar arguments would determine whether you wanted to see all the books written by each author or if you preferred to group all books of a specific type regardless of the author. This hierarchical approach to the data distinguishes pivot tables from regular tables.

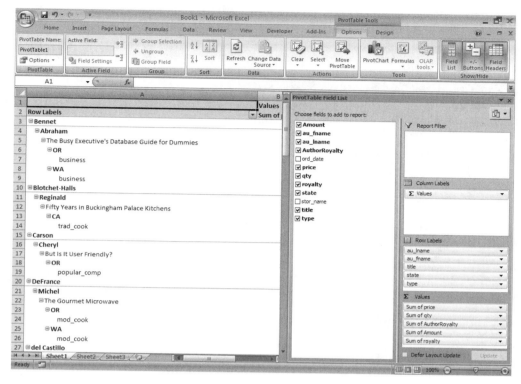

Figure 8-27. *Default layout of data in a pivot table*

If you decide that you want to create a different hierarchy after you have selected the fields, you don't have to start over again. Simply find the field in either the **Row Labels** or **Values** box and click it to display the drop-down field menu. Options in the menu allow you to move the field up or down in the list, or even directly to the top or bottom. You can also move fields between the other three areas or remove fields from display entirely.

As to the different areas where pivot tables place fields by default, Excel assigns label and date type fields to the **Row Labels** bin. It then assigns numeric type data automatically to the **Values** bin and assumes that you want to sum the values here. This may not be what you want. You can move all the fields from the **Values** bin to the **Row Labels** bin. In all cases, be aware of any implied hierarchy in the order of the fields in the **Row Labels** area.

Formatting a Pivot Table to Look Like a Worksheet

When you have the fields you want to display selected and in the order you want, you can begin formatting the pivot table so it looks like a spreadsheet. Begin by selecting the **PivotTable Tools Options** Ribbon. Then from the **PivotTable** section, click **Options**. The **PivotTable Options** dialog box, shown in Figure 8-28, consists of five tabs. Select the tab **Layout and Format** if it does not appear by default. On this page, locate the following two options and check them if necessary:

- **Autofit column widths on update**

- **Preserve cell formatting on update**

Then click the **Data** tab and set the drop-down value in the last option to **None** for the property **Number of Items to retain per field**. You generally should not retain items deleted from the data source without a good reason.

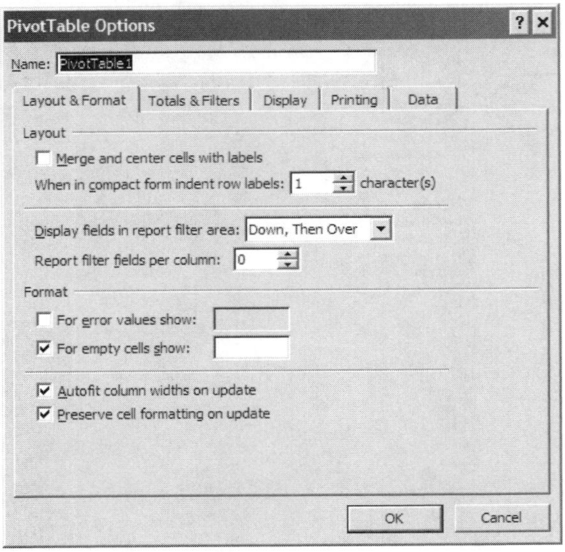

Figure 8-28. *Setting the pivot table options*

Also on the **Options** Ribbon, the **Show/Hide** group on the right allows you to turn the field list on or off, hide or show the expand/collapse buttons associated with each unique group value, and hide or show the field headers. Typically, I prefer to hide the field headers because they display the original field names from the table or view. Unless you created meaningful alias names for all the fields, these names may be somewhat cryptic. Therefore, rather than display these names to the user, I hide the headers, and then insert another row at the top of the pivot table and enter my own column headers there.

Next, open the **PivotTable Tools Design** Ribbon and locate the **Layout** group. In the major buttons of this group, make the following changes:

In **Subtotals**, select the option **Do Not Show Subtotals**, unless you want to create subtotals for groups.

In **Grand Totals**, select **Off for Rows and Columns**, unless you want grand totals for columns, in which case select **On for Columns Only**.

In **Report Layout**, select **Show in Tabular Form** to create the appearance of a normal column and row table.

On this Ribbon, you can also select a pivot table style if you prefer. When you choose a pivot table style, you can use the **PivotTable Style Options** group to determine whether special formatting should apply to headers and whether to apply row or column banding to make the table more readable.

After making all of these changes, your pivot table should look similar to Figure 8-29.

	First Name	Last Name	Book Type	Book Name	State	Quantity	Book Price	Revenue	Royalty %	Royalty Amount	K	L
1	First Name	Last Name	Book Type	Book Name	State	Quantity	Book Price	Revenue	Royalty %	Royalty Amount		
2	Abraham	Bennet	business	The Busy Executive's Database Guide	OR	10	19.99	199.9	10	19.99		
3					WA	5	19.99	99.95	10	9.995		
4	Akiko	Yokomoto	trad_cook	Sushi, Anyone?	CA	20	14.99	299.8	10	29.98		
5	Albert	Ringer	psychology	Is Anger the Enemy?	CA	10	10.95	109.5	12	13.14		
6						75	10.95	821.25	12	98.55		
7					WA	3	10.95	32.85	12	3.942		
8						20	10.95	219	12	26.28		
9				Life Without Fear	WA	25	7	175	10	17.5		
10	Ann	Dull	popular_comp	Secrets of Silicon Valley	CA	50	20	1000	10	100		
11	Anne	Ringer	mod_cook	The Gourmet Microwave	OR	15	2.99	44.85	24	10.764		
12					WA	25	2.99	74.75	24	17.94		
13			psychology	Is Anger the Enemy?	CA	10	10.95	109.5	12	13.14		
14						75	10.95	821.25	12	98.55		
15					WA	3	10.95	32.85	12	3.942		
16						20	10.95	219	12	26.28		
17	Burt	Gringlesby	trad_cook	Sushi, Anyone?	CA	20	14.99	299.8	10	29.98		
18	Charlene	Locksley	psychology	Emotional Security: A New Algorithm	WA	25	7.99	199.75	10	19.975		
19	Cheryl	Carson	popular_comp	But Is It User Friendly?	OR	30	22.95	688.5	16	110.16		
20	Dean	Straight	business	Straight Talk About Computers	CA	15	19.99	299.85	10	29.985		
21	Innes	del Castillo	mod_cook	Silicon Valley Gastronomic Treats	CA	10	19.99	199.9	12	23.988		
22	Johnson	White	psychology	Prolonged Data Deprivation: Four Cas	WA	15	19.99	299.85	10	29.985		
23	Livia	Karsen	psychology	Computer Phobic AND Non-Phobic In	WA	20	21.59	431.8	10	43.18		
24	Marjorie	Green	business	The Busy Executive's Database Guide	OR	10	19.99	199.9	10	19.99		
25					WA	5	19.99	99.95	10	9.995		
26				You Can Combat Computer Stress!	CA	35	2.99	104.65	24	25.116		

H ◀ ▶ H \ Sheet1 \ Sheet2 \ Sheet3 \ ℗ \

Figure 8-29. *Formatted pivot table shown in Excel*

Publish Your Formatted Workbook

To publish your workbook, click the **Office Button** and position your mouse over the **Publish** option to display the options shown in Figure 8-30. Click **Excel Services** to prepare the workbook for SharePoint.

Figure 8-30. *Publishing an Excel workbook to SharePoint*

As before, when you published an Excel spreadsheet to SharePoint, you must specify the library where you want to save the document as shown in Figure 8-31. This should be a library that your SharePoint administrator has already defined as a trusted library using Excel Services. Be sure that you select the option **Open in Excel Services** located at the bottom of the **Save As** dialog box when you publish the workbook. Also, if you have multiple worksheets in the workbook, you can select which sheets you want users to have access to by clicking the **Excel Services Options** button and selecting which sheets to publish.

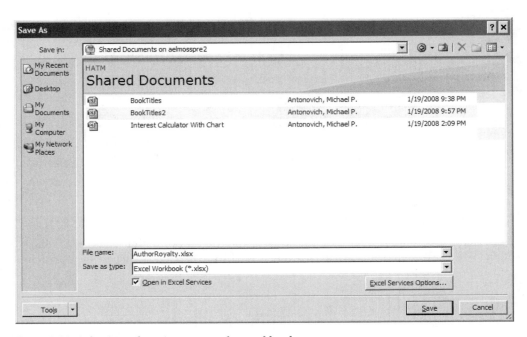

Figure 8-31. *Selecting a location to save the workbook*

When you click **Save**, Excel sends the workbook to SharePoint and opens the workbook in your browser as shown in Figure 8-32. If you already have a workbook in the selected library with the same name as the current workbook, Excel prompts you to replace the existing workbook. Select **Yes** to replace the current workbook when publishing an update.

	A	B	C	D	E	F	G	H	I	J	K	L
									Royalty	Royalty		
1	First Name	Last Name	Book Type	Book Name	State	Quantity	Book Price	Revenue	%	Amount		
2	Abraham	Bennet	business	The Busy Executive's Database Guide	OR	10	19.99	199.9	10	19.99		
3					WA	5	19.99	99.95	10	9.995		
4	Akiko	Yokomoto	trad_cook	Sushi, Anyone?	CA	20	14.99	299.8	10	29.98		
5	Albert	Ringer	psychology	Is Anger the Enemy?	CA	10	10.95	109.5	12	13.14		
6						75	10.95	821.25	12	98.55		
7					WA	3	10.95	32.85	12	3.942		
8						20	10.95	219	12	26.28		
9				Life Without Fear	WA	25	7	175	10	17.5		
10	Ann	Dull	popular_comp	Secrets of Silicon Valley	CA	50	20	1000	10	100		
11	Anne	Ringer	mod_cook	The Gourmet Microwave	OR	15	2.99	44.85	24	10.764		
12					WA	25	2.99	74.75	24	17.94		
13			psychology	Is Anger the Enemy?	CA	10	10.95	109.5	12	13.14		
14						75	10.95	821.25	12	98.55		
15					WA	3	10.95	32.85	12	3.942		
16						20	10.95	219	12	26.28		
17	Burt	Gringlesby	trad_cook	Sushi, Anyone?	CA	20	14.99	299.8	10	29.98		
18	Charlene	Locksley	psychology	Emotional Security: A New Algorithm	WA	25	7.99	199.75	10	19.975		
19	Cheryl	Carson	popular_comp	But Is It User Friendly?	OR	30	22.95	688.5	16	110.16		
20	Dean	Straight	business	Straight Talk About Computers	CA	15	19.99	299.85	10	29.985		
21	Innes	del Castillo	mod_cook	Silicon Valley Gastronomic Treats	CA	10	19.99	199.9	12	23.988		
22	Johnson	White	psychology	Prolonged Data Deprivation: Four Cas	WA	15	19.99	299.85	10	29.985		
23	Livia	Karsen	psychology	Computer Phobic AND Non-Phobic In	WA	20	21.59	431.8	10	43.18		
24	Marjorie	Green	business	The Busy Executive's Database Guide	OR	10	19.99	199.9	10	19.99		

Figure 8-32. *The Excel workbook displayed using Excel Services in SharePoint*

Working with the Report Center

The Report Center is a site definition found in the Enterprise template group installed by MOSS 2007. While most people will probably implement the Report Center from their top-level site, you can create it as a subsite under any other site.

The Report Center serves as a central location for storing many of the document types previously discussed, including Excel-based reports, lists, connections to data sources, and document libraries of many types. It supports all the page templates you have already seen and the web parts already discussed, including the Excel web part. However, it includes a special list specifically for building Key Performance Indicators (KPIs) that you will explore here. In the balance of this chapter, you will examine how to use the Report Center to create a single place to publish Excel spreadsheets, build dashboards, and display scorecards.

Introduction to KPIs

KPIs provide a visual communication tool that shows progress toward a goal. Each item in a KPI list measures one item. Each item has a desired goal value. The list can then show the current value of that item and compare it to the goal. Based on ranges of values defined by the person building the KPI, you can then display a color-coded status icon illustrating how well the current value compares to the desired value.

Project teams, managers, and businesses use KPIs to gain a quick visual check on the progress of their projects, to determine whether employees are meeting production goals or whether sales are meeting expectations. KPIs can quickly illustrate whether you are ahead, behind, or on schedule with whatever business factors the KPI measures.

KPI Types Defined

There are four basic types of KPIs available within SharePoint, depending on the source of the data used to create them. While the data source may differ, the basic look and method of using KPIs does not differ.

- **SharePoint lists**: You can use existing SharePoint lists to develop KPIs. For example, suppose you track issues at your company using an issue tracking list. By using simple counts, you can compare the number of outstanding issues to a desired goal for your help desk to see how well they handle incoming calls. For more complex issues, you could track the time needed to resolve issues by your programming staff and compare the average elapse time to a desired goal.

- **Excel workbooks**: You can link a KPI to an Excel workbook. Updated workbook data can then drive the current value in the KPI. Using the Excel web part on the same page, you can display a detailed list of the data backing up the KPI.

- **SQL Server Analysis Services**: Analysis Services can also provide information to create KPIs. This method can supply tracking data from systems maintained in SQL Server. With a little work, you can build performance information in a table and then use that information through Analysis Services to create SQL performance KPIs.

- **Manual data**: If you do not have a formal way to collect data using one of the preceding methods, you can always manually enter the goal and its current value in this KPI type.

Creating a KPI List

Creating a KPI list follows many of the same steps used when creating other list types. You begin by going to the site where you want to create the KPI list, which in this case is your Report Center site. Once there, click **Site Actions** and then select **View All Site Content**. If your Report Center displays the **Quick Launch** menu, you might be able to click the **View All Site Content** link from the top of this menu.

Next, click **Create** on the **All Site Content** page. On this page, locate the **Custom List** group and then click the **KPI List** option within this group. The KPI list creation page only requires a few configuration fields as shown in Figure 8-33.

Supply a name for the list and enter an optional description. For the example here, I want to create a KPI list to track problem calls. Therefore, I suggest the name **Problem Calls**. After providing a description for the list, choose the **No** radio button under **Display this list on the Quick Launch?**. Finally, click the **Create** button to build the list.

Opening the KPI list, you can see that the default columns for each item include a column named **Indicator**, which will describe the KPI. The **Goal** column represents the minimum acceptable value for the item that represents success for the KPI item. The **Value** column represents the current measured value for the item. Finally, the **Status** column displays an icon that visually indicates whether the item has achieved the desired goal.

HATM > HATMReports > Create > New
New

Name and Description

Type a new name as you
want it to appear in
headings and links
throughout the site. Type
descriptive text that will
help site visitors use this
list.

Name:

Problem Calls

Description:

This KPI will track the number of
active issues as well as the number
of issues resolved. It also displays
a KPI listing the status of major
corporate applications.

Navigation

Specify whether a link to
this list appears in the
Quick Launch.

Display this list on the Quick Launch?

○ Yes ⦿ No

[Create]   [Cancel]

Figure 8-33. *Creating a KPI list*

Creating a KPI List with Manually Entered Information

To see how to define a KPI, click the down arrow to the right of the **New** option in the list's
menu bar. Figure 8-34 shows that this menu lets you select from the four different data source
KPIs. If you click the **New** button, not the drop-down arrow, SharePoint assumes you want to
create the default KPI type, one using a SharePoint list. Let's begin with the manually entered type.

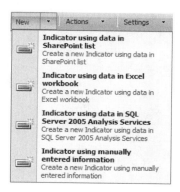

| New ▼ | Actions ▼ | Settings ▼ |

Indicator using data in SharePoint list
Create a new Indicator using data in SharePoint list

Indicator using data in Excel workbook
Create a new Indicator using data in Excel workbook

Indicator using data in SQL Server 2005 Analysis Services
Create a new Indicator using data in SQL Server 2005 Analysis Services

Indicator using manually entered information
Create a new Indicator using manually entered information

Figure 8-34. *Selecting the type of indicator*

The first property of an item in this list is called **Name** on this screen, but it appears in the
Indicator column when you display the KPI list. You must supply this property. The **Description**
property that explains the purpose of the indicator remains optional. However, you might
want to document here whether high values or low values represent success. Then using the
optional **Comments** section, enter an explanation of how you measure the current value for
this item and perhaps even how you selected the status range values. Figure 8-35 shows the
first part of the page defining the properties of a KPI item.

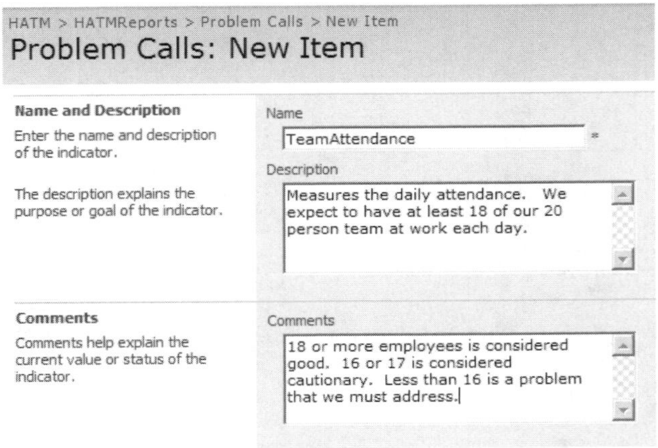

Figure 8-35. *Defining the name and description properties of the indicator*

Next, you must enter the current value for the indicator. Because you have selected a manual indicator, you must open and edit this item each time the value changes. Since this example tracks attendance, you will probably find yourself doing this daily.

Figure 8-36 also shows that you have to define the rules for the status icon. You can choose to represent better values by higher or lower values. In the case of attendance, higher values represent better values. Therefore, let's assume that you have met your attendance goal when 18 or more employees out of 20 come into work each day. If only 16 or 17 employees arrive, you want to raise a warning to management. If fewer than 16 employees arrive, you want to display the danger icon.

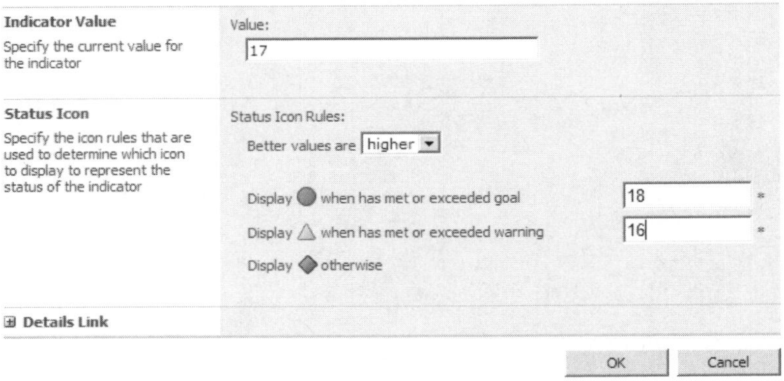

Figure 8-36. *Defining the indicator value and status rules*

After defining the KPI, click **OK** to see how the KPI appears. Figure 8-37 displays the KPI list with a single indicator showing that you might have the start of an absentee problem.

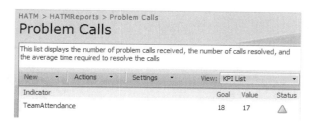

Figure 8-37. *Viewing the resulting indicator in the list*

If you want to see what happens when you change the current value of the indicator, click the KPI item and select **Edit**.

Creating a KPI List Using a SharePoint List

Let's now look at a KPI indicator that uses a SharePoint list. I've already created a SharePoint list that tracks the number of active application systems. Suppose I define success as having at least 90% of our systems running, and that I define failure as having less than 80% of our systems running. (OK, I know that may be low for your organization. You can, of course, enter your own numbers.)

Rather than track this information manually, suppose further that you have a SharePoint list named **Systems Supported** that includes an item for each application. Furthermore, suppose that this list has a field named **Status** defined as a choice field type with three possible values: **OK**, **Repairs**, and **Down**. You can use this list to supply the data for the KPI. That way, by maintaining the status in **Systems Supported**, the KPI indicator will update automatically.

Figure 8-38 shows the full properties list for this KPI item. The new options begin with the **Indicator Value** section. In this area, you must enter the name of the SharePoint list and view that you want to use to calculate the KPI value. Notice that you can then calculate the current KPI value in one of three ways:

- Simply total the number of list items in the selected view.

- Calculate the percentage of list items with a specific value in the view based on a Boolean expression.

- Calculate using all list items in the view.

In this case, you want to calculate the percentage of systems that have a **Status** field value of **OK**. However, if you had a list that included the amount of time a system was down, you could sum the down time across all systems for the time period represented by the view.

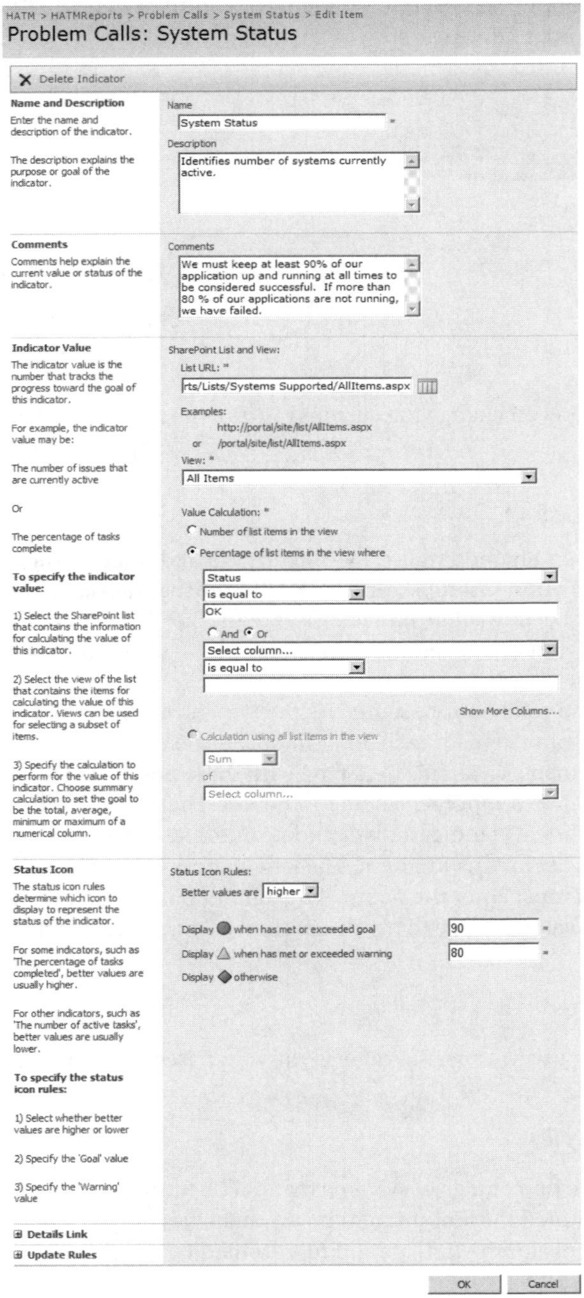

HATM > HATMReports > Problem Calls > System Status > Edit Item

Problem Calls: System Status

✕ Delete Indicator

Name and Description
Enter the name and description of the indicator.

The description explains the purpose or goal of the indicator.

Name

System Status

Description

Identifies number of systems currently active.

Comments
Comments help explain the current value or status of the indicator.

Comments

We must keep at least 90% of our application up and running at all times to be considered successful. If more than 80 % of our applications are not running, we have failed.

Indicator Value
The indicator value is the number that tracks the progress toward the goal of this indicator.

For example, the indicator value may be:

The number of issues that are currently active

Or

The percentage of tasks complete

To specify the indicator value:

1) Select the SharePoint list that contains the information for calculating the value of this indicator.

2) Select the view of the list that contains the items for calculating the value of this indicator. Views can be used for selecting a subset of items.

3) Specify the calculation to perform for the value of this indicator. Choose summary calculation to set the goal to be the total, average, minimum or maximum of a numerical column.

SharePoint List and View:

List URL: *

rts/Lists/Systems Supported/AllItems.aspx

Examples:
    http://portal/site/list/AllItems.aspx
  or /portal/site/list/AllItems.aspx

View: *

All Items

Value Calculation: *

○ Number of list items in the view

● Percentage of list items in the view where

Status

is equal to

OK

○ And ● Or

Select column...

is equal to

              Show More Columns...

○ Calculation using all list items in the view

Sum

of

Select column...

Status Icon
The status icon rules determine which icon to display to represent the status of the indicator.

For some indicators, such as 'The percentage of tasks completed', better values are usually higher.

For other indicators, such as 'The number of active tasks', better values are usually lower.

To specify the status icon rules:

1) Select whether better values are higher or lower

2) Specify the 'Goal' value

3) Specify the 'Warning' value

Status Icon Rules:

Better values are higher

Display ● when has met or exceeded goal   90

Display ⚠ when has met or exceeded warning   80

Display ◆ otherwise

⊞ **Details Link**
⊞ **Update Rules**

OK   Cancel

Figure 8-38. *Defining an indicator based on a SharePoint list*

Creating a KPI List from an Excel Workbook

Next, if you use an Excel workbook to supply your indicator values, you must supply the URL of the workbook published on your SharePoint site using Excel Services. Then you must enter the address of the cell to use for the value or reference the cell by a cell name. If you click the icon to the right of the value, the pop-up window displays the workbook and lets you select the cell to use not just for the **Indicator Value**, but also for the **Indicator Goal** and the **Indicator Warning** values. In fact, you can click the workbook icon next to any of these three values on the main property page for the KPI item to return to the workbook to verify or select new cells to use for these values. This does not mean that you must use cell values for the **Indicator Goal** or **Indicator Warning**. You can enter manual numbers for these values. Figure 8-39 shows just this portion of the KPI item properties, as the other properties have already been reviewed in discussing the previous KPI types.

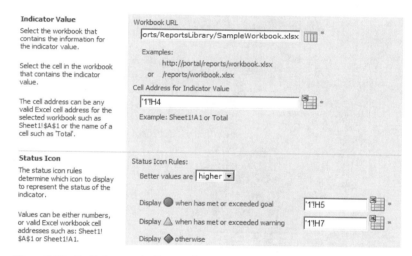

Figure 8-39. *Defining an indicator based on an Excel workbook*

Creating a KPI List from SQL Server 2005 Analysis Services

Finally, when defining a KPI using SQL Server 2005 Analysis Services, you must begin by defining the data connection to the data cube. You must store this data connection in a data connection library within your site. Remember that the Report Center supports a data connection library for this purpose. You must then select the Analysis Services KPI to use. If the KPI has other KPIs that contribute to its value, you can choose to include them in the current KPI list. Figure 8-40 shows the property page for an Analysis Services-based KPI.

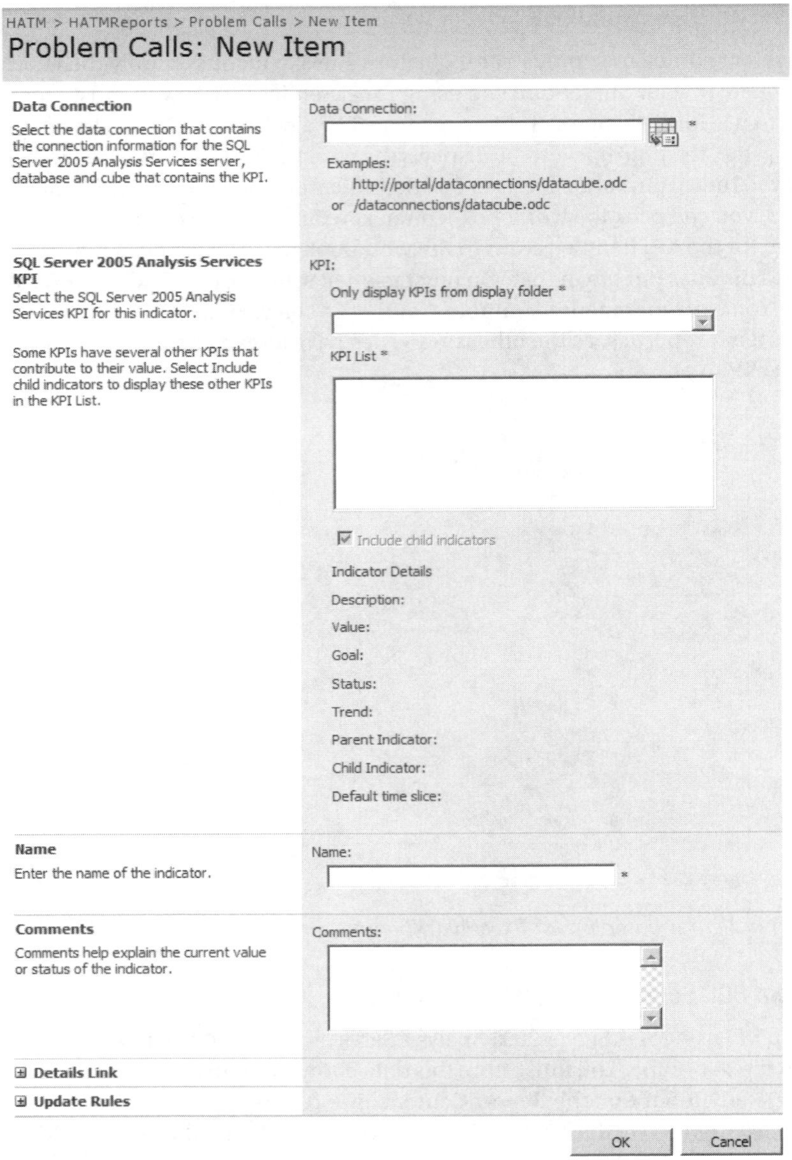

HATM > HATMReports > Problem Calls > New Item
Problem Calls: New Item

Data Connection

Select the data connection that contains the connection information for the SQL Server 2005 Analysis Services server, database and cube that contains the KPI.

Data Connection:

Examples:
http://portal/dataconnections/datacube.odc
or /dataconnections/datacube.odc

SQL Server 2005 Analysis Services KPI

Select the SQL Server 2005 Analysis Services KPI for this indicator.

Some KPIs have several other KPIs that contribute to their value. Select Include child indicators to display these other KPIs in the KPI List.

KPI:

Only display KPIs from display folder *

KPI List *

☑ Include child indicators

Indicator Details

Description:

Value:

Goal:

Status:

Trend:

Parent Indicator:

Child Indicator:

Default time slice:

Name

Enter the name of the indicator.

Name:

Comments

Comments help explain the current value or status of the indicator.

Comments:

⊞ **Details Link**

⊞ **Update Rules**

OK   Cancel

Figure 8-40. *Defining an indicator based on SQL Server Analysis Services*

Creating Dashboards with Excel and KPIs

What is a dashboard? Within SharePoint, you can define a dashboard as any web page that displays business information. Often dashboards use graphics to display data, but they don't have to include graphics. What they do have to do is show trends that can help identify problems, opportunities, or decision points. Some people might refer to this ability as an at-a-glance health check for a business of its key indicators. But the fact is you can use dashboards for tracking project progress, employee satisfaction, customer purchasing trends, and many more things. The value of a good dashboard lies in its ability to help management make decisions that benefit the corporation.

Building a Dashboard from the Dashboard Template in the Report Center

So how can you make a dashboard in SharePoint? First, open your Report Center site and click the option **Reports** or **Dashboards** in the **Quick Launch** menu. It does not matter which option you select since both take you to the **Reports** library. Once you have the **Reports** library open, open the **New** drop-down menu. Do not just click **New**, because SharePoint may assume that you want to add a report to the library. From the drop-down menu, click the option **Dashboard Page**.

As shown in Figure 8-41, you begin defining your dashboard by supplying a page name and a page title. You can also optionally enter a description. Notice that you cannot edit the next two fields in the **Location** section. SharePoint defines the document library as a reports library, and you cannot change it unless you have multiple reports-type libraries. Unless you have defined a folder structure for this library (remember earlier discussions about creating folders to better organize your files), the folder also defaults to the top-level folder. Of course, if you have defined a folder structure, you can select any of your existing folders from this drop-down. This is another reason why you should plan out your folder structure before beginning to add documents to your libraries.

■**Tip** Of course, if you do procrastinate building out your folder structure until after you have already created documents, all is not lost. You can simply switch to the Windows Explorer view of your library by using the option **Open with Windows Explorer** in the **Actions** drop-down menu. There you can drag and drop documents between folders and even create new folders.

In the next section, **Create Link in Current Navigation Bar**, you can determine whether to create an entry in the **Quick Launch** menu. Here you have three options of which section to add the dashboard: **Reports**, **Dashboards**, and **Resources**. Let's just think of these three options as categories of special web pages for now.

In the **Dashboard Layout** section, you can choose from three different layouts, which basically differ by the number of columns in the layout. Each layout actually represents a page template specially designed for dashboards and combines by default KPI lists, Excel web parts, text areas, contact information of the person creating the page, and more.

The last option lets you create a new KPI list automatically. If you let SharePoint generate a new KPI list for you, it will name the list using a combination of the current page name followed by the text "KPI Definitions." You can also create a dashboard using an existing KPI list, or you could decide not to include a KPI list at all on the dashboard. What? A dashboard without a KPI list?

Actually, despite calling the web page a dashboard and leading you to think that it is something special, it is not. The dashboard template provides nothing that you cannot re-create starting from a blank web part page with the same number of web part zones.

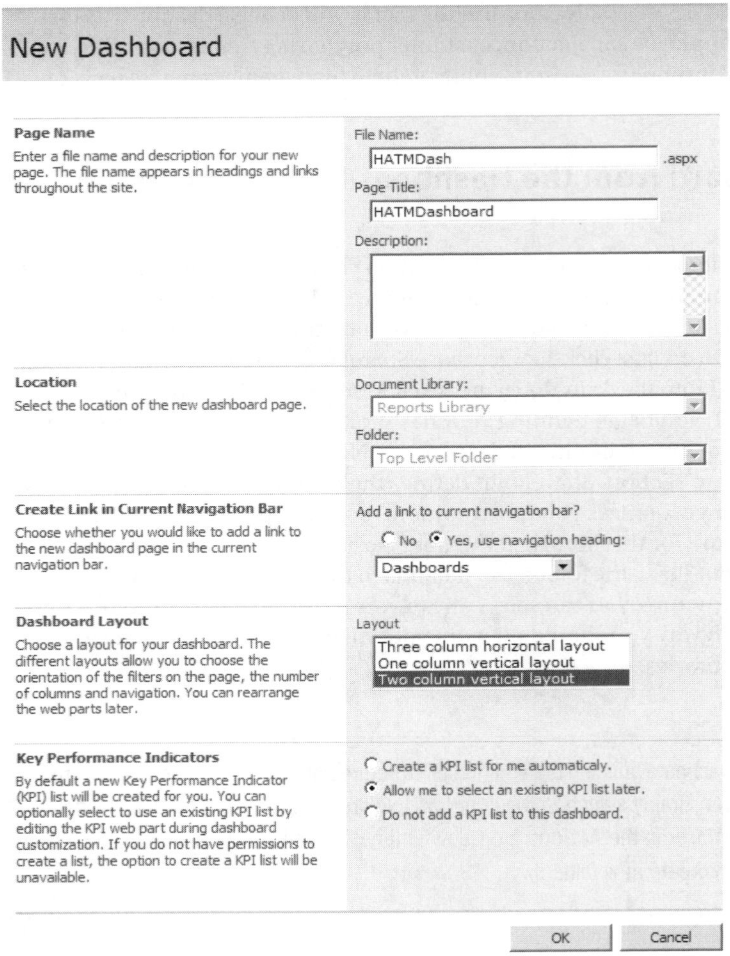

Figure 8-41. *Creating a two-column dashboard document*

So why create the dashboard this way? It can save you a little time by preplacing common web parts used by dashboards on a web page and then placing that page in a separate navigation group in the **Quick Launch** menu.

Organizing Web Parts in the Dashboard Web Part Zones

So let's continue looking at what you get when you create a two-column dashboard. Figure 8-42 shows the initial two-column web page. This page actually places each of the web parts in its own web part zone. These zones include

- Top Left zone

- Top Right zone

- Middle Left zone

- Middle Right zone

- Bottom Left zone

- Bottom Right zone

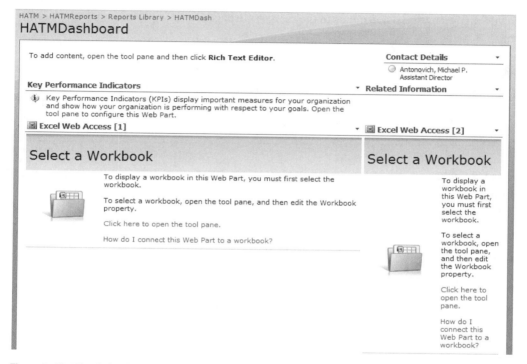

Figure 8-42. *The default dashboard page created by SharePoint*

You can just imagine what you would get with a three-column dashboard. Actually, don't imagine, go ahead and try it. You can always delete the page if you do not want to keep it.

If you do not want to use all of these web parts, no problem; just edit the page and close them. If you don't like the way SharePoint lays out the page, just edit the page and drag and drop the web parts to locations you do like. Want different web parts? Just click **Add a Web Part** found at the top of each web part zone, and select a web part from the list of available web parts. Remember that you can create "new" web parts by defining new lists using any of the list templates available. While Microsoft provides a collection of commonly used web parts with SharePoint, you can go online and find free or relatively inexpensive web parts to do all sorts of things. And if you still cannot find the web part that will do what you want, you can always go down the hall to the den of programmers the company keeps around for emergencies and ask them to build a web part for you using Visual Studio. If your company does not employ a den of programmers, you can find many consultants through the Internet that can build that web part for you.

Adding KPIs to Your Dashboard

Let's continue on by modifying the Key Performance Indicators web part found in the Middle Left web part zone. If you do not have the page in **Edit** mode, do so now by selecting **Edit Page** from the **Site Actions** drop-down menu. With the page in **Edit** mode, open the drop-down menu associated with the **Edit** button and select the option **Modify Shared Web Part**. When you do this, an option panel opens to the right of the page.

■**Note** If you click **Modify Shared Web Part** and do not see the option panel, it may be that your screen is not wide enough. You could go out and buy a new 24" wide-screen panel. And as much fun as that might be, the easier solution is to look for the horizontal scrollbar at the bottom of window. You should see that you can drag the elevator button in the bar to the right to bring the option panel into view.

Figure 8-43 shows the top portion of the option panel. This section usually includes most of the unique properties for the current web control. Most option panels also have sections named

- **Appearance**

- **Layout**

- **Advance**

SharePoint typically leaves these other sections closed until you want to see them by clicking the box with the plus sign to the left of the section name.

Figure 8-43. *Selecting a KPI list to display*

First, you must define the KPI list you want to display in the web part's first option. You can enter the relative URL for this list beginning with the root of your site. Or you could click the icon to the right of the field for a simpler way to create this reference. This icon lets you search your site for the KPI list as shown in Figure 8-44. When you find the list you want to use, double-click it, or click it once and click the **OK** button to select the list.

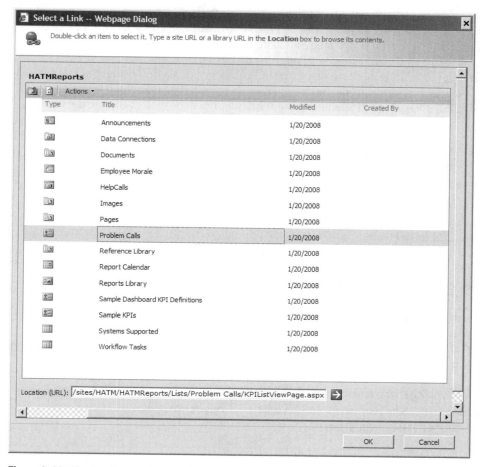

Figure 8-44. *Navigating to the KPI list rather than entering its URL manually*

The second option, **Change Icon**, lets you do exactly that. You can choose from four different icon styles for your visual status indicators as shown in Figure 8-45. You have already seen the default indicators in several of the past figures. The **Checkmarks** consist of colored circles with either a checkmark, exclamation point, or X in their centers. The **Flat** icons consist of plain colored circles with no symbols. Finally, the **Traffic Lights** consist of black boxes with a green, yellow, or red "bulb" in them. If you want to see these for yourself, select any of the icon types and then click the **Apply** button at the bottom of the option panel. The **Apply** button updates the contents of the edited web part but leaves the option panel open.

Figure 8-45. *Changing the KPI status icon*

Figure 8-46 shows the configured KPI list: **Problem Calls**, which you built in part earlier. Notice that the list, even in **Edit** mode, displays the list's menu selections. Right from this screen, you can open the **New** drop-down menu and add a new indicator to the list. You can also open the **Actions** menu and change the icons, reset the order of indicators, and update their values. The reset order of indicators option places the indicators in alphabetical order. The last feature, to update values, can be especially useful when working with data that changes frequently. If you have manually entered KPI values, this option does not allow you to change the values.

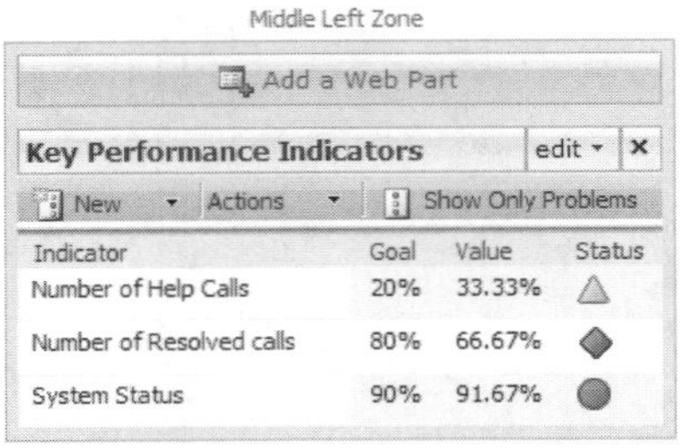

Figure 8-46. *Displaying the KPI list*

The last option in the list's menu lets you display only problem indicators. If you have a long list of indicators, for which most are OK, you can help management focus on problem issues by only displaying the indicators that need attention.

Note The KPI menu items remain visible after you publish the page so that users viewing the page also have access to them. Using permissions, you can control which users can change the KPI lists, making the list read-only for the vast majority of users.

As you move your mouse over the indicators, a drop-down box arrow appears to the right of the indicator text. When you open this menu, you will find options that let you edit the properties of the item, assuming you have the appropriate permissions. You can also move individual indicators up and down in the list, creating a custom order.

In the bottom right of the page, I have removed the Excel web part, replacing it with the KPI Details web part. This web part also works with an existing KPI list, which you must specify in its option panel. In this case, you must not only supply the URL for the KPI list as you did in the last web part, but also identify the specific indicator that you want to display. Again, you can select from the four icon styles for the **Status** field. Figure 8-47 shows the options for the web part as well as the web part itself after clicking the **Apply** button.

Finally, I've made several other changes to the dashboard page, as shown in Figure 8-48. These include

- Adding some basic text to the Content Text web part in the Upper Left zone

- Adding the graphical results of a survey on employee morale to the Middle Left zone

- Adding a reference to a published Excel workbook to the Excel web part in the Lower Left zone

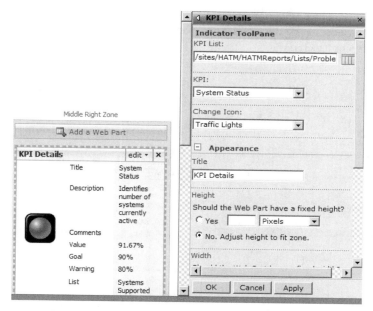

Figure 8-47. *Showing details of one indicator using the KPI Details web part*

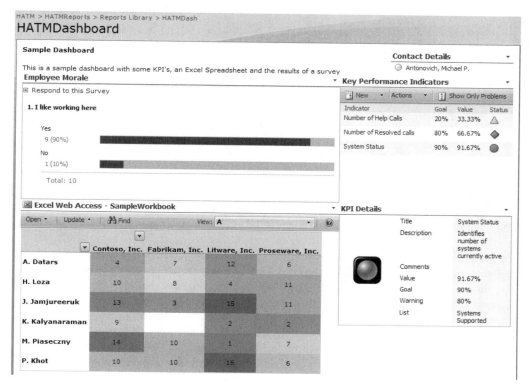

Figure 8-48. *Final dashboard page*

Finally, to illustrate the point that there is nothing special in a dashboard that you cannot create from a blank web page by adding the same web parts, Figure 8-49 shows a web page created from scratch using the same web parts.

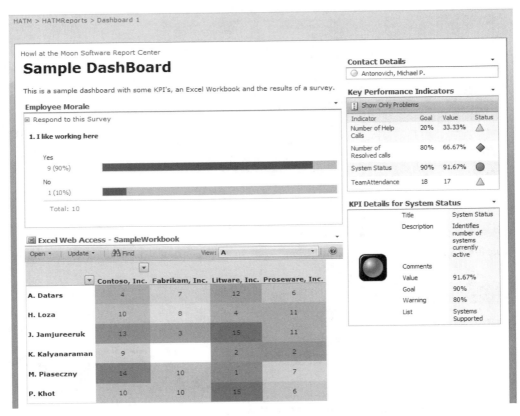

Figure 8-49. *Equivalent page created starting from an empty web page*

Summary

This chapter started by asking whether Excel was the weakest link in the Microsoft Office lineup of products in terms of collaboration with SharePoint. In the previous chapter, you saw that a key feature of sharing data between two systems, synchronization, had been deprecated in the most recent version of Excel. And while I did show a way to recover from this weakness, it still may have felt that Excel did not contribute to collaboration as thoroughly as some other products.

So I kicked off this chapter by showing how you can publish a static Excel workbook to a SharePoint site. Once published, a service called Excel Services could open and display that Excel workbook in your browser with virtually no lost of visual fidelity compared to Excel itself. This feature allows users of your site who do not have Excel installed on their local computers to share in the data from the workbook, at least by viewing it. But a static workbook does not allow interaction.

Next, I introduced the concept of parameters to allow a published workbook to become a little more dynamic. Visitors to your site can supply their own values to the parameters and then recalculate the spreadsheet using those values.

Then you took a look at Report Center sites. A new feature examined here called KPIs provides a way to quickly and visually show important measurable factors in an organization. When management sets a goal level for each factor, they can then measure the actual value of the factor and compare it to the goal. Depending on how well the actual value compares to the goal, the KPI list can display a status icon that at a glance shows which key factors have been met and which need further attention by management.

I then closed out the chapter by combining the ability to display Excel workbooks on a web page along with other web parts, such as the KPI list, to give management a dashboard, a single-screen view of the status of factors that they find important to the success of their organization. While SharePoint provides a dashboard template that can give you a head start in building such a web page, I ended by showing that you could create the same basic web page from a blank web page that has access to the same web parts.

So in closing, with the help of Excel Services, Excel may not be the weakest link after all. It certainly displays some interesting abilities that you might be able to take advantage of in your organization to help management view protected versions of your workbooks. The decision is yours.

CHAPTER 9

■■■

An Introduction to Creating Forms with InfoPath

I know many people who have installed Microsoft Office 2003 or 2007 on their desktop machines. On practically a daily basis, they open and use MS Outlook and MS Word. They may even use MS Excel, MS PowerPoint, and occasionally MS Access. But many of them never noticed a largely undiscovered tool named InfoPath, which first became part of the Microsoft Office Suite in 2003 and has been significantly enhanced in 2007.

InfoPath is important to your SharePoint implementation because it brings an easy-to-use form design tool based on XML (Extensible Markup Language) to the desktop and your browser. With it, you can gather data from users without having to write applications, and you can then save that data in XML files, databases, or SharePoint lists.

The reason InfoPath works well with SharePoint is that it is based on XML technology just like the rest of Microsoft Office 2007. When InfoPath saves a form, it creates an XSN file. This file acts like a cabinet (CAB) file to hold a collection of files needed by the form. These files include XML Schema Definition (XSD) files and Extensible Stylesheet Language (XLS) files that provide a formal definition of the XML data, such as element names, data types, and attributes for each field used in a form. InfoPath also uses XSL Transformation (XSLT) files to define different views of the same data or subsets of the data. Because the form data is stored in XML, you can start building a form from an existing XML data schema, or you can begin with a blank form and let InfoPath build the data schema for you.

Perhaps all these strange-sounding technologies scare some people away from using Info-Path. However, you really do not need an in-depth knowledge of these technologies to create and use InfoPath forms, as I will show in this chapter.

You will explore InfoPath's design environment, which includes a rich set of controls for building forms that can be displayed through your browser and thus within SharePoint. It includes all the popular controls needed for forms, ranging from standard text boxes, lists, and date pickers, to repeating and optional sections, attachments, hyperlinks, and more. Rather than building ASP pages to collect data on your internet, you can skip most of the programming tasks for simple data-gathering applications by creating an InfoPath form and then publishing it in a library on your site. Users can access your form template and fill in their data online. You can then save the data collected by an InfoPath form locally in an Access table, SQL Server database, or even a SharePoint list.

InfoPath also lets you add workflows to forms using Windows Workflow Foundation and published through SharePoint. Workflows allow you to define a work process for the form. For example, after you fill in an absence request form, you probably need to submit that form to your supervisor. He must then sign the document before forwarding it to your department secretary. The secretary then enters the information into your payroll system. You can automate this entire process to pass the form from one person to next, sending e-mails to each recipient that notify that person of a task to complete. And because workflows are tracked by SharePoint, you can always tell where in the workflow a document is. Together with SharePoint, InfoPath can help improve the efficiency of your work processes.

In this chapter, you will see how easy it is to create an InfoPath form from scratch, as well as how to take existing Microsoft Word and Microsoft Excel documents and convert them to InfoPath forms. You will also look at how to work with different data sources. This will give you the foundation you need to publish these forms within SharePoint, which is covered in Chapter 10, so that all users of your site can access these forms and fill them in.

Why You Should Use InfoPath

I don't know many organizations that do not collect data for their business from customers, potential customers, suppliers, partners, or their own employees. Forms have always provided a standardized way to collect information, ensuring that all employees collect all necessary information in a consistent manner. Sometimes companies simply store this information on the paper form used to collect it. However, often this data must be entered into a computer system by armies of data entry clerks.

Using paper forms to collect information exposes the process to several types of errors. First, if the user handwrites the data into the original form, there could be a problem interpreting the handwriting. Second, even if the data entry clerk can clearly read the data on the form, she still could create errors when she enters the data into a computer system through simple typing mistakes. For example, suppose someone fills in an application form for a car or home loan. Whether due to the applicant's poor writing or a typing error made by a data entry clerk, bad data could be sent to the credit bureau, resulting in the denial of the loan request.

Also, many business processes use a collection of forms to complete a transaction such as buying that car or home. Typically, several fields appear on all of these forms such as the name of the people involved in the transaction, their addresses, phone numbers, work locations, and perhaps other fields as well. Each time the person collecting this information has to reenter the information, there is one more chance for the data to be entered incorrectly. With fully integrated electronic forms, once the person collecting the data enters the information, subsequent forms can retrieve the data and prefill repeated fields, making the entire process run faster and with less chance of errors.

As mentioned in the first section, you can publish InfoPath forms through the Internet, allowing people not just inside your company, but also outside your company to view, print, and fill in the form. With the increasing use of mobile devices such as BlackBerry handhelds, you might want to create forms that users can fill in via one of these mobile devices. You can even fill in InfoPath forms offline. Once you download a form, you can disconnect from the Internet and fill in the form over one or more work sessions. When you complete the form, you can reconnect to the Internet and submit it.

Similar to mobile users, InfoPath forms also support Tablet PC users by allowing users to directly write with their tablet pens to fill in the form fields. InfoPath can then automatically convert this "ink" into text. You might even allow Tablet PC users to add hand-drawn sketches to illustrate information, such as what you might include in a traffic accident report used by the police.

Another benefit of using a tool like InfoPath forms comes from the ability to share the resulting data with other Office applications. You can even send forms via e-mail and Outlook, export the data to MS Excel, and then pump the data into an Access or SQL Server database.

By having users fill in forms electronically, you can help ensure that they enter correct data by validating the data as they enter it. By using validation rules on individual form fields, you can prevent bad data from getting into your database. The cost of correcting data entry errors increases dramatically the further through the process the bad data travels. Therefore, flagging bad data as users enter it can save time and money by prompting users to immediately correct their mistakes.

Completing forms online rather than on paper also appeals to those interested in going "green." For others, a more important benefit might be that use of less paper for forms saves money. Your company can buy less paper, cut printing costs, and not have to build and main-tain storage facilities to keep the completed forms.

Because InfoPath forms allow you to show and hide different sections of a report, you might be able to combine several similar forms into a single form and then provide a way for users to show or hide the portions they need or don't need to work with. Different views on the same data allow you to collect all the data needed with a single form, and then, through different views, show subsets of the data to different users within your organization based on what they need to see rather than sending them the entire form.

Exploring the InfoPath Interface

Let's first examine the InfoPath interface a little. When you open InfoPath, a dialog box pops up that lets you decide how to start. On the left side of this screen, you can see three groups of options to help you start using InfoPath. The first option group, called **Form categories**, allows you to select from recently used forms, a favorite form, or all forms. You can change the number of recently used forms that display by opening the **Options** dialog box under **Tools**. In the **General** section of the **General** tabbed page, the first option defines whether to display recently used forms at all, and when you do display them, the number of entries that InfoPath retains.

You control the forms added to the **Favorites** option. The easy way to add a form to your favorites begins by clicking the next option in this group, **All Forms**. First click the form you want to add to your favorites to select it. Then, using the **Form Tasks** list on the right side of this window, click **Add to Favorites**. This action adds the selected form to the **Favorites** category.

The second group allows you to open a form. Previous forms that you saved appear in this list, as well as an option to search your computer for additional forms. Selecting a form from this group opens the form as if you wanted to fill it in. If you still need to work on the form's design, you need to go to the next option group.

The third group includes options to design a form. The first option, **Design a Form Template**, opens a wizard that helps you create a new form, as you will see in the next section. The second option, **Import a Form**, lets you begin a new form by using either an MS Excel workbook or an MS Word form. The final option lets you begin customizing one of the sample forms included with InfoPath. When you select this last option, several forms may appear in the central panel of this dialog box. If none of these forms meet your needs, rather than immediately starting to design a form from scratch, click the **Form Templates on Office Online** link at the bottom of the column in the left panel. This option takes you to the **Microsoft Office Online Templates** site. Take a few moments to search the available templates here for InfoPath templates. Starting from an existing template will save you time over creating your template from scratch.

■**Tip** Use the **Filter by Product** option on the left side of the **Microsoft Office Online Templates** page to show only InfoPath templates.

Creating a Simple Form

For this example, assume that you did not find a template that you could download and customize. Therefore, you decide to create a new form from a blank template. Select the option **Design a Form Template**, as shown in the left column of Figure 9-1 just prior to clicking this option.

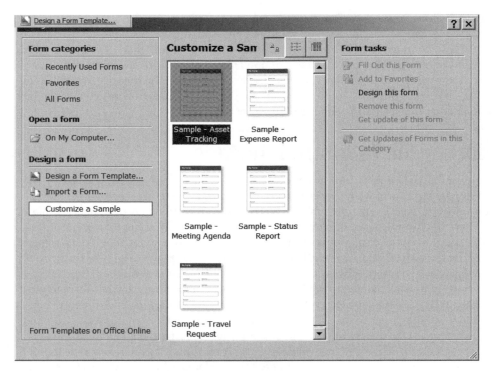

Figure 9-1. *InfoPath's Getting Started dialog box*

■Note After you have created a form and saved it, you can reopen the form using one of the options in the first group or perhaps the second group, and then select **Design this form** from the **Form tasks** panel in the rightmost column of the **Getting Started** dialog box.

After you click the option to design a form template, a new pop-up dialog box appears to ask you to further define what exactly you want to design. This dialog box, displayed in Figure 9-2, shows that the default option allows you to create a new form from a blank template that builds the data source while you design the form. This dialog box also displays four other options.

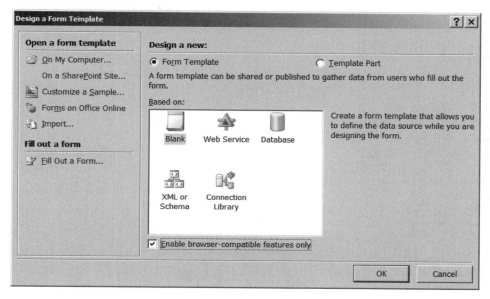

Figure 9-2. *Identifying the data source for the form template*

The **Web Service** option assumes that you want to design a form that queries and submits data to a *web service*. A web service can be thought of as an application that uses XML to transfer information between a client and a server. The **Database** option lets you build a form template that queries and submits data to an Access or SQL database. The **XML or Schema** option starts a form by using an existing XML document or XML schema as the data source. Finally, the **Connection Library** option enables you to search a Microsoft Office server for a data connection that you will use with your form template. This last option also lets you connect to a SharePoint server.

Notice the check box **Enable browser-compatible features only**. If you want your form to work within a browser, you should select this check box. It will limit the controls that you can select from to those that browser-compatible forms support. This chapter will primarily focus on browser-enabled forms for use with SharePoint. However, I will also mention some of the other features for forms that are not browser based.

To first focus on the basics of building a form, let's start with the default blank form that builds the schema while you design the form. When you click **OK**, InfoPath presents you with a blank design screen along with the **Design Tasks** panel on the right side of the window. The **Design Tasks** panel, shown in Figure 9-3, contains all the tools you need to create a form. It breaks these tools into six task groups and organizes them sequentially top to bottom in roughly the order you typically need to work with them. Before continuing with the creation of our simple example form, the **Request for Absence Report,** let's take a look at the actions available in each of these groups.

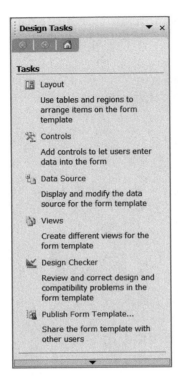

Figure 9-3. *The Design Tasks panel defines available actions when designing a form.*

The Task Group: Layout

Layout controls provide structure to the form and make it easier to place other controls more accurately on the page. Without using tables to provide structure for placing other controls, InfoPath, like HTML-based web pages, defaults to a flow layout when placing controls on a page. This means that as you add controls to the page, InfoPath tries to place them as close to the top-left corner of the page as possible. It begins by placing the first control in the upper-left corner of the page. It then tries to place the next control to the immediate right of the first control, also at the top of the page. If it determines that the new control cannot fit in the remaining space on the line, it then continues again on the left side below the leftmost control of the current line, beginning a new line.

Sometimes this works for what you need to do. However, most times, you need more structure to your pages to place controls at specific positions. At these times, you can turn to the **Layout** section to add tables and regions to your form so that you can arrange controls on the page the way you want to rather than the way the default flow layout attempts to place them.

■**Caution** Regions only apply to InfoPath forms that are not browser compatible. As a result, I will not discuss them further here.

The browser-compatible **Layout** section has two groups of options, shown in Figure 9-4. The first group lets you place various predefined tables on the form. To start a page, you might want to use the **Table with Title** option. This option creates a simple two-row, one-column table with a very thick line (6 pt) to divide the rows. You may want to use this option to create a title for the top of the form, and then use the second row to hold a nested table that you will split into columns and rows for the rest of the form's content. The most useful table layout to further define your overall form structure is the **Custom Table** option, which lets you define the number of columns and rows for the table.

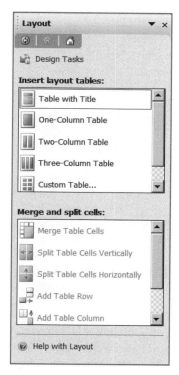

Figure 9-4. *Layout options for a web-based form*

■**Tip** Want to increase the height of a row? Place the cursor after the last character in the cell and press **Shift+Enter**.

■**Tip** To change the color of a table cell, place the cursor in the cell and click the right mouse button. Select the option **Borders and Shading**. Click the **Shading** tab and select a new color or even no color if your form uses a background color or image.

■**Tip** To change the color or style of a border on the table, click anywhere within the table. You should see a small gray square in the upper-left corner of the form. Right-click this square and select the option **Borders and Shading**. Click the **Borders** tab. Select the line style, color, and width of the line. Then by either using the buttons in the **Presets** section or clicking the buttons or individual lines in the border diagram, set the table border lines.

HOW DO YOU DECIDE HOW MANY COLUMNS YOU NEED?

When laying out your form using tables, you need to determine how many columns you need in your table. To determine how many columns you need, you need to know what goes into a column. Let's suppose you plan on adding a few text boxes with labels before them to aid users in knowing what information to place in each text box. Typically, you should place the label before the text box in a separate column from the text box itself. This technique gives you more control over the spacing between the label and the text box. Thus you already need two columns for one field.

Then if you want two text boxes on the same line such as for first and last name, you might need three or four columns depending on whether each text box has its own label. In such cases, many form designers recommend that you place a spacer column between the two sets of columns. By adding a spacer column, you can easily control the amount of space between the text box of the first column set and the label of the second column set, even when you use right-justified label text.

Thus you can see that the number of columns you need for a typical form can grow quite rapidly. You can see that you may need as many as five table columns in one row of two data columns and eight table columns for three data columns in the next row. How can you create a table to handle the situation in which every row requires a different number of columns? By splitting and merging cells or by inserting individual tables for each row.

The second set of options in the **Layout** panel lets you merge and split cells. To merge cells, you select two or more cells by clicking the first cell and dragging through the cells you want to include. You can select cells vertically, horizontally, or both at the same time when you merge cells. When you merge the cells, the interior cell walls disappear, and you end up with a single large cell.

Similarly, you can split cells horizontally or vertically. Simply select the cell you want to split, and select one of the split options. If you need to split a cell both horizontally and vertically at the same time, use the **Custom Split** option.

Finally, this second section also allows you to add rows and columns to the table in case you misjudged your requirements when creating the table. Of course, if you merely want to add another row to the end of your table, just place the cursor in the rightmost cell of the last row in the table and press that Tab key. Similarly, you can delete rows by dragging through them to select them and pressing the Delete key.

When you design a form for the Web, those are the only options you have available. If other people who have InfoPath on their desktops will be using your form, you can add two additional layout controls found in a third layout group. The first is a scrolling region. This control allows you create a form in which you can place more controls in a scrollable region than would normally fit in the same vertical space on a page. However, an even better use for a scrolling region is to hold repeating tables. Because a repeating table can have any number of rows, you cannot predict the total vertical space needed by the table on a form. However, by defining a scrolling region, you limit the visual area on the screen for the table. Then by using the automatically supplied scrollbars, you can scroll through the repeated sections of the table as necessary. The second layout control you can use is a horizontal region. When you place two horizontal regions side by side on your form, they will resize automatically to fill in the available space when you resize the form.

The Task Group: Controls

The **Controls** section of the **Task** group displays all the controls that you can place on your form. The number of controls you have available depends on the how you deploy the form. If you plan on web-enabling your form, your control choices diminish. Table 9-1 lists the controls by section and whether they appear in web-enabled forms or InfoPath forms only.

Table 9-1. *InfoPath Controls*

Control Name	InfoPath Control	Web-Enabled Control
Standard		
Text Box	X	X
Drop-Down List Box	X	X
List Box	X	X
Check Box	X	X
Button	X	X
Rich Text Box	X	X
Combo Box	X	
Date Picker	X	X
Option Button	X	X
Section	X	X
Repeating and Optional		
Optional Section	X	X
Repeating Table	X	X
Master/Detail	X	
Numbered List	X	
Multiple Selection List	X	
Repeating Section	X	X
Horizontal Repeating Table	X	
Bulleted List	X	

Table 9-1. *InfoPath Controls (Continued)*

Control Name	InfoPath Control	Web-Enabled Control
Plain Text	X	
File and Picture		
File Attachment	X	X
Ink Picture	X	
Picture	X	
Advanced		
Hyperlink	X	X
Vertical Label	X	
Horizontal Region	X	
Repeating Choice Group	X	
Repeating Recursive Section	X	
Expression Box	X	X
Scrolling Region	X	
Choice Group	X	
Choice Section	X	

I will not spend a lot of time talking about each of these controls here. You can find excellent coverage of many of these controls in the book *Pro InfoPath 2007* by Philo Janus (Apress, 2007). Before I give you a step-by-step list of what you must do to re-create the **Request for Absence Report** featured in this chapter, let's look at some of the properties of the controls available to you when building an InfoPath form.

First, to view the properties of any control, right-click the control after adding it to the form (you can double-click or click and drag the control to position it on the form within a table). From the drop-down menu, select the **Properties** option at the bottom of the list.

The check box and option button controls have an interesting property that many may not suspect if they are familiar with these types of controls from other programming languages. When you add a check box control to a form, you would expect that each check box would support a Boolean value of **True** or **False** or perhaps the integer variation on this of **1** or **0**. However, you if open the **Properties** dialog box and select the **Data** tab, you can change the data type associated with the check box. Notice that the control supports several different types of values ranging from text, to integers, to dates, to even hyperlinks. You still can only save two values, and both values must have the same data type. However, if you would rather save one of two possible dates, depending on whether the user selects the option, or one of two possible decimal values, you can. Figure 9-5 shows an example where a check box returns the discount to be applied to a sale depending on whether the user clicks a check box asking whether the buyer has a frequent buyer card. In this case, the frequent buyer card holder gets an extra 10%.

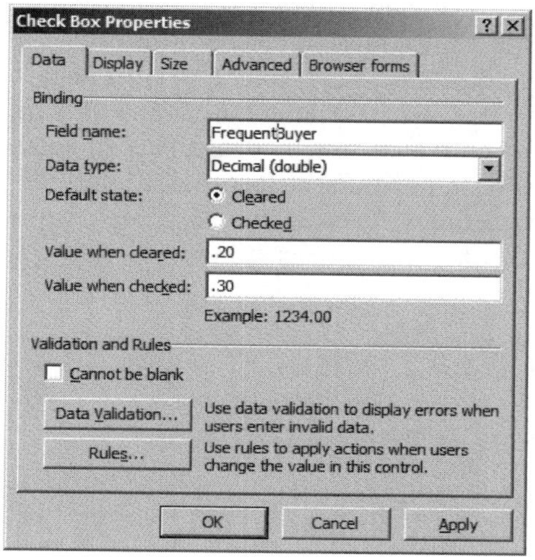

Figure 9-5. *Using other data types in check boxes*

Similarly, the option button control returns a single value no matter how many buttons you associate with the instance of this control. By default, these buttons return an integer ranging from 1 to *n*, where *n* represents the number of option buttons in the group. However, you can return letters, text strings, whole numbers, decimals, or dates instead.

Another interesting feature of controls, *conditional formatting*, lets you change the appearance of the control's contents based on a condition that you define as a Boolean expression. You can access this feature by right-clicking the control and selecting **Conditional Formatting**. Figure 9-6 shows an example of a conditional formatting rule that displays negative values of the control in red.

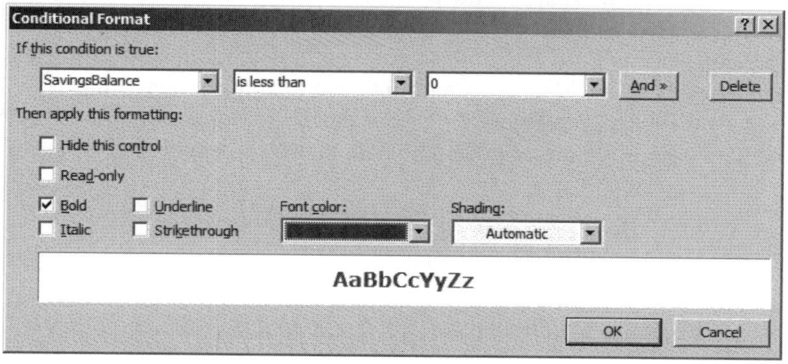

Figure 9-6. *Applying a conditional format to a text box*

You can define more than one conditional formatting rule. For example, suppose you have an absence form that includes a field for the number of hours the employee is requesting to have off. You might want to use one color to indicate requests of less than 8 hours versus a different color for requests of greater than one week. If you only had those two conditional formatting expressions, it would not matter which expression appeared first because the tested hour range does not overlap. However, if you add a third expression to color the hours field when the requestor asks for less than or equal to 40 hours, you have a potential conflict with the conditional formatting for requests of less than 8 hours. InfoPath executes rules in sequential order and stops after the first successful rule. Therefore, if the form executes the 40-hour rule first, it will not execute the 8-hour rule and incorrectly formats the field. Therefore, you have to make sure that InfoPath executes the 8-hour rule first by placing it physically before the 40-hour rule as shown in Figure 9-7.

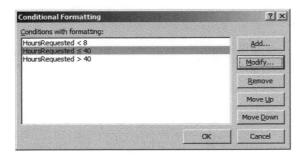

Figure 9-7. *Multiple condition expressions must be ranked.*

You can also apply data validation rules to any field. Using data validation to identify bad data values at the form level before submitting data to the data source allows the user entering data into the form to immediately correct problems. Updating bad data after submitting it to a data source or even at a later time generally requires more time and expense than immediately addressing it.

A validation rule requires a Boolean expression that identifies values that you do not want to accept. You can then define a tooltip to explain the problem as well as a message. However, messages only work with non-web-based forms. When the user enters a value for which the Boolean validation expression returns **True**, InfoPath surrounds the offending field with a red dashed box. As the user places his mouse over the offending field, the tooltip then indicates why the value has been flagged as shown in Figure 9-8. If you design the form as a non-web-based form, the user also sees a pop-up message when he tries to leave the field after entering an incorrect value.

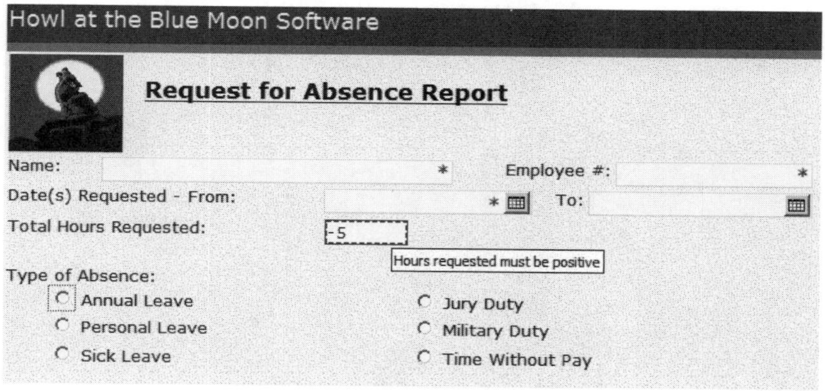

Figure 9-8. *Data validation catches bad data as it's entered.*

The last feature of controls examined here is the ability to add rules to your form that can display messages, set values of other controls, and even execute other actions based on the values entered into the control. You begin defining a rule much like you did for the last two features, by defining a Boolean condition specifying when you want the rule to fire. Then you can define an action. Possible actions include the following:

- Show a dialog box message (not available for web-based forms).

- Show a dialog box expression (not available for web-based forms).

- Set a field's value.

- Perform a query using a data connection.

- Submit form data using a data connection.

- Open a new form to fill out (not available for web-based forms).

Each action requires additional configuration data. For example, to show a dialog box message, you must supply a text message that you want to appear. On the other hand, to set a field's value, you must identify which field on the current form you want to set and the value you want use.

As with conditional formatting, you can specify multiple actions, and also like conditional formatting, you must carefully specify the order of the actions. However, unlike conditional formatting, InfoPath runs all actions in the order you specify them.

The Task Group: Data Sources

The **Data Sources** task group lets you examine your data sources. In the case where you build the data source while you build the form, the **Data Source** panel displays the name of each field you added along with selected properties of the field as shown in Figure 9-9.

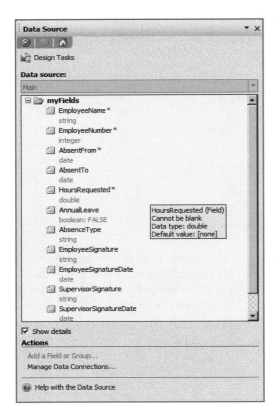

Figure 9-9. *Viewing the data source structure*

If you use a different data source such as an Access or SQL database, you will see the fields used in those respective databases.

The Task Group: Design Checker

The **Design Checker** panel is especially useful when you design a web-based form to be used with InfoPath Forms Services. It identifies and lists any errors on your form that will prevent your form from working properly. It also lists warnings such as the definition of validation messages for some of your form's fields. While InfoPath Forms Services cannot display valida-tion messages, defining them in your form definition does not create a fatal error condition when you display the form, because web-based forms simply ignore this extra information. On the other hand, if the Design Checker identifies an error, you should fix the indicated error before publishing the form template. Figure 9-10 shows sample results of the Design Checker.

By default, the Design Checker validates the form as if it were running within a standard browser or InfoPath 2007. However, if you click the link **Change Compatibility Settings**, you can validate the form against the earlier InfoPath 2003 edition or directly against a server running InfoPath Forms Services such as a SharePoint MOSS site.

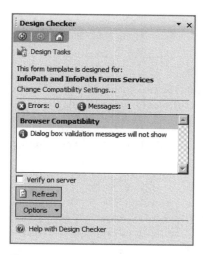

Figure 9-10. *Design Checker identifies errors and warnings before publishing a form.*

The Task Groups: Views and Publish Form Template

I will defer discussion of views for the section "Defining InfoPath Views" found later in this chapter. Chapter 10 will discuss publishing form templates.

Steps to Build the Request for Absence Report

Here are the steps to re-create the **Request for Absence Report** shown earlier in Figure 9-8:

1. With a blank form open, make sure the **Layout** group is displayed in the **Design Tasks** panel on the right side of the screen. If not, you can open it from InfoPath's **View** menu.

2. Add the **Table with Title** control to the blank form by simply clicking it.

3. Click in the top row of this table and enter the company name **Howl at the Blue Moon Software**.

4. Click in the second row of this initial table to move the insertion bar. It is often difficult to guess how many rows your form will need ahead of time. Therefore, I recommend either sketching your form on paper first or working on one section at a time. Use this second method to expand your form one row at a time as needed.

5. Click the **Layout** option **Add Table Row**. You should now see two blank rows under the title row of the table.

6. Click back in the first of the two blank rows and click the layout option **Split Table Cells Vertically** so you can place the company logo in the left cell and the report title in the right cell.

7. To add the company logo, click in the left cell of this two-cell row, and then click the **Insert Picture** button in InfoPath's **Standard** toolbar.

> **Note** The **Insert Picture** button looks like a mountain range with the sun over the mountain peaks.

8. From the **Insert Picture** dialog box opened by the **Insert Picture** button, navigate to and select an image you want to use as the company logo. (I recommend an image that is 90 pixels or less in height.)

9. Place your mouse over the dashed vertical line separating the left and right cell on this line, and shrink the left cell width so it is just large enough for your logo plus a small amount of space (5–10 pixels) so your logo does not run directly against the report name in the right cell.

10. Click inside the right cell and type the form's title: **Request for Absence Report.** After entering the text, select it and change the style to bold, underlined, 14 pt Verdana (or the font of your choice) by either using the options in the **Formatting** toolbar or opening the **Font** dialog box found in the **Format** menu drop-down.

11. Next, right-click anywhere in the report name cell and select **Table Properties**. From the **Table Properties** dialog box, click the **Cell** tab, and in the **Vertical Alignment** section, click the **Center** button.

12. Click **Apply** and then **OK** to accept your changes.

13. Click in the last row and again add another row, but this time, add it by clicking the **Insert** button in the **Tables** toolbar and selecting the option **Rows Below**. This method also adds a row to the bottom of the table. Repeat this operation two more times.

14. Click within the first blank row. Then select **Custom Table** from the **Insert layout tables** section of the **Layout** group.

15. In the **Custom Table** dialog box, enter **4** as the number of columns and **1** as the number of rows. Click **OK** to create the table. This adds a table inside the existing table row. Thus, you can build nested tables. I'll explain why that is important in a moment.

16. In the first column of this new child table, enter the text **Name:**.

17. Place your cursor in the second column of this table.

18. Click the down arrow to the right of the group title **Layout** in the **Design Tasks** panel on the right side of the screen to display a drop-down menu, and select the **Controls** group.

19. From the **Controls** group, click **Text Box** from the **Insert controls** section.

20. Right-click in the text box added to the table and select the option **Text Box Properties.** The text box control displays a dialog box with five tabbed pages. Here you can change many of the text box properties, ranging from its name, to the data type it contains, default values, validation clauses, and rules. You can also change the way the control is displayed, its size, accessibility, and postback settings. Change the control's name to **EmployeeName** on the **Data** tab page.

21. Next, click the **Size** tab and change the **Width** setting to 100% by entering **100** in the first text box, and then selecting **%** from the drop-down. This allows the text box to expand and contract automatically as the cell width is changed. Click **OK** to accept your changes.

22. Next, click in the first cell again, and then place the mouse pointer over the vertical line between the first and second cells. Press the mouse button and hold it while you drag the vertical line left or right to resize the label cell to eliminate excess space between the label and the text box.

23. Repeat steps 19 through 22 to add the text box **EmployeeNumber** to the fourth cell in this row.

24. Clicking in the next blank row, switch back to the **Layout** group and insert another custom table having four columns and one row.

25. In the first column of this new child table, enter the text **Date(s) Requested - From:**.

26. In the third column of this table, enter the text **To:**.

27. Place your cursor in the second column of this table.

28. Click the down arrow to the right of the group title **Layout** in the **Design Tasks** panel on the right side of the screen, and select the **Controls** group.

29. From the **Controls** group, click **Date Picker** from the **Insert controls** section.

30. Open the date picker's properties dialog box. Change the control's name to **AbsentFrom** and select the check box **Cannot be blank** from the **Validation and Rules** area of the **Data** tab. Next, click the **Size** tab and change the **Width** setting to 100% by entering **100** in the first text box, and then selecting **%** from the drop-down. Then click **OK** to close the dialog box.

31. Add another date picker to the fourth cell in this table named **AbsentTo** following the same properties defined in step 30.

32. Again, you can click in any cell and then click and drag on either vertical bar between it and an adjacent cell to change the size of the selected cell. Notice that when you change the size of a cell in this row of the form, it does not affect the cell sizes in the first row with the employee name and number. That is because you added two independent child tables, one in each row of the parent table. Had you simply added a single custom table with four columns and two or three rows, all cells in the same column would have to maintain the same width. You will see this in the next section of the form.

33. Finally, click in the next blank row of the form. (There should be two blank rows yet from step 13. If not, add another blank row to the parent table first.) This time, insert a custom table with two columns and one row.

34. In the first column of this new child table, enter the text **Total Hours Requested:**.

35. In the second column of this table, add a text box named **HoursRequested**.

36. Open the text box properties dialog box and check the box **Cannot be blank** in the **Validation and Rules** section.

37. Click the **Data Validation** button, and in the resulting dialog box, click the **Add** button. In the dialog box that then appears, define a validation condition. To define a validation condition, create a Boolean expression that evaluates to **True** when it represents the error condition. In this case, to prevent negative values for the hours requested, select the field **HoursRequested** from the first drop-down combo. Then select **is less than** from the second drop-down combo. In the third drop-down, select **Type a number** and then enter **0**. You could enter additional Boolean expressions here by clicking the **And** button, but for the purposes of this example, you will not. Next, enter text for a ScreenTip and a message in the appropriate text fields. A ScreenTip displays when you position your mouse over a field when the field detects an error during the filling in of the form. The message displays when the validation expression succeeds, indicating an invalid entry. Remember that you are validating by exception. Note, however, that messages do not display when building a browser-based form. Click **OK** three times when you are done to return to the form.

38. Again, you can adjust any of the cell widths before continuing by clicking first in the cell that you want to adjust, and then clicking the vertical dotted line between that cell and an adjacent cell and dragging it to a new position.

39. You have now finished the first section of the form. To begin the second section of the form, add another row and place the text **Type of Absence:** in this row.

40. Add two more rows to the base table.

41. Click in the row after the text entered in step 39. Then, returning to the **Layout** group in the **Design Tasks** panel, select the **Custom Table** control. This time, create a table with three rows and three columns.

42. Drag the vertical line between the first and second column to reduce the width of the first column to about one-quarter inch. Notice that no matter from which row in the table you click and drag this vertical line, the line moves for all three rows in the table. That is the difference between adding a single-row table and a multiple-row table.

43. Click in the second column of the first row, and then select the **Option Button** control from the **Insert controls** section of the **Controls** group.

44. In the **Insert Option Buttons** dialog box, change the number of option buttons to **6**, and then click **OK**. This places all six buttons in this one cell, stretching the height of the row as necessary for all to fit, but don't panic.

45. Select each button by dragging through it (include both the button's label and the circle part of the button), and then drag it to one of the other empty cells in columns two and three of this three-row table. When you are done, you should have one button in each cell in columns two and three.

46. Now right-click any of the buttons and select **Option Button Properties**. Change the field name to **AbsenceType**. You only have to do this to one of the buttons because they must all have the same name.

47. Next, check the value of the property **Value when selected** for each of the option buttons. By default, these are numbered from **1** to *n*, where *n* is the number of buttons. These values also happen to be strings as defined by the **Data Type** property. You can provide other values if you prefer, including using a different data type. However, the data type of all buttons in a group must be the same. I left these numbered **1** through **6** as **Text** (string) data type values.

48. After you have checked the properties of the option buttons, select the label associated with each button by dragging through it with your mouse, and then provide a different label for each button to help the user select the one she wants. Table 9-2 shows each label and value I used.

Table 9-2. *Option Button Labels and Values*

Value	Label
1	Annual Leave
2	Personal Leave
3	Sick Leave
4	Jury Duty
5	Military Duty
6	Time Without Pay

49. When you are done changing the properties of the option buttons, you may need to adjust the row height of the first row where all the buttons originally appeared. You can also adjust the column widths.

50. Next, click in the last row of the form, adding another row if desired, and insert another table for signatures and dates. This custom table should have four columns and two rows.

51. In the first row, add the label **Employee Signature** to the first column, and place a text box with the name **EmployeeSignature** in the second column.

52. In the first row, add the label **Date** to the third column, and place a date picker with the name **EmployeeSignatureDate** in the fourth column.

53. In the second row, add the label **Supervisor Signature** to the first column, and place a text box with the name **SupervisorSignature** in the second column.

54. In the second row, add the label **Date** to the third column, and place a date picker with the name **SupervisorSignatureDate** in the fourth column.

Wow! That was a lot of work, but you have completed the **Request for Absence Report**, and you did it without writing a single line of code.

Migrating Your Existing Word Forms into InfoPath

Suppose you already have a form created using MS Word. You may have spent a great deal of time creating the formatting of that form to make it look exactly the way you want. Or maybe you found the perfect form template on Microsoft's template site, but the site only had a Word version of it. In either case, you definitely do not want to re-create that form from scratch. So how can you import that Word form into InfoPath without a lot of extra work?

I'm going to start with a form template downloaded from Microsoft's site named **Petty Cash Receipt**, which is shown in Figure 9-11. While this form is fairly simple, it demonstrates the concepts needed to convert a Word template to an InfoPath form. The original version of this form template includes three receipts on a page. I've removed the two extra receipts so you can focus on just a single copy of the form.

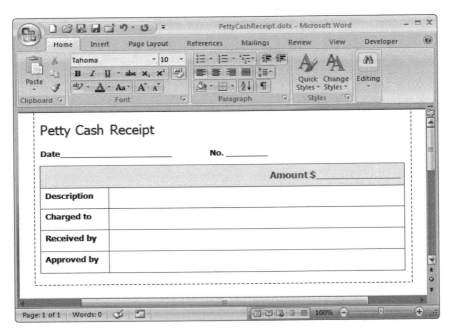

Figure 9-11. *Petty Cash Receipt form in MS Word*

■**Note** I've replaced the fields that were in this template with simple underlines for the **Date**, **No.**, and **Amount** fields, as the field types used will not automatically convert to InfoPath and need underlines as hints. The need for this step will become apparent when I describe how InfoPath determines the location of fields in a Word document.

When you have a Word template exactly as you would like it, save it as a template file (with the extension .dot or .dotx) in a directory where you can find it later, and then close Word.

Next, open InfoPath and choose the option **Import a Form** from the left pane of the **Getting Started** dialog box. This action opens the **Import Wizard**. From this wizard, you can import either an Excel workbook or a Word document. In this case, select **InfoPath importer for Word documents** as the source and click **Next**.

The second page of the **Import Wizard** prompts for the name of the file to import. You can either directly enter the file name or use the **Browse** button to locate the file through Window's standard **Open** dialog box. But first, let's click the **Options** button to look at the **Options** dialog box.

The **Options** dialog box lets you import just the form layout. You might do this if you want to custom define the form's fields. The second option imports both the form layout and the form fields, converting the fields as best it can based on the field properties in Word. The last option imports the basic form layout, but lets you customize the conversion of the form fields when it brings them into InfoPath. Choose this option when one or more of the following conditions exist in your Word document:

- You must convert existing Word form fields to InfoPath controls.

- You must detect repeating tables.

- You must detect rich text areas.

- You must convert empty underlined areas to text boxes.

- You must convert empty spaces after colons to text boxes.

- You must convert empty table cells to text boxes.

- You must convert table cells containing label text to text boxes.

- You must convert brackets around multiple spaces to text boxes.

- You must convert brackets around single spaces to check boxes.

For the purpose of this demonstration, select the custom conversion option to specifically convert empty underline areas, areas after colons, and empty table cells to text boxes as defined in the **Petty Cash Receipt** template.

After specifying the file to import and selecting your options, click the **Finish** button to begin the conversion. When the conversion finishes, the wizard displays one last page, informing you whether the conversion completed successfully or not.

■Note You cannot have the template open in Word while you convert it to an InfoPath form.

A conversion can also complete successfully with issues. When this happens, you can review these issues using the **Design Checker** and correct them in InfoPath. Figure 9-12 shows the results of converting the **Petty Cash Receipt** form.

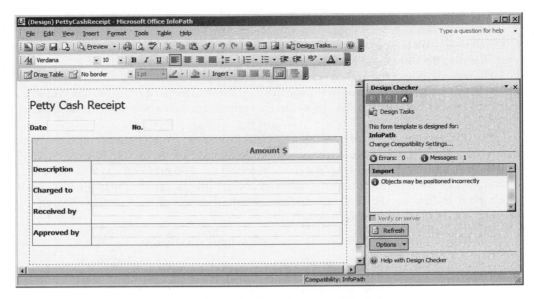

Figure 9-12. *Converting the Petty Cash Receipt form into an InfoPath form*

■Tip When InfoPath converts underline characters to fields, it names the fields generically: **Field1**, **Field2**, etc. However, when InfoPath converts a blank area after a colon to a field, it uses the text to the left of the colon as the field name.

Once you have converted your Word template to InfoPath, use the **Design Checker** to see whether there are any problems you need to resolve. In this case, the only message in the **Design Checker** states that objects may be positioned incorrectly. You might also want to go into some of the fields to add data validation, conditional formatting, or other rules.

Migrating Your Existing Excel Workbook into InfoPath

As with MS Word forms, you may have existing forms in Excel that you want to use with Info-Path. Or maybe you found the perfect form template on Microsoft's template website, but the site only had an Excel version of it. In either case, you definitely do not want to re-create that form from scratch. So how can you import that Excel workbook into InfoPath without starting from a blank form?

I'm going to start with an Excel form template downloaded from Microsoft's site named **Donation Receipt**, which is shown in Figure 9-13. While this form is fairly simple, it demonstrates the concepts needed to convert an Excel template to an InfoPath form. The original version of this form template includes three receipts on a page. I've removed the two extra receipts in order to work with just a single copy of the form. Don't be afraid to modify the forms you download before you convert them to InfoPath. They may contain duplicates of the form because they have been designed to print on standard 8.5"-by-11" sheets of paper.

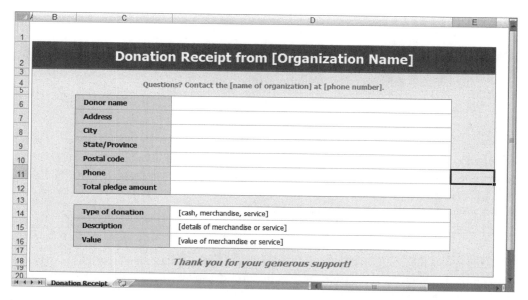

Figure 9-13. *Donation Receipt form as an Excel document*

Note The Excel form contains several cells that have prompting text enclosed in brackets ([ ]). The Info-Path **Import Wizard** will not convert these areas to fields, but rather will leave them as text. To convert these to fields, you may want to remove the text, at least in the three cells at the bottom of the form. You can leave the placeholders in the header and subheader text to be replaced when the form is used.

When you have an Excel workbook exactly as you would like it, save it as an Excel template (with extension .xlsx) in a directory where you can later find it, and then close Excel.

Next, open InfoPath, and choose the option **Import a Form** from the left pane of the **Getting Started** dialog box. This action opens the **Import Wizard**. From this wizard, you can import either an Excel workbook or a Word document. In this case, select **InfoPath importer for Excel workbooks** as the source and click **Next**.

The second page of the **Import Wizard** prompts for the name of the file to import. You can either directly enter the file name or use the **Browse** button to locate the file through Windows' standard **Open** dialog box. But first, let's click the **Options** button to look at the **Options** dialog box.

The **Options** dialog box lets you import just the form layout. You might do this if you want to custom define the form fields. The second option imports both the form layout and the form fields, converting the fields as best it can based on the field properties in Excel. The last option imports the basic form layout, but lets you customize the conversion of the form fields when it brings them into InfoPath. Choose this option when one or more of the following conditions exist in your Excel document:

- You have repeating tables.

- You have cells containing formulas that you want to convert to text boxes.

- You have cells containing numeric data rather than just string data.

- You have cells referenced by formulas in other cells.

- You have empty cells within a grid that displays cell borders.

Tip If you have a fairly complex form, InfoPath may not be able to easily determine which empty cells to convert to text boxes. In Excel, you can provide InfoPath with hints by turning on the borders for cells that you want to convert to text boxes. This provides the same type of effect as underlines, brackets, and colons do in MS Word. You can see the borders defined in Figure 9-13.

After specifying the file to import and selecting your options, click the **Finish** button to begin the conversion. When the conversion finishes, the wizard displays one last page, informing you whether the conversion completes successfully or not.

Note You cannot have the template open in Excel while you convert it to an InfoPath form.

A conversion can complete successfully with issues. When this happens, review these issues using the **Design Checker** and correct them in InfoPath. Figure 9-14 shows the results of converting the **Donation Receipt** form.

You can see in Figure 9-14 that during the conversion process, several unexpected things occurred that you may want to modify. First, the conversion process changed the background colors of the form's cells. Second, the form appears to include a few additional columns and rows. With a little work, you can select the excess table rows and columns and delete them. Then to change the background color of cells to more closely match the original, begin by selecting cell ranges that you want to change. Then right-click the selected cells and click **Borders and Shading** in the drop-down menu. In the dialog box that appears, you may have to click the **Shading** tab to pick the color used to shade the cells. From this page, you can either select one of the existing colors or click the **More Colors** option at the bottom of the color list. This selection opens the **Color Picker** dialog box. Here you can select a color from a larger list of defined colors, or you can custom blend a color using the area on the right to mix the color you want. When you find a color you like, be sure to click the button **Add to Custom Colors** so you can reuse the same color for other cell areas that you may still need to select. With these changes, the InfoPath form now looks like the one shown in Figure 9-15, which closely resembles the original Excel workbook form.

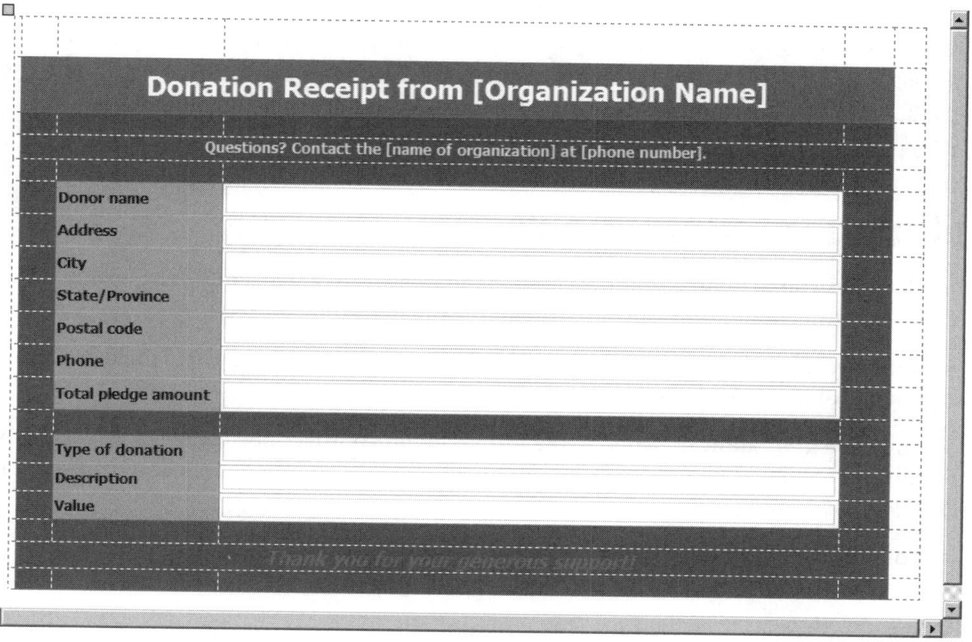

Figure 9-14. *Raw converted Excel form*

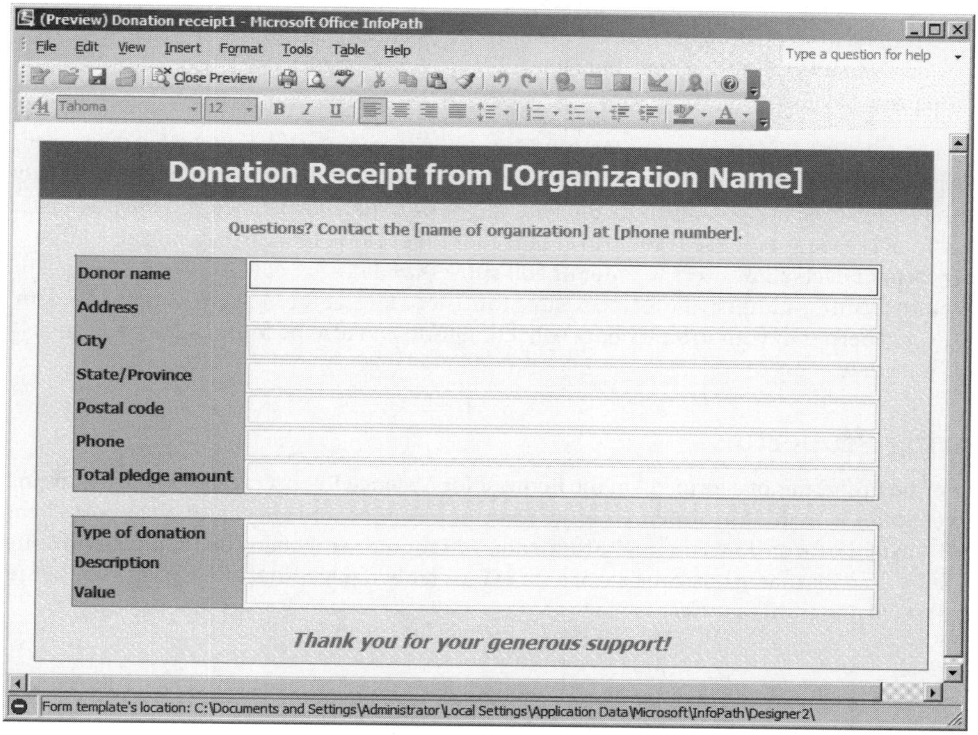

Figure 9-15. *After cleaning up the InfoPath form*

Note InfoPath converts all blank cells to text boxes. However, you can change the control type by right-clicking the control and selecting a different control type from the secondary slideout menu that appears when you position your mouse over **Change to**.

Defining InfoPath Views

InfoPath allows you to define multiple views in the same form against different subsets of the data. Views can serve multiple purposes including the following:

- You have a very large form and decide to divide it into smaller pages to make it more manageable to those entering data.

- You have a workflow attached to the form and the approver needs read-only access to most of the fields, with perhaps the ability to update a comment field and to accept or reject the form.

- You have different people who work on different sections of the form, and they only need to see the part of the form they are responsible for.

- You have different people who have access to the form, but who do not need to see all the data in the form. Perhaps they do not have the rights to see all the data.

- You want to define a separate print view for a form, perhaps to change the controls used to represent the data, thus making the output easier to read and use. You can hide this view from users entering data, but allow them to automatically use it when they attempt to print the form.

You may have additional reasons for wanting multiple views. But no matter what the reason, the technique for building those views begins the same way. I suggest you first build the master form that collects all the possible data that you might want to collect. Once you have a master form, which is a view in of itself, you can create additional views that display subsets of that master form or even allow users to enter or edit subsets of data.

Before creating another view of an existing form, let's look at the view properties of a form. The view properties of your primary data collection form can also be found in all additional views you create.

Viewing Properties

To view the properties of a form, open the **Request for Absence Report** created at the beginning of this chapter. With this form open, click the **View** menu option and select **View Properties** near the bottom of the drop-down menu that appears. You should see a dialog box similar to the one in Figure 9-16. This dialog box consists of a set of four tabbed pages that allow you to configure several visual and print features.

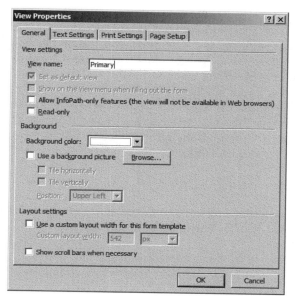

Figure 9-16. *General tab of the View Properties dialog box*

The **General** tab includes basic settings for the view beginning with the **View name**. By default, InfoPath names the views **View_1**, **View_2**, etc. However, these default names do not really describe the purpose of the page. Even if you plan on having only a single view or maybe a view for editing data and a view for printing it, providing a more descriptive name can help you later remember why you created multiple views for the same data source.

Note that you can create a view that allows all InfoPath features, including features not generally available when displaying a form in a web browser. Using this capability on one of your views means that you can create one view for web browsers and a separate view for users who use the form directly from their installation of InfoPath on their desktops.

As you add more views, you can select which view to use as the default view, as well as whether you want to display a menu of available views to the user during data entry. Finally, the **View settings** section allows you to define a view that provides read-only access to the data.

In the **Background** section, you can define a background color for the form or even paint the background with an image. When using an image for the background, you may need to tile the background. A common tiling technique defines a horizontal ribbon image that, when tiled, vertically gives the illusion of a larger background image that repeats to create a page of any length.

In the **Layout settings** section, you can define a standard-width page. You probably want to use this option when creating a view for printing data. You can also choose to use scrollbars when necessary within the form.

The **Text Settings** page in the **View Properties** dialog box lets you change the font and font characteristics for any controls listed in the list box on the left. When you change the font settings through this dialog box, you update the font in every instance of the selected control throughout your form for the current view. For controls that appear frequently through your form, this method of changing the font characteristics saves time over changing the font characteristics of each control instance.

The **Print Settings** page allows you to set the print characteristics of the view. The first option on this page lets you select another view to use instead of the current default view when the user attempts to print this view. You can also change the print orientation, include headers and footers, define the number of copies, and select which pages should be printed if not all of them. When defining headers and footers, InfoPath includes autotext to display the date and/or time you print the form. You can also include page numbering for longer views.

The **Page Setup** page lets you preset the printer that the current view uses as well as the paper and margins. By using this page, users do not have to worry about how to select a network printer or which paper tray to use, or how large the margins should be. You can preset all these options for them so they only need to print the view and then go to the printer to retrieve it.

Generating Your Second View

Now that you know the basic properties of views, let's create a second view for the **Request for Absence Report** that shows only the names of the people who will be absent, the dates they have requested, and the total number of hours.

To create a new view, open the **View** drop-down menu from the InfoPath menu bar and select **Manage Views**. It opens the **Views** task panel on the right side of the window. Figure 9-17 shows this task panel.

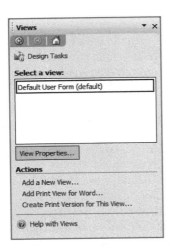

Figure 9-17. *The Views task panel lets you add a new view.*

The top of the task panel begins with a list of your views. In Figure 9-17, the views list only has a single view. Notice that you can also explore the view properties by selecting the view you want and the clicking the **View Properties** button from this task panel.

Beneath the list of views, you will find three actions. The first action lets you create a new view that other users can interact with on the screen. The second action creates a view to send data to Word. The last action lets you create a print version for the view. Let's create a new view for managers to see a summary of absences by clicking **Add a New View**.

First, InfoPath asks you to supply a name for this new view. For this example, name the view **Management Absence Summary**. When you click **OK**, InfoPath displays a blank form for you to create your form. The following list steps through the creation of this second view:

1. Open the **Layout** tasks panel and select the **Table with Title** option from the **Insert Layout Tables** section.

2. Change the title text to **Management Absence Summary**.

3. Using the **Split Table Cells Vertically** option in the **Merge and Split Cells** group, split the second row of the table into six cells.

■**Tip** You can also use the **Custom Split** option.

---

4. Switch to the **Data Source** panel to display the fields associated with this form.

5. Drag the **EmployeeNumber** field to the first cell in the second row.

6. Drag the **EmployeeName** field to the second cell in the second row.

7. Drag the **AbsentFrom** field to the third cell in the second row.

8. Drag the **AbsentTo** field to the fourth cell in the second row.

9. Drag the **HoursRequested** field to the fifth cell in the second row.

10. Drag the **AbsenceType** field to the sixth cell in the second row. With all fields now added to the second row, you might want to resize some of the cells. Also notice that by dragging the fields from the **Data Source** panel into the cell, you automatically get the name of the field, not just the field's control. You can edit these labels.

11. Right-click each of the date cells and select **Change To** from the drop-down menu. In the submenu, select **Text Box**. This changes the display type of these two fields.

12. Right-click each of the cells in the second row and select **Text Box Properties** from the drop-down menu. In the pop-up dialog box, click the **Display** tab and check the option **Read-only**.

13. Open the **Controls** panel and add a text box control to the **Absence Type** cell after the other controls. By default, InfoPath names this control **Field1**.

14. Right-click the **AbsenceType** text box to open the drop-down menu, and select the option **Conditional Formatting**.

15. In the **Conditional Formatting** dialog box, click **Add**.

16. Define the conditional format condition: **AbsenceType is greater than 0**. Also click the check box for **Hide this control**. Then click **OK** twice to save this conditional format. Basically, you want to use this conditional format to hide the **AbsenceType** control when the form displays. You do not want to see the integer value that this field holds. Rather, you want to see text that describes the absence type. However, you cannot do this directly in this field. But you can use the **AbsenceType** field to create a set of rules that place appropriate user-friendly text in the text box named **Field1**.

17. Right-click the **Absence Type** field and select **Rules**. Currently, this field contains a number stored as a string that represents the option button selected from the main data entry absence form.

18. In the **Rules** dialog box, click the **Add** button to add a rule.

19. In the **Rule** dialog box, click the **Set Condition** button.

20. In the **Condition** dialog box, define the first rule as **AbsenceType is equal to "1"**. To enter a text value of 1, select **Type text** from the value drop-down box, and then enter a **1** in the resulting text box that replaces the drop-down. Click **OK** to set this condition.

21. Click the **Add Action** button. In the **Action** dialog box, select the action **Set a field's value**. For the **Field**, click the button to the right of the text box, select **Field1**, and click **OK**. In the **Value** text box, enter the text **Annual Leave**, since this text represents the type of leave associated with the type value of **1**.

22. Click **OK** twice to save your first rule.

23. Repeat the last five steps to add rules for the other five option buttons defined as follows:

- 2: **Personal Leave**
- 3: **Sick Leave**
- 4: **Jury Duty**
- 5: **Military Duty**
- 6: **Time Without Pay**

24. Close the **Rules** dialog box by clicking **OK**.

Now return to the **Default** form view by opening InfoPath's **View** drop-down menu and click **Preview**. Enter some sample data into the form. Then open the **View** drop-down menu again, selecting the **Management Absence Summary** view this time. You should see a form that looks something like Figure 9-18.

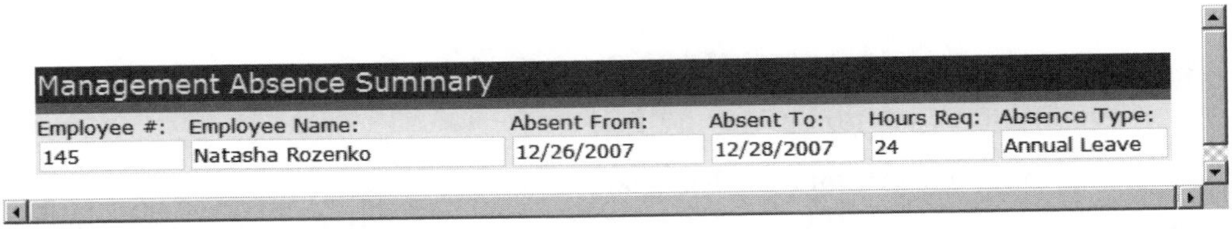

Management Absence Summary					
Employee #:	Employee Name:	Absent From:	Absent To:	Hours Req:	Absence Type:
145	Natasha Rozenko	12/26/2007	12/28/2007	24	Annual Leave

Figure 9-18. *Management summary view of absences*

Notice that only one text box appears in the **Absence Type** column. The text box **Field1** appears with the text assigned to it by the rule created in the **AbsenceType** text box control, which you conditionally hide.

Hopefully, this simple example gives you some ideas of how you can create different views from the same form.

Building Data Connections for Forms

In the first part of this chapter, you saw how to create a basic form that generates XML data files when you submit the form's data. But you can also create an InfoPath form that uses SQL or Access tables as both the source and the destination for data from a form. To do that, you need to create a data connection from the form to the database. Actually, you need two connections, one to select data from the database, and a second to update the database. This section explores the steps needed to created a data connection to a SQL Server database, which you will then use in the next section to build a form to view and update data from one of the tables in that database.

To begin, select the option **Design a Form Template** from the **Getting Started** menu when you open InfoPath. This opens the dialog box shown in Figure 9-19.

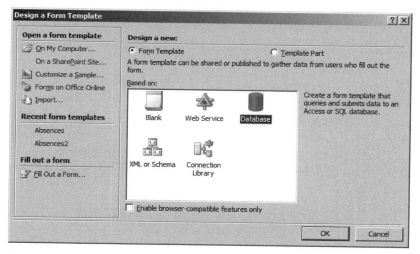

Figure 9-19. *Beginning a form template with a SQL Server data connection*

In this dialog box, select the form template based on a **Database**. Also, make sure that you do not select the option **Enable browser-compatible features only**. If you do leave this option checked, the resulting form can read data from the database, but it cannot submit data back to it.

When you click **OK**, the **Data Connection Wizard** opens. At this point, your only option appears at the top of the form, allowing you to select the SQL Server or Access database you want to use as your form's data source. Click the **Select Database** button to continue.

InfoPath then opens the **Select Data Source** dialog box, shown in Figure 9-20. This dialog box may show existing connections having an extension of .odc. If you do not know the details behind these existing connections, you probably need to create a new connection by double-clicking either **+NewSQLServerConnection.odc** or **+Connect to New Data Source.odc**.

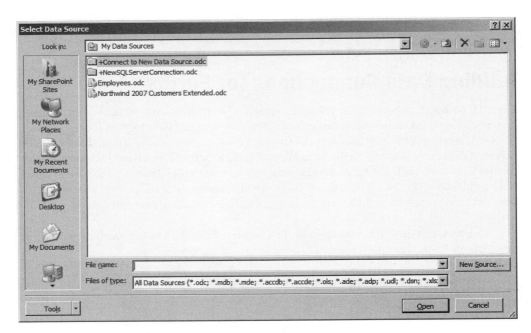

Figure 9-20. *List of available data sources*

■**Note** If you want to connect to an Access database, you should double-click the option **+Connect to New Data Source.odc**. This action opens a dialog box that lets you select from a variety of data sources, depending on what data sources you have already defined on your machine. While it may be tempting to select a data source other than SQL Server or Access just because you may see it on this list, these other data sources will not work with InfoPath at this time.

For this example, you will use the AdventureWorks database running on SQL Server 2005 and will therefore select the option **+NewSQLServerConnection.odc**. This action opens another dialog box titled **Welcome to the Data Connection Wizard** as shown in Figure 9-21.

You need to know the name of the SQL Server you want to connect to before you continue. If you are not sure, check with your database administrator. If you are running SQL Server on your development machine, you could reference the server with the generic name of localhost. However, if you then publish your form on a network share rather than your local machine, the form will not be able to resolve the reference to localhost. It is always better to specifically name the server you want to use, as shown in Figure 9-22.

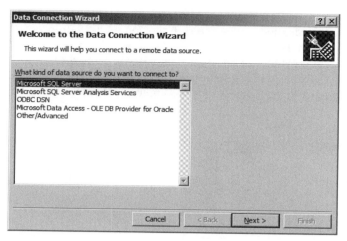

Figure 9-21. *Choosing the type of data source you want to create*

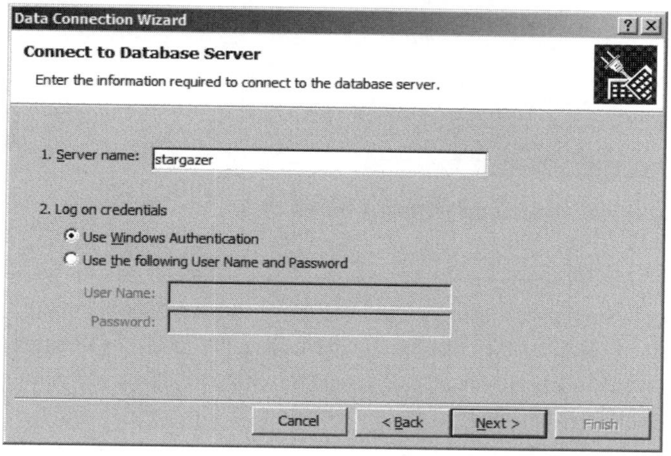

Figure 9-22. *Defining a database server connection*

If you use a central Domain Controller to log in to your machine and validate you on your corporate network, or even if you are running everything on your high-powered desktop workstation, you can continue to use Windows Authentication as your logon credentials. You can also use a specific SQL Server user name and password if your SQL Server security has been set to mixed mode. However, when you use SQL credentials, the operating system passes your logon information over the network using clear text, making it much less secure than Windows Authentication, which does not. If you do use a SQL Server user name and password, at least use a strong password. Strong passwords incorporate at least three of the following types of characters: uppercase letters, lowercase letters, numbers, and symbols. Passwords should have at least 8 characters. Microsoft recommends 14 characters or more.

After specifying a database server, the **Data Connection Wizard** goes to the server and retrieves the names of all the databases defined on that server. It then populates a drop-down list on the next screen of the wizard with these database names. You must select which database you want to use in this connection. When you select the database you want, the wizard populates the list at the bottom half of this screen with the names of the tables in the database. Figure 9-23 shows the wizard defining a connection to the table DimEmployee in the database AdventureWorksDW.

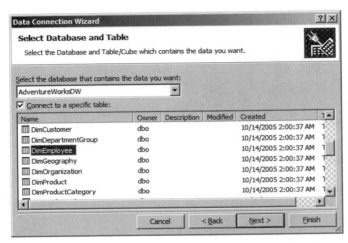

Figure 9-23. *Dialog box for selecting the database and table you want to use*

Note When working with InfoPath, you eventually must select a single table to work with on your form. However, you can create a generic connection to just the database by not checking the check box **Connect to a specific table**. Then each time you select the connection, before you can continue creating your form, InfoPath pops up a dialog box asking you to select a table.

Next, the wizard prompts you to save the data connection file. You can accept the default file name or provide your own. In either case, you should include your own description as well as a friendly name for the connection. You can also supply keywords that can help you search for the connection you want. However, most people do not have enough connections to make this a required step. More importantly, choose a name for the file that clearly defines what data it accesses. Figure 9-24 shows the file name selected for this example's connection.

When you click **Finish**, you are returned to the first screen of the **Data Connection Wizard**. However, now the lower portion of the screen displays the data source structure. If you see only the table name, make sure to select the check box **Show table columns**. You should see the fields in the table, each with a check box before it. Check the box of each field you want to use in your form. If you do not need the field, do not check it. Including only the fields you need in your form helps the query execute faster when retrieving data. Figure 9-25 shows an example of selecting only a few of the available fields from the DimEmployee table.

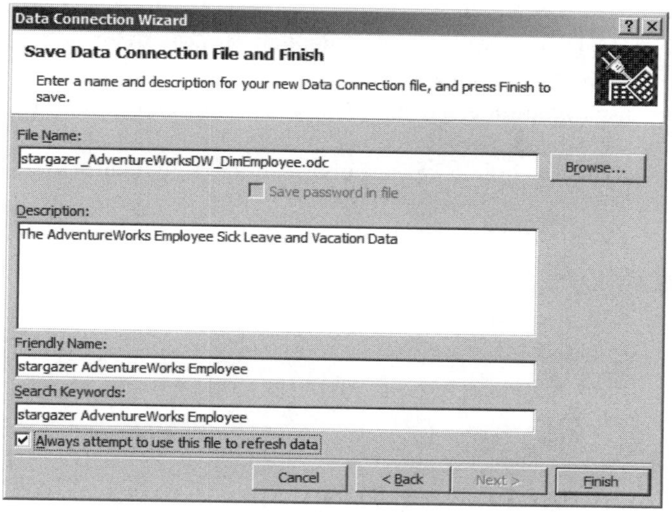

Figure 9-24. *Defining the data connection name*

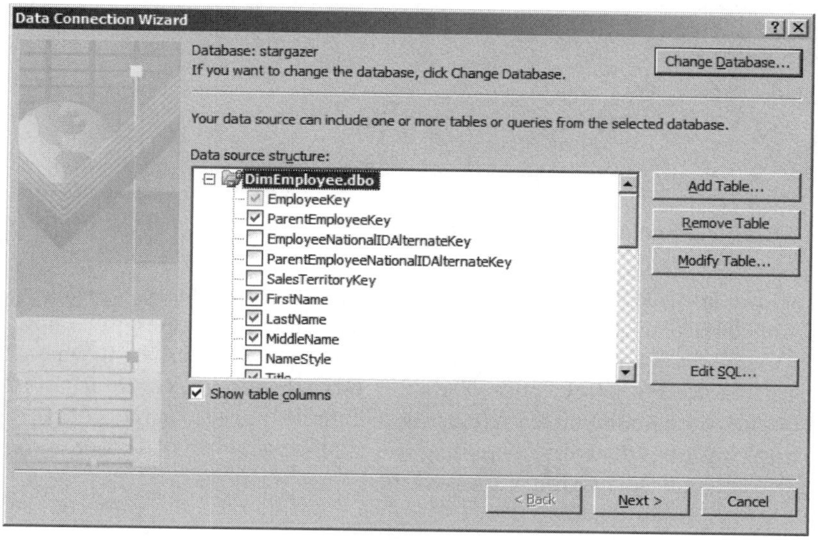

Figure 9-25. *Selecting fields to retrieve from the table*

Note that the field **EmployeeKey** has a selected check box before it, but that the check box is dimmed so that you cannot select or deselect it. This occurs because you must include primary key fields when you want to either select specific records to display or update data. Without the primary key, you cannot submit any changes you make to the fields of a displayed record, because SQL Server would not know which record to update.

An interesting option at this point is the ability to add another table to your data source structure by clicking the **Add Table** button. You can select from any of the tables in the database defined by the connection. However, you will need to link the tables selected. Therefore, you might use this feature to define parent-child relationships between tables. You can then use InfoPath forms to display data from the parent record in individual controls and display the child data in repeating tables or repeating sections.

When you click **Next**, the wizard displays one final screen. This screen lets you enter a name for the primary data connection used to select data from the database for the form. If you defined a non-web-based form, you can also supply a name for the submit connection. Figure 9-26 shows this dialog box.

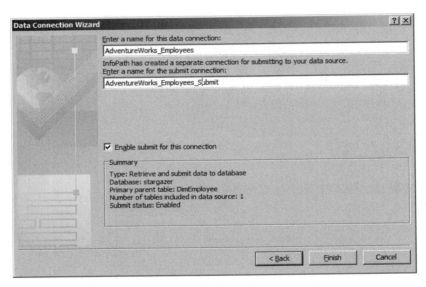

Figure 9-26. *Naming the retrieve and submit data connections*

At this point, you have finished defining your connection for the current form. However, you can reuse the connection for additional forms. In that case, simply select the connection from the list described earlier in Figure 9-20. If the connection points to the database in general (no table selected), you first need to select a table. Then the rest of the process continues from the point in which you select the fields you want to use and enter the name of a data connection(s). The next section continues the story of creating your SQL-based form at the point just after you have finished using the **Data Connection Wizard**.

Connecting InfoPath Forms to Data

Having made it through the definition of the data connection, InfoPath generates a default form for working with the data. This default form, shown in Figure 9-27, has three sections.

The top section uses the **Title and Table** layout control you saw earlier. Here you can enter a title for the form. You can also include content for the form here. But before doing that, let's look at what you can do with the other two sections.

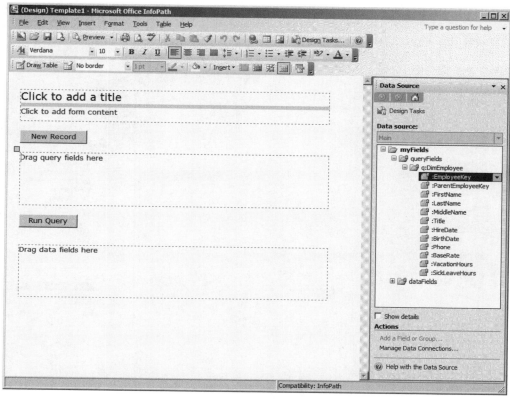

Figure 9-27. *Selecting a query field(s) for the form's data retrieval*

The second section is called the *query section* because here you can drag fields that you want to use to query the database. Your first thought might be to use the primary key for the main table as the query field. In fact, if you look back at Figure 9-27, you can see the screenshot shows me in the process of dragging the primary key for the DimEmployee table, **EmployeeKey**, from the list of query fields in the **Data Source** panel to the query section of the form. While using the primary keys is not a bad choice, you can actually use any field to query the database. Using fields that correspond to indexes in the database helps the performance of the query, but even that is not strictly necessary.

In the third section, you place data fields. Again, InfoPath provides an easy way to do this. Simply expand the dataFields folder in the **Data source** list on the right. If you want to include all the fields, simply drag the table d:DimEmployee to the third section, as shown in Figure 9-28. However, if you only want a subset of the available fields, open the d:DimEmployee folder to access the individual fields, dragging each one individually over to the third section of the form.

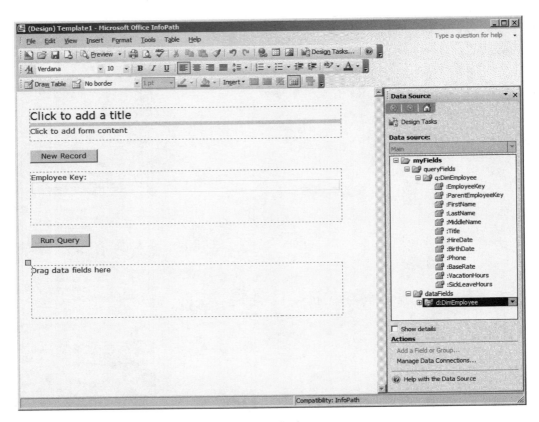

Figure 9-28. *Selecting the data fields to display in the form*

After dragging the entire table to the third section, InfoPath asks whether you want to place the data in a repeating table or a repeating section with controls. In this case, because the table only has a relatively small number of fields, you might choose to use a repeating table. A repeating table works best when you plan to display multiple records from a query.

On the other hand, if you want to work on a single record at a time, or if you have a large number of fields, or if any of the fields consist of large text areas, you might want to use the repeating section with controls. Initially, InfoPath adds all the controls vertically down the form. If you want to provide additional structure to this section, perhaps by adding a table within the section to position the individual controls, you must do that manually.

No matter how you lay out the fields, you can control many of the properties of the controls as you saw earlier, including converting the control types of some fields or adding conditional formatting, rules, and data validation. Figure 9-29 shows the resulting form template designed to display a list of employees with their vacation and sick leave balances.

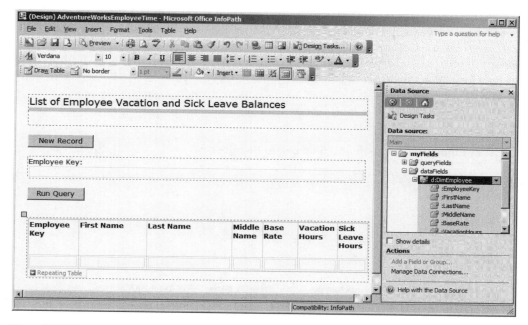

Figure 9-29. *Inserting the data fields in a repeating table*

To see how this template works, click the **Preview** button in the toolbar. This opens a new window with the form displayed as it would appear when someone opens it. In Figure 9-30, you can see that a single **Employee Key** value has been entered. When you click the **Run Query** button, the select query built in to the **Data Connection Wizard** picks up the fields defined in the query section of the report and uses them to return a filtered set of data. Since the **Employee Key** serves as the primary key to the table, supplying a valid key value returns a single record.

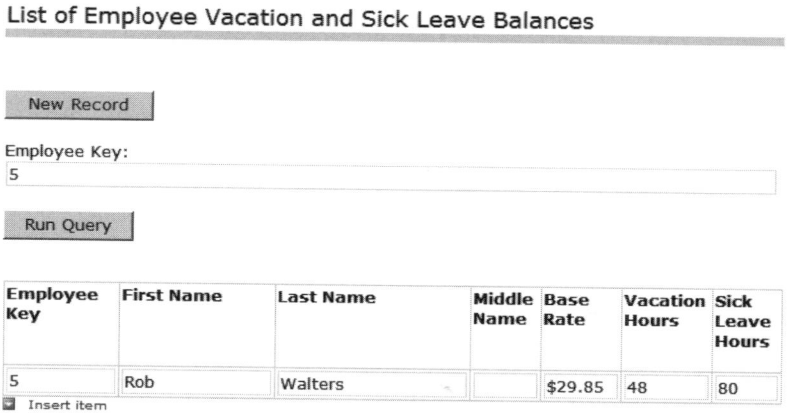

List of Employee Vacation and Sick Leave Balances

New Record

Employee Key:
5

Run Query

Employee Key	First Name	Last Name	Middle Name	Base Rate	Vacation Hours	Sick Leave Hours
5	Rob	Walters		$29.85	48	80

Insert item

Figure 9-30. *Querying the form data using a single field, the table's primary key*

Perhaps a more interesting result appears when you click the **Run Query** button without entering any value for the **Employee Key**. In this case, the query performs no filtering on the data retrieved, thus returning the entire table as shown in Figure 9-31. I would not recommend doing this on a large table with millions of records. In fact, InfoPath warns that returning all the records for a table can take some time. On the other hand, it can be quite useful for a small set of data.

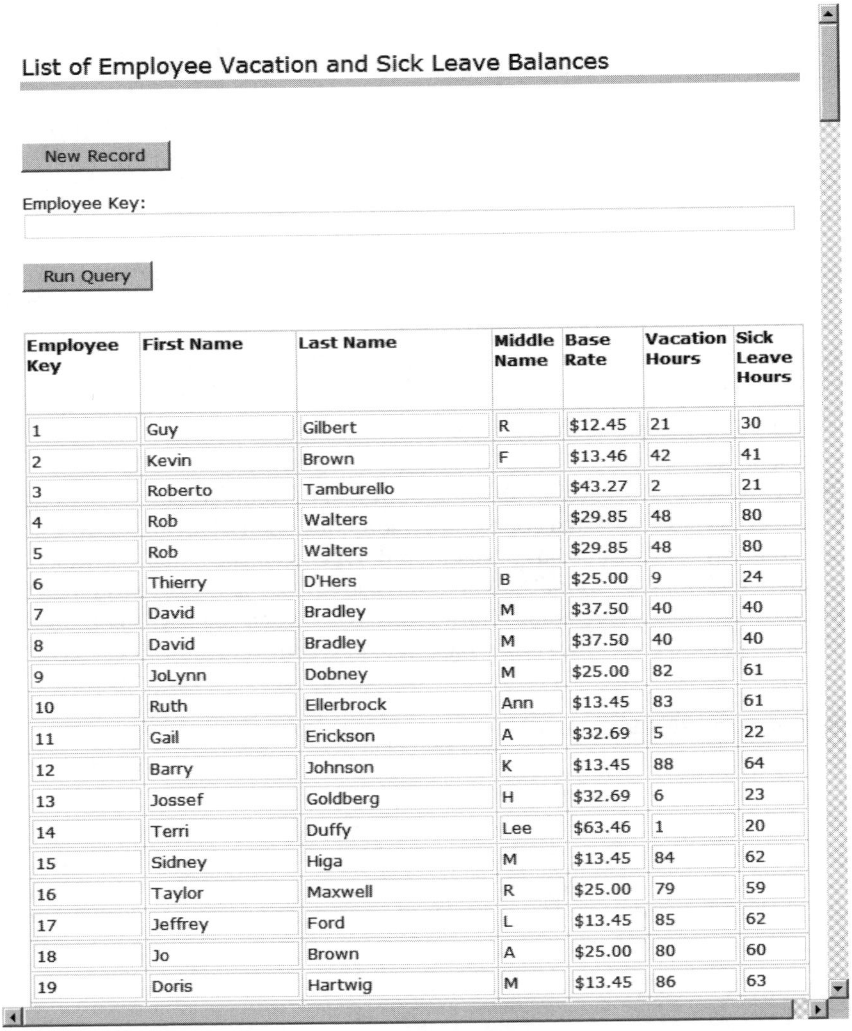

List of Employee Vacation and Sick Leave Balances

New Record

Employee Key:

Run Query

Employee Key	First Name	Last Name	Middle Name	Base Rate	Vacation Hours	Sick Leave Hours
1	Guy	Gilbert	R	$12.45	21	30
2	Kevin	Brown	F	$13.46	42	41
3	Roberto	Tamburello		$43.27	2	21
4	Rob	Walters		$29.85	48	80
5	Rob	Walters		$29.85	48	80
6	Thierry	D'Hers	B	$25.00	9	24
7	David	Bradley	M	$37.50	40	40
8	David	Bradley	M	$37.50	40	40
9	JoLynn	Dobney	M	$25.00	82	61
10	Ruth	Ellerbrock	Ann	$13.45	83	61
11	Gail	Erickson	A	$32.69	5	22
12	Barry	Johnson	K	$13.45	88	64
13	Jossef	Goldberg	H	$32.69	6	23
14	Terri	Duffy	Lee	$63.46	1	20
15	Sidney	Higa	M	$13.45	84	62
16	Taylor	Maxwell	R	$25.00	79	59
17	Jeffrey	Ford	L	$13.45	85	62
18	Jo	Brown	A	$25.00	80	60
19	Doris	Hartwig	M	$13.45	86	63

Figure 9-31. *Retrieving the entire table when no query field is specified*

But even if you have millions of records, you could add query fields to limit records to a reasonable number. In the case of your employee file, you might want to see employees only from a specific department.

■**Tip** As you can see by the examples provided, the query values can only exactly match values in the table. You can get around this limitation by creating a view in the database that combines the data you want, including the addition of calculated fields. For example, if you want to list employees with more than 100 hours of combined vacation and sick time, you could create a Boolean field in the view that resolves to **True** if the sum of vacation and sick hours exceeds 100. Then in your InfoPath form, you can include this field in the query section and check for a value of **True**.

Creating and Reusing Form Sections with Template Parts

Most programmers practice code reusability. Form designers can also benefit from reusing common groups of controls, especially when those controls require extensive formatting. Info-Path provides a way to build groups of controls that you can later reuse in other templates. In this example, you will build a template for a customer's mailing address so you can use it in a variety of forms, including the order shipment page of an order manifest. In fact, this page uses the template part twice, once for the mail-to address and once for the bill-to address.

You start the process of building a template part similar to that of building a template form. Click **Design a Form Template** from the **Getting Started** dialog box when you start Info-Path. From the **Design a Form Template** dialog box, select the option button **Template Part**. Select the **Blank** template part and click **OK**. Figure 9-32 shows this dialog box.

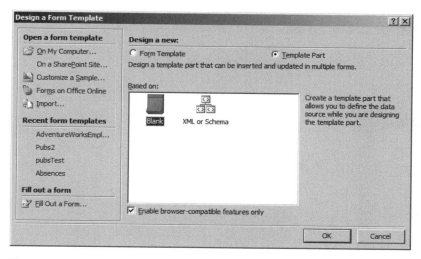

Figure 9-32. *Designing a template part*

■**Caution** If you plan on using the template in browser-compatible forms, be sure to select the option **Enable browser-compatible features only** before clicking **OK**.

> **Note** When designing a template part, you must begin with a blank template or an existing XML schema. However, you can change the binding for the template part controls after you add it to another form to bind the controls to other data sources.

When InfoPath opens the blank template design area, you should notice that you have all the design tools in the **Design Tasks** panel to create a form layout, add controls to that layout, define data sources, and run your design through the **Design Checker**. You do not have the ability to create multiple views for the template part. However, in any form that you add the template part, you can create alternative views. You also do not have the options associated with publishing the form, because you cannot publish a template part, since it is not meant to represent an entire form by itself.

Figure 9-33 shows the completely designed template part. It contains several required fields and several optional fields. While most of these fields consist of simple text boxes with little formatting, the **State** field uses a drop-down listbox that includes the names of all the states. You can add information for a drop-down manually (as was done for this example), read it from the form's data source, or use an external data source. You can even change the data source after you drop the template part onto a form that you later design. Therefore, you might create a minimal list box, one with only a few entries for testing purposes, if you know that the data source for the form you plan on building later can retrieve values for the list either from the data source itself or from another external data source.

Figure 9-33. *Completed template part showing drop-down state list*

When you have finished the template part, test it using the preview mode. Then save the completed part to a directory of your choice.

■**Tip** If you plan on designing a large number of forms, keeping your reusable template parts in a separate directory on your design machine or a network share, if you are only one of several form designers, helps organize your template parts.

After you have saved it, open the **Controls** panel and click the hyperlink beneath the list of **Insert Controls**: **Add or Remove Custom Controls**. This action opens the dialog box shown in Figure 9-34.

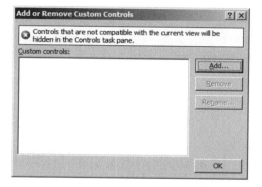

Figure 9-34. *Custom control list page*

Click the **Add** button to add the control you just created.

■**Note** You must save the template part first. This dialog box does not assume that you want to add the currently open template part.

From this menu, you can add either a template part or an ActiveX control. In this case, you want to select the **Template Part** option and click **Next**.

The dialog box next asks for the file location of the template part. Enter the full directory path where you saved the completed part manually, or use the **Browse** button to locate and select the file. When you click the **Finish** button, the final page of the dialog box shows the name assigned to the custom control and the version. Clicking the **Close** button on this page closes the dialog box and returns you to the **Add or Remove Custom Controls** page shown in Figure 9-35, where you can see that your custom template part has been added successfully.

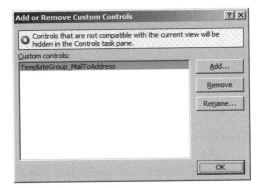

Figure 9-35. *Add or Remove Custom Controls dialog box showing the new template part*

The next time you open InfoPath to design a new form or even to modify the design of an existing one, you will see in the **Custom** section of the **Controls** panel the new template part you created and saved. Figure 9-36 shows the **Addresses** page of the **Order Shipping Informa-tion** form. On this page, you need to have two possible addresses. The first address represents the mailing address for the customer, while the second address lists the customer's billing address. Most larger businesses provide centralized ordering services for their remote locations. Therefore, while you may ship an order to one address, you may need to send the bill for the order to an entirely different address.

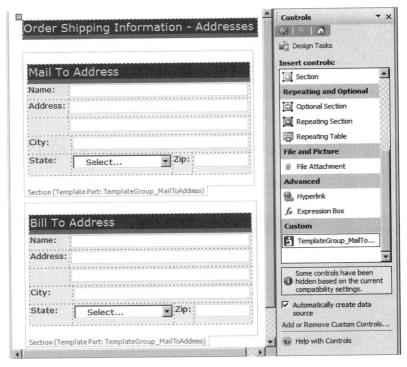

Figure 9-36. *Completed Addresses page for the Order Shipping Information form*

In this case, you added the same custom template part twice to the same form. However, you can also add this same control to other forms. In each case, you can customize the formatting of the fields, the label data, the binding information for the controls, and even the data source for the drop-down list box. Template parts can be as simple as this one or significantly more complex. The point is that they provide reusability within form design, which also results in uniformity in the way similar information appears and works.

Summary

In this chapter, you explored some of the basic features of InfoPath, in the process learning how to create a simple form that saves submitted data as XML files, create forms that work with tables in SQL Server, and create and use reusable template parts. InfoPath provides more features than I could cover in such a short amount of space. Fortunately, other books such as *Pro Info-Path 2007* by Philo Janus (Apress, 2007) can help you further explore the details of InfoPath.

The next chapter dives deeper into using InfoPath specifically with SharePoint, allowing you to use lists to both populate your drop-down form lists and submit data. You will also look more closely at form libraries within SharePoint to store your forms and then use Forms Services to display the forms within a browser.

CHAPTER 10

■■■

Publishing InfoPath Forms in SharePoint Libraries

In the last chapter, you saw how easily you can build InfoPath forms and use InfoPath to enter data into such forms. When examining those forms, the text primarily focused on using forms created and saved in a single location, even if that location was on your local computer. However, unlike data files for other Office products such as Word, Excel, PowerPoint, or Access, you cannot simply copy an InfoPath form to another person's computer and then open and use it. You have to publish the form either to that user's computer or to a network file share that other people in your organization can access, the latter being preferable to the former.

However, even if these users have access to the network file share, perhaps not everyone that needs to enter data into that form may have a copy of InfoPath installed on their computers. To be really useful, you need to create forms that anyone can use, preferably through a SharePoint library. SharePoint allows you to store InfoPath forms in libraries and then use them via InfoPath Forms Services. However, there is a cost for this ability to display forms using your web browser: you must compromise your design by avoiding the use of some of InfoPath's features that Forms Services does not support.

In this chapter, we will look further at publishing forms, both to network file shares and form libraries, using SharePoint to allow more users to access them.

Publishing InfoPath Forms to a Network File Share

The easiest way to publish your InfoPath forms, and perhaps your only way to publish them if you do not have InfoPath Forms Services running on your SharePoint server, uses a simple network file share. A *network file share* is any directory on your network that people in your organization can access from their local computers.

Anyone with InfoPath on their local computer can open the published forms and enter data using them. They can then save a copy of their data back to the same directory. Let's see how this works by using one of the forms created in the last chapter, the **Request for Absence Report**.

If you start by saving your InfoPath form to a network file share from the very beginning of its design life, you may not need to worry about this step. You already have the form template saved where others can access it. However, this is probably not the case. Most likely, you save the form to your local hard drive at intervals as you work on it, just in case you lose power. You also might save the form locally on a regular basis because you simply do not have enough time to finish working on it in a single development session.

No matter where you save your form as you develop it, there will come a day when you complete your work. Then you need to publish the form someplace where others can access and use it.

After you have finished designing your form, you need to publish the form to a network file share that all authorized users can access to open and use the form. You cannot simply perform a file copy of the form from your local computer drive to the network file share, because InfoPath embeds the URL of the template in the definition of the template and the data files created by filling in the template. Therefore, you need to publish the final form to its shared location.

To begin publishing a form, select **Publish** from InfoPath's **File** menu option while you have the form open in **Design** mode as shown in Figure 10-1. The **Publish** option not only makes sure that you can save the file to a new shared location, but also brands the copy of the template placed there with that new file location.

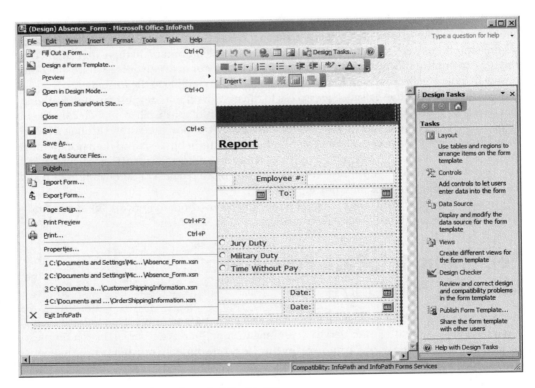

Figure 10-1. *Publishing a form from InfoPath's File menu*

If you haven't saved your finished form before attempting to publish it, you may first get the pop-up **Save As** dialog box asking you to save the form. This copy of the form is your design master copy. Do not confuse it with the published version of the form that others will access. It is important to keep a copy of your design master in case you need to go back to it and make changes. You can then republish the modified form, replacing the published version of the form.

After saving a design master copy of your form, the first page of the **Publishing Wizard**
appears. When you publish an InfoPath form, you have the option of four different destina-
tions as shown in Figure 10-2. The first option lets you publish the form to a SharePoint library.
Notice that this option says that you can publish to SharePoint with or without Forms Services.
If you publish to a SharePoint server that does not support Forms Services, then SharePoint
acts as a file storage and sharing location. Earlier in this book, I mentioned that SharePoint
integrates with most of the Microsoft Office products and allows you to open the document
directly in the appropriate Microsoft Office product. That statement holds true for InfoPath as
well. If you save an InfoPath form to a standard document library in SharePoint, anyone with
InfoPath can navigate to the library, right-click the form's name, and select the option to open
the form using InfoPath. That user can then use InfoPath to display the form and fill it in.

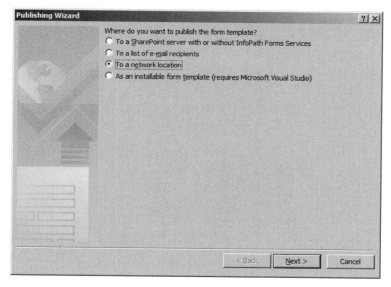

Figure 10-2. *Publishing to a network location if you do not want to use SharePoint*

A problem, of course, exists for those users who do not have InfoPath on their local machine.
They cannot open the form using InfoPath. For them, Forms Services provides that ability to
open InfoPath forms within a browser window without the aid of InfoPath. I will return to this
option in the section "Using InfoPath Forms Services for Customers Without InfoPath" later in
this chapter.

The second option allows you to send the form to a group of e-mail recipients. They can
then open the e-mail, fill in the form, and send back their entered data. But let's assume for
now that you do not want to be the person who has to send everyone an e-mail when they need
to get a copy of the form to enter the data.

The third option lets you publish the form to a network location. From there, anyone with
InfoPath on their local machine can open the template, fill it in, and save the resulting data
back to a separate data file in the same or different directory. Let's examine this option in more
detail.

Publishing a Form to a Network Location

If you decide to publish to a network location, you must enter the URL of that location. When you click **Next** in the page shown in Figure 10-2, the next page of the **Publishing Wizard** asks for the URL, as shown in Figure 10-3. You can provide a fully qualified URL beginning with the name of the server. You can also publish the file using a mapped drive letter to make it easier to reference the URL. If you use a mapped drive letter, InfoPath and the operating system automatically converts this to the full URL for you.

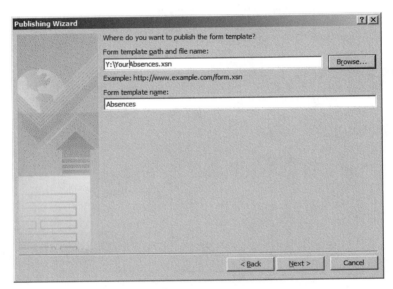

Figure 10-3. *Identifying the location and file name of your published network form*

■**Tip** You can test publishing to a network location by creating a mapped drive letter to a directory on your local machine. Let's say you have a directory named C:\Absences. To create a mapped drive to this directory, open Windows Explorer, open the **Tools** menu, and select **Map Network Drive**. In the resulting dialog box, first select a drive letter that you want to use. Then enter the folder name, adding your computer name as a reference and changing the drive share. A drive share defaults to the letter of the drive followed by a **$**. For example, on my computer, I might enter **\\stargazer\c$\absences**.

After specifying the form template path and file name you want to use, you must also supply the name of the template. This name does not have to be the same as the name you used while you were developing the form on your local machine or the file name in which you save it.

On the next page of the wizard, shown in Figure 10-4, you have the opportunity to enter a different path that users might use to access the form from the location specified on the last page. This option may be useful if you have defined public URLs, perhaps because you are using reverse proxy publishing or load balancing in a SharePoint farm scenario. On the other hand, if all users can access the file folder where you will publish your form using the same name you entered in the previous screen, just click **Next**.

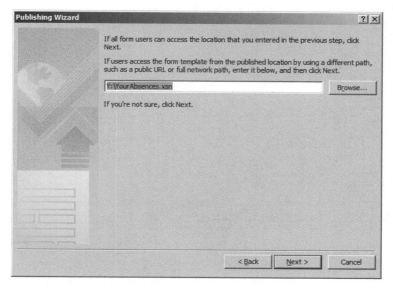

Figure 10-4. *Providing an alternative URL for users to access the published form*

The last page of the wizard displays the information you entered, including the form name, the path you will use to publish the form, and the path all other users will use to access the form. When you click **Publish**, InfoPath writes your form to the designated location. It then adds the two check boxes to the wizard's page, as shown in Figure 10-5, that let you send the form to e-mail recipients or open the form template from the published location.

Notice the reference to **Security Level** in this figure. By default, InfoPath sets the security level for a form to **Restricted**. A Restricted security level limits the form to accessing content only from within the form itself. This means the form cannot use any of the following features:

- Custom dialog boxes

- Custom task panes

- Data connections

- Human workflow services

- Linked pictures

- Microsoft ActiveX controls

- Managed code and script

- Print view for Microsoft Office Word 2003

- Roles based on Active Directory directory service

- Rules associated with opening forms

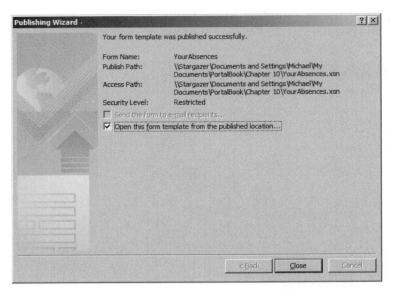

Figure 10-5. *After publishing the form, open the form to verify it.*

There is a second security level, Domain security, that allows forms to access content stored in the form itself, as well as

- Data in the same domain as the form

- Data in domains included in the trusted sites zone in Internet Explorer

- Content in the local computer and local intranet zone of Internet Explorer

Finally, the Full Trust security level allows a form to access data in itself, in the same domain as the form, and in other domains where it has access. It also provides access to files and settings on the computer. You can grant Full Trust to a form if you digitally sign a form with a trusted root certificate. Your system administrator can help generate certificates that allow you to install and use Full Trust forms.

Using Your Published Form

When you use a mapped drive, InfoPath assumes that the form resides on a server. Therefore, when you attempt to open the form template from its published location, Microsoft Office flags the action as a potential security concern and displays the message shown in Figure 10-6. Since you are working on drives within your network, you typically can ignore this notice.

Figure 10-6. *InfoPath displays a security warning when you open a server-based form.*

If you checked the option to open the form after publishing it, as shown earlier in Figure 10-5, you may also see the **Form Template Conflict** dialog box, shown in Figure 10-7. This dialog box appears because InfoPath assigns each template created a unique ID, and in this case, I am using the same box on which I developed and saved the initial template to now access the published version of the form. This ID exists in both the locally saved copy of the form and the published version. When you attempt to open the template from the published site, InfoPath recognizes that this ID also exists in a version of the template on your computer and displays this dialog box. It gives you the option to replace the form template on your computer if the conflicting template is more recent and comes from a trusted source. You can keep the template on your computer and open it by clicking the button **Keep Form Template on Your Computer**. This option allows you to retain your local version of the template, and InfoPath opens it rather than the published version. On the other hand, other users will not see this dialog box when they directly access the published version and can use the published template when they open it.

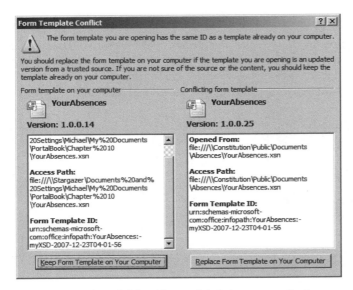

Figure 10-7. *InfoPath identifies multiple instances of a form.*

Saving Your Completed Form

Once you have opened the form, proceed to fill in the fields as illustrated in Figure 10-8. Because you have opened the form using your local copy of InfoPath, when you are done, you must use the **Save** or **Save As** option in the **File** menu to save your results. (Actually, both options display the **Save As** dialog box.)

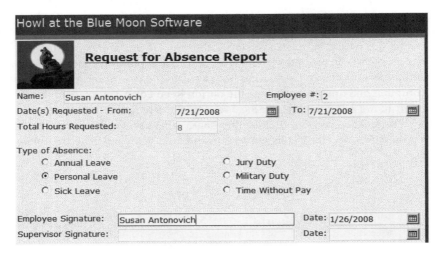

Figure 10-8. *Opening a form for use within InfoPath*

Notice in the **Save As** dialog box that the file type being saved is XML, not XSN. When you save your completed form, you do not actually resave the form. Instead, you save just the data entered in the form along with the necessary information to tell InfoPath where to find the form template to redisplay the data. You can save the XML file in any directory. Because Info-Path saves information on how to find the form template, you do not have to save the data file in the same directory as the form template.

Figure 10-9 shows an example of the contents of an XML file after opening and saving a set of data from a Windows Vista computer that can access the published form. You can see that it contains information to identify the location of the form template (four lines from the top in this figure). It then displays all the fields and their values as XML elements.

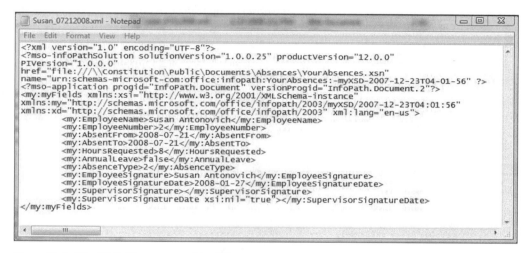

Figure 10-9. *The XML file generated by filling in an InfoPath form*

If you were to double-click the data file, even after moving it to another location, the Windows operating system would use the information in the XML file to recognize the data as coming from an InfoPath form. It would then open InfoPath from your local machine and use the information in the XML file to locate and open the template. Finally, it would load the data from the XML file into the opened template. If you have a local version of the template, and it is different from the version used to create the data file, InfoPath would again display the conflict dialog box shown earlier in Figure 10-7, allowing you to update your version.

Thus you can publish an InfoPath form to a network share where others can open the form, fill it in, and save the results to the same or different directory. Each person who fills in the form creates his own XML file. Because the user has direct control over defining the resulting data file name, you might want to give some consideration to defining standards ahead of time. For example, it might make sense to have everyone name data files created by the **Request for Absence Report** by using the person's name followed by an underscore character, and then the first date in the date range of the absence. However, any consistent method followed by all users would serve the purpose of organizing your files.

Using InfoPath Forms Services for Customers Without InfoPath

Suppose you don't want to publish your forms to a network file share because it requires the form users to have InfoPath on their desktop, and not everyone in your organization has Info-Path installed. If you have InfoPath Forms Services installed on your SharePoint server, you can publish your templates to document libraries. Users can then access the forms from the library just like they would access other document types.

You can specify in the library whether to attempt to open the file using the appropriate client application or to open it in the user's web browser. Of course, if you do not have Forms Services, you can still publish your form to the library, and users can open the form using their local copy of InfoPath. But with Forms Services, you can give users the choice of whether they want to open the document in InfoPath or directly within their browser.

Publishing to a SharePoint Server

Using the **Request for Absence Report** again from the previous section, let's republish the form, but instead of choose the network share option, choose the SharePoint option, as shown in Figure 10-10.

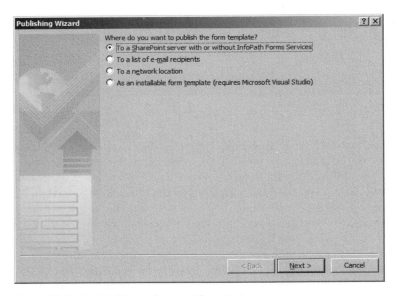

Figure 10-10. *Publishing a form to SharePoint*

Next, enter the SharePoint site where you want to publish the form. You need to enter the URL of the library for the site you want to use. You can navigate to it as long as you can enter the URL of the site itself. Figure 10-11 shows the next page of the **Publishing Wizard**, where you can specify just the name of your SharePoint site or InfoPath Forms Services site.

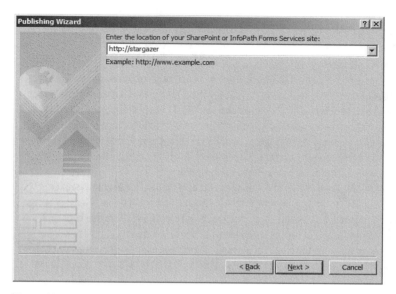

Figure 10-11. *Identifying the site where you want to publish the form*

On the next page of the wizard, shown in Figure 10-12, you must first specify whether you want users to fill out the form using a browser or if you want them to download the form and open it with a local copy of InfoPath.

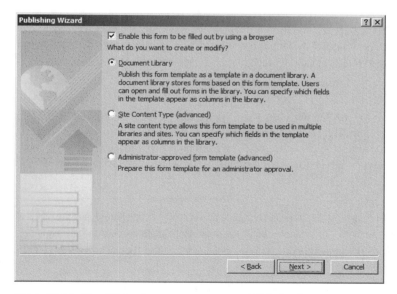

Figure 10-12. *Identifying how you want to publish the form*

VALIDATING YOUR FORM BEFORE PUBLISHING

Before beginning the process of publishing your form, you should have InfoPath verify that the form does not contain any features that browsers do not support. You can do this by selecting **Form Options** under the **Tools** menu. In the **Category** list, select **Compatibility**. On the right side of the screen, select if necessary the option **Design a form template that can be opened in a browser or InfoPath**. To verify the compatibility of the form with InfoPath Forms Services, enter the name of your SharePoint server in the text box in the **Browser compatibility** section. For example, I would enter `http://stargazer` for my server. When I save the form, InfoPath automatically adds the rest of the URL, transforming my entry to `http://stargazer/_vti_bin/ FormsServices.asmx`. Click **OK** to accept your changes to **Form Options**.

Then open the **Design Tasks** panel if you do not already have it open and select **Design Checker**. It may take a few moments for InfoPath to verify your form. However, when it finishes, it displays a set of errors and messages. You must fix errors before you can publish the form if you want Forms Services to be able to open the form. However, messages tell you of noncritical concerns that you can ignore or address without affecting whether Forms Services can open the form. For example, a message warning you that dialog box validation messages will not show merely reminds you that dialog box validation messages can only appear when you open the form with InfoPath.

Next, on this same page of the wizard, you must select from three choices for publishing your form. The first option lets you publish the form to a document library. If your form only has declarative functionality, you can publish the form usually without assistance to a document library and begin using it as long as Forms Services has already been activated for the site.

■**Note** *Declarative functionality* means that the form supports basic conditional formatting that may change the form's appearance, alter the visibility of individual controls, or change the read-write state of controls.

When you first get started working with InfoPath, I generally recommend that you publish each form template to a new library. However, you will see in the section "Working with a Library That Has Multiple Content Types" that you can publish more than one template to a single library using content types, which the second option on this page of the wizard foretells.

■**Tip** When deciding whether to make more than one template available in a single library, ask the users of the library if that makes sense to them. For example, while you might include a gas-mileage-only expense form in the same library as more extensive trip expense forms, you probably would not include either of these with a vacation or absence request form.

Finally, use the last option on this page when you have a form that requires administrator approval. Form templates that use managed code or data connections usually require the assistance of your SharePoint administrator to set up. These forms also typically require Full Trust or at least Domain trust to run, since the data is not self-contained in the form.

For this example, I will run you through publishing the **Request for Absence Report** to a standard document library, since it does not used managed code or reference external data.

On the next page of the wizard, shown in Figure 10-13, you can choose to publish the form to either a new library or an existing library. If you choose to publish to an existing library, you can select from the available libraries found on the SharePoint server listed at the bottom of this page of the wizard.

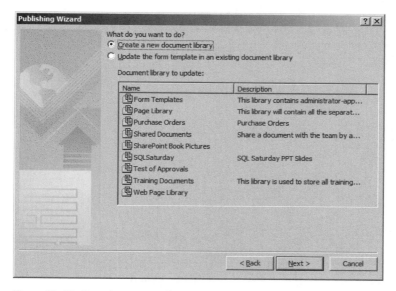

Figure 10-13. *Creating a new document library at the same time you publish the form*

You may be tempted to try to publish your form to an existing document library by clicking the second option button in Figure 10-13, and then selecting a library from the list. However, if you do not first configure the document library to accept InfoPath forms, it will reject the update. You can only update existing document libraries that already have an InfoPath form defined as the default content type. On the other hand, this list also displays form libraries to which you can directly publish your form. Unfortunately, there is no easy way to tell from this list which libraries are defined as document libraries and which might be defined as form libraries.

So you might think that you can simply cancel the **Publishing Wizard** at this point, switch to SharePoint, and manually create a new document library. However, when you create a new document library from within SharePoint, you do not get an InfoPath document as a default template type. This is because unlike Word, Excel, and several other template options that SharePoint does include, a blank InfoPath form is not an option. While you could accomplish this task by creating a new content type first, building the document library, adding the content type to the library, and then making that content type the default for the library, that entails a lot of extra steps.

You could also create a form library, which is essentially a specialized document library designed to handle XML data created from form templates. A form library uses a Microsoft

InfoPath document as its default template type. You could then update the template of that form library in this step.

The easiest method of publishing a new form is to just select the first option shown earlier in the page in Figure 10-13, and let InfoPath do all the necessary work to create a new document library based on the InfoPath form you want to publish.

In fact, choosing that option prompts you for the name of the document library along with a description. You can see this on the next page of the **Publishing Wizard**, shown in Figure 10-14.

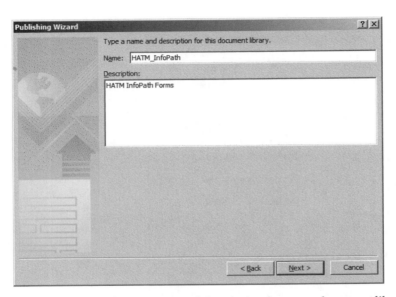

Figure 10-14. *Providing a name and description for a new document library*

Defining Metadata for the Document Library

When creating a new document library, SharePoint wants to know what additional columns you want to associate with the library. SharePoint gives you the option of adding any of the fields from the InfoPath form as columns. Displaying the major form fields as columns makes it easier to scan through the saved data files after using the form to see important information without having to open each data file individually.

■**Tip** Recall from Chapter 7, which covered managing SharePoint lists in Excel, that you can export the metadata from a document library to a spreadsheet. Since the metadata from this library represents data from completing the forms, you can use the resulting Excel spreadsheet to process the data to display groupings, subtotals, totals, averages, etc.

Figure 10-15 shows that InfoPath recognizes most of the simple data fields and automatically adds them to the list of potential columns in the document library it creates. If you want to check whether the form has any additional fields that you might want to display as a column, click the **Add** button to the right of the dialog box.

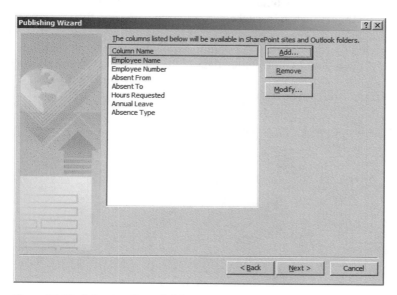

Figure 10-15. *Selecting form fields to appear as columns in the library*

When you click the **Add** button, the **Select a Field or Group** dialog box appears, as shown in Figure 10-16. If you scroll through the list of available fields, you can select any field from the form not already included in the column list already selected in Figure 10-15. Notice that you can also use this opportunity to rename any form field that may have an abbreviated or complex name with a more descriptive name, which will then display in the column header of the library.

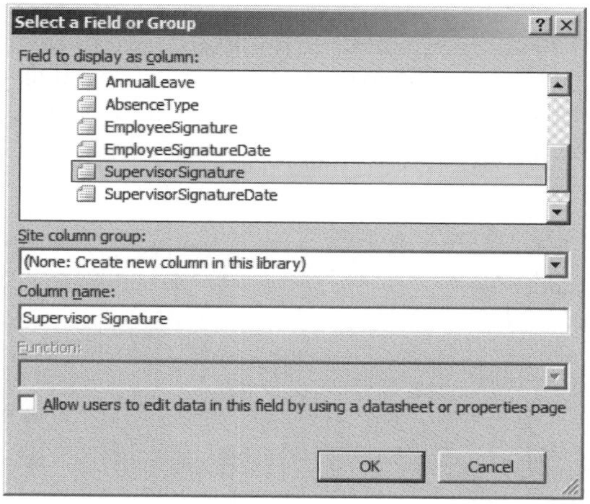

Figure 10-16. *Adding a column or changing its name*

If you decide not to include any of the columns that InfoPath preselected, you can remove them from the column list before you build the library by selecting them in the list shown earlier in Figure 10-15 and then clicking the **Remove** button. You can even update the column names of the fields that InfoPath preselected by clicking the column name and then clicking the **Modify** button.

When you have all the columns defined that you want to extract from the form, click the **Next** button on the page to proceed to the confirmation page of the **Publishing Wizard**, shown in Figure 10-17. This page displays a summary of the configuration information for the library. If you click **Publish** to continue, InfoPath builds the new document library in SharePoint.

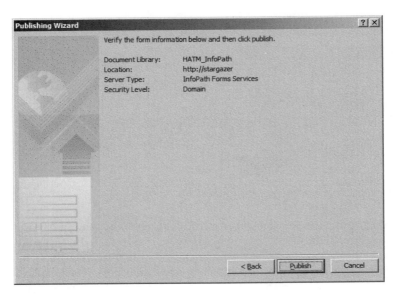

Figure 10-17. *Verifying action parameters before publishing the form*

It may take a few seconds for InfoPath to create the new document library. However, when it finishes, it refreshes this page of the wizard, giving you the option to send the form as an e-mail to users or to open the document library. Figure 10-18 also shows that you can open the form in a browser, but you have a few more library settings to look at first.

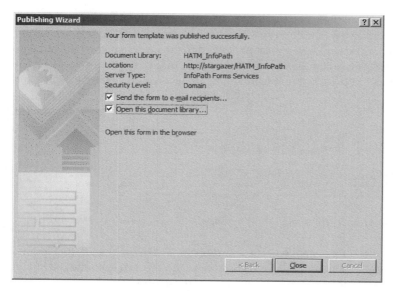

Figure 10-18. *Verifying the published form by opening it or sending it in an e-mail*

Additional Library Settings

Open the **Settings** drop-down menu for the library and click **Form Library Settings**. Then
select **Advanced Settings** under the **General Settings** group. You will see that the **Document
Template** has been set to HATM_InfoPath/Forms/template.xsn. The first part of this name is the
name of the document library. Think of the next part of the path, Forms, as a directory where
the library stores all its templates. Then the file name, template.xsn, is the name of the default
template, which in this case is an InfoPath template, based on its extension of .xsn.

   So how do you know that this file is the form that you began with? You could click **New**
back on the library's menu to show that the default new document for this library opens a
blank copy of the form. You could also click the **Edit Template** link immediately beneath the
Template URL on the **Advanced Settings** page. Because the extension of the current template
is .xsn, this action opens the template in InfoPath. It first pops up a dialog box to tell you that
you can update the form template. However, you must save the form locally and then republish it to this library to update it. Republishing the form does not affect any of the existing data
records created with the older version of the form.

Caution The fact that the existing data records are not affected by publishing a new version of the form
is not the same as saying that the data will work with the new form. Deleting or renaming fields can cause an
apparent loss of data when the new form attempts to display an old data file.

If you click the **Close** button in Figure 10-18 after selecting the option to open the document library, SharePoint opens the new library as shown in Figure 10-19. Of course, the library starts out empty. So you may be wondering what happened to the form that you published to this library. It is there. However, rather than becoming an entry in the library as would happen if you simply tried to upload a document to the library, it has become the default template for the library.

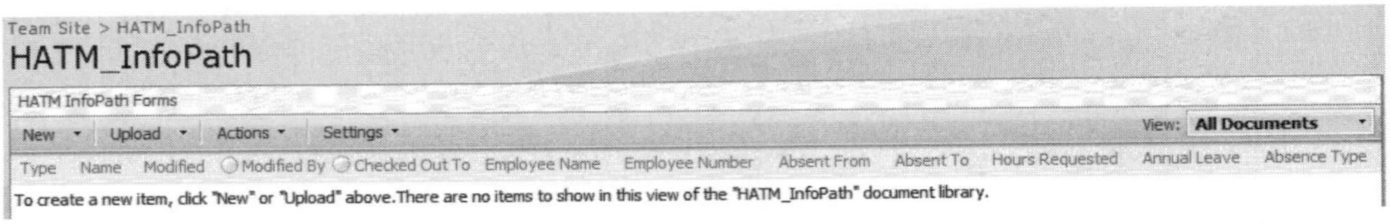

Figure 10-19. *New document library for a form showing the custom columns from the form*

You may have also noticed that when you click **Settings** in the library header, the option said **Form Library Settings**, not **Document Library Settings**. Don't worry. Even though SharePoint said it was creating a document library, it actually created a form library, which as I said earlier is a special type of document library to handle InfoPath's XML-based forms. This library will work perfectly for your forms.

While you are in the **Advanced Settings** page, look at the next section, named **Browser-enabled Documents**. This setting lets you choose whether to open documents in a browser or client application for those documents that support both modes. By default, SharePoint assumes you want to open all documents in their client application. Therefore, for a form library, you will want to change the default setting to **Display as a Web page** so that users can fill in the form online. Figure 10-20 shows this setting.

Browser-enabled Documents

Specify how to display documents that are enabled for opening both in a browser and a client application. If the client application is unavailable, these documents will always be displayed as Web pages in the browser.

Opening browser-enabled documents

○ Open in the client application

● Display as a Web page

Figure 10-20. *Changing the default display setting to Display as a Web Page to view the page in your browser*

Finally, if you plan on adding more than one form to this library, you need to change the setting for the first option, **Content Types**. By changing the value of this option to **Yes**, you allow the library to support multiple content types, where each content type is a different form. If you plan to use only a single form type within this library, leave this setting at **No**, although setting it to **Yes** will not hurt anything either.

With the **Custom Send To Destination** setting, you can set a name and URL to which to send a copy of the form. You may want to do this if you need to have users send a copy of their form data to a second location after they have saved it to the library. Other options include the ability to turn on or off the **New Folder** command in the **New** menu and the ability to determine whether to include this library in search results. Figure 10-21 shows the top portion of the **Advanced Settings** page.

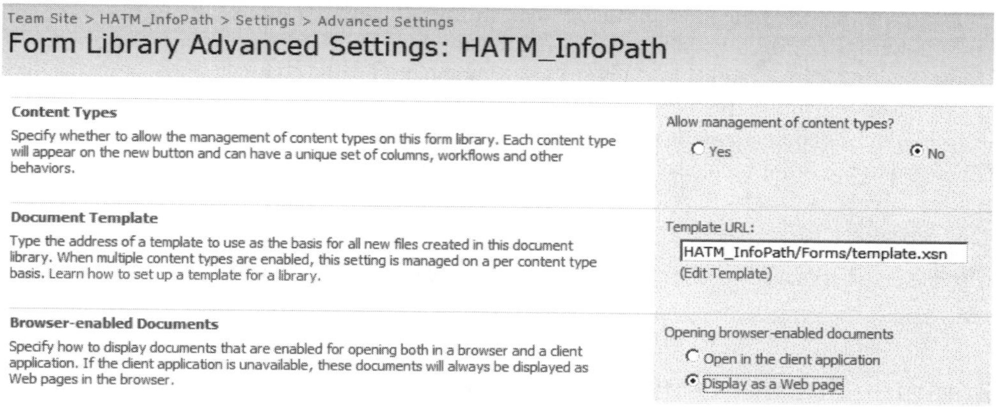

Team Site > HATM_InfoPath > Settings > Advanced Settings

Form Library Advanced Settings: HATM_InfoPath

Content Types

Specify whether to allow the management of content types on this form library. Each content type will appear on the new button and can have a unique set of columns, workflows and other behaviors.

Allow management of content types?

○ Yes   ◉ No

Document Template

Type the address of a template to use as the basis for all new files created in this document library. When multiple content types are enabled, this setting is managed on a per content type basis. Learn how to set up a template for a library.

Template URL:

HATM_InfoPath/Forms/template.xsn

(Edit Template)

Browser-enabled Documents

Specify how to display documents that are enabled for opening both in a browser and a client application. If the client application is unavailable, these documents will always be displayed as Web pages in the browser.

Opening browser-enabled documents

○ Open in the client application

◉ Display as a Web page

Figure 10-21. *Deciding whether you want to manage multiple content types in the current library*

Using the Published Form

Click **OK** to save your changes in the **Advanced Settings** page. Then click the library name in the breadcrumb area to display the library list again. So if the form itself does not appear in the library, what does appear in the library? Let's see what happens when you use the default form template to enter some data. Click the **New** button in the library header to open an instance of the form. Figure 10-22 shows the form displayed not in InfoPath, but in the browser.

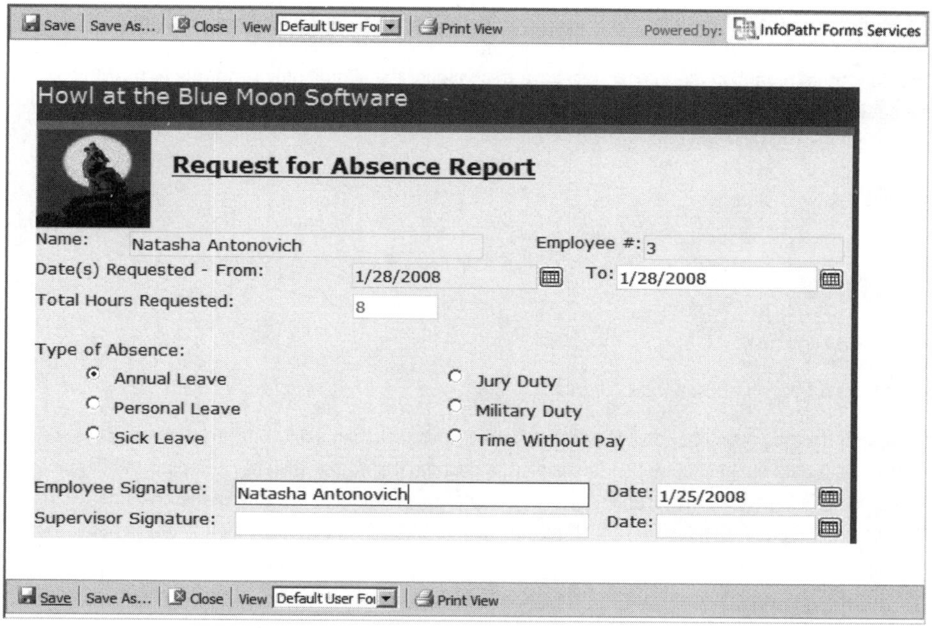

💾 Save │ Save As... │ 🗒 Close │ View Default User Fo ▾ │ 🖨 Print View   Powered by: 🗂 InfoPath Forms Services

Howl at the Blue Moon Software

Request for Absence Report

Name: Natasha Antonovich   Employee #: 3

Date(s) Requested - From: 1/28/2008   📅   To: 1/28/2008   📅

Total Hours Requested: 8

Type of Absence:

◉ Annual Leave   ○ Jury Duty
○ Personal Leave   ○ Military Duty
○ Sick Leave   ○ Time Without Pay

Employee Signature: Natasha Antonovich   Date: 1/25/2008   📅
Supervisor Signature: Date: 📅

💾 Save │ Save As... │ 🗒 Close │ View Default User Fo ▾ │ 🖨 Print View

Figure 10-22. *Displaying the form using Forms Services in your browser*

The appearance of the form in the browser mimics the appearance of the form within InfoPath, with the addition of a header and footer toolbar. This toolbar displays options such as **Save**, **Save As**, **Close**, **Views**, and **Print View**. For shorter forms, displaying the same toolbar at the top and bottom of the form may seem redundant. However, for larger forms, displaying the toolbar in both places can be very useful, saving the user from having to scroll from one end of the form to the other to access the options.

■**Tip** For entering data into a form, you typically do not need the **Views** command.

Changing Submit Options for a Form

If you want to change the options displayed on these toolbars or to suppress one or the other of the toolbars, you need to open the **Tools** menu while displaying the form in **Design** mode in InfoPath. In this menu, select **Form Options** to open a dialog box that lets you set many of the form's options. Because of the number of options, InfoPath groups the options by category. The categories appear in a list along the left side of this dialog box. Select the **Browser** category if not already selected. In the **Toolbars** section of this set of options, you can determine which toolbars to display and the commands that appear on the toolbars. You cannot choose different commands for the top toolbar compared to the bottom toolbar.

CONFIGURING SUBMIT OPTIONS FOR A FORM

To use the **Submit** command in the toolbar, you have to configure the submit options for the form. You can find these options by selecting **Submit Options** from the **Tools** drop-down menu. You can configure submit options to send a copy of the form data to

- E-mail

- A separate SharePoint document library

- A web service

- A hosting environment

- A connection from a data connection library

The **Submit Options** dialog box also provides options to create custom actions using either rules or code. You can even use a data connection option to specify the document library you want to employ and define a file name based on fields within the form, such as the employee's name and the date of her absence. This would eliminate the need for the user to remember the file naming convention discussed in this section.

Saving the Data from a Form

After completing the form as shown in Figure 10-22, you need to save your data. You can click the **Save** or **Save As** option. Both options open the **Save As** dialog box if you began with an instance of a new form. The **Save As** dialog box, shown in Figure 10-23, assumes that you will save the data from the form in the current library. However, it prompts for a file name. You can enter any name here. Defining a naming convention may help you locate different instances of the form data. For example, Natasha filled in the **Request for Absence Report**, shown previously in Figure 10-22, to take a day off on January 28, 2008. Therefore, by combining the user's name with the date she requested to have off, you create a meaningful name that helps to identify the user and the date she requested to have off.

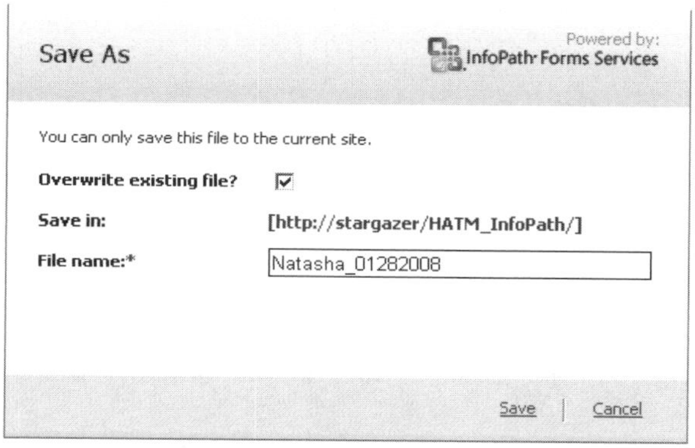

Figure 10-23. *Saving the data from filling in a form using Forms Services*

When you click **Save**, InfoPath Forms Services saves a copy of the form data in the library. When you look at the library's contents, you will now see an entry having the name just entered in the **Save As** dialog box as the file name. You will also see some other common library columns such as

- **Type**

- **Modified** (which displays the date modified)

- **Modified By**

- **Checked Out By**

In addition to these columns, you can see the other columns that you selected earlier in the **Publishing Wizard**. If you decide you want to change which columns appear in the list, you can select **Form Library Settings** from the **Settings** menu. In the **Columns** section, click the option **Add from existing site columns** found beneath the list of currently used columns.

Figure 10-24 shows the first entry in the library.

Team Site > HATM_InfoPath
HATM_InfoPath

HATM InfoPath Forms

New ▾	Upload ▾	Actions ▾	Settings ▾									View:	**All Documents** ▾
Type	Name		Modified	◯ Modified By	◯ Checked Out To	Employee Name	Employee Number	Absent From	Absent To	Hours Requested	Annual Leave	Absence Type
🗎	Natasha_01282008 I NEW		1/25/2008 10:22 PM	STARGAZER\administrator		Natasha Antonovich	3	1/28/2008	1/28/2008	8	No	1

Figure 10-24. *This library shows a new item containing the form's output data file.*

Like entries in other libraries, you can position your mouse over the item **Name** field to display a drop-down list of options. This list, shown in Figure 10-25, includes options to view and edit the properties, manage permissions, edit the form data, delete the entry, send the data to another location, check out the file, and create an alert if the file changes.

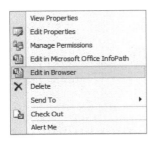

Figure 10-25. *This item drop-down lets you open the form data in InfoPath for Forms Services.*

To prove that this file is only the data, select the **Edit Properties** option in the file's drop-down menu. The only editable property is **Name**. While you can change the main part of the name, you cannot change the extension, which you can see defaults to .xml. If you were to open it, this XML file would look similar to the one shown earlier in Figure 10-9.

Notice also that the drop-down menu has two **Edit** options. The first option lets you edit the data file using a copy of Microsoft Office InfoPath from your desktop. If you make changes to the data on the form using InfoPath, you must select **Save** from the **File** menu in InfoPath to save the data changes back to the data file. If you use the second edit option to open a copy of the data file in your browser using InfoPath Forms Services, you can make changes to the data on the form and then click **Save**, not **Save As**, unless you want to create a second data instance with a new name.

In either case, it may at first appear that the metadata for the data file does not update. Remember that SharePoint uses web pages. To update the metadata, simply click your browser's **Refresh** button, and the metadata should reflect any changes you made to the data.

Publishing a Form to a Content Type

In this section, you will see how to publish a form to a site content type. With a site content type, you can easily add the form as a content type to any library in the site or its subsites. Therefore, if you have a form that users need to access from many different sites, publishing the form as a content type may be the fastest way to make it available across multiple libraries. It will also let you manage any future changes from a central location.

Just like publishing a form to a specific library, you need to begin with the form open in **Design** mode in InfoPath. Then select **Publish** from the **File** menu. On the first page of the **Publishing Wizard**, select the option **Site Content Type (advanced)**, as shown in Figure 10-26.

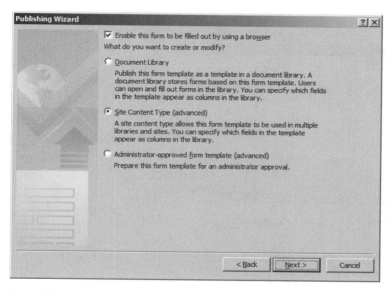

Figure 10-26. *Publishing your form as a content type to your SharePoint site*

When you click **Next**, the second page of the wizard asks what you want to do. You can create a new content type if this form has never before been published as a site content type. However, you should select the **Update an existing site content type** option if you previously published the form and need to republish the form due to changes in it. Notice that when you update a content type, SharePoint must update all libraries that use that content type. If you have used it in several libraries, this process could take some time. However, it also shows how you can manage multiple libraries that use the content type from one place.

On the bottom half of the page of this wizard, shown in Figure 10-27, you must select what you want to base the content type on. For a new form, select the generic content type **Form**.

As with all objects, when you add a site content type, you must provide a name and description for that content type. You must supply a unique name. The description, although optional, should be entered to help users identify what the content type supports. Figure 10-28 shows the minimal entries for these two properties, assuming that you began with the **Absentee** form as the source for the content type.

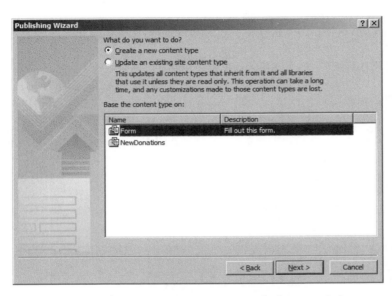

Figure 10-27. *Creating a new content type or updating an existing one*

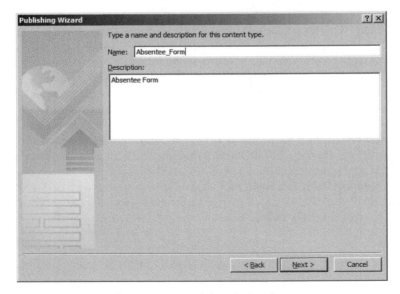

Figure 10-28. *Providing a name and description for a new content type*

Next, Figure 10-29 shows that you must specify the name of the site where you want to publish the form. For this example, I will publish the form in the root site of my SharePoint server, so I will enter the URL http://stargazer/.

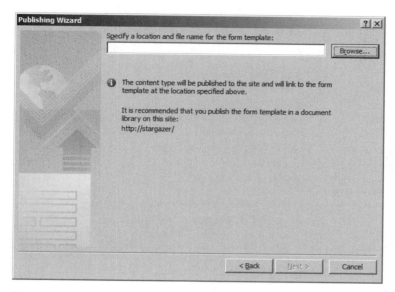

Figure 10-29. *Specifying the site where you want to publish the content type*

When you click **Next**, SharePoint displays the names of all the libraries that you can access from the requested site (see Figure 10-30). Note that the availability of the form directly relates to the site hierarchy. When you add a content type to a site, all child sites also have access to that content type. Therefore, if you want all of your SharePoint sites to use a specific form, you need to add that content type to the highest level from which you want to use it. For that reason, you may want to simply publish the content type to your top-level site.

Notice that both form libraries and document libraries appear in Figure 10-30. This can be confusing, as you have to remember which libraries have been created as document libraries, as opposed to form libraries. When you save the form template (in XSN format), you must save it in a document library if you plan on saving the source in SharePoint so others can access it. You should only use form libraries when you publish the form. A document library can hold any type of file. However, the form library is customized to work with XML documents based on one or more form templates defined as content types for that library. The form library stores a single copy of the form template (XSN) and multiple copies of the associated data files (XML) for each time someone fills it in.

After you select a document library where you want to store the source, Figure 10-31 shows that you must enter a name for the form template. You can name the template anything you want.

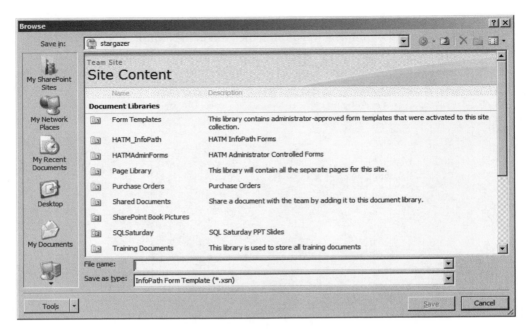

Figure 10-30. *Selecting an initial library to use a content type*

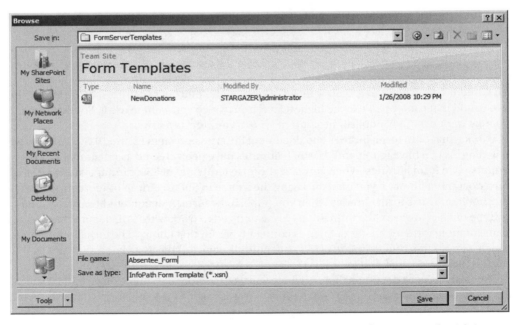

Figure 10-31. *You can publish the content type to a form library so others can work with it.*

On the next page of the **Publishing Wizard**, you have the opportunity to define which fields from the form you want to use as columns or metadata in the libraries where you will use this content type. You do not have to select all the fields. However, remember from earlier chapters that you can export metadata from a SharePoint library to an Excel spreadsheet. This capability can be very useful to perform analysis of the collected data without having to resort to a programming language.

Using the buttons shown in Figure 10-32, you can include additional form fields as columns, remove some of the columns, and modify the column names, perhaps providing a more descriptive name if the form's fields were not particularly well named.

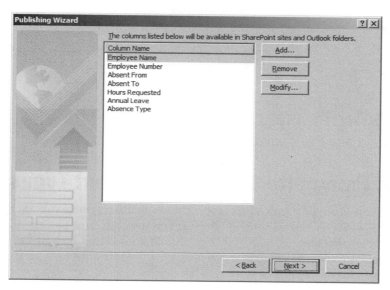

Figure 10-32. *Selecting the form fields you want to publish as columns in a library*

When you are finished defining which fields you want to display as columns, click the **Next** button to proceed to last page of the **Publishing Wizard** before InfoPath actually publishes the content type. Figure 10-33 shows a summary of the collected parameters. If everything looks correct, complete the publishing of the content type by clicking the **Publish** button.

The actual publishing process may take a few seconds. However, when it completes, two links appear on this page that let you either manage the content type or open the content type as a form in your browser to review how it looks.

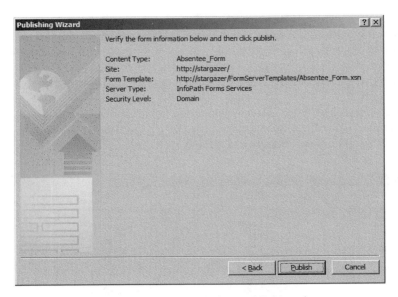

Figure 10-33. *Verifying your settings before publishing the content type*

Installing and Using Site Collection Content Types

After you publish a form as a content type, you have to specify the form library where you want to use that content type. However, published content types become available to all libraries in not only the current site where that library resides, but also all child site libraries. So how can you tell an existing library to use your new content type?

Adding a Content Type to a Library

Open the specific library where you want to use the content type. Select the option **Document Library Settings** from the **Settings** menu option at the top of the library. If you have not previously gone into the **Advanced Settings** to allow the library to manage content types, you need to do that first. While there, decide whether you want SharePoint to open your form content types using the content type's client application (InfoPath in this case), or to open the form in your web browser.

When you close the **Advanced Settings** page, you should see a section within the **Settings** page with the title **Content Types**. Initially, a document library supports a document content type, meaning Word. However, by clicking the link **Add from existing site content types**, you can add other available content types to the library, as shown in Figure 10-34. While you can view content types from all groups, forms created in InfoPath can be found in the Microsoft Office InfoPath group. After finding the content type you want to use, you can either double-click its name to add it or single-click it and click the **Add** button. You can add multiple content types to the current library while on this page before clicking **OK** to exit.

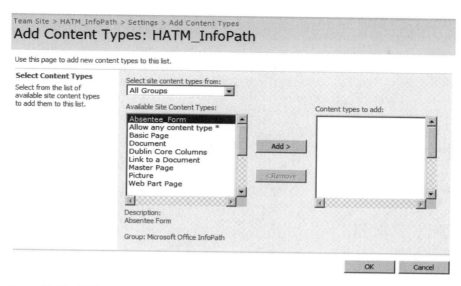

Figure 10-34. *Adding an available content type to another library/list*

Returning to the **Settings** page, you should see your new content types listed in the **Content Types** area. Notice that by default, all content types activated have a check in the column **Visible on New Button**. This means that when you open the library's **New** drop-down menu, you can choose from these content types to create a new document. However, if the user simply clicks the **New** button itself, he will get an instance of the default document or form identified by the **Default Content Type** column.

Changing the Default Content Type

To change the default content type, click the hyperlink beneath the content type table: **Change new button order and default content type**. Figure 10-35 shows the **Content Types** section of the **Settings** page with the second hyperlink at the bottom of the image selected to change the content type order and default content type.

Content Types

This document library is configured to allow multiple content types. Use content types to specify the information you want to display about an item, in addition to its policies, workflows, or other behavior. The following content types are currently available in this library:

Content Type	Visible on New Button	Default Content Type
Form	✔	✔
NewDonations	✔	
Absentee_Form	✔	

▫ Add from existing site content types

▫ Change new button order and default content type

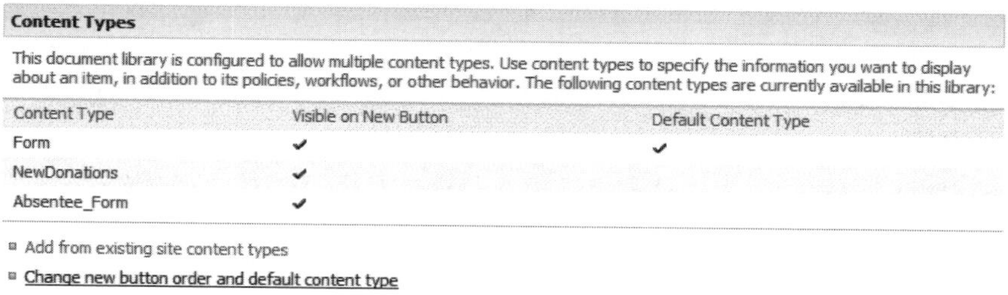

Figure 10-35. *Libraries can have multiple content types, but only one default type.*

When you go to the page that displays the active content types for the current library, you can identify the order of the content types by the numbers in the drop-down boxes on the right side of the screen. These numbers define the order of the content types when you open the **New** drop-down list. The content type, identified as number 1, becomes the default content type used by the library. Figure 10-36 shows the process of making the **Absentee_Form** the default content type by moving it to the first position in the list.

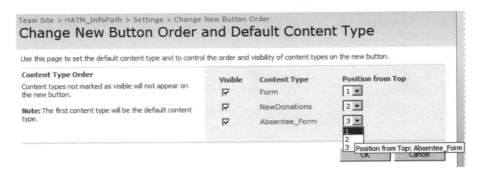

Figure 10-36. *Selecting the default content type by moving it to the top of the list*

When you return to the library list and open the **New** drop-down list, you see all the available content types for the library. Figure 10-37 shows that this library has three possible content types to choose from, but that the content type at the top of the list, **Absentee_Form**, acts as the default content type.

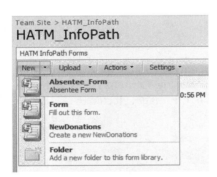

Figure 10-37. *Choosing a content type from the New drop-down menu*

Working with a Library That Has Multiple Content Types

If you have defined multiple content types for a library, you probably also have unique columns that refer to each of those content types. This probably also means that for any given row in the library, only a few of the columns actually have values. While a few of those columns may be common across more than one content type, most are unique to a single content type. Rather than create a confusing display in which the user has to horizontally scroll through blank columns to find the data she needs for a specific item in the library, you could create individual views for each content type.

When you create individual views for each content type the library uses, you can customize the columns used, the sort criteria, filters, and other view properties. To display only the items for one specific content type in each view, look for a field in each content type that always has a value for that content type but no other content types. You can compare that field to a blank or zero depending on the field type, thus determining whether to include that item in the view. If you do not have a unique column you can reference to identify the content type, you may need to consider adding either a custom column that you can manually update or, better yet, a field in the form of each content type that includes a default value. However, it will probably be rare that a content type does not contain at least one required field that can serve as the filter field for the view.

Building Custom Workflows for InfoPath Forms Using SharePoint Designer

While SharePoint Designer is not a part of either the WSS 3.0 or MOSS 2007 installation, nor is it included with any of the current versions of Microsoft Office, it is a great tool for working with SharePoint that most administrators and designers typically will require. While SharePoint Designer can trace its roots back to the days of Microsoft FrontPage, it provides much more functionality than FrontPage. One of those areas of new functionality pertains to the creation of workflows for InfoPath forms published to a web page.

What Is a Workflow?

Let's begin by first briefly defining the term workflow. A *workflow* is a repeatable process that uses specific resources to perform defined actions when certain conditions exist. An example of a process that requires a workflow can be seen when an employee at a company requests vacation time. Basically, the employee begins the process by filling in a form requesting specific time off, detailing the number of hours and which days he wants off. Upon completion, the employee typically needs to e-mail or carry the form to his immediate supervisor for approval. Of course, the supervisor has several options on how to act on the request:

- The supervisor can approve the request and forward it on to the clerical staff to enter the information into the company's payroll system.

- The supervisor can reject the request and send a notification of the rejection back to the employee with or without explanation as to why she rejected it.

- If the request for time off is over a specific number of hours or exceeds the number of hours that the employee currently has available, the request may need to be forwarded to the next level of management, where the process of approval or rejection begins again.

These steps define a relatively simple process, or workflow, that a vacation request might go through. Within SharePoint, you will want to model this workflow so the document passes from the employee to his immediate supervisor or manager and eventually to the payroll department. In terms of publishing web pages, a similar workflow might take pages from the creator, to editors, to reviewers, and finally to approvers.

The example of the vacation request workflow illustrates a relatively simple sequential workflow. However, you can model complex workflows with intricate branching conditions and actions performed by individuals and by the computer system. The key advantage of software-driven workflows is that the users can focus on the tasks and not get distracted by thinking about the process steps.

Perhaps you haven't thought of attaching workflows to your libraries and lists before, but when you begin to publish forms on your site, the need for workflows becomes apparent. In many business situations, you must route a completed form to one or more additional parties for review, additional data, or approval. Sure, you could simply save the form or other document in a SharePoint library and then separately notify the next person that she needs to access the document to do her part of the process. But there are problems with this manual technique of passing documents along a process, some of which include the following:

- The more steps/people that become involved in the process, the harder it becomes to track the status of the document.

- Directly notifying the next person to process the document means that you have to manually create an e-mail to him and that you must know to whom to send it.

- If you must perform an action, you must know exactly what action to perform and how to respond to any result.

Automated workflows improve efficiency by taking the guesswork out of what to do next. Furthermore, SharePoint Designer's ability to create workflows with no coding makes it easy for anyone familiar with creating rules in products like Outlook to handle e-mail to apply similar skills to building a workflow.

Beginning a Simple Approval Workflow

To illustrate the concept of building a workflow for a form, let's build a simple approval work-flow for a bid request form. I will keep this process relatively simple while showing how easy it is for you to build workflows for your libraries.

To begin a new workflow, open SharePoint Designer from your **Start** menu. Before you can start a new workflow, you have to select the site where you want to work. If you have not used SharePoint Designer previously, you will have to open a site by selecting the option **Open Site** from the **File** menu. Otherwise, you may be able to select the site from the **Recent Sites** menu option, also in the **File** menu. If you do not see the site in **Recent Sites**, you may still see a reference to it in the **Open Site** option. In any case, you can use the **Open Site** option to enter the URL of the site to open it. For example, for my server, I might enter

```
http://stargazer
```

Next, select **New** also from the **File** menu and select **Workflow**. Designer may display a message informing you that it is downloading necessary data from the server. This process can take a varying amount of time, depending on the speed of your network. This menu option opens the dialog box shown in Figure 10-38. In this menu, you must provide a name for the workflow. When you add a workflow to a SharePoint site using SharePoint Designer, you can attach it to a specific list, as you will do here. You can select in which list to install the workflow by selecting it from the drop-down of all the lists in the selected site.

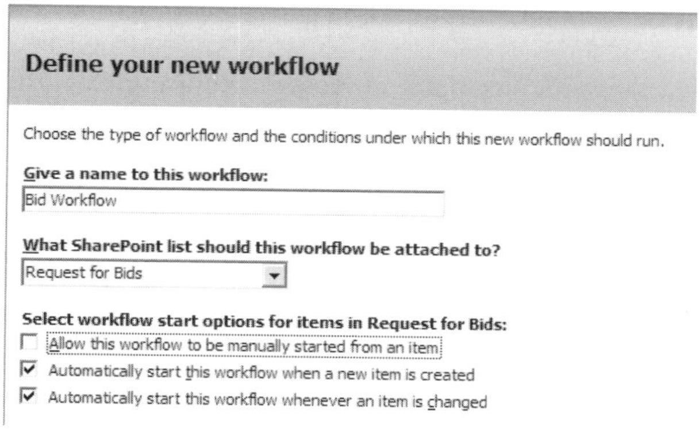

Figure 10-38. *Creating a new workflow using SharePoint Designer*

The last section of this page lets you choose how and when you want to start the workflow for the selected list. If you check the first check box, the user must start the workflow manually for the item. Use this option only if you do not need to start the workflow when an item is added or changed, and only if the average user will know when to and when not to start a workflow. For example, you may want the user to be able to create items in a list or library while she works on them over several sessions without starting a workflow until she finishes working on the item. Only at that time will the user want to start the workflow on the completed item.

The second check box tells SharePoint to automatically start the workflow whenever someone creates a new item in the select list. This means that even if the user has not finished entering the item but wants to save what he did so he can finish at a later time, the mere fact that he saved his temporary work will fire off the workflow. If users typically complete the entry of all data for the form in a single session, maybe you do want to select this option to start the workflow when they create the item.

The third check box starts the workflow whenever an item changes. This feature can help ensure that users do not make changes to items without starting an approval process. Otherwise, users might submit an initial item, get it approved, and then return to edit the item without needing approval of their changes.

INITIATION BUTTON

The **Initiation** button lets you create a simple form that appears at the start of a workflow in which you can prompt the user to enter values for parameters that the rest of the workflow can use. However, the workflow only prompts the user for these values if you start the workflow manually. Otherwise, the workflow uses default values that you define for each parameter.

You can also define local variables for the workflow using the **Variables** button. Local variables allow you to carry data from one step to another step. You must define a name for the variable as well as the variable type with this option. Then in the workflow steps, you can use the **Set Workflow Variable** action to store a value from one step for an item that you can retrieve in another step.

When you click **Next**, you can begin the first step of the workflow as shown in Figure 10-39. SharePoint Designer provides a default name for each step beginning with "Step" followed by a sequential number. However, you can change the step name to some more meaningful text such as **Send E-mail to Approver**.

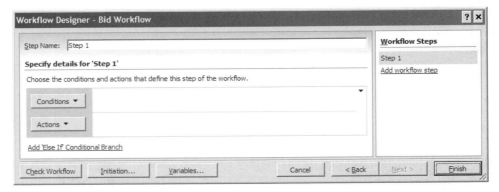

Figure 10-39. *Workflows have steps containing actions executed based on conditions.*

Defining Workflow Details

Each step consists of one or more sets of details. Each detail consists of a condition and an action that you want the workflow to perform when the condition evaluates to **True**. Condition statements are optional. If you want to execute a specific action every time the workflow runs, you can skip the condition and go directly to the **Actions** button. Therefore, let's first look at the **Actions** button.

When you click the **Actions** button, a drop-down list of possible actions appears, as shown in Figure 10-40. As you can see from the list, you have quite a set of options available. In fact, there are so many options that the drop-down includes an option at the bottom to show more actions than you can see in the initial list.

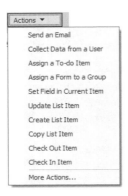

Figure 10-40. *Selecting from the available actions drop-down list*

In this case, you want to build a simple approval workflow. Therefore, the first action you want the workflow to perform when a user saves a new item to the list is to send an e-mail to the approver for the list. Therefore, select the first option: **Send an Email**.

Configuring an E-mail Message

This option then displays the skeleton command for the e-mail action shown in Figure 10-41 in the text area to the right of the buttons. Each command has one or more placeholder text strings that you can replace with data. In this case, the placeholder contains the text **Email this message**. Notice that the words "this message" in the placeholder appear as a link. This formatting tells you that you can customize the information that appears at this point in the command.

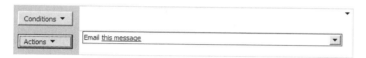

Figure 10-41. *Creating an action that sends an e-mail message*

Clicking the link for this placeholder opens a dialog box to define the e-mail message shown in Figure 10-42. Here you can enter the e-mail address of a person directly, or you can click the button to the right of the text box on the **To:** line to select from the users or user groups known to the SharePoint site. For example, if you have a group defined as **Approvers**, you can select this SharePoint group, rather than the e-mail address of an individual, to receive the e-mail. This is usually the preferred solution over entering individual e-mail addresses as shown in this figure, because you can easily e-mail multiple people who have the approver permission, letting any one of them approve the item. Also, if you hard-code an individual's e-mail address in a workflow, and that person leaves the organization, the workflow will fail until you edit the workflow and replace the invalid e-mail address with a new e-mail address. By referencing a group, you simply have to maintain the group's membership. This also applies to the **CC:** line of the e-mail. By default, the **FROM:** address for the e-mail can be set in the **Central Administration**'s **Operations** page. Go to the **Outgoing e-mail settings** option and update the **From Address** field.

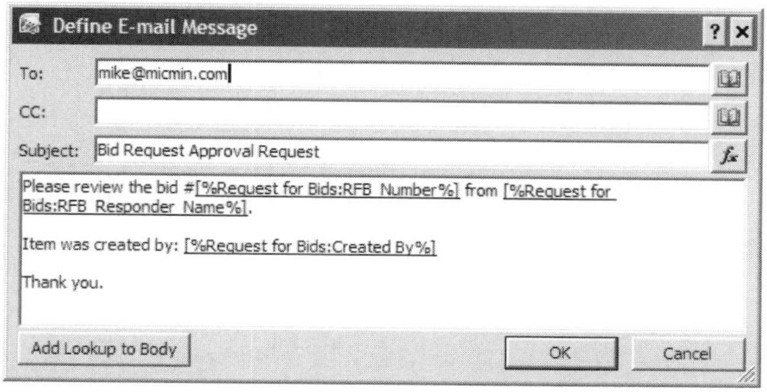

Figure 10-42. *Defining the properties and content of the e-mail message*

Next, you can enter a text string to appear in the **Subject** field. You can enter a simple text string as shown in Figure 10-42, or at any point within the text string, you can click the function button found to the right of the **Subject** field. This opens a dialog box that lets you look up a value from a variety of sources ranging from fields in the current item, to fields in other lists. If you choose to use a value from another list, you must identify the item and the field from the list that you want to use.

In fact, the body of the message in Figure 10-42 shows several reference fields. In the first paragraph of the body, the string [**%Request for Bids:RFB Number%**] retrieves the value from the **RFB Number** column of the current item and inserts it into the string. Similarly, it also retrieves values from the column **RFB Responder Name** and the column **Created By**. In this way, you can create a custom message that tells the e-mail recipient more than just that she has something to approve on the portal. You can provide specific information to tell her exactly what she needs to approve. You can even provide a link to the list so that the user does not have to try to remember the URL and then navigate to the required list, all of which takes extra time for the approver. By displaying the URL in the e-mail to the approver, you increase the approver's efficiency.

When you click **OK**, SharePoint Designer returns you to the **Step** page, shown in Figure 10-43, where you can add more actions.

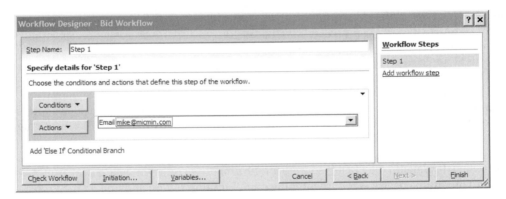

Figure 10-43. *Actions without a condition always execute.*

Adding Multiple Actions

You can have multiple steps each with individual actions, or you can have a single step with multiple actions. Suppose you decide to add another action to this step to log the workflow into the **History** list. To do this, click the **Actions** button a second time, and click the option **Log to History List**, as shown in Figure 10-44. For this action, you can specify the exact text you want to add to the log.

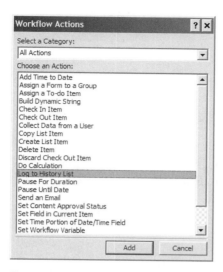

Figure 10-44. *Adding actions from the full action list*

Next, add a third action telling the workflow to wait until the approval process changes from **Pending** to another value. The need for this action may not be obvious until you consider that workflows execute from beginning to end once they start without pausing, unless you tell them to pause. In fact, currently the workflow defined here will execute as soon as an item is added or changed in the list where the workflow has been attached. It starts by sending an e-mail to the person or group defined in the **TO:** portion of the e-mail definition and then creates a log entry. In the next step, you want to determine whether the approver sets the item's status to **Approved** or **Rejected**. If you do not put a pause or wait action at the end of step 1, step 2 will immediately execute without giving the approver time to even look at the item. Therefore, you need to add an action telling the workflow to wait at this point until the item's status changes from its initial value of **Pending**.

Adding Conditions to Actions

To be complete, you can add a condition that defines when you want even the actions in step 1 to execute. In this case, you only want to send an e-mail to the approver when a document has the status of **Pending**. If you have a list with versioning turned on, this allows you to save intermediate values without triggering a workflow, because they have the status of **Draft** and only receive a status of **Pending** when the user submits them for approval.

To add this condition, click the **Conditions** button for the first step. From the drop-down list, shown in Figure 10-45, select the option **Compare Request for Bids field**.

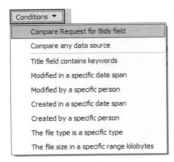

Figure 10-45. *Conditions define when to execute the actions in the step.*

When you select this option, the command skeleton in the condition that appears to the right of the condition button says

If `field equals value`

In this case, you see that SharePoint Designer underlines three of these words. When you click the first word, **field**, you can select which field you want to compare from the current list item. Depending on the field that you select, the drop-down list that appears when you click the word **value** changes. SharePoint Designer reads the definition of the list, and if the selected field has a limited number of possible values, it only displays those values. For fields that can have any value, SharePoint Designer lets you enter the value directly in the text box. You can even reference a value from another object such as another list on the site.

Even the word **equals** between field and value can be changed by clicking it, providing you with different comparison options. If necessary, you can build multiple conditions in which you can connect each condition, using either an **AND** or an **OR** connection.

Figure 10-46 shows one possible way to complete the first step of the approver workflow. It sends the approver an e-mail and logs the start of the workflow when a new or edited document with the status of **Pending** appears in the list.

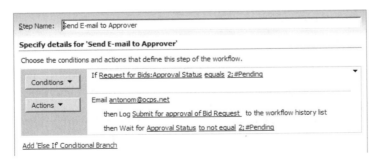

Figure 10-46. *One way to define the step to send an e-mail to an approver*

Adding Additional Steps

By clicking the hyperlink **Add workflow step** in the panel on the right side of SharePoint Designer, which shows the **Workflow Steps**, you can define what you want the workflow to do when the approver changes the status of the item to either **Approved** or **Rejected**.

For this step in the workflow, let's define a condition that checks whether the **Approval Status** field of the current item equals **Approved**. When it does, let's send an e-mail back to the person who created the item, informing him that the item has been approved.

Begin by clicking the **Conditions** button and select the option **Compare Request for Bids field** as you did for the condition in the first step of this workflow. Then select the field **Approval Status** and compare it to the value **Approved**.

Next, create an action that sends an e-mail. In the e-mail dialog box, click the **Select Users** button on the far-right side of the **To:** field and select **User who created current item** from the list of available users and groups list, as shown in Figure 10-47.

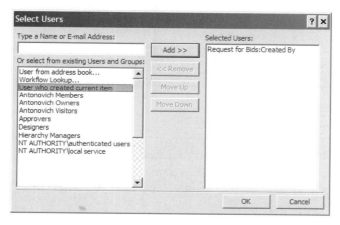

Figure 10-47. *Using dynamic properties to define an e-mail's To: field*

In this step, you need to have a second condition, because the approver can either accept or reject the item. The first condition/action set defines what to do when the approver approves the item. But next you must define what you want the workflow to do when the approver rejects the item.

To do this, click the hyperlink **Add 'Else If' Conditional Branch** found at the bottom of the **Specify Details** panel. You will see a new **Conditions** and **Actions** set of buttons. Click the **Conditions** button and define the Boolean expression that compares the **Approval Status** to the value of **Rejected**. Next, click the **Actions** button to send the user who created the current item an e-mail informing him that the approver has rejected the item.

■**Tip** An interesting process you can create places all pending items of a specific type in an initial pending list. When a user creates an item in this list, it starts a modified approval workflow. In this workflow, add an action to the **Approved** step to copy the list item to a different list, an approved item list, followed by another action to delete the current item from the current list. If the approver rejects the item, you can leave the item in the pending list.

Figure 10-48 shows one possible way to build the second step in this approval workflow.

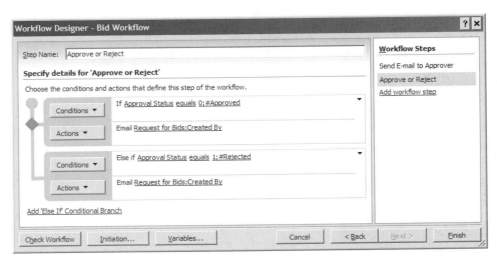

Figure 10-48. *Defining the approver's possible actions*

■**Tip** If you ever create your workflow steps out of order, you can easily rearrange their order by positioning your mouse over the right side of the step name in the **Workflow Steps** panel until the drop-down arrow appears. Click this arrow, and then select either the **Move Step Up** option or the **Move Step Down** option.

■**Tip** If you miss a step, just add the step to the end of the steps. Then using the previous tip, move it up in the list of steps to the spot where it belongs.

■**Tip** If you decide you no longer need a workflow step, open the drop-down list of step options as described in the previous tips and select the **Delete Step** option.

Restructuring Your Conditions

If you add a conditional branch that you later decide you no longer need, you can click the down pointing arrow to the upper right of any of the existing conditional branches to display a drop-down menu. From this menu, you can move conditional branches up or down in the sequence of branches. Remember that workflows evaluate branches sequentially from top to bottom by default, with the first branch that returns a **True** result for its condition being chosen to execute its actions. You also have options in this menu to add new branches, delete the current branch, or change the way the workflow executes conditional branches to execute them all in parallel rather than sequentially.

If you have a condition or action with multiple statements, you can also change the order of these statements by clicking anywhere on the line of the statement other than on a hyperlink to select the condition or action. To the right appears a drop-down button that, when clicked, displays a menu letting you move the current action or condition up or down or even delete it. Therefore, even if you miss a condition or action, you can simply add it to the bottom of the list of actions or conditions in the appropriate conditional branch, and then move it to the position where it needs to appear.

■**Tip** One of the conditions you can use compares the file size to a specific range in kilobytes. You can use this condition to automatically set the approval status to **Approved** or **Rejected** along with sending appropriate e-mail messages to users attempting to add large files to lists.

■**Tip** Another condition you can use compares the file type to a specific type. By including a series of conditions joined with an **OR** connector, you can limit the ability of users from uploading specific file types to lists and libraries.

When you finish defining the steps in your workflow, save the workflow by clicking the **Finish** button in the lower-right corner of the SharePoint Designer. This action saves the workflow to SharePoint and specifically attaches it to the list specified when you started the workflow definition. The next time a user adds an item to the list, the workflow initiates and sends an e-mail, such as the one shown in Figure 10-49, to the person or group defined in the **To:** field.

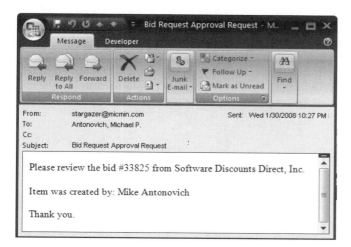

Figure 10-49. *An example of the e-mail received by the approver*

While this section introduces you to the ability of SharePoint Designer to create workflows, you can create workflows quite a bit more complex than the one shown here. If you find that you need to perform actions that SharePoint Designer does not support, you can also create workflows using Visual Studio and add custom coding for individual forms; in addition, you can create workflows that can be installed at the site's collection level and then applied across multiple lists and libraries. If you have programming skills and would like to learn more about creating workflows using Visual Studio, you may want to check out the book *Pro SharePoint Solution Development: Combining .NET, SharePoint and Office 2007* by Ed Hild with Susie Adams (Apress, 2007).

Summary

In this chapter, you looked at different ways to publish a form created with InfoPath. You started by looking at publishing the form to a network share. This solution may work adequately for those organizations in which only a few people need to use the form and have InfoPath installed on their desktop machines. The major limitation of this method is that the form and its data are static files. Furthermore, forms published this way cannot participate in large automated workflows without substantial custom development, and who has time for that?

Next, you looked at publishing a form directly from InfoPath to a SharePoint library. You can even create a new library for the form at the same time that you publish it. You can also use this method to update the form template of existing libraries. When publishing a form to a library, you can include fields from the form as column data in the library, making it easy to see the form's information. By exporting the library metadata to an Excel spreadsheet using techniques discussed in Chapter 7, you can further analyze the data collected from the forms using a tool you are familiar with.

If you need to use a form with more than one library or more than one site, you can publish the form as a content type to a site. Content types published to a site become available to libraries not only in that site, but also in any child sites. By publishing to the top-level site of the site collection, you can make the content type available to all sites in the collection.

Finally, I introduced you to the use of SharePoint Designer to create workflows. While SharePoint Designer replaces Microsoft FrontPage as Microsoft's web page designer, SharePoint Designer offers more than just web page creation. It supports the ability to visually create workflows that you can associate with specific lists/libraries in your SharePoint site. It uses a nonprogramming approach with point-and-click options to build the workflow. SharePoint Designer then attaches the workflow to the selected list so you don't have to do any configuration to make the workflow operate with your form in your SharePoint library.

CHAPTER 11

■ ■ ■

Peer-to-Peer Collaboration with Groove

If you are wondering what Groove is, you are not alone. Groove gets the award as the newest and least known addition to the Microsoft Office Suite. Groove provides you with a personal collaboration area where you can bring together small teams from within or even outside your company. You can even invite friends and neighbors into your collaboration site. Within your site, you can

- Share documents

- Create calendars

- Participate in discussions

- Publish forms

- Track issues

- Hold meetings

- Share pictures

- And more

Most importantly for you, one of Groove's tools lets you share files between a SharePoint document library and a Groove-based file tool.

The fact that you can do all of these things without involving your IT department or hiring outside consultants puts you in control of sharing information with people outside of your normal network, extending your ability to collaborate with anyone having Internet access. You don't have to worry about firewalls, servers, or security. And since you can invite anyone to join your Groove-based collaboration site and share your files, you can communicate with anyone who has Internet access. You can even use your Groove account from multiple computers as a way to share files between your machines at work and at home.

However, the greatest advantage of Groove is that it can allow you to work with temporary employees or consultants who need to share files and be involved in meetings. Because of their short-time status, your IT department may choose not to add them to the authenticated users of your corporate network. Groove can help you collaborate with them anyway.

Getting into the Groove

First, you may already have Groove. If you own either the Enterprise or Ultimate editions of Microsoft Office 2007, you already own Groove. If you have not installed it yet, go back to your installation disks and modify your options to install it. If you have one of the other versions of Microsoft Office 2007, you can still obtain Groove as a stand-alone application.

Once installed, you can choose from two ways to begin using Groove:

- Create your own workspace.

- Be invited to participate in someone else's workspace.

Actually, you must do one other thing first. You must create a Groove account with at least one identity so others can find you or so you can create a workspace yourself. Your Groove account resides on your computer and holds your identity along with references to workspaces to which you belong, contact information for other members in your workspace, "keys," and information about the devices you use.

CREATING YOUR GROOVE ACCOUNT

When you first start using Groove, the **Account Configuration Wizard** opens, as shown in the following screenshot, giving you the option of creating a new Groove account or using an account you may already have, perhaps from another computer. Let's assume for now that you want to create a new account.

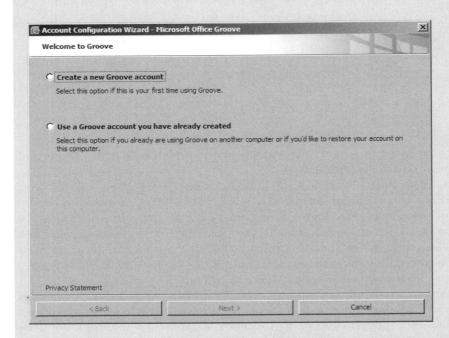

The next screen asks whether you have a Groove Account Configuration Code. The first two options, shown in the following screenshot, relate to corporations who may be hosting a Groove server internally and have an administrator who supplies accounts. Let's assume this is not the case and that you want to create a noncorporate account by choosing the last option.

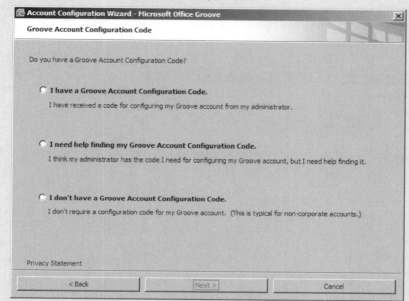

The wizard will then prompt you for your name, your e-mail address, and password information, as you can see in the following screenshot. It uses this information to create an account to identify you and to allow you to access the workspaces where you become a member.

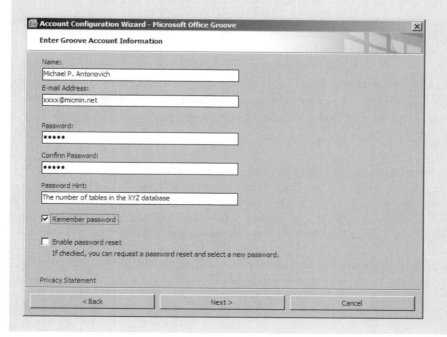

After a few moments, the following screen will appear, through which you can choose to list your new Groove account in the Public Groove Directory where others can find you. Or, you can keep your account private. If you keep your account private, you can still become a member of a workgroup by having others directly invite you by sending an invitation to your Groove e-mail address. You can also now create your own workspace and invite others to join it.

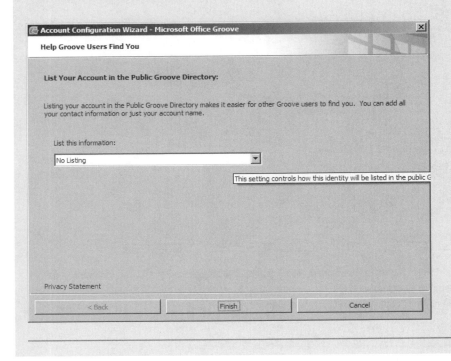

Tip You can create a new account for Groove anytime if you already have Groove installed on your computer by right-clicking the **Groove** icon in the task bar of your computer and selecting the **New Account** option. It will open the wizard described in the sidebar "Creating Your Groove Account."

When you open Groove for the first time, you can create your first workspace by clicking the **New Workspace** link on the Groove **Launchbar** as shown in Figure 11-1.

In the dialog box that pops up, you must name your workspace as well as choose the workspace type. To follow the examples in this chapter, choose the **Standard** workspace and click **OK**. After a few moments, your first workspace appears and should look like the one shown in Figure 11-2.

Before taking a deeper look at the details of the Groove workspace, let's see how you can invite someone to your workspace and how you would accept someone else's invitation to his workspace.

Figure 11-1. *Opening the Groove Launchbar*

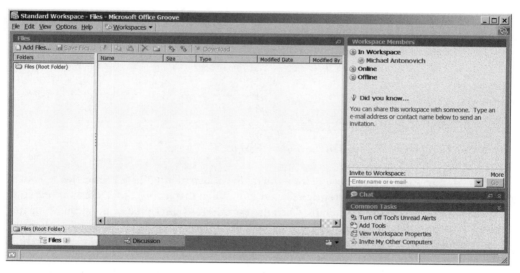

Figure 11-2. *A new Groove workspace*

Once you have a workspace, you can invite others to it directly from the workspace itself. Referring back to Figure 11-2, notice the prompt **Invite to Workspace** on the right side of the image. After clicking it, you can enter the e-mail address of a person you want to invite to your workspace. If you use Windows Messenger and are logged in, you can also open the drop-down list by clicking the down arrow button and selecting one of your Messenger contacts by name. If you want to invite more than one person to your site, clicking the **More** link displays a dialog box where you can specify any number of people to invite at one time. When you have entered the e-mail addresses of those you want to invite, click the **Go** button to send them an e-mail invitation to your workspace.

Figure 11-3 shows the dialog box that appears when you send a message. Notice that in addition to specifying the e-mail addresses of each new person you want to invite to your workspace, you can select each user's role in your workspace. By default, people you invite to your workspace receive the role **Participant**. This role gives them the ability to do anything on the site except change the roles of other members. In other words, they can add and remove tools and invite new members to your workspace. On the other hand, the **Guest** role does not have any of these permissions. People with the **Guest** role can only read information from the workspace. Finally, anyone with the **Manager** role can do everything a participant can plus modify the permissions assigned to each of the roles.

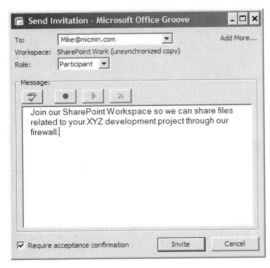

Figure 11-3. *Completing the Send Invitation dialog box*

The **Manager** role can also select from the main Groove menu **File ➤ Properties ➤ Tool** to display the properties of the currently selected tool. When displaying a tool's properties, you may see a dialog box with several tabs. Click the **Permissions** tab to see what permissions the tool supports. On this page of the dialog box, you must first select the role for which you want to edit permissions. Then check or uncheck the box before each specific permission to customize the role.

You can also include a message with your invitation informing the other person why she has received the invitation. Before clicking the **Invite** button, check the box **Require acceptance confirmation**.

At this point, Groove sends an e-mail similar to the one shown in Figure 11-4 to each invitee. As each one accepts the invitation, you will receive an e-mail reconfirming the invitation. This occurs even if you do not check the **Require acceptance confirmation** box.

As shown in this figure, the invitee can accept the invitation in two different ways. If he has never used Groove and does not have a copy of it, he can choose the first option, which allows him to download a free trial version of Groove. If the invitee already has Groove, he can accept the invitation to the workspace using the second link. In either case, a message is sent back to the person who invited him to confirm the acceptance. Groove tries to send this message back via the Groove infrastructure. Therefore, the first person should monitor her Groove account for incoming messages.

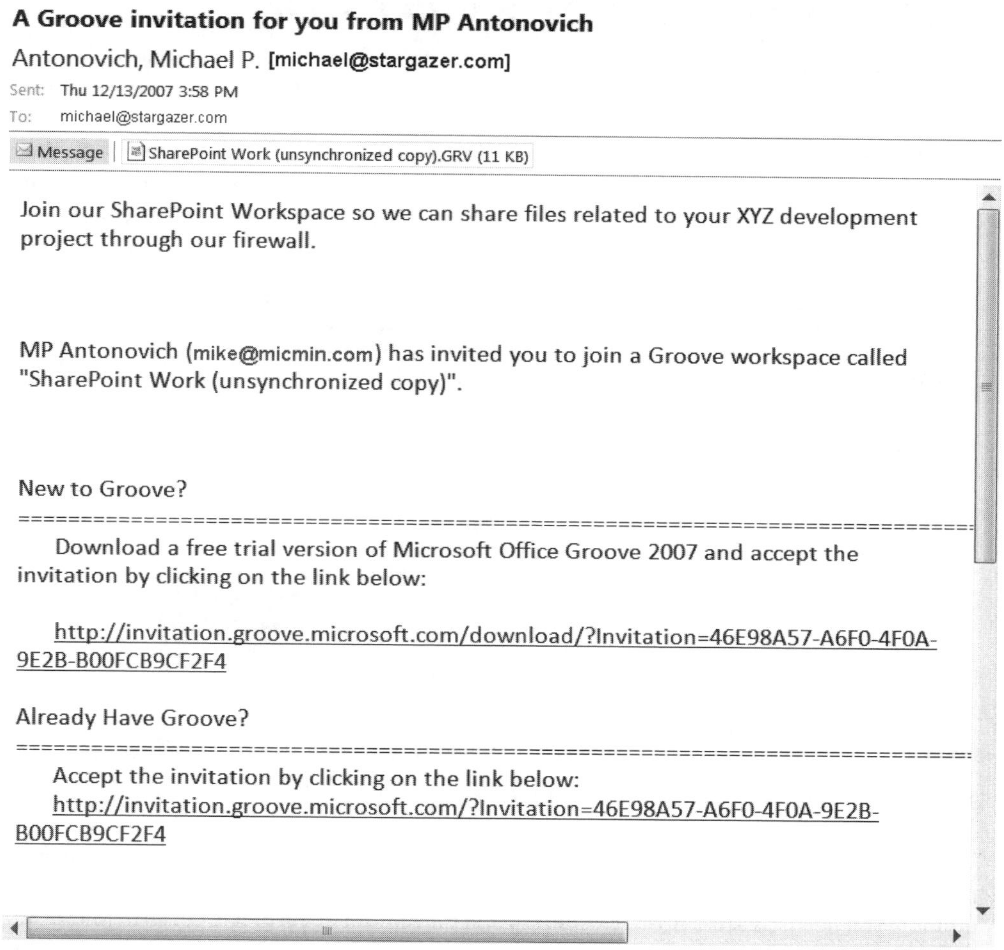

A Groove invitation for you from MP Antonovich

Antonovich, Michael P. [michael@stargazer.com]

Sent: Thu 12/13/2007 3:58 PM
To: michael@stargazer.com

⊠ Message | 📄 SharePoint Work (unsynchronized copy).GRV (11 KB)

Join our SharePoint Workspace so we can share files related to your XYZ development project through our firewall.

MP Antonovich (mike@micmin.com) has invited you to join a Groove workspace called "SharePoint Work (unsynchronized copy)".

New to Groove?
===
    Download a free trial version of Microsoft Office Groove 2007 and accept the invitation by clicking on the link below:

    http://invitation.groove.microsoft.com/download/?Invitation=46E98A57-A6F0-4F0A-9E2B-B00FCB9CF2F4

Already Have Groove?
===
    Accept the invitation by clicking on the link below:
    http://invitation.groove.microsoft.com/?Invitation=46E98A57-A6F0-4F0A-9E2B-B00FCB9CF2F4

Figure 11-4. *Responding to an invitation to join a workspace*

Incoming messages and other actions that you must respond to appear in a box that is displayed in the lower-right corner of the screen when you hover your mouse over the **Groove** icon in the notification area of the task bar. When a message first appears, it slides up above the task bar and flashes. The notification area includes an envelope icon when a new message is waiting. When you see the incoming message with the invitee's acceptance, click it to open the **Confirm Acceptance** dialog box. Within the dialog box, click the **Confirm** button to complete the process. As each invitee accepts your invitation to your workspace, his name appears in the **Workspace Members** list on the right side of the window.

A Quick Look at Groove's Other Tools

I will not spend time covering all of Groove's features here. That would take us beyond the scope of how to use Groove with SharePoint. However, it might help you appreciate the power of Groove if I quickly describe the major tools Groove makes available in your workspace.

To add a tool to your workspace, open the **Tools** menu using the button found on the bottom-right side of the workspace that looks like a white page with a green plus sign in its upper-left corner. Figure 11-5 shows Groove's available tools above the **Tool** button.

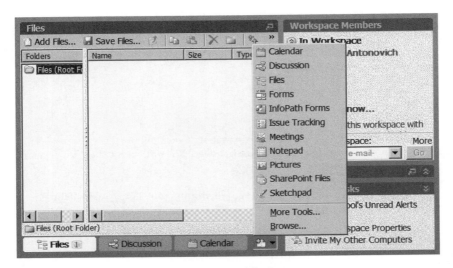

Figure 11-5. *Tools available to Groove out of the box*

If you do not see all these options, click the **More Tools** option at the bottom of the list. This option displays a dialog box that shows the tools available to you. If you still do not find everything you need, click the **Browse Online** link at the bottom of the tool list to go to Microsoft's Groove site to find additional tools, or you can simply perform a search on the Internet using your favorite search engine on the term "Groove Tools." For example, I found a free Groove tool that displays RSS feeds in Groove.

Chat

The first Groove feature that you might want to explore in more detail, even before trying out some other tools, is the Chat capability. Using Groove, you can chat with any member currently in your workspace. If he is online, but not in the workspace, you can send that user a message by clicking his name and then clicking **Send Message** in the **Common Tasks** panel. You can also send messages to offline members. However, they will not receive the message until after the next time they go online.

Pictures

The Pictures tool lets you include images saved in JPG and BMP formats to your workspace and share them with other members. Once loaded into Groove, you can rename the image, export another member's image to your local hard drive, delete the image from Groove, and navigate between images. You cannot edit images directly within Groove.

Sketchpad

The Sketchpad tool allows you to create simple sketches using drawing tools such as Pencil, Line, Rectangle, Ellipse, Polygon, and Textbox. One interesting feature of this tool is that it lets you begin with a background image (JPG or BMP) and then draw over the top of the image. You may find this capability useful to annotate images that you share with other members. However, the tool does not provide a way to export the final sketch. Even the copy-and-paste feature only works within Sketchpad, although you can copy and paste your sketch additions from one sketch page to another.

■**Tip** If you have a third-party screen capture application or if you use Vista, you can use the Snipping tool to capture the screen and crop the image before saving the image to a file or pasting it into another application.

Notepad

The Notepad tool allows you to record text notes. Each note must have a title or name. Within the body of the note, you can add only text, just like with the Notepad tool in the operating system. However, this tool adds more text formatting capability, including font colors, font styles, and font sizes. It also allows you to specify different line justifications by paragraph and to create indented and bulleted sections. To access features like hyperlinking to other sites and spell checking of your text, right-click anywhere in the text area while editing your note, and select the appropriate option from the pop-up menu.

Discussion

The Discussion tool takes the Notepad tool and adds the ability to respond to specific topics or create your own topic. You might even think of the Discussion tool as a structured chat feature that does not require members to be online, much less to be in the workspace to participate. Of course, resyncing of responses only occurs when the member returns to an online state. In some ways, the Discussion tool creates an environment that resembles a blog in that each member can post new topics in a particular discussion at any time. They can also return to existing topics to add responses to the topic or even to add responses to responses. Groove tracks responses in a tree-like structure, indenting each response level a small amount to show the relationship. A small box with a plus or minus sign appears to the left of each topic or response that has a child response. You can click this box to alternately show and hide the rest of the tree beneath that point. If you have no interest in a topic, you can minimize the space it uses by clicking the box to close all responses in that branch. Finally, discussion entries support rich text formatting as well as the ability to add hyperlinks to the text and spell checking.

Files

The Files tool allows you to drag files and even folders from your local desktop or mapped drives and drop them into Groove's Files folder. This tool provides an easy way to share non-SharePoint documents with other members of your workspace. In addition to the typical properties you expect from a directory of files, Groove adds a **Modified By** column to tell you the name of the last person who modified the file. Unlike SharePoint, Groove does not display an indicator when someone else is editing a file. However, Groove recognizes edit conflicts and saves additional copies of the file by appending the name of the person making the changes to the end of the file name. Finally, Groove does not synchronize file changes back to the original folder from which you copied the file. If you want to have a copy of the changed file, you must drag the file back from the Groove folder to your desktop folder.

Calendar

The Groove Calendar tool supports a subset of the features found in Outlook. You can display its calendar in month, week, or day mode. You can add appointments to the calendar defining a subject, a start date and time, an end date and time, and details about the appointment. However, you cannot create recurring events. Nor can you create appointments with specific members of your workspace. Perhaps more importantly, you cannot transfer appointments between Outlook and Groove and keep them synchronized. However, if you need to track appointments related to the members in your workspace, especially if those members work outside of your organization, this tool may meet your needs.

Issue Tracking

The Issue Tracking tool lets you list tasks/issues that you or other members of your workspace need to address and allows you to track their status. When entering the original issue, you can specify a title for the issue as well as a category and subcategory to group your issues. You can also track who reported the issue and include a rich-text description of the issue. On the issue's **Status** page, you can identify the person and/or organization responsible for the issue as well as provide a status, priority, and a rich-text comment area.

However, before you start entering issues, you need to spend time prefilling the drop-down tables used by issue tracking. These include tables that identify the originating organization and individual, the organization and individual the issue is assigned to, the issue categories and subcategories, the priority levels, and status levels. By prefilling these drop-downs, you can select values from these lists when you enter an issue or the response to an issue.

When a member of your workspace responds to an issue, she adds a separate response entry to the issue, which Groove prepopulates with selected data from the issue. They can then add a detailed description of the work they performed to resolve the issue using the rich text editor. They can also add attachments to their response. Any file can become an attachment. Therefore, you might want to capture screen images of the changes made and attach them to the response, documenting how to fix this issue should it recur.

Meetings

The Meetings tool allows you to create meeting sites, define the attendees for the meeting, create an agenda, keep minutes of the meeting, and post action items from the meeting. Begin by selecting **New Meeting** from the menu to create a meeting. This action opens a **New Meeting** dialog box, which consists of five tabbed pages. The first page, defined by the tab **Profile**, allows you to define a subject for the meeting, as well as the start and end dates, a location, and details for the meeting. You can even include attachments for the attendees to review before the meeting.

The second tab, **Attendees**, opens the **Attendees List**, letting you add meeting attendees. This list only includes the names of members of your workspace. From the attendees, you can select a chairperson as well as a minutes taker. The **Notes** section on this page might, for example, be useful for documenting why you did or did not select specific meeting attendees.

The third tab, **Agenda**, lets you define an agenda for your meeting. With so much time being spent in meetings, most professionals appreciate getting an agenda for the meeting ahead of time so they can determine what the meeting will cover, allowing them to better prepare for the meeting. Again, you can include attachments specific to agenda items so that attendees can review the documents ahead of time and come to the meeting prepared to discuss them.

The **Minutes** tab gives the minutes taker a place to document what was discussed at the meeting and record any major decisions made. To help the minutes taker, you can copy the agenda from the **Agenda** tab. That way, the minutes taker already has the major topic areas and can simply fill in the details after each section.

The **Actions** tab lets you document the action items decided on during the meeting. Each action item has a name, an owner, a status, and a priority. However, when you edit the details of the action item, you can also add attachments as well as detailed notes about the action. The project leader or the person who called this meeting may then reference this section to ensure that all actions decided upon during the meeting occur in a prompt fashion.

Unlike SharePoint's meeting workspace, the Groove Meetings tool does not integrate back into Outlook or even into the other Groove tools. Thus the meeting attendees do not have alerts to notify them when a meeting that they must attend has been scheduled. Furthermore, action items do not appear in the assignee's to-do task list in Outlook. However, if you hold virtual meetings in which attendees are members of your workspace, but may not be members of your organization and may furthermore physically reside in different locations, states, or even countries, Groove may be a tool to facilitate conducting virtual meetings.

Forms

Groove comes with a few different ways to create forms. The Forms tool lets you create custom document forms that members of your workspace can fill in. You can complete most form designs without resorting to coding or development skills. Forms support several different types of fields, styles, and views. Groove can import data from XML, CSV (comma-delimited files), and several other formats. Similarly, you can export data from Groove to binary, regular XML, CSV, Microsoft Office Excel, tabular text, and structured text files. For the developer, you can also use the Groove Web Services API to programmatically access other back-end systems.

Groove stores the records you create through use of your form in the workspace. You can use forms to edit those records. You can also use views to sort and display the data. If you have development skills, you can further customize your forms with custom styles, macros, and scripting.

Finally, you might choose to use the Groove Forms tool because not all members of your workspace may have InfoPath 2007, which is required by the InfoPath Forms tool. Another good reason for using the Groove Forms tool might be because you need a multiform solution that uses a hierarchical relationship, such as the forms used in the Discussion tool, to create topic and response forms. You can model even more complex relationships between parent and child forms. Finally, your form can use data from another form as a lookup in the current form.

Creating forms can be quite a complex process and goes beyond the scope of this chapter. However, Microsoft has several online articles that further explore the use of Groove forms.

InfoPath Forms

The InfoPath Forms tool uses the InfoPath Form Designer to create forms. As with regular Info-Path forms, you can have multiple views for displaying or collecting form records. One of the advantages of using the InfoPath Forms tools is that you can create forms that you can use outside of Groove with users who have InfoPath or that you want to publish on a SharePoint site. Also, InfoPath Forms support repeating controls and groups as well as the **Ink Picture** control, features not found in the Groove Forms tool.

If you already have an InfoPath form, you may be able to import the form into Groove. There are, however, a few settings and restrictions that apply. For example, you must set the **Property Promotion** of the fields you want to use before importing the form to Groove. This can be set in the **Forms Options** of the InfoPath form. Other restrictions and settings include the following:

- You can only import forms from InfoPath 2007 templates.

- You must set the **Submit Options** from the **Tools** menu so the form sends data to the hosting environment.

- You must deselect the check box that displays the **Submit** menu, as Submit is not a feature available within Groove.

- You must set the **Security Level** in the **Security and Trust** category of the **Form Options** to **Restricted**.

- You must set **Versioning** in the **Forms Options** to **Automatically upgrade existing forms**.

- On this same page, you must deselect the option **Allow form users to choose whether to upgrade**.

- Groove does not support Information Rights Management (IRM).

- Groove does not support the custom task panel, menu, or toolbar integration.

You might use Groove's InfoPath Forms tool if you already have a form similar to the one you want in Groove already created as a Microsoft Office Word document or Excel workbook, since InfoPath 2007 supports a wizard to convert these file types to InfoPath forms. You might also use the InfoPath Forms tool if you already have an XML data file using the W3C XML schema language to create the form.

SharePoint Files

The SharePoint Files tool adds features to the standard Groove Files tool that allow you to interact and synchronize files between Groove and SharePoint. Groove only supports WSS 3.0 and MOSS 2007 or better. The rest of this chapter focuses on how to use Groove's two file tools.

Sharing Your Files Using Groove: Simple Group Collaboration

Let's explore the basic Files tool. This tool allows you to share any file you have on your desktop or can access from a network drive. You simply have to open Windows Explorer, find the file, and drag and drop it into the Files folder as shown in Figure 11-6.

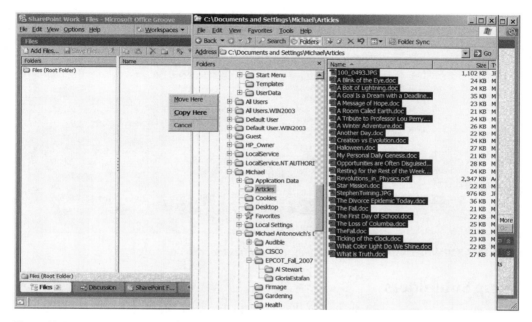

Figure 11-6. *Dragging and dropping files to Groove's Files tool*

In addition to using drag and drop to populate your Groove Files root folder, you can use the **Add Files** button found in the **Files** toolbar. When you click this button, Groove displays an **Add Files** dialog box that allows you to navigate through your directory structure, looking for files you want to add from your local drive or network drives to which you have access. When using this method, you can select multiple files by dragging through them if they appear contiguous in the list. If the files you want to transfer appear scattered through a directory, you can press and hold the Ctrl key while you click individual files to select them.

After you copy the files into the Files tool, Groove synchronizes the Files tool with all other members of the workspace. This may take a few seconds until every other member of the workspace sees the same file list. Everyone else's view of the new files, however, displays a small yellow square with a red asterisk-like symbol in the upper-left corner, as you can see in Figure 11-7. This symbol indicates that the file has recently been added by another member of the workspace and that you have not yet opened or read it.

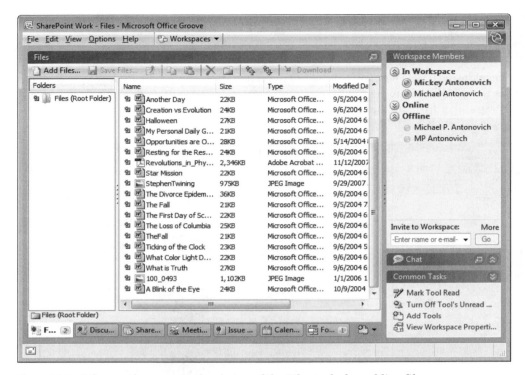

Figure 11-7. *Other workspace members' view of the Files tool after adding files*

Using Subfolders

Notice also that in this case, you copied all the files to the root folder named Files. Clearly, if everyone in your workspace continues to do this, you will soon have difficulty finding any file in the growing file list. However, not only can you create subfolders beneath the root folder, you can also create subfolders beneath subfolders. Suppose you create two folders under the root folder named Images and Short Stories. To do this, click the Files folder to select it. Then click the **Create New Folder** button from the **Files** toolbar, displayed as a folder icon with an asterisk in the upper-right corner.

■Tip You can see these button names when you hover over the icons in the **Files** toolbar.

This action creates a new folder within the selected folder. Supply the folder name in the dialog box, Images in the case of the first subfolder and Short Stories for the second subfolder. In addition to these two new folders, under Short Stories, add another subfolder named Articles.

Now that you have a folder hierarchy started, you might want to move some of the files that you originally dropped into the root folder to one of these other subfolders. Your first inclination might be to drag and drop files from the root folder into one of these new subfolders. Unfortunately, you cannot do that.

What you can do though is go to the root folder and select the file you want to move by clicking it. Then in the **Files** toolbar, select the **Copy Selected Item(s) to the Clipboard** button, displayed as the icon with two slightly offset pages. This action places a copy of the file on the clipboard.

Next, open the subfolder where you want to add the file. Click the **Paste Item from Clipboard** button, displayed as the icon with a page offset from a clipboard. At this point, you have two copies of the item, one in the current folder and one in the original folder.

If you do not want to keep a copy of the file in both folders (and I don't recommend that you do because it can be confusing if different updates occur to both copies), return to the original folder, click the original file to select it, and then click the **Delete selected item** button displayed as an X in the toolbar.

If you have many files to move, this process can be tedious at best. However, it serves as a good reminder that you should plan out your folders before you start copying files to Groove so that you can copy them to the desired folder right from the beginning.

Editing Your Shared Files

If you do not have any other workspace members currently in the workspace and you have a quick change, you can edit a file by double-clicking its name.

■**Note** As with SharePoint and even Windows Explorer, double-clicking a file to open it in **Edit** mode only works as long as you have an application compatible with that file type.

Suppose you have a Word document that you want to edit. After you finish making your changes, select **Save** from the menu displayed by clicking the **Office Button**. Then close Word. When you display the Groove window again, you should see a pop-up menu asking you to save your changes to Groove. Figure 11-8 shows this dialog box.

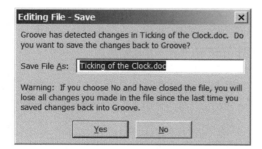

Figure 11-8. *Dialog box to save file changes back to Groove*

Notice the warning that if you do not choose to save the changes back to Groove immediately, you will lose all the changes you made since the last save. This happens because unlike SharePoint, Groove does not keep a copy of the file in a local drafts folder, which allows you to work offline and then synchronize your changes at a later time.

Dealing with Conflicts

So what happens if someone else enters the workspace and attempts to make a change to the same file you have open in **Edit** mode? The first person to save her changes wins, so to speak. Let's suppose that this other person saves her changes before you. When you attempt to save your change, you get a conflict dialog box similar to the one shown in Figure 11-9 where two people made a change to the file `Ticking of the Clock.doc`.

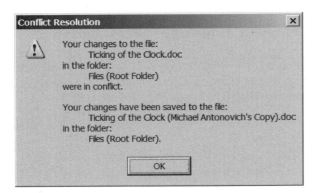

Figure 11-9. *Conflict Resolution dialog box from Groove*

Notice that Groove does not give you an option to resolve the conflict. Rather, it takes the approach of saving your changes to a second copy of the file, adding your name enclosed in parentheses to the end of the original file name. If you want to resolve the differences between your version of the document and the one that someone else saved before you, you must do that manually. If the document is a Word document, you can use Microsoft Word's ability to compare two documents to show the differences. However, for most other applications, you may have to perform a manual comparison of the documents to find and evaluate their differences.

Unfortunately, the Groove Files tool does not support check-out and check-in of documents to help protect your files from others who might make changes to the same document as you.

■**Tip** Before you begin editing a document, you might want to consider opening the **Chat** window and typing a message that you are about to edit a specific file. When you send your chat message, the **Chat** window on the right side of the workspace expands, showing your message to all members currently in the workspace. If anyone else is in the middle of editing the same document, that person can notify you before you get started.

Deleting Files

Finally, you can delete files from the Groove Files tool at any time by clicking the file to select it and then clicking the **Delete Selected Item** icon from the toolbar. In this way, you can delete individual files, groups of files, or entire folders. However, unlike SharePoint, Groove does not have a Recycle Bin to protect you from accidental deletions. Although you or another member of the workgroup may have an original copy of each of the documents from the time when they were first added, these versions probably do not have the changes added since that time, unless someone specifically saved a newer copy of the file.

Saving Files

As mentioned in the previous section, changes made to shared files exist only in the Groove folder. If you want to back up the changes, you need to copy the file(s) back to your local drive or a network drive. You can do this by selecting the file(s) and then clicking the **Save Files** button in the **Files** toolbar. This action displays a dialog box, shown in Figure 11-10, that allows you to specify where to save the selected file(s) by choosing an existing directory or by making a new folder. In this figure, I tell Groove to save the selected file(s) in the Documents folder of the current Vista user (Michael).

Figure 11-10. *Selecting a local folder in which to save a file*

Creating a New File

It is possible to create a new file from the Groove Files tool. To do this, open the **File** menu in the Groove toolbar and select the **New** option. This action opens a submenu that allows you to open a new folder, as well as new files of several types as shown in Figure 11-11. The file types you see in your menu depend on what applications you have installed on your desktop. In this case, I might decide to create a new Microsoft Office Word document.

When you create a new file, a new entry appears in the currently selected folder with the default name **New Microsoft Office Word Document**. You should immediately change this name to one more appropriate for your new document. Then double-click the document name to open it in the appropriate client application.

■**Tip** Select the folder first before selecting the **New** option from the **File** toolbar.

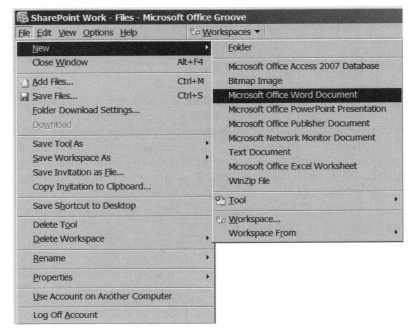

Figure 11-11. *Selecting a file type when adding a new file*

Setting Up a SharePoint Document Library Connection

Now that you have seen how to work with files added to Groove's basic Files tool, let's take a look at how you can access the **Shared Documents** library from a SharePoint site within Groove's SharePoint Files tool. To begin, open the **Tools** menu and select **SharePoint Files** from the list of tools.

This action first opens a welcome screen to the SharePoint Files tool that is different from the opening screen for the other tools. To set up Groove to use SharePoint, you must provide additional information about where to find the SharePoint files. Therefore, Groove starts a wizard to help configure the tool and connect it to a SharePoint library. Click the **Setup** button on this wizard's first screen to continue.

The wizard now displays a dialog box that asks you to select a document library or folder. Your dialog box should look similar to Figure 11-12.

In Windows XP, you can select your SharePoint library from the list of previous network places you have visited. If you have not previously visited the library you want to connect to, you must enter the URL of the library in the **Address** field at the bottom of the dialog box. In Windows Vista, you may have to enter the library's URL anyway, because Vista does not support a Network Places folder.

You must select a document library or a folder within a document library. Interestingly, you can also select a picture library. But the real advantage of working with Groove comes from sharing files from your SharePoint document libraries with people who do not have access to your SharePoint site, such as outside consultants on your project.

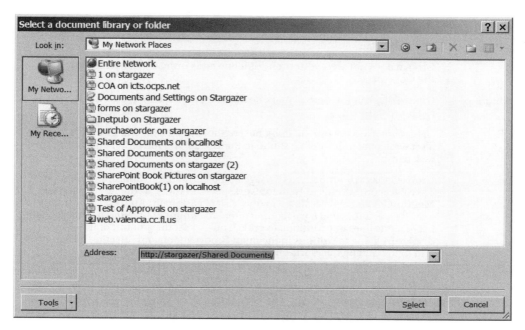

Figure 11-12. *Opening My Network Places to select a SharePoint library*

If you have several document libraries that you want to share, you can open multiple instances of the SharePoint Files tool, one for each document library to which you want to connect. You cannot connect to multiple libraries from a single instance of the tool, as each instance of the tool can only support a single connection definition.

Setting Permissions for the SharePoint Files Folder

Once you have created your SharePoint Files instance, you may want to review the properties that members with different roles have within the instance. As mentioned earlier, every tool within Groove has its own set of properties. Furthermore, every instance of a tool has its own unique set of properties and permissions. To view and edit these properties, follow these steps:

1. Open Groove's **File** menu and position your mouse over **Properties**.

2. Click **Tool** in the **Properties** submenu.

The resulting dialog box consists of three tabbed pages: **General**, **Alerts**, and **Permissions**.

The **General** properties page tells you basic information about the tool. The **Alerts** page lets you set the unread alert level for the tool. By default, Groove sets most tools to an **Auto** setting. What does **Auto** mean, and what other settings are possible? Table 11-1 explains the four possible alert settings for file workspaces.

Table 11-1. *Alert Settings for File Workspaces*

Alert Level	Alert Definition
Off	Groove does not alert you when someone adds unread information to the workspace.
Medium	Groove displays the unread mark next to the unread item (a yellow box with a red asterisk).
High	Groove displays the unread mark next to the unread item and displays a pop-up alert with a possible audible sound in the Windows notification area above the task bar.
Auto	Groove looks at your pattern of usage and determines an appropriate alert level. This level corresponds to **High** for workspaces that you frequently visit and to **Medium** for workspaces that you only visit occasionally. Auto can also auto-dismiss alerts that you have ignored after an amount of time has passed so your list of alerts does not continue to grow. You can set the amount of time alerts display by going to **Options** in the main Groove menu and selecting **Preferences** and then opening the **Alerts** tab.

Unread files represent either a new file that someone has uploaded to the workspace or a file that someone has just edited. Alerts typically appear in a small box that pops up in the lower-right side of the task bar known as the Windows notification area. However, when you set alerts to **High**, you can also choose to associate a sound file with the alert.

In addition to getting alerts when someone posts a new file or when someone updates an existing file, you can also receive an alert when a member of your workspace enters the tool. Again, with this alert, you can associate a sound file. This feature can be especially useful in tools such as the Discussion tool and the Meetings tool to let you know when someone enters the tool.

The **Permissions** properties page lets you change permissions associated with different roles. The drop-down list lets you select the role for which you want to review permissions. The area beneath this selection lists the permissions associated with the current tool. For the **Files** tools, these permissions include the following:

- **Synchronize** (SharePoint Files tool only)

- **Add files/subfolders**

- **Modify files**

- **Modify own files**

- **Delete files/subfolders**

- **Delete own files/subfolders**

- **Modify permissions**

To the left of each permission, you will find a check box that you can check or uncheck to determine whether the selected role has that permission. By default, the **Manager** role has all the permissions available for the current tool. On the other hand, the **Guest** role includes none of the permissions. However, you could grant guests limited rights such as the ability to create and edit their own documents within a tool such as the Discussion tool. Of course, all roles have permission to view the data in all tools. By default, the **Participant** role cannot modify permissions (because participants could then change anything managers set) and cannot delete files or subfolders other than ones that the participant creates. You might want to make this role more restrictive by taking away all delete rights or perhaps the ability to modify files. Unfortunately, you do not have the ability at this time to create additional roles and can only modify the permissions of the three predefined roles.

Working on SharePoint Documents Offline

The SharePoint Files tool also helps users who may need to work on documents while not connected to the Internet. Perhaps you need to finish working on a set of documents, but your company does not allow VPN access from outside the company walls to its intranet or to collaboration sites where you save your working documents. Of course, you could stay at work to finish working on those files. But an increasing number of people today are finding that they can be just as productive, if not more so, from home. There they can minimize distractions from coworkers, meetings, and the guy in the next cube with his constant interruptions to tell you about the impossible play his favorite team for this week made in the game he watched last night.

Perhaps you want to work on the files from home to put a few last minute finishing touches on them. Maybe you need to work on the files while you fly cross-country to a meeting the next day. No matter what the reason, you may not always be able to access your documents online. In these cases, Groove lets you work on documents placed in your SharePoint drafts folder. However, you want to be sure that no one else can modify your document while you work offline. Then, when you return to an online state, you can synchronize your changes back to the Share-Point source library. Therefore, Groove allows you to check out and then check back in documents in your SharePoint `Files` folder just like you can from directly within SharePoint itself.

Protecting Changes with Check-Out and Check-In Along with Versioning

At least when you are online and using Groove, you can easily tell whether other members of your workgroup are also online. When you work offline, you have no way of knowing not only whether others members of your workgroup are logged in to Groove, but also whether they are simultaneously editing the very file you have open for editing. Borrowing a feature you have seen in SharePoint, you can prevent others from editing the files you want to work on offline through the use of the Check-Out and Check-In features.

You can use Groove's Check-Out feature while online and connected to your SharePoint site to retrieve the latest copy of a document and place it within Groove. Then you can later access and safely edit the document from Groove's SharePoint `Files` folder while offline. By "safely," I mean that you can edit a document exclusively, preventing other users from making simultaneous changes to the same document. If you remember from earlier chapters, the Check-In and Check-Out features of SharePoint give you exclusive control over a document.

To check out a document within Groove, you could return to SharePoint and check it out from the library directly. However, Groove allows you to check out a document from the

SharePoint Files tool itself. Just right-click the file you want to check out while you are still connected to the Internet and the SharePoint server. Select the **Check In/Check Out** option from the drop-down menu and then select **Check Out from SharePoint**, as shown in Figure 11-13.

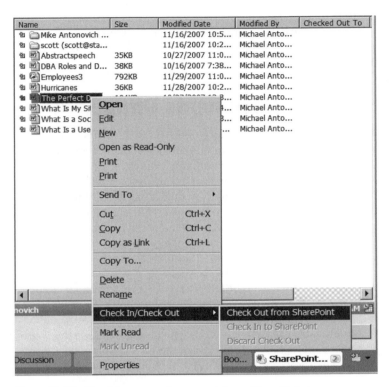

Figure 11-13. *Checking out a document from SharePoint*

This action marks the document in the SharePoint library as checked out. You can verify this by going to the **Shared Documents** library and checking whether the icon has the green box in the lower-right corner with the white arrow identifying the document as checked out. You should also see a column in the SharePoint **Files** window entitled **Checked Out To**. In this column, Groove displays the name of the person who has the file checked out. You can now disconnect from the network and make your changes, knowing that no one else can make changes to the document until you check it back in—or can you?

While it is true that you have checked out the file as far as SharePoint is concerned, the file is checked out to Groove, not to you. That means that any member connected to the workspace can open and edit the document, even while you already have it open in **Edit** mode. Then when you both try to save your individually edited copies, Groove recognizes a conflict. It stores the first copy saved back to the original file name. However, it stores the second copy saved to a separate file that begins with the name of the original file, but adds the name of the other member who edited the file enclosed in parentheses to the end of the name.

You must manually resolve the differences between these copies of the original file before you check in the file to the SharePoint library. Depending on the software application used to create the file, this process varies from relatively easy to very difficult. For example, if you use Word 2007, you can use the document **Compare** feature to help identify changes in each document and to merge individual changes together into a final document.

Collaborating with People Outside Your Organization

One the advantages of creating a Groove workspace is that you can invite anyone who has Internet access to become a member of your workspace and share files on it. One of the disadvantages of creating a Groove workspace is that you can invite anyone who has Internet access to become a member of your workspace and share files on it.

If those statements confuse you just a little, consider that when you create a personal collaboration space with Groove, you have total responsibility for who you invite into your workspace. If you use Groove to invite other company employees from outside of your department to a Groove site you create for your project because your departmental SharePoint collaboration site does not allow anyone from outside of the department to view, much less, edit department files, then Groove can serve as a positive factor.

While you might exercise care when deciding who you want to invite into your workspace, by default, anyone with the **Manager** or **Participant** role can invite others into your workspace. Some of these people may not be people that you would choose to invite into your workspace. Of course, if you have the **Manager** role, you can simply uninvite them. But with potentially dozens of members, you may not even know who recently became a member of the workspace without periodically reviewing the member list.

Not only can you use Groove to collaborate with members of other departments who cannot see your collaboration site, but you can also use it to collaborate with people outside your organization. A prime candidate for external users to your Groove site might be consultants hired to assist on a project. In this case, corporate policy may prevent these people from accessing internally hosted SharePoint sites. Yet to effectively work with these people, you need to share documents, set up meetings, have discussions, track issues, etc. Groove satisfies this need and can help organize your project and its activities.

Unfortunately, if these external consultants have the default **Participant** role, they can add others to your workspace. Again, this could occur without your necessarily knowing about it until after they have caused problems in your site or accessed information that was not suppose to be public.

Finally, consider the fact that documents added to your Groove workspace could contain macros that harbor viruses. One thing you should do if you plan to let people from outside your company share files on your Groove site is to turn virus scanning on. You can do this by opening the **Options** drop-down menu in the main Groove menu and selecting **Preferences**. In the **Preferences** dialog box, click the **Options** tab. Locate the **File Settings** tab at the bottom of this page and select the option **Scan incoming and outgoing files for viruses**. At this time, Groove only officially supports integrated virus scanning when you use Norton Antivirus Personal Edition 2002 or higher.

Synchronizing Files Between Groove and SharePoint Document Libraries

Groove creates a copy of the files from the SharePoint library locally when you add a SharePoint Files tool to your workspace. As you or other members of your workspace make changes to the files in this tool, Groove stores the changes in a local log file. It does not immediately send the changes back to SharePoint. In addition, anyone with access to your SharePoint site and with rights to edit files in your document libraries can also make changes to these file versions, which do not immediately get published to Groove. Therefore, you need to periodically synchronize both sets of files.

Only the **Synchronizer** role has the necessary rights and options to perform this synchronization. I will talk more about this role in the next section. However, for now, assume that you created the SharePoint Files instance in your workspace. The member who creates this instance becomes the synchronizer by default. You can tell whether you have the **Synchronizer** role by opening the SharePoint Files tool and looking at the bottom of the workspace. On the left side of the bar, immediately beneath the folder and files sections, you will find the label **Synchronizer** as shown in Figure 11-14. If your name follows this label, you are the synchronizer. Also in the bar, but on the right side, you can see the date and time of the last synchronization. If several days have passed since this date, you probably should synchronize the data. Even if you know that no members have been in the Groove site, you may still need to refresh changes to these files from their SharePoint libraries.

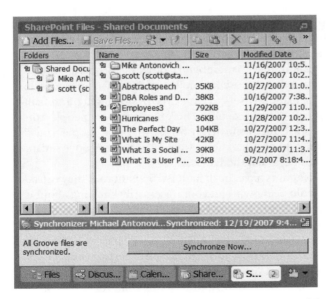

Figure 11-14. *The Synchronizer panel shows the name of the synchronizer and the time of last synchronization*

How can you tell when you need to synchronize your Groove files? The area immediately beneath the bar just discussed has a message on the left side that provides a hint of the file status. Table 11-2 lists possible messages and what they mean.

Table 11-2. *Synchronization Messages*

Status Message	Meaning
All Groove files are synchronized.	This message typically means only that Groove does not have any changes that it needs to synchronize with SharePoint. SharePoint, on the other hand, may have pending changes that Groove needs to receive but knows nothing about.
All Groove files are synchronized. Synchronization errors.	This odd message occurs when Groove successfully synchronizes all files or thinks it has. However, perhaps due to different allowable file types between SharePoint and Groove, there may be a SharePoint file that Groove cannot download.
There are unsynchronized changes in this tool.	This message occurs when Groove has unsynchronized changes to one or more files.
There are unsynchronized changes in this tool. Synchronization errors.	This message occurs when synchronization errors occur between Groove and SharePoint.

Also in this panel area, you can find a single large button with the label **Synchronize Now**. You can click this button at any time to manually synchronize Groove with SharePoint. You can also choose **Synchronize Now** from Groove's **Edit** drop-down menu.

If you select the option to manually synchronize the files in Groove with SharePoint, a dialog box pops up named **Preview Synchronization**. This dialog box shows pending changes by listing the name of the file and the action required.

If there is a conflict between changes made to a file in SharePoint and its corresponding file in Groove, Groove displays an **Action of Conflict** for the corresponding file. It also enables the **Resolve** button found in the lower-left corner of this dialog box. This dialog box displays a message in the text area immediately above the buttons along the bottom telling you that the change will not be synchronized. When you click the **Resolve** button, the **Resolve Conflict** dialog box appears, as shown in Figure 11-15.

This dialog box gives you the choice of keeping either the SharePoint or the Groove version of the file. Just click the radio button to select which version you would like to keep, and then click the **OK** button. Unfortunately, this dialog box does not provide any details about the differences between these two versions of the file. You could click **Cancel**. This action just stops the synchronization. You might choose this option so you can open both versions of the document to examine the differences between the two file versions. However you accomplish it, you must resolve this conflict between the different versions of the file before you can synchronize the files. Unfortunately, that also means that other members of the workspace cannot get files they need synchronized until you resolve your conflict.

■**Note** If you attempt to synchronize files without resolving outstanding conflicts, a **Synchronization Errors** link appears. You can click this link to display the errors. In this case, you must manually resolve the conflicts.

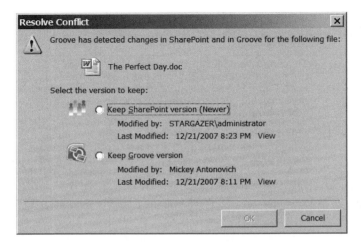

Figure 11-15. *Resolve Conflict dialog box*

If no conflicts occur, the synchronization proceeds without further delay. The time required to perform the synchronization varies depending on the number of files and changes made in SharePoint or Groove since the last synchronization.

DETERMINING WHAT FILE TYPES GROOVE ALLOWS

Groove will not allow you to share just any file. In fact, Groove restricts quite a few file types that it deems potentially dangerous. These include file types that could launch viruses or other malware into your system. To see a list of the restricted file types, open the **Options** drop-down menu from the main Groove menu. From this menu, select **Preferences**. In the **Preferences** dialog box, click the **Security** tab. On this page, find the **File Restrictions** section and click the link **View restricted types**. You will see a list that includes the following file types:

*.ade, *.adp, *.app, *.asp, *.bas, *.bat, *.cer, *.chm, *.cmd, *.com, *.cpl, *.crt, *.csh, *.der, *.exe, *.fxp, *.hlp, *.hta, *.inf, *.ins, *.isp, *.its, *.js, *.jse, *.ksh, *.lnk, *.mad, *.maf, *.mag, *.mam, *.maq, *.mar, *.mas, *.mat, *.mau, *.mav, *.maw, *.mda, *.mdb, *.mde, *.mdt, *.mdw, *.mdz, *.msc, *.msh, *.msh1, *.msh2, *.msh1xml, *.msh2xml, *.mshxml, *.msi, *.msp, *.mst, *.ops, *.pcd, *.pif, *.plg, *.prf, *.prg, *.ps1, *.ps1xml, *.ps2, *.ps2xml, *.psc1, *.psc2, *.pst, *.reg, *.scf, *.scr, *.sct, *.shb, *.shs, *.tmp, *.url, *.vb, *.vbe, *.vbs, *.vsmacros, *.vsw, *.ws, *.wsc, *.wsf, *.wsh, *.xnk

Unfortunately, there is no way to use the interface to turn off or on individual file types included in this restriction list. Groove either restricts or allows files with extensions from this entire list depending on the setting of the check box on the **Security** page labeled **Block restricted file types**.

Scheduling Synchronization

In addition to manually starting synchronization, you can automatically request synchronization to occur. To do this, click the icon that looks like a calendar at the end of the bar mentioned earlier with the synchronizer's name. This opens a dialog box, shown in Figure 11-16, that allows you to choose between manually starting synchronization and scheduling it.

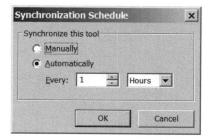

Figure 11-16. *Setting the synchronization schedule*

Even if you do not have rights to start synchronization, you will still see the **Synchronization Schedule** dialog box. You just will not be able to make changes to the schedule. If you have the **Synchronizer** role and you decide to set a schedule, click the **Automatically** option. Then select how often you want synchronization to occur. You can choose either hours or days. With hours, Groove limits you to a value between 1 and 24 hours inclusive. If you choose the unit of days, Groove limits you to a value between 1 and 21 days inclusive.

Managing Synchronization

Groove records all changes to SharePoint documents in a log file. Groove tracks not only changes made to documents, but also which members of the workspace have received those changes to their locally stored versions of the documents. Groove can synchronize changes among the members whenever they come back online.

However, if one or more members fail to log in to Groove at least once a month, and the files experience fairly heavy editing, this log may become too large to easily synchronize between the members. When this happens, a yellow alert icon appears next to the workspace in the **Launchbar** as a way of notifying the other members that the log file has grown to over 100MB.

The workspace manager can resolve this problem by suspending a member from the workspace. He can also uninvite members from the workspace. The option to perform either action appears in the **Common Tasks** panel of the workspace for members with the **Manager** role.

When a manager suspends a member, Groove stops saving changes for this member and clears the log of pending changes. When that user next attempts to open the workspace, she will see a message informing her that Groove no longer synchronizes her workspace copy. In fact, the user must request a reinvitation to the workspace to resynchronize her copy of the workspace.

Tip To restore a suspended member, you do one of two things:

Uninvite him, and then send a new invitation to him.

Download a copy of the synchronized workspace data from another computer or member.

If the manager decides to uninvite the member whose inactivity has caused the problem with the log, that member will be unable to open the workspace the next time she tries to enter it. You must reinvite that user to your workspace again before she can regain access to the shared files.

Who Is the Synchronizer?

At least one member of the workspace must have the following rights in order to instantiate the Groove SharePoint tool:

- Rights to access the desired SharePoint document library.

- Permission to send and receive changes to the SharePoint library. Typically, this must include the ability to add, edit, and delete items.

- Permission within Groove to synchronize with SharePoint. This permission belongs by default to the **Manager** and **Participant** roles, but not to the **Guest** role. Furthermore, participants may not have the ability to delete files other than their own. In this case, Groove displays warnings during synchronization when file deletions fail.

Any workspace member with all these characteristics has the ability to be the synchronizer, but only one member can hold the role of **Synchronizer** at a time. The member who instantiates the SharePoint Files tool becomes the first synchronizer. You can see the name of the synchronizer in the lower-left corner of the window beneath the folders list as shown in Figure 11-17. Also on this line to the right is the date and time that Groove last synchronized the files.

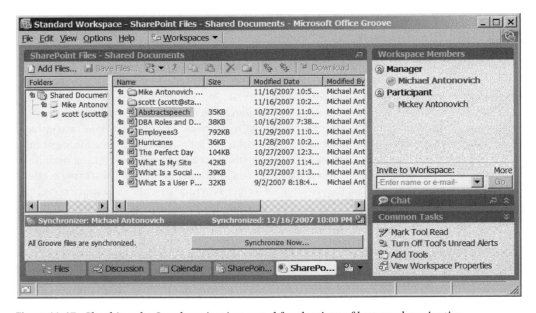

Figure 11-17. *Checking the Synchronization panel for the time of last synchronization*

If the current synchronizer no longer wants the responsibility of the **Synchronizer** role, he cannot initiate the transfer of the role to someone else. On the other hand, other members of the workspace who qualify for the role can request to become the synchronizer. The current synchronizer can then either pass on the role to this person or reject the request and retain the role. To request the role, the workspace member must open the **Edit** menu and select **Synchronize Now**. This opens the dialog box shown in Figure 11-18.

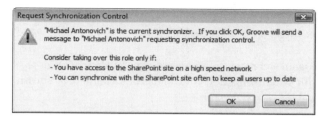

Figure 11-18. *A person in the Participant role requesting synchronization control*

If you click **OK** from this dialog box, Groove sends a message to the current synchronizer requesting control over synchronizing. Remember that you should only make this request if you have the necessary permissions on the SharePoint site. It also helps to have a high-speed network connection, especially if the libraries have a large number of files or the files are large. If you choose to assume this role, remember also that other members of the workspace then depend on you to keep the files synchronized. If you do not keep the files up to date, you can be assured that someone else will request to take the role away from you.

If you have the **Manager** role within Groove, you will also see a button labeled **More** in the lower-left corner of this dialog box, not shown in Figure 11-18, that allows you to take synchronization control away from the current synchronizer without sending a request. Use this option only if you know that you cannot reach the current synchronizer because she is out of the office or perhaps no longer belongs to the workspace.

If you are the synchronizer and someone requests control from you, you will get the message through Groove's message facility. When you click this message, a **Synchronization Control Request** dialog box appears, as shown in Figure 11-19. This dialog box tells you that another member of the workspace has requested to become the synchronizer. You can choose to surrender the role and approve his request, giving that member immediate control. You can defer the decision until a later time, or you can simply deny the request. If you select the **Approve Later** option, the **Synchronization Control Request** dialog box closes, but the message remains in the Windows notification area. You can reopen it by clicking the message once again. Of course, if you deny the request or merely delay your decision, you may want to immediately start a synchronization, or that member will probably send another request for control.

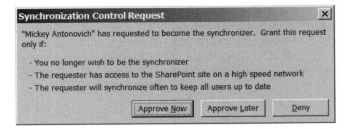

Figure 11-19. *Responding to the synchronization control request*

If you deny the control request, the requester receives a message through Groove's message facility informing him that his request for synchronization control has been denied, as shown in Figure 11-20.

Figure 11-20. *Denying a synchronization control request*

If you approve the control request, the requester receives a message through Groove's message facility approving the request for synchronization control, as shown in Figure 11-21. At this point, he should see the synchronizer's name change on his screen, and he can perform a manual synchronization by clicking the **Synchronize Now** button.

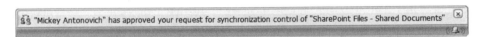

Figure 11-21. *Approving a synchronization control request*

If you start receiving frequent requests for synchronization control, you may want to more frequently synchronize the files if you have been performing the synchronization manually. If you scheduled synchronization to occur on a regular basis, you may want to shorten the time interval between synchronizations or switch from manually starting the synchronization process to automatically running it every so many hours or days as needed.

Summary

In this chapter, you looked at one of the newest additions to the Microsoft Office family of tools, Groove. Groove allows you to build your own personal collaboration network without needing a server or any special administration tools. As a peer-to-peer collaboration application that only requires Internet access to work, Groove allows you to create collaboration workspaces that include not only people that you work with, but also anyone with Internet access.

While many of the tools that Groove offers sound a lot like similar tools in SharePoint or even Office itself, Groove does not provide integration with most of these other tools at this point. Nor does it integrate its tools with corresponding Microsoft Office products like Share-Point does. The only major exception occurs in the area of SharePoint document libraries.

Groove can share files between a SharePoint document library and itself, allowing workspace members access to files that they may not have direct access to through your SharePoint site. Of course, you should always be careful who you allow to access shared document files.

You can work with files in your Groove folders even when you are not connected to the Internet. However, working offline increases the potential danger of having two or more people edit the same document at the same time. The ability to check out a SharePoint document may limit other SharePoint users from accessing and changing the document while you have it open in Groove, but it does not prevent other Groove users in your workspace from editing the same document simultaneously. While Groove recognizes potential conflicts when you attempt to save your changes, you must then determine how to reconcile your changes with those made by someone else.

If you create a SharePoint Files section within Groove, you automatically become the synchronizer for that section. As synchronizer, you have total control over how often to synchronize the files in your Groove site with those in SharePoint. Other members of your workspace may not agree with the synchronization frequency you choose and may challenge your authority by requesting to become the synchronizer. You can continue to hold on to this responsibility, or you can relinquish it to another user who has appropriate rights to perform the task.

Despite a few shortcomings, when properly used, Groove can greatly aid you in sharing documents as well as calendars, issue lists, discussions, and other features with people you work with. Especially interesting is its ability to work outside of your corporate firewalls, allowing you to provide collaboration capability with external workers and consultants. Combining this ability with Groove's SharePoint Files feature allows you to provide access to documents you normally store in SharePoint to external workers, thus making Groove an auxiliary tool to augment your SharePoint implementation.

■■■

CHAPTER 12

Additional Supporting Libraries

This last chapter will examine three final library types that I have not touched on previously. These three libraries are typically not used by themselves, but are most often used in a support capacity with other SharePoint and Microsoft Office functionality. Two of these libraries can only be found in MOSS 2007. Therefore, if you work with a WSS 3.0 site, you will not be able to use these libraries, but you may want to read through the sections covering these libraries anyway to see what you are missing. Hopefully, through the use of the included figures, you can still gain a good understanding of how these libraries can benefit your organization.

The first library type is a special implementation of a document library used for records management that only MOSS 2007 supports. However, you might be interested in records management if you need to archive time sheets, absence requests, purchase requests, performance evaluations, and other documents that your department or company must retain. Typically, records management provides long-term storage for documents created originally in other libraries.

The second library type is the picture library, which you first saw in Chapter 3; I'll give you a deeper look at it here. While the most common use of a picture library may be to support content pages, you can maintain picture libraries that are nothing more than libraries of pictures that anyone can view. For that reason, I will show you the different ways you can upload and view your pictures in this library.

The final library type you will examine is the slide library. This library is also only found in MOSS 2007 and works specifically with PowerPoint slide presentations. If you have groups of people that must work together on presentations, a SharePoint slide library may be the easiest way for them to share slides and easily build new presentations based on pulling together slides from other presentations along with their own slides.

So let's get started by looking at creating a records management system.

Creating a Records Management System to Archive Your Documents

Increasingly, today's organizations spend more time managing records than they did just a few years ago. Regardless of whether the reason for retaining more records comes from the fear of litigation or the need to meet new government requirements, more records are retained than ever before and must be managed so that they can be easily retrieved when needed. To meet this need, MOSS 2007 adds a Records Center template to the list of Enterprise sites. You might argue that even the basic SharePoint features already serve as a central repository for records by providing departments and management with a single place to create, process, and store data. SharePoint's collaboration features facilitate the easy creation of multiple sites for departments and project groups, with each one potentially supporting multiple document libraries. But flexibility can also bring chaos. In fact, it might not take long before you find your organization's records scattered across multiple sites.

> ■**Tip** Microsoft has released a Resource Kit to enable SharePoint 2007 to become DoD 5015.2 Chapter 2 compliant. This update affects the management of records and their permissions, e-mail, and support for complex retention rules. Additional information can be found at `http://www.microsoft.com/sharepoint/capabilities/ecm/dod5015.mspx`.

A Records Center provides a central repository for long-term storage of records after the department or project no longer actively needs them. In addition to determining what to do with documents from a department or project after projects complete, you may also require records retention as part of your organization's auditing and/or compliance requirements. You might also need to archive records for historical reporting or even tax purposes. Regardless of why you think you need a centralized store for your long-term retention of records, Share-Point's Records Center site can help.

To keep the illustrations relatively simple, let's focus on one type of document in a single document library. Suppose your organization has decided that it needs to archive each Request for Bid (RFB) document on your new SharePoint site. Let's see how a Records Center site can satisfy this need.

Creating Site Columns

Assuming that the need to store RFB documents is a new requirement, you have the opportunity to think through how you want to handle them. For example, rather than letting each manager create his own RFB format each time he needs to send out a new RFB, you could provide a common template that everyone could use. You could then create a library that uses that template as its default document type. Furthermore, by using a common RFB, you could create metadata specific to the RFB so that, when you display that metadata in a library, you could quickly view key information about each RFB record. Finally, after a project ends or the item ordered arrives and is accepted, you can archive the original RFB into a Records Center.

Let's start the process by creating a set of site columns that you can reuse when defining content types. Remember that you can add site columns to libraries as metadata so that when you display a list of the items in the library, you can quickly see important information about each item. Suppose you want to create the following site columns to associate with each Request for Bid:

- **RFB_Number**

- **RFB_Due_Date**

- **RFB_Responder_Name**

- **RFB_Response_Amount**

To create a new site column, follow these steps:

1. Open the **Site Actions** menu.

2. Select **Site Settings**.

3. Click **Site Columns** in the **Galleries** column of the **Site Settings** page.

4. In the **Site Column Gallery**, click **Create**.

5. Enter the column name and select a column type.

6. Enter other information as needed to define the column such as defaults, valid value ranges, etc.

For example, you might define the **RFB_Number** column as a numeric field, the **RFB_Due_Date** field as a date and time field, the **RFB_Responder_Name** as a single line of text, and the **RFB_Response_Amount** as currency. As you enter your first column definition, you must choose to place your new columns in an existing column group or create a new group. Using a new group might make it easier to locate columns related to a content type. Figure 12-1 shows the creation of the **RFB_Group** for RFB-related columns at the same time that you define the properties for the **RFB_Number** column.

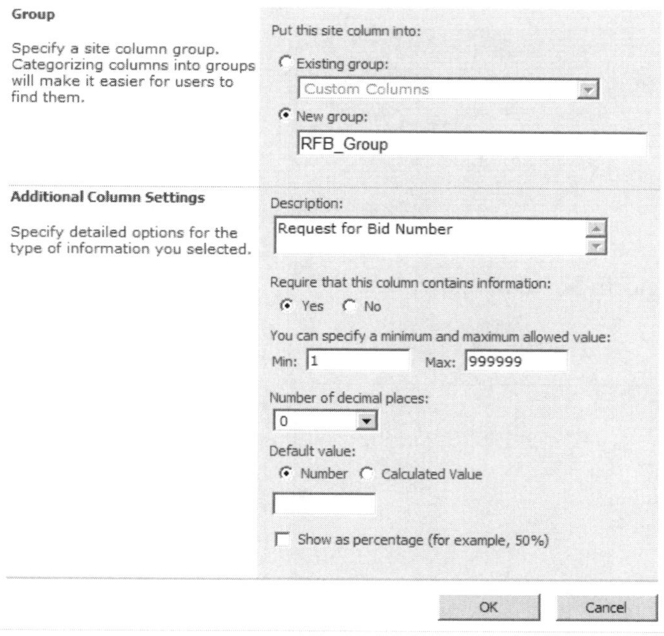

Figure 12-1. *Creating a new site column group while adding a site column*

Similarly, define the rest of the site columns, reusing the **RFB_Group** to organize them. After you finish adding all the fields, you should see all the new columns you added to the **RFB_Group** by selecting just that group in the **Site Column Gallery**. Figure 12-2 shows the new site columns in the **RFB_Group**.

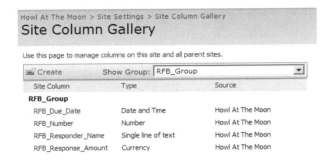

Figure 12-2. *New site columns in the RFB_Group*

Creating a Content Type for RFB Documents

Using a common form for RFB documents not only saves time when creating a new RFB by providing a predefined format, but also helps employees fill in and evaluate forms due to the consistency with which the data appears. Therefore, your next step is to create a basic RFB template using Word that you can then add to the SharePoint library so that each time a user creates a new document, she begins with a common and accepted form for entering the form details. Figure 12-3 shows an example of such a simple word template for the company Howl at the Moon Software, Inc.

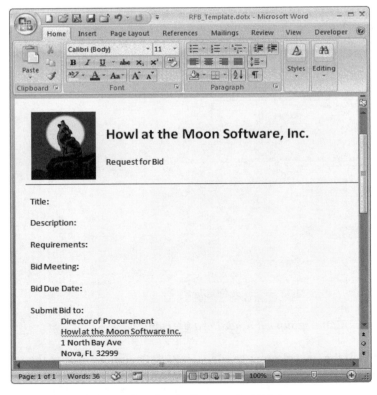

Figure 12-3. *Word template for the Request for Bid document*

To use this Word template as the default template in SharePoint, follow these steps:

1. Open the **Site Actions** menu.

2. Select **Site Settings**.

3. From the **Site Settings** page, select **Site content types** from the **Galleries** section as shown in Figure 12-4.

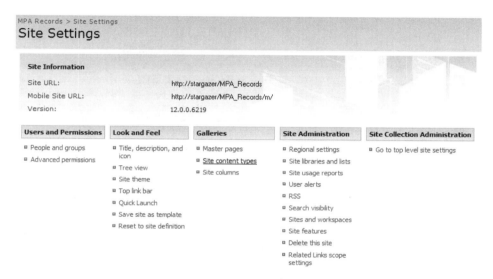

Figure 12-4. *Creating a new site content type*

4. From the **Site Content Type Gallery**, select the **Create** link in the header area of the gallery as shown in Figure 12-5.

Figure 12-5. *Creating a new content type from the Site Content Type Gallery*

5. Within the **New Site Content Type** dialog box, enter a name for your new content type. For example, you may want to abbreviate the name for the content type as RFB.

6. Next, supply a description for the content type so everyone knows the purpose of the new content type.

Notice that in this section, you can also determine from which content group and specific content type you want to inherit the new content type. In the case of the RFB, the most logical content type to inherit from is the **Document** type in the **Document Content Types** group.

You can also determine in which group to place the new content type, including creating a new content type group if you feel that the differences in the new content type warrant its own group.

7. To finish the definition of the content type, click the **OK** button. Figure 12-6 shows the definition of the RFB content type.

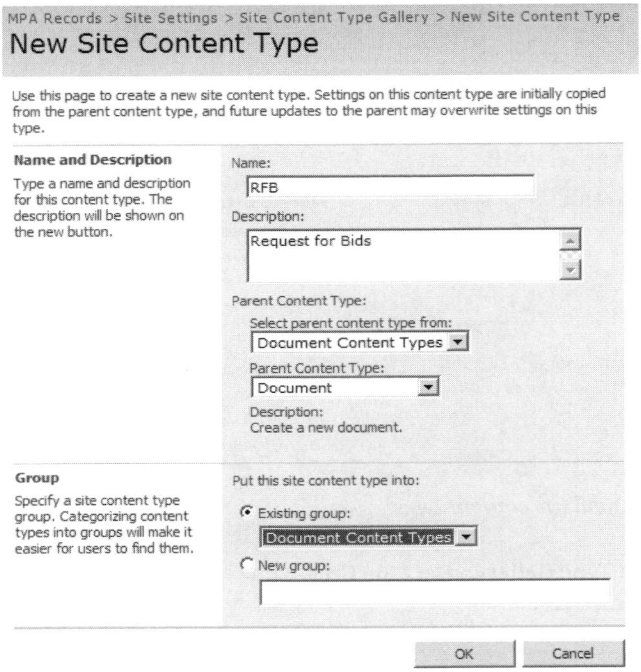

Figure 12-6. *The site content type RFB defined*

You should now see a content type definition page similar to Figure 12-7. On this page, you can define additional settings for this content type.

The most important additional setting at this point is the one that associates the Word template with the content type. Therefore, before setting any other properties, click the **Advanced Settings** link found in the **Settings** section. This option opens a page that allows you to associate a new or existing document template with the current content type. Figure 12-8 shows the RFB content type being associated with a document template previously created and saved as G:\Chapter 12\RFB_Template.docx.

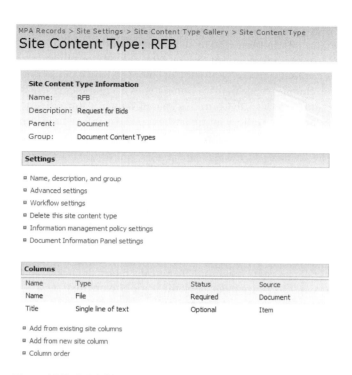

Figure 12-7. *Initial site content type definition*

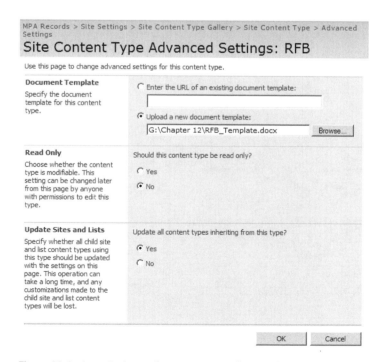

Figure 12-8. *Associating a document template with the content type*

You can also determine at this time whether anyone can modify the content type and whether you want sites and lists that use this content type to be updated. When you create a new content type, the setting of this latter option does not matter. However, if you modify an existing content type on which other content types have already been based, you can use this option to determine whether to cascade changes made here to content types in child sites and lists.

When you are done, click **OK** to return to the **Site Content Type: RFB** page. Alternatively, simply click the breadcrumb **Site Content Type Gallery** found at the top of the image to return to the gallery. You should now see the new content type listed in your selected type group.

Creating a Site Library to Collect RFB Documents

Now that you have site columns defined along with a content type for the documents you plan to create, you can associate them with an existing document library or create a new one. Let's assume you want to create a separate document library to hold RFB documents created by your department. Go to the department or project site where you want to create the library, which must be in the same site collection as the content type, since content types are scoped to site collections. There you can either click **Create** from the **Site Actions** menu or click **Create** from the **View All Site Contents** page. On the **Create** page, click the option to create a new document library. In either case, you should see the **New Library** page, as shown in Figure 12-9. This page allows you to assign a name and description to the new library as well as navigation and version history settings. In the **Document Template** section, select an existing template from the drop-down list such as a Word 97-2003 document.

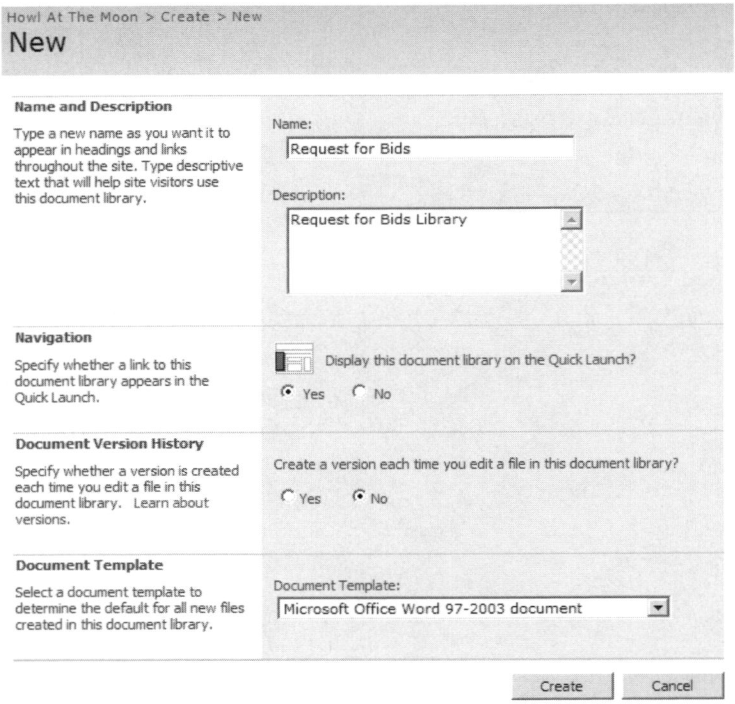

Figure 12-9. *Creating the working library*

SharePoint creates the library and displays the empty library list, but you still have configuration settings to apply to the library. Therefore, with the new library open, select the option **Document Library Settings** from the **Settings** menu option. Select **Advanced Settings** from the **General Settings** option group. In the resulting settings page, locate the section titled **Content Types** and select the option to allow management of content types, as shown in Figure 12-10.

Howl At The Moon > Request for Bids > Settings > Advanced Settings

Document Library Advanced Settings: Request for Bids

Content Types

Specify whether to allow the management of content types on this document library. Each content type will appear on the new button and can have a unique set of columns, workflows and other behaviors.

Allow management of content types?

⦿ Yes   ○ No

Figure 12-10. *Turning on management of content types for the working library*

Click **OK** to accept your changes in the **Advanced Settings** page. Returning to the **Settings** page for the library, look again at the section called **Content Types**. This section lists the content types this library can use. By default, document libraries support the **Document** content type. If no template has been associated with this content type, it opens the Word file `template.doc`, which displays a default blank Word document when the user clicks the **New** button. Figure 12-11 shows the customization page for the Request for Bids library.

Howl At The Moon   Welcome Antonovich, Michael P. ▾ | My Site | My Links ▾ | ⓘ

Howl At The Moon

Home | MyBlog   Site Actions ▾

Howl At The Moon > Request for Bids > Settings

Customize Request for Bids

List Information

Name: Request for Bids
Web Address: http://stargazer/Request for Bids/Forms/AllItems.aspx
Description: Request for Bids Library

General Settings	**Permissions and Management**	**Communications**
▫ Title, description and navigation	▫ Delete this document library	▫ RSS settings
▫ Versioning settings	▫ Save document library as template	
▫ Advanced settings	▫ Permissions for this document library	
▫ Audience targeting settings	▫ Manage checked out files	
	▫ Workflow settings	
	▫ Information management policy settings	

Content Types

This document library is configured to allow multiple content types. Use content types to specify the information you want to display about an item, in addition to its policies, workflows, or other behavior. The following content types are currently available in this library:

Content Type	Visible on New Button	Default Content Type
Document	✔	✔

▫ Add from existing site content types
▫ Change new button order and default content type

Figure 12-11. *Adding a new content type*

To add a new content type, click the option **Add from existing site content types** at the bottom of this section. The subsequent page shows the available content types. Scroll through this list, select the RFB content type created earlier, and click **Add**. Figure 12-12 shows that you want to add the content type RFB to the current library. When you click **OK**, SharePoint adds this content type to the library.

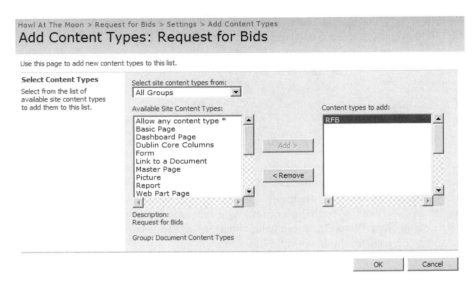

Figure 12-12. *Selecting the content type to add*

After adding this new content type, the blank Word document content type, **Document**, still appears as the default type. While the drop-down menu for the **New** button in the library now shows both content types, **RFB** and **Document**, clicking the **New** button itself assumes that you want to create an instance of the default content type. Rather than default to a blank Word document, you want to default to a blank RFB form that already has your organization's header on it as well as formatted sections for the RFB contents.

SharePoint provides two ways to promote your RFB form to become the default type replacing the blank Word document. You could simply delete the default content type. If you never want users to create a generic Word document in this library, this may be your best choice. However, if you want to leave your options open, you could change which content type acts as the default. You can do this by clicking the link **Change new button order and default content type**, as shown in Figure 12-13.

The page to change the content type order works much like the page used to change the order of columns in a view. You see a separate row for each content type. To the left of the content type name appears a check box that lets you determine whether users of the library can see that content type. To the right of the content type name, you see the relative order of the content types. The first content type becomes the default content type. So the second way to make the RFB content type the default type for this library requires that you simply change its numeric position to **1**, as shown in Figure 12-14.

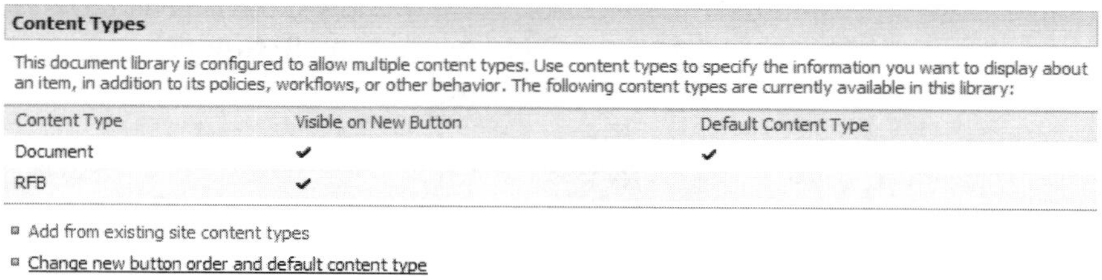

Content Types

This document library is configured to allow multiple content types. Use content types to specify the information you want to display about an item, in addition to its policies, workflows, or other behavior. The following content types are currently available in this library:

Content Type	Visible on New Button	Default Content Type
Document	✔	✔
RFB	✔	

▫ Add from existing site content types
▫ Change new button order and default content type

Figure 12-13. *Viewing the content types for the library*

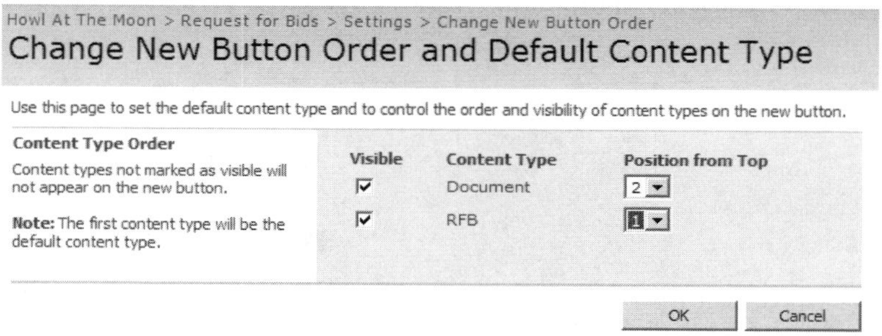

Howl At The Moon > Request for Bids > Settings > Change New Button Order

Change New Button Order and Default Content Type

Use this page to set the default content type and to control the order and visibility of content types on the new button.

Content Type Order	**Visible**	**Content Type**	**Position from Top**
Content types not marked as visible will not appear on the new button.	☑	Document	2 ▾
Note: The first content type will be the default content type.	☑	RFB	1 ▾

OK   Cancel

Figure 12-14. *Changing the default content type for the library*

When you return to your library's **Standard View** and open the **New** drop-down menu, you will see that it supports two different content types, **RFB** and **Document**. Figure 12-15 shows this drop-down menu. Notice that the order of the content types matches the order selection made in Figure 12-14. From this drop-down, you can select either content type or even create a new folder. However, if you simply click the **New** button rather than open the drop-down list, SharePoint uses the default content type and opens the RFB template, allowing you to create a new bid.

Figure 12-15. *Selecting from content types when adding a new document*

Before you leave this document library, you have one more thing to do. If you already went back to the **Standard View** to see the **New** menu, return to the **Settings** page for the library. Scroll down to the **Columns** section. Earlier I mentioned that you could create site columns that could be applied to libraries. Beneath the list of current columns used by the library, click the link **Add from existing site columns**. This link displays the window shown in Figure 12-16. To see only the columns associated with Request for Bids, select the **RFB_Group**.

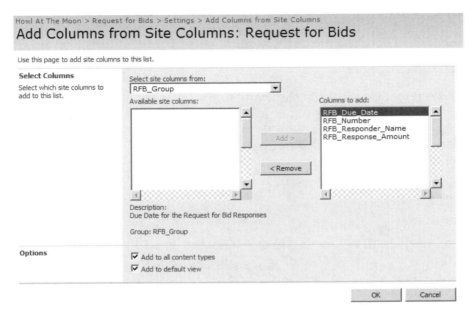

Figure 12-16. *Adding columns to library metadata from the site columns group RFB_Group*

You can now add each of the columns one at a time from the list on the left to the list on the right by clicking it once to select it and clicking the **Add** button. You can also double-click a column name to move it from one box to another. If you have a lot of columns to select, you might find it faster to begin by clicking the first column name. Then while holding down the **Shift** key, click the last column name, followed by clicking the **Add** button.

After you have added all four columns to the second list box, consider the two options at the bottom of the dialog box. The first option, **Add to all content types**, adds the selected site columns to each of the content types in the library. If you do not want to do this, remove the check from the check box. In this example, you probably would not want to add these columns to the document content type. The second option adds the site columns to the default view.

If you do not want to add the site columns to all content types, you can still add the site columns to specific content types by performing the following steps:

1. From the library's **Settings** page, click the content type you want to modify.

2. From the **List Content Type** page, click the link **Add from existing site or list columns** beneath the **Columns** list.

3. The **Select Columns** group defaults to **List Columns** to display any columns included in the list, but not in the current content type. If this list shows the RFB columns, move them to the list box on the right the same way as previously described.

4. Click the **OK** button to complete the addition of the columns to the content type.

You should now see the RFB columns included in the **Columns** section as shown in Figure 12-17.

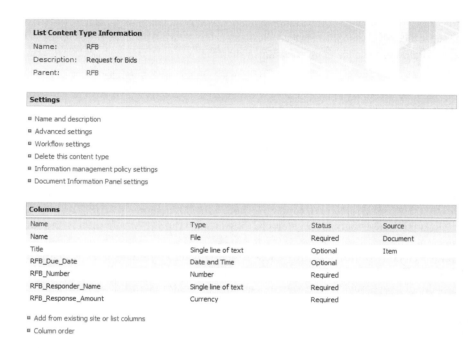

Figure 12-17. *Site columns added to the RFB content type*

If you return to the **Settings** page for the library using the breadcrumbs at the top of the page, you will also see the new columns in the **Columns** section, as shown in Figure 12-18. The **Used In** column shows which content types use each of the user-defined columns.

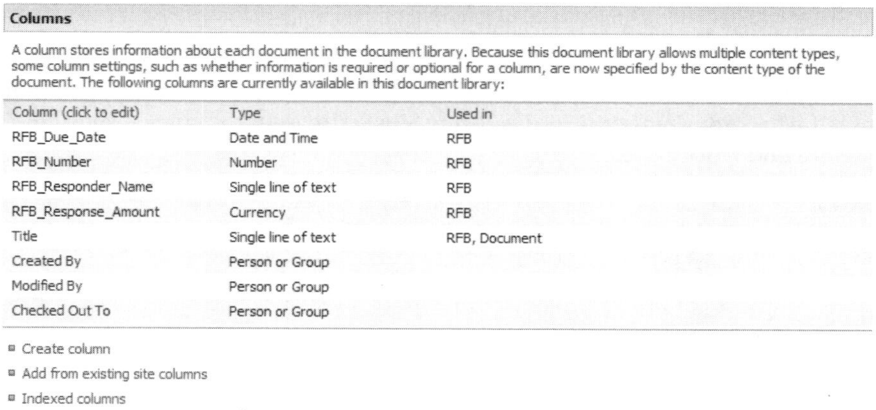

Figure 12-18. *Library metadata after adding site columns to only the RFB content type*

Now that you have a document library for creating documents based on your custom content type for bid requests, let's look at the next step: creating the **Records Center** site.

■**Note** You may need the help of your SharePoint administrator to complete this portion of the setup, as you may not have administrative rights to the **Central Administration** site.

Creating the Records Center Site

If you have the necessary permissions to create new sites, open the **Site Actions** menu and select **Create**. From this dialog box, click **Sites and Workspaces**, found in the **Web Pages** group. When the **New SharePoint Site** page appears, enter a title and description for the new site. The title appears in the header of the site. The description also appears in the header when supplied.

Next, supply a URL name for the site. Developers often use an abbreviated version of the site title for the URL, leaving out spaces or replacing them with underscores. Using shorter URL names makes it easier to enter them later when creating links to the site or referencing the site to upload objects.

The **Template Selection** option lets you choose from many different templates available in your SharePoint installation. While MOSS 2007 or WSS 3.0 will install all the templates shown in this book, advanced users may choose to install additional custom templates. SharePoint groups similar templates together so that in this section, you see a tabbed page in which each tab corresponds to one or more related templates. Both WSS 3.0 and MOSS 2007 support the templates found in the tabs **Collaboration** and **Meetings**. MOSS 2007 then adds the **Enterprise** and **Publishing** tabs. To continue creating your records management system, open the **Enterprise** tab and select **Records Center**, as shown in Figure 12-19.

For this subsite, you can choose to use the same user permissions as the parent site, or you can define unique permissions. While you may choose to create your Records Center as the top level of a separate site collection, if you have a small installation, you may choose to create the Records Center as a subsite, as shown here. In either case, most site administrators will probably decide to create unique permissions for the Records Center primarily because fewer people need access to the Records Center, and even those who do typically require more rights than they usually have on other sites.

Finally, as with any subsite, you can define the navigation options, including whether to include the site in the top link bar of the parent site. If you select **No** for this option, you can still locate and enter the Records Center site by displaying **Site Settings** for the current site and looking under **Sites and Workspaces**.

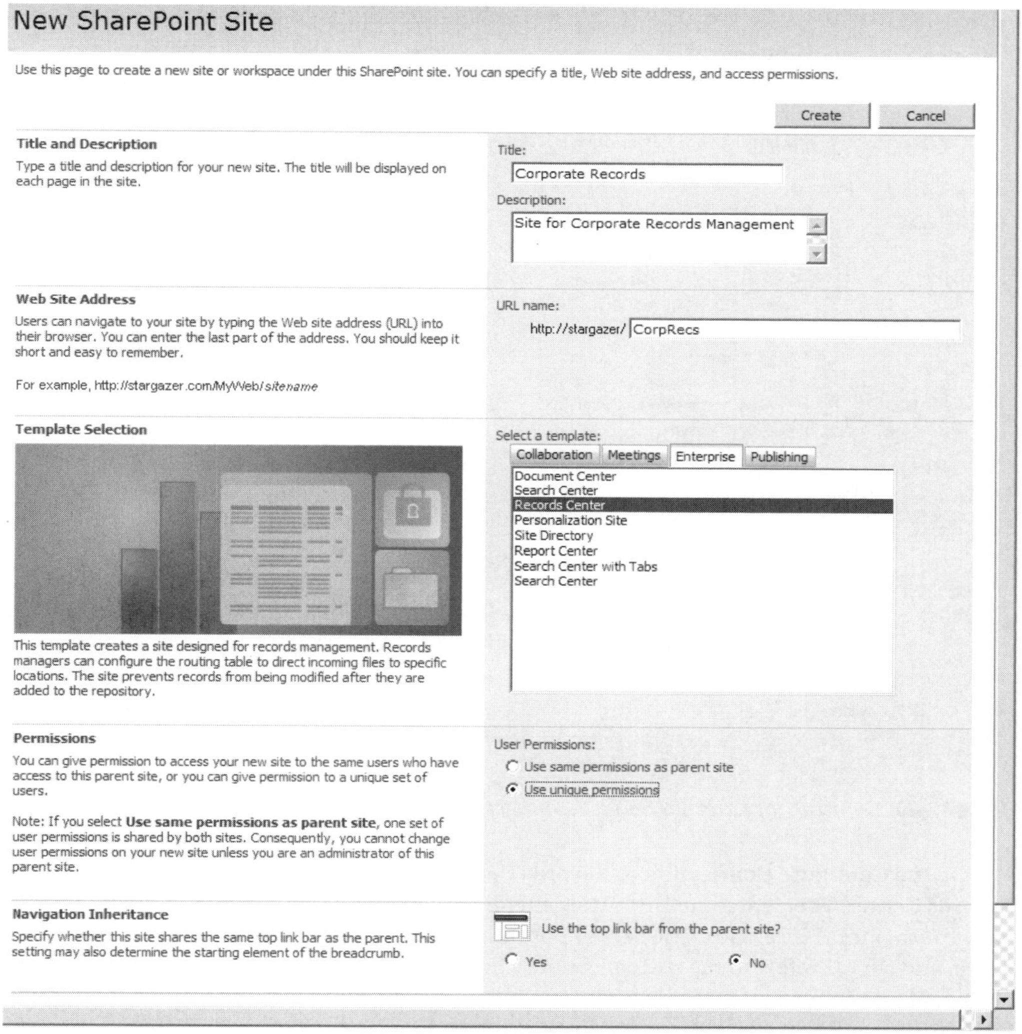

New SharePoint Site

Use this page to create a new site or workspace under this SharePoint site. You can specify a title, Web site address, and access permissions.

[Create]   [Cancel]

Title and Description

Type a title and description for your new site. The title will be displayed on each page in the site.

Title:
Corporate Records

Description:
Site for Corporate Records Management

Web Site Address

Users can navigate to your site by typing the Web site address (URL) into their browser. You can enter the last part of the address. You should keep it short and easy to remember.

For example, http://stargazer.com/MyWeb/*sitename*

URL name:
http://stargazer/ CorpRecs

Template Selection

This template creates a site designed for records management. Records managers can configure the routing table to direct incoming files to specific locations. The site prevents records from being modified after they are added to the repository.

Select a template:

| Collaboration | Meetings | Enterprise | Publishing |

Document Center
Search Center
Records Center
Personalization Site
Site Directory
Report Center
Search Center with Tabs
Search Center

Permissions

You can give permission to access your new site to the same users who have access to this parent site, or you can give permission to a unique set of users.

Note: If you select **Use same permissions as parent site**, one set of user permissions is shared by both sites. Consequently, you cannot change user permissions on your new site unless you are an administrator of this parent site.

User Permissions:

○ Use same permissions as parent site
◉ Use unique permissions

Navigation Inheritance

Specify whether this site shares the same top link bar as the parent. This setting may also determine the starting element of the breadcrumb.

Use the top link bar from the parent site?

○ Yes   ◉ No

Figure 12-19. *Creating the Records Center site*

Creating the External Service Connection

The first step in configuring the Records Center site that you just created involves creating an **External Service Connection**. You must perform this step from the **Central Administration** site for the Records Center site. Log in to the **Central Administration** site and switch to the **Application Management** page using the tabs at the top of the site. On this page, select **Records Center** under the **External Service Connections** section, as shown in Figure 12-20.

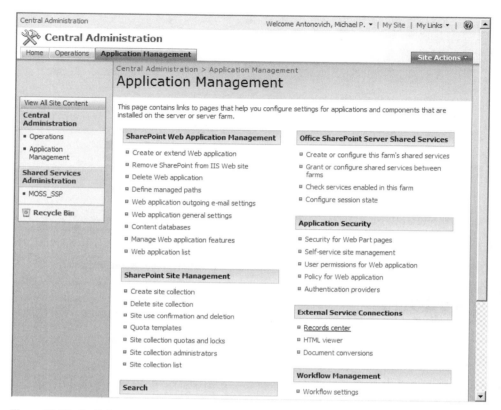

Figure 12-20. *Defining an External Service Connection for the Records Center*

On the **Configure Connection to Records Center** page, select the option **Connect to a Records Center**. Then enter the URL. The generic version of the URL is `http://server/portal/_vti_bin/officialfile.asmx`. The `server` portion, of course, refers to your SharePoint server's name, and `portal` refers to the site collection. The last portion of this URL refers to a program file that directs items sent to the Records Center to a web service that builds the Records Center folder for the archived file. You cannot just copy files from other site libraries into the Records Center. Instead, each file sent to the Records Center generates its own folder identified by the date and time that you created it. This folder contains the archived document, along with a folder for properties and audit history.

Finally, enter a display name for the Records Center and click **OK**. This name will be used by your end users to send documents to the Records Center. Figure 12-21 shows the **External Service Connection** definition for my Records Center named **HATMRecs**.

Figure 12-21. *Defining the connection URL and display name*

Creating the Archival Library in the Records Center

Next, open the Records Center and create a document library. Supply a unique name for the library as well as an optional description. When you click **OK**, SharePoint opens the new library. Select **Document Library Settings** from the **Settings** drop-down menu, and select **Information Management Policy Settings** from the **Permissions and Management** group of options, as shown in Figure 12-22.

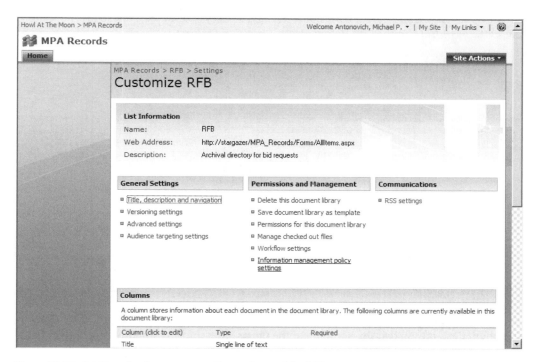

Figure 12-22. *Adding the document policy to the archival library*

If you have multiple content types in the library, you must select the content type for which you want to define a policy. After you select a content type, you will see a screen that lets you specify a policy for files of that type in the library, as shown in Figure 12-23. If you previously created an information management policy under site collection policies for your Records Center site, you can associate it now with this library by clicking the option **Use a site collection policy**. Then, using the drop-down box, select the policy that you want to use. Figure 12-23 shows the selection of an existing policy named **Bid Policy**.

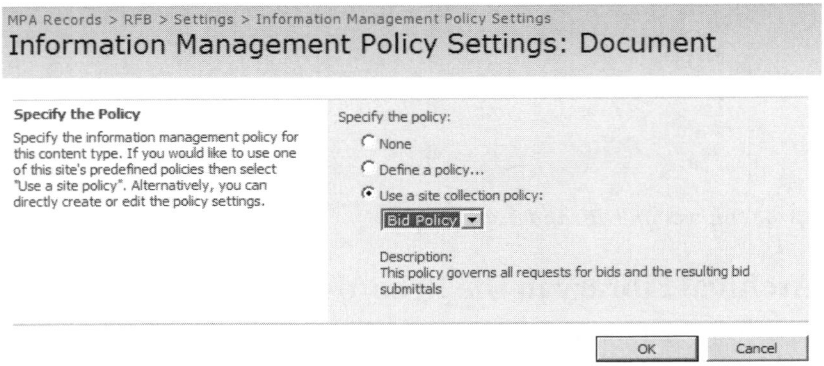

Figure 12-23. *Selecting from existing policies*

Creating a Policy for the Archival Library

On the other hand, if you have not previously created a policy, select the **Define a policy** option. Click **OK** to continue to the **Edit Policy** screen, shown in Figure 12-24.

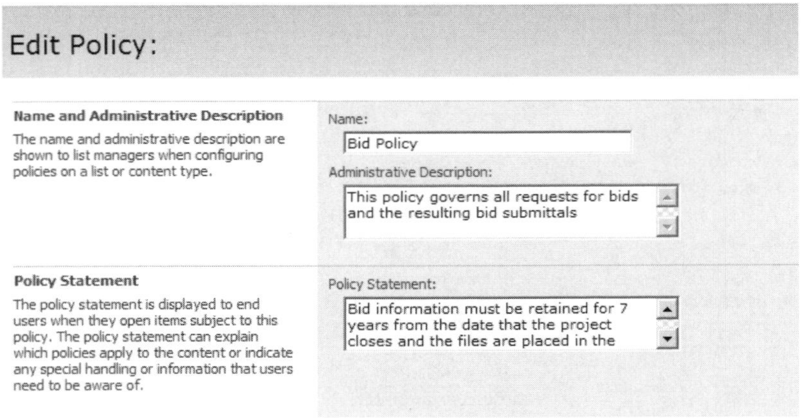

Figure 12-24. *Beginning of a policy definition*

Begin the policy definition by providing a name and description for the policy. The policy statement describes in text the handling of the file or other information that users might be interested in.

▌**Note** The policy statement does not actually create an action against the file.

You might also want to check the **Enable Auditing** option, shown in Figure 12-25, which tells SharePoint to audit specific events, such as each time someone views the items in the list, edits the items, checks the items out, or moves, copies, or deletes the items.

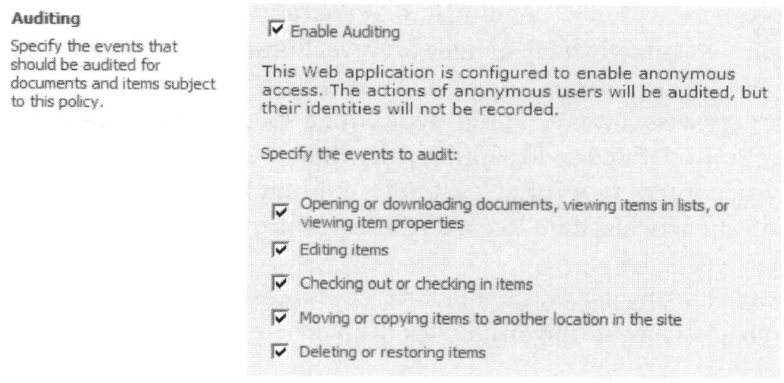

Auditing

Specify the events that should be audited for documents and items subject to this policy.

☑ Enable Auditing

This Web application is configured to enable anonymous access. The actions of anonymous users will be audited, but their identities will not be recorded.

Specify the events to audit:

☑ Opening or downloading documents, viewing items in lists, or viewing item properties
☑ Editing items
☑ Checking out or checking in items
☑ Moving or copying items to another location in the site
☑ Deleting or restoring items

Figure 12-25. *Enable auditing in a policy*

The **Expiration** section, shown in Figure 12-26, defines a retention period for the items in the library. If your company requires you to keep bid requests for 7 years after the file has been archived, select the **Enable Expiration** check box. This action adds fields to the form that let you specify a retention period. For example, you could define the retention period as a time period based on the file's creation date plus 7 years. The creation date here refers to the date you add the file to the Records Center.

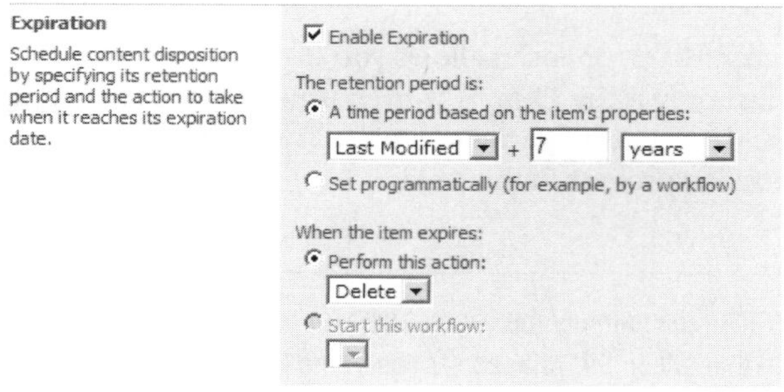

Expiration

Schedule content disposition by specifying its retention period and the action to take when it reaches its expiration date.

☑ Enable Expiration

The retention period is:
⦿ A time period based on the item's properties:
[Last Modified ▼] + [7] [years ▼]
○ Set programmatically (for example, by a workflow)

When the item expires:
⦿ Perform this action:
[Delete ▼]
○ Start this workflow:
[▼]

Figure 12-26. *Enabling expiration actions in a policy*

You can also specify what happens when the item does expire. The first option lets you perform an action such as a delete. This moves the file to the Record Center's Recycle Bin, where the administrator for the site can permanently delete it or restore it if necessary. You can also start a workflow for the document based on the workflows defined for the site.

Other options include the ability to assign barcodes to each document or item, which could then be used to track printed copies of the document. You can also provide labels with the document that it includes when it is being printed.

Creating a Record Routing Rule

The last step in setting up your Records Center involves creating record routing instructions. Without record routing, SharePoint would not know what to do with records sent to the Records Center. You can have as many record routing rules as you have content types defined. Each rule can then treat each content type individually, sending it to a separate archival library with its own policy. In this simple example, you only have a single archival library, but you can have any number.

The record routing rule therefore associates a content type with a specific library in the Records Center. By default, SharePoint defines an exception rule when the record sent to the Records Center does not have a content type, or at least not a content type with an associated rule. It sends these records to the **Unclassified Records** library for further processing by the Records Center administrator.

Figure 12-27 shows the **Record Routing** list. By default, SharePoint displays this list on the Records Center's home page. To create a new routing rule, click the **New** button in the menu bar.

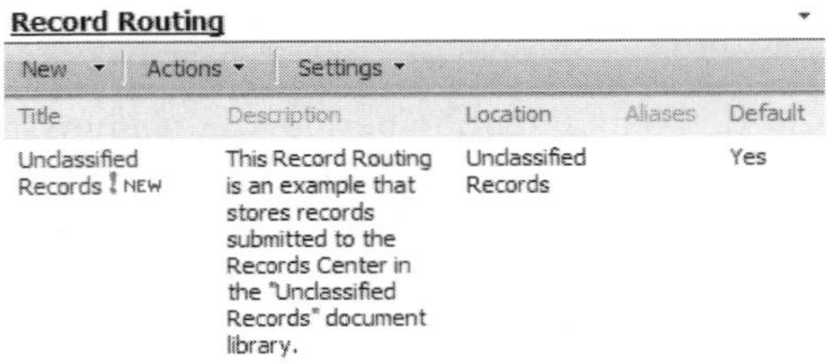

Figure 12-27. *Viewing the Record Routing rules list*

When the next screen, shown in Figure 12-28, opens, it allows you to define a new record routing rule. The first property you must supply is the **Title**. However, unlike titles in many of the other SharePoint objects, this title field has a very special meaning. You should enter the name of the content type you want the rule to process in this field.

■**Tip** Actually, you could provide a title other than the name of the content type, as long as you specified all the content types that you want to handle with this rule in the **Aliases** section of the **Record Routing** form.

In the **Description** field, you can provide information to the site user about this rule. The **Location** property also has a very special meaning. The value for this property must be the name of the library in the Records Center where you want to send records processed by the Records Center with the content type specified by this rule. The **Aliases** property allows you to supply the names of additional content types that you want to process with this rule, allowing you to use a single rule for more than one content type.

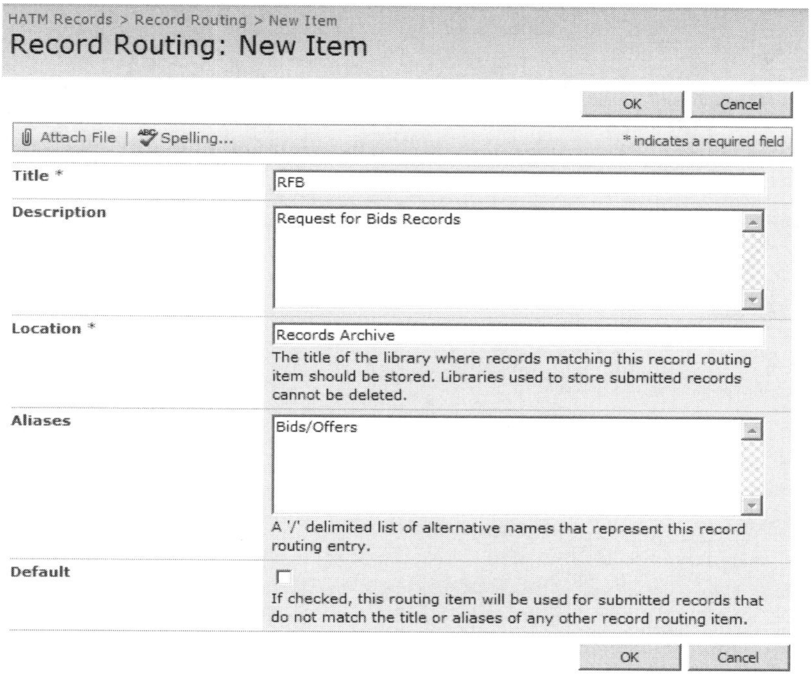

HATM Records > Record Routing > New Item
Record Routing: New Item

	OK	Cancel

📎 Attach File | 🏷 Spelling...   * indicates a required field

Title *	RFB
Description	Request for Bids Records
Location *	Records Archive
	The title of the library where records matching this record routing item should be stored. Libraries used to store submitted records cannot be deleted.
Aliases	Bids/Offers
	A '/' delimited list of alternative names that represent this record routing entry.
Default	☐
	If checked, this routing item will be used for submitted records that do not match the title or aliases of any other record routing item.

	OK	Cancel

Figure 12-28. *Defining a new record routing rule*

Finally, you can define which rule you want to use as the default rule when the submitted record's content type does not match the title or aliases. There can only be one default rule. Setting one default rule automatically deselects any other rule as a default.

Archiving Your Documents

Now that you have completed the setup for the Records Center, let's return to the working library where you can define an RFB document. Figure 12-29 shows a document using the Request for Bids template. Notice that the site columns added to this content type appear as document properties at the top of the document as you edit it.

After saving this sample document, you can now test the archival process from the working library to the Records Center. If you configured everything correctly, you can open the working library and position your mouse over the file you want to archive to open the drop-down menu for the document. Moving your mouse to the **Send To** option opens a submenu, as shown in Figure 12-30. This submenu now contains the entry **Records Center**. If you do not see this entry or if you see an entry with a different name, then you did something different when defining the **External Service Connection** discussed earlier. Since this information must be configured in the **Central Administration** site, you may need to contact your SharePoint administrator for assistance at this point.

Select the **Records Center** option to begin the archival process. After a few seconds, a pop-up dialog box should tell you that the copy of the file to the Records Center succeeded.

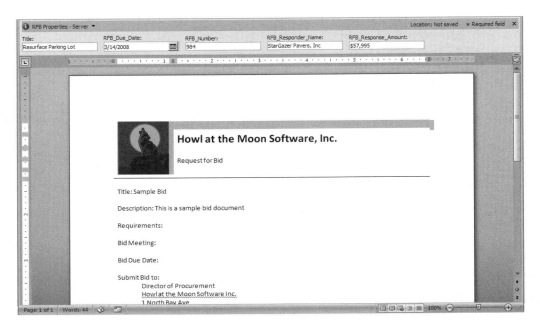

Figure 12-29. *Sample of a new RFB document*

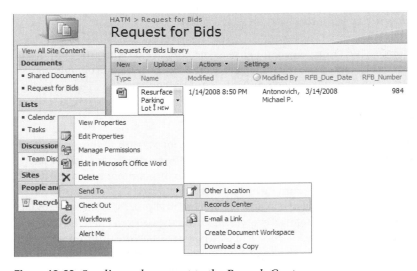

Figure 12-30. *Sending a document to the Records Center*

■**Note** A copy of the file remains in the working library. You can delete this copy if you do not need it further, but only after verifying that the copy operation to the Records Center succeeds.

If you now go to the Records Center, you should see the folder created for the newly archived file as shown in Figure 12-31. This folder has a name created by concatenating the date along with the time that you sent the document to the Records Center.

Figure 12-31. *Archived document folder*

If you double-click this folder, you should see the document that you archived along with one or more folders. The first folder you should see is a `Properties` folder. The second folder you may see is an `Audit` folder. If you open the `Properties` folder, you will see a single file. Opening that file displays the properties of the archived document as shown in Figure 12-32.

HATM Records > Records Archive > 2008-01-15T01-52-16Z > Properties > Resurface Parking Lot_SXAQKI
Records Archive: Resurface Parking Lot_SXAQKI

| 🖉 Edit Item | ✗ Delete Item | 🗃 Manage Permissions | 🗐 Manage Copies | 🔒 Check Out | 🗐 Version |

Name	Resurface Parking Lot_SXAQKI
Title	
Exempt from Policy	No exemption. Exempt from policy...
Original Expiration Date	
Expiration Date	1/14/2015 8:52 PM
Hold Status	Item is not on this hold. Add to a hold...

Version: 0.1
Created at 1/14/2008 8:52 PM by System Account
Last modified at 1/14/2008 8:52 PM by System Account

Figure 12-32. *Archived properties of the document*

This brief introduction to using the Records Center only covers the basics of how to build and use a Records Center. You may need to consider many additional factors before creating a Records Center for your organization.

Creating a Picture Library in SharePoint

Picture libraries in SharePoint can be used to share pictures with other users of your site. A library lets you view, organize, share, and edit common graphics. The ability to create a slide show from a picture library may let you share your pictures with coworkers. However, the most important purpose of a picture library is to supply files for web pages that contain images, icons, or pictures of any sort. To do this, you must first store the picture files in your picture library, where SharePoint web pages can find them.

To create a picture library within your SharePoint site, if you do not already have one, select the **Create** option from the **Site Actions** menu. On the **Create** page, find **Picture Library** under the **Libraries** category, as shown in Figure 12-33, and click it.

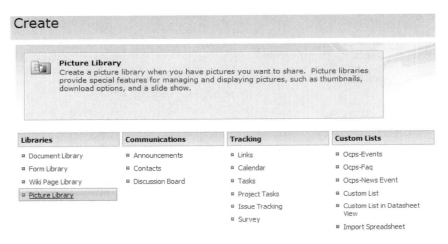

Figure 12-33. *Selecting Picture Library from the Libraries group*

When creating a new picture library, as with any other library, list, or web page, you must name it. Names consist of alphanumeric strings that can include spaces, although some people would agree with me in not recommending spaces. I suggest replacing spaces with underscores for readability. In any case, the name must be unique within your web site.

You can also provide an optional description. If you do provide a description, it will appear when you open the library above the library's menu.

Next, choose whether you want the picture library to appear in the **Quick Launch** area. Typically, if you have a picture library primarily to share pictures with other members of your team, you would add it to the **Quick Launch** area so that others can access it easily. However, if your picture library only exists to serve pictures to web pages or to provide icons for pages, other members of your site probably have no need to regularly access the library, and thus you should not include it in the **Quick Launch** area. If you use a picture library for both purposes, you probably need to rethink your design and split your pictures into two or more libraries so that only pictures you really want other members to share exist in libraries that appear in the **Quick Launch** area.

Finally, you can determine whether SharePoint tracks versions of your pictures each time you save a new picture with the same name. If the image consists of time-sensitive information that someone might need to go back to earlier versions to view, then by all means include versioning. However, for most uses, tracking picture versions does not make sense, especially considering the size requirements of most pictures. Figure 12-34 shows the properties screen of a new picture library.

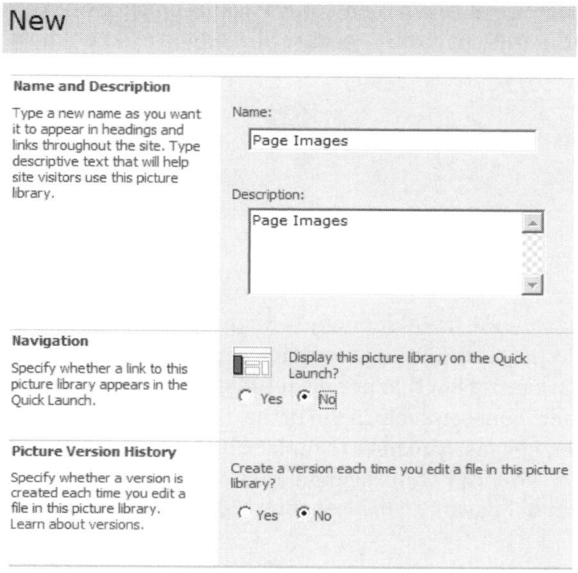

New

Name and Description

Type a new name as you want it to appear in headings and links throughout the site. Type descriptive text that will help site visitors use this picture library.

Name:

Page Images

Description:

Page Images

Navigation

Specify whether a link to this picture library appears in the Quick Launch.

Display this picture library on the Quick Launch?

◯ Yes ◉ No

Picture Version History

Specify whether a version is created each time you edit a file in this picture library. Learn about versions.

Create a version each time you edit a file in this picture library?

◯ Yes ◉ No

Figure 12-34. *Setting the properties of the picture library*

KEEPING THE SIZE OF YOUR IMAGES UNDER CONTROL

The first and most obvious goal is to keep your images as small as possible. Different formats of the same image can result in greatly different file sizes. Usually, JPG or GIF files result in the smallest files. If you need an image that is only 100 pixels square, don't save an image that is 300 by 300 pixels, and then just let the page formatting "shrink" the image down. This process may display a smaller image, but the physical image size in bytes remains the same. Also, it is not just the physical storage on your server you need to be concerned about. The larger your image files become, the longer it takes to download those images to a browser, making your web site appear slower than it should.

Another technique to reduce the size of your image files is to reduce their color depth. Often the color depth of digital camera images far exceeds what is necessary when displaying the image on a web page. Usually, you can reduce the color depth from 32 bit to 16 bit or even less with no perceptible difference in the image. If you work with GIF files representing drawings rather than photographs, you can often reduce the color depth down to a mere 256 colors or less.

Finally, check whether your graphics program has a way to change the number of dots per inch (dpi). Most pictures displayed on a web page appear quite nicely with only 75 dpi.

One tool to help you modify the sizes of your images is the Microsoft Office Picture Manager. It can handle most of your resizing and image modification needs.

Once you have created your picture library, you can open it either by clicking its name in the **Quick Launch** menu if you placed it there or by clicking **View All Site Content** in the **Quick Launch** menu and locating your library within the **Picture Library** group.

Within your picture library, you may want to organize your pictures into different folders and perhaps even different subfolders. To create a folder, click the **New** button in the menu bar as shown in Figure 12-35. Notice that the new drop-down menu only has this one option. You cannot create a new picture from within a SharePoint library because SharePoint does not host its own graphics design tool.

Figure 12-35. *Giving your library structure by adding folders*

When you create a new folder, you must name it. Folder names can have up to 128 alphanumeric characters and can contain blank spaces. While you can place periods within a folder name to perhaps represent a hierarchy, you cannot put that period at the start or the end of the name. Nor can you put two period characters consecutively in the name. SharePoint also does not allow most special characters. However, because you have to replace blank spaces with the string %20 in URL references to the library, you may want to avoid blank spaces or replace them with underscore characters, as shown in Figure 12-36. After entering a name, click **OK** to create the folder.

New Folder: Page Images

	OK	Cancel

✎ Spelling...   * indicates a required field

Name .   Mystery_Images

	OK	Cancel

Figure 12-36. *You must give folders names.*

You do not have to fully define your folder structure before starting to use your picture library. While you may not anticipate every need for the picture library and thus not be able to fully build out the file structure for the library ahead of time, leaving the file structure up to the users could also result in a very disorganized structure, maybe even one in which all pictures appear in just one folder.

Deciding when to add a picture to an existing folder and when to create a new folder for the picture is a lot like saving a file in your local or network drive. Get a group of people together, and you typically end up with several different suggestions for the structure. Some members of your SharePoint site might feel it best to separate images by topic. Others might want to save images by how they get used within the site such as by page. Still others might want to save images based on who uploaded them. The best recommendation I can give you is that any organization is better than no organization, as long as you follow it consistently. Choose a method to structure your pictures within a library, publish the method so anyone using the library knows how to store and search for images, and then stick with that method. You might even include your file structure logic in the description of the library where every site member can read it.

Uploading Pictures to SharePoint Using Picture Manager

Now that you have a picture library, you probably want to save pictures to it. Accessing the **Upload** menu of the open picture library shows you have two options for uploading pictures: one for uploading individual images and one for uploading multiple images. In reality, you can select either option because even the **Upload Picture** option allows you to upload multiple images, and the **Upload Multiple Pictures** option does not fail if you only select a single image to upload. Figure 12-37 shows the **Upload** menu.

Figure 12-37. *Uploading pictures individually or in groups*

Uploading Single Images

From the upload page shown in Figure 12-38, you can upload a single image by manually entering its fully qualified name. A more reliable way to reference a picture you want to upload to ensure that you not only spell it correctly, but also get the syntax for the URL correct begins with the **Browse** button. Clicking the **Browse** button displays a standard **Choose File** dialog box common to many Windows applications. From here, you can navigate through the directories of not only your local machine, but also the directories of any network drive that you have rights to view.

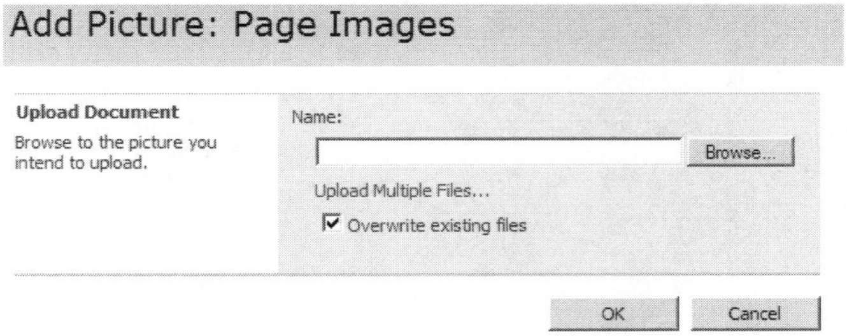

Add Picture: Page Images

Upload Document	Name:
Browse to the picture you intend to upload.	[ ] Browse...
	Upload Multiple Files...
	☑ Overwrite existing files

OK   Cancel

Figure 12-38. *Here you can enter the URL for the picture or locate it with Browse.*

When you find the file you want, click the file name and then click the **Open** button. You can also just double-click the file name. The **Choose File** dialog box passes the URL for the image back to the **Add Picture** dialog box.

Before clicking **OK**, you can choose to check the box next to **Overwrite existing files** if you want to automatically override any pictures in the library with the same name. If you do not check this box, and SharePoint discovers that the file you are uploading has either already been uploaded or at least has the same name as a file already in the library, the upload fails with an error. The error message identifies the file by name. You can simply rename one of the images and try to upload the picture again.

Selecting a single file to upload opens a page that lets you immediately update the default metadata associated with a picture in a picture library. Figure 12-39 shows this page. You can change the name of the file used by the library. You do not have to keep the same name as the original file. You can also specify a title for the picture. Next, you can specify the date and time the picture was taken. Not all pictures need this type of information, but for pictures that might be related to specific times, you can document that information here. SharePoint uses the description field as alternative text when you place the picture on a web page and the viewer of the web page has turned graphics off. Applications for the seeing impaired can sometimes read the alternative text associated with pictures. In either case, a good description of the image could help people who do not see the picture. Finally, you can specify keywords for the picture that the search engine can use to locate specific images.

Figure 12-39. *Defining a picture's metadata as soon as you upload it*

■**Tip** You can also create content types for picture libraries just as with other libraries. Those content types can have unique column definitions that can include, remove, or modify the default columns used by the default picture library.

Uploading Multiple Images

If you want to upload multiple files, rather than enter a file name in the first text box or click the **Browse** button, click the option **Upload Multiple Files**. This option works a little differently for picture libraries than it does for shared document libraries. Rather than showing a directory tree of the files on your local drive, it opens Microsoft Office Picture Manager, which I will discuss further in the next section. You can also get to this same point by selecting the **Upload Multiple Pictures** option from the **Upload** drop-down menu.

   In either case, if you attempt to upload a file with a name that already exists in the library, Microsoft Office Picture Manager pops up an error message that displays four options:

- **Replace File**: This option replaces only the file that raises the current error message. If other files marked for upload also have duplicate names, you will have to address each one separately.

- **Replace All**: This option replaces not only the file that raises the current error message, but also any other files that have a duplicate name in the current upload batch without further prompting.

- **Skip File**: This option skips the current duplicate file from the upload batch and continues with the next file. It continues through the rest of the pictures marked for uploading unless it finds another duplicate. If so, it displays the error dialog box again to let you decide on an action for that file.

- **Cancel Upload**: This option cancels the upload at this point. Files already uploaded remain uploaded, but Microsoft Office Picture Manager will not attempt to upload any of the additional files in the set of selected files.

   This ability to handle file name conflicts during upload might be a good reason to use the Microsoft Office Picture Manager, even when you only want to upload a single file. But there are several other advantages to using this tool to upload your pictures.

Using the Microsoft Office Picture Manager

The ability to preview a thumbnail of the available images in any directory of your local drive is another advantage of the Microsoft Office Picture Manager, shown in Figure 12-40. The panel on the left lets you navigate to any folder on your local drive and view thumbnails of the pictures found there.

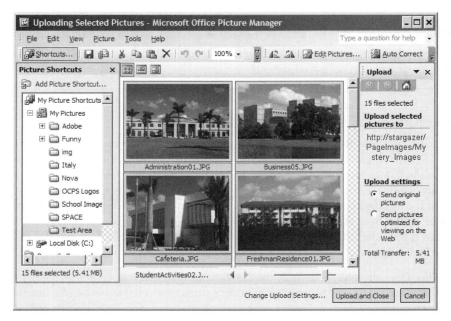

Figure 12-40. *Using Microsoft Office Picture Manager to preview and upload pictures*

The center panel displays thumbnails of each image found in the selected directory. You can change the size of the thumbnails by using the slide control at the bottom right of this panel. Along the top of the center panel, you should see three icons that allow you to select between three different view modes. The first icon displays each image as a thumbnail with the name of the image immediately beneath it. The second view option, called the **Filmstrip View**, uses the top half of the center panel to display the currently selected image. The rest of the images appear across the bottom half of the panel in a single row. You can move from one image to the next by clicking one of the visible images in the filmstrip area at the bottom, or you can click the left and right pointing arrows found in the control area in the middle of the central panel. An example of this view appears in Figure 12-41.

The third and final option, called the **Single Picture View**, shows only a single picture at a time from the selected library (see Figure 12-42). Beneath the picture, you will find a control bar. Starting from the left side of the control bar, you will see the name of the picture file, navigation buttons that allow you to move to the previous or next image in the directory, and a zoom slide bar that lets you change the size of the displayed image.

You will most likely select pictures to upload from the **Thumbnail View**. When you click an image, the **Upload** panel on the right side of the screen tracks the number of files you have selected, the name of the library that it will upload the image to, whether it will send the original picture, and whether it will optimize the picture for viewing on the Web. As you might expect, this setting helps reduce the file size for images with millions of colors such as photographs, but it can also substantially reduce the size of even captured screen images. You can easily see the difference in size by alternately clicking the two option buttons in the **Upload Settings** section and checking the value displayed beneath them after the label **Total Transfer**. The **Total Transfer** value can also give you an idea of how "expensive" in terms of file size it would be to display a collection of images on your web pages.

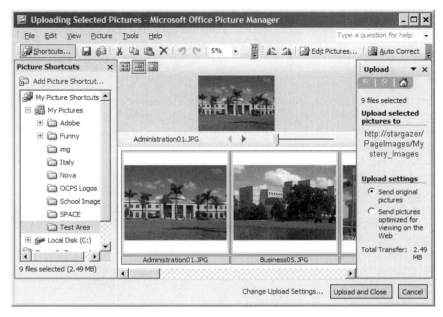

Figure 12-41. *Displaying pictures in a folder using the Filmstrip View*

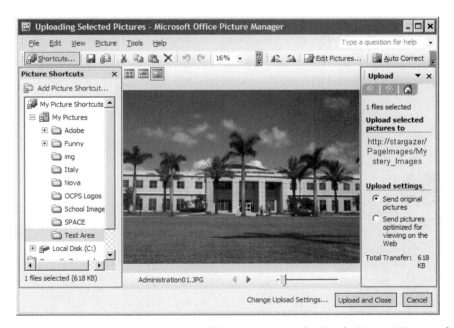

Figure 12-42. *Seeing larger versions of the image using the Single Picture View mode*

■ **Tip** If you do not see the **Upload** panel, click the text **Change Upload Settings** found at the bottom of the Microsoft Office Picture Manager window to the left of the **Upload** and **Cancel** buttons.

You can select multiple images to upload in the **Thumbnail View** by clicking the first picture you want, and then while holding down the **Shift** key, clicking the last picture. This includes all of the intermediate pictures, starting at the topmost picture selected, and then proceeding from left to right, top to bottom, to the bottommost picture.

If you only want to transfer selected pictures from a folder, click the first picture you want, and then while holding down the **Ctrl** key, click each of the additional pictures you want.

Finally, you can also use the mouse to click and drag through the images. The only limitation, which you may find inconvenient at times, is that you can only select images from a single directory as part of a single upload. If you want to upload images from multiple directories, you must select and upload files from each directory separately.

When you have selected your images, click the **Upload and Close** button to begin the transfer of the files to your SharePoint picture library. Depending on the number of pictures you have selected and their individual sizes, this could take a few seconds to complete.

Using Windows Explorer to Upload Pictures

Another way to upload pictures to your picture library begins by switching the view of your picture library to open it with Windows Explorer. You can find this option in the **Actions** drop-down menu as shown in Figure 12-43.

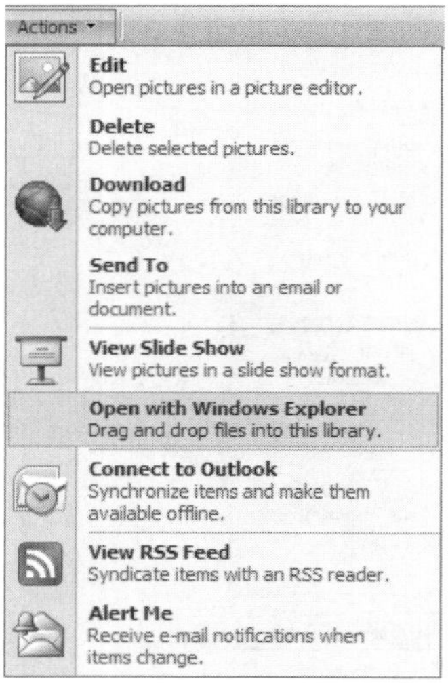

Figure 12-43. *Switching to the Windows Explorer view mode*

■ **Tip** You can also open the **View** drop-down and change from the **All Pictures** view to the **Explorer View**.

Then open an instance of Windows Explorer from your operating system's **Start** menu. You may want to resize the SharePoint library window and the Windows Explorer window so that you can view both windows side by side. Next, navigate to the directory in Windows Explorer that contains the pictures you want to upload, and select them individually or as a group. With your pictures selected, click and drag the selection over to the SharePoint library area and release the mouse button, as shown in Figure 12-44.

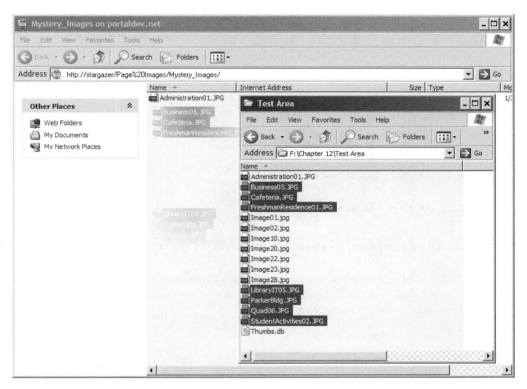

Figure 12-44. *Using drag and drop to transfer pictures*

Downloading Images from Your Picture Library

Earlier, I covered how to display pictures from a picture library on a web page. But if end users of your SharePoint site can view your picture library, they can download the images to their local hard drives. Not only do picture libraries provide an alternative to sending pictures as e-mail attachments to people, but they also have some ability to control the size of the downloaded image. Figure 12-45 shows the **Page Images: Download Pictures** page displayed by selecting the **Download** option in the **Action** menu. Notice that you can download one of three different sizes for the selected pictures: full size, preview size, and thumbnail. This figure shows thumbnails of the two pictures selected before choosing the **Download** option.

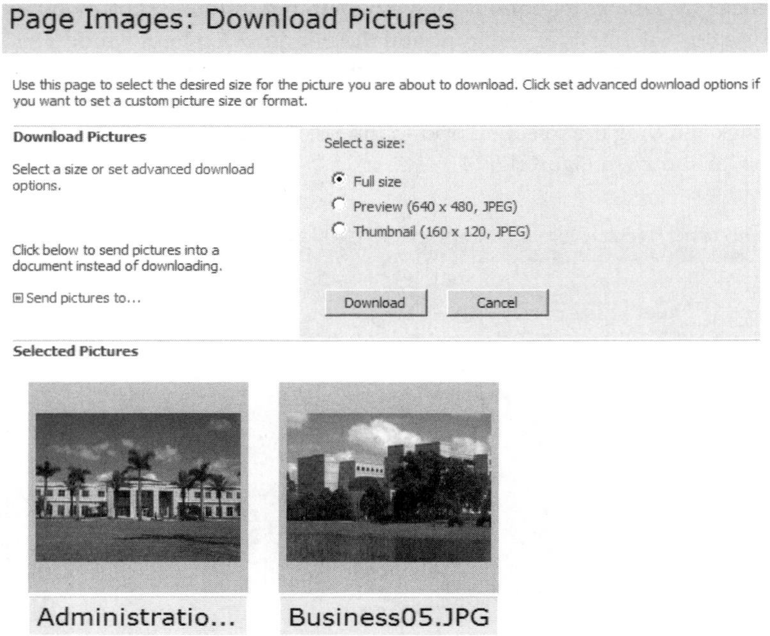

Figure 12-45. *Selecting the size of the pictures to download*

By default, SharePoint downloads the images as saved. However, if you click the **Set Advanced Download Options** link, you can choose a different format for the pictures. SharePoint supports converting pictures to the following format types:

- JPEG Interchange Format (*.jpg)

- Tagged Image File Format (*.tif)

- Windows Bitmap (*.bmp)

- Graphics Interchange Format (*.gif)

- Portable Network Graphic (*.png)

You can choose the final size of the image from a larger selection of predefined sizes. You can also create your own custom-sized image by either specifying the width and height of the image in pixels, which gives you independent scaling of the horizontal and vertical image size, or by specifying a percentage to stretch both the horizontal and vertical size. The page in Figure 12-46 specifies retaining the original format and size of the images to be downloaded.

When you click the **Download** button, you must still identify the directory where you want to place the pictures. You can do this either by entering the directory name in the check box or by locating the directory by clicking the **Browse** button to look for it. If you specify a directory that does not exist, SharePoint displays a message box that allows you to create it.

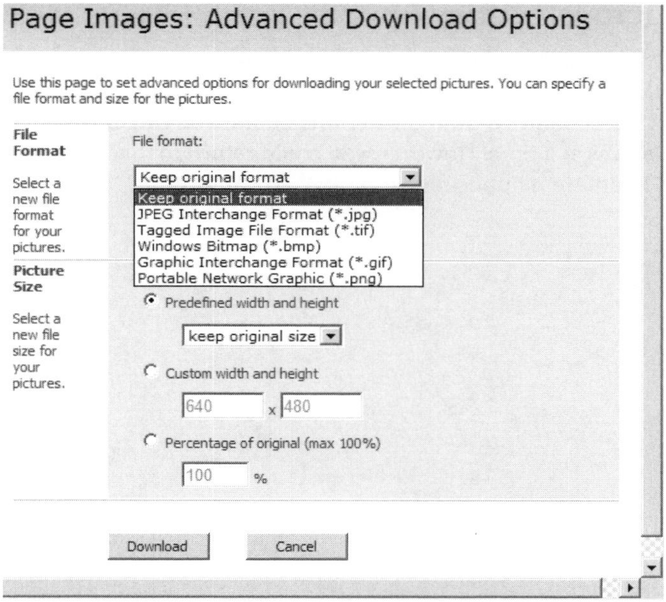

Figure 12-46. *Choosing a file format for downloaded images*

By default, SharePoint assigns the downloaded pictures the same name they have in the picture library. However, you can rename the pictures as you download them by supplying a base name to which SharePoint adds a numeric value to uniquely name each image. Figure 12-47 shows that it will download the images to a directory named My Pictures\Page Images. It also will rename each picture included in the download beginning with the text **Buildings** and then appending a number starting with **01**.

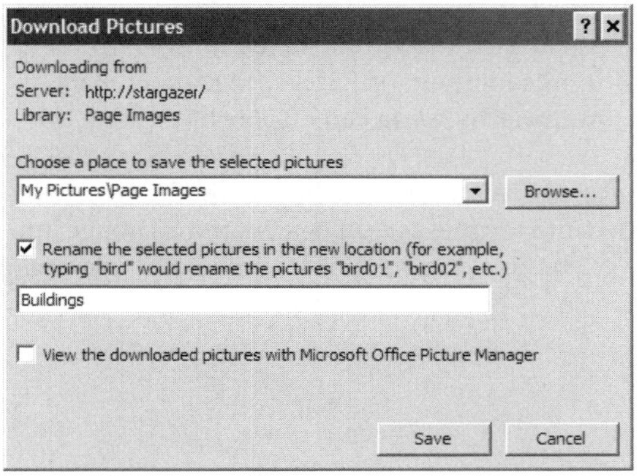

Figure 12-47. *Defining where to save images and how to name them*

Sending Images to a Microsoft Office Application

Rather than download the image, you could send the image to one of four Microsoft Office applications. Figure 12-48 shows the dialog box that appears after you select one or more of the pictures from the library and then select **Send To** from the **Actions** menu. You can only select one of the Microsoft Office applications at a time. However, you could return to this option several times to resend the image to different applications.

Figure 12-48. *Sending a picture to an Outlook message*

If you currently have a Microsoft Office file open such as a Word document, the name of the document appears in the drop-down box found beneath the label **Insert into an open file**. In fact, if you have more than one Word or PowerPoint file open, you can insert the graphics into any of them by selecting the one you want from the drop-down list. If you do not have any open Office files, this option appears disabled.

Even if you have a recognized file open, you can still send the selected images to a new Outlook message, Word document, PowerPoint presentation, or Excel spreadsheet. Each possible output destination has its own set of options, which you can display by clicking the **Options** link.

When sending the images in an Outlook message, you must first decide whether you want to send the images as attached files or embedded into the message. If you embed an image into the message, you get to choose the preview size. Possible output sizes for embedded pictures include

- **Thumbnail (160 x 160 pixels)**

- **Postcard (448 x 336 pixels)**

- **Large Postcard (640 x 480 pixels)**

You can then determine the layout of the images in the message. You can either use a table layout, which allows multiple images in a row, or save a single image to a single row. Figure 12-49 shows an example of the **Options for Sending Pictures** dialog box used to save the selected pictures as previews within the message using the postcard image size and a table layout.

Figure 12-49. *Selecting options for displaying an image in an Outlook message*

▌**Note** The table shows no borders by default. If you want to display the borders between and around the pictures, right-click between any of the pictures and select **Table Properties** from the pop-up menu. In the **Table Properties** dialog box, select **Borders and Shading**. In the **Borders and Shading** dialog box, click the **Borders** tab if necessary and then select the borders or individual lines you want.

When you send the pictures to a Word document, a PowerPoint presentation, or an Excel workbook, you can set only the image size. You can choose from the following sizes:

- **Original size**

- **Document – Large (1024 x 768 pixels)**

- **Document – Small (800 x 600 pixels)**

- **Web – Large (640 x 480 pixels)**

- **Web – Small (448 x 336 pixels)**

- **E-mail – Large (314 x 235 pixels)**

- **E-mail – Small (160 x 160 pixels)**

Don't think that you can only use the first three size options just because you want to send the pictures to a Word document. You can use any of these seven sizes when sending a picture to a Word document, PowerPoint presentation, or Excel workbook.

▌**Note** While selecting a size smaller than the original picture SharePoint shrinks the larger picture to the size indicated. However, it will not stretch a smaller picture to a larger size.

Viewing the Pictures in a Picture Library

You have several ways to view the pictures in your library. The first way, shown in Figure 12-50, shows the **Detail View** of the pictures. This default view only shows the item type (a picture in this case), the picture name, the picture size in pixels, and the file size. These image properties tell you a lot about the picture, but they do not show you what the picture looks like. However, you can easily remedy that by clicking the view drop-down in the upper-right corner and selecting the **Modify This View** option. Among the available data columns you will find these three columns: **Preview**, **Thumbnail**, and **Web Preview**. Each of these columns can display the picture. Use the **Thumbnail** column for most list views because it requires the least amount of space, especially for libraries with larger images. There are also columns to track the date of the picture, keywords used by the search engine, versions, check-in status, and more.

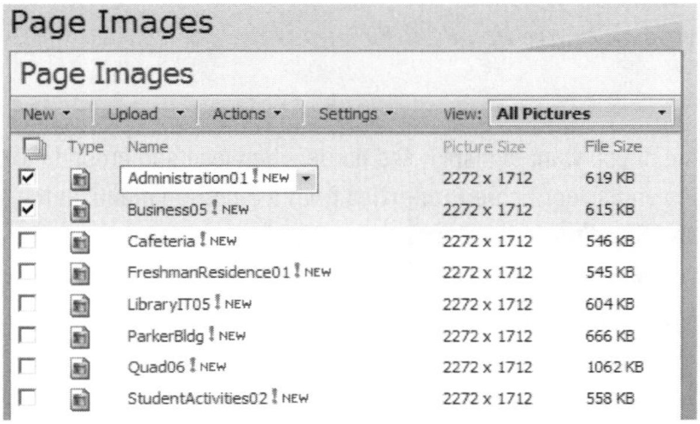

Figure 12-50. *Viewing picture library contents using Detail View*

■**Note** If you attempt to edit an image, SharePoint tries to open a picture editor such as Microsoft Office Picture Manager.

To change the picture view, return to the **View** drop-down. Notice that the first item in the drop-down, **All Pictures**, has a right pointing arrow to the right of the name. As with other menus, this symbol indicates that this item has a second flyout menu. As you position your mouse over this text, you should see a flyout menu with the options **Details**, **Thumbnails**, and **Filmstrip**. Select **Thumbnails** to see an image like the one shown in Figure 12-51.

Notice the check boxes to the left of each item's name. You must select one or more of the pictures by clicking these boxes to perform an action on the pictures such as **Delete**, **Download**, or **Send To**.

This figure shows thumbnails of each image in the library in a table-like structure spanning from left to right, top to bottom. If you resize your windows, the number of pictures in each row automatically adjusts based on the available space.

Figure 12-51. *Viewing picture library contents using the Thumbnails view option*

The third view option under **All Pictures**, **Filmstrip**, displays the pictures in a filmstrip mode. This mode displays up to five thumbnail-sized images across the top of the screen. Each of these thumbnails has a check box before the name just like the **Thumbnails View**, allowing you to select images from this view before opening the **Actions** menu to perform an action on them. It then displays one of the images in a larger format in the bottom half of the screen as shown in Figure 12-52. Below this larger image, you will see the image name and a description if you provided one when you uploaded the image.

■**Note** No matter how wide you can make the window on your monitor, the filmstrip at the top can display only a maximum of five images. Then a vertical bar appears with a green arrow button on either the left, the right, or both sides, indicating the presence of additional images. To bring those images into view, click the green arrow to scroll through the filmstrip.

The **Selected Pictures** option in the **View** menu supports the same three subviews as the **All Pictures** option, except that it only displays the images you have selected by clicking the check box before the image names.

Figure 12-52. *Viewing picture library contents using Filmstrip View*

The **Explorer View** option, shown in Figure 12-53, rounds out the list view options. This option shows the pictures using icons representing the file type. This view allows you to copy and paste images between this view and Windows Explorer.

■**Caution** If you copy and paste pictures from Windows Explorer to your picture library using this method, remember that you may need to go back into each image to add the additional metadata that Windows libraries do not store or provide.

When you click an image in the picture library, SharePoint displays it in a preview form that displays not only the picture, but also the supporting metadata for the image, as shown in Figure 12-54. From this view, click **Edit Item** to open the edit form for the picture. There you can change the picture's name, title, date taken, description, and keywords.

Figure 12-53. *Using Explorer View to drag and drop images between folders*

Figure 12-54. *Edit preview window for an image*

■**Tip** Keywords can help your search engine find pictures, since searches only work on text and would otherwise have no way to identify pictures.

You can also delete the picture, modify the permissions for the picture, manage copies of the picture, check out the picture to exclusively edit it, and set alerts that can tell you when someone else edits or deletes this specific picture.

One last picture viewing option appears in the **Actions** menu of the library. Figure 12-55 shows an example of the picture library after selecting **View Slide Show** from the **Actions** menu.

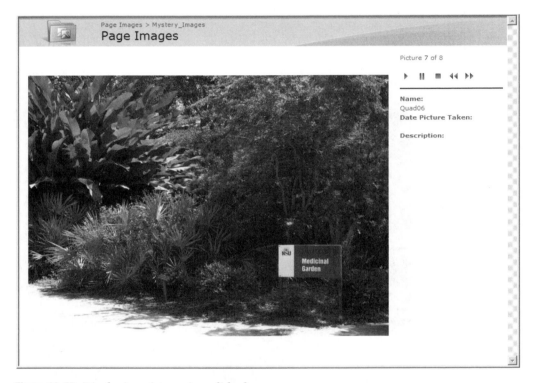

Figure 12-55. *Displaying pictures in a slide show*

While picture libraries work great with static pictures, they do not work well with Power-Point slides. Therefore, Microsoft adds a special library in MOSS 2007 specifically to handle PowerPoint slides. The next section explores that library.

Creating a Slide Library in SharePoint

This chapter closes by taking a look at the slide library. This library resembles the picture library in that it stores images. However, it has been specifically customized to store the individual slides from a PowerPoint slide presentation. You can use the slide library to simply store your slide presentations. However, a more powerful use of this library is to store common slides that your employees can subsequently use in their presentations. Perhaps the slides depict the history of your organization or its products. Maybe you have a set of slides with brief bios of your principal corporate officers. Some slides might represent technical data about your products or services. Whatever the slides may contain, you might want to store the slides in a common shareable location so that others can easily include those slides while putting together a custom presentation or while making a presentation to a potential customer or client.

MOSS 2007 adds slide libraries to the available library types in SharePoint. To create a slide library, begin by clicking the **Create** option in the **Site Actions** drop-down menu. Then, as shown in Figure 12-56, select **Slide Library** from the **Libraries** column in the **Create** page.

Figure 12-56. *Creating a slide library for PowerPoint slides*

The settings page for the new library then appears. You must specify a name for the library. If you also include a description, that description appears beneath the library name when you open the library.

As with other libraries, you can decide to include the library in the **Quick Launch** menu. If you want most users to access this library, you probably want to add it to the **Quick Launch** menu. However, even if you do not include it there, you can also get to the library by clicking the **View All Site Content** option in the **Quick Launch** menu and then looking for the library under the section **Document Libraries**.

■**Note**   I know you are probably saying to yourself that there should be a section titled **Slide Libraries**. At the very least, you might have expected to find the slide library under the picture libraries, which it closely resembles. For that reason, take special note that slide libraries fall into the **Document Libraries** grouping when viewing **All Site Content**.

Finally, you can choose to track versions of images added to this library. Unlike picture libraries, which often do not need versions, many people find tracking versions of slides important. If you need to track slide versions, select **Yes** under the **Slide Version History** section.

Figure 12-57 shows a library created to store slides from a recent SQL Saturday presentation. This library does not appear in the **Quick Launch** menu and does not track versions of the slides.

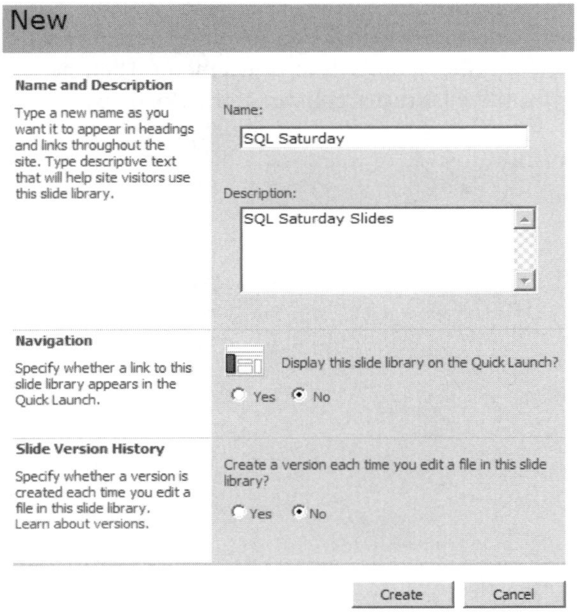
New
Name and Description
Type a new name as you want it to appear in headings and links throughout the site. Type descriptive text that will help site visitors use this slide library.
Name:
SQL Saturday
Description:
SQL Saturday Slides
Navigation
Specify whether a link to this slide library appears in the Quick Launch.
Display this slide library on the Quick Launch?
Yes No
Slide Version History
Specify whether a version is created each time you edit a file in this slide library.
Learn about versions.
Create a version each time you edit a file in this slide library?
Yes No
Create
Cancel

Figure 12-57. *Defining metadata for a slide library*

After clicking the **Create** button, you will see your new empty slide library. Before you start uploading slides into your library, you might want to think about the structure you want to create for your slides. Do you really want to store all your slides under a single folder or list? Would it make more sense to group some slides together, separating them from other slides? Of course, you could create separate slide libraries to store slides for different purposes. However, you can achieve the same results while making it easier to transfer slides between areas by using a folder structure for your slides, much like you create a folder structure to store files on your hard drive.

When you click the **New** option in the library menu bar, as shown in Figure 12-58, the only option that you will see, **New Folder**, allows you to create a new folder from your current location in the library. Starting from the library root, you can create a set of folders for different types of slides.

New
New Folder
Add a new folder to this document library.

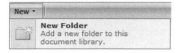

Figure 12-58. *Organizing your slides with folders*

When you select this option, SharePoint presents you with a very simple form to enter the name of the folder. Folders have no additional properties other than their names. In Figure 12-59, I show a folder named TSQL_CASE_Statements being created.

SQL Saturday: New Folder

	OK	Cancel

🐝 Spelling...   * indicates a required field

Name *	TSQL_CASE_Statements

	OK	Cancel

Figure 12-59. *Folders must have names.*

You can add other folders under the library root in a similar fashion. By double-clicking a folder, you can open it and add a subfolder within it.

Uploading Pictures to Your Slide Library from PowerPoint 2007

While you do not have to complete your entire folder structure before beginning to add pictures to the folders, you should have at least a fairly good idea of the initial folders you need. Once you have your folders, you have two ways to publish your slides from PowerPoint. You can start from your slide library and upload them, or you can start from PowerPoint 2007 and publish them.

Uploading Your Slides

The first way to load slides into your new slide library begins by selecting the option **Publish Slides** from the **Upload** menu. This option begins the process of copying slides from an existing PowerPoint presentation to the library as shown in Figure 12-60.

Figure 12-60. *Publishing your PowerPoint slides to your library*

When you start from SharePoint, SharePoint opens an instance of PowerPoint on the client machine and pops up the **Browse** dialog box to help you locate the PowerPoint presentation file and open it. After selecting a presentation, the **Publish Slides** dialog box appears that displays all the slides in the presentation as a list consisting of a small thumbnail of each slide, the name of the file that contains the slide, and a short description of the slide.

■**Note** SharePoint takes the slide description from the slide title area.

To the left of each thumbnail, a small check box allows you to select which slides you want to upload. If you want to upload all the slides, click the **Select All** button at the bottom of the window. If you decide to change your selection, you can either unselect the slides by clicking their check boxes again or simply click the **Clear All** button to start over. Once you have selected the images that you want to publish, you can verify the name of the slide library you will add them to by checking the contents of the **Publish To** box at the bottom of the dialog box. If you need to change this library, you can manually update this text or use the **Browse** button to navigate to a different location.

Finally, click the **Publish** button to transfer the PowerPoint slides to SharePoint. Figure 12-61 shows several slides being published to the **SQL_Saturday** library.

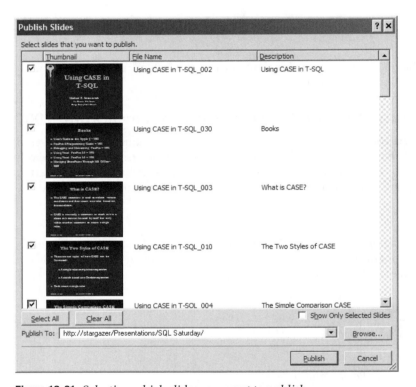

Figure 12-61. *Selecting which slides you want to publish*

Publishing Your Slides from PowerPoint 2007

The second way to transfer slides into your library begins from PowerPoint 2007 and publishes the slides to SharePoint. To do this, open your PowerPoint presentation and then from the **Office Button**, click **Publish**. The **Publish** submenu provides several ways for you to publish your presentation to other people. Select the option **Publish Slides** as shown in Figure 12-62.

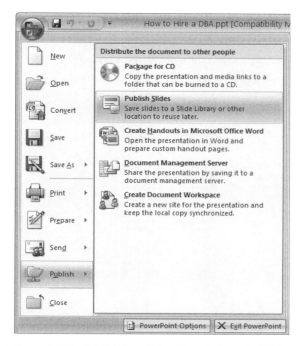

Figure 12-62. *Publishing slides directly from Publisher 2007*

PowerPoint then opens the same dialog box shown earlier in Figure 12-61 that displays all the slides in the current slide show. To select a slide, you must click the check box to the left of each slide to indicate which slides you want to publish. You do not have to publish all slides in the presentation deck, but you must select at least one before the **Publish** button at the bottom of the dialog box activates.

Before you can publish the slides, you must specify where you want to publish them. When you start from the slide library, SharePoint provides this information to you. However, starting from PowerPoint means that you must enter the URL of an existing SharePoint library in the **Publish To** text box. If you do not know the exact name of the library, you can enter just the root URL to the SharePoint site and then use the **Browse** button to drill down further into the site to locate the folder. However, the folder must already exist. The **Publish Slides** dialog box cannot create a new slide folder for you automatically. When you click **Publish**, PowerPoint transfers the slides from your local presentation deck to the specified SharePoint library.

Viewing and Performing Actions on Your Slides

Once you have published the slides in the library, they appear in the library list as shown in Figure 12-63. Like most lists, you can customize this list by opening the view drop-down menu and selecting the **Modify This View** option. However, the default view provides several useful pieces of metadata about the slides.

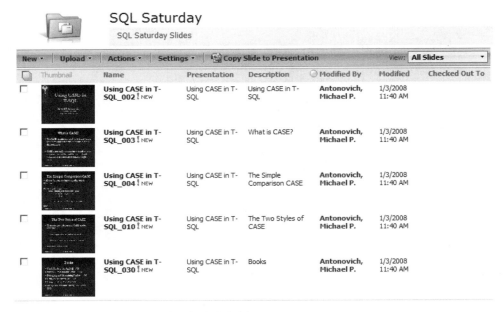

Figure 12-63. *Viewing your published slide library*

The list begins with a small thumbnail image of the slide. Following this column, you can find the slide name, taken from the title area of the slide. Immediately after this column, you can find the name of the presentation that contains the original slide. Also on this default view, you can see who last modified the slide, when she modified it, and the name of the person who has the slide checked out if applicable.

■**Tip** Slide libraries also use content types. Therefore, you can create your own content type definition for slide libraries.

As with picture libraries, a check box precedes each slide, allowing you to select on which slides you want to perform specific actions. When you open the **Actions** menu, as shown in Figure 12-64, you will not find as many options as for the picture library.

For example, you can delete slides from your library by selecting which slides you want to remove and then selecting the **Delete Slides** option from the **Actions** menu. Notice that the **Actions** menu does not provide options to edit slides, change their permissions, or work with them in any other way. I will come back to that in a moment.

The **Actions** menu does contain an option to change the view to a **Datasheet View** to allow you to quickly make mass changes to multiple properties in one or more of the slides without having to edit the properties of each image individually. It also includes the **Windows Explorer** view. This view allows you to easily move slides between folders in your slide library. However, if you attempt to move them to a directory on your local disk drive, SharePoint will create a separate PowerPoint presentation file for each slide copied.

Figure 12-64. *Viewing available actions for slide libraries*

■**Tip** To move an image from one library folder to another, click the image in the **Windows Explorer** view and press Ctrl+C. Then navigate to the destination folder and paste it there by pressing Ctrl+V. You can also use the **Windows Explorer** view to delete folders that you no longer want. Some people also find it easier to build out their folder/directory structure using the **Windows Explorer** view.

So if the **Actions** menu does not provide options to work with individual images in the library, how can you work with these images? Simply position your mouse over the name of the image you want to work with. An arrow for a drop-down menu appears to the right of the name. Click this arrow to display the item menu, as shown in Figure 12-65.

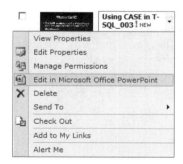

Figure 12-65. *Editing an individual slide from the library*

From this menu, you can view and edit the item's properties, manage its permissions, edit it using Microsoft Office PowerPoint (this option requires you to have PowerPoint installed on your local machine), delete the item, download the slide, and send the slide to an e-mail address or other location. You can also check out the image just like you would check out a Word document before editing it so that others cannot edit the slide while you have it checked out. Finally, there are options that allow you to add the slide to My Links, a feature of MOSS, or create an alert to receive an e-mail when someone changes or deletes this slide.

As useful as all these features may sound, the real power feature is still in the library menu bar. That feature allows you to copy slides from your library to a new or existing PowerPoint presentation.

Copying Slides from Your Slide Library to PowerPoint Presentations

As mentioned at the beginning of this discussion on slide libraries, you may want to use slide libraries to store commonly reused slides so that anyone in your organization creating a new PowerPoint presentation can import the existing slide rather than create the slide from scratch. To do this, refer back to the library menu bar and the option **Copy Slide to Presentation**, as shown in Figure 12-66.

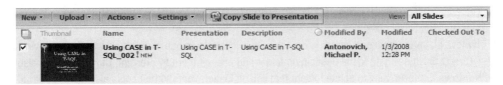

Figure 12-66. *Selecting a slide to copy to a PowerPoint slide presentation*

Before selecting this option, select the slides you want to insert into the new or existing presentation by checking the box to the left of each desired slide. You should also first open the PowerPoint presentation into which you want to add the slide(s) from the library. When you click **Copy Slide to Presentation**, SharePoint opens the dialog box shown in Figure 12-67. In this dialog box, you can specify whether you want to add the selected slide(s) to a new presentation or an open presentation. If you want to copy the slides to an existing presentation, the drop-down box displays the names of all presentations you currently have open. While typically you will only have one presentation open, the one you want to add the slide into, you could have several presentations open and then add the slides to each of the presentations by repeating the process described here, selecting a different presentation from the drop-down list each time.

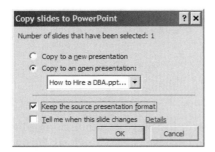

Figure 12-67. *Defining how to copy slides*

You can also decide to keep the source presentation format. This option retains the formatting of the slide as seen in the slide library. However, because this formatting may differ from the formatting used in the presentation, you may want to deselect this option so that PowerPoint reformats the slide using the current master format scheme used by the presentation you are copying the slide into.

The last option in this dialog box allows PowerPoint to retain a link to the slide library so that it can notify you when changes occur to the slide in the SharePoint slide library.

When you click **OK**, SharePoint copies the selected slides from the library to the end of the referenced presentation. At this point, you can use all the features of PowerPoint to manipulate the slide further and to reposition the copied slides within the presentation.

Figure 12-68 shows a single slide copied from the sample slide library TSQL_CASE_Statements to the end of an existing presentation. After being added to the presentation, you can click the slide and drag it to a new position within the presentation if you do not want it at the end.

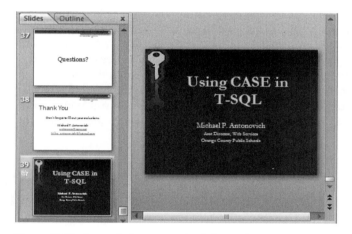

Figure 12-68. *PowerPoint appends slides to the end of the show.*

Summary

In this chapter, you examined three supporting SharePoint libraries. The first library, the Records Center, is the most complex library implementation presented in this book, although it starts from the basic document library. It requires coordination between at least two different sites, a working document site and an archival site, with libraries in each using content types, site columns, and configuration settings made through SharePoint's **Central Administration** site. However, it provides organizations with a powerful tool to archive documents to protect their most important information.

In learning how to build a records management system, you saw how to create reusable site columns. You also created a Word-based site content type and then made it the default content type for the library. To create the Records Center site, you needed to define an External Service Connection through the **Central Administration** site. You set up a policy on what to do with records after adding them to the Records Center, and you also saw how to create a record routing rule.

You then took a second look at the picture library, which you employed in earlier chapters as the source for images used on web pages. The chapter dived deeper into its ability to serve as a central warehouse for your organization's images, which can then be shared and viewed online through built-in **Filmstrip View** modes. You also looked at the use of the Microsoft Office Picture Manager tool and how it serves as a tool when adding and editing pictures in the picture library. Finally, you saw how to export pictures to several Microsoft Office products, changing the picture type as well as some of its other characteristics.

But the picture library does not solve all of your organization's image needs, especially if your organization uses Microsoft PowerPoint to create both internal and external presentations. The slide library adds features to the basic picture library specifically to support PowerPoint slides. You can use it to store and display slide presentations. But its real power comes into play when you use it to share common slides with other people who can download them into their own PowerPoint presentations.

And that wraps up this book introducing you to how you can begin to integrate your use of Microsoft Office products with SharePoint. I hope you gained an appreciation for how to integrate the Microsoft Office tools that you already know with SharePoint. SharePoint collaboration will change the way you and the rest of your organization work. The ability to share and work with document libraries and lists from any location where you have Internet access lets you work anywhere, anytime. This universal access to your information gives your organization the ability to decentralize the way your staff works, increasing their productivity while maintaining the integrity of the information they use. In the office, at home, or on a business trip, you are no longer far from your corporate data when you integrate your daily activities through SharePoint.

Index

A

Access
data formats, 215
exporting data from, to SharePoint, 215–217
forms and reports
changing table used by form, 213
creating, 237–245
controlling availability of, 252–259
data connection to, 365–370
lists
copying list data to, 214–215
exporting SharePoint lists to, 211–224
importing SharePoint lists directly from, 223–224
linking list data to, 214
linking SharePoint lists to, 225–229
offline lists within, 246–252
mass updates using, 227–229
multivalued fields and, 230–236
recovering deleted records, 259–260
replacing existing table, 212
reusing saved exports, 222
synchronizing data in tables, 213–214
transfer issues, 218–224
autoincrement fields, 218–219
with duplicate lists, 220
with Outlook tasks, 221

with referential tables, 220
validation rules, 219–220
acquiescence bias, 65
actions, in workflows, 414–418
adding conditions to, 417–418
adding multiple, 416–417
creating, 415
sending e-mail message, 415–416
Actions button, 414–416
Add new announcement link, 75
Add Web Parts dialog box, 110
agenda list, 69
Alert Me feature, 87, 193
alerts, 55
for change notifications, 193–197
configuring, 194–196
correcting or modifying, 196–197
for list changes, 87–89
turning on, 193
All Site Content page, 72
Allow multiple values check box, 230
alternative text, for images, 104
Analysis Services, 318, 323–324
anchor tags, 114
Announcement list, 54–55
anonymous access, 13
approvals, for document versions, 48–50, 128–129

archival library

defining document policy for, 471–474

record management system for, 455–477

atomicity, 230

autoincrement fields, 218–219

autonumber field, 219

AutoRecovery, frequency for, 138

■B

Basic Meeting Workspace template, 7

Blank Meeting Workspace template, 7

Blank Site template, 5

blog sites, 156

account creation, 160–161

blog post creation, 159–162

creating, 157–158

defining categories for, 158–159

editing, 162

publishing entries to, 159–162

setting permissions, 162–164

Blog template, 6

branding, 155

■C

cabinet (CAB) files, 335

calendar list, 59

Calendar tool, in Groove, 432

calendars

changing calendar items, 182

copying and moving items between, 183

creating new Outlook, 179

deleting items from, 183–184

overlaying, 180–181

restoring deleted items, 183–184

synchronizing between SharePoint and Outlook, 176–184

cells

changing color of, 341

merging, 342

splitting, 342

See also tables

Central Administrator site, 11

central tendency bias, 65

Chat tool, in Groove, 430

check boxes, 86, 344–345

Check in link, 191

Check-In/Check-Out feature, 36–41, 136, 268

editing web pages with, 123–126

in Groove, 443–445

linked lists and, 227

in Outlook, 188–191

overriding checked-out documents, 40–41

choice type columns, 230, 233–234

code reusability, 375

collaboration, peer-to-peer, 423–453

conflict resolution, 444

with external users, 445

file sharing, 435–439

file synchronization, 446–450

protecting document changes, 443–445

setting permission for, 441–443

See also Groove

Collaboration Portal template, 11

collaboration site templates, 3–6

Blank Site, 5

Blog, 6

Document Workspace, 5

Team Site, 4–5

Wiki Site, 6

color depth, of images, 479

columns

adding, to synchronize with Outlook, 170

choice type, 230, 233–234

content type, 410–411

displaying form fields as, 394–395

in forms, 342

indexed, 97

lookup type, 230, 234

multivalued

creating 230–234

filtering, 233

opening list with, 234, 235

reasons not to use, 236

site, 82–83

spacer, 342

See also tables

communications lists, 53–56

Announcements list, 54–55

contacts, 55

discussion board list, 56

concurrency problems, 36, 140. *See also*
conflict resolution

conditional formatting, of controls, 345–346

conditions

adding to actions, 417–418

restructuring, 420–422

in workflows, 414

Conditions button, 417

conflict resolution

in Groove, 438, 444, 447–448

with linked data, 226–227

update conflicts, 171–173, 250–253

when working offline, 250–252

contacts lists, 55

deleting contacts, 173–174

moving contacts between, 175–176

recovering deleted contacts, 174–175

synchronizing Outlook and SharePoint,
167–176

update conflicts, 171–173

Content Approval setting, 126

Content Editor web part, 111–113, 115

content pages

adding hyperlinks to, 104

adding images, 103–104

adding tables to, 105

adding to site, 99–101

copying Word documents to, 104–105

customization of, 155

editing, with Check-In/Check-Out,
123–126

placing content on, 101–106

publishing, 126–129

recovering from Recycle Bin, 130

as web pages, 99

web part pages, 107–119

See also web pages

Content Query web part, 108

content types

adding to library, 408–409

changing default, 409–410

creating, in Records Center, 458–462

installing and using, 408–411

multiple, 398, 410–411

name and description for, 404

publishing form to, 403–407

setting for document library, 463–466

site collection, 408–411

Contents list, 5

Contribute permission level, 14

controls, form, 343–347

    check boxes, 86, 344–345

    conditional formatting, 345–346

    properties of, 344

    reusing, 375–377

custom forms, 241–244

custom lists

    building, 77–82

    exporting Excel data to, 269–275

    saving as template, 71

Custom Send To Destination setting, 398

■D

dashboards

    adding KPIs to, 328–332

    creating, 324–332

    defined, 324

    organizing web parts in, 326–327

data

    editing linked, 226–227

    list, 214–215

    manual, and KPIs, 318–321

    offline, 188–193, 246–252

    synchronizing, 213–214, 249–250

Data Connection Library, 13

Data Connection Wizard, 365–370

data connections

    building, for forms, 365–370

    creating external, with Excel workbooks, 306–311

data sources

    choosing type of, 367

    for forms, 347–348

    list of available, 366

    viewing external, in Excel worksheets, 305–317

Data Sources task group, 347–348

data types, 273, 344–345

data validation

    applying to form fields, 346–347

    of InfoPath forms, 392

database views, with Excel worksheets, 309–311

databases

    connecting InfoPath forms to, 370–375

    naming, 211

    See also Access

Datasheet View

    displaying documents in, 30–32

    editing documents from, 34–35

declarative functionality, 392

Decision Meeting Workspace template, 7

default page, of site, 2

deletions, recovering from Recycle Bin, 50–51, 130, 174–175, 183–184, 259–260

Design a Form Template, 337–339, 375

Design Checker, 348, 356, 392

Design permission level, 14

Design Task group, 339–340

    Controls section, 343–347

    Data Sources section, 347–348

    Designer Checker section, 348, 356, 392

    layout controls, 340–343

Detail View, of images, 492

Discard My Changes button, 251–252

discussion board list, 56

Discussion tool, in Groove, 431

Display as a Web page option, 398

document archives. *See* archival library

Document Center template, 8

document libraries, 9, 12

    accessing from Groove SharePoint Files tool, 440–441

    archival. *See* archival library

    adding, 19–21

        content type to, 408–409

        documents to, 22–25

        Excel workbook to, 289–290

        site columns to, 466–468

    advanced settings, 397–399

    alerts for changes in, 193–197

    changing default template for, 23

    content type

        adding, 408–409

        changing default, 409–410

        multiple, 410–411

        publishing to, 405

        setting, 463–466

    creating, 21, 393–394, 462–468

    defining metadata for, 394–397

    defining properties for, 19–20

    documents

        adding, 22–25

        checking in, 39–40

        checking out, using Outlook, 188–190

        displaying, 154

        editing, 33–36, 140–145

        publishing to, 45–48

        saving, 140–145

        types, 133

        uploading, 26–30

    dragging and dropping files into, 32

    vs. lists, 262

    menu creation, 108

    publishing to

        content type, 405

        documents, 45–48

        forms, 381, 390–402

    referencing documents in, from Office, 139

    stored as lists, 53

    for storing web pages, 100

    synchronizing files between SharePoint and Groove, 446–450

    URLs for, 296

    viewing, from Windows Explorer, 136

Document Management panel, 144, 151–154, 190–191

document policy, 472–474

document templates. *See* templates

document versions. *See* versions

Document Workspace template, 5

documents

    adding to library, 22–25

    approval status of, 46–48

    changing sort order of, 29

    checking in/out, 36–41, 136, 191, 268

    concurrency problems, 36, 140

    creating, 22

default properties for, 24–25

displaying

    changing settings for, 398

    in Datasheet View, 30–32

    in Windows Explorer, 32

editing, 33–36, 136–138, 140–145, 267

filtering, 29–30

locking of, 35–36

managing, with Document Management panel, 151–154

metadata, 149–150

opening from within Office, 134–139

opening in browser, 398

publishing to document library, 45–48

recovering from Recycle Bin, 50–51

saving to document library, 140–145

searching, 154–156

sorting/filtering, 31–32

uploading, 26–30, 147–149

workflow management, 48–50

working with offline

    using Groove, 443–445

    using Outlook, 188–193

workspaces, 6, 143–145

.docx files, 164–165

DoD 5015.2 Chapter 2 compliance, 456

Domain Security level, 386

Draft Item Security setting, 126

drafts, storage, 137

Drafts folder, 190

drop-down lists, 86

dual list boxes, 231

duplicate lists, 220

■**E**

e-mail

    alerts, 55

    configuring, 415–416

    enabling, 208

    sending links in, 209

    sending to groups, 207

    sending to lists, 207–209

    See also Outlook 2007

Excel

    advantages of publishing, 287–288

    data transfer between SharePoint and, 268

    displaying imported lists in, 264–265

    exporting a list from SharePoint to, 261–269

    exporting data from, to custom list, 269–275

    introduction of, 261

    linking list in, to SharePoint, 280–284

    list views in, 266

    synchronization with SharePoint, 276–280, 282–283

    Table Tools tab, 268–271

    tables, exporting, 271–274

    viewing exported data from, in SharePoint list, 274–275

Excel 2003

    creating list in, 277

    exporting SharePoint lists to, 276–277

    exporting worksheets, to SharePoint, 277–279

    synchronization and, 276–279

Excel 2007

    defining tables in, 281

    lack of synchronization in, 279–280

Excel Services

configuring, 288–289

defining parameters for Excel forms, 293–300

publishing to, 289–292, 295–300, 315–317

reasons to use, 287–288

viewing external data in, 312–313

viewing uploaded Excel documents, 300

Excel Web Access web part, 301–305

Excel worksheets/workbooks

adding comments, 294

adding to document library, 289–290

cell names, 294–295

creating external connection with, 306–311

creating KPI list from, 323

defining parameters for, 292–300

defining table within, 270–271

display options, 296–298

exporting metadata to, 407

formatting pivot tables to look like, 313–315

importing SharePoint lists to, 311–313

KPIs and, 318

migrating to InfoPath, 356–360

navigating, 291–292

publishing, 289–292, 295–300, 315–317

refreshing, 292

viewing data from external sources in, 305–317

viewing uploaded, 300

Explorer View option, 494–495

export tasks, 221

Export to Spreadsheet option, 262

Extensible Stylesheet Language (XLS) files, 335

external data sources, viewing in Excel worksheets, 305–317

External Service Connection, 469–471

External Table Data group, 268–269

F

file formats

allowed by Groove, 448

for images, 488

Word 2007, 164–165

XML, 164–165

File in Use dialog box, 141, 152

file permissions. *See* permissions

file sharing, in Groove, 435–439

file synchronization, in Groove, 446–450

conflict resolution, 447–448

management of, 449–450

scheduling, 448–449

status messages, 447

Files tool, in Groove, 431, 435–439

adding files to, 435

creating new file, 439

deleting files, 438

dragging and dropping to, 435

editing shared files, 437

saving files, 439

using subfolders, 436–437

Filmstrip View option, 494

filters, list, 96

form fields, 394–395

form libraries, 12, 393

advanced settings, 397–399

publishing content type to, 405–406

Form Services. *See* InfoPath Form Services

Form Template Conflict dialog box, 387–388

form templates, 392

Form Wizard, 237–238

forms. *See* InfoPath forms

Forms tool, in Groove, 433–434

Full Control permission level, 14, 16, 18

Full Trust security level, 386

■**G**

Galleries option, 15

Gantt charts, 62–63

Global Links Bar, 5

Groove

   account creation, 424–426

   adding files to, 435

   check-in/check-out of documents in, 443–445

   collaborating with external users, 445

   conflict resolution, 438, 444, 447–448

   creating files, 439

   deleting files, 438

   editing files, 437

   file sharing, 435–439

   file synchronization, 446–450

   file types allowed by, 448

   getting started with, 423–429

   Guest role, 428

   inviting others to join, 427–428

   Manager role in, 428

   message notification, 429

   Participant role, 428

   protecting document changes, 443–445

   responding to invitations to join, 429

   saving files, 439

   setting permissions for SharePoint Files folder, 441–443

   SharePoint Files tool, 440–441, 443–450

   Synchronizer role, 446, 450–452

   tools, 430–450

   viewing and editing properties, 441–443

   using subfolders, 436–437

   working with documents offline, 443–445

   workspace, 427–428

Group By section, 96

groups, 13–18

   creating, 15

   defining, 18

   managing permissions of, 16–18

   Members, 14

   Owners, 14, 16, 18

   sending e-mail to, 207

   site owner, 13

   Visitors, 13–14

Guest role, in Groove, 428

■**H**

Help link icon, 5

HTML (hypertext markup language)

   modifying generated, 113–114

   Word document converted to, 117

hyperlinks

   adding to content pages, 104

   e-mailing, 209

   using in lists, 266–268

■**I**

ID field, 218–219

images

   adding to content pages, 103–104

   alt text for, 104

   downloading from picture library, 487–489

   file formats, 488

   sending to Office application, 490–491

size, 479, 491

tracking versions of, 478

uploading

to picture library, 103–104

to slide library, from PowerPoint, 499–504

viewing

in picture library, 492–496

in slide show, 496

Import Data dialog box, 264

Import Wizard, 355–357

indexed columns, 97

InfoPath

defining views, 360–365

files used by, 335

interface, 337–338

introduction to, 335–336

reasons to use, 336–337

XSN files, 335

InfoPath forms

adding workflows to, 335

browser-compatibility of, 339

building custom workflows for, 411–422

connecting to data, 370–375

controlling availability of, 252–259

controls for, 343–347, 375–377

creating Access, from lists, 237–245

creating simple, 338–353

custom, 241–244

data connections for, 365–370

data sources for, 347–348

data validation rules for, 346–347

declarative functionality, 392

defining rules for, 347

defining views for, 360–365

Design View, 240–241

display settings for, 398

error checking, 348, 356

example, 349–353

interface, 337–338

layout controls, 340–343

migrating

Excel workbooks to, 356–360

Word forms to, 354–356

naming, 238,–239

publishing

to a content type, 403–407

to document libraries, 390–402

to network file share, 381–389

to network location, 384–386

to SharePoint library, 381

to SharePoint server, 390–394

query section of, 371, 374–375

reasons to use, 336–337

reusing, with template parts, 375–379

saving data from, 401–402

saving, 238–239, 388–389

security levels for, 385–386

server-based, 387

Split Form, 239–241

subforms, 241–244

submit options for, 400

templates for, 338–339

using published, 387–400

validating, 392

XML files generated from, 389

InfoPath Forms Services, 381, 390–402

InfoPath Forms tool, in Groove, 434

information access, 2

Information Rights Management (IRM), 434

Initiation button, 413

Internet Explorer 7.0, adding RSS feed to, 198–200

IQY files, 262–264

issue tracking list, 63–64, 185

Issue Tracking tool, 432

▪K

Key Performance Indicators (KPIs), 70
    adding to dashboard, 328–332
    introduction to, 317–324
    list creation, 318–324
        from Analysis Services, 323–324
        from Excel workbook, 323
        with manual data, 319–321
        using SharePoint list, 321
    types of, 318

▪L

Languages and Translators list, 70

layout controls, 340–343

libraries
    displaying, using web parts, 118–119
    form, 12, 393, 397–399, 405–406
    picture, 477–496
    records management, 455–477
    sending e-mail to, 207–208
    slide library, 496–505
    types, 11-13
    See also document libraries

Likert scale, 65

Limited Access level permissions, 16

Link to data on the SharePoint site option, 235

linked data, editing, 226–227

links
    adding to content pages, 104
    e-mailing, 209
    using lists in, 266–268

links list, 57–58, 154

list data, 214–215

list views
    changing, 60
    default, 80, 95
    defining, 93–95
    deleting, 93
    filtered, 96–97
    for mobile devices, 97

lists
    adding columns to, 78–79
    adding items to, 75–76, 81–82
    alerts for changes to, 87–89
    built-in types, 53–70
    choices in, 86
    contacts, 55, 167–176
    creating, 70–75
    creating Access forms and reports from, 237–245
    custom, 71, 77–82, 269–75
    defining master-detail relationships between, 119–122
    defining views for, 93–95
    display options in Excel, 264–265
    displaying, using web parts, 118–119
    drop-down, 86
    duplicate, 220
    editing linked, 226–227

exporting

    to Access, 211–224

    from Excel to custom, 269–275

    to Excel, 261–269, 276–277

    transfer issues, 218–224

hyperlinks in, 266–268

importing

    SharePoint to Excel, 311–313

    from Access, 223–224

issue tracking, 63–64, 185

KPI, 70, 317–324

Languages and Translators, 70

vs. libraries, 262

limits on, 80

linking, 225–229, 280–284

mass updates to, using Access, 227–229

modifying columns in, 83–87

MOSS 2007, 70

multivalued fields in, 230–236

naming, 77

offline, within Access, 246–252

recovering deleted records, 259–260

removing items from, 211

RSS feeds for, 89–93

sending e-mail to, 207–209

site columns, 82–83

sorting and filtering, 96–97

tasks, 60–61, 154, 184–188

templates for, 70–74

tracking, 57–68

use of, 53

Look and Feel option, 15

lookup column type, 230, 234

lookup tables, 230, 235

M

Main Content area, 5

Manager role, in Groove, 428

manual data, KPIs and, 318–321

mapped drive letter, 384

mass updates, using Access, 227–229

master pages, customization of, 155

master-detail relationships, 119–122

Meeting templates, 6–8

Meetings tool, 432–433

Members group, 14

menus, for document libraries, 108

message status indicators, 26

metadata

    defined, 145

    defining for document library, 394–397

    editing, 227

    exporting to Excel, 407

    mass updates to, 227–229

    uploading existing documents and, 147–149

    using, with document information panel, 146–147

    working with document, 149–150

Microsoft Access. *See* Access

Microsoft Excel. *See* Excel

Microsoft Office applications

    opening SharePoint document from within, 134–139

    sending images to, 490–491

    See also specific applications

Microsoft Office 2003, 133–134

Microsoft Office 2007, 133–134

Microsoft Office Excel Security Notice dialog box, 263

Microsoft Office Excel Web Query File, 262–264

Microsoft Office Picture Manager. *See* Picture Manager

Microsoft Outlook. *See* Outlook

Microsoft PowerPoint. *See* PowerPoint

Microsoft SharePoint Server 2007 (MOSS 2007), 3, 8–11, 70. *See also* SharePoint

Microsoft Word. *See* Word 2007

Modify Shared Web Part option, 328

Move to SharePoint Site Issues table, 218

mover boxes, 231

Multipage Meeting Workspace template, 8

multivalued fields

    creating, 230–234

    in lists, 230–236

    schema for, 236

My Network Places folder, 134

■N

Name Manager button, 295

Navigation Bar, 5

network file share

    defined, 381

    publishing InfoPath forms to, 381–389

News Site template, 11

Notepad tool, in Groove, 431

■O

object types, 3

objects, 3

Office applications. *See* Microsoft Office applications

offline data

    conflict resolution, 250–252

    editing options, 138

    synchronizing changes to, 249–250

working with

    in Access, 246–252

    in Groove, 443–445

    in Outlook, 188–193

online mode, returning to, 249–250

Open in Browser button, 269

option button control, 344–345

Outlook 2003, 167

Outlook 2007

    adding RSS feed to, 201–204

    adding tasks lists to, 185–187

    calendar synchronization, 176–184

    creating new calendar, 179

    e-mailing links, 209

    integration of, 167

    Office files preview feature, 190

    RSS reader, 198–206

    sending e-mail to lists, 207–209

    sending image to, 490–491

    synchronizing contacts lists, 167–176

    tasks, 217

        editing, 187–188

        for exporting Access data, 221

        synchronization, 184–188

    working with offline content in, 188–193

    See also e-mail

Owners group, 14, 16, 18

■P

page title bar, modifying, 108–110

pages. *See* content pages; web pages

paging controls, for viewing Excel worksheets, 291

Participant role, in Groove, 428

performance issues, 80

Permission Levels option, 16

permissions

    adding new levels, 16–18

    assign level to users, 14–15

    for blogs, 162–164

    Contribute level, 14

    Design level, 14

    Full Control level, 14–18

    in Groove, 441–443

    Limited Access Level, 16

    managing, 16–18

    Read level, 13–14

Personalization Site template, 9

picture libraries

    adding to Quick Launch area, 478

    creating, 477–496

    downloading images from, 487–489

    folder structure, 479–480

    previewing pictures, with Picture
        Manager, 483–486

    sending images to Office application,
        490–491

    uploading images to, 103–104, 481–483,
        486–487

    viewing pictures in, 492–496

Picture Library, 12

Picture Manager, 479

    previewing pictures with, 483–486

    uploading pictures using, 481–483

pictures. *See* images

Pictures tool, in Groove, 430

pivot tables, 312–315

policy definition, creating, 472–474

PowerPoint

    copying slides to, from slide library,
        504–505

    uploading pictures from, to slide library,
        499–504

primary keys, 219, 371

project tasks list, 61–62

Properties button, Excel, 269

Publishing Portal template, 11

Publishing Site template, 10

Publishing Site with Workflow template, 10

publishing sites, 9–11

Publishing Wizard, 383–384, 390

PUBS database for SQL Server 2005, 306

■Q

queries

    creating, 228

    of databases, for forms, 371, 373–375

Quick Launch menu, 5, 478, 497

■R

radio buttons, 86

Read permission level, 13–14

record routing rules, 474–475

records

    recovering deleted, 259–260

    viewing modified, 248

Records Center template, 8, 455

records management system (Records
    Center), 9, 455–477

    archival library creation, 471–474

    archiving documents in, 475–477

    creating, 468

creating content type for documents, 458–462

document library creation, 462–468

external service connection for, 469–471

site column creation, 456–458

record routing instructions for, 474–475

sending documents to, 475–477

uses of, 456

Recycle Bin

recovering deleted items from, 50–51, 130, 183–184, 259–260

restoring contacts from, 174–175

settings for, 130, 174

referential tables, issues with transferring, 220

Refresh button, Excel, 268, 275

relational databases, 219

Report Center

dashboards and, 324–332

KPIs and, 317–324

site template, 9

working with, 317

Report Library, 13

reports

controlling availability of, 252–259

creating Access, from lists, 237–245

Resolve Conflicts dialog box, 251

Restricted Security level, 385–386

Retry All My Changes button, 252

Retry My Changes button, 252

Reviewing Pane button, 153

Rich Text Editor, 101–106

RSS feeds

adding to Internet Explorer, 198–200

adding to Outlook, 201–204

creating, for lists, 89–93

deleting items from, 204–205

subscribing to, 198–206

viewing list items not in, 205–206

RSS reader, in Outlook, 198–206

■S

saved exports, reusing, 222

Search Center site template, 8

Search Center with Tabs site template, 9

Search feature, 5, 154–156

security levels, for InfoPath forms, 385–386

server-based forms, security warnings for, 387

Shared Documents library, 19, 22

accessing from Groove SharePoint Files tool, 440–441

uploading documents to, 26–30

SharePoint administrator, 13

SharePoint Designer, 155, 411–422

SharePoint documents. *See* documents

SharePoint Drafts folder, 137

SharePoint Files tool, 434, 440–450

SharePoint libraries. *See* document libraries; libraries

SharePoint lists. *See* lists

SharePoint sites. *See* sites

Site Actions menu, 5, 15

Site Administration option, 15

Site Collection Administration option, 15

site collection content types.
See content types

site collections, 2–3

site columns, 82–83

site content type, 403–407

Site Directory template, 9

site members, adding new, 154

site owner group, 13

Site Settings page, 15–16

sites

adding content pages to, 99–101

anonymous access to, 13

changing appearance of, 155

configuring for automatic check-out of
pages, 124

creating, 2–3

customizing, 15–16

default page, 2

Enterprise, 8–9

hierarchy of, 2

publishing pages to, 126–129

publishing, 9–11

searching, 154–156

templates, 3–11

upload limits for, 28

Sketchpad tool, in Groove, 431

slide libraries, 496–505

copying slides from, to PowerPoint,
504–505

creating, 497–498

defining metadata for, 498

folder structure for, 498–499

including in Quick Launch menu, 497

performing actions on slides in, 502–504

uploading pictures to, from PowerPoint,
499–504

viewing slides, 501–502

Slide Library, 13

social desirability bias, 65

Social Meeting Workspace template, 7

Source Editor, viewing HTML in, 114

spacer columns, 342

Split Form, 239–241

SQL 2000 PUBS database, 306

SQL databases, 3, 365–370

SQL Server 2005 Analysis Services, 318,
323–324

SQL Server Express, 3

SQL statements, 213

Standard View

checking out document in, 37–38

editing Word documents from, 33–34

subforms, 241–244

Submit command, 400

Submit Options dialog box, 400

subsites, 2

survey list, 64–68

synchronization

add-in, for Excel, 280

with Excel, 276–280, 282–283

file, 446–450

with Outlook, 176–188

Synchronizer role, in Groove, 446, 450–452

■T

table borders, changing color/style of, 342

Table Tools tab, 268–271

tables

    adding to content pages, 105

    cells

        changing color of, 341

        merging, 342

        splitting, 342

    defining, with Excel worksheet, 270–271

    exporting Excel, 271–274

    laying out form, 340–343

    linking, with multivalued fields, 236

    lookup, 230, 235

    number of columns in, 342

    parent-child relationships between, 241

    pivot, 312–315

    primary keys, 219

    referential, 220

task synchronization, between SharePoint and Outlook, 184–188

tasks, creating Outlook, 217

tasks lists, 60–61, 154

    adding to Outlook, 185–187

    approval process for, 187–188

    editing, from Outlook, 187–188

    uses of, 184

Team Site template, 4–5

template parts, for reusing forms, 375–379

templates

    changing default, for document library, 23

    collaboration site, 3–6

    creating lists based on, 70–75

    dashboard, 325–326

    document, 21

    Enterprise, 8–9

    library, 11–13

    meeting, 6–8

    of object types, 3

    publishing sites, 9–11

    web page, 74

text formatting features, 101–102

themes, changing, 155

thread view, of discussion board list, 56

Thumbnails View option, 492–493

Title area, 5

title bars, page, 108–110

tracking lists, 57–68

    agenda list, 69

    calendar list, 59

    issue tracking list, 63–64

    links list, 57–58

    project tasks list, 61–62

    survey list, 64–68

    tasks list, 60–61

Translation Management library, 12

■U

Unlink button, Excel, 269

update conflicts

    in Access tables, 250–252

    in contacts lists, 171–173

URLs, for document libraries, 296

user interface, InfoPath, 337–338

Users and Permissions option, 15

V

validation rules

    for form fields, 346–347

    transfer issues and, 219–220

Variables button, 413

Version History option, 41–42

version numbers, 40, 126

Versioning settings, 48–49

versionless mode, 126

versions

    adding comments to, 128

    approval for, 128–129

    Groove and, 443–445

    history of, 130

    picture, 478

    promoting prior version to current, 43–44

    publishing, 45–47, 126–127

    resynching, after editing offline, 191–193

    retrieving from backup, 127

    tracking, 41–42, 126

    of web pages, 124–126, 130

View Properties dialog box, 360–362

views

    adding columns to, 25

    database, 309–311

    defining InfoPath, 360–365

        for form properties, 360–362

        generating second, 362–365

    list, 60, 80, 93–97, 266

Views task panel, 362

Visio Pivot Diagrams, 268

Visitors group, 13, 14

Vista, references to sites visited in, 135–136

W

web pages,

    adding hyperlinks to, 104

    adding images to, 103–104

    automatic check-out of, 124

    copying content from Word documents, 117

    creating, 99–101

    editing, with Check-Out/Check-In, 123–126

    including Excel documents in, 301–305

    naming, 107

    opening in new window, 113–114

    placing content on, 101–106

    publishing, 126–129

    recovering, from Recycle Bin, 130

    retrieving from backup, 127

    SharePoint sites as, 73

    templates for, 74

    versions of, 124–126, 130

web part pages

    adding content to, 111–113

    adding functionality to, 107–117

    adding to web part zones, 110–111

    adjusting appearance of, 115–116

    creating, 107–108

    editing properties of, 118

    modifying generated HTML, 113–114

    page title bar, 108–110

web part zones, 5

    adding web parts to, 110–111, 326–327

    displaying libraries and lists using, 118–119

web parts

adding to web part zones, 110–111, 326–327

Content Editor, 111–115

Content Query, 108

Excel Web Access, 301–305

web servers, image location and, 103–104

web services, 339

web-enabled forms

controls for, 343–344

error checking, 348

Welcome menu, 5

Wiki Page Library, 12

Wiki Site template, 6

Windows Explorer

displaying documents in, 32

opening SharePoint document from, 135–136

uploading pictures using, 486–487

Windows SharePoint Services (WSS), 3. *See also* SharePoint

Windows Workflow Foundation, 335

Word 2007

compatibility with, 24

creating blog posts with, 159–162

default file format, 164–165

opening SharePoint document from, 137

Word documents

2003 vs. 2007, 29

copy and pasting text from, 117

copying text from, 104–105

editing, 33–34, 140–145

saving, 142–145

searching, 154–156

See also documents

Word forms, migrating to InfoPath, 354–356

workflows

actions in, 414–418

adding steps to, 418–420

adding to forms, 335

building (example), 412–414

configuring e-mail message, 415–416

custom, for InfoPath forms, 411–422

defined, 411–412

defining details, 414–415

managing document, 48–50

rearranging steps in, 420

restructuring conditions in, 420–422

saving, 421

variables for, 413

working with, 10

working offline, 247–248, 250–252. *See also* offline data

workspaces, 6, 143–145

▪**X**

XLSB files, 289

XLSX files, 289

XML (Extensible Markup Language), 335

XML files, 164–165, 389

XML Schema Definition (XSD) files, 335

XSL Transformation (XSLT) files, 335

XSN files, 335

You Need the Companion eBook

Your purchase of this book entitles you to buy the companion PDF-version eBook for only $10. Take the weightless companion with you anywhere.

We believe this Apress title will prove so indispensable that you'll want to carry it with you everywhere, which is why we are offering the companion eBook (in PDF format) for $10 to customers who purchase this book now. Convenient and fully searchable, the PDF version of any content-rich, page-heavy Apress book makes a valuable addition to your programming library. You can easily find and copy code — or perform examples by quickly toggling between instructions and the application. Even simultaneously tackling a donut, diet soda, and complex code becomes simplified with hands-free eBooks!

Once you purchase your book, getting the $10 companion eBook is simple:

❶ Visit **www.apress.com/promo/tendollars/**.

❷ Complete a basic registration form to receive a randomly generated question about this title.

❸ Answer the question correctly in 60 seconds, and you will receive a promotional code to redeem for the $10.00 eBook.

THE EXPERT'S VOICE™

2855 TELEGRAPH AVENUE | SUITE 600 | BERKELEY, CA 94705